THE ENCYCLOPEDIA OF
CONSPIRACIES AND CONSPIRACY THEORIES

Michael Newton

☑®
Checkmark Books®
An imprint of Facts On File, Inc.

For Harold Weisberg

The Encyclopedia of Conspiracies and Conspiracy Theories

Copyright © 2006 by Michael Newton

Checkmark Books
An imprint of Facts On File, Inc.
132 West 31st Street
New York NY 10001

Library of Congress Cataloging-in-Publication Data

Newton, Michael, 1951–
The encyclopedia of conspiracies and conspiracy theories / by Michael Newton.
p. cm.
Includes bibliographical references and index.
ISBN 0–8160–5540–8 (hc: alk. paper)—ISBN 0–8160–5541–6 (pbk: alk. paper)
1. Conspiracies—Encyclopedias. I. Title.
HV6275.N49 2004
364.1'03—dc222004004284

Text design by Erika K. Arroyo
Cover design by Nora Wertz

Printed in the United States of America

VB FOF 10 9 8 7 6 5 4 3 2 1

This book is printed on acid-free paper.

Contents

Preface

Black's Law Dictionary defines a conspiracy as "a combination or confederacy between two or more persons formed for the purpose of committing, by their joint efforts, some unlawful or criminal act." That is it, in a nutshell—and the marvel of modern journalism is that virtually any suggestion of an active conspiracy provokes knee-jerk charges of "paranoia," "eccentricity," or outright "delusional insanity."

In fact, we are surrounded by conspiracies each day, around the world, in every walk of life. Each time a pair of thieves goes shoplifting, it is a conspiracy. Wherever prostitutes and pushers meet with johns and junkies, conspiracies thrive and multiply. Each time a bribe is offered and accepted, anywhere criminals or corrupt politicians plot illicit backroom deals for their own benefit, wherever police ignore the commission of crime—there lies conspiracy.

Illegal plots are hatched within the best and worst of families, in seedy bars and Fortune 500 board-rooms, at the Pentagon and in the nests of radicals who scheme against the government. The White House has been both a target and a hotbed of conspiracy in modern times. Some famous (or notorious) organizations are conspiratorial by definition—the Mafia, the Ku Klux Klan, and the CIA are only three examples out of thousands. Other institutions, though created to deter illegal actions, have themselves become corrupted over time, committing more crimes than they solve. Some individuals and institutions are the authors *and* the targets of conspiracies: The late President John F. Kennedy provides a case in point. In fact, it may be said that active plotters, by virtue of their lifestyles, are most likely to become the focus of hostile conspiracies (a lesson some leaders of organized crime have learned only during the final moments of their violent lives).

The fact that thousands of conspiracies exist and have been amply documented does not mean, of course, that every theoretical conspiracy is true. Some are absurd, transparently ridiculous, or even physically impossible. A number of the plots detailed within these pages seem to be half tawdry jest and half distilled insanity. Unfortunately for the critics of "conspiratorial thinking," some of the silliest plans are also among the best-documented, confessed by their authors and verified from declassified government files.

Who, in real life, would plot to embarrass a national leader by dusting his clothes with depilatory powder to make his hair fall out? Or by lacing his favorite cigars with hallucinogenic drugs to make him babble incoherently on television? Who would ever think to kill a famous skin diver by planting explosive seashells along his favorite beach? What twisted mind would surgically implant microphones inside a stray cat and then release the cat on the grounds of a hostile embassy?

The answer to all four of those questions is the same: the CIA. Within living memory, our "master spies" devoted countless hours and untold taxpayers' dollars to these and other bizarre schemes: "remote viewing" by psychic spies, mind control via LSD, and assembly-line production of hypnotized "robot" assassins. By 1976, in the wake of Watergate, the Vietnam War and congressional hearings on illegal domestic surveillance, citizens in the Land of the Free had to ask themselves if there was any difference between truth and illusion, between conspiracy and government business as usual.

As conspiracies vary in scope and intent, so the selection of topics for the work in hand has been arbitrarily confined to *significant* conspiracies and conspiracy theories. The author defines that term to mean any plot (or suspected plot) that involves or affects large numbers of people, or that, while having a limited direct impact, still inspires widespread interest or comment. An example of the first variety would be the Iran-contra conspiracy, in which two successive presidents violated federal law, obstructed justice, and condoned illegal sale of weapons and narcotics to pursue an outlawed terrorist campaign abroad. The latter might include a claim that John Dillinger (America's most famous outlaw of the 1930s) escaped his final shootout with police and left a hapless double to die in his place. Both plots pervert the course of justice, one threatening the very soul of the republic, with the other being a mere sideshow, and both are offered here—if nothing else, for sheer variety.

As indicated by this volume's title, some conspiracies detailed within its pages may exist only in theory, lacking any sort of "smoking gun" that would permit indictment, trial, and conviction of suspected plotters—where, in fact, conspirators are even named. Inclusion of those theories here, *as theories,* does not constitute endorsement either by the author or his publishers. In every case, the allegations have been previously published elsewhere; those sources may be found in the work's extensive bibliography.

In a similar vein, while legal definitions of *conspiracy* require the plotting of a crime, society accepts a broader meaning that includes any covert combination against the public interest, whether or not laws are broken. Thus, it may not be a crime to pay off inventors and suppress their inventions—a superefficient carburetor, say, or a cure for AIDS—but such actions clearly fall within the wider defini-

tion of *conspiracy,* and allegations of such actions are included here. Likewise, while some hoaxes, practical jokes, and publicity stunts stop short of crossing the line into fraud, their impact on society may be profound and deleterious, thus warranting inclusion here.

Entries in this encyclopedia are alphabetically arranged. They include short biographies of conspirators and victims, profiles of conspiratorial organizations and movements, brief histories of nations that have spawned or suffered from conspiracies (and which has not?), descriptions of specific conspiratorial events, and general essays on social, political, or religious movements of a conspiratorial nature. The appearance of a name or term in SMALL CAPITALS denotes a subject with its own discrete entry in the text. "Blind" entries also direct the reader to entries containing information on the subject listed (e.g., Billy the Kid—See UNDEAD OUTLAWS). The bibliography is limited to sources published or translated in the English language, and while extensive, it is by no means exhaustive. Most of the works listed there contain their own bibliographies, replete with further leads to this or that conspiracy theory.

Thanks are due to Dave Frasier at Indiana University for his generous assistance with various points of research. Every effort has been made to make the work in hand as timely and complete as possible, but conspiracy theories evolve and mutate with the speed of e-mail in this Internet age. Readers are invited to submit corrections and any pet conspiracy theories of their own to the author in care of Facts On File. Barring a request for anonymity, any material used in future editions of this work will be publicly acknowledged.

Entries A–Z

ABBAS, Abu (1948–2004)

One of the world's most notorious terrorists prior to the advent of Osama bin Laden (see BIN LADEN FAMILY), Abu Abbas was born in 1948 in a Syrian refugee camp for Arabs who were expelled from ISRAEL. He studied at Damascus University and was recruited by the Popular Front for the Liberation of Palestine in 1968. After guerrilla training in the Soviet Union, Abbas joined the newly formed Palestine Liberation Front and engaged in bitter conflict between rival Palestinian groups in LEBANON. He subsequently allied himself with Yasser Arafat and Arafat's Palestine Liberation Organization (PLO). In 1981, Abbas was credited with planning the hangglider attack on an oil refinery at Haifa, Israel. A year later, when the PLO was exiled to Tunisia, Abbas was elected to the group's ruling executive committee. In October 1985 U.S. authorities named Abbas as the mastermind of the *Achille Lauro* hijacking, during which an American hostage was murdered. Abbas negotiated the surrender of four hijackers in that case and joined them on a flight to Tunisia, where they were supposed to be "disciplined" by PLO leaders. That flight was intercepted by U.S. warplanes, with Abbas and the hijackers jailed by Italian authorities, but Abbas was released to Yugoslavia on October 12, 1985. From there, he reportedly flew to Baghdad, IRAQ. An Italian court subsequently convicted Abbas in absentia and sentenced him to life imprisonment, but he remained in hiding until 1996 when Israeli authorities permitted him to settle in the Gaza Strip as part of the endless Middle East "peace process." Abbas publicly embraced nonviolence, while U.S. and Italian authorities ignored him. U.S. troops captured Abbas in April 2003 after they invaded Baghdad as part of OPERATION IRAQI FREEDOM. His death in U.S. custody was announced in February 2004, with jailers blaming his demise on natural causes while the late prisoner's widow called his death an assassination.

AFGHANISTAN

Darius I and Alexander the Great were the first conquerors to visit Afghanistan, followed by Muslim invaders in the seventh century, Genghis Khan (13th century) and Tamerlane (14th century). Four hundred years later, the "great game" between England and RUSSIA for control of central Asia sparked three Afghan Wars (1839–42, 1878–80, and 1919). Britain was victorious, granting Afghani independence in 1919, and the monarchy of Emir Amanullah was founded in 1926.

The Afghan front remained peaceful until the cold war prompted King Mohammed Zahir Shah to accept financial aid from the Soviet Union. A royal cousin, Mohammed Daud Khan, dethroned the king in 1973 and was himself unseated by rival Noor Taraki five years later. Taraki and successor Babrak Karmal tried to establish a Communist state, but

Islamic rebels (*mujahideen*) violently opposed the move. Fearing defeat, Karmal requested Soviet military aid; Moscow responded with a full-scale invasion in December 1979.

Enter the United States, with heavy covert aid for the *mujahideen* (whose ranks included Osama bin Laden and the future leaders of AL-QAEDA). Armed and trained by the CENTRAL INTELLIGENCE AGENCY (CIA) and U.S. Special Forces, financed in equal parts by U.S. aid and international HEROIN sales, the *mujahideen* waged bloody guerrilla war against the Russians until April 1988, when diplomats from the United States, the Soviet Union, Afghanistan, and PAKISTAN agreed to cut off foreign support for Afghani combatants. Russian troops withdrew in February 1989, leaving the pro-Soviet regime of President Najibullah in nominal command of the nation. Islamic rebels deposed Najibullah in April 1992 and then turned on each other as rival drug-dealing warlords battled for supremacy. Amid the chaos, a group of extreme Muslim fundamentalists (the Taliban) seized the capital in September 1996 and imposed a system of religious statutes that included death by stoning for adultery and severing of hands for theft. By 1998 the Taliban controlled 90 percent of Afghanistan, though its regime was recognized only by Pakistan, SAUDI ARABIA, and the United Arab Emirates.

Global isolation made Afghanistan a fertile breeding ground for radical groups and heroin smugglers. Bin Laden and al-Qaeda used Afghanistan as a launching pad for acts of TERRORISM, culminating in the PENTTBOM attacks of September 11, 2001, whereupon President George W. Bush invaded the country and unseated the Taliban regime (missing bin Laden in the process). U.S. conduct during that military action—dubbed "Operation Enduring Freedom"—remains highly controversial. Several hundred Afghan prisoners of war were transferred to a U.S. military base in Cuba, where they remain today without criminal charges being filed; the White House refuses to identify the captives. One prisoner who was released, Pakistani national Mohammad Sagheer, claimed in November 2002 that some 7,000 POWs died in U.S. custody before or during transportation to the mysterious "Camp X-Ray" in Cuba. Meanwhile, military action continues in "liberated" Afghanistan, where a U.S. air strike killed 50 members of a wedding party in Oruzgan Province in 2002. Another tragic "accident" occurred in April 2003 when American planes bombed a residential district in eastern Afghanistan, killing 11 civilians.

Curiously, while U.S. spokesmen claimed that suppression of Afghanistan's heroin network was a major secondary goal of Operation Enduring Freedom, drug smuggling has *increased* dramatically since the U.S. invasion in 2001. By February 2002 Afghanistan supplied an estimated 75 percent of the world's total heroin supply, and 90 percent of all heroin found in Great Britain. According to various sources including the UNITED NATIONS, Afghan heroin production *decreased* by 91 percent under Taliban rule and then soared again in the wake of the U.S. invasion, until Afghanistan surpassed MYANMAR as the world's foremost producer of opium and its illicit derivatives. U.S. authorities have no comment on the curious trend, except to note (in May 2003) that "most of the heroin that winds up in New York City comes from COLOMBIA." Critical observers note disturbing parallels between Afghanistan and VIETNAM, where CIA agents and their warlord clients collaborated on heroin smuggling throughout the 1960s.

The situation remained volatile in the first half of 2005 when an unsubstantiated report in *Newsweek* claimed that U.S. soldiers had desecrated copies of the Koran at the Guantánamo Bay prison camp in order to intimidate prisoners. The article sparked riots in Afghanistan and other parts of the Muslim world that resulted in several deaths and extensive property destruction. *Newsweek* later retracted the article when no evidence could be located to backup the claim and it appeared their initial source was unreliable. Much of the Muslim world reacted to the retraction with skepticism.

See also BIN LADEN FAMILY; BUSH DYNASTY.

AFRICAN National Congress

The African National Congress (ANC) was created at Bloemfontein, SOUTH AFRICA, on January 8, 1912, to defend the rights of the nation's black majority from dominant racist whites. Its first campaign was limited to opposing passage of the 1913 Land Act, which barred black Africans from owning land in broadly defined "white areas" of South Africa. That effort failed, and the ANC stagnated until 1944 when a new and more militant ANC Youth League was organized by activists Nelson Mandela, Oliver Tambo, and Walter Sisulu. The revitalized ANC sponsored nonviolent mass action against South

Africa's increasingly racist legislation, forging an alliance to that end in 1947 with the Natal Indian Congress and the Transvaal Indian Congress.

In 1948, neofascist elements with ties to the lately defeated THIRD REICH organized South Africa's National Party to inaugurate a sweeping system of apartheid (Afrikaans for "separateness" of the races), and the next four years saw black rights steadily erode on all fronts. In June 1952 the ANC joined other antiapartheid groups for a Defiance Campaign of civil disobedience, but that effort was scuttled in April 1953 by a new law banning protest meetings. In June 1955 a "Congress of the People" held at Kliptown, near Johannesburg, adopted the Freedom Charter that would henceforth serve as the primary document of opposition to apartheid. Sweeping arrests in 1956 jailed 156 leaders of the ANC and allied groups, but all were acquitted at their "treason trial" in 1961. ANC leader Albert Luthuli won the Nobel Peace Prize in 1960, but the ANC was soon outlawed in South Africa, its members driven underground by accusations of TERROR-ISM and sedition.

Once banned from legitimate discourse, the ANC had no choice but to adopt armed struggle as a method to depose apartheid. In 1961, its leaders organized Umkhonto we Sizwe (Spear of the Nation) to wage war against the racist power structure in South Africa. Nelson Mandela was arrested in 1962 and sentenced to life imprisonment, along with Walter Sisulu and other ANC leaders, at trial in 1964. Oliver Tambo subsequently established the ANC's government in exile, fielding an estimated force of 6,000 guerrillas from bases in ANGOLA, MOZAM-BIQUE, and ZAMBIA. The ANC forged close ties with the banned South African Communist Party, and its central party document, the Manifesto of the Azanian People, described the ANC's primary goal as the destruction of "racial capitalism" in South Africa.

Three decades of struggle and repression climaxed on February 2, 1990, when President F.W. de Klerk lifted the ANC's ban. Nelson Mandela won the Nobel Peace Prize in 1993, and majority rule was restored to the nation in 1994. That April, the ANC won a landslide victory in South Africa's first integrated election, to become the nation's ruling party. Mandela served as president until 1999, when he was succeeded by Thabo Mbeki. The ANC also holds an elected majority in eight of the country's nine provinces.

A curious sideshow to mainstream activities involves the controversial career of Nelson Mandela's ex-wife. Winnie Mandela was charged with attempted murder in 1991, following the disappearance of a young bodyguard whose torture and death she allegedly ordered. In the absence of a corpse, she was acquitted of the primary charge, but jurors convicted her of kidnapping. The court imposed a suspended sentence for that offense, but Mrs. Mandela's legal problems continued. On April 25, 2003, she was convicted on 43 counts of fraud and 25 counts of theft, receiving a five-year prison term. Court watchers predicted that she would serve a maximum of eight months in jail.

AGENT Orange

"Agent Orange" was the code name used for a powerful herbicide employed by the U.S. military during the VIETNAM War. The name derives from an orange band painted around metal drums that contained the product. Although initially developed in the 1940s, it was not seriously tested for application in tropical climates until the early 1960s. By 1971, when its use was discontinued, an estimated 20 million gallons of Agent Orange were sprayed in Vietnam, either by hand or (more commonly) in mass drops from aircraft. (The motto of one airborne chemical unit: "Only You Can Prevent Forests.")

Agent Orange was a 50–50 mix of two chemicals, commonly known as 2,4–D and 2,4,5–T. The combined product was mixed with kerosene or diesel fuel before dispersal in widespread "deforestation" campaigns. A variant form (dubbed "Orange II" or "Super Orange"), used in Vietnam during 1968–69, combined chemicals 2,4–D and 2,4,5–T. Early health concerns surrounding Agent Orange focused on contamination of the product with TCDD, a form of dioxin related to the dibenzofurans and pcb's. Some dioxins occur in nature and may be harmless, but TCDD has produced a wide variety of diseases in lab testing on animals, including several ailments fatal to humans.

Beginning in the late 1960s, Vietnamese natives complained that Agent Orange and other military defoliants were killing livestock and producing birth deformities in humans. The Pentagon ignored those claims and likewise struck a pose of denial in the postwar years when U.S. veterans displayed abnormally high rates of cancer and other diseases linked to TCDD exposure. Finally, on January 23, 2003, the Veteran Affairs Department acknowledged a link between Agent Orange and chronic lymphocytic leukemia (CLL), granting an extension of government benefits to veterans suffering from that disease. Speaking for the government, Secretary Anthony Principi said, "It's sad that we have to presume service connection, because we know that [veterans] have cancer that may have been caused by their battlefield service. But it's the right thing to do." And while the "right thing" came too late for veterans who died of CLL and similar diseases prior to 2003, Veterans Affairs (VA) doctors announced their expectation of finding 500 new CLL cases per year among Vietnam vets.

At the time of the VA's belated announcement, 10,000 Vietnam survivors were under treatment for illness related to Agent Orange, Super Orange, or the 13 other defoliants widely used during the Asian war. The other compounds, all used between 1962 and 1964, included: "Blue" (cacodylic acid), Bromacil, Dalapon, Dinoxol (mixing 2,4–D and 2,4,5–T), Diquat, Diuron, "Green" (2,4,5–T), Monuron, "Pink" (2,4,5–T), "Purple" (2,4–D and 2,4,5–T), Tandex, Trinoxol (2,4,5–T), and "White" (a formulation of Picloram and 2,4–D).

AGHORA cult

Described by investigators as "a very open society," the Aghora sect of the Hindu religion is nonetheless one that would surprise most westerners for its practice of ritual cannibalism. In June 2003 Reuters News Service reported the experience of Mike Yon, a Florida native and ex-Green Beret who visited India in search of ideas for a book he was planning. On September 5, 2002, Yon was present when an Israeli tourist drowned in the Ganges River near Rishikesh. A team of Israeli divers sent to recover the body found another Caucasian corpse instead, and Yon watched with dive-team leader Yigal Zur as a member of the Aghora cult approached the bloated body, placed a coin on the dead man's exposed liver, and then tore off a piece of flesh and ate it on the spot.

Widespread stories persist that the Aghoris are not mere scavengers but may be active predators in the mold of the Thugs who terrorized India from the 12th century until the latter 1800s. Like the Thugs, Aghoris worship Kali, the dark god of Hinduism, and they also revere Shiva (god of destruction and reproduction). As

Yon told Reuters, "I heard rumors that European and American tourists were being taken. It sounds ludicrous, but where it is in India, anything goes." As Yon explained the cult's philosophy, white foreigners are viewed as possessing great Shakti—a creative energy that Hindus believe flows directly from God. "If you sacrifice a rich or powerful person," Yon explained, "they have more Shakti. Children have more Shakti because they haven't lived long."

Yon discovered that the sect is not confined to India but also thrives in Nepal. Bribes of whiskey—consumed by cultists as a sacrament—led Yon to an American convert, 52-year-old Texas native Gary Stevenson, now known as Kapal Nath. Adorned with dreadlocks, tattoos and a set of tom-toms made from infant human skulls, Nath sipped his liquor from a hollowed skull while briefing Yon on the proper method of cooking human flesh. "I like to take a fresh body, you know," Nath told Yon, "maybe even an Israeli, cook 'em barbecue." The technique, Nath explained, involved a "big, big bucket of barbecue sauce, paintbrush, roller, you know."

Yon emerged from the interview with a disturbing view of Hinduism's darker side. "The amazing thing," he told Reuters, "is that they are doing it there in the open. A policeman was burning the body of his neighbor and cracked open the skull to release the soul. The policeman gave Nath some of the brains to eat." Human brains, in fact, topped Nath's list of favorite foods. A self-confessed serial killer, Nath admitted multiple murders during a conversation that Yon taped for posterity. His first victim, long before joining the cult, was apparently a man he shot in San Francisco sometime in the 1970s. Nath also boasted of stalking human prey on the Hawaiian island of Oahu, where he lived from 1978 to 1994. As Yon recalled, "He said he liked to eat the brain and heart. He said human meat has the same taste as pork."

AGNEW, Spiro (1918–1996)

A son of Greek immigrants born in Baltimore on November 9, 1918, Spiro Agnew received a law degree from the University of Baltimore in 1947. In 1962, campaigning as a reformer, he was elected chief executive of Baltimore County. Four years later, Agnew was elected governor of Maryland. Republican presidential candidate RICHARD NIXON chose Agnew as his running mate in 1968.

That campaign was well advanced when President LYNDON BAINES JOHNSON (LBJ) heard rumors of a Republican effort to sabotage peace negotiations on the VIETNAM War. Specifically, Anna Chennault—a Chinese-born Republican activist and leader of Concerned Asians for Nixon—was suspected of urging South Vietnamese leaders to stall the peace talks. Johnson ordered a FEDERAL BUREAU OF INVESTIGATION (FBI) investigation, which included wiretaps and physical surveillance on Chennault. Three days before the election, on November 2, 1968, FBI eavesdroppers heard Chennault advise a South Vietnamese politician that his country would "get a better deal" from Nixon in the new year. Asked if Nixon knew what she was doing, Chennault replied, "No, but our friend in New Mexico does." Coincidentally or otherwise, Spiro Agnew spent that afternoon in Albuquerque, making campaign speeches.

J. EDGAR HOOVER, himself a staunch Nixon supporter, reported the conversation to President Johnson on November 6. Furious, LBJ telephoned Nixon—already the president-elect—and chastised him for meddling in U.S. foreign policy. Hoover subsequently reported the FBI investigation of Agnew and Chennault to Nixon, placing full blame on the Johnson White House.

If Agnew took offense at the snooping, he covered it well. During the next four years, employed primarily as Nixon's mouthpiece for stinging attacks on the press, "radical liberals," and other targets drawn from the White House enemies list, Agnew repeatedly sought Hoover's help in preparing his inflammatory speeches, once requesting "especially graphic incidents" from classified files with which to smear his critics. A phone call placed on May 18, 1970, for instance, solicited FBI assistance in defaming Rev. Ralph Abernathy, a civil rights activist and leader of the Southern Christian Leadership Conference. Hoover described the call in a memo: "The Vice President said he thought he was going to have to start destroying Abernathy's credibility, so anything I can give him would be appreciated. I told him that I would be glad to."

Exposure of the WATERGATE scandal in 1972 spelled political doom for Spiro Agnew. Journalists investigating the Nixon administration discovered that Agnew had been taking bribes since 1962 from engineers and architects pursuing government contracts in Maryland. The payoffs had continued after he became vice president, and Agnew persistently failed to report the income on his tax returns. Meeting with Nixon on August 6, 1973, Agnew proclaimed himself innocent of any wrongdoing, but his days were numbered. On October 10, 1973, he resigned in disgrace, pleading "no contest" the same afternoon on one count of income tax evasion dating from 1967. Agnew was fined $10,000 and placed on three years' probation. Following his resignation, Agnew told friends that he had been threatened by unnamed persons at the Nixon White House and stated, "I feared for my life." He never spoke to Nixon again, but he described the events in a memoir titled *Go Quietly or Else* (1980). Agnew died in 1996.

AIDS

The deadly disease known as AIDS—Acquired Immune Deficiency Syndrome—was first officially reported in 1981 from the United States, though most authorities believe that it originated in Africa. (Some claim that the first case, unrecognized at the time, may have surfaced as early as 1969.) The human immunodeficiency virus (HIV) that causes AIDS was identified in 1983, and reliable tests for the virus were perfected two years later. The virus is transmitted by exchange of bodily fluids, chiefly via sex, transfusions of infected blood, or sharing contaminated hypodermic needles. There is presently no cure for AIDS, though various drugs retard its advance in some patients. AIDS kills by leaving its victims open to attack by various "opportunistic" diseases that are normally repelled by healthy immune systems. At the end of 2001, the World Health Organization reported that AIDS had killed 24.8 million victims worldwide; another 40 million persons were infected, more than half of them (28.1 million) residing in sub-Saharan Africa.

What is the origin of HIV? Reporter William Carlsen, writing for the *San Francisco Chronicle*, notes that "[i]n the early years of the AIDS epidemic, theories attempting to explain the origin of the disease ranged from the comic to the bizarre: a deadly germ escaped from a secret CIA laboratory; God sent the plague down to punish homosexuals and drug addicts; it came from outer space, riding on the tail of a comet." Today, the official line traces HIV to a population of African apes that were infected with a similar virus, which somehow jumped the normal "species barrier" to attack human beings. Still unexplained is the means by which a mutated simian disease suffered by heterosexual black Africans spanned the Atlantic in the 1970s to infect predominantly gay, Caucasian victims in North America. Those yawning gaps in medical knowledge invite sinister speculation, and conspiracy theories are fed by tantalizing bits of evidence from the public (or not-so-public) record.

On June 9, 1969, a high-level biological research administrator for the U.S. Defense Department, Dr. Donald MacArthur, appeared before a House subcommittee on military appropriations, seeking funds for a new line of research. "Within five to ten years," MacArthur testified, "it would probably be possible to make a new infective microorganism which would differ in certain important aspects from any known disease-causing organisms. Most important of these is that it might be refractory to the immunological and therapeutic processes upon which we depend to maintain our relative freedom from infectious disease. Should an enemy develop it, there is little doubt that this is an important area of potential military technological inferiority in which there is no adequate research program." Congress funded MacArthur's research—and AIDS surfaced in Africa a decade later, during 1977–78.

Coincidence?

On July 4, 1984, a New Delhi newspaper called the *Patriot* published the first accusation that AIDS was created as a weapon by the U.S. Army. Citing articles from an official army research publication on "natural and artificial influences on the human immune system," *Patriot* reporters claimed that scientists from the Army Biological Warfare Laboratory at Fort Detrick, Maryland (known since 1969 as the National Cancer Institute's Frederick Cancer Research Facility), scoured Africa to find "a powerful virus that could not be found in Europe or Asia." When located, the *Patriot* claimed that material "was then analyzed at Fort Detrick and the result was the isolation of a virus that causes AIDS."

Army spokesmen branded the *Patriot* report an example of "infectious propaganda" from RUSSIA, but the story would not die. In 1986, two French-born scientists living in East Germany, Jakob and Lilli Segal, published a pamphlet titled *AIDS: USA Home-Made Evil.* The document, circulated widely in Europe and Africa, claimed that HIV is a genetically engineered hybrid of the visan virus (source of a brain disease borne by sheep) and a virus dubbed HTLV-I

(known as a cause of cancer in white blood cells). Army denials persisted, but Col. David Huxsoll created further doubt in February 1987 with a public announcement that "studies at army laboratories have shown that the AIDS virus would be an extremely poor biological warfare agent." (Huxsoll later denied ever making that statement; the reporter who quoted him maintains that his report was accurate.)

If gays were targeted for a secret biowarfare blitz, how and when did it happen? In 1978, more than 1,000 nonmonogamous gay men received experimental hepatitis B vaccinations at the New York Blood Center in Manhattan, sponsored by the Centers for Disease Control and the National Institutes of Health. The first U.S. cases of AIDS were recorded among New York gays in 1979; by 1985, 64 percent of the original CDC-NIH test group in Manhattan were dying from AIDS. At the same time, two other "new" diseases surfaced among Manhattan homosexuals. One, a herpes virus now believed to cause Kaposi's sarcoma (also known as "gay cancer") is closely related to a cancer-causing herpes strain studied in U.S. animal research labs a decade before AIDS appeared. The other, an infectious microbe christened *Mycoplasma penetrans,* attacks the patient's circulatory and respiratory systems. Its origin remains officially unknown.

AIR America

Once the largest unofficial airline in the world, Air America evolved from a makeshift operation in the 1930s when Gen. Claire Chennault's "American Volunteer Group" was dispatched to aid CHINA in its long war against JAPAN. In December 1941 the PEARL HARBOR attack eliminated any vestiges of feigned U.S. neutrality, but the covert tradition died hard. In 1947, the CENTRAL INTELLIGENCE AGENCY (CIA) and the State Department used the framework of Chennault's old group to create Civil Air Transport (CAT), operating a fleet of aircraft to assist Nationalist Chinese forces in their war against the communist troops of MAO ZEDONG. With the Red victory, CAT moved its headquarters to TAIWAN, continuing support for "Free China" while operating routine passenger flights throughout Southeast Asia. The Korean War (1950–53) found CAT pilots flying more covert missions on behalf of "democracy." The end of that "police action" brought diversification, with CAT elements operating as Southern Air Transport,

Air America, and Air Asia Ltd. Mercenary pilots hired with U.S. taxpayers' money flew various illicit (and unrecorded) missions, including support for FRANCE in its losing battle to maintain control of Indochina (today VIETNAM, LAOS, and CAMBODIA).

In the 1960s, as the United States assumed the French imperial burden in Vietnam, the CIA consolidated its various client airlines under the single logo of Air America. Most of the pilots were military veterans, responding to advertisements for "the most highly skilled, adventurous, and patriotic aviation personnel who could be found." Air America's motto was "Anything, Anytime, Anywhere"—a catchall that included illegal supply flights from Vietnam into Laos and Cambodia, as well as transportation of HEROIN shipments from Asia's "Golden Triangle" to the United States. Air America officially disbanded in 1975 with the fall of Saigon. Twelve years later on May 30, 1987, former CIA Director William Colby dedicated an Air America Memorial at the University of Texas in Dallas.

ALBANIA

Located on the eastern shore of the Adriatic Sea, Albania was ruled from ancient times successively by Rome (to A.D. 535), the Byzantine Empire (535–1444), and the Ottoman Turks (1446–1912). It was then, and remains today, one of the poorest European nations. A ravaged battlefield in World War I, Albania emerged from that conflict to declare itself a republic, but Muslim strongman Ahmed Zogu proclaimed himself president in 1925 and then switched his title to king (Zog I) three years later. He ruled until 1939, when Benito Mussolini's fascist government annexed Albania. Near the end of World War II, in 1944, Communist guerrillas led by Enver Hoxha liberated Albania from Italian occupation.

Unfortunately for natives who expected liberty, Hoxha was a devotee of Soviet dictator JOSEPH STALIN and emulated Stalin's brutal methods of suppressing dissent. In 1961 Hoxha broke with RUSSIA over personal and political differences with Nikita Khrushchev, forging a new alliance with the Chinese government of MAO ZEDONG. With Mao's death in 1978, Hoxha was set adrift, pursuing his own dead-end policies that left Albania the most impoverished and isolated country in Europe. Ramiz Alia succeeded Hoxha in 1985, and public faith in COMMUNISM remained strong, despite the nation's failed economy.

Reds won a decisive victory in the March 1991 elections, even as the Soviet Union collapsed, but a general strike and riotous street demonstrations soon forced the ruling cabinet to resign. A change of names and public policy failed to carry 1992's election for the former Communist (now Socialist) Party, as Dr. Sali Berisha became Albania's first elected president.

Unfortunately, Albania's democratic experiment failed in early 1997 when a series of shady pyramid schemes collapsed, robbing gullible investors of $1.2 billion in savings. The furious dupes turned their wrath on the government, which had naively endorsed the swindlers. Rioting destroyed Albania's fragile infrastructure, while rebels and organized gangsters turned the country into a free-for-all shooting gallery. A multinational force of 6,000 peacekeepers arrived to restore a semblance of order and supervise elections that ousted President Berisha from office. Trouble continued for Albania at the turn of the new millennium. Ethnic cleansing in neighboring SERBIA drove 440,000 Albanian expatriates back to their ancestral homeland. Since then, a witch's brew of political dissension, minority rebellion, organized crime, and economic instability has frustrated efforts to create a functioning democracy in this troubled land.

ALEPH   See AUM SHINRIKYO.

ALEXANDER I (1888–1934)

Alexander I had ruled as king of Yugoslavia for 13 years, by the time an assassin took his life on October 9, 1934. The king was in Marseille, riding in an open car with French foreign minister Louis Barthou, when Croatian nationalist Petrus Kaleman leaped onto the vehicle's running board and killed both men with close-range fire from an automatic rifle. Kaleman, in turn, was seized and fatally beaten by security police; another 40 persons were injured when mounted guards charged into a crowd along the parade route. Detectives of the French Sûreté declared the double murder the result of a conspiracy among Croatian rebels. As a result of the slayings, the League of Nations established two international conventions to combat political TERRORISM in 1937: The Convention for the Prevention and Punishment of Terrorism "criminalized" attacks on heads of state and other "internationally protected persons," while the Convention for the Creation of an International Criminal

Court sought to enforce those regulations. However, since few nations (including the United States) ratified either convention, they had no legally binding effect.

ALEXANDER II (1818–1881)

Czar Alexander II ruled RUSSIA with an iron hand for 26 years before he was assassinated on March 1, 1881. The murder was carried out by members of a radical group called *Narodnya Volya* ("The People's Will"), organized with an estimated 500 members in 1875. Czar Alexander was traveling by coach to view the wreckage of a recent *Narodnya Volya* bombing in St. Petersburg, when suicide bomber Ivan Grinevetsky attacked the royal coach, killing himself along with his target. Various conspirators, including ringleader Sophia Petrovskaya, were soon rounded up by police, convicted at a perfunctory trial, and speedily hanged. In addition to Czar Alexander, other Russian officials who were slain by *Narodnya Volya* included the governor-general of St. Petersburg and a chief of the dreaded OKHRANA.

ALGERIA

Beginning in the seventh century B.C., Algeria has been pillaged by successive invaders including Romans, Vandals, Hafsids, Merenids, assorted pirates, Spaniards, Arabs, and Turks. French soldiers conquered the country in 1830, and Algeria was named an "integral part" of FRANCE in 1848. French colonists put down roots with a vengeance, brutally resisting when a nationalist uprising in 1954–55 escalated into full-scale war between France and Algeria's National Liberation Front (FLN). President Charles de Gaulle opened peace negotiations in 1962, prompting renegade elements of the French army—calling themselves the OAS (Secret Army Organization)—to plot de Gaulle's assassination. Acts of TERRORISM in Algeria and France failed to stop Algerian independence in July 1962, but FLN victory did not end the violence.

Ahmed Ben Bella was elected premier in October 1963, but his regime was overthrown on June 19, 1965, by military forces under Col. Houari Boumediene. Boumediene promptly suspended Algeria's constitution in a bid to "restore economic stability," but the resultant military government was not a typical right-wing junta. Recalling their revolutionary roots, Algeria's new leaders welcomed radicals from around the world—including members of the BLACK PANTHER PARTY, the IRISH REPUBLICAN ARMY, and various Palestinian groups engaged in war against ISRAEL—to train at desert camps described by U.S. spokesmen as "schools for terrorism."

Algeria's first-ever parliamentary elections were held in December 1991, but army leaders invalidated the results after members of fundamentalist Islamic Salvation Front (FIS) won a majority of votes. That autocratic move plunged the nation into bloody civil war, which continues to the present day. Chief among the current rebel factions is the Armed Islamic Group (GIA), headquartered on the Mitidja Plain outside Algiers (lately dubbed the "Triangle of Death"). Estimated body counts for the latest Algerian conflict range from 100,000 to 250,000 or more. Wholesale slaughter of civilians has flourished since February 1997 when GIA leaders vowed to "slash the throats of all apostates and their allies." Observers briefly hoped for peace with Abdelaziz Bouteflika's ascension to the presidency in April 1999, but conflicts with the military have emasculated Bouteflika's administration. Despite a facade of democracy, Algeria is essentially a military dictatorship with Islamic militants and a long-disaffected Berber minority engaged in perpetual rebellion.

ALIEN abductions

Since the mid-1960s a sizable body of literature has developed purporting to describe or debunk the alleged phenomenon of humans being kidnapped and detained by the (apparently extraterrestrial) occupants of unidentified flying objects (UFOS). Believers in the alien abduction phenomenon range from self-described abductees to psychiatrists and professors at prestigious universities. Their critics—some with equally impressive scientific credentials, others simply professional naysayers—insist that such reports are the result of deliberate hoaxes or mental illness, with the latter (typically long-distance) diagnoses running the gamut from FALSE MEMORY SYNDROME to full-blown psychosis.

Reports of UFOs—which may be any airborne object unidentified by its immediate observers—are as old as human history. "Close encounters" with UFO pilots or passengers are a more recent phenomenon, with reports from Europe and North America apparently beginning in the 19th century.

The best-known cases of alleged alien abduction include the following:

September 1961—Barney and Betty Hill reportedly experienced a "missing time" phenomenon while driving near Portsmouth, New Hampshire. Under hypnosis they later recalled an alien abduction that included medical experiments. Their case went public in 1966 in a two-part series in *Look* magazine and in John Fuller's book *The Interrupted Journey*. The case was subsequently dramatized in a made-for-television movie, *The UFO Incident*.

January 25, 1967—Betty Andreasson was allegedly taken by five-foot-tall aliens from her home in South Ashburnham, Massachusetts, while relatives stood paralyzed and helpless to assist her. She later recovered fragmentary memories of the event.

December 3, 1967—Police Sergeant Herbert Schrimer lost consciousness after seeing a UFO in Ashland, Nebraska, and woke with "a red welt on the nerve cord" behind one of his ears. Two months later, under hypnosis, Schrimer described his conversation with "a white blurred object" that descended from the UFO.

October 11, 1973—Mississippi residents Charles Hickson and Calvin Potter were night fishing along the Pascagoula River when they allegedly sighted a UFO and were carried aboard by three of the craft's occupants. They were released 20 minutes later, after the aliens told them, "We are peaceful. We mean you no harm." Hickson reportedly passed a polygraph test administered by private investigators on October 30 and appeared on Dick Cavett's TV talk show in January 1974. Parker, meanwhile, shunned publicity and moved out of state.

November 5, 1975—Logger Travis Walton was allegedly beamed aboard a hovering UFO near Heber, Arizona, in full view of six coworkers. He was found five days later, nude and incoherent, but later recovered fragmentary and horrific memories of his captivity aboard the UFO. In Walton's absence the six witnesses (suspected by police of murdering Walton and hiding his body) sat for polygraph tests. Five were rated "truthful" in their description of the incident, while the sixth—a convicted felon—yielded "inconclusive" test results. The incident was later dramatized in the motion picture *Fire in the Sky* (1993).

August 26, 1976—Four fishermen were allegedly abducted by aliens near Allagash, Maine. Their case was later detailed by author Ray Fowler in *The Allagash Abductions* (1994)—and may well have inspired Stephen King's best-selling novel *Dreamcatcher* (2001).

December 1977—Bloomington, Indiana, resident Debbie Jordan was reportedly abducted from her home. A decade later, author Budd Hopkins described the incident in his book *Intruders* (1987). Jordan maintains an Internet Web site with details of the case at www.debshome.com.

1987—Best-selling science-fiction author Whitley Strieber published *Communion*, the first of several "nonfiction" books detailing his own alleged experience with alien kidnappers. Strieber's background (and the profits derived from his books) prompted skeptics to suggest a long-running hoax.

September 1990—Three anonymous witnesses (said to include an elected official and two government agents) allegedly saw a woman "floating" from a 12th-story apartment window in Manhattan, accompanied by three small aliens who steered her levitating body toward a hovering UFO. When all were safely aboard, the craft nose-dived into the East River. Author Budd Hopkins reported the case in his book *Witnessed* (1996).

By June 1992 the alien abduction phenomenon was regarded seriously enough in some circles to rate a five-day conference at the Massachusetts Institute of Technology (MIT), chaired by MIT physicist David Pritchard and Harvard psychiatrist John Mack. One topic of discussion was the so-called missing embryo/fetus syndrome (ME/FS) that was reported by some female subjects who claim unexplained and prematurely terminated pregnancies following their abductions. Although such incidents are "now considered one of the more common effects of the abduction experience," according to author David Jacobs in his book *Secret Life* (1992), a report to the MIT conference found no confirmatory evidence. "By now," Dr. John Miller told the gathering, "we should have some medically well-documented cases of this, but we don't. Proof of a case of ME/FS has proved entirely elusive."

The same is apparently true of other physical "evidence" reported by alleged abductees. Such phenomena as bloody noses, cuts, bruises, burns, and "scoop marks" are cited as proof of alien contact, but all have plausible explanations in everyday life. Various subjects report surgical implants in their heads or other parts of their bodies, but again none are confirmed. Alleged abductee Richard Price submitted a tiny object, surgically removed from his penis, for testing at MIT as a suspected "alien implant." Laboratory analysis concluded that the object consisted of "successive layers of human tissue formed around some initial abnormality or trauma, occasionally accreting fibers of cotton from Price's underwear that became incorporated into this artifact as the tissue hardened."

Such verdicts do not faze believers, including many who suspect an intergalactic conspiracy of silence surpassing anything seen on *The X-Files*. In 1998, author Ann Druffel published a book titled *How to Defend Yourself Against Alien Abduction,* with the recommended defensive techniques including mental and physical struggle, "righteous anger" and "protective rage" (both "best employed before the onset of paralysis"), and prayers to divine entities (named by Druffel as "the most powerful technique yet discovered" for repelling alien kidnappers). If simple attitude proves ineffective, Druffel's readers are advised to employ various flowers, herbs, crucifixes, metal fans, and "bar magnets crossed over the chest" to discourage abduction. Failure to be kidnapped by a snatch squad from beyond the stars presumably suggests that the repellents are effective.

ALPHA 66

Alpha 66 ranks among the most violent and most notorious of the Cuban-exile groups devoted to overthrowing FIDEL CASTRO's regime in Havana. Official histories of the organization claim it was founded in PUERTO RICO sometime in the latter part of 1961. The group's cryptic name allegedly combines the first letter of the Greek alphabet (marking "the beginning" of exile campaigns against Castro) with the number of men present at its founding (66).

Throughout 40-odd years of arson, bombing, murder, and futile commando raids against CUBA, Castro has charged—and U.S. intelligence "insiders" privately agree—that Alpha 66 enjoys covert support from the FEDERAL BUREAU OF INVESTIGATION (FBI),

the CENTRAL INTELLIGENCE AGENCY (CIA), and other organs of the U.S. government. (In 1976, Alpha 66 leader Antonio Veciana Banch told the CHURCH COMMITTEE that his group was actively supported by the CIA from 1960 to 1973, during which time the group participated in CIA-MAFIA plots to kill Castro.) That relationship has not always been a friendly one, however. Following the BAY OF PIGS fiasco, Attorney General Robert KENNEDY staged raids against exile training camps run by the CIA in conjunction with elements of the Mafia, the KU KLUX KLAN, and other criminal groups. Antipathy toward President John Kennedy was so pronounced among right-wing Cuban exiles that they remain prime suspects in the 1963 JFK ASSASSINATION, and members of Alpha 66 were questioned in 1977 by the HOUSE SELECT COMMITTEE ON ASSASSINATIONS.

While acts of TERRORISM linked to Alpha 66 could fill a hefty volume of their own, prosecutions in the United States have been few and far between. Five armed members of the group were captured in Cuba in December 1968, but U.S. authorities made no effort to punish Alpha 66 for violating neutrality laws. Two years later in September 1970, Cuban authorities announced the capture of nine more Alpha 66 commandos on the island. Terrorist actions in Cuba continued through the 1990s—including three drive-by shootings at the same Havana hotel between March 1994 and May 1995—while the FBI professed inability to find the men responsible. Similar failure resulted in various crimes committed on U.S. soil, thereby strengthening the widespread belief that Alpha's efforts were endorsed from Washington. The group remains active today, claiming chapters in various U.S. cities with large Cuban-American populations.

al-Qaeda See under *Q.*

AMERICA First Committee

Established in September 1940, the America First Committee (AFC) was ostensibly an isolationist group opposed to U.S. involvement in World War II. Although its membership included prominent Americans of every political stripe, the group's public tone was set by inclusion of outspoken bigots including Henry FORD and one-time hero aviator Charles Lindbergh. Both men were bitter racists and anti-Semites: Ford had spent the 1920s reviling Jews in his newspaper, the *Dearborn Independent,* while Lindbergh was compromised by visits to Nazi GERMANY, where he fathered three illegitimate children and accepted a medal from Reichsmarshal Hermann Göring in October 1938. A public endorsement from Jew-baiting Rev. Charles Coughlin in April 1941 cinched the AFC's reputation as a thinly veiled pro-Nazi propaganda vehicle. Lindbergh himself confirmed that judgment in a speech at Des Moines, Iowa, where he declared that the "three most important groups who have been pressing this country toward war are the British, the Jewish, and the Roosevelt administration." Soon after, in another public statement, Lindbergh said that "the Jewish people are a large factor in our movement toward war."

Flagrant bigotry notwithstanding, the AFC attracted some 800,000 members to 450 local chapters by autumn 1941. Many recruits were die-hard enemies of the NEW DEAL, seeking any vehicle to punish Franklin Roosevelt for "socializing" America. Some sources claim that the AFC formally dissolved on December 11, 1941, four days after the Japanese raid on PEARL HARBOR, but Lindbergh and company seemed unaware of that fact when he addressed an audience of 50 AFC members in New York City on December 17. Wound up to fever pitch by the U.S. declaration of war against Germany and JAPAN, Lindbergh railed that there was "only one danger in the world, namely, the Yellow Danger." Japan and CHINA (at war with Tokyo for the past decade, now America's ally) were really "allied together against the white race," Lindbergh claimed, lamenting that Washington had missed a chance to use Germany "as a weapon against this alliance." (Lindbergh's genius apparently did not extend to recognizing Germany's alliance with Japan against the United States.) Instead of joining ADOLF HITLER to preserve a white world, Lindbergh ranted, U.S. troops were "fighting on the side of the Russians and Chinese." Worse yet, he said, Washington had "no plan and does not know what it is fighting for."

The federal government knew whom Lindbergh supported, however. On February 23, 1934, FEDERAL BUREAU OF INVESTIGATION Director J. EDGAR HOOVER reported to Roosevelt that the AFC was funded by Nazi supporters, including Axel Wenner-Gren, a pro-German financier in Sweden. As recently as November 1941, Hoover noted, AFC spokesman (and former Wisconsin governor) Robert La Follette had called for violent revolution by "fearless red-blooded Americans to overthrow the government." Such revelations, coupled with the extremist remarks of AFC leaders themselves, combined to destroy the group's once-substantial public influence by 1943.

AMERICAN Indian Movement

Patterned after the California-based BLACK PANTHER PARTY, the American Indian Movement (AIM) was organized in Minneapolis during the summer of 1968. As chapters spread across the country, AIM began to garner national attention. Members participated in the 1969 occupation of Alcatraz Island, though AIM did not initiate the move. A 1972 "Trail of Broken Treaties" march on Washington, D.C. climaxed with presentation of a 20-point solution paper to President RICHARD NIXON. The following year, a 71-day occupation of Wounded Knee, South Dakota, included violent clashes with the FEDERAL BUREAU OF INVESTIGATION (FBI) and U.S. Army, and the government-sponsored vigilante group GUARDIANS OF THE OGLALA NATION (GOON), resulting in exposure of the FBI's illegal tactics. A total of 1,162 persons were finally arrested, including 562 siege participants and 600 others detained across the country for supporting AIM. Of the 1,162 initially jailed, only 185 were finally indicted, some of them on multiple felony charges. Trials spanned the next two years, but the most important was the trial of AIM leaders Dennis Banks and Russell Means in 1974. Each defendant was charged with 13 counts, including arson, burglary, criminal conspiracy, theft, interfering with federal officers, and possession of illegal weapons. Judge Fred Nichol ultimately dismissed all charges, lamenting from the bench that "the FBI I have revered so long, has stooped so low." Nichol added:

Although it hurts me deeply, I am forced to the conclusion that the prosecution in the trial had something other than attaining justice foremost in its mind. . . . The fact that the incidents of misconduct formed a pattern throughout the course of the trial leads me to the belief that this case was not prosecuted in good faith or in the spirit of justice. The waters of justice have been polluted, and dismissal, I believe, is the appropriate cure for the pollution in this case.

Still, the GOON campaign of TERRORISM continued at Pine Ridge for another two years. On June 26,

1975, a shootout occurred on the reservation between FBI agents and members of AIM, claiming the lives Agents Jack Coler and Ronald Williams, along with AIM member Joe Killsright. On November 25, 1975, a federal grand jury indicted four AIM members for the Coler-Williams murders. Defendants Darelle Butler, James Eagle, and Robert Robideau were already in custody, while 31-year-old Leonard Peltier remained at large. Canadian police captured Peltier at Hinton, Alberta, on February 6, 1976, and extradited him to the United States on December 18. At trial, defendants Butler and Robideau admitted firing on Coler and Williams, but they claimed that the G-men had started the shootout; jurors acquitted both men on July 16, 1976, accepting their plea of self-defense. Prosecutors dropped all charges against James Eagle on September 8, 1976, leaving Peltier as the only defendant in the case. At his trial, beginning in March 1977, the government claimed Peltier alone had shot both agents, killing them execution style with rifle bullets fired at point-blank range. To prove that case, prosecutors illegally suppressed an FBI memo of October 2, 1975, stating that Peltier's weapon "contains a different firing pin than that in [the] rifle used at [the] . . . scene." Deprived of that exculpatory evidence, jurors convicted Peltier on April 18, 1977. Six weeks later, on June 1, 1977, Judge Paul Benson sentenced Peltier to two consecutive life terms. Today, many FBI critics still regard his trial as a deliberate frame-up.

AIM remains active today, though its programs rarely make national headlines. FBI harassment has presumably ceased, though members still recall an off-the-record comment from one G-man after Wounded Knee: "Half the stuff that went on out there isn't even on paper." In 2000 FBI Director Louis Freeh lobbied publicly (and successfully) to discourage President Bill Clinton from pardoning Leonard Peltier.

See also CLINTON, BILL AND HILLARY.

AMERICAN Legion

Organized by veterans of the First World War in 1919, the American Legion was created to promote "100% Americanism"—defined by its founders as militant opposition to all things "radical" or "Bolshevik." Violence quickly followed, with at least five deaths resulting by year's end, as legionnaires attacked unfriendly editors, suspected communists, or union strikers. The early legion plainly favored FASCISM, as witnessed by its 1923 pledge of honorary membership to Italian dictator Benito Mussolini. Two years later, national commander Alvin Owsley granted a newspaper interview that included threats to overthrow the U.S. government.

> *"If ever needed [said Owsley], the American Legion stands ready to protect our country's Institutions and ideals as the Fascisti dealt with the destructionists who menaced Italy!"*
> *"By taking over the Government?" he was asked.*
> *"Exactly that," he replied. "The American Legion is fighting every element that threatens our democratic government—Soviets, anarchists, IWW, revolutionary Socialists and any other 'Red.'. . . . Do not forget that the Fascisti are to Italy what the American Legion is to the United States."*

Nine years later, in the spring of 1934, high-ranking legionnaires attempted to carry out Owsley's threat, operating through a front group called the AMERICAN LIBERTY LEAGUE. On the eve of World War II, legion commanders announced their plan to organize a civilian spy network, keeping track of perceived "subversives" from coast to coast. Attorney General Robert Jackson sidetracked the vigilante campaign by authorizing the FEDERAL BUREAU OF INVESTIGATION (FBI) American Legion Contact Program, whereby some 40,000 legionnaires were recruited as "confidential national defense informants," reporting gossip about their coworkers and neighbors. So successful was the program, filling J. EDGAR HOOVER's private files with much information he might otherwise have missed, that it was continued until 1966.

From the 1940s onward, legionnaires provided Hoover's most dependable forum for speeches attacking communists, civil rights activists, antiwar protesters, and other enemies of the FBI, but collaboration was not always peaceful. The legion's super-patriots took themselves too seriously at times, as during the McCarthy era of the early 1950s. In 1953 Hoover ordered Inspector Cartha DeLoach to join the legion and "straighten it out." DeLoach enlisted, rising swiftly to become a post commander, department commander, and then national vice-commander. Legionnaires wanted to elect him as their national commander in 1958, but Hoover vetoed the move, deeming the top post "too political." Instead, DeLoach became chairman of the legion's national public-relations commission, ensuring that any public criticism of Hoover or the FBI was met by immediate protest from legion posts nationwide, scripted by ghost writers in the FBI's Crime Records Division.

AMERICAN Liberty League

In July 1933 retired U.S. Marine Corps Maj. Gen. Smedley Butler received a visit from two prominent AMERICAN LEGION officials, William Doyle and Gerald MacGuire, requesting that Butler campaign for election as the legion's next national commander. The thoughtful legionnaires assured Butler that cash had been collected to finance his campaign, yet Butler demurred when the pair produced a speech for him to deliver at the legion convention in Chicago, including demands for a U.S. return to the gold standard. A year later, MacGuire approached Butler again, this time hailing the role military veterans had played in bringing FASCISM to GERMANY and ITALY. MacGuire asked Butler to lead a veteran's march on Washington, where they would stage a coup d'état against President Franklin Roosevelt and save the United States from a "communist menace."

Although convinced that "the whole affair smacked of treason," Butler requested further details. MacGuire spelled out a plan to seize the government by force and install a suitable strongman in the White House. The plotters had $3 million in hand, with more on tap whenever they needed it, MacGuire said. "Is there anything stirring yet?" Butler asked. "Yes, you watch," MacGuire replied. "In two or three weeks, you will see it come out in the papers."

Two weeks later, in August 1934, the American Liberty League was publicly launched by a coalition of right-wing financiers and politicians known for strident opposition to Roosevelt's NEW DEAL. Included were directors and officers of U.S. Steel, General Motors, STANDARD OIL, J.C. Penney, Montgomery Ward, Goodyear Tire, Mutual Life Insurance, and the members of the wealthy DUPONT family. After MacGuire approached him a third time, Butler told his story to FEDERAL BUREAU OF INVESTIGATION Director J. EDGAR HOOVER, followed by an appearance before the HOUSE COMMITTEE ON UN-AMERICAN ACTIVITIES. No leaders of the league were called to testify, but exposure of the group's plans in media reports caused prominent backers to distance themselves from the group. A half-baked scheme to run Georgia governor (and KU KLUX KLAN ally) Eugene Talmadge for president died on the drawing board, and the league dissolved in 1936.

AMES, Aldrich Hazen (1941–)

The son of a CENTRAL INTELLIGENCE AGENCY (CIA) officer, born June 26, 1941, Aldrich Ames worked summer jobs for the agency in his teens and joined full-time in February 1962. He quickly mastered Russian and distinguished himself in handling matters related to the Soviet Union. Lust intervened to sidetrack his career in 1981 while Ames was assigned to Mexico City. There, he met and fell in love with Maria del Rosario Casas Dupuy, a cultural attaché with the Colombian embassy who persuaded Ames to divorce his wife and marry her. Ames soon discovered that his salary could not satisfy Maria's expensive tastes, and his quest for additional money led him to become a mercenary Russian "mole" within the CIA.

Between 1985 and his arrest on February 21, 1994, Ames earned more than $2.5 million by selling classified information to Russian spies, his betrayal continuing beyond the 1991 collapse of the Soviet Union. Aside from delivering thousands of CIA documents, Ames also identified 25 Russian nationals employed as spies by the CIA or the FEDERAL BUREAU OF INVESTIGATION (FBI). All were arrested by the KGB, with at least 10 subsequently executed. Those losses belatedly prompted a joint CIA-FBI investigation, beginning in 1991, but both agencies somehow ignored Ames's extravagant lifestyle until May 1993 when he was betrayed by a KGB defector. G-men then placed Ames under close surveillance, including phone taps, searches of his household trash (revealing notes from a Russian contact), and retrieval of information stored on his computer. Ames and his wife were both indicted on April 26, 1994, Ames quickly striking a bargain on Maria's behalf. The couple pleaded guilty to various charges on April 28, Ames receiving a sentence of life without parole for conspiracy and tax fraud, while Maria received a sentence of five years and three months. Both the FBI and the CIA were widely criticized for their apparent negligence in plugging the deadly intelligence leak.

ANARCHISTS

In its purest form, anarchism is the belief that all forms of government should be abolished. Historically, some anarchists have gone beyond mere advocacy and have attempted to secure their goal by physical attacks on prominent officials in Europe and the United States. Before the advent of Bolshevism with the Russian Revolution of 1917, "radicals" and "enemy aliens" in the United States were likely to be branded *anarchists* regardless of their actual philosophy. The same label was also broadly applied to social reformers and labor organizers, just as a later generation of activists would be falsely branded *Communist*.

America's anarchist panic dated from 1880 with the onset of a major immigration wave from ITALY. On May 4, 1886, the Chicago Haymarket bombing killed eight policemen and an uncertain number of civilians and injured more than 260 others at a rally for striking workers. Eight alleged anarchists were convicted of conspiracy, though evidence proved that none of them had thrown the bomb. Fear of anarchism increased with each reported act of violence. In 1900, Italian anarchist Gaetano Bresci left his adopted home in New Jersey to assassinate King Umberto I of Italy. The following year, anarchist Leon Czolgosz shot and killed President William McKinley in Buffalo, New York. McKinley's successor, Theodore Roosevelt, created the Bureau of Investigation (later, the FEDERAL BUREAU OF INVESTIGATION [FBI]) and signed legislation to stifle the anarchist press in 1908. Four years later, two immigrant labor organizers were framed on murder charges (but were finally acquitted) during a textile strike at Lawrence, Massachusetts. Colorado's Ludlow massacre of 1914 prompted three anarchists to plot the murder of

In 1901, anarchist Leon Czolgosz (left) assassinated President William McKinley (right), and the murder sparked widespread fear of anarchists in the United States. (Author's collection)

Emma Goldman (left) was among those deported to Russia in 1919 along with another advocate of violent revolution, Alexander Berkman (right). (Author's collection)

industrialist John D. ROCKEFELLER (and thus sparked creation of the New York City bomb squad). Two more anarchists were arrested (some say framed) in New York the following year for plotting to blow up St. Patrick's Cathedral.

"Progressive" president Woodrow Wilson reserved some of his harshest words and legislation for "enemy aliens" on the eve of America's entry into World War I. The bolshevik revolution of 1917 gave nativists a new reason to tremble, but communism and anarchism (or "syndicalism") were confused in many minds, including that of a fledgling clerk at the JUSTICE DEPARTMENT named J. EDGAR HOOVER. War's end brought no cessation of violence, as a wave of strikes and riots sparked fears of an anarchist revolt in the United States.

Those fears were exacerbated in April 1919 when 29 bombs were sent through the mail to various prominent targets around the United States. The first was detected and disarmed on April 28 at the home of Seattle mayor Ole Hanson (who had recently used troops to crush a strike by 60,000 shipyard workers). The next day, in Atlanta, a parcel bomb exploded at the home of former U.S. Senator Thomas Hardwick, maiming one of his servants. During the next week, 34 more bombs were intercepted and defused without further injury. Their targets included Frederick Howe (commissioner of immigration at Ellis Island); Senator Lee Overman (chairman of a series of recent hearings on the bolshevik menace); Supreme Court Justice Oliver Wendell Holmes, Jr.; U.S. Postmaster General Albert Burlson; Secretary of Labor William Wilson; Attorney General A. Mitchell Palmer; federal judge Kenesaw Landis (who had sentenced IWW leaders to prison); and two living symbols of unfettered capitalism, J.P. MORGAN and John D. Rockefeller.

The bombers tried again on the night of June 3, 1919. This time they delivered their "infernal devices" by hand and all detonated, but the only casualties were two of the bombers themselves. In Washington, D.C., a blast outside the home of Attorney General Palmer damaged houses within a two-block radius, shredding the bodies of two clumsy saboteurs who would remain forever unidentified. Other bombs rocked targets in Boston; Cleveland; New York City; Newtonville, Massachusetts; Paterson, New Jersey; Philadelphia; and Pittsburgh, without further injury. Handbills were found at most of the bombing scenes, signed by "The Anarchist Fighters." Palmer and J. Edgar Hoover struck back with a vengeance between November 1919 and January 1920 with a series of coordinated dragnet raids designed to capture and deport alleged "enemy aliens." Thousands were arrested without warrants or specific charges from coast to coast, but fewer than 600 were finally deported; most were released without so much as an apology for their detention and occasional subjection to brutal "third-degree" tactics in custody. The sweeping PALMER RAIDS produced no suspects in the 1919 bombing, and publicity surrounding the fiasco boomeranged against Palmer in Congress, where exposure of his vigilante tactics doomed his presidential ambitions and soon drove him from office in disgrace. (Hoover dodged the axe and lived to raid another day, concocting fables that he had "deplored" the raids, although surviving documents prove that he personally organized and supervised every aspect of the events.)

On September 16, 1920, a horse-drawn wagon filled with dynamite and iron sash weights exploded outside the Wall Street offices of J.P. Morgan in Manhattan. Its detonation, timed to coincide with a lunchtime exodus of workers from buildings in the financial district, instantly killed 30 victims and injured at least 300 (of whom 10 more would die from shrapnel wounds). Hundreds of windows were shattered, some as far as a quarter-mile from ground zero. William Flynn, chief of the U.S. SECRET SERVICE (and soon to be director of the FBI), denied that the bombing was an attempt to murder Morgan, even then vacationing in Europe. "This bomb was not directed at Mr. Morgan or any individual," Flynn declared. "In my opinion it was planted in the financial heart of America as a defiance of the American people. I'm convinced a nationwide dynamiting conspiracy exists to wreck the American government and society." As for the authors of that conspiracy, veteran Red-hunter Flynn had no doubts: they were the same anarchists blamed for the still-unsolved bombings of 1919. Attorney General Palmer arrested William ("Big Bill") Haywood, boss of the radical Industrial Workers of the World, "as a precaution," but no evidence was found linking Haywood or his "Wobblies" to the crime.

ANDERSON, Jack (1922–)

Born in 1922, newsman Jack Anderson first gained national prominence in the late 1940s when he joined Drew Pearson at the *Washington Post,* helping to produce the nationally syndicated "Washington Merry-Go-Round" column. Ironically, Anderson owed his position to J. EDGAR HOOVER, who informed Pearson that his former aide (Andrew Older) was a communist. Pearson promptly fired Older and hired Anderson to replace him. Anderson, in turn, became friendly with Senator Joseph McCarthy, funneling information from Pearson's private files to McCarthy without Pearson's knowledge. Although forewarned that the files contained unverified allegations, McCarthy quoted the information as factual, thereby losing Anderson's support. In 1951, after publicly questioning the use of FEDERAL BUREAU OF INVESTIGATION (FBI) agents to escort McCarthy's secretary on a visit to Hawaii, Anderson and Pearson were placed on the bureau's "no contact" list.

Despite that ostracism, the columnists still praised Hoover effusively through the 1960s until the relationship finally soured in 1968, when Pearson and Anderson began to investigate Senator Thomas Dodd, a former G-man and the FBI's unofficial mouthpiece on Capitol Hill. FBI agents tried to foil that investigation by stealing some of Anderson's mail, the theft later acknowledged by U.S. Postmaster General Lawrence O'Brien. The columnists retaliated with a December 1968 article in *True* magazine, predicting that America was witnessing "the last days of J. Edgar Hoover." The piece ascribed Hoover's "sainthood" to "40 years of planted press notices," without mentioning that Anderson and Pearson had participated in the charade.

FBI surveillance of Anderson continued into the 1970s, joined by agents of the CENTRAL INTELLI-

GENCE AGENCY (CIA), the INTERNAL REVENUE SERVICE, and military intelligence. Anderson turned the tables by interviewing Hoover's neighbors and raiding his garbage cans, reversing the standard FBI "trash cover" to report on Hoover's favorite brand of soap and liquor. Anderson won a Pulitzer Prize for his coverage of Washington scandals in 1972, prompting members of RICHARD NIXON's staff (including former FBI agent G. Gordon Liddy) to plot Anderson's assassination. Several methods were discussed, including an LSD-induced car crash and a simulated mugging, before the White House ruled that murder was "too severe a sanction." Instead, Nixon aides asked Hoover to help them discredit Anderson. Hoover cheerfully agreed, denouncing Anderson as "the lowest form of human being to walk the earth," a "journalistic prostitute," and "the top scavenger of all columnists" who would "go lower than dog shit for a story."

On May 1, 1972, Anderson's column branded Hoover "the old curmudgeon of law enforcement," detailing decades of FBI harassment against MARTIN LUTHER KING, JR., and others. Furious, Hoover ordered an investigation to identify Anderson's sources within the bureau, but he never learned the results. Next morning, the FBI director was found dead at his home in Washington, D.C. Anderson subsequently became the first U.S. reporter to expose the CIA's long-running plots to murder Cuban leader FIDEL CASTRO.

ANGLICAN Church

The Anglican Church (or Church of England) was created in 1536 when King Henry VIII dissolved all monasteries and abbeys of the CATHOLIC CHURCH throughout Britain. The rift with Rome resulted in equal parts from a growing Protestant movement in England and from Henry's personal quarrel with the pope (who refused to permit even royal divorces). The Anglican creed followed British colonists to Canada and there became a tool of imperial racism, as thousands of aboriginal children were forcibly installed in church-run "residential schools." Those sectarian institutions worked overtime to break ties between captive students and their native culture, imposing new language, religious creeds, dress codes, and a view of history in which their ancestors were "heathen savages." Many children in the Anglican residential schools were also subjected to sadistic

abuse in the guise of discipline—and to sexual predation which the church long ignored and then actively denied until the cover-up unraveled in the 1970s and 1980s. An official church apology for the abuse in 1998 failed to mollify surviving victims, 12,000 of whom filed a total of 4,500 civil lawsuits seeking monetary damages. In autumn 2002 Anglican leaders agreed to settle out of court: The church agreed to pay victims of the residential school system a total of $25 million. The relatively simple resolution of those claims, while long delayed, stands in sharp contrast to the ongoing scandals surrounding the Catholic Church's protection of PEDOPHILE PRIESTS on four continents.

ANGOLA

The arrival of Portuguese explorers in 1482 spelled disaster for native inhabitants of this nation in southwestern Africa. Soon, Angola became a major source of slaves for PORTUGAL's huge colony of BRAZIL. Rigid colonial rule and brutal suppression of dissent continued through World War II and the 30 years of civil war that followed. Major nationalist groups battling against the colonial regime included the Popular Movement for Liberation of Angola (MPLA), the National Front for the Liberation of Angola (FNLA), and the National Union for the Total Independence of Angola (UNITA). Portugal finally granted Angolan independence in 1975, and the dominant MPLA has controlled the new government ever since, but opposition from UNITA leaders sparked a new civil war that continues to the present day. RUSSIA and CUBA supported the Marxist MPLA government with aid and troops until 1989, while U.S. arms and aid were funneled to UNITA through the CENTRAL INTELLIGENCE AGENCY (CIA). Angola thus became a proxy battlefield for rival superpowers, much as SPAIN had been during its civil war in the 1930s. The UNITED NATIONS supervised free elections in 1992, declaring victory for MPLA incumbent president José Eduardo dos Santos. UNITA contender Jonas Savimbi instantly declared the process fraudulent and resumed armed struggle against the ruling regime. Although (allegedly) deprived of CIA financing, until his death in a gun battle in February 2002, Savimbi controlled 80 percent of Angola's diamond supply, and funded his struggle via outlawed sale of "conflict diamonds" on the global black market.

ANIMAL Liberation Front

The Animal Liberation Front (ALF) was organized in New York City in the early weeks of 1979. Officially, it comprises a loose-knit network of autonomous local units, each of which (in ALF's own words) "carries out direct action against animal abuse in the form of rescuing animals and causing financial loss to animal exploiters, usually through the damage and destruction of property." Such actions are illegal by definition and thus constitute conspiracy, although ALF spokespeople deny the existence of a true organization, maintaining that "any group of people who are vegetarians or vegans and who carry out actions according to ALF guidelines have the right to regard themselves as part of the ALF." A list of ALF actions, taken from the group's own Internet Web site, includes the following:

March 14, 1979—Two dogs, one cat, and two guinea pigs were taken from the New York University Medical Center's lab in New York City.

June 15, 1981—ALF activists in Toronto, Canada, liberated 21 experimental animals from a laboratory at the Hospital for Sick Children.

May 1984—ALF commandos caused $60,000 property damage at the University of Pennsylvania's Head Injury Laboratory, escaping with 60 hours of videotape that was later released as a movie entitled *Unnecessary Fuss,* which proved so disturbing to viewers that funding for the program was ultimately slashed.

January 1, 1985—Canadian ALF activists rescued a rhesus monkey and three cats from a lab at the University of Western Ontario (in London), leaving the facility with $600 in property damage.

April 1985—Nearly 1,000 lab animals were liberated from the University of California at Riverside. An estimated $700,000 in property damage was reported. The intruders escaped with lab documents and videotapes (later released to the media).

October 26, 1986—264 animals were liberated from a breeding facility at the University of Oregon, with $120,000 estimated damage inflicted on the school laboratory.

April 6, 1987—ALF arsonists struck the Animal Diagnostics Laboratory at the University of California in Davis, destroying the lab and damaging 20 university vehicles. Authorities estimated the damage at $5.1 million.

April 2, 1989—Nocturnal raiders took 1,231 lab animals from a Veterans Administration Hospital at the University of Arizona in Tucson. Spray painting and fires set in two laboratory offices caused a total of $500,000 damage.

April 24, 1989—ALF claimed credit for arson fires that inflicted $10,000 damage on three meat markets in Vancouver, British Columbia. Hycrest Meats and Robson Gourmet Meats were closed forever by the fires, while Nazare Meat spent four months in renovation.

August 1991—ALF's "Operation Bite Back I" targeted the U.S. Department of Agriculture (USDA) Fur Animal Research Facility at Washington State University. Intruders liberated 23 animals and inflicted $150,000 damage to research facilities.

August 13, 1991—ALF claimed credit for a break-in at Bustad Hall on the Washington State University campus, where 18 experimental animals were freed from their cages. Substantial damage was inflicted to lab facilities and research records.

December 14–15, 1991—The Billingsgate Fish Company suffered $100,000 in damage overnight when ALF commandos vandalized the plant and torched three delivery vehicles.

December 22, 1991—An anonymous phone call linked ALF to an arson fire that destroyed a building at the Malecky Mink Ranch in Yamhill, Oregon. The ranch owner, who collaborated with state researchers on various projects, claimed that his business was destroyed.

February 28, 1992—ALF arsonists set fire to a research office at Michigan State University and vandalized a lab where mink were kept, inflicting $100,000 in property damage. Medical research data spanning three decades was lost in the raid.

June 6, 1992—ALF raiders in Edmonton, Alberta, struck the University of Alberta's Ellerslie Research Station, rescuing 29 cats and inflicting $100,000 in property damage. Stolen files documented the lab's purchase of animals from illegal sources.

October 24, 1992—ALF claimed responsibility for a fire at a coyote farm run by researchers from Utah State University. Damage was estimated at $100,000.

May 10, 1994—ALF took credit for an arson fire that forced evacuation of 1,000 workers from the Carolina Biological Supply Company (CBSC) in Burlington, North Carolina. CBSC is one of the largest U.S. suppliers of animals for lab research and dissection in schools.

October 1994—ALF's first fox liberation campaign struck the McEllis Fur Farm at Pleasant View, Tennessee, sparing an estimated 25 foxes from certain death in the name of "fashion."

October 2, 1995—Raiders struck the Dargatz Mink Ranch near Chilliwack, British Columbia, destroying crucial breeding documents and releasing 2,400 mink into the wild.

November 12, 1996—ALF arsonists leveled the Alaskan Fur Company in Minnesota. Company spokespeople pegged total damages at $250,000 for the building and $2 million for lost furs.

April 4, 1997—The Don Kelly Chinchilla Farm in Texas was raided by ALF commandos, liberating 10 chinchillas for placement in private homes.

April 26, 1997—More than 50 activists were jailed after storming the Yerkes Regional Primate Center at Emory University in Atlanta. Police battled the crowd with Mace and tear gas, charging those arrested with various criminal counts.

May 30, 1997—"Operation Bite Back II" climaxed with a record theft of 10,000 mink from the Arritola Mink Farm at Mount Angel, Oregon.

July 21, 1997—ALF arsonists caused $1 million in damage to Cavel West, a horse-rendering plant in Redmond, Oregon, that provided tissue to the Pacific Coast Tissue Bank in Los Angeles. Medical procedures at Pacific Coast were postponed indefinitely.

July 5, 1998—Raiders at Cornell University (in Ithaca, New York) liberated dozens of woodchucks, releasing them into the wild. The intruders also removed data cards from the cages, destroyed crucial ledgers, and left vials of serum to spoil at room temperature.

November 13, 1998—ALF activists liberated 6,000 mink from the Rippin Fur Farm near Aldergrove, British Columbia. At the same time, breeding files collected during a 70-year period were destroyed.

April 5, 1999—Activists struck research facilities at the University of Minnesota, stealing 116 lab animals, ransacking a dozen separate labs, and destroying equipment valued in the millions of dollars.

Those actions, while among the most spectacular, are merely the tip of ALF's iceberg. Between 1979 and 1993, JUSTICE DEPARTMENT spokespersons claimed that at least 313 raids of various kinds were carried out against various targets in the name of animal rights across the United States. No final tabulation is available for Canada or for Britain's similarly active ANIMAL RIGHTS MILITIA. The actions continue to this day on all fronts.

ANIMAL Rights Militia

The Animal Rights Militia (ARM), an ally of the ANIMAL LIBERATION FRONT (ALF), was organized in England during the early 1980s and subsequently expanded to North America. While emulating the ALF's tactics of liberating captive animals and causing economic damage to its targets, ARM spokespeople maintain that the ALF "does not go far enough with regards to direct action. More effective victories can be achieved with poisoning hoaxes, and other such strategies." Acknowledged ARM actions include:

1984—A poison hoax in England targeting the Mars candy company, which "performed horrific tooth-decay experiments on animals with no signs of stopping." ARM threats of poisoned candy forced mass recalls of various Mars products, inflicting "huge financial losses" on the company and prompting abandonment of the offensive experiments.

September 1, 1987—ARM claimed credit for California arson fires that destroyed a paper products warehouse and caused $100,000 damage to San Jose Veal Inc.

November 26, 1987—The same California arsonists caused $230,000 damage to the Ferrara Meat Company, destroying a barn filled with hay and grain.

January 2, 1992—ARM activists initiated a poison scare against Cold Buster candy bars in Canada. The bar's inventor, Larry Wang, was named by ARM spokespeople as a participant in cruel animal experiments at the University of

Alberta. Development of the candy allegedly included 16 years of animal research. The ARM poison scare forced a recall of candy valued in excess of $1 million.

April 23, 1992—ARM commandos equipped with red paint celebrated the International Day for Laboratory Animals by vandalizing the home of Hans Fibiger, an animal researcher at the University of British Columbia.

August 10, 1994—ARM raiders in the United Kingdom coordinated detonation of incendiary devices at the Edinburgh Woolen Mill, Nurse's fur store, C.H. Brown's saddlery and leather shop, Westworld Leather Goods, and Madison's leather shop.

August 24, 1994—ARM incendiary bombings around England caused $4 million damage at two leather shops, a fishing tackle shop, the Cancer Research Fund Shop, and an outlet of the Boots the Chemist chain (targeted as supporters of animal testing).

September 16, 1994—Further British incendiary attacks caused an estimated $4 million damage at the Linsley Brothers sport shop, the Imperial Cancer Research Foundation store, and two more Boots the Chemist outlets. Boots subsequently sold off its pharmaceutical division to avoid further incidents.

December 23, 1994—Another ARM poison hoax rocked Vancouver, British Columbia. Activists falsely claimed to have injected frozen turkeys with rat poison, placing the contaminated poultry in various Safeway and Save-on-Food markets throughout the city. Turkeys valued at $1 million were recalled, while Turkey Producers Co-op reportedly suffered major revenue losses.

January 15, 1998—ARM activists in Uppsala, Sweden, raided laboratories owned by Bio Jet Service, liberating 92 guinea pigs slated for experimentation at Uppsala University. The breeder, Gothe Olofsson, announced that he was giving up the trade in laboratory animals.

ANSLINGER, Harry (1892–1975)

A Pennsylvania native who was born in 1892, Harry Anslinger went to work for the U.S. War Department in 1917 and then shifted to the U.S. Treasury Department in 1926. Appointed commissioner of PROHIBITION in 1929, he served barely a year in that position before he was named commissioner of narcotics in 1930. Anslinger thereafter led the Federal Bureau of Narcotics (FBN) until his retirement in 1962, campaigning for stricter drug laws and harsh enforcement.

A perennial lightning rod for J. EDGAR HOOVER's wrath, Anslinger invited that reaction in various ways. He courted national publicity, and Hoover blamed Anslinger for using copycat initials to name his agency (although the "FBI" label was not adopted until 1935, five years after the FBN's creation). The greatest bone of contention was Anslinger's public warnings of an international drug-dealing MAFIA. Strong evidence supported Anslinger's contention, but Hoover was incapable of any compromise with enemies, a stance that led him to deny the very existence of organized crime. Deputy Attorney General William Hundly recalled, years later, that Hoover "got in a big pissing match with Harry Anslinger over at Narcotics, who he didn't like, and Anslinger had the Mafia coming up out of the sewers the same way Hoover had the communists coming up out of the sewers. So Hoover got himself locked into saying there was no Mafia."

That claim proved humiliating over time. Anslinger tapped exiled Mafioso CHARLES "LUCKY" LUCIANO's telephone in December 1946, exposing narcotics traffic from Europe to America. Four years later, he cooperated with Senator Estes Kefauver's investigation of organized crime, while Hoover and the FBI remained aloof. In 1957, following the mass arrest of Mafia bosses at Apalachin, New York, congressional investigator Robert Kennedy demanded FBI files on the various gangsters identified and then infuriated Hoover by delivering the information to Anslinger's FBN, where Kennedy thought prosecution was more likely to result. (In fact, Kennedy found that the FBN had files on all 70 of the arrested mobsters, while the FBI had thin dossiers on only 30.) While Hoover belatedly ordered illegal phone taps on various "top hoodlums," Anslinger recruited the U.S. Coast Guard, INTERNAL REVENUE SERVICE, and U.S. Customs officers to interdict narcotics shipments.

Anslinger retired from the FBN in 1962 and published a book, *The Murderers*, that detailed the growth of international drug cartels since the

1920s. He remained outspoken on the subject until his death in 1975.

See also KENNEDY DYNASTY.

ANTARCTICA

Antarctica is the fifth-largest continent on Earth, with a total area of 5.4 million square miles. It is a world of ice where no recorded temperature has ever topped 59° Fahrenheit, and the record low (from July 21, 1983) is –129°F. Despite the presence of small research stations, Antarctica is officially uninhabited—but was it always so?

In 1959, while performing research at the Library of Congress, Professor Charles Hapgood (Keene College, New Hampshire) discovered a map drawn by Orontheus Phynius in 1531. It pictured Antarctica with rivers and mountains but without its trademark mile-thick glaciers. A similar map of an ice-free Antarctica was published in 1737 by Philippe Boiche, a member of the French Academy of Science. In fact, Boiche depicted the southernmost continent as two great bodies of land divided by water in the same region where the Transantarctic Mountains are shown on modern maps. Boiche's vision was affirmed in 1958 when modern cartographers revealed that Antarctica is, in effect, an icebound archipelago of large islands.

How did mapmakers of the 16th and 18th centuries present such a strikingly different picture of Antarctica? Conspiracy theories advanced in this realm typically involve some variation of the "ancient astronauts" theme, though intimations of a link to lost Atlantis or the mythic HOLLOW EARTH are also popular. From those beginnings theorists generally invoke a global conspiracy of silence, masking The Truth (as they see it) about planet Earth, its beginnings, and the origins of humankind.

ANTHRAX conspiracies

Anthrax is a spore-forming bacillus that is deadly to humans and is transmitted in three different forms: cutaneous (contracted through the skin), gastrointestinal (ingested orally while eating), and pulmonary (inhaled by its victims). Various countries, including the United States, have stockpiled anthrax since the early 1930s, constantly experimenting and refining the disease to make it more effective as a biological weapon. In recent years, the FEDERAL BUREAU OF INVESTIGATION (FBI) has twice investigated plots to use anthrax within the country, as a terrorist weapon, with unfortunate results in both cases.

The United States suffered a tragic brush with anthrax in 2001. Between October 4 and November 21, at least 46 residents of the eastern United States tested positive for exposure to anthrax, after a series of infected letters were mailed to various media outlets and government offices. Five of those victims died: two Washington postal workers, an employee of a Florida tabloid, a New York hospital employee, and an elderly Connecticut woman. Despite a massive nationwide investigation, including a $1 million reward offer for information leading to the arrest of persons responsible for the anthrax mailings, the case remains unsolved today. FBI failure to crack the case, despite unprecedented effort and publicity, opened the bureau to harsh criticism from Congress, the media, and the U.S. public at large.

In August 2002 *Newsweek* magazine reported "intriguing new clues" in the bureau's search for the anthrax killer(s). According to that report, tracking dogs employed to screen a dozen possible suspects "went crazy" at the Maryland home of Dr. Steven Hatfill, a 48-year-old scientist once employed at an army bioweapons-research lab. *Newsweek* dubbed Hatfill "eccentric . . . [f]lamboyant and arrogant," proclaiming that FBI agents were "finally on the verge of a breakthrough" in the case. Hatfill was placed under round-the-clock surveillance and subjected to a polygraph test (which he reportedly passed), and his home was searched twice without revealing evidence of any criminal activity. Still, that did not prevent Attorney General JOHN ASHCROFT from publicly branding Hatfill "a person of interest" in the case, refusing to define the term when challenged by Hatfill's attorneys. Hatfill held a press conference to declare his innocence on August 11, 2002; two days later his attorney filed complaints with the bureau's Office of Professional Responsibility, alleging misconduct in Hatfill's case. On September 4, 2002, Hatfill was fired from his job at Louisiana State University's biomedical laboratory, after JUSTICE DEPARTMENT officials barred him from working on projects funded by federal grants. In May 2003 G-men acting on "a tip" dredged a pond near Hatfill's home and again came away empty-handed. Disposition of Hatfill's lawsuit against the FBI and Justice Department was pending as this volume went to press.

APOLLO Project

On July 20, 1969, millions of people around the world watched in awe as U.S. astronaut Neil Armstrong stepped from his spider-legged spacecraft to set foot on the Moon. It was, as Armstrong proclaimed to the television cameras, "One small step for man, one giant leap for mankind."

Or was it?

In 1991 author Bill Kaysing announced his "discovery" that there was, in fact, no Moon walk—not on Armstrong's flight nor on any of the subsequent Apollo missions claimed by National Aeronautics and Space Administration (NASA). The events were not filmed in space, Kaysing said, but rather on a military soundstage in Nevada (perhaps at supersecret AREA 51). In Kaysing's view, the whole Apollo program came down to a "$30 billion swindle," incorporating "programmed astronauts," some "well-faked photographs," and bogus Moon rocks, sold to the world with "the help of father-figure [Walter] Cronkite as the journalistic goat." In place of proof, Kaysing posed pointed questions, which NASA has thus far declined to answer. They include:

- Why are no stars visible in photos of the jet-black lunar sky?
- If the Moon's surface is dusty enough to show deep footprints, why did the lunar lander's rocket dig such a shallow crater—and why is there no dust on the spacecraft's legs?
- If Armstrong was the first human to set foot on the Moon, why was a shoeprint visible at the base of the ladder as he filmed his own original descent?
- If the Moon was proved sterile after the first Apollo landing, why did astronauts from later missions spend long terms in quarantine?
- In Kaysing's own words, "Why did so many astronauts end up as executives in very large corporations?"

Kaysing believes the "fake" Moon landings were staged after NASA discovered that its years of expensive research and planning were all for nothing and that the Moon walk was impossible; scientists thereupon allegedly joined forces with members of the MAFIA in LAS VEGAS to fake the various Apollo missions, thereby avoiding criticism and potential cancellation of their meal tickets. The scenario includes empty spacecraft launched from Florida and crashing back to Earth in the Antarctic, while astronauts are flown to the Nevada movie set and bogus Moon rocks are concocted in a high-tech ceramics kiln. Curiously, a film with a similar theme, *Capricorn One,* was released by Hollywood in 1978—13 years before Kaysing published his treatise on NASA's great scam.

In 1999 a public-opinion poll revealed that 11 percent of the U.S. population doubted that astronauts had ever set foot on the Moon. That margin reportedly jumped to 20 percent in 2001 after the Fox TV network twice broadcast a program titled *Conspiracy Theory: Did We Really Land on the Moon?* On September 9, 2002, in Beverly Hills, aging astronaut Buzz Aldrin assaulted a heckler half his age after the man brandished a Bible, asking Aldrin to swear that he had walked on the Moon.

Throughout the mounting controversy, NASA maintained stony silence, refusing to debate skeptics concerning the Apollo project's validity. As late as 2001 NASA's response to the controversy consisted of a one-line memorandum: "Apollo: Yes, we did." Then, on October 30, 2002, newspapers across the United States reported that NASA had retained Houston author and aerospace engineer James Oberg (for $15,000) to write a book debunking critical claims. "Ignoring it," Oberg told reporters, "only fans the flames of people who are naturally suspicious." Stephen Garber, NASA's acting chief historian, weighed in with the opinion that Oberg's 30,000-word manuscript "is not going to convince the people who believe in these myths. Hopefully, it'll speak to other people who are broad-minded." The book, Garber said, would expose "space myths writ large [and will] look at some of these broader issues of how these myths get initiated and promulgated."

The ink was barely dry on that announcement when, nine days later, NASA announced cancellation of Oberg's book. An unnamed NASA spokesperson told reporters that "the project stirred up too much ridicule." Instead of the reported $15,000 advance, Oberg would receive $5,000 "for work already done." Oberg, for his part, vowed to find another publisher. "I'm writing the book anyway," he told reporters, "and now commercial publishers are interested. We live in a time teeming with conspiracy theories, and people, especially teachers, have little to help train students in critical thinking."

AQUINO, Benigno (1932–1983)

In the 1970s Benigno Aquino led political opposition to U.S.-supported dictator FERDINAND MARCOS in the PHILIPPINES. After three years of political exile in the United States, Aquino returned to his homeland on August 21, 1983, and was murdered on arrival by Manila airport employee Rolando Galman. Filipino security forces killed Galman on the spot, and authorities soon proclaimed him the proverbial "lone gunman." Dogged investigators soon uncovered evidence of a conspiracy within the corrupt Filipino army, however, and 25 officers (including Gen. Fabian Ver, army chief of staff) were charged with Aquino's murder. A court acquitted the defendants on December 2, 1985, but the resultant scandal propelled Aquino's widow into a political race against Marcos (ironically supported by the army). Marcos fled the country in February 1986, absconding with an estimated $3 billion in loot.

ARAB Communist Organization

Little is known of the Arab Communist Organization's (ACO) beginnings. Its first known action, on August 14, 1974, was a bombing that damaged the U.S. pavilion at the Damascus International Fair in SYRIA. Two weeks later, in LEBANON, ACO members attacked the American Life Insurance Company's office at Sidon. On September 14 another Damascus bombing targeted a building planned for use by the U.S. Information Agency. That same month, ACO members robbed a bank in Tyre, Lebanon, escaping with $68,400. Back in Damascus, on October 10, 1974, an ACO bombing on the eve of a visit by U.S. Secretary of State HENRY KISSINGER killed one person and wounded another at a National Cash Register office. Subsequent attacks targeted a Lebanese mineral water firm in Beirut (November 1974); two Beirut banks ($66,000 stolen in December 1974; $438,000 in February 1975); a British-owned department store in Beirut (bombed twice, in December 1974 and January 1975); the Jordanian and Egyptian embassies in Damascus (January 1975); American Life's offices in Tyre (February 1975) and Kuwait (April 1975); and an International Telephone and Telegraph (IT&T) office in Beirut (May 1975). Leaders of the group were arrested and sentenced to life imprisonment in Syria in 1975 (with the survivors finally paroled in 2002). ACO members were briefly suspected in the June 1976 kidnap-murder of U.S. Ambassador Francis Meloy and his chauffeur in Beirut, but the culprits in that case were never caught. Alternate theories in the case blame members of the Palestine Liberation Organization and the Popular Front for the Liberation of Palestine.

AREA 51

Area 51 is a supersecret U.S. Air Force base at Groom Lake, Nevada, buried at the heart of the Nevada Test Site (60-odd miles northwest of Las Vegas). It figures prominently in most conspiracy theories involving unidentified flying objects (UFOs) and government suppression of alien technology that was allegedly collected since the Roswell UFO crash of 1947. Unauthorized personnel are strictly banned from the region and are subject to arrest for trespassing. Popular rumors (and a dramatic episode of *The X-Files* TV series) suggest that intruders on the site are brutally "debriefed" and may be subject to memory-erasure treatments prior to their release (if, in fact, they do not simply "disappear"). U.S. Air Force spokespersons dismiss such stories as fantasy, noting that Area 51 *was* the scene of prolonged testing involving "stealth" aircraft, a circumstance that may have contributed to local UFO sightings. President George W. Bush confirmed the covert base's sinister reputation for many observers in September 2002 when he exempted Area 51 from federal environmental legislation that required disclosure of classified information concerning local operations.

See also BUSH DYNASTY.

ARGENTINA

South America's second-largest country was "discovered" by SPAIN in 1516 and colonized thereafter, with the usual impact on aboriginal people. Argentineans broke with Spain to establish their own government in 1810, finally declaring independence on July 9, 1816. The country remained neutral during both World Wars, though strongman leader Juan Perón welcomed Axis investments throughout World War II and offered sanctuary to many THIRD REICH fugitives accused of WAR CRIMES. Perón's popular wife—Eva Duarte de Perón ("Evita")—doubled as de facto minister of health and labor, forging close ties with labor unions, but her death in 1952 and Perón's increasing authoritarianism produced a military coup that drove Perón from power in 1955. Military juntas ruled Argentina for most of the next 18 years, before Juan Perón returned to power by popular demand in 1973. He died the following year, leaving his fourth wife (Isabel Martínez de Perón) as the Western Hemisphere's first female chief of state.

The honeymoon was short-lived, as Argentina teetered on the brink of chaos. In 1975, incidents of right- and left-wing TERRORISM claimed at least 700 lives. Strikes and public demonstrations paralyzed the government, while the cost of living rose 355 percent. On March 24, 1976, Lt. Gen. Jorge Rafael Videla seized power and declared martial law, launching Argentina's infamous "dirty war" to suppress all dissent. During the next 17 years, the Argentine Commission for Human Rights (operating from Geneva, SWITZERLAND) would tabulate 2,300 political murders, more than 10,000 political arrests, and the disappearance of another 20,000 to 30,000 persons.

While violence by dissident groups soon declined, the economy remained chaotic, and Argentina's military rulers lived at constant risk from their comrades. Field Marshal Roberto Viola deposed Videla in March 1981, and was later ousted in turn by Lt. Gen. Leopoldo Galtieri. In April 1982, Galtieri invaded the British-held Falkland Islands and then resigned in disgrace two months later after England handed Argentina a humiliating defeat. Gen. Reynaldo Bignone succeeded Galtieri, scheduling popular elections for 1983 as inflation hit 900 percent.

A return to democracy has thus far done nothing to improve Argentina's disastrous economy. Mass infusions of $21.7 billion from the International Monetary Fund in 2001 likewise failed to end the country's crippling recession—or to prevent Argentina from defaulting on $155 billion in foreign debts. The nation's former dictators sought to shield themselves from prosecution with blanket amnesty laws passed in 1986–87, but courts have found various loopholes allowing prosecution of the worst offenders. In July 2002, ex-Gen. Galtieri and 42 other military officers were indicted for the torture-slayings of 22 leftist rebels during the long "dirty war." Former naval officer Ricardo Cavallo, the latest defendant, was extradited from Mexico in June 2003 to face charges of genocide and terrorism.

The most bizarre skeleton in modern Argentina's closet may be the fate of several thousand children taken by the state from parents who "disappeared" in the 1970s. Years later, investigators from Conadi (the National Commission for the Right to Identity) discovered that the children were kidnapped and adopted by members of the ruling junta. As Conadi explains: "The baby thefts were carried out as part of a systematic plan. Some babies were abandoned in city parks or hospital clinics, but most were placed in the hands of military officers and other members of the regime and their families, who raised them as their own."

ARMENIA

In successive centuries, Armenia (in the southern Caucasus, bounded by AZERBAIJAN, GEORGIA, IRAN, and TURKEY) was conquered in turn by Greeks, Romans, Persians, Byzantines, Mongols, Arabs, Ottoman Turks, and Russians. Turks proved the worst rulers, occupying Armenia from the 16th century through World War I. Demonstrations of Armenian nationalism prompted Turkish massacres of thousands in 1894 and 1896, but the worst slaughter began in April 1915 and continued throughout the "war to end all wars." During that four-year campaign of annihilation, now widely regarded as the first 20th-century example of genocide, Turkish rulers ordered deportation of the entire Armenian population to the desert wastes of SYRIA and Mesopotamia. Most (non-Turkish) historians agree that 600,000 to 1.5 million victims were slain in that early campaign of "ethnic cleansing."

Following Turkey's defeat in World War I, an independent Armenian republic was established in May 1918, but invaders from RUSSIA throttled the short-lived democracy in November 1920. In March 1922 Armenia became part of the Transcaucasian Soviet Socialist Republic. Fourteen years later, it was "liberated" as a separate Soviet Republic, and remained under Moscow's thumb until the Soviet Union collapsed in 1991. Meanwhile, in 1988, Armenia began a six-year war with Azerbaijan for control of the disputed Nagorno-Karabakh enclave, that conflict costing another 30,000 lives before Azerbaijan emerged victorious in 1994.

Political conspiracy and violence continue in Armenia to the present day. Prime Minister Vazgen Sarkissian and six associates were assassinated on October 27, 1999, when gunmen opened fire in Parliament. Aram Sarkissian was appointed to succeed his murdered brother, but his outspoken opposition to President Robert Kocharian led Kocharian to replace him as prime minister with Andranik Markaryan in May 2000.

ARMY of God

This loose-knit coalition of religious zealots, devoted to eliminating legalized abortion in the United States, made its first appearance in August 1982 when self-styled members kidnapped Dr. Hector Zevallos and his wife from their home in Illinois. Dr. Zevallos, the operator of a women's clinic in Granite City, was held captive for six days until he promised to stop performing abortions. (Ringleader Don Anderson received a 30-year prison sentence for that crime; he subsequently earned another 30-year stretch for torching two Florida clinics.) Since that incident, the Army of God (AOG) has claimed credit for various acts of TERRORISM across the United States, generally bombings, arson, and other acts of vandalism against women's clinics. Convicted clinic bomber Michael Bray describes himself as "chaplain" of the group while simultaneously denying any culpable knowledge of its ongoing criminal activities. Some critics argue that the AOG does not exist, per se, but that its name is simply invoked by perpetrators of various violent crimes in a bid to make the scattered "pro-life" movement seem well organized. In 1997–98 letters signed by the AOG claimed credit for fatal bombings in Atlanta and Birmingham, subsequently linked to neo-Nazi fugitive Eric Rudolph. Following an Atlanta gay-bar bombing linked to Rudolph in February 1997, a letter signed by the AOG announced: "We declare and will wage total war on the ungodly communist regime in New York and your legislative-bureaucratic lackey's [sic] in Washington. It is you who are responsible and preside over the murder of children and issue the policy of ungodly preversion [sic] that[']s destroying our people. . . . Death to the NEW WORLD ORDER." Despite this and similar pronouncements through the years, spokesmen for the FEDERAL BUREAU OF INVESTIGATION (FBI) in Washington have declared that its "Terrorist Section does not consider the 'Army of God' as a terrorist group, and therefore no FBI investigation appears warranted at this time." In 2001 the group was blamed for sending dozens of hoax ANTHRAX mailings to clinics across the United States.

ARNOLD, Benedict (1741–1801)

A Connecticut native who was born January 14, 1741, Benedict Arnold was named for an ancestor who served as governor of Rhode Island. In 1775, prior to the official outbreak of the American Revolution against England, Arnold was commissioned as a captain in the Massachusetts governor's Second Company of Guards. Bouts of illness, quarrels with rival militia officers, and perceived shabby treatment by his commanders soon grated on Arnold's nerves. Though pleased with a promotion to colonel, Arnold was humiliated by a failed attempt to seize Québec and landed in court on a charge of plundering Montreal's stores. Exonerated on that count, he was given a fleet of 15 ships with orders to oust British troops from Fort Ticonderoga. Though successful, Arnold lost 10 of his ships in the battle, seething in the face of more public criticism. Further embarrassed by the promotion of younger subordinates, Arnold resigned

Benedict Arnold became America's first notorious traitor during the Revolutionary War. (Author's collection)

in July 1777. He soon changed his mind, and while Congress took him back, Arnold lost his seniority in the hot-headed gesture. Further quarrels with his commanders, a wound suffered during the Saratoga campaign, and an expensive new wife (mollified by the income from shady business deals) led Arnold to betray his country in May 1779. British spies offered him £10,000 and a commission in the redcoat army for assistance in defeating the upstart colonials. Arnold responded with plans for the capture of West Point, New York, but a courier was captured, and his treason was revealed. Arnold escaped and was rewarded for his treachery with land in Canada, plus pensions for himself, his wife, and his five children. Arnold tried his hand at shipping, but no one would really trust a turncoat, and he found himself nearly friendless in Canada. His business subsequently failed, and he died, nearly forgotten, in 1801.

ARYAN Brotherhood

Arguably the largest and most violent of U.S. PRISON GANGS, the Aryan Brotherhood (AB) was organized at California's San Quentin Prison in 1967. It evolved from a series of white-supremacist jailhouse cliques in the 1950s and early 1960s, including groups called the Bluebirds, the Nazi Gang, and the Diamond Tooth Gang. It was initially established to protect white inmates from violence by nonwhite gangs, primarily the MEXICAN MAFIA. Today, the AB has members in prisons throughout the United States, while those on the outside (however briefly on parole) engage in a variety of criminal activities that include wholesale theft, the manufacture and sale of illegal drugs, and contract murder.

As suggested by its name, the AB is a far-right, racist, and anti-Semitic group that nurtures intense hatred of Jews and nonwhite minorities. In addition to the "AB" logo, its heavily tattooed members traditionally sport swastikas, the lightning-bolt symbol of the Nazi SS, shamrocks, the Satanic numerals *666*, and various expressions of "White Pride." In prisons where gangs are theoretically banned, AB members meet and plot their crimes under the guise of holding Odinist religious ceremonies (an ancient Scandinavian belief system adopted since the 1990s by many neo-Nazis who reject "Jewish" Christianity). This marks a change from 1980s when most AB members publicly espoused the CHRISTIAN IDENTITY creed (maintaining that Anglo-Saxons are God's chosen people, while Jews are literally children of Satan).

Violence is habitual with AB members. In August 1993 AB member Roy Slider was convicted of assaulting a black prison guard, Thomas Davis, in Ohio. A year later, in October 1994, AB disciple Donald Riley drew a life prison term in Houston, Texas, for the murder of a black Marine Corps veteran. Between 1996 and 1998 an AB "reign of terror" at California's Pelican Bay State Prison included six murders. In April 1997 AB member John Stojetz was convicted of murdering a black teenage inmate at an Ohio state prison. In 1998 when black victim James Byrd, Jr., was dragged to death behind a pickup truck near Jasper, Texas, two of those arrested for the crime were self-declared AB members who were festooned with racist tattoos. During commission of the crime, one of the killers gleefully declared, "We're starting *The* TURNER DIARIES early."

ASBESTOS

This fibrous mineral had few industrial applications until its fire-retardant properties were discovered in the 1890s, whereupon its use expanded rapidly. Another decade passed before physicians recognized the first of several respiratory diseases resulting from exposure to asbestos—whereupon its chief producers shifted into cover-up mode. A brief chronology of the 90-year battle follows.

1918—An officer of Prudential Insurance declares that life-insurance companies will no longer cover asbestos workers, due to "health-injurious conditions of the industry."

1930—The Johns-Manville Company, a leading asbestos producer, produced and suppressed a report detailing job-related fatalities among asbestos workers.

1932—A letter from the U.S. Bureau of Mines informed asbestos manufacturer Eagle-Picher: "It is now known that asbestos dust is one of the most dangerous dusts to which man is exposed."

1933—Physicians employed by Metropolitan Life reported that 29 percent of the workers in one Johns-Manville plant have asbestosis ("white-lung disease"). The firm settled lawsuits filed by 11 dying employees on the condition that their attorneys agreed never again to "directly or indirectly participate in the bringing of new actions against the Corporation."

1934—Executives of Johns-Mansville and Raybestos-Manhattan edited an article on asbestos written by a Metropolitan Life physician, downplaying the perils of asbestos dust to humans.

1935—Officers of Johns-Mansville and Raybestos-Manhattan order the editor of *Asbestos* magazine to cease publication of critical pieces.

1936—While combining to sponsor research on the health risks of asbestos dust, a consortium of major producers retains exclusive control over disclosure of all findings.

1942—A secret internal memo circulated to Owens-Corning executives described "medical literature on asbestosis . . . scores of publications in which the lung and skin hazards of asbestos are discussed."

1943—The president of Johns-Mansville privately denounced the executives of a competing asbestos company as "a bunch of fools for notifying employees who had asbestosis." When a subordinate inquired, "Do you mean to tell me you would let them work until they dropped dead?" the CEO replied, "Yes. We save a lot of money that way."

1944—A survey of 195 asbestos miners, conducted by Metropolitan Life, found 42 suffering from asbestosis.

1951—Having sponsored yet another medical report on asbestos, executives of several leading producers removed all references to cancer from the document before publication.

1952—Johns-Mansville executives reject a plea from their company's medical director, Dr. Kenneth Smith, that warning labels be attached to products containing asbestos. Smith later testified under oath, "It was a business decision as far as I could understand. . . . [T]he corporation is in business to provide jobs for people and make money for stockholders and they had to take into consideration the effects of everything they did and if the application of a caution label identifying a product as hazardous would cut into sales, there would be serious financial implications."

1953—The safety director for National Gypsum penned a letter to Indiana's Division of Industrial Hygiene suggesting that mixers of acoustic plaster wear respirators "because of the asbestos used in the product." Company executives deemed the letter "full of dynamite" and ordered its interception. A subsequent memo revealed that company agents "succeeded in stopping" the letter, which "will be modified" before mailing.

1964—A study published in the *Journal of the American Medical Association* demonstrated that asbestos workers display an abnormal incidence of asbestosis, mesothelioma, and lung cancer.

1966—An executive of Raybestos-Manhattan declared, "We feel that the recent unfavorable publicity over the use of asbestos fibers in many different kinds of industries has been a gross exaggeration of the problems. There is no data available to either prove or disprove the dangers of working closely with asbestos."

1971—The U.S. government issued its first standard for asbestos exposure.

1973—The Environmental Protection Agency (EPA) banned spray-on asbestos insulation as hazardous to health.

1977—Attorneys representing disabled asbestos workers uncovered correspondence revealing that major producers had suppressed information on the dangers of their product since the 1930s.

1978—A judge in South Carolina, presiding over a lawsuit against Owens-Corning Fiberglas® Corporation, acknowledged "a conscious effort by the [asbestos] industry in the 1930s to downplay or arguably suppress, the dissemination of information to employees and the public for fear of the promotion of lawsuits."

1979—The EPA announced its intent to ban all forms of asbestos for the good of public health.

1982—Johns-Manville filed for bankruptcy protection against civil litigation.

1986—After seven years of delay, the EPA published its proposed rule banning all use of asbestos.

1989—A full decade after its initial proposal, the EPA ban took effect.

1991—Asbestos producers won a federal lawsuit, resulting in court-ordered revocation of the EPA's 1989 asbestos ban.

1994—Washington tightens asbestos-exposure standards while permitting its continued use in certain circumstances.

1997—FRANCE banned importation of asbestos, prompting the government of Canada (an asbestos exporter) to file complaints of alleged "free trade" violations with the World Trade Organization in 1998.

1999—Florida's Supreme Court finds that Owens Corning willfully concealed evidence of health hazards posed by asbestos. The court's ruling says: "It would be difficult to envision a more egregious set of circumstances . . . a blatant disregard for human safety involving large numbers of people put at life-threatening risk."

2000—At trial in Albany, New York, 12 individual defendants and two corporations pleaded guilty to criminal violations of federal asbestos restrictions. At the same time, a Syracuse grand jury indicted a 15th defendant for money laundering and violations of the Clean Air Act.

ASHCROFT, John (1942–)

John Ashcroft is the son and grandson of fundamentalist Pentecostal ministers who carried that conservative upbringing through law school and into the political arena, first as a failed congressional candidate in 1972 and then as Missouri's state auditor (1973–75), state attorney general (1976–85), and governor (1985–93). He was elected to the U.S. Senate in 1994, proving so unpopular with his constituents that he lost his 2000 reelection bid to an opponent who died before election day. A longtime friend and ally of the Bush family, Ashcroft was considered for the post of U.S. attorney general in 1991, but he was ultimately deemed too controversial. President George W. Bush had no such qualms in 2001, although Ashcroft was admittedly his second choice. Confirmed despite stiff opposition from minorities and civil libertarians, Ashcroft vowed that his religion would have no impact on his performance in office—and then spent $8,000 for a drape to hide a bare-breasted statue of Justice at his headquarters in Washington.

Ashcroft avoided any major controversy until the terrorist attacks of September 11, 2001, whereupon he unleashed a national campaign of arrests unequaled since the PALMER RAIDS of 1919–20. He also campaigned for new powers in the realm of domestic surveillance, achieved with passage of the USA PATRIOT ACT, but Congress stopped short of granting Ashcroft's fondest wishes: authority to unilaterally detain and deport on suspicion alone any aliens branded "suspected terrorists," elimination of deportation hearings, and waiver of appeals from deportation orders.

Despite his commitment to pursuing terrorists, on December 7, 2001, Ashcroft issued an order forbidding FEDERAL BUREAU OF INVESTIGATION agents from checking the names of suspected terrorists against federal firearms-purchase records. Former JUSTICE DEPARTMENT attorney Mathew Nosanchuk bluntly accused Ashcroft and his aides of "rejecting their own authority and acting as lawyers for the gun lobby." At the same time, Ashcroft tried to work behind an airtight screen of secrecy. While in the Senate, during 1998, he had accused Attorney General Janet Reno of "stonewalling" when she withheld federal prosecutors' memos from Congress; in 2002 Ashcroft claimed the same privilege for himself, prompting the chairman of the House Judiciary Committee to express "concern that you have one standard for a Democrat attorney general and another standard for yourself." Ashcroft, unfazed by criticism, dismissed public fears that his nationwide crusade might threaten civil rights, responded in terms reminiscent of J. EDGAR HOOVER: "To those who scare peace-loving people with phantoms of lost liberty, my message is: your tactics only aid terrorists, for they erode our national unity and diminish our resolve." Beset by lawsuits from all sides, Ashcroft continued his demands for greater power. He resigned as attorney general in January 2005.

See also BUSH DYNASTY.

ASSASSINS cult

The first agents of militant Islam in the Middle East were members of a neo-Ismailite sect, formed by Caliph-Imam al-al-Mustansir and his son Nizar in EGYPT sometime in the mid-11th century. Nizar was driven from Cairo by rivals at court, finding support among Ismailite converts in the mountains of Persia (now IRAN). There, while Nizar remained the movement's figurehead, true power resided with Hassan ibn-al-Saabah, leader of the Persian Ismailites. In

1090 Hassan's warriors captured the mountain stronghold of Alamut, where Hassan installed himself and soon became known as the Old Man of the Mountain. Alamut—also known as the Eagle's Nest—provided a fortuitous vantage point for observation and interdiction of Christian invaders during the centuries of the Crusades.

According to Marco Polo, who visited Alamut in 1271, the stronghold included fabulous gardens, occupied by lovely women whom the reigning cult leaders used to good advantage. Simply put, cult members would be drugged with hashish and then carried into the garden, where they woke among nubile beauties who were willing to satisfy any sexual demand. After they were drugged a second time, the soldiers found themselves "back" at Alamut, where the Old Man informed them that they had been granted a glimpse of Paradise—the very afterlife awaiting any disciple who died in service of Allah. So emboldened, the Assassins—from *hasashhim,* "users of hashish")—feared no danger when they were dispatched to kill targets chosen by their leader. Many of the victims were crusaders, but rival Muslim leaders also fell before the cult's onslaught, and the Assassins also served as mercenary contract killers if the price was right.

By the late 11th century, the cult had outposts in SYRIA and had converted the prince of Aleppo, Ridwan ibn-Tutush (d. 1113). By 1140 Assassins had captured mountain fortresses throughout northern Syria, including Masyad, al-Kahf, al-Qadmus, and al-'Ullayqah. Where Christian invaders failed to curb the cult, Mongol invaders finally succeeded, routing the Assassins from Masyad in 1260. Twelve years later, the Mamluk Sultan Baybars dealt the cult a final blow with mass arrests and executions. Still, some members of the sect reportedly escaped to India—where they may have resurfaced as thugs in the 13th century.

ASTRAZENECA

On June 20, 2003, leaders of the giant pharmaceutical company AstraZeneca pleaded guilty in Washington, D.C., on a felony charge of health-care fraud and agreed to pay $355 million in settlement of criminal and civil accusations filed against the company. Those charges claimed that AstraZeneca engaged in a nationwide plot to market illegally Zoladex, a prostate-cancer drug, by bribing 400 doctors across

the United States to prescribe the company's product to patients. The bribes included financial grants, employment of some doctors as "consultants," free travel and entertainment, plus countless free samples of Zoladex (worth hundreds of dollars each)—which the doctors then billed to Medicare or other federal health programs. AstraZeneca's $355 million settlement included a $64 million criminal fine, $266 million to settle civil accusations from the U.S. government, and $25 million to settle accusations that the firm defrauded various Medicaid programs that were partially administered by various state governments. AstraZeneca's settlement marked the largest U.S. fine for health-care fraud since October 2001 when leaders of Tap Pharmaceutical Products paid $875 million to settle charges in a nearly identical conspiracy.

ATF See BUREAU OF ALCOHOL, TOBACCO, AND FIREARMS.

ATLANTA Police Department

From 1915 to 1961 Atlanta, Georgia, was the national headquarters of the KU KLUX KLAN (KKK), which remained violently active in the city even after its largest faction sought whiter pastures in Alabama under Governor GEORGE WALLACE. For many years, Atlanta's police department was infested with Klansmen, including officers of command rank. Racist governors Eugene and Herman Talmadge encouraged Klan infiltration of Georgia law enforcement, and local policeman Sam Roper served as Imperial Wizard of the state's dominant KKK faction in 1949–53. Some critics went so far as to claim that Klan membership was a prerequisite for employment with the Atlanta Police Department, and while that may not have been literally true, the case of Officer "Trigger" Nash suggests the extent to which KKK sentiments subverted honest enforcement of law in Atlanta (and throughout Georgia at large).

On November 1, 1948, Officer Nash—whose nickname derived from his propensity for shooting blacks—was one of several police officers who addressed a Klan meeting in Atlanta. He was greeted with applause that night "for killing his thirteenth nigger in the line of duty" a few days earlier. According to the minutes of that gathering:

Trigger Nash, also a policeman, got up and made a talk and said he hoped he wouldn't have all the honor of killing the niggers in the South, and he hoped the people would do something about it themselves.

Infiltrator Stetson Kennedy noted that Nash and his fellow patrol officers faced no censure for their open expressions of homicidal racism. Furthermore, Kennedy charged, the Atlanta Police Department made a habit of suppressing evidence whenever KKK "wrecking crews" committed murders, bombings, and other crimes within city jurisdiction.

A generation later, racist malfeasance of another kind was charged in the case of alleged serial killer Wayne Williams. Convicted on dubious evidence in the murders of two adult ex-convicts, Williams was publicly branded as the "Atlanta child killer" who was responsible for the murders of 30-odd victims since 1979. Critics of the murder investigation noted that Atlanta police (then led by a black chief and mayor) seemed intent on crafting an arbitrary list of victims, excluding some cases while others were illogically included, suppressing eyewitness statements that named an alternate (Caucasian) suspect in one of the slayings attributed to Williams. Years after Williams was convicted and sentenced to life in prison, records from the FEDERAL BUREAU OF INVESTIGATION and the Georgia Bureau of Investigation revealed that Klansmen had been suspects in the murders before Williams was arrested, but those files—including transcripts of an apparent confession in one case—were "lost" in favor of jailing a black defendant (and thus avoiding potential race riots in Atlanta).

AUM Shinrikyo

JAPAN is world renowned as a haven for bizarre alternative religions, but none in recent memory has sparked more controversy—or spawned more lethal violence—than the sect known as Aum Shinrikyo ("Supreme Truth Society"). Organized in 1989, the cult was later linked to a triple murder committed in its first year of operation; six years later, its leaders were jailed for a mass-murder plan designed to bring about the ultimate apocalypse.

Aum's founder, Shoko Asahara, was born Chizuo Matsumoto in 1955. His vision was poor from childhood, and he attended a school for the blind before moving to Tokyo in 1976. Early acquaintances recall his childhood obsession with money and power. Years later, in Tokyo, he founded a yoga school and was jailed on charges of selling phony medicine. With that rap behind him, he shifted his focus to religion in 1989, launching Aum Shinrikyo with 10 disciples who dubbed the myopic messiah their "venerable master." Before the year was out, Aum drew complaints from the parents of young recruits. Several families pooled resources and hired attorney Tsutsumi Sakamoto to sue the cult. In November 1989 Sakamoto, his wife, and their 14-month-old son vanished without a trace. Six years elapsed before their remains were found, in September 1995, resulting in murder charges against Asahara and company. By then, Aum's venerable master had more pressing problems on his hands. After years of preaching imminent apocalypse—most recently a forecast that 90 percent of the world's urban population would die in poison gas attacks by 1997—Asahara had decided to give prophecy a helping hand.

In June 1994 seven residents of Matsumoto were killed and more than 200 were injured when deadly sarin nerve gas was released in a residential neighborhood. Developed by German scientists in the 1930s, sarin is among the world's deadliest chemical compounds. Authorities investigating the attack found evidence of sarin by-products near Aum Shinrikyo's headquarters in Kamikuishiki, 100 miles southwest of Tokyo, but there was insufficient evidence for criminal charges, and the case remained officially unsolved.

Nine months later, on March 20, 1995, unknown persons released another blast of sarin on the Tokyo subway during morning rush hour. This time, 12 persons were killed, with more than 5,500 treated for nonfatal injuries. Two days later, police raided Aum headquarters in Kamikuishiki, but Asahara and his chief lieutenants had already fled. Four cultists were arrested, but the real surprise was in the evidence retrieved: two tons of chemicals for making sarin—enough, in fact, to kill at least four million people; $7 million in cash; gas masks; and cult publications including Asahara's prediction of impending gas attacks throughout the world. Another 50 cultists were in residence, most of them severely malnourished, but they were released by police.

Shoko Asahara was still at large on March 24 when he showed up on national television, denying any role in the Tokyo gas attack. His sincerity was questioned three days later when police found a chemical lab concealed at an Aum Shinrikyo shrine near Mount Fuji. On March 29 Aum cultists were named as suspects in the near-fatal shooting of Japan's top law-enforcement officer, Takaji Kunimatsu, and two more cultists were jailed on March 31 for carrying explosive chemicals. On April 7, 1995, illegal firearms were seized from a vehicle owned by the sect.

Asahara, for all his protestations of innocence, was still predicting disaster—most recently, mass deaths in Tokyo that were expected to occur on April 15. The date passed without incident, but four days later, in Yokohama, 300 persons were injured when poisonous phosgene gas was released in the city's main railroad terminal. On April 21 two dozen more victims were hospitalized by a gas attack in a Yokohama shopping center. The following week, Japanese authorities announced that two army sergeants, both members of Aum Shinrikyo, had warned Asahara before the police raids in March.

The dragnets and terror continued. On May 4, 1995, police arrested cult attorney Yoshinebu Aoyama as a suspect in the gas attacks. Days later, an alert cleaning woman for the Tokyo subway system discovered gas bombs with sophisticated trigger mechanisms—enough gas, police said, to kill 10,000 people. On July 4 cyanide canisters were found at another Tokyo train station, but the devices were successfully disarmed. Australian police reported that cult members had apparently tested their gas on Aussie sheep at a remote farm in the Outback.

By that time, more than a dozen cultists were in custody, facing various charges related to the gas attacks. Asahara himself was arrested on May 15 and was soon indicted with six others on murder charges stemming from the March subway attack. On June 20 one of his disciples who was still at large hijacked an airliner with 350 persons aboard, demanding the immediate release of "venerable master" Asahara, but police stormed the plane and disarmed him without loss of life.

On October 5, 1995, Japanese news sources reported that Shoko Asahara had confessed involvement in the Tokyo subway attack and various other crimes. One of Asahara's aides, Masahiro Taming, surrendered to police three days later, facing charges of attempting to murder Tokyo's governor. On October 30 a Japanese court officially ordered the disbandment of Aum Shinrikyo. Slow-motion murder

trials proceeded during the next eight years with multiple convictions, but Asahara's trial was still in progress during 2003 with the defendant alternately sleeping in court or mumbling incoherently in what detractors called a pretense of insanity designed to spare him from a death sentence.

As for Aum Shinrikyo, it was revived as "Aleph" in February 2000, offering apologies to the families of its victims, coughing up cash settlements from the millions of yen its members earn selling computer parts throughout Japan. The reborn sect claims 1,650 members, including 300 in RUSSIA, recently visited by cult leader Fumihiro Joyu. Unimpressed by Aum's about-face, U.S. Secretary of State Colin Powell formally labeled Aleph a terrorist organization in 2001. A few months later, in January 2002, five Russian members, led by Dmitri Sigachev, were jailed on charges they had plotted to bomb various Japanese cities and thereby secure Asahara's freedom.

AUSTRIA

In 1867 the Austrian empire merged with HUNGARY to become a dual monarchy under Emperor Franz Joseph I, a belligerent ruler who joined GERMANY, TURKEY, and BULGARIA as part of the Central Powers in 1914. When BLACK HAND rebels assassinated Archduke Franz Ferdinand that summer, the alliance plunged Europe—and later the world—into World War I. That conflict left Austria in political and economic chaos after 1918. A new constitution established parliamentary democracy in November 1920, but members of a growing Nazi Party soon agitated for another alliance with Germany. Chancellor Engelbert Dollfuss imposed a dictatorship in 1933 to block the spread of Nazism, but Nazis assassinated him on July 25, 1934. German troops invaded Austria in March 1938, and ADOLF HITLER declared its union with Germany (the Anschluss) as part of the THIRD REICH.

After World War II, the victorious Allies declared Austrians a "liberated" people, but fond memories of the Reich lingered on. Neo-Nazi groups thrived after Austria regained full independence on May 15, 1955, and their influence continues to the present day. In June 1986 former UNITED NATIONS secretary-general Kurt Waldheim was elected president in a campaign marked by controversy over his alleged links to Nazi WAR CRIMES in YUGOSLAVIA. In February 2000 the conservative People's Party formed an alliance with the extremist Freedom Party led by Jörg Haider, a racist xenophobe known for public remarks that praised wartime Nazi policies. Haider's fascist views prompted sanctions against Austria by other members of the European Union, and while he resigned from the party in May 2000, Haider remained an influential adviser. The Freedom Party–People's Party coalition crumbled in September 2002, with Haider striking off to form a new and more extreme vehicle for his political ambitions. The struggle for control of Austria's soul and body politic continues.

"AXIS of Evil"

In the latter part of 2001, while American troops were engaged in toppling the government of AFGHANISTAN, U.S. President George W. Bush publicly blamed the world's terrorist crisis on an "Axis of Evil," including the nations of IRAQ, IRAN, and North KOREA. Lee Hamilton—former chairman of the House Foreign Affairs Committee, now head of the Woodrow Wilson International Center—noted that Bush's turn of phrase "was a very effective phrase for rallying the American public" after the PENTTBOM attacks of September 11, 2001. Critics promptly branded the label both illogical and irrelevant: Iraq and Iran had been mortal enemies since the 1970s, while North Korea had no ties to either Middle Eastern nation— and none of the countries singled out by Bush had any link to the 9/11 raids. By late 2002 Hamilton acknowledged that Bush's name-calling "has made diplomacy more difficult in the months since [9/11] and probably exacerbated the dangers that he was seeking to contain." Lumping the three disparate nations together also made it more difficult for Bush to explain the U.S. invasion of Iraq (based on unsupported claims that Baghdad possessed weapons of mass destruction) while pursuing diplomatic negotiations with North Korea (which boasts of its nuclear arsenal). In fact, while right-wing allies still employ the term *Axis of Evil* in their calls for a continuing global war on TERRORISM, Bush himself has not uttered the phrase since August 2002. Professor David Houck, a linguistics expert at Florida State University, analyzed Bush's rhetoric in an interview with *USA*

Demonstrators in New York City protesting the war in Iraq carry a sign featuring the likenesses of Vice President Dick Cheney, President George W. Bush, and Attorney General John Ashcroft under the words "Axis of Evil." (Corbis)

Today. While acknowledging that "Axis of Evil" was "a shorthand phrase that does a lot of work," Houck also noted its primary shortcoming: "The trouble is that 'evil' doesn't leave a lot of room for negotiation. How do you negotiate with evil?"

See also BUSH DYNASTY.

AZERBAIJAN

Azerbaijan, located on the western shore of the Caspian Sea at the southeast extremity of the Caucasus, was ceded to RUSSIA by Persia (now IRAN) through the Treaty of Gulistan (1813) and the Treaty of Turkamanchai (1828). The country declared independence from Russia in May 1918, following the Bolshevik Revolution, but Red Army forces reconquered Azerbaijan two years later. It was annexed into the Transcaucasian Soviet Socialist Republic in 1922 and then was reestablished as a separate Soviet republic in 1936. Finally, Azerbaijan once again declared independence from the collapsing Soviet Union in August 1991.

Freedom hardly ended the nation's troubles, however. In 1988, Azerbaijan and ARMENIA went to war for control of the Nagorno-Karabakh enclave, a struggle that cost 30,000 lives before Azerbaijan emerged victorious in 1994. Current prime minister Artur Rasizade was elected two years later, in a process labeled "seriously flawed" by international observers. Economic woes verging on national bankruptcy may be alleviated by Western investment in Azerbaijan's vast OIL reserves, valued in the trillions of U.S. dollars, but long-running dissension over the route of a new oil pipeline has thus far stalled the country's black gold bonanza. In July 2001 Iranian warships chased two Azerbaijani oil-exploration ships out of disputed Caspian waters, thus exacerbating conflict over petroleum rights.

BACKWARD masking

Backward masking (BM) is the process of recording words or music backward to include a secret message on recordings that can only be deciphered by playing the tape or CD backward. In the 1980s BM became a point of heated controversy: TELEVANGELISTS, politicians, and private groups such as the Parents Music Resource Center alleged deliberate "brainwashing" of children by using hidden plugs for sex, drugs, and SATANISM. Arguments ranged from flat denials to bizarre allegations of a global conspiracy involving thousands of executives, performers, and technicians in the music industry. The truth, as usual, lay somewhere in between.

It is a fact that BM *does* exist and has for many years. In 1969 the Beatles planted backward lyrics on their *Abbey Road* album, hinting at Paul McCartney's death as a morbid publicity stunt. Popular singers David Bowie and Meat Loaf Aday have acknowledged using BM on their albums but deny any sinister intent. In 1990 Rob Halford (lead singer for the heavy-metal band Judas Priest) told reporters that BM "has been going on for 30 or 40 years."

The question then must be: To what effect? BM critics—typically fundamentalist Christians or politicians seeking their support—see demons inside every album. In April 1986 Ohio minister Jim Brown convinced local teenagers to burn their records of TV's *Mr. Ed*'s theme song, somehow persuading them (and their presumably mature parents) that the rever-

sal of "A horse is a horse" yields "Someone sang this song for Satan." The Arkansas state senate passed a ban on BM in 1983, while Congress defeated a similar federal bill. In 1990 performers Judas Priest and Ozzy Osbourne faced lawsuits from parents who claimed that the performers' music had driven their sons to commit or attempt suicide, but the defendants prevailed in both cases.

BAHAMAS

Christopher Columbus "discovered" the Bahamas (not North America) on October 12, 1492. A nightmare of slavery and sadism ensued for the Arawak natives, who were soon wiped out. A notorious haven for pirates by the early 17th century, the Bahamas remain so today. Mobster MEYER LANSKY paved the way for large-scale casino gambling before England granted the islands internal self-rule in 1964, and the tourist traps now flourish. The scenic islands also serve as a way station for South American COCAINE and HEROIN en route to the United States and Europe. Pervasive government corruption ensures that few shipments are seized and that visiting felons (at least those with money) are rarely molested.

BAHRAIN

This rocky archipelago in the Persian Gulf was ruled by various invaders from the fourth century A.D.

until its final master (Britain) granted full independence on August 14, 1971. OIL was found in Bahrain in the 1930s, but its wells are expected to run dry early in the 21st century. Efforts to diversify the national economy have been frustrated by bloody sectarian fighting between rival Shi'ite and Sunni Muslims. Women voted for the first time in February 2001, throwing their weight behind a constitutional monarchy, but the immensely rich al-Khalifa family still owns most of Bahrain's wealth.

BALTIMORE Police Department

During the years 1966–82, law enforcement in Baltimore, Maryland, was dominated by Police Commissioner Donald Pomerleau, a die-hard enemy of perceived "subversives" who also used the police department to punish his personal critics. Pomerleau launched the Baltimore Police Department's (BPD) Red Squad—also known as the Inspectional Services Division (ISD)—on July 1, 1966, with officers trained by the FEDERAL BUREAU OF INVESTIGATION (FBI) and U.S. Army Intelligence to ferret out "enemies" of the state. ISD's chief, Maj. Maurice DuBois, was himself an FBI agent for 20 years before he joined the BPD. Under such leadership BPD engaged in a wide range of illegal surveillance and harassment directed at black or "leftist" organizations. A primary target was the BLACK PANTHER PARTY (BPP), earmarked for destruction by the FBI and the BPD alike.

Pomerleau and DuBois saw their chance to crush the local BPP in early 1970 when a human skeleton was unearthed in Baltimore. The city's medical examiner reported that the deceased was a white male, 25–30 years old, who died of a drug overdose. Unsatisfied with that bland result, BPD shipped the remains to the FBI crime lab, where technicians "positively" identified the corpse as 20-year-old Eugene Anderson, a black BPP member allegedly killed by a close-range shotgun blast. In April 1970, 17 Panthers and white attorney Arthur Turco were charged with murdering Anderson, allegedly because they thought he was a police informer. The indictment followed a meeting between Baltimore's district attorney and U.S. Attorney General John Mitchell, who was subsequently jailed for his role in the WATERGATE conspiracy. The prosecution's three witnesses, all paid BPD/FBI informers, were granted immunity from

prosecution and placed on salary for the duration of the trial, but they failed to earn their money. "Key witness" Mahoney Kebe was so confused at trial that the judge ejected him from court and ordered his testimony stricken from the record. A new district attorney ultimately dismissed all charges against the defendants, while admitting that his predecessor was guilty of "improper prosecution practices." The Maryland state senate investigated complaints of BPD's abusive conduct in 1975, and its December report sustained most of the charges made by various harassment victims. Three years later, state lawmakers passed new legislation that restricted police surveillance and granted citizens access to information contained in their files. With his spying activities curtailed, Commissioner Pomerleau resigned in 1982, two years before the expiration of his term in office.

BANGLADESH

Formerly East PAKISTAN, this segment of India's historic Bengal region was widely separated from the Muslim state of West Pakistan when INDIA was partitioned in 1947. Religion aside, people of the two Pakistans had nothing in common, prompting East Pakistan to declare independence (as Bangladesh) in March 1971. Nine months of civil war and deadly famine then ensued, climaxed by India's intervention to defeat West Pakistan in December 1971. Since then, a relentless series of famines and natural disasters have ravaged the country, climaxed in 2002 by a deadly arsenic crisis. Authorities say that 3–4 million wells that were dug by the UNITED NATIONS as part of a "safe-water program" in the 1970s now contain dangerous levels of arsenic. At last count, 35 million persons were plagued by ailments ranging from skin lesions to cancer and diabetes.

BAPBOMB

Birmingham, Alabama's, Sixteenth Street Baptist Church has a long history of involvement in the black civil rights movement. In 1946, after it hosted a meeting of the Southern Negro Youth Congress, police commissioner EUGENE "BULL" CONNOR visited the pastor and warned him that if such activities continued, God—acting through the KU KLUX KLAN—might "strike the church down." Seventeen years later, when the church served as a rallying point for demonstrators led by Dr. MARTIN LUTHER KING, JR., that threat was realized. On Sunday, September 15, 1963, a powerful bomb rocked the church. Four adolescent girls—Addie Mae Collins, Denise McNair, Carole Robertson, and Cynthia Wesley—were killed in the blast; a fifth, Sarah Jean Collins, was permanently blinded in one eye.

Klan members were the prime suspects, with several names provided by Gary Rowe, a FEDERAL BUREAU OF INVESTIGATION (FBI) informant in the KKK since 1960. Director J. EDGAR HOOVER called the investigation—code named BAPBOMB—the bureau's most intensive manhunt since the killing of JOHN DILLINGER; yet it was marked from the beginning by what journalist Diane McWhorter aptly calls a "leisurely pursuit of witnesses." When local police sought information on prime suspect Robert Chambliss, a violent Klansman known to his friends as "Dynamite Bob," G-men falsely reported that they had mounted constant surveillance on Chambliss's home the night before the bombing and observed nothing irregular. Results of FBI polygraph tests on Chambliss and other Klan suspects were likewise withheld from Birmingham authorities, perhaps because Connor's police force was known to be heavily infiltrated with Klansmen. Governor GEORGE WALLACE "beat the Kennedy crowd to the punch" soon after the bombing when suspects Chambliss, Charles Cagle, and James Hall were charged with misdemeanor counts of possessing unregistered dynamite. All three were convicted and sentenced to six months in jail, their sentences suspended by the court. A few days later, James Hall joined Rowe (and countless other Klansmen) on the FBI's payroll as a full-time informant, vowing to help solve the BAPBOMB case.

In 1964 the bureau obtained tape recordings of Klansman Thomas Blanton, Jr., discussing details of the church bombing with his wife in their home. Later reports claimed the tapes were "barely audible" without computer enhancement, unavailable in the 1960s, but the issue remains contested today. Before year's end, G-men knew beyond doubt that the bombers were Blanton, Chambliss, Herman Frank Cash, and Bobby Lee Cherry. In 1965 Hoover ruled out prosecution on grounds that chances of conviction by an Alabama jury were "remote." A five-year federal statute of limitations officially closed the case in 1968, yet FBI historian Robert Kessler contends that "the investigation continued until 1971."

Be that as it may, the Blanton tapes and other BAPBOMB evidence went into storage after Hoover's death in 1972, and FBI headquarters made no initial offer of assistance until five years later when Alabama Attorney General Bill Baxley reopened the investigation. Finally, after Baxley threatened to hold a Washington press conference with survivors of the four slain girls, G-men released a portion of their file on Robert Chambliss, while withholding all material on Blanton and the other bombers. Chambliss was indicted for murder in September 1977 and convicted two months later, largely on the testimony of a niece who heard him boasting of the crime in 1963. Chambliss received a life prison term with a 10-year minimum before parole; he died in custody in 1985.

Accounts vary as to what the FBI did next. Robert Kessler maintains that Birmingham agent-in-charge G. Robert Langford reopened the BAPBOMB case in 1993 "without telling headquarters" and that he subsequently "found" the Blanton tapes (allegedly mislaid and forgotten since 1972). An alternate report, published in April 2000, claimed that the FBI reopened its investigation in 1997 after the chance discovery of "new and credible" evidence—that is, the tapes maintained in bureau files since 1964. In either case, bomber Herman Cash died in 1994 without facing criminal charges. A grand jury convened to study the case in November 1998, its review culminating in the May 2000 arrest of aging Klansmen Blanton and Cherry on charges of first-degree murder. Even then, controversy endured: Cherry claimed that G-men had offered to reduce the charges if he would "lie" under oath about Blanton; Blanton's daughter told reporters, "The FBI told dad, 'We're going to pin it on somebody. We don't care who.'" Agent Craig Dahle of the Birmingham field office denied the charges, telling reporters, "It wouldn't happen that way."

Thomas Blanton was convicted of murder on May 1, 2001, and sentenced to life imprisonment. A year later, on May 22, 2002, Bobby Cherry was convicted and received an identical sentence. In the wake of Blanton's conviction, Bill Baxley voiced outrage at the FBI's long suppression of recordings and other evidence in the case: "What excuse can the FBI have for allowing Mr. Blanton to go free for 24 years with this smoking-gun evidence hidden in its files?" he asked. "If we had had those tapes, we would have unequivocally been able to convict Blanton [in 1977]. The FBI, for all intents and purposes, gave a 'get out of jail free card' to Tommy Blanton." Former assistant attorney general John Young recalled of the 1977 Chambliss prosecution, "[The FBI] denied having any more evidence than what they gave us, and it was hard enough getting what we got." Director Louis Freeh agreed, calling the BAPBOMB case "a disgrace to the FBI" and telling the media, "That case should have been prosecuted in 1964. It could have been prosecuted in 1964. The evidence was there."

Agent Dahle, in Birmingham, told reporters that there was "no easy answer" to Baxley's questions but insisted, "I think it is wrong to assert that there was any effort to block anything." Newsman Kessler blamed the whole thing on simple ignorance: "Instead of withholding evidence from Alabama Attorney General Baxley in 1977, as Baxley claimed, the FBI did not realize it had the material." While that assertion strained credulity, Kessler went even further, giving the bureau credit for Alabama's state prosecution of Tom Blanton: "Because of the tenacity of Langford . . . and . . . others involved," Kessler wrote, "the FBI had brought to justice a man who had blown up four girls because of the color of their skin."

See also KENNEDY DYNASTY.

BARBIE, Klaus (1913–1991)

An avid supporter of ADOLF HITLER and the genocidal THIRD REICH, Klaus Barbie served as chief of the GESTAPO in occupied FRANCE during 1942–44. In that capacity, the "Butcher of Lyon" supervised executions of at least 4,000 persons, deported another 7,500 to certain death in concentration camps, and tortured countless others. Captured by U.S. authorities in Germany after the war, Barbie was recruited to serve the CENTRAL INTELLIGENCE AGENCY (CIA) as part of Operation Paperclip, a scheme whereby Nazi intelligence officers were shielded from WAR CRIMES prosecution while helping the CIA fight COMMUNISM in Europe. (The Nazi sadist's contributions to "world freedom" remain classified.) French extradition warrants were rejected while Barbie served the United States (1947–51), and the CIA afterward relocated Barbie's family to BOLIVIA, where he enjoyed the protection of pro-Nazi dictator Hugo Banzer Suárez and

the CATHOLIC CHURCH's archbishop in La Paz, Abel Antezana. Living affluently as "Klaus Altmann," Barbie served as a leader of the Nazi underground movement in South America, reportedly communing regularly with fugitive MARTIN BORMANN. His cover was blown in 1973, but Bolivian authorities stalled extradition to France for another decade. In the meantime, INTERPOL's chief officer in Bolivia was fired on corruption charges for aiding Barbie's concealment. On his return to France in 1983, Barbie launched a campaign of legal delays that postponed his trial until May 1987. He was convicted of mass murder two months later and sentenced to life imprisonment. Barbie died in prison of leukemia on September 25, 1991.

BARBIE® dolls

Critics who denounce the Mattel Toy Company's famous Barbie® dolls as tools of a global conspiracy are less concerned with Mattel's acknowledged $1.5 billion sales than with Barbie®'s impact on youngsters who play with the well-endowed plastic material girl. As outlined on various Internet Web sites, the Barbie® conspiracy involves long-term brainwashing of girls (or children generally) to accept a body image that is unattainable without extensive plastic surgery, while craving a kind of parasitic "bimbo" lifestyle. Mattel executives deny promoting any such message, either consciously or otherwise, and in 1997 filed a lawsuit against the Danish band Aqua over Aqua's dance tune "Barbie Girl." (Lyrics included "I'm a blonde bimbo girl in a fantasy world / Dress me up, make it tight, I'm your dolly.") Although Mattel sued primarily for copyright infringement—Aqua's advertising used the same "electric pink" employed in Barbie® ads for decades—lawyers for the firm made it clear that they were fighting for Barbie®'s reputation. That lawsuit was dismissed, and appellate judge Alex Kozinski later noted that the original 1950s Barbie® resembled a "German streetwalker" before it was revamped into a long-legged all-American girl with a "fictitious figure." The U.S. SUPREME COURT rejected Mattel's final appeal in January 2003. Meanwhile, the company's announced plan to introduce "smart" Barbie® dolls drew ridicule from critics nationwide. As one put it, "Making smart Barbies is like making G.I. Joe a conscientious objector."

BAYER Corporation

In June 2003 several U.S. hemophiliacs filed a class-action lawsuit against the Bayer pharmaceutical company, alleging that Bayer (and others) deliberately exposed patients to AIDS and hepatitis C by selling medicine manufactured from the blood of ailing, high-risk donors. The lawsuit, filed in San Francisco, alleges that Bayer engaged in DRUG DUMPING, distributing tainted blood-clotting products in Asia and Latin America during 1984–85, after notice of infected products blocked their sale in the United States. Attorney Robert Nelson, speaking for the plaintiffs, said, "This is a worldwide tragedy. Thousands of hemophiliacs have unnecessarily died from AIDS and many thousands more are infected with HIV or hepatitis C." Defense attorneys replied with a statement saying, "Bayer at all times complied with all regulations in force in the relevant countries based on the amount of scientific evidence available at the time." The firm added that "decisions made 20 years ago should not be judged by today's scientific knowledge." No verdict had been rendered in the case at press time for this volume.

BAY of Pigs invasion

In 1960 Vice President RICHARD NIXON proposed a plan (dubbed Operation Zapata) to topple the regime of Cuban leader FIDEL CASTRO by means of a military invasion. President Dwight Eisenhower approved the scheme and authorized CENTRAL INTELLIGENCE AGENCY (CIA) planning of the assault, but his second term ended in January 1961, and Nixon's presidential hopes were dashed by the election of John Kennedy. With enthusiastic support from his brother (and attorney general) Robert, Kennedy decided to proceed with Nixon's plan and thus restore "freedom" to CUBA. The CIA's "army" consisted of 1,500 Cuban exiles, including 200 former soldiers who had fought Castro under deposed dictator Fulgencio Batista (14 of them fugitives from outstanding murder charges in Cuba). The force trained in GUATEMALA, with U.S. arms and equipment, operating on the theory that suffering Cubans would rise against Castro en masse when the first shots were fired. The invaders' target was the Bahia de Cochinos (Bay of Pigs) on Cuba's southern coast. They landed on April 17, 1961, but found no welcoming committee of the Cuban people. Instead, they were instantly betrayed by locals loyal to Castro, and

a Cuban military force closed in to crush the landing team. By April 20, 1,197 invaders had been captured, and most of the others were dead (including four CIA pilots). Embarrassed by the fiasco, President Kennedy drew criticism from all sides, including complaints from Cuban exile leader José Miró Cardona that the invasion was doomed by Kennedy's failure to provide air support. In December 1962 Castro released 1,113 of the prisoners in exchange for $53 million in food and medicine raised by private U.S. donations. The Bay of Pigs debacle marked Cuba's first-ever victory against U.S. imperialism, and many theorists today believe it was a motivating factor in the 1963 JFK ASSASSINATION.

See also KENNEDY DYNASTY.

BCCI conspiracy

Founded in the 1970s by Middle Eastern financiers Agha Hasan Abedi and Swaleh Naqvi, the Bank of Credit and Commerce International (BCCI) swiftly spun a global net of shady deals involving (among others) the CENTRAL INTELLIGENCE AGENCY (CIA), the MAFIA, international drug dealers, Arab terrorists, and the usual cast of corrupt politicians (many of them influential leaders of the U.S. Democratic Party). Volumes could be written about BCCI's crimes, but a December 1992 report from the U.S. Senate fairly summarized the bank's illicit transactions.

BCCI's unique criminal structure . . . was an essential component of its spectacular growth, and a guarantee of its eventual collapse. The structure was conceived by Abedi and managed by Naqvi for the specific purpose of evading regulation or control by governments. It functioned to frustrate the full understanding of BCCI's operations by anyone.

Unlike any ordinary bank, BCCI was from its earliest days made up of multiplying layers of entities, related to one another through an impenetrable series of holding companies, affiliates, subsidiaries, banks-within-banks, insider dealings and nominee relationships. By fracturing corporate structure, record keeping, regulatory review, and audits, the complex BCCI family of entities created by Abedi was able to evade ordinary legal restrictions on the movement of capital and goods as a matter of daily practice and routine. In creating BCCI as a vehicle fundamentally free of government control, Abedi developed in BCCI an ideal mechanism for facilitating illicit activity by others, including such activity by officials of many of the governments whose laws BCCI was breaking.

BCCI's criminality included fraud by BCCI and BCCI customers involving billions of dollars; money laundering in Europe, Africa, Asia, and the Americas; BCCI's bribery of officials in most of those locations; support of terrorism, arms trafficking, and the sale of nuclear technologies; management of prostitution; the commission and facilitation of income tax evasion, smuggling, and illegal immigration; illicit purchases of banks and real estate; and a panoply of financial crimes limited only by the imagination of its officers and customers.

Among BCCI's principal mechanisms for committing crimes were its use of shell corporations and bank confidentiality and secrecy havens; layering of its corporate structure; its use of front-men and nominees, guarantees and buy-back arrangements; back-to-back financial documentation among BCCI controlled entities, kickbacks and bribes, the intimidation of witnesses, and the retention of well-placed insiders to discourage governmental action.

The BCCI facade suffered its first major crack in 1988 with a Florida indictment for laundering drug money, but even then federal prosecutors failed to grasp the enormity of BCCI's crimes, including infiltration and ownership of major U.S. banks. Operating in 73 nations and bribing officials in each, BCCI took full advantage of endemic corruption in ARGENTINA, BANGLADESH, BOTSWANA, BRAZIL, CHINA, COLOMBIA, the CONGO, GHANA, GUATEMALA, INDIA, JAMAICA, KUWAIT, LEBANON, Mauritius, MOROCCO, NIGERIA, PAKISTAN, PANAMA, PERU, SAUDI ARABIA, SENEGAL, SRI LANKA, SUDAN, SURINAME, the United States, ZAMBIA, and ZIMBABWE. By the time it finally collapsed in the 1990s with a handful of its ranking leaders prosecuted for various crimes, BCCI had paved the way for a new millennium of corporate corruption. As summarized by Senate investigators:

Unanswered questions include, but are not limited to, the relationship between BCCI and the Banco Nazionale del Lavoro; the alleged relationship between the late CIA director WILLIAM CASEY and BCCI; the extent of BCCI's involvement in Pakistan's nuclear program; BCCI's manipulation of commodities and securities markets in Europe and Canada; BCCI's activities in India, including its relationship with the business empire of the Hinduja family; BCCI's relationships with convicted Iraqi arms dealer Sarkis Sarkenalian,

Syrian drug trafficker, terrorist, and arms trafficker Monzer Al-Kassar, and other major arms dealers; the use of BCCI by central figures in the alleged "OCTOBER SURPRISE," BCCI's activities with the Central Bank of Syria and with the Foreign Trade Mission of the Soviet Union in London; its involvement with foreign intelligence agencies; the financial dealings of BCCI directors with Charles Keating and several Keating affiliates and front-companies, including the possibility that BCCI related entities may have laundered funds for Keating to move them outside the United States; BCCI's financing of commodities and other business dealings of international criminal financier Marc Rich; the nature, extent and meaning of the ownership of other major U.S. financial institutions by Middle Eastern political figures; the nature, extent, and meaning of real estate and financial investments in the United States by major shareholders of BCCI; the sale of BCCI affiliate Banque de Commerce et Placement in Geneva, to the Cukorova Group of Turkey, which owned an entity involved in the BNL Iraqi arms sales, among others.

BELARUS

Belarus (also known as White Russia) has been variously claimed throughout its history by Lithuania, POLAND, and RUSSIA. It suffered more than most nations in World War II, with seesaw battles between JOSEPH STALIN's Red Army and ADOLF HITLER's Wehrmacht, played out on its swampy soil. When the Soviet CHERNOBYL power plant exploded in 1986, 70 percent of its nuclear fallout landed in Belarus, causing epidemic cancer and related illnesses. Belarus declared independence in August 1991, but its people had no taste for freedom. A new treaty with Russia in April 1997 stopped just short of a political merger. President Aleksandr Lukashenko (in power since January 1994) runs an authoritarian state that is widely denounced for its human-rights violations in the Stalinist mode. Accused of fielding death squads that have murdered dozens of dissidents since the late 1990s, Lukashenko was nonetheless reelected (under highly suspicious circumstances) on September 9, 2001.

BELGIUM

Since 57 B.C., a series of conquerors ranging from JULIUS CAESAR to ADOLF HITLER have used Belgium as the gateway for attacks on more inviting parts of

Europe. At the same time, Belgian kings acquired an African empire that they pillaged brutally with utter disregard for the welfare of aboriginal peoples. Belgian control of the Congo and Ruanda-Urundi (now RWANDA and BURUNDI) was not relinquished until 1960–62, after a final spasm of warfare along racial lines. Belgium has been rocked by incessant scandal since 1991 when a deputy prime minister was slain by still-unidentified contract killers. In 1996 disclosure of the Marc Dutroux child-sex-and-murder ring revealed a morass of perversion and government corruption that had permitted predatory killers to act with near impunity. Two years later Belgian statesman and former NATO official Willy Claes was convicted of bribery. In 1999 public officials confessed to concealing evidence that most of Belgium's poultry was contaminated with cancer-causing dioxin. New prime minister Guy Verhofstadt began sweeping reforms that same year, but his efforts were overshadowed by Belgium's odd claim of "universal jurisdiction" over WAR CRIMES, allegedly permitting Belgian courts to extradite and try citizens of any nation for atrocities committed anywhere on Earth. A cast of suspects led by President George W. Bush staunchly denied Belgian jurisdiction outside its own borders, and Belgium scrapped the law on July 12, 2003, in a bid to keep U.S. goodwill.

See also BUSH DYNASTY.

BELIZE

Sandwiched between MEXICO and GUATEMALA in Central America, Belize was ruled, or "supervised," by England (as British Honduras) until September 21, 1981. Guatemala delayed recognition of Belize's national sovereignty for another decade, and it still claims rights to more than half of Belize. Negotiations before the Organization of American States has thus far failed to resolve the conflict, leaving an atmosphere ripe for subversion, spying, and crossborder guerrilla raids.

BERIA, Lavrenty Pavlovich (1899–1953)

A native of GEORGIA who was born in 1899, Lavrenty Beria trained as an architect but later devoted himself to the Communist Party and served in its SECRET POLICE. He met Russian dictator JOSEPH STALIN on vacation in 1931 and there earned Stalin's gratitude by foiling an assassination attempt.

(Later, some claimed Beria staged the event himself in order to win Stalin's favor.) By 1938, Beria was the chief of Stalin's NKVD (later the KGB), and he was ultimately blamed for the deaths of millions in Russia's various purges. A closet pedophile whose crimes against children were covered by Stalin's protection, Beria earned a reputation as a ruthless tyrant who "got things done," trusted with Stalin's most important jobs (including development of RUSSIA's early nuclear weapons). At Stalin's death in 1953, many Russia watchers assumed Beria would be the nation's next supreme leader, but he had made too many enemies during those past 15 years. Before year's end a group of rivals led by Nikita Khrushchev conspired to have Beria jailed and executed as an "enemy of the state."

BIG Seven

The "noble experiment" of PROHIBITION created the first national crime syndicate in U.S. history as various local and ethnic bootlegging gangs joined forces to minimize bloodshed and maximize profits. Before the web of crime spread nationwide, however, an experimental prototype was tested by mobsters on the East Coast. That alliance, known as the Big Seven, was created in 1926–27; members included: (1) the "Bug and Meyer Mob" under Benjamin "Bugsy" Siegel and MEYER LANSKY; (2) New York's dominant MAFIA faction, led by CHARLES "LUCKY" LUCIANO and John Torrio; (3) the Joe Adonis gang in Brooklyn; (4) the dominant gang in northern New Jersey, led by Abner "Longy" Zwillman and Willie Moretti; (5) southern New Jersey's crime lord, Enoch "Nucky" Johnson; (6) New England mobster Charles "King" Solomon (operating from Boston with Joseph Kennedy); and (7) the Philadelphia syndicate run by Irving Wexler (also known as "Waxey Gordon"), Irving "Bitzy" Bitz and Harry Stromberg (also known as "Nig Rosen"). This group served as the nucleus of future "crime conventions" held in 1929–34, at which alliances with gangs from Florida to Chicago and California were solidified to mutual advantage. Allies from the Big Seven also ensured Luciano's victory in his 1931 war to modernize the American Mafia and depose the old guard of "mustache Petes." Its members would remain dominant figures in organized crime through the 1950s—and in Lansky's case, long after that.

See also KENNEDY DYNASTY.

BIKO, Stephen Bantu (1946–1977)

The founder of SOUTH AFRICA's "black consciousness" movement was born in 1946 and became an outspoken critic of the nation's racist apartheid system from childhood. Expelled from his first school for "antiestablishment" activity, Biko later organized the South African Students' Organization while attending segregated classes at the University of Natal Medical School. Three years later, in 1972, he was among the founders of the Black People's Convention, working to merge 70-odd different civil rights groups from different parts of South Africa. The all-white government "banned" Biko in 1973 with a decree that forbade any travel outside his hometown in the Eastern Cape Province. Undeterred, he founded the Zimele Trust Fund to assist political prisoners and their families. That effort sent Biko to jail for brutal interrogation on four occasions between August 1975 and September 1977. The last session proved fatal, with a savage beating inflicted by Biko's jailers on September 7. Police surgeons recommended hospital treatment on September 11, but Biko's jailers moved him to the Pretoria Central Prison instead, where he died one day later, lying naked and untreated on the concrete floor of his cell. Minister of Justice James Kruger initially claimed that Biko died from a self-imposed hunger strike, remarking that the news of Biko's death "left him cold." Kruger's lie was discarded after an inquest revealed Biko's head injuries, but the magistrate in charge deemed the wounds accidental. Following the collapse of apartheid, Biko's family sued the state for damages in 1979 and settled out of court for R65,000 ($25,000). Three doctors involved in Biko's case were initially cleared by the South African Medical Disciplinary Committee but then were mildly censured for their negligence in 1985. The police officers who murdered Biko in jail sought and received amnesty in 1997 from the troubled nation's Truth and Reconciliation Commission.

BILDERBERG group

Little is known about the origins of this shadow organization that was thought by some to secretly control the daily course of major events throughout much of the world. Some accounts say the group was founded in the early 1950s by Prince Bernhard of the Netherlands, while others speak of secret meetings held at England's Oxford University in 1940. Some observers call the group Marxist even as others proclaim it the last bastion of neoimperial capitalism. Whatever their political leanings, many associates of the group also belong to the TRILATERAL COMMISSION and the COUNCIL ON FOREIGN RELATIONS (not to mention some with strong connections to the CENTRAL INTELLIGENCE AGENCY). A clique of such low profile that it has no formal name, the Bilderberg group takes its public label from the Bilderberg Hotel in Oosterbeek, Holland, where journalists first discovered the group's existence in 1954. While the group maintains a headquarters in Leyden, it has no formal membership. Rather, secret invitations are sent to suitable candidates for once-yearly strategy sessions convened at plush resorts around the world. *Asia Times* described the group as follows in May 2003, shortly before it convened at Versailles:

> *The Bilderberg club is regarded by many financial and business elites as the high chamber of the high priests of capitalism. You can't apply for membership of such a club. Each year, a mysterious "steering committee" devises a selected invitation list with a maximum 100 names. . . . Participants and guests rarely reveal that they are attending. Their security is managed by military intelligence. But what is the secretive group really up to? Well, they talk. They lobby. They try to magnify their already immense political clout, on both sides of the Atlantic. And everybody pledges absolute secrecy on what has been discussed.*
>
> *The Bilderberg mingles central bankers, defense experts, press barons, government ministers, prime ministers, royalty, international financiers and political leaders from Europe and America.*
>
> *Guests this year . . . Queen Beatrix of the Netherlands, Queen Sofia and King Juan Carlos of Spain, and high officials of assorted governments. The Bilderberg does not invite—or accept—Asians, Middle Easterners, Latin Americans or Africans.*

Other past or present U.S. power players with confirmed links to the group include Bill Clinton, David Rockefeller, HENRY KISSINGER, U.S. Secretary of Defense Donald Rumsfeld, and Henry Ford II. Whatever the true thrust of its hidden agenda(s), the Bilderberg group's near-obsessive secrecy and ties to every major government on earth ensures that it will be the object of conspiracy theories as long as it exists.

See also CLINTON, BILL AND HILLARY.

BILLY the Kid   See UNDEAD OUTLAWS.

BIN LADEN family

The best-known member of this affluent Saudi Arabian clan is Osama bin Laden, founding father of AL-QAEDA and the reputed mastermind of a five-year TERRORISM campaign that culminated in the catastrophic PENTTBOMB attacks of September 11, 2001. Few Americans know the rest of bin Laden's family or recognize its strong economic ties to the BUSH DYNASTY spanning more than a decade. Bush–bin Laden family ties date from the 1970s, but they were not revealed until 1990's public exposure of the international BCCI CONSPIRACY. Houston businessman James Bath was a major BCCI stockholder and personal friend of George W. Bush, whom he met while both served in the Texas Air National Guard. As explained by *Time* magazine reports, Bath initially "made his fortune by investing money for [Sheikh Kalid bin] Mahfouz and for another BCCI-connected Saudi, Sheikh bin Laden" (Osama's father). Among the firms receiving bin Laden money from 1977 onward was Arbusto Energy, an oil company founded by "Dubya" Bush. A decade later, when Bush and Rath moved on to another oil company, Harken Energy, Salem bin Laden (Osama's brother) negotiated access to oil fields in Bahrain, thus granting the Bushes another multimillion-dollar windfall.

In the United States, meanwhile, financial assets of the Saudi Binladen Corporation (SBC) were managed by the Carlyle Group—one of the world's largest arms dealers and a majority shareholder in such firms as the Seven-Up Company and the Federal Data Corporation (sole supplier of air traffic-control surveillance systems to the U.S. Federal Aviation Authority). Carlyle earns $12 billion minimum per year, managed by an executive team that includes Frank Carlucci (former deputy director of the CENTRAL INTELLIGENCE AGENCY (CIA) and secretary of defense under President RONALD REAGAN) and James Baker II (secretary of state under President George H. W. Bush). Carlyle's overseas representatives include George H. W. Bush and former British prime minister John Major. In 2003 Carlyle would reap more billions by supplying most of the hardware to coalition forces for OPERATION IRAQI FREEDOM.

While his family and the Bush clan were growing rich together in the 1990s, Osama bin Laden turned to terrorism in the name of Islamic fundamentalism, seeking to destroy ISRAEL and its global allies. Following the August 1998 al-Qaeda bombings of two U.S. embassies in Africa, President Bill Clinton ordered the CIA to take bin Laden "dead or alive," but the agency failed to carry out the contract. Clinton told the press in September 2001, "At the time we did everything we can do. I authorized the arrest and, if necessary, the killing of Osama bin Laden and we actually made contact with a group in AFGHANISTAN to do it." Theorists explain the CIA's failure to bury Osama in various ways, ranging from institutional incompetence to sinister intervention by members of the Bush family. George H. W. Bush, they recall, was director of the CIA in 1976–77 and maintained his ties to the agency as vice president (1981–89), as president (1989–93), and as a paid spokesman for the Carlyle Group.

Soon after the January 2001 inauguration of President George W. Bush, CIA and FEDERAL BUREAU OF INVESTIGATION (FBI) insiders claim they received

During a search-and-destroy mission in the Zhawar Kili area of Afghanistan, U.S. Navy SEALs (SEa, Air, Land) found valuable intelligence information, including this Osama bin Laden propaganda poster located in an al-Qaeda classroom, January 14, 2002. (Reuters/Corbis)

direct orders from the White House to "back off the bin Ladens." Whether that fiat included Osama (an FBI "Top Ten" fugitive since 1996) may never be known, but the global manhunt for bin Laden fared no better under Bush than it had under Clinton. After the 9/11 attacks, when U.S. forces invaded Afghanistan with the specific intent of capturing or killing al-Qaeda's leaders, bin Laden escaped once again and remains at large to this day, issuing periodic communiqués to the faithful from exile in parts unknown. Avid supporters of the Afghani invasion were confused by subsequent White House announcements that bin Laden's apprehension "is not a priority" and by news that President Bush himself had aborted a plan to kill bin Laden with missile-firing drone aircraft in January 2001 after the CIA allegedly pinpointed his location in Afghanistan.

See also CLINTON, BILL AND HILLARY.

BIRMINGHAM Police Department

Birmingham, Alabama, was once described as "the most segregated city in America," a place where the color line was drawn so starkly that black and white witnesses in court swore oaths on different Bibles. From RECONSTRUCTION through the 1960s, Birmingham was a hotbed of unfettered KU KLUX KLAN violence, nicknamed "Bombingham" by black residents who suffered 50-odd unsolved dynamite attacks (including the lethal BAPBOMB incident) between 1948 and 1966. To find out why such crimes remained unsolved, we need look no further than the Birmingham Police Department (BPD).

Like every other police department worldwide, the BPD served major interests in its city, in this case Birmingham's "Big Mules" of industry. That support included "suppression of labor unions and "communists" of all sorts, along with blacks who forgot "their place" in lily-white southern society. Under public safety commissioner EUGENE "BULL" CONNOR (1941–53, 1957–63) the BPD and city fire department were little more than tools for enforcing white supremacy. The BPD's Intelligence Division mounted nonstop surveillance on civil rights activists, yet never seemed to notice when their homes were bombed or strafed with gunfire. Detective Sergeant Tom Clark, a specialist in "racial matters," was Connor's personal liaison with the KKK and helped arrange (with FEDERAL BUREAU OF INVESTIGATION collusion) the May 1961 Klan assault on

FREEDOM RIDE participants in Birmingham. Two years later, after black witness Roosevelt Tatum saw a Birmingham policeman (Car 22) deliver a bomb to a black-owned motel, FBI agents stepped in to save the day, slapping Tatum with perjury charges that sent him to prison for 12 months. Connor's minidictatorship ended in 1963, but routine police harassment of black activists and organizations continued into the late 1970s, including illegal surveillance, wiretaps, and opening of mail.

BLACK Dragon Society

This militaristic, ultranationalist secret society of JAPAN traced its roots to the tumultuous 1868 Meiji Restoration, which dissolved the nation's traditional samurai class. Following a failed revolt against the emperor in 1877, disaffected samurai organized various secret societies, which merged in February 1881 as the Black Ocean Society (Genyosha). The group's first president, Hiraoka Kotaro, owned the richest opal mines in Japan. Obsessed with plans for an invasion of KOREA, Black Ocean members seduced, bribed, and blackmailed various government officials to support the plan, assassinating several who refused. A network of brothels in Japan, CHINA, and other Asian countries served the Genyosha by collecting intelligence and providing blackmail ammunition against politicians and other prominent targets. By 1890 the organization received more financial support from the Ministry of War than from private donors, and it enjoyed a special status with the Home Ministry (which used Genyosha goons to attack leftists and other political opponents).

In 1894 the Black Ocean's terrorist campaign sparked the Sino-Japanese War, resulting in Japanese victory over China. At the same time, turning its sights against RUSSIA, the group changed its name to the Black Dragon Society (Kokuryukai). The group's driving goal was to extend Japanese influence throughout Asia and the world at large. To that end, the society recruited members ranging from government ministers and military leaders to opium smugglers and professional killers. Hundreds of members were taught to speak Russian and were then dispatched into Siberia and Mongolia as spies for Japan. That intelligence network played a large role in the Russo-Japanese War, climaxed by Russia's defeat in 1905. Black Dragon leaders next broadened their target to encompass "Greater East Asia," a goal emphasized by nationalists during Japan's "national reconstruction" in the 1930s. Once again, acts of terrorism precipitated war—this time in Manchuria—and politicians who opposed the Black Dragon Society (including Prime Minister Inukai Tsuyoshi) were marked for assassination. The campaign culminated in 1936 with a military revolt, and while that uprising failed, Black Dragon members and supporters retained enough influence to guide Japan through the portentous years ahead to an alliance with ADOLF HITLER and the PEARL HARBOR attack that brought the United States into World War II.

BLACK Friday conspiracy

To finance the U.S. Civil War (1861–65), President Abraham Lincoln issued millions of dollars in paper currency—dubbed "greenbacks"—that were secured by the credit of the federal government. In the event of Union victory, greenback holders believed the paper currency would be redeemed with GOLD. They were still waiting for that payback in 1869 when a group of speculators led by "robber barons" Jay Gould and James ("Jubilee Jim") Fisk set out to corner the U.S. gold market. Realizing that cooperation from President Ulysses Grant was crucial to their success, Fisk and Gould paid Grant's brother-in-law, financier Abel Corbin, $25,000 to lobby against the sale of government gold reserves. Corbin persuaded Grant to name Daniel Butterfield as assistant U.S. treasurer, presumably unaware that Butterfield had agreed to tip Fisk and Gould in advance of any government gold sales.

On September 20, 1869, Fisk and Gould began to purchase large stocks of gold on the open market, thus boosting the price from $20 to $162 per ounce during the next three days. President Grant reacted to the move by ordering the sale of $4 million in

Robber baron Jim Fisk (left) was a prime mover in the "Black Friday" gold conspiracy, while Jay Gould (right) was a cohort who escaped punishment for his role in the scandal. (Author's collection)

government gold on September 24—"Black Friday"—thereby puncturing the "gold bubble" and causing prices to plummet. Fisk and Gould, forewarned of Grant's move by Butterfield, sold short and made millions from the crisis. (Butterfield himself made $35,000 by selling gold short on Black Friday.) With scandal brewing Fisk issued a series of statements implicating President Grant and his wife in the conspiracy, which in turn prompted a congressional inquiry led by Representative (later president) James Garfield. Democrats sought to elicit testimony from Grant, his wife, and Abel Corbin's spouse, but those petitions were defeated in the House by a Republican majority. Creditors pursuing Fisk and Gould were stymied by a blizzard of injunctions from TAMMANY HALL, leaving Butterfield alone to suffer dismissal from his treasury post. Historians remain divided on Grant's complicity in the Black Friday plot.

BLACK Guerrilla Family

This all-black PRISON GANG was organized in 1966 at California's San Quentin Prison by BLACK PANTHER PARTY member GEORGE JACKSON. Unlike other prison gangs that focus primarily on drug sales and/or racial warfare behind bars, the Black Guerrilla Family (BGF) was born with (and maintains today) a strong political ideology incorporating black revolution against the U.S. government. (As is common with revolutionary groups, the BGF soon quarreled with Black Panther chiefs, and the two groups became bitter enemies.) Many present members of the gang were once affiliated with the Panther Party or its more militant offshoot, the Black Liberation Army. The highly organized BGF accepts any black inmates (except homosexuals) who accept the group's philosophy. Candidates must be sponsored by members in good standing, and they are investigated by screening committees that investigate the inmate's background, criminal record, and relationship to his sponsor. Once accepted, members swear a "death oath" vowing lifelong allegiance to the BGF. Gang structure includes a central executive committee, "field generals," captains of squads, lieutenants, and soldiers. Membership declined in the 1980s and then enjoyed a resurgence with enrollment of imprisoned street gang members such as CRIPS AND BLOODS. Many BGF members display tattoos with the gang's initials, plus crossed sabers

or shotguns and black dragons sitting astride prison towers. BGF members are mortal enemies of the neo-Nazi ARYAN BROTHERHOOD.

BLACK Hand(s)

Historically, the "Black Hand" name was applied to two distinct and separate groups. The first, hardly an organization at all, was a loosely knit network of Italian terrorists and racketeers (including some members of the MAFIA) who extorted money from their fellow countrymen. The technique involved crude threatening notes with a demand for cash, "signed" with the imprint of a hand in black ink. Failure to pay up on time typically brought reprisals in the form of arson, bombing, vandalism, beatings, mutilation, or murder. When large numbers of Italians migrated to the United States after the Civil War, Black Hand extortionists came with them and continued their activities in cities ranging from New Orleans to Chicago and New York. Few convictions were obtained in Black Hand cases because the victims and their families were commonly too frightened to report the crimes or to testify against their persecutors. Simple passage of time doomed the Black Hand rackets in America, as PROHIBITION gave the ethnic gangs a new source of fabulous income, while advancements in fingerprint technology made Black Hand notes a one-way ticket to prison.

The *other* Black Hand was a Serbian nationalist group, organized in May 1911 to reverse AUSTRIA's recent annexation of BOSNIA AND HERZEGOVINA. The organization's formal name was *Ujedinjenje ili Smrt* (Union or Death), but members emulated Italy's freelance terrorists by adopting a black handprint as their logo. Membership approached 2,500 by 1914, including many Serbian army officers and Crown Prince Alexander, all sworn to the goal of creating a "Greater Serbia" by any means available. New members swore "before God, on my honor and my life, that I will execute all missions and commands without question. I swear before God, on my honor and on my life, that I will take all the secrets of this organization into my grave with me." The group's last great coup was the June 1914 assassination of Archduke Franz Ferdinand in Sarajevo, which in turn sparked a chain of events that unleashed World War I. Most leaders of the Black Hand were in jail by May 1917 when a show trial sentenced seven ranking officers to death. The group itself was banned by law one month later, by which time its surviving members were immersed in the bloody business of surviving in their war-torn homeland.

BLACK Hundreds

During the Russian Revolution of 1905 leaders of the czarist SECRET POLICE organized various reactionary groups to fight dissidents at the grass-roots level. The largest of those groups was the League of the Russian People, more commonly known as the Black Hundreds. (*Black,* at the time—and in parts of Europe today—was deemed the opposite of *Red,* or revolutionary.) The league's membership included landowners, bureaucrats, police officers, and relatively "wealthy" peasants. Its philosophy was promonarchy, antirevolutionary, and anti-Semitic. Mass slaughter of Jews had been common in RUSSIA since the 1881 assassination of Czar ALEXANDER II, and the Black Hundreds continued that brutal tradition. Jews bore the brunt of violence by the Black Hundreds through 1911, prompting thousands of survivors to flee Russia entirely. Ironically, in March 1917, most of the league's 3,000 members joined the left-wing Bolshevik Party led by VLADIMIR LENIN, and some later rose to prominence in the Soviet government, including leadership positions in the KGB.

BLACK Muslims   See NATION OF ISLAM.

BLACK Orchestra

"Black Orchestra" was the GESTAPO code name for a group of conspirators within the German army who plotted to overthrow ADOLF HITLER during World War II. The group gained a powerful ally in February 1944 when Hitler demoted the chief of his intelligence service, Admiral Wilhelm Canaris. Black Orchestra members made several abortive attempts on Hitler's life, but their best effort came in July 1944 with a time-bomb secreted in Hitler's command bunker during a general staff meeting. Days before the attempt, Canaris learned that SS chief HEINRICH HIMMLER suspected a plot, but the conspirators proceeded with their plan despite the admiral's warning. Three of Der Führer's aides died in the blast, but Hitler suffered only minor injuries and launched a purge of suspected traitors. The Black Orchestra conspirators were soon identified, brutally tortured, and

hanged from meat hooks with piano-wire nooses. (Hitler reportedly filmed the executions to enjoy them repeatedly.) Admiral Canaris was confined at Flossenberg concentration camp until March 1945 when he was hanged on Hitler's order, his nude body left to rot on the scaffold.

BLACK Panther Party for Self-Defense

The Black Panther Party was organized in October 1966 by Huey Newton and Bobby Seale, two students at Merritt College in Oakland, California. Combining Maoist politics with the teachings of MALCOLM X, they devised a party program that included freedom, full employment, decent housing, improved educational facilities, liberation of all black men held in American prisons, exemption from military service for all blacks, and "an immediate end to police brutality and murder of black people." To the latter end, Panthers armed themselves and "patrolled" police in the ghetto, advising black prisoners of their constitutional rights. Soon, spokesmen of STUDENTS FOR A DEMOCRATIC SOCIETY hailed the Panther Party as "the vanguard of an anticapitalist revolution involving the whole of American society."

FEDERAL BUREAU OF INVESTIGATION (FBI) Director J. EDGAR HOOVER seems to have taken that overblown rhetoric seriously, describing Black Panthers as the single greatest threat to America's internal security. Reports suggest that there were never more than 1,200 Panthers nationwide, but many white police and politicians shared Hoover's view, exacerbated by a series of violent clashes in late 1967 and early 1968. In November 1968 Hoover ordered FBI field offices "to exploit all avenues of creating . . . dissension within the ranks of the BPP"; he also demanded "imaginative and hard-hitting counterintelligence measures aimed at crippling the BPP." California G-men engineered a shooting war between Panthers and members of the rival United Slaves (U.S.) organization, using informants and agents provocateurs on both sides to keep the action going. At least four Panthers were killed by U.S. gunmen before the feud ended, mute testimony to the claim of ex-Agent Wesley Swearingen that "Hoover wanted the Panthers in jail or dead." A similar effort in Chicago sparked violence between the Panthers and members of a volatile street gang, the Blackstone Rangers. Between December 1967 and December 1969, at least 28 Panthers were killed by police or rival militants—many of whom, on closer inspection, proved to be FBI hirelings.

Prosecution was another angle of attack, although with less certain results. In 1969 alone 348 Panthers were jailed across the United States on various felony charges, costing the party more than $200,000 in bail premiums. In April of that year G-men and New York police charged 21 Panthers with conspiracy to commit murder and arson, but all were finally acquitted at trial. A month after those arrests, on May 15, 1969, Hoover issued a memo commanding all agents to "destroy what the BPP stands for." In Detroit agents drafted spurious extortion letters in the party's name, addressed to local businessmen. In Los Angeles FBI informant MELVIN SMITH provided information on a nonexistent cache of weapons, prompting police to raid the local Panther office in December 1969. Four days later members of the CHICAGO POLICE DEPARTMENT used a floor plan drawn by G-men and informant WILLIAM O'NEAL to raid the home of party leader FRED HAMPTON, riddling him with bullets as he lay asleep in bed. In 1972 G-men and informants joined forces with the LOS ANGELES POLICE DEPARTMENT to frame Panther Elmer ("Geronimo") Pratt on a false murder charge.

The FBI's Panther hunt did not end with Hoover's death in May 1972 or with the party's subsequent dissolution. Imprisoned Panthers were still subject to surveillance and harassment under the bureau's PRISACTS (Prison Activists) program which targeted "extremist, revolutionary, terrorist, and subversive activities in penal institutions." PRISACTS was launched in 1974 "with the primary goals of promoting liaison and cooperation between the FBI and prison administrators nationwide relative to above elements, and to generally provide for two-way exchange of information."

G-men also pursued the scattered party veterans still at large, including ex-Panther Joanne Chesimard. Linked to robbery and a shootout in New Jersey during May 1973, Chesimard was indicted for a wide range of East Coast crimes, but courts dismissed three cases, and juries acquitted her in two others. Finally convicted on the original counts in March 1977, she escaped from prison in November 1979 and surfaced in Cuba eight years later to promote her autobiography. Huey Newton also fled to Cuba, dodging charges for the murder of an Oakland prostitute in 1974; he then returned in 1977 to face trial. Two juries failed to reach a verdict in the case.

Newton was killed in Oakland on August 22, 1989, in what police described as a drug dispute. A member of the rival BLACK GUERRILLA FAMILY was convicted of Newton's murder in 1991.

BLACK September

This Arab terrorist group took its name from the bloody events of September 1970 when King Hussein of JORDAN turned his army against Palestinian militant groups operating against ISRAEL from Jordanian soil. Bitter fighting ensued before thousands of refugees fled into LEBANON, SYRIA, and IRAQ. Some researchers claim Black September was an ultramilitant branch of FATAH, the military wing of the Palestine Liberation Organization (PLO) led by Yasser Arafat. The group's most infamous action occurred in September 1972 when masked gunmen invaded the Olympic Village in Munich, GERMANY, killing 11 Israeli athletes and coaches. Israel's WRATH OF GOD hit teams pursued alleged leaders of the group through 1973, killing several in Europe and various points in the Middle East. While the mopping up was still in progress, one of the group's alleged founders, Abu Daoud, told Jordanian journalists, "There is no such thing as Black September. Fatah announced its operations under this name so that Fatah would not appear as the direct executors of the operations." The last known "action" claimed by Black September was a December 1973 radio broadcast from Jordan, threatening to kill HENRY KISSINGER during a tour of the Middle East.

BOHEMIAN Club

Allegedly founded in 1883, the Bohemian Club is described by some conspiracists as a collection of "secret world leaders" on a par with the ILLUMINATI, the BILDERBERG GROUP, or the TRILATERAL COMMISSION. Prominent Americans identified (in unsubstantiated Internet reports) as members of the group include Nelson ROCKEFELLER, HENRY KISSINGER, and various past presidents, among them Theodore Roosevelt, Herbert Hoover, and RICHARD NIXON. Meetings are supposedly held each July at Bohemian Grove, a plot of redwood forest along the Russian River, near San Francisco in northern California's Sonoma County.

Most information available on the Bohemian Club comes from spokesmen of a self-styled "avenging posse," the Bohemian Grove Action Network (BGAN), which strives to expose the club's alleged subversive activities. Supposed eyewitness reports from BGAN infiltrators describe "80 percent of the Bohemians in a state of intoxication so advanced that many of them had fallen insensible among the ferns," yet conspiratorial business presumably continues—and is said to be occult in nature. One supposed club ritual, dubbed the Banishment of Care, includes the burning of a giant effigy, apparently photographed from a distance by BGAN spies in 2003. Internet researcher Alex Jones maintains that the ritual is a celebration of Molech (or Moloch), a pagan god reviled by authors of the Old Testament.

Jones also suggest that club members have, at some time in the past, indulged in human sacrifice. His "evidence" allegedly consists of two "rediscovered photos depicting scenes from early 20th-century Bohemian Grove gatherings"—though, in fact, they are undated and contain no landmarks to identify the sparsely-wooded setting(s). One photo depicts the apparent hanging of a man (or mannequin) dressed in a suit, his face concealed by a drooping hat. It resembles a typical lynching photo and contains no solid clues as to when or where it was taken. The second shot reveals a group of men surrounding a male figure lying prostrate on a wooden table. Jones maintains that the recumbent form "is clearly a black child or a midget," though in fact simple comparison shows him to be roughly as tall as those surrounding the bier.

What do the photos prove? What is their source? Do they portray authentic homicides, or were they staged? In either case, where and when were they taken? What evidence do they reveal of any occult ritual? How are the alleged killers identified as members of the Bohemian Club? Such questions mean little to dedicated conspiracists. The mystery—and public controversy—will doubtless persist.

BOLIVIA

Spanish invaders decimated Bolivia's indigenous peoples in the 16th century, soon reducing them to slavery. Some of the colonists lost interest as mineral wealth dried up in the latter 17th century and as Bolivia won independence in 1825 (taking its name from liberator Simón Bolívar). Feuds with neighbors resulted in loss of substantial territory to CHILE (1879–84), BRAZIL (1903), and PARAGUAY (1932–53), while the incessant border warfare destabilized Bolivia's government. In 1965 Bolivian rebels aided by fighters from CUBA launched a revolution, but the movement was crushed by native troops and CENTRAL INTELLIGENCE AGENCY agents two years later. Bolivia's halting progress toward democracy was stalled by imposition of a military junta (1980–82), but the subsequent election of a leftist government did little to reform the country. Regular strikes paralyzed the economy, while much of Bolivia's natural wealth was either wasted or funneled through black-market outlets. The one growth industry, COCAINE, produced pervasive corruption in government and law enforcement. President Hugo Bánzer (1997–2002) allegedly made "significant progress" toward curbing drug traffic, but eradication of coca plunged many Bolivian farmers into abject poverty.

BONAPARTE, Napoleon (1769–1821)

Once the emperor of France and arguably the most powerful man in all of Europe, Napoleon Bonaparte (born Buonaparte) died in exile on the island of St. Helena at age 51 on May 5, 1821. Initially, his death was blamed on stomach cancer, which had also claimed the lives of his father and two sisters. Another 150 years passed before Bonaparte's death was reexamined by Swedish dentist Sten Forshufvud, whose study of Napoleon's last days convinced him that the ex-emperor had died from slow poisoning with arsenic. Chemical analysis of Napoleon's hair seemed to confirm the diagnosis, leading Forshufvud to publish his findings in 1961. Three decades later, another student of Napoleon, Ben Weider, reached the same conclusion and named Count Charles Tristan de Montholon as the actual killer (allegedly prompted by the Comte d'Artois, who became King Charles X of the French in 1824). A different verdict was delivered in by a team of French scientists in 1999, however. While confirming that Napoleon's remains contained 15 parts of arsenic per million (five times the "safe" level), the analysts concluded that Napoleon absorbed the toxin from "such things as hair products, wallpaper, ash from wood fires or glue." If the arsenic had been ingested orally, the team declared, Napoleon's death "would have been much quicker"—an argument blandly ignoring the Forshufvud/Weider theory that Bonaparte was poisoned slowly over time with small doses of arsenic to simulate natural death. The ultimate conclusion, affirming the 19th-century cancer diagnosis, predictably failed to persuade conspiracy theorists that Napoleon died from natural causes.

BORMANN, Martin (1900–?1945)

The son of a former Prussian soldier, Martin Bormann, who was born in 1900, dropped out of school to work as a farm laborer and then served with a German artillery unit in World War I. In the early 1920s he espoused NATIONAL SOCIALISM and joined the far-right Rossbach Freikorps, participating in acts of Nazi TERRORISM. In March 1924 Bormann received a one-year prison term as an accomplice of RUDOLF HESS in the brutal murder of Walther Kadow (Bormann's former elementary school teacher). Upon release, he rose swiftly through the Nazi ranks, serving as second-in-command to Deputy Führer Hess. At the same time, he administered ADOLF HITLER's personal finances, and ascended to supplant Hess in May 1941 after Hess made his mysterious one-way flight to England. Dubbed Hitler's "Brown Eminence" during the remainder of World War II, Bormann was regarded by some observers as the true master of the brutal THIRD REICH. Author William Stevenson, in *The Bormann Brotherhood* (1973), contends that Bormann blackmailed Hitler, suppressing evidence that Hitler murdered his niece and lover, Geli Raubal, in September 1931. Be that as it may, no covert machinations could save the crumbling Nazi Reich in 1945 as Allied troops advanced on Berlin from all sides. With Hitler and other high-ranking Nazis, Bormann must have known he would be prosecuted for WAR CRIMES and the atrocities of the HOLOCAUST. According to official histories, Bormann fled the Führerbunker on April 30, 1945, acting on Hitler's order "to put the interests of the nation before his own feelings" and save himself to carry on the fight from exile.

What happened next remains a point of heated controversy. Hitler's chauffeur, Erich Kempka, claimed that Bormann was killed by artillery fire while fleeing Berlin in a tank. Artur Axmann, a leader of the Hitler Youth, told a different story, insisting that Bormann committed suicide and that he (Axmann) saw Bormann's body lying on a Berlin street on May 2, 1945. Nonetheless, between December 1945 and September 1946, Allied investigators heard "strong rumors" that Bormann was alive and well in AUSTRIA, SPAIN, ARGENTINA, and ITALY. The Nuremberg war-crimes tribunal treated him as living and sentenced Bormann to death in absentia on October 1, 1946. Five months later, a Swiss newspaper reported that Bormann was living in the Alps and plotting the rise of a FOURTH REICH. In May 1948 John Griffiths, a businessman living in URUGUAY, told U.S. authorities that Bormann was hiding in Argentina. President Harry Truman ordered a FEDERAL BUREAU OF INVESTIGATION investigation, but J. EDGAR HOOVER's report of September 8, 1948, claimed that no trace of Bormann could be found.

A West German court declared Bormann legally dead on January 30, 1954, but the controversy resurfaced in 1962 when a Peruvian newspaper claimed that Bormann had died in PARAGUAY on February 15, 1959. (The alleged attending physician denied any knowledge of Bormann.) In 1965 German prosecutors excavated a site in Berlin where Bormann's remains were allegedly buried, but they came up empty handed. Seven years later, construction workers digging on the same spot allegedly unearthed a skeleton said to be Bormann's, but the find only made matters worse. Between December 1972 and April 1973 German authorities released photographs of four distinctly different skulls, each in turn "positively" declared to be Bormann's. On that weird note another court issued Bormann's second legal-death notice, but Nazi-hunters remained unconvinced.

BOSNIA and Herzegovina

Once known to Roman invaders as Illyricum, the modern Federation of Bosnia and Herzegovina is a triangular patch of territory in the Balkans, best known for endless ethnic and religious feuds between its Bosnian, Croat, and Serbian inhabitants. Serbian nationalists touched off World War I in 1914 by assassinating AUSTRIA's Archduke Franz Ferdinand at Sarajevo. Absorbed by YUGOSLAVIA in 1929, the region was occupied by ADOLF HITLER's Nazi troops in 1941. Jew-hating locals learned new genocidal tricks during the HOLOCAUST, which served them well a half-century later. The fractured nation declared independence from Yugoslavia in December 1991, and a brutal war of "ethnic cleansing" erupted the following year, marked by atrocities on both sides (Muslim-Croats vs. Serbs) during the next four years. At the peak of conflict, reports surfaced that various warlords or independent felons were using the carnage to produce commercial SNUFF FILMS.

That charge remains unproved, but sluggish WAR CRIMES trials continue at The Hague, where more than 100 defendants stand indicted. A Bosnian Serb commander, Gen. Radislav Drstic, was convicted in August 2001 for killing 8,000 Muslims at Srebrenica, in 1995. The trial of former Serbian president SLOBODAN MILOSEVIC continues at this writing (in May 2005).

BOTSWANA

After being overrun by Zulus (1820s) and then by Boers from Transvaal (1870s), aboriginal San tribesmen of Botswana were "protected" by the British Empire from 1885 to 1965, emerging from colonial rule as Africa's first true democracy in September 1966. Although maintaining superficial good relations with white neighbors Rhodesia and SOUTH AFRICA, Botswana harbored black rebels from both countries and suffered repeated incursions by white troops hunting "subversives." High unemployment and stratified socioeconomic classes combined to produce a deepening recession in the 1990s. At the same time Botswana suffered the world's worst devastation from AIDS. By 2001, 350,000 of its 1.6 million people were infected, and half of the population between ages 25 and 29 was rated terminally ill. Ambitious pronouncements that new health programs will prevent any new AIDS infections by 2016 have yet to be tested.

BOY Scouts of America

A self-styled patriotic and religious movement whose members take an oath to "God and country," the Boy Scouts of America (BSA) was sued in 1990 by the parents of a seven-year-old boy in Illinois. The boy was rejected as a Cub Scout because of both his agnosticism and his refusal to pronounce the religious portion of the scout oath. Discrimination was claimed; BSA spokespersons defended their group as a private order, immune to federal civil rights laws that demand equality of treatment in any "place of public accommodation." A federal district court accepted that argument in May 1993, and the U.S. SUPREME COURT declined to review the case seven months later. BSA leaders hailed the verdict as a victory for Christian values, but some of those same leaders left much to be desired where morality and ethical behavior were concerned.

Scouting originated in England, with Robert Baden-Powell's creation of the Boy Scout Movement. Although himself a closet pedophile who collected nude photos of boys, Baden-Powell publicly voiced the opinion that child-molesting scoutmasters should be flogged. In practice, though, his attitude was very different, and he allowed two of his top aides—H. D. Byrne and Robert Patterson—to resign quietly after both were exposed as serial offenders with dozens of victims. To the end of his days, Baden-Powell was known for his "extreme reluctance to discuss the perennial problem posed by homosexual scoutmasters."

The BSA was organized by publisher William Boyce with help from Baden-Powell in 1910. By that time, the Scout Movement in England had established a "Gray List" of adults banned from scouting for various reasons, including pedophilia, that was used (theoretically) to screen incoming scoutmasters. In 1911, after one short year of operation, the BSA created its own "Red Flag List," known at headquarters as the Ineligible Volunteer Files. Those banned from scouting are not exclusively pedophiles—the list has ranged over time from political "undesirables" to convicted killers—but child molesters represent a substantial portion of those excluded. According to statistics revealed in various lawsuits, some 4,000 adults were banned from scouting between 1971 and 1991, with at least 1,800 of those dismissed as sexual predators. James Tarr, head of the BSA from 1979 to 1984, admitted that pedophilia has "been an issue since the Boy Scouts began."

It should not be assumed, however, that 1,800 child molesters were arrested or convicted of molesting boy scouts during 1971–91. Far from it. In fact, BSA leaders have done everything within their power—including lies under oath—to protect the movement's "good name." Time after time, as amply documented in Patrick Boyle's *Scout's Honor* (1994), BSA leaders suppressed evidence of criminal activity to preserve scouting's public image. Each and every one of the 4,000 adults banned from scouting in 1971–91 received a personal letter from BSA headquarters, vowing that "this decision [to reject or expel a scoutmaster] and the reasons for it will be kept confidential." In a 1988 Virginia lawsuit, the judge demanded all Ineligible Volunteer Files compiled on pedophiles from 1975 through 1984, and BSA attorneys delivered 231 dossiers. A year later, in

California an identical judicial demand was issued for all such files spanning the past 20 years. This time the BSA produced only 180, but the judge had already perused a week-long series in the *Washington Times* that identified 416 files. Slapped with a heavy punitive fine, BSA leaders claimed they "misunderstood" the court's original order, producing another 1,691 pedofiles, for a grand total of 1,871.

It should not be presumed that lawsuits have changed much (if anything) within the world of Scouting. In January 2003 police in Christchurch, New Zealand, went to arrest scoutmaster Roland Harding at his home on charges of molesting four boys and found their suspect dead in an apparent suicide. Three weeks later, a 66-year-old former scoutmaster in Guelph, Ontario, pleaded guilty to charges of molesting three scouts. In June 2003 a report published in *USA Today* revealed that "at least 25" members of the BSA's Law Enforcement Explorers program—assigned to work with various U.S. police departments—had been sexually abused during the past three years. A dozen of those victims had been molested during the past 12 months in California, Tennessee, and Texas. Once again the old refrain was trotted out: "Sponsors have promised to reform the program." Critics suggest that after nearly 100 years, the reforms should be completed.

BRAZIL

PORTUGAL claimed the territory of modern Brazil in 1500, staking out its sole New World colony in a hemisphere dominated by SPAIN and England. Colonial rule was as disastrous for aboriginal people here as in other parts of the Western Hemisphere, but independence came earlier with a revolution in 1820. Brazil fought with the victorious Allies in both World Wars, but its military leaders seemed to learn more from their FASCIST enemies than from Western democracies. In 1961, after President João Goulart nationalized a Brazilian IT&T subsidiary and took other steps to prevent U.S. corporations from looting the nation, CENTRAL INTELLIGENCE AGENCY leaders conspired with native military officers to topple the civilian government. Their coup was successful in 1964, establishing a brutal police state that endured for 20 years, sustained by the torture and murder of dissidents. Popular elections resumed in January 1985, but corruption continued, forcing the resignation of President Collor de Mello in December 1992.

Economic woes continued into the 21st century, and national bankruptcy was only prevented by a $30 billion loan from the International Monetary Fund in August 2002. In June 2003 Brazilian lawmakers obtained copies of a secret report prepared by the U.S. NATIONAL SECURITY AGENCY in 1974. The document (National Security Study Memorandum 200) detailed plans to target 13 developing nations for intensive efforts to promote sterilization as a means of population control. Brazil was singled out because it "clearly dominates the continent demographically" and might achieve "a growing power status . . . over the next 25 years." Brazil's Ministry of Health charged that 44 percent of all Brazilian females between the age of 14 and 55 had been permanently sterilized by U.S.-funded doctors since the program began.

BROOKINGS Institution

The Brookings Institution is a private nonprofit organization that seeks to improve the performance of American institutions, the effectiveness of government programs, and the quality of U.S. public policy. Since 1916 when it began life as the Institute for Government Research (renamed for St. Louis philanthropist Robert Somers Brookings in 1927), the group has functioned as "a bridge between scholarship and public policy," researching various critical subjects and critiquing government efforts to cope with various problems. Its stated goals include "bringing new knowledge to the attention of decisionmakers and affording scholars a better insight into public policy issues."

Such efforts are predictably unwelcome to dogmatic regimes that operate covertly in defiance of the law. President RICHARD NIXON, obsessed with pursuit of those who had leaked the so-called Pentagon Papers to various newspapers in 1970, decided that "liberal Democrats" at the Brookings Institution had played some role in the affair. The evidence: a paper reviewing U.S. involvement in the VIETNAM War, written for Brookings by ex-Pentagon employee Leslie Gelb. White House conspirator Charles Colson wrote a memo to Nixon aide John Ehrlichman on July 6, 1971, saying in part: "It looks to me like we may soon expect another installment in the Pentagon Papers written by the same authors but doubtless more up to date. . . . In my opinion this should be promptly investigated."

Robert Somers Brookings founded the Washington institute that Watergate conspirators plotted to destroy in 1972. (Author's collection)

to presidential counsel John Dean. Dean, in turn, warned Ehrlichman against pursuing the "insane" conspiracy, and Ehrlichman allegedly ordered Colson to forget the plan. Colson, for his part, denies any knowledge of the plot (though a friend later told author J. Anthony Lukas that Colson may have suggested the plan as "a joke").

BULGARIA

Absorbed by the Roman Empire in the first century A.D., the territory of modern Bulgaria was subsequently invaded by Goths, Huns, and Bulgars (in 679). Ottoman Turks overran the country in 1396 and ruled it ruthlessly until 1908. Initially an ally of aggressor GERMANY in both World Wars, Bulgaria turned on ADOLF HITLER in 1944 and established a Communist regime. During the cold war, Bulgaria was known as RUSSIA's most slavish ally, and many of the KGB's expendable assassins were Bulgarians. Todor Zhikov, general secretary of the Bulgarian Communist Party, resigned in 1989 after 35 years in power. His successor scheduled free elections for May 1990; the Communist Party won a surprise victory and promptly renamed itself the Bulgarian Socialist Party. Voters defeated the Communist/Socialist slate in October 1991, electing Bulgaria's first noncommunist government in 47 years, but the nation's economy continued its downward spiral amid revelations of rampant corruption and organized crime.

See also COMMUNISM.

White House "plumber" John Caulfield later claimed that he was summoned to Colson's office in the second week of July 1971 and there informed that President Nixon recognized "a high priority need to obtain papers from the office of a gentleman named Leslie Gelb" at the Brookings Institution. Colson also had a plan, according to Caulfield: "The suggestion was that the fire regulations in the District of Columbia could be changed to have the FBI [FEDERAL BUREAU OF INVESTIGATION] respond to the scene of any fire in the district and that if there were to be a fire at the Brookings Institute [*sic*] that the FBI could respond and obtain the file in question from Mr. Leslie Gelb's office." While no specifics were discussed, Caulfield inferred that he was being told to set the fire himself.

Caulfield, himself no stranger to criminal activity, reportedly deemed the plan "asinine" and reported it

BULL, Gerald Victor (1928–1990)

An American citizen born at North Bay, Ontario, in 1928, Gerald Bull suffered a loveless childhood, raised by an aunt after his mother died and his father left for parts unknown. Still, he excelled in school and was rated a virtual genius, earning his Ph.D. from the University of Toronto at age 23. By that time he was already obsessed with the idea of building giant guns that could propel satellites into outer space, a vision fueled in equal parts by childhood readings of Jules Verne and study of the giant field guns used by Germany to bombard Paris during World War I.

Bull took the first step toward realizing his vision when he joined the Canadian Armament and Research Development Establishment (CARDE), involved throughout the 1950s with problems of supersonic aerodynamics for aircraft and missiles.

Supersonic wind tunnels were expensive to build, so Bull devised an alternative method of testing: In lieu of constructing vast tunnels, he proposed using cannon to fire models down a test range at supersonic speed. The early tests were successful, and at age 31 Bull was promoted to lead CARDE's aerophysics department. A loathing for bureaucratic red tape drove Bull to a series of unapproved media interviews, which in turn alienated his superiors, and he was dismissed from CARDE two years later in 1961.

Briefly adrift in private life, Bull soon found support from the Pentagon, the CENTRAL INTELLIGENCE AGENCY (CIA), and the Canadian Defense Department for a new experimental program dubbed Project HARP (High-Altitude Research Program), created to study large guns and high-altitude ballistics. Initial testing was done in subterranean tunnels on land that Bull purchased along the Vermont-Quebec border. Free-flight tests were later conducted on the island of Barbados, where giant projectiles were lobbed over the Atlantic, peaking at an altitude of 108 miles.

Diversion of military funds for the ongoing Vietnam War doomed Bull's project and once again left him without official sponsors. Before the bitter end, Bull transferred HARP's assets to his own company—Space Research Corporation (SRC)—operating from an 8,000-acre spread in rural Vermont. By the 1970s CIA contacts had placed Bull in touch with government representatives from SOUTH AFRICA, CHINA, and IRAQ, but those connections ultimately landed Bull in jail. American relations with South Africa's racist apartheid regime were severed in the latter 1970s, and U.S. corporations were banned from doing business with Johannesburg. Bull ignored the restrictions until he was arrested for smuggling 30,000 artillery shells to South Africa via the West Indies. A guilty plea on that charge brought Bull a six-month jail term, despite a federal prosecutor's recommendation that Bull serve no time in custody. The conviction left Bull bankrupt and desperate. On release from prison he moved to Brussels, seeking any clients who would keep his dream afloat financially.

By 1981 Bull had a new deal with Iraq, by then immersed in a marathon war with neighboring IRAN. Rumors persist that Bull met personally with Saddam Hussein, then a favorite client of the Pentagon and the REAGAN-BUSH White House for his opposition to Iran. According to journalist David Silverberg, Hussein was so taken with Bull's presentation that he "downed a bottle of Johnny Walker Red and called up his cronies in the middle of the night, insisting that they rush right over to hear Bull." Be that as it may, Bull soon found himself at the helm of Project Babylon, designing a "supergun" for Iraq that would sport a 120-meter barrel and tip the scales around 4.2 million pounds. A model of the giant weapon was displayed in May 1989 at the Baghdad International Exhibition for Military Production. On the side, Bull also helped Iraq design a multistage missile that would have permitted long-range strikes against Hussein's enemies.

At 6:20 P.M. on March 22, 1990, as Bull paused to unlock the door of his sixth-floor apartment in Brussels, an unknown assassin shot him three times in the back with a silencer-equipped pistol. Bull collapsed to the floor, where two more shots were fired into the back of his head at close range. Killed instantly, he lay bleeding on the floor for 20 minutes before police arrived. Bull's briefcase lay untouched nearby, containing various papers, financial documents, and close to $20,000 in cash. Within days of the murder, Saddam Hussein declared in a speech from Baghdad, "A Canadian citizen with U.S. nationality came to Iraq. He might have benefited Iraq. I don't know. They say the Iraq intelligence service is spread over Europe, but nobody spoke of human rights of the Canadian citizen of U.S. nationality. After he came to Iraq, they killed him."

ISRAEL was the immediate prime suspect in Bull's murder because Israel was committed to retarding weapons-development programs in Iraq and other hostile Arab states. Alternate scenarios blame the Iranian government (known enemies of Iraq), British intelligence, and the CIA. The British theory, advanced by journalist Walter De Bock in 1998, claims that Prime Minister Margaret Thatcher ordered Bull's murder because he was taking lucrative Iraqi arms contracts away from British firms. (As support for his claim, De Bock noted that reporter Jonathan Moyle was murdered in Chile on March 31, 1990—eight days after Bull's assassination—while investigating claims of secret British military trading with Iraq.) American involvement in the murder was suggested by Canadian journalist Dale Grant, reporting that Michael Bull "broached the idea that the CIA did it, because his father was applying for a U.S. pardon of his arms-smuggling conviction." Two years later, former SRC employee

Christopher Cowley told the House of Commons that he and Bull had briefed the CIA and Britain's MI5 on the progress of Project Babylon as it proceeded. While convinced that Israel was responsible for killing Bull, Cowley "speculated that the CIA must have been tipped off by the MOSSAD [Israeli intelligence] and thus had acquiesced in the assassination."

Project Babylon disintegrated after Bull's death, which was doubtless the intention of his killer(s). SRC immediately closed its doors, and the employees scattered. Iraqi forces invaded neighboring KUWAIT on August 2, 1990, and U.S.-led forces responded with aerial attacks in January 1991, climaxed by a swift land offensive the following month. Bull's superguns were located and destroyed by UNITED NATIONS weapons inspectors in the wake of the Gulf War. No suspects have yet been identified in Dr. Bull's murder.

BUREAU of Alcohol, Tobacco, and Firearms

The U.S. government has taxed alcoholic beverages since 1791, but the Treasury Department's modern Bureau of Alcohol, Tobacco, and Firearms (BATF) properly traces its lineage to the PROHIBITION Bureau that was active between 1920 and 1933. That unit was briefly transferred to the JUSTICE DEPARTMENT in June 1933, merging with the FEDERAL BUREAU OF INVESTIGATION (FBI) to create a new Division of Investigation, but its life ran out with Repeal six months later. After the demise of Prohibition's "noble experiment," Treasury created a new Alcohol Tax Unit to pursue recalcitrant bootleggers. (As late as 1963, 5,500 suspects were charged with distilling or selling untaxed alcohol; the number dropped to 75 in 1979.) Guns were added to the mix in 1934 with passage of the National Firearms Act (which taxed, but did not ban, such "gangster weapons" as machine guns, silencers, and sawed-off shotguns). The federal Gun Control Act of 1968 extended those taxes to "destructive devices," but BATF remained a division of the INTERNAL REVENUE SERVICE until July 1972 when it became a separate agency at Treasury. That same year witnessed passage of the Federal Bombing Statute, which divided jurisdiction in explosives cases as follows:

- U.S. Postal inspectors are responsible for mail bombs and bombings of post offices;

- The FBI investigates all bombings of federal property other than post offices or Treasury facilities;
- BATF takes primary responsibility for all other bombings *unless* the incidents are officially designated as acts of TERRORISM, in which case G-men assume control of the investigation.

In a nation where the phrase "gun control" sparks acrimonious debate from coast to coast, BATF was bound to be a controversial agency. It did not help that John Caulfield, appointed by President RICHARD NIXON to lead BATF, was soon exposed as a hush-money bagman in the WATERGATE scandal. In 1979 BATF's critics told the U.S. Senate that "75 to 80 percent of BATF cases brought [to trial in Maryland and Virginia] involved defendants who had no criminal intent, but were enticed by bureau agents into violating technical requirements, which the defendants did not know existed." President RONALD REAGAN hoped to dismantle the unit entirely, thus repaying political debts to the National Rifle Association, but he succeeded only in cutting BATF's budget and human resources.

Still BATF endured, often struggling in an adversarial relationship with the FBI. As BATF historian James Moore reports, "The FBI has had a deep and lasting impact on the ATF, and the effects were clearest and most destructive in terrorist cases." According to the BATF, conflict arose primarily when G-men manipulated their definition of *terrorism* to avoid unwanted cases (notably those involving antiabortion violence and the KU KLUX KLAN) or when they claimed credit for cases solved by BATF agents. Moore describes 10 such cases with 50 defendants, in which bureau spokesmen claimed credit after the fact.

Two of the FBI's most embarrassing cases from the 1990s began as BATF operations. The first, from Idaho, involved a four-year BATF campaign to entrap neo-Nazi Randy Weaver in illegal arms transactions. When he was finally charged and refused to surrender, agents of the U.S. Marshals Service were sent to arrest him, sparking a shootout that killed Weaver's son and a federal officer. The FBI's SWAT took over at that point, and matters quickly went from bad to worse, resulting in the death of Weaver's wife and a $3.1 million settlement to her survivors. Eight months later, another BATF squad attacked the Branch Davidian religious sect near Waco, Texas. Six persons died in the clash, and G-men moved in for a siege that ended with the fiery deaths of nearly 80 more on April 19, 1993.

After the catastrophic PENTTBOM attacks of September 11, 2001, as President George W. Bush sought to reorganize America's "homeland security" apparatus, there were renewed calls for BATF's relocation from Treasury to Justice. FBI spokesmen hailed the proposed move on November 12, 2002, with a press release that read:

> The FBI supports the proposed transfer of the criminal enforcement authorities of the Bureau of Alcohol, Tobacco, and Firearms (ATF) to the Department of Justice (DOJ). We have been working closely with the DOJ and with the Treasury Department to ensure that any legislation effectuating such a transfer would preserve the ATF's existing criminal and regulatory enforcement authorities.

The department was transferred in January 2003. In addition, its name was changed to the Bureau of Alcohol, Tobacco, Firearms, and Explosives.

See also BUSH DYNASTY.

BURNETT, Alfred (fl. 1970)

A twice-convicted felon in Seattle, Alfred Burnett was awaiting trial on robbery charges in January 1970 when he was suddenly released from the Kings County jail despite objections from his parole officer. Burnett subsequently pleaded guilty in that case but remained at large, again despite the parole officer's demand that he be jailed for failure to appear for sentencing on another charge. The FEDERAL BUREAU OF INVESTIGATION's (FBI) Seattle field office overruled Burnett's parole officer in each case, naming Burnett as an informant who supplied the bureau with "valuable information" on ghetto violence and the BLACK PANTHER PARTY. More specifically, he was assigned to locate Jimmy Davis, a Panther suspected of involvement in one or more recent bombings.

Burnett never located Davis, but he compromised by targeting a friend of Davis's, 22-year-old VIETNAM War veteran Larry Ward. After some haggling, Ward apparently accepted Burnett's offer of $75 to plant a bomb at Seattle's Hardcastle Realty Company on the night of May 14, 1970. Burnett supplied the bomb but then alerted G-men and police to the impending crime. According to his later statements, "The police wanted

a bomber and I gave them one." Burnett insists that he "distinctly told them it was Ward instead of [Davis]" and "that he was unarmed." Be that as it may, when Ward arrived on foot at Hardcastle Realty carrying Burnett's bomb, he was surrounded by Seattle squad cars and killed in a barrage of gunfire. Adopting a remorseful pose after the fact, Burnett maintained, "I didn't know Larry Ward would be killed."

Seattle police were equally surprised—that is, if we believe their later statements (although the city's mayor had publicly advocated killing bombers as a "deterrent" to future attacks). John Williams, chief of the Seattle Police Department's intelligence unit, blamed FBI agents for Ward's death. "As far as I can tell," Williams told Senate investigators, "Ward was a relatively decent kid. Somebody set this whole thing up. It wasn't the police department." FBI agents protected Burnett, now marked as an informer, by securing his transfer from state prison to federal custody.

BURNS, William J. (1860?–1932)

A Baltimore native who was born "around 1860" and raised in Ohio, William Burns worked briefly as a SECRET SERVICE agent (and later chief) before retiring in 1909 and founding his own Chicago-based William J. Burns International Detective Agency. In 1910 Burns was credited with solving the bombing of the *Los Angeles Times*, though some critics called the case a frame-up. A year later, according to reports filed by Attorney General George Wickersham, Burns stacked the trial juries of Oregon Senator John Mitchell and Representative John Williams with political enemies, thus securing dubious convictions on land-fraud charges. Before the United States entered World War I, Burns was also employed as an agent of British Intelligence.

Despite that checkered background—or perhaps because of it—Burns was tapped by Attorney General HARRY DAUGHERTY (a personal friend) on August 18, 1922, to head the Bureau of Investigation. Burns took office four days later, while young J. EDGAR HOOVER was promoted to serve as the bureau's first assistant director. That same afternoon G-men in Michigan illegally raided a meeting of the Communist Party, seizing membership records and other documents. That action set the tone for Burns's tenure as director, during which the bureau was used as a partisan political weapon, pursuing "radicals" and labor unions, breaking strikes, maintaining files on Democratic congressmen, and generally protecting the corrupt regime of President WARREN HARDING.

Burns also kept files on the party affiliations and political connections of his agents, whose number increased from 346 to 441 at the end of his tenure. (Clerical staff decreased by 78 during the same period, for an overall net increase of 17 bureau employees.) Some of the new G-men were hired as favors to influential politicians; others were drawn from the ranks of private-detective agencies, notorious as corrupt strikebreakers. When Congressman Oscar Kellar objected to bureau involvement in a national railroad strike, G-men raided his office in September of 1922. A year later, in the midst of the Teapot Dome scandal, Burns and Hoover sent agents to investigate the administration's leading critics, Montana senators Thomas Walsh and Burton Wheeler.

While Hoover later took pains to distance himself from Burns, he also learned a great deal from the aging director—including the use of scare tactics

William J. Burns brought a background of corruption and brutality to government as an early leader of the FBI. (Author's collection)

and dubious statistics to milk appropriations from Congress. Hoover accompanied Burns on his various trips to Capitol Hill, where Burns warned credulous lawmakers of the latest "menace" and impressed them with news of the bureau's achievements. In 1922, for instance, Burns told the House Appropriations Committee that Bolshevik strategy in America—

principally consists of urging the working man to strike, with the ultimate purpose of bringing about a revolution in this country. . . . Radicalism is becoming stronger every day in this country. They are going about it in a very subtle manner. For instance, they have schools all over the country where they are teaching children 4 and 5 years old, and they are organizing athletic clubs through the country. I dare say that unless the country becomes aroused concerning the danger of this radical element in this country, we will have a very serious situation.

Where finances were concerned, Burns fell back on the Dyer Act to claim that G-men had "recovered" thousands of stolen cars across the United States (most of them retrieved in fact by local police). Playing a tune that Hoover would echo for the next 50 years, Burns told the House in 1922, "The value of automobiles recovered by our service amounts to more than our appropriation."

The Teapot Dome investigation snowballed after President Harding's sudden death in August 1923, and Burns was one of those called before Congress to explain his behavior. Burns admitted using G-men to investigate Senators Walsh and Wheeler, but the interrogation skirted his apparent role in the May 1923 shooting death of JUSTICE DEPARTMENT employee Jess Smith. Attorney General Harlan Stone demanded Burns's resignation on May 9, 1924, and after a brief spell of defiance, Burns complied the next day, replaced as director by J. Edgar Hoover. (The modern FEDERAL BUREAU OF INVESTIGATION's Internet Web site erroneously claims that Burns remained in office until June 14, 1924.)

Resignation did not end his involvement with the Teapot Dome conspirators, however. When the trial of ex-Secretary of the Interior Bernard Fall finally opened in October 1927, Burns (now back at the helm of his detective agency) was hired to shadow the jurors. A mistrial was declared, and Burns narrowly escaped conviction on a charge of criminal contempt. The near-miss drove him into retirement at Sarasota, Florida, where he passed his final years penning "true" accounts of his more famous cases. At his death, on April 14, 1932, the *Washington Post* hailed Burns as "probably the most famous individual in the detective business during his active years."

BURUNDI

The original inhabitants of Burundi were pygmies who now comprise 1 percent of the nation's population. Ruled by GERMANY through World War I, the region was ceded to BELGIUM in 1923, when the League of Nations broke up German East Africa. Belgian colonists exacerbated ethnic rivalries by forcing blacks to carry I.D. cards denoting them as Hutu or Tutsi. On gaining independence in 1962, Burundi became a monarchy under Tutsi king Mwami Mwambutsa IV. The nation's Hutu majority rebelled in 1965, prompting brutal Tutsi reprisals. Mwambutsa was deposed by his son, Ntaré V, in 1966, and a military junta (also led by Tutsi) seized power a few months later. A civil war killed 100,000 Hutu in 1970–71 while successive military coups in 1976 and 1987 heightened ethnic tension in Burundi. Another 20,000 Hutu were slaughtered by Tutsi mobs in August 1988. Pierre Buyoya, a Tutsi, was defeated in Burundi's first democratic election, which installed a Hutu—Melchior Ndadaye—as president in June 1993, but he died in a coup before year's end. Burundi's next Hutu president, Cyprien Ntaryamira, was killed with RWANDA's president when rebels shot their plane down on April 6, 1994. The Tutsi-dominated army seized power in July 1996, again installing Pierre Buyoya as leader but ethnic clashes continued, claiming 200,000 lives by late 2002. The military leadership has not been officially recognized but that of Pierre Buyoya has. Various peace negotiations have thus far failed to halt the black-on-black campaigns of "ethnic cleansing."

BUSH dynasty

The patriarch of this political dynasty—as wealthy and influential as the more "liberal" KENNEDY clan—was Samuel Prescott Bush (1863—1948), a New York native who made millions as president of the Buckeye Steel Casting Company (1907–27), first president of the National Association of Manufacturers, and a charter member of the U.S. Chamber of Commerce. In 1929–33 he was a close adviser to President Herbert Hoover, whose hands-off approach to the financial crises ushered in the Great Depression.

The Bush family suffered no pangs of hardship during that era, as Prescott Sheldon Bush (1895–1972) expanded into banking. (He also inaugurated the family's ties with Yale University and the super-secret SKULL AND BONES Society.) Prescott was a director and major shareholder in the United Banking Corporation (UBC), which in turn purchased the Consolidated Silesian Steel Corporation from Nazi industrialist Fritz Thyssen. Herr Thyssen obtained many of his workers from the Auschwitz concentration camp (not yet converted to a full-time slaughterhouse for Jews), and exposure of that enemy link in 1942 prompted U.S. authorities to seize UBC and two other Bush-managed firms (Holland-American Trading Corp. and Seamless Steel Equipment Corp.) in October 1942 under terms of the federal Trading with the Enemy Act. The stigma of helping finance ADOLF HITLER did not prevent Prescott Bush from serving in the U.S. Senate (1955–63), although he lost his first political race in 1950.

Meanwhile, George Herbert Walker Bush (1924–) had returned from World War II a hero, decorated for airborne action against the same THIRD REICH supported by his father's investments. A Yale graduate and Skull and Bones loyalist, George soon expanded the family's portfolio to include Texas OIL fields. Twice defeated in campaigns for the U.S. Senate (1964, 1970), Bush finally settled for a seat in the House (1967–71) and then served as U.S. representative to the UNITED NATIONS (1971–73), chairman of the Republican National Committee (1973–74), U.S. liaison to China (1974–75), and director of the CENTRAL INTELLIGENCE AGENCY (1976–77). A failed Republican presidential candidate in 1980, Bush accepted the consolation prize of serving as RONALD REAGAN's vice president (1981–89). In that capacity he worked overtime to cement Reagan's ties with the INTERNATIONAL BROTHERHOOD OF TEAMSTERS and helmed the first U.S. War on Drugs, condemned by U.S. Coast Guard spokesmen as "an intellectual fraud." As Reagan's successor in the White House (1989–93), Bush invaded PANAMA and launched the GULF WAR against IRAQ, but domestic fumbles doomed him to a one-term presidency. In the end, his staunchest supporters on the far right wound up

President George W. Bush sits with his wife Laura during morning church services at the National Cathedral in Washington, D.C. Behind Bush (left to right) are his father, former President George Bush, his mother Barbara, his daughters Jenna and Barbara, and his mother-in-law Jenna Welch. (Corbis)

suspecting Bush of treason after his public references to a NEW WORLD ORDER inspired a host of fresh conspiracy theories. Before leaving office, Bush pardoned six of his comrades in the IRAN-CONTRA CONSPIRACY and engineered the taxpayer bail-out of son Neil's Silverado Savings and Loan company, one of the prime offenders in the national SAVINGS AND LOAN SCANDAL.

Neil Mallon Bush (1955–) never tried his hand at politics, but his brothers made up the difference. George Walker Bush (1946–)—commonly called Dubya to distinguish him from father George—

attended Yale as a Bush "legacy" and completed his obligatory term with Skull and Bones. The war in VIETNAM threatened Dubya's health and welfare upon graduation, but his family arranged for George, Jr., to serve his country stateside in the Texas Air National Guard. The uniform proved too confining, and Dubya literally vanished during the last 12 months of his military service, later spinning contradictory yarns about that missing year while his commanding officers assured reporters that he had not been at his post. For whatever reason no charges were filed, leaving Dubya to dabble in oil and professional baseball while he sought his true calling. Those ventures prompted an SEC investigation on charges of insider trading. Again, no charges were filed, but a formal statement from the SEC warned: "It must in no way be construed as indicating that the party has been exonerated or that no action may ultimately result." Dubya changed directions in 1994, campaigning successfully to become governor of Texas. During his term in office (1995–2000), Texas led all other U.S. states in executions of prison inmates and in spiraling environmental pollution.

While George, Jr., made his mark in Texas, brother John Ellis ("Jeb") Bush (1953–) was staking out the family's claim in Florida. Jeb broke the clan's tie with Yale, preferring the University of Texas, but he otherwise maintained tradition by his involvement in dubious real-estate transactions (including defaulted loans) and his losing race for the Sunshine State's governorship in 1994. Successful on his second try four years later, Jeb Bush presided over a regime that was second only to Texas in execution of prisoners and attempts to sink oil wells in protected nature preserves. Jeb's alleged manipulation of ballots during Dubya's first presidential campaign posed one of the major controversies in a still-disputed ELECTION 2000, but the family prevailed (with help from five Republican SUPREME COURT justices) to put George, Jr., in the White House.

As president, Dubya swiftly wiped out the hard-won national economic surplus and charted a course toward record deficit spending, while calling for tax cuts to benefit the richest 2 percent of Americans. He also ordered federal agents to "back off" investigations of the Saudi Arabian BIN LADEN FAMILY, long-standing financial allies of the Bush dynasty. That move backfired with the PENTTBOM attacks of September 11, 2001, masterminded by AL-QAEDA leader Osama bin Laden, but Bush rallied by invading AFGHANISTAN and pushing passage of the USA PATRIOT ACT in the name of "enduring freedom." While the United States sank deeper into recession, Bush next declared media war against a mythical AXIS OF EVIL, allegedly including mortal enemies IRAQ and IRAN with isolationist North KOREA. In 2003 Bush launched OPERATION IRAQI FREEDOM to unseat SADDAM HUSSEIN, but the advance claims that Iraq possessed "weapons of mass destruction" were soon proved false. That glitch notwithstanding, Dubya seemed intent on waging his reelection campaign in the guise of a warrior, donning military garb to pose with combat veterans 30 years after evading his own stint of military duty.

See also KENNEDY DYNASTY.

CAMBODIA

When FRANCE colonized Southeast Asia in 1863, it merged the modern nations of Cambodia, LAOS, and VIETNAM into an artificial unit dubbed French Indochina. In Cambodia the invaders seized all but ceremonial powers from the Hindu Khmers who had ruled Cambodia since A.D. 600. French extraction of rubber and other raw materials was interrupted by JAPAN in World War II. France reluctantly "liberated" Cambodia in 1949, though full military independence was not achieved until 1955. The royal Norodom family sought to remain neutral in Vietnam's war with the United States, but Vietnamese rebels sought sanctuary in Cambodia, pursued by U.S. troops under President RICHARD NIXON. Pressure from indigenous communists (Khmer Rouge) prompted a military coup by Gen. Lon Nol in March 1970. Khmer Rouge forces under Pol Pot seized power in April 1975, inaugurating a four-year campaign of genocide against native Cambodians. Vietnamese troops deposed Pol Pot in January 1979, but he fought on from hiding until 1997, while various coups disrupted the Cambodian government. (Finally captured and sentenced to house arrest for his crimes, Pol Pot died on April 15, 1998.) UNITED NATIONS efforts to establish a WAR CRIMES tribunal failed in February 2002. Cambodian officials vowed to handle the matter themselves, but Prime Minister Hun Sen—himself a former Khmer Rouge member—has thus far done nothing to punish his former colleagues.

CAMDEN 28   See HARDY, ROBERT W.

CAMORRA

While the MAFIA restricts "made" membership to persons of Sicilian ancestry, the Camorra criminal society is composed of mainland Italians. Details of its history are deliberately obscure, but the Camorra's roots are traceable to the Garduna, a Spanish secret society transplanted to Italy when Spain seized Naples in the 16th century. Blood oaths and secret signs were employed, and a Grand Ruling Council based in Naples supervised the operations of small units led by *caporegimes* (a term shared with the rival Mafia, frequently shortened to *capo*). Whereas the early Mafia was chiefly a rural organization, the Camorra enjoyed an urban power base, frequently using the CATHOLIC CHURCH as a cover. Sporadic warfare between the Camorra and the Mafia increasingly turned toward collaboration after World War II. By the 1970s Camorra gangsters on the Italian mainland worked hand-in-hand with the Mafia's heroin smugglers. More recently, authorities have claimed links between the Camorra and the RUSSIAN MAFIA in smuggling of contraband that includes weapons-grade nuclear material.

CAMP Van Dorn massacre

By any standards, the U.S. Army's 364th Infantry Regiment (Colored) was one of the most controversial

Allied military units created during World War II. Consisting entirely of black soldiers but commanded by white officers, the 364th was initially stationed in Arizona, but a mass transfer was ordered after unruly behavior there produced a rash of complaints. May 1943 found the regiment at Camp Van Dorn, outside Centreville, Mississippi. Despite strictly segregated quarters, the men of the 364th were soon in trouble again, accused of looting a shop on the base. On May 30, Pvt. William Walker was fatally shot by white military police officers, allegedly while trying to seize one of their weapons in an angry confrontation. Following that incident U.S. Army files confirm that Col. John F. Goodman ordered the firing pins removed from all weapons that were carried by men of the 364th. What happened next remains a point of heated controversy more than 60 years after the fact.

According to author Carroll Case, disturbances at Camp Van Dorn continued until July 4, 1943, when military police surrounded barracks occupied by soldiers of the 364th and slaughtered some 1,200 men with concentrated small-arms fire. Case heard the story first from an ex-MP, a blatant racist identified as Bill Martzall (deceased in 1989), who said:

> We were riding in weapons carriers and were armed with .45-caliber machine guns. We were told to wait until dark and to report to the black camp. It was located near the Engineering Division close to the railroad. Some other troops armed to the teeth joined us. We pulled up to the black camp and ordered the 364th out into this area. I remember that one of the nigger soldiers threw a brick and hit one of the MPs in the eye. I don't know if he lost his eye or not because all hell broke loose. We were ordered to let them have it. We had the whole area sealed off—it was like shooting fish in a barrel. We opened fire on everything that moved, shot into the barracks, shot them out of trees where some of them were climbing, trying to hide. We shot every nigger we could find. The screaming, yelling and begging was horrible.

Two other locals, Luther Williams and W. M. Ewell, corroborated the story. Williams had been a Wilkinson County firefighter in 1943, while Ewell was a civilian employed in the camp laundry. Both described a "makeshift morgue" at Camp Van Dorn, with "hundreds and hundreds of bodies stacked up like hogs, almost as high as the ceiling." The corpses were allegedly removed aboard a special train for burial at some unknown location.

When Case's book was published in 1998, cast in the form of a novel with a short nonfiction preface, U.S. Army spokespersons dismissed it as a flight of fantasy. In December 1999 an official report was published, intended "to put to rest any concern that these alleged events were even remotely possible." According to that document, "All of the nearly 4,000 men who were assigned to the 364th Infantry in 1943 have been traced to their separation from military service." Leaders of the NAACP expressed concern with the results of the investigation. "We aren't saying the Army is wrong," spokesman John White told reporters, "but we don't have the personnel here to confirm what they found. We are saying we need a third party to offer an objective look at the matter. If the Justice Department signs off on the Army report, we will be satisfied."

Neither Attorney General Janet Reno nor successor JOHN ASHCROFT displayed any inclination to investigate the claims. Case's publisher, Rusty Denman, challenged the army's version of events, comparing Camp Van Dorn to the long-denied Korean War massacre at NO GUN RI. For years the army denied any record of that event, Denman noted, "And then—boom!—there it is."

CANCER cures

It is an article of faith among many conspiracists that one or more sure-fire cures for cancer have been discovered over the past century, only to be callously suppressed by leaders of the mainstream medical establishment. The names most often mentioned as oppressed benefactors of humankind include:

Harry Hoxsey, grandson of farmer John Hoxsey, who allegedly discovered an herbal cure for cancer in horses around 1840. The Hoxsey treatment was refined in time, handed down from father to son within the family, until grandson Harry went public with his miracle cure a century later. The Hoxsey treatment combines ingestion of a tonic (including red clover, licorice root, and other natural ingredients) with external application of a salve made from bloodroot, antimony trisulfide, and zinc chloride. According to Hoxsey and his supporters, the combination is effective in reversing most forms of cancer, but it has been branded quackery and effectively suppressed by leaders of the American Medical Association (AMA).

Royal Raymond Rife, a scientist who spent 20 years tracking the cause of cancer across the United States and Europe, finally isolating a microorganism he dubbed the "BX virus." In the course of his research, Rife also allegedly learned how to kill BX and reverse its effects among "terminal" patients. The results of his research were published in 1931, endorsed by a panel of researchers at the University of Southern California—until the AMA closed ranks to censor all future reports and hound Rife into obscurity.

Gaston Naessens, a Canadian researcher who developed a camphor derivative called "714-X," allegedly capable of reinforcing the human immune system to defeat cancer, AIDS, and other "incurable" diseases. AMA leaders are cast as the villains once again in a campaign of persecution that saw Naessens branded a quack and indicted on various felony counts in 1985. He was acquitted of all charges in December 1989, but his "fraudulent" cure is still banned.

Why would anyone—much less a panel of prominent physicians—suppress effective cures for cancer and other deadly diseases? The obvious answer is *greed.* Research and treatment of cancer is a multibillion-dollar global industry. If patients could be cured with items readily available at any health-food store, huge yearly profits would be lost to doctors, hospitals, health-insurance carriers, and PHARMACEUTICAL COMPANIES around the world. The countless scandals of modern medicine, from DRUG DUMPING to Medicare fraud and needless surgery, makes it clear that modern healers are no strangers to avarice. As for the so-called cancer cures touted and banned over the past 160 years, only the inventors and their patients know if any were truly effective.

CARLOS the Jackal (1949–)

Arguably the world's most infamous terrorist before Osama BIN LADEN, Carlos the Jackal was born Ilich Ramirez Sanchez in 1949. The son of a wealthy Venezuelan physician devoted to COMMUNISM, Ramirez enjoyed lavish affluence in his youth while being schooled in the rhetoric of proletarian revolu-

tion. Educated in RUSSIA under KGB tutelage, he was dispatched to the Middle East in the early 1970s, for paramilitary training with Palestinian commandos. There in the desert camps, Ramirez became "Carlos." (The "Jackal" tag was added later, after police found a copy of the novel *Day of the Jackal* in one of his abandoned hideouts.) Much deliberate mystery surrounds his subsequent movements, and there is no hard evidence to support claims that Carlos participated in BLACK SEPTEMBER's lethal attack on the 1972 Munich Olympics. Carlos probably assassinated Lord Edward Seiff in Britain on December 30, 1974, before moving on to conduct a series of bombings and rocket attacks against pro-Israeli targets in France. Almost cornered in Paris in 1975, Carlos shot his way out of the trap, killing two French police officers and a Palestinian informer. That December Carlos led the team that invaded an OPEC conference in Vienna, killing three persons and escaping with 42 hostages to LIBYA. Accounts differ on whether Carlos then remained in Libya as a guest of MUAMMAR AL-QADDAFFI or returned to France, perhaps leading the 1982 rocket assault on a French nuclear reactor. Before year's end, French police jailed his wife, Magdalena Kopp (a terrorist with ties to the German Red Army faction). Kopp ultimately served five years in prison, despite a series of terrorist attacks designed to win her freedom. International heat drove Carlos underground, perhaps in SYRIA, but rumors circulated in the early 1990s that SADDAM HUSSEIN might bring him out of retirement for raids on U.S. interests. In 1994 Carlos was finally arrested, reportedly while recuperating from testicular surgery to improve a low sperm count. At his trial in 1997, Carlos received a life prison term for three of his suspected 80-plus murders.

CARTER, Asa Earl (?–1979)

Alabama native "Ace" Carter studied journalism at the University of Colorado and tried his hand as a radio disc jockey in Colorado before settling on a career as a full-time white supremacist. Employed at a Birmingham radio station in 1955, he sparked protests with anti-Semitic broadcasts that were aired during Brotherhood Week and was fired from his job. Moving on to the segregationist CITIZENS' COUNCIL, Carter soon quarreled with Alabama leader Sam Englehardt and resigned to organize a local faction of the KU KLUX KLAN. Six members of his group assaulted singer Nat "King" Cole at a Birmingham concert in April 1956, based on Carter's claim that Cole was "a vicious agitator for integration." In January 1957 Carter was jailed for shooting two of his own Klansmen after they questioned his handling of KKK money. Eight months later, four of his followers kidnapped and castrated black handyman Edward Aaron as part of a Klan initiation ceremony. The four were sentenced to 20-year prison terms but received early parole from Governor GEORGE WALLACE, who employed Carter as his chief speechwriter. In that capacity Carter penned Wallace's infamous "Segregation Forever" speech, including a promise to "stand in the schoolhouse door" if black students enrolled at Alabama colleges. In later life Carter reinvented himself as a best-selling author. Taking the name "Forrest" Carter (after 1860s KKK leader Nathan Bedford Forrest), he wrote the novel *Gone to Texas,* later filmed with Clint Eastwood as *The Outlaw Josey Wales.* Next, he fabricated Cherokee grandparents to write *The Education of Little Tree* (ironically including a loving portrait of a Jewish peddler). Carter would not live to see his final book become a 1990s cult phenomenon, however. He died in 1979, allegedly from a heart attack, but ambulance attendants say he choked to death on vomit following a drunken fistfight with his son.

CASEY, William (1913–1987)

William Casey launched his long career in covert operations in 1941 during World War II as an agent for the OFFICE OF STRATEGIC SERVICES (OSS). Following ADOLF HITLER's defeat, Casey stayed on with the OSS in Europe to spearhead PROJECT PAPERCLIP, recruiting "ex"-Nazis for the new struggle against COMMUNISM. Retiring from the intelligence game to private legal practice in 1946, Casey represented various CENTRAL INTELLIGENCE AGENCY (CIA) members and front groups in the 1960s before President RICHARD NIXON tapped him to chair the U.S. Securities and Exchange Commission. Subsequent SEC leaders have distanced themselves from Casey's regime, some remarking that under his leadership the body's initial's might have stood for "See Everything Crooked." With top aide Stanley Sporkin, Casey instituted a policy of "enforcement actions" that served primarily to keep Casey's name in headlines, while 95 percent of the SEC lawsuits instituted were "settled" within 48 hours. (Casey's immediate

superior, Senator Harrison Williams, was later driven from his post as chairman of the Senate Banking and Finance Committee after he accepted bribes from undercover FEDERAL BUREAU OF INVESTIGATION agents in the ABSCAM sting operation.) Casey served as RONALD REAGAN's presidential campaign manager in 1980, engineering the OCTOBER SURPRISE, and he was rewarded with appointment to serve as director of the Central Intelligence Agency. Stanley Sporkin was named the CIA's general counsel and joined Casey to plot the covert contra war of TERRORISM against the lawful government of NICARAGUA. When Congress banned that crusade, Casey-Sporkin plunged headlong into the IRAN-CONTRA CONSPIRACY with Vice President George H. W. Bush. Before that scandal publicly erupted, Reagan appointed Stan Sporkin to serve as a federal judge in Washington, D.C. (where he remained on the bench for 18 years). William Casey died from a malignant brain tumor in early 1987 shortly before he was scheduled for questioning by senate investigators in the Iran-contra case. In death he became the perfect scapegoat for the politicians who had pulled his strings at CIA headquarters.

See also BUSH DYNASTY.

CASOLARO, Joseph Daniel (?–1991)

Prior to August 1991, few persons outside Washington, D.C., recognized the name of 44-year-old freelance journalist Danny Casolaro. His life—and what some call his quixotic quest—only achieved significance for conspiracy theorists after Casolaro was found dead in the bathtub of a hotel room in Martinsburg, West Virginia, wrists slashed with a single-edged razor blade. In the rented room, police found beer bottles, a half-empty bottle of wine, a shattered drinking glass, and a handwritten note reading "God will let me in." Dr. James Frost, West Virginia's deputy chief medical examiner, found "nothing inconsistent with suicide" in Casolaro's death, but relatives and close friends insist he was murdered.

Why? And by whom?

Before his death, Casolaro was obsessed with revealing the details of a global megaconspiracy, tracking a single thread that allegedly linked such diverse plots and scandals as the OCTOBER SURPRISE of 1980, the IRAN-CONTRA plot of Presidents RONALD REAGAN and George H. W. Bush, and the BCCI banking network. In death, he left behind unfinished proposals for a book titled *The Octopus,* described by Casolaro as "the most explosive investigative story of the 20th century." As described in Casolaro's synopsis: "This story is about a handful of people who have been able to successfully exploit the secret empires of espionage networks, big oil, and organized crime. This octopus spans the globe . . . to control governmental institutions in the United States and abroad."

Unfortunately, Casolaro left no details of the plot(s) behind. Relatives say he was traveling to meet a source in West Virginia when he died, but Casolaro had not named the individual. The files he carried with him everywhere were not found in his hotel room or at his home. From all appearances his months of research on a book that never went to press produced no detailed notes, no interviews on tape, no photocopied documents. That circumstance, as much as any other, fuels speculation that Casolaro was killed to prevent revelations of what "They" had done and/or planned to do in the future.

See also BUSH DYNASTY.

CASSIDY, Butch   See UNDEAD OUTLAWS.

CASTRO, Fidel (1926–   )

Fidel Alejandro Castro Ruz was born on August 13, 1926, at Mayari, CUBA. He graduated from Havana's Colegio Belen in 1945 and auditioned for the New York Yankees as a prospective pitcher (rejected) before earning his LL.D. from the University of Havana in 1950. Castro practiced law for two years and then joined the revolution against U.S.-supported dictator Fulgencio Batista. After leading an assault on the Moncada Barracks at Santiago de Cuba, he was imprisoned for two years (1953–55) and then exiled to MEXICO and the United States. Embarrassed by Batista's corruption and brutality, leaders of the CENTRAL INTELLIGENCE AGENCY (CIA) offered Castro their covert support, and he returned to Cuba with renewed zeal for the revolution. (The CATHOLIC CHURCH excommunicated Castro in 1955, though whether for his politics or his divorce cannot be ascertained.) Batista fled the island in 1959, and Castro assumed control of Cuba, first as prime minister (1959–76) and then as president (1976–present). He soon disappointed U.S. leaders by jailing or deporting MAFIA bosses who ran Havana's casinos and by nationalizing Cuba's natural resources. Deprived of aid from Washington, Castro turned to RUSSIA and declared himself a communist. CIA leaders joined right-wing Cuban exiles to plot an invasion of Cuba, resulting in the BAY OF PIGS fiasco (1961). Repeated CIA-Mafia efforts to murder Castro failed in the 1960s, but terrorist raids against Cuba continued for decades, carried out by U.S.-based groups such as ALPHA 66 and Omega 7. Many researchers believe the covert war on Cuba led directly to the JFK ASSASSINATION of 1963, but they disagree on whether Castro or his enemies killed President John Kennedy. Castro, meanwhile, remained in power as this volume went to press, the longest-serving head of state in the Western Hemisphere.

See also COMMUNISM; KENNEDY DYNASTY.

CATHOLIC Church

It is difficult for us to grasp in modern times with the ecclesiastical chaos of rival creeds, but for more than a millennium following the alleged death of JESUS CHRIST, there was only one Christian church on Earth. Purportedly organized by the 11 loyal apostles, with Peter generally identified as the first pope, the new sect expanded from its Middle Eastern roots by word of mouth. Church leaders spent their first 500 years debating and revising doctrines, ratifying some "holy" texts while discarding others, translating pagan festivals into Christian "holy days" for the sake of acceptance by Rome's emperors. That empire's collapse provided church leaders with their first great opportunity for seizing power, as frightened and disoriented people sought solace from their faith. Before the church could rule, however, it had to destroy its opponents—and that task would consume the next 1,300 years.

First came a purge of all "ungodly" knowledge that conflicted with the church's narrow and self-serving tenets. In 391 Christians burned the great library at Alexandria, destroying an estimated 700,000 scrolls. "Dark Ages" descended on Europe as similar actions followed wherever the pope held sway. Even Greek and Roman medical texts were declared "heretical," leaving humanity vulnerable to a plague that killed an estimated 100 million persons in the sixth century. (The 12th-century Black Death, by contrast, killed about 27 million.) Under church leadership from the sixth to the 16th centuries, "medicine" was largely restricted to prayer and bleeding, a combination that virtually guaranteed death from any significant illness. Still, the plague was good news for church leaders as terrified peasants flocked to find relief from "God's judgment." As its influence expanded, so the church accumulated ever-growing wealth—by sale of ecclesiastical offices or priestly "indulgences" (free passes for sin), sometimes by brute seizure of coveted lands and property from "heretics." As papal power increased, so the occupation of pope became increasingly hazardous. Indeed, the rapid turnover in popes—10 between 891 and 903 alone—sparked rumors of assassination within the Vatican itself.

The church suffered its first great rift in 1054 when Rome's pope quarreled with church leaders in Constantinople and the latter defected to create their own Eastern Orthodox Church. Instant "heretics" by definition, Eastern Orthodox believers joined Muslims and Jews on the papal hit list when the first Crusade was launched in 1095. Those "holy" wars against an ever-shifting cast of "infidels" dragged on until 1291, killing tens of thousands (some historians say millions) in a brutal series of seesaw campaigns for control of the "Holy Land." The fighting meant more loot for Rome, while on the home front, equally brutal campaigns were mounted against religious dissenters. The Albigensian Crusade, launched by Pope Innocent III in 1208, slaughtered an estimated 1 million Cathar heretics in France. At least 60,000 died in the siege of Beziers alone; when a captain asked the pope's field commander how his men should distinguish Catholics from Cathars, the commander replied, "Kill them all, for God knows his own." Persecution of dissidents and other unfortunates was formalized in 1231 when Pope Gregory IX established the Inquisition. That saintly murder machine spread worldwide during the next 400 years, reaching as far as the Americas and India (where 3,800 "infidels" were murdered at Goa for rejecting Jesus). Women were also favored targets in a series of collateral witch hunts that spanned roughly three centuries from 1450 to 1750. Sexual abuse and torture added a new twist to saintly sadism in those cases, as whole European districts were depopulated of females. (The perversity of inquisitor Foulques de Saint-George was so notorious that residents of Toulouse took the unusual and dangerous step of gathering evidence against him.)

If there was any doubt about the Vatican's desire to rule the world, Pope Boniface erased it with the bull (decree) *Unam Sanctum* in 1302. That proclamation read:

> *Therefore, if earthly power errs, it shall be judged by the spiritual power . . . but if the supreme spiritual power errs it can be judged only by God, and not by man. . . . Therefore we declare, state, define and pronounce that it is altogether necessary for salvation for every human creature to be subject to the Roman pontiff.*

With global domination on the table, it was no surprise that sundry papal candidates aggressively pursued the throne of Rome. That contest produced the Great Schism, wherein dueling popes reigned at Rome and Avignon between 1378 and 1417. The separate papal lines had no quarrel about Christian dogma or ritual but struggled fiercely for control of the "one true church's" political and financial power until the contest was finally resolved in Rome's favor.

Discovery of the New World in 1492 gave the church new chances for winning souls at gunpoint. Spanish and Portuguese conquistadors traditionally approached native tribes in the Western Hemisphere with a printed order from Rome—the *Requermiento* (requirement)—demanding that all present abandon their traditional beliefs and accept Jesus on the spot under pain of execution or enslavement. Naturally, since the "Indians" spoke neither Spanish nor Portuguese, they were fair game for slaughter, and Roman priests were among the first to claim shackled survivors as slave labor for their missions and plantations. Back in Europe, meanwhile, papal authority was challenged by a new breed of dissidents (or Protestants) led by Martin Luther. Henceforth, both branches of Christianity would persecute Jews and witches, but they would also kill each other in a series of clashes that included the ST. BARTHOLOMEW'S DAY MASSACRE (10,000 Protestants slaughtered in France) and the Thirty Years' War (1618–48) that involved six nations and the Holy Roman Empire. In North America, sectarian conflict took the form of conspiracy theories targeting JESUIT monks and anti-Catholic agitation by members of the KNOW-NOTHING MOVEMENT and the KU KLUX KLAN.

Controversy surrounding the Catholic Church has not subsided in modern times. Religion was a major issue for Catholic presidential candidates Al Smith (1924, 1928) and John Kennedy (1960), while some

Protestant sects and institutions still teach believers that the pope is the Antichrist and the "Beast of Revelation." During World War II and the HOLOCAUST, Pope Pius XII charted a course of accommodation with ADOLF HITLER that protected church property while ignoring the wholesale slaughter of Jews and other minorities. (In 2003 Pius XII was nominated for sainthood.) Sectarian violence often overshadows political issues when members of the IRISH REPUBLICAN ARMY clash with Protestant groups such as the Ulster Defense Association in Northern Ireland. Rome's stance on abortion and contraception (both banned by papal decree) provides theological support for such terrorist groups as the ARMY OF GOD. Within the church itself, ongoing scandal surrounds the Vatican's handling (some say coddling) of PEDOPHILE PRIESTS and the so-called rehabilitation programs offered by groups such as the SERVANTS OF THE PARACLETE. By 2003 hundreds of priests in the United States and Europe stood accused of sexual offenses while their superiors often seemed more intent on protecting the church's reputation than the minds and bodies of its loyal parishioners. On the financial side, persistent scandal dogs the VATICAN BANK and its alleged ties with organized-crime groups including the MAFIA and the CAMORRA. As long as religion remains a bone of contention between human beings, the world's largest and richest church will doubtless be a lightning rod for criticism and suspicion.

See also KENNEDY DYNASTY.

CENTRAL African Republic

This landlocked nation of equatorial Africa was ravaged by slave traders from the 16th to the 19th century. FRANCE occupied the territory in 1894, expanding by 1910 to create French Equatorial Africa (including portions of the Congo and modern Gabon). A 1946 rebellion forced the French to grant self-government, and 12 years later residents of the district voted to become an autonomous republic within the French community. President David Dacko declared independence from France in August 1960, aligning the country with CHINA before a military coup deposed him in December 1965. New ruler Jean-Bédel Bokassa declared himself Emperor Bokassa I in December 1976, and the country was renamed the Central African Empire. Brutality and repression marked the "new" regime and continued

through two more coups (in September 1979 and September 1981). By the 1990s a crippled economy prohibited payment of government salaries, and the army revolted in 1996. Prime Minister Ange-Félix Patassé requested French troops to crush the rebellion, and UNITED NATIONS peacekeepers arrived in 1998 to quell ongoing bloodshed. In September 1999 Patassé defeated rival André Kolingba in an election that was marred by charges of massive fraud. Troops from LIBYA and the Congo helped Patassé survive a coup by Kolingba supporters in May 2001, followed by bloody reprisals against the insurgents.

CENTRAL Intelligence Agency

Near the end of World War II, William Donovan suggested to President Harry Truman that the OFFICE OF STRATEGIC SERVICES (OSS) or some similar group should continue operations during peacetime. Truman agreed but bypassed Donovan for leadership of the new CIA when it was created in 1947. A year later, the agency's charter was expanded from mere intelligence gathering to include "covert actions," though the CIA was specifically barred from operating inside the United States—a restriction that has seldom (if ever) restrained America's "spooks" from spying when and where they please.

By 1953 when Allen Dulles took charge of the CIA, simple intelligence gathering had lost its allure. The agency—or "The Company," as it is often called—was ready and willing to embark on a more aggressive phase of covert operations. Under Dulles and his successors, *covert operations* were defined as activities "conducted or sponsored by this Government against hostile foreign states or groups or in support of friendly foreign states or groups but which are so planned and executed that any U.S. Government responsibility for them is not evident to unauthorized persons and that if uncovered the U.S. Government can plausibly disclaim any responsibility for them."

During the next two decades, operating on the razor's edge of "plausible deniability," the CIA would plunge headfirst into murky waters throughout the world. A few of its known illegal operations include: toppling the duly elected governments of GUATEMALA and CHILE; installing the shah of IRAN as absolute dictator and supporting his terrorist regime for another quarter-century; conducting covert proxy wars in LAOS, ANGOLA, and elsewhere in the name of "anti-COMMUNISM"; launching the disastrous BAY OF PIGS INVASION in a failed effort to unseat FIDEL CASTRO in CUBA; plotting with leaders of the MAFIA to murder Castro; planning "executive action" (that is, murder) against other heads of state throughout the Third World; collaborating with organized crime in Europe and the Far East to suppress native dissidents; pursuing MIND-CONTROL experiments through use of LSD, hypnosis, and other means; smuggling heroin to the United States aboard AIR AMERICA flights; arming "contra" terrorists to overthrow the elected government of NICARAGUA, and spearheading the IRAN-CONTRA CONSPIRACY; arming Muslim rebels (including Osama bin Laden) to fight Soviet forces in AFGHANISTAN; arming SADDAM HUSSEIN during IRAQ's long war with Iran; and conducting decades of illicit domestic surveillance and "disinformation" campaigns that included bribing journalists, infiltrating college campuses, spying on political candidates, and harassing political dissenters. The latter operations were conducted both in collaboration with the FEDERAL BUREAU OF INVESTIGATION (FBI), and sometimes in opposition to the JUSTICE DEPARTMENT's authorized domestic snoopers. Since 2001 domestic spying by the CIA has been approved and vastly expanded under terms of the USA PATRIOT ACT.

The net result of those covert activities, spanning more than a half-century, has been predominantly negative. From the Bay of Pigs to untimely reports of Osama bin Laden's "death," the CIA has embarrassed its political masters time and time again. (Most recently, President George W. Bush used the agency as his scapegoat when journalists exposed his false justifications of OPERATION IRAQI FREEDOM.) CIA agents left their clumsy fingerprints on every phase of the WATERGATE scandal, and a later generation bungled efforts to predict (and thus prevent) the catastrophic PENTTBOM attacks of September 11, 2001. The agency has also suffered mightily from "blowback"—the phenomenon in which a group or nation armed and funded by the CIA turns and attacks the guiding hand. (Saddam Hussein, Osama bin Laden, and PANAMA's Manuel Noriega provide three classic examples.)

Given the CIA's long record of highly public failures, some critics suggest that its operations have little to do with "intelligence," however we define that term. Others suggest that it is not too late to follow through on President John Kennedy's reputed 1963 plan to "dismember" the agency and "scatter it to the winds" (a plan foiled, coincidentally or otherwise, by the JFK ASSASSINATION). CIA apologists grant that The Company has made "a few mistakes"—after all, its leaders and agents are "only human"—but they claim that untold good has also been accomplished by unsung heroes acting in the best interests of "God and country." Unfortunately, those supposed good deeds are shrouded by the same cloak of secrecy that covers everything else about the CIA, including the size of its annual budget.

That very secrecy, coupled with the CIA's known crimes, ensures that conspiracy theories will always dog the agency's covert footsteps. Some of the more durable theories include CIA involvement in the RFK ASSASSINATION, the murders of Dr. MARTIN LUTHER KING, JR., and MALCOLM X, invention of the AIDS virus, creation and widespread ghetto distribution of crack COCAINE, toppling President RICHARD NIXON by means of fabricated Watergate evidence, the murder of JOHN LENNON, and suppression of "the truth" concerning UFOS. At age 51 and counting, only one thing can be said with certainty about the CIA: Nothing said by any spokesman for the agency should be accepted at face value.

See also BIN LADEN FAMILY; DULLES BROTHERS; KENNEDY DYNASTY.

CERMAK, Anton Joseph (1873–1933)

A native of Bohemia (now the CZECH REPUBLIC) and born in 1873, Anton Cermak immigrated to Chicago and worked as a street vendor (known as "Pushcart Tony") before he discovered the wonders of urban ward politics. Rising swiftly through Democratic Party ranks, Cermak served as an Illinois delegate to the party's national conventions in 1924, 1928, and 1932. He failed to win a U.S. Senate seat in 1928, but was elected mayor of Chicago two years later. Although portrayed in Windy City mythology as a crusading reformer, Cermak was known among local mobsters as Ten-Percent Tony for the flat rate of bribes he demanded. (He also ran a thriving real estate business, profiting hugely from insider tips he received from members of the state legislature.) Curiously, once installed in office, Cermak severed ties with the powerful Al Capone mob and forged alliances with rival gangster Roger Touhy (local boss of the INTERNATIONAL BROTHERHOOD OF TEAMSTERS). For that treachery Cermak paid the ultimate price. On February 15,

1933, while attending a campaign rally with presidential candidate Franklin Roosevelt in Miami, Cermak was shot by Giuseppe Zangara, a former sharpshooter with the Italian army. When his Chicago secretary rushed to Cermak's hospital bedside, Cermak said, "So you survived all right. I thought maybe they'd shot up the office in Chicago, too." He lingered for three weeks until gangrene and pneumonia claimed his life on March 6. Zangara was billed in the press as a lone-nut assassin who failed in a bid to kill Roosevelt, but Chicago judge John Lyle later declared, "Zangara was a MAFIA killer, sent from Sicily to do a job and sworn to silence." Sixty years after Zangara's execution, SECRET SERVICE files released under the Freedom of Information Act revealed that the gunman had been jailed for bootlegging in 1929 and subsequently lost huge sums to mob-owned racetracks in Florida, working off part of his debt as a drug-smuggling "mule." Conspiracists note the similarity between Zangara's case and those of "lone assassins" in the JFK and RFK ASSASSINATIONs and the murder of Dr. MARTIN LUTHER KING, JR.

CHAD

Three rival kingdoms surrounded Africa's Lake Chad by the 16th century, but all were conquered by Sudanese warlord Rabih al-Zubayr between 1883 and 1893. French invaders toppled Rabih in 1900 and 10 years later absorbed the territory into French Equatorial Africa. Chad became a separate colony in 1920, was admitted to the French community in 1946, and finally achieved independence in August 1960. President Ngarta Tombalbaye died in a coup, in 1975. Successor Gen. Félix Malloum soon faced rebels in a civil war financed from LIBYA. In 1977 Libya seized a strip of territory in Chad, prior to launching a full-scale invasion two years later. Libyan leader MUAMMAR AL-QADDAFFI proposed a formal merger of nations in January 1981, but Chad refused, so Libyan troops withdrew before year's end. They returned for another try in 1983, supporting antigovernment rebels led by Goukouni Oueddei, while France sent troops to defend current ruler Hissen Habré. In 1990 Habré's government was toppled by the Patriotic Salvation Movement, which suspended Chad's constitution and dissolved the legislature. PSM leader Idriss Déby soon faced violent opposition from a new Movement for Democracy and Justice (MDJC). Clashes continue, despite a cease-fire agreement in January 2002.

CHALLENGER shuttle disaster

At 11:40 A.M. on January 28, 1986, the space shuttle *Challenger* was launched from Kennedy Space Center in Florida. Seventy-three seconds into the flight, a global TV audience watched, horrified, as the spacecraft erupted into a giant fireball and plummeted back toward splashdown in the Atlantic. All seven astronauts aboard were killed, and while investigators later blamed a defective "O" ring for permitting an explosive fuel leak, conspiracy theories abound. As with the subsequent COLUMBIA SHUTTLE DISASTER, theories include an act of sabotage or TERRORISM, intervention by extraterrestrials to prevent further space exploration by earthlings, and a mundane cover-up of negligence among planners and technicians of the National Aeronautics and Space Administration (NASA). Thus far, none of the claims has been substantiated.

CHAPPAQUIDDICK incident

On the night of July 18, 1969, a black Oldsmobile sedan plunged off a narrow bridge on Chappaquiddick Island, Martha's Vineyard, Massachusetts. Submerged, the car was not found until the morning of July 19. Inside it authorities discovered the corpse of 28-year-old Mary Jo Kopechne, a former secretary to murdered U.S. Senator Robert Kennedy. Soon after that grim discovery, Senator Edward Kennedy entered the Edgartown police station on Martha's Vineyard and confessed that he had driven the car. At the time, "Ted" Kennedy was considered a Democratic frontrunner for president in 1972, but the Chappaquiddick scandal doomed any hopes that he cherished for occupying the White House. A series of evasive and contradictory statements left many questions surrounding the accident forever unanswered, despite Kennedy's guilty plea to charges of leaving the accident scene. He received a two-month suspended jail sentence, and while some observers denounced the wrist-slap as a prime example of political corruption, others question whether Kennedy was even in the car when it crashed. Conspiracist R.B. Cutler maintains that the Chappaquiddick incident was an "ambush" and "political assassination" of Kennedy, carried out by the CENTRAL INTELLIGENCE AGENCY to bar yet another Kennedy from seeking the presidency. As for Kopechne's bereaved mother, she told reporters in July 1969, "I am satisfied with Kennedy's statement and hope he decides to stay in the Senate." Kennedy fulfilled that wish, remaining in office as this volume went to press.

See also KENNEDY DYNASTY.

CHASE Manhattan Bank

Founded and owned by the ROCKEFELLER family, Chase Manhattan Bank (formerly Chase National) moved closer to becoming the world's richest bank in September 2000 with its bid to buy out rival J.P. MORGAN. That step prompted journalists to review Chase's corporate history, and what they found was a sordid record of cashing in on human misery. Before World War II Chase and parent company STANDARD OIL (now Exxon) financed ADOLF HITLER's rise to power in GERMANY and assisted him in building Europe's most powerful army. Both Chase and Standard Oil were major stockholders in I.G. FARBEN, the German chemical company that built the Auschwitz death camp and invented Zyklon-B nerve gas to facilitate extermination of "undesirables" during the HOLOCAUST. Farben reciprocated by purchasing masses of Standard Oil stock. The symbiotic relationship did not end with the U.S. entry into World War II but rather flourished despite legislation banning trade with the fascist enemy. Before Hitler's defeat, Chase/Standard operatives helped the Nazi elite smuggle stolen assets worth billions of dollars to friendly banks in SWITZERLAND and South America.

Supporting the THIRD REICH was more than simply good business for Chase executives: for some, it was also a labor or love. Family patriarch John D. Rockefeller ranked among the world's foremost promoters of "eugenics," the pseudoscience of "race betterment" by selective breeding. Auschwitz "Angel of Death" JOSEF MENGELE was among the eugenics experts funded by Rockefeller endowments. Today, operating as the Manhattan Institute—founded by former CIA director WILLIAM CASEY—Chase/Rockefeller supports such "scholars" as Charles Murray (whose opus *The Bell Curve* claims blacks are genetically and intellectually inferior to whites). The Manhattan Institute also pioneered theories of "compassionate conservatism" which

were touted in modern times by President George W. Bush. (Statements from Bush declare the Manhattan Institute second only to the Bible as a guiding influence on his political philosophy.) The Rockefeller-owned Museum of Modern Art in New York City still proudly displays works of art that were looted from Jewish families en route to Hitler's death camps.

In December 1998 Holocaust survivors named Chase, J.P. Morgan, and seven French banks as defendants in a lawsuit seeking to recover assets stolen from victims of Hitler's regime before and during World War II. According to affidavits filed in support of that class-action lawsuit, the defendants "froze and blocked Jewish accounts during the period of the Nazi occupation in France, depriving Jewish families of the financial means to flee France." Chase's Paris branch, supported by headquarters in New York, displayed "excessive zeal" in enforcing anti-Jewish laws and was held in "very special esteem" by Nazi puppet rulers of the Vichy French regime. Court papers also claimed that Chase nearly doubled its deposits under German rule in France from 27 million francs in 1942 to 50 million in 1944. Chase spokesmen told reporters that their firm had been engaged in "settlement talks" with the World Jewish Congress for several weeks and lamented the filing of an "unnecessary" lawsuit. The brief embarrassment did not prevent Chase from purchasing Morgan in 2000 to become J.P. Morgan Chase. Critics note that the corporate logo bears a strong resemblance to a "modified swastika."

See also BUSH DYNASTY; FASCISM; FARBEN INDUSTRIES.

CHECHNYA

With the Soviet Union's collapse in 1991, this southern "republic" of the USSR campaigned for full independence. Russian troops sealed the borders in December 1994 and replaced Prime Minister Viktor Chenomyrdin with a pliable successor, but rampant organized crime and a plummeting economy guaranteed further trouble, and guerrilla warfare continued through 1996. In 1998, Russian leader Boris Yeltsin sacked Prime Minister Sergei Kiryenko and restored Chenomyrdin to tentative power. Warfare resumed in 1999 with some 215,000 Chechen refugees driven into neighboring Ingushetia. Russian troops captured the Chechen capital (Grozny) in December 2000 and

Rows of body bags containing bodies of dead hostages lie for identification at a morgue in the town of Vladikavkaz, September 4, 2004. At least 322 people, including 155 children, died during the bloody end to a hostage-taking at a school in the southern Russian town of Beslan, near Chechnya. (Sergei Karpukhin/Reuters/Corbis)

thus declared "victory," but fighting continues, while members of the "Chechen Mafia" expand their rackets throughout Europe and beyond.

CHENEY, Dick (1941–)

Nebraska native Richard Bruce (Dick) Cheney was born in 1941 and moved to Wyoming as a child with his family. He briefly attended Yale University (1959–60) before earning his bachelor's and master's degrees from the University of Wyoming (1965–66). He abandoned his Ph.D. studies in 1969 to pursue right-wing Republican politics. Under President RICHARD NIXON, Cheney served as "special assistant" to the Office of Economic Opportunity (1969–70),

White House staff assistant (1971), and assistant director of the Cost of Living Council (1971–73). When Nixon resigned in disgrace, Cheney moved on to serve as vice president of Bradley, Woods & Company, a New York investment research firm (1973–74), and then returned to Washington under President Gerald Ford as deputy assistant to the president (1974–75) and White House chief of staff (1975–77). Next, Cheney was elected to the House of Representatives from Wyoming (1979–89), where he distinguished himself as one of only two congressmen opposing a federal ban on armor-piercing "cop killer" bullets.

Cheney left Congress to serve President George H. W. Bush as secretary of defense (1989–93) and then became chief executive officer of the Halliburton Company, a major U.S. energy conglomerate. He earned more than $36 million from Halliburton in 2000, but Cheney was worth every cent to the firm. Under his leadership, Halliburton increased its government contracts by 91 percent (to $2.3 billion) and qualified for nearly $2 billion in federal loans. At the same time, Halliburton admitted to $100 million in "accounting irregularities" and signed contracts with two of the world's top "state sponsors of TERRORISM" (LIBYA and IRAQ). In 2000 when Cheney left private enterprise to seek the vice presidency under George W. Bush, Halliburton donated $1.8 million to the Republican Party. Soon after his inauguration, Cheney met with leaders of the OIL, natural gas, and nuclear power industries to assemble a "wish list," which was then recast as the Bush administration's national energy policy. The resulting scandal from that escapade (including Cheney's involvement with ENRON) found Cheney withholding 13,500 pages of Energy Plan documents from congressional investigators, pleading "executive privilege" in the face of subpoenas and court orders. The PENTTBOM attacks of September 11, 2001, distracted Congress from the inquiry, and Halliburton returned to the government trough in 2003, reaping a secret, no-bid $7 billion contract to pump oil and fight fires in Iraq after Bush launched OPERATION IRAQI FREEDOM. When questioned about the sweetheart deal on *60 Minutes*, Halliburton's spokesman managed to keep a straight face while claiming that Cheney's influence had "zero impact" on the terms of their secret contract. (In December 2003 it was revealed that Halliburton had overcharged U.S. military forces an average of $1.60 per gallon on fuel pumped and processed in Iraq.) Cheney is a member of COUNCIL ON FOREIGN RELATIONS and the TRILATERAL COMMISSION.

See also BUSH DYNASTY.

CHERNOBYL disaster

On April 26, 1986, cooling systems failed at the Chernobyl nuclear reactor, 50 miles north of Kiev in the Soviet UKRAINE. As described in subsequent reports, a series of technical errors caused water to run low and overheat in various cooling components, creating an explosion that shattered the reactor's 1,000-ton lid, set fire to the facility, and unleashed a deadly cloud of radioactive fallout on the surrounding countryside. For weeks thereafter helicopters fought the fire by dumping sand and lead into the shattered reactor. A second major blaze erupted on May 23, requiring further desperate efforts. Meanwhile, radiation spread throughout Ukraine and across much of Europe.

The Chernobyl body count may never be known. Russian authorities did not acknowledge the disaster until April 28, when monitors at a power plant in Sweden detected large doses of radiation in the air and suspected a leak at their own facility. Within 36 hours of the explosion 300 persons were treated for serious radiation sickness, and more than 100,000 were evacuated from their homes. In 1991 the Canadian Broadcasting System claimed 10,000 to 15,000 immediate deaths; various sources projected long-term losses from cancer and other diseases, ranging as high as 125,000. Apologists for the nuclear industry, meanwhile, claim that only 48 verified deaths have occurred thus far, with an additional 800 cases of thyroid cancer reported in children.

Chernobyl conspiracy theories do not concern the incident's death toll, however, but rather Russian claims that it was accidental. The Soviet Union's collapse in 1991 has done nothing to mollify lifelong anticommunists who believe that Russian commissars still plot world domination on behalf of a slightly revised "evil empire." As one Internet Web site summarizes the case (noting the "rather profound connections [Chernobyl] had to astrology and biblical prophecy"):

The Chernobyl disaster in the Soviet Ukraine . . . was no accident. To the contrary, it was a sick, intentional experiment conducted by the "former" Communist government in Moscow to garner knowledge about the effects of radioactive contamination. For what reason? To prepare to fight and survive a global nuclear war.

The clincher, in that view, is Kosvinskiy Mountain, an underground control and command center similar to those scattered throughout the United States, that Russian authorities constructed in 1996. "Why would this be so," the conspiracists ask, "unless the Kremlin is planning to fight a nuclear war?"

See also COMMUNISM.

CHIANG Kai-shek (Jiang Jieshi) (1887–1975)

A native of CHINA's Zhejiang province who was born in 1887, Chiang Kai-shek studied in JAPAN, including military training with the Japanese Imperial Army. While there he joined Dr. Sun Yat-sen's United Revolutionary League, forerunner of the Kuomintang (KMT), which opposed the reigning Ming dynasty. In 1911 when rebels rose against the Manchu dynasty, Chiang returned home to join in the action. A Chinese republic was established in 1912, but Chiang disliked new leader Yüan Shih-kai (Yuan Shikai) and worked during the next four years to topple him. When Sun Yat-sen (Sun-Yixian) established a new government in 1917, Chiang served as his military aid, using the post to cement his ties with various TRIAD criminal syndicates. Sun's death in 1925 left Chiang the dominant KMT leader. He continued Sun's policy of collaboration with China's Communist Party until 1927 when Chiang reversed himself and launched a bloody purge of Reds nationwide. By 1928, with Red leaders MAO ZEDONG and Zhou Enlai in hiding, Chiang assumed ultimate power as head of the KMT government and "generalissimo" of all Chinese military forces.

Chiang's honeymoon was short lived. Communist resistance sparked new purges in the 1930s, driving the Red Army into its historic Long March by 1934. Simultaneously, Chiang's old mentors from Japan invaded Manchuria (1931) and then China itself (1937). With the outbreak of World War II Chiang became supreme commander of Allied forces in the Chinese theater of operations. Victory over Japan brought no peace, however, as fighting resumed between Communists and KMT forces. Chiang's government collapsed in 1949, and he fled off-shore to TAIWAN, where he established a Chinese government in exile. Supported by Triad drug money and

U.S. aid to "Nationalist China," Chiang spent the rest of his life rattling sabers, calling for "reunification" of China (under his command), and scheming with Western intelligence agencies to subvert the Beijing regime. Secure as president for life on Taiwan, he ruled a modest empire of corruption until his death in 1975.

See also COMMUNISM.

CHICAGO Police Department

Best known until 1968 for its corrupt alliance with organized crime, the Chicago Police Department has also been extremely active in political surveillance—so active, in fact, that author Frank Donner once dubbed Chicago "the national capital of police repression." Official conflict with ANARCHISTS and labor unions dates from the 19th century; later targets of surveillance and harassment included the Communist Party and the Industrial Workers of the World. FEDERAL BUREAU OF INVESTIGATION (FBI) agents kept abreast of those campaigns and cooperated when they could while ignoring (and publicly denying) the existence of syndicated crime in the Windy City. Occasional insults, such as G-man Melvin Purvis's decision to capture JOHN DILLINGER without informing local police, never truly jeopardized the joint pursuit of persons and organizations that were branded "subversive."

By 1960 Chicago's intelligence unit had collected files on 117,000 "local individuals," plus 141,000 out-of-towners and some 14,000 suspect organizations. Subjects included the STUDENTS FOR A DEMOCRATIC SOCIETY and its offshoot Weatherman Underground, the Southern Christian Leadership Conference and various organizations opposed to the VIETNAM War. Agents of the FBI's Chicago field office frequently shared information with police, as in Chicago's 1966 campaign against JOIN (Jobs or Income Now), which climaxed with a raid on the group's office. Two years later, televised incidents of police brutality during the Democratic National Convention shocked America. (Congressional investigators dubbed the incident a "police riot.") At the same time, in 1968–69, police collaborated with the FBI's illegal COINTELPRO operations against the Blackstone Rangers and the BLACK PANTHER PARTY. Armed with floor plans drawn by an FBI informant, Chicago police invaded the home of Chicago Panther chief FRED HAMPTON in December

1969 and killed him while he slept. (It now appears that Hampton was drugged before the raid by the same bureau informant who sketched his apartment for police.)

In 1970 the Chicago police department had 382 officers assigned to its intelligence unit, 49 committed full-time to investigation of "subversive" activities (as opposed to actual crimes). Citywide more than 1,000 federal, state, and city agents were engaged in undercover operations, spending an estimated $2 million that year in pursuit of alleged traitors. Chicago's Subversive Activities Unit received a broader mandate in 1971, ordered "through covert and overt activity," to gather intelligence on all "organizations and individuals which present a threat to the security of the country, state, or city." That mandate was renewed in 1973, with a special "dirty tricks" campaign inaugurated in 1974 to "neutralize" various targets by causing them "to cease or change direction." Exposure of illicit activities embarrassed the department in 1974, and by year's end police spokespeople admitted destroying files on 1,300 organizations and 105,000 individuals (thus concealing the names of 220 informants). No surveys of police surveillance have been made since the 1970s, but minority groups and civil libertarians suggest that the problem is ongoing. Mundane corruption continues, meanwhile: In January 2003 three Chicago cops were charged with conspiracy to distribute COCAINE.

See also COMMUNISM.

CHICAGO 7

The year 1968 is described by some historians as the United States' most tumultuous year since the Civil War. Disaffection over the long-running war in VIETNAM mounted throughout 1966–67, with mass demonstrations organized by groups including STUDENTS FOR A DEMOCRATIC SOCIETY (SDS), the National Mobilization Committee to End the War in Vietnam (MOBE), Vietnam Veterans Against the War, and the Youth International Party (YIP). Those protests peaked in August 1968 when delegates to the Democratic National Convention gathered in Chicago to select their presidential candidate. Officers of the CHICAGO POLICE DEPARTMENT, encouraged by Mayor RICHARD DALEY, responded with brute force (dubbed a "police riot" by members of a congressional investigative committee). In the wake of that chaotic week, on March 20, 1969, federal prosecutors indicted eight defendants on charges of conspiracy to violate the Anti-Riot Act of 1968. Those charged included:

Abbie Hoffman, 32-year-old leader of the Youth International Party, self-described "orphan of America" and "child of Woodstock Nation"

Jerry Rubin, radical cofounder of the YIP

David Dellinger, 54-year-old chairman of MOBE, described by prosecutors as "the chief architect of the conspiracy"

Rennie Davis, 29-year-old national director of community organizing programs for the SDS

Thomas Hayden, cofounder of the SDS, author of that group's famous Port Huron Statement, and "chief ideologue" of the antiwar movement

John Froines, 32-year-old industrial chemist with a Ph.D. in toxicology, charged with manufacturing stink bombs for the protesters

Lee Weiner, teaching assistant in sociology at Northwestern University, likewise charged with making "incendiary devices" (stink bombs)

Bobby Seale, cofounder of the BLACK PANTHER PARTY, who briefly visited Chicago during the convention but participated in none of the advance planning for protests. Prosecutors apparently included him on the list to link the other defendants with Seale's prior radical statements

Trial of the Chicago 8 before Judge Julius Hoffman began on September 24, 1969. By October 29 profane outbursts from Seale prompted Hoffman to order him bound and gagged in the courtroom. Protests against that action left defense attorneys cited for contempt, but Seale's case was finally severed from the others on November 5, reducing the list of defendants to seven. Jurors began deliberations on February 14, 1970, and returned with verdicts four days later. Defendants Froines and Weiner were acquitted on all counts, while the other five were convicted. On May 11, 1972, the Seventh Circuit Court of Appeals reversed Judge Hoffman's contempt convictions against all defendants and their lawyers. Six months later, on November 21, the same court voided all convictions in the case. Charges were dismissed against Bobby Seale, and a Connecticut jury acquitted him on unrelated charges of murdering a suspected FEDERAL BUREAU OF INVESTIGATION

informer in the Panther Party. Abbie Hoffman was charged with COCAINE violations in 1974 and spent seven years as a fugitive, finally surrendering to a work-release program in 1981–82; he committed suicide in April 1989. Tom Hayden married actress Jane Fonda, later serving in the California state assembly (1982–92) and state senate (1992–2000). Dave Dellinger was arrested in August 1998 at age 83 while demonstrating outside a nuclear power plant.

CHILE

Chile's aboriginal Inca and Arucano rulers were brutally deposed by Spanish invaders in the 16th century. Rebel leaders Bernardo O'Higgins and José de San Martín threw off the Spanish yoke in 1818. A series of wars with PERU and BOLIVIA (1836–39, 1879–83) expanded Chile's territory while leaving Bolivia forever landlocked. Industrialization began prior to World War I and prompted creation of dissident communist groups. Chile's president during World War II was initially pro-Nazi, but he shifted allegiance midstream to support the victorious Allies. Marxist president Salvador Allende Gossens was elected to office in September 1970 and swiftly formed alliances with CUBA and CHINA. Prompted by U.S. investors (with IT&T chief among them), President RICHARD NIXON and aide HENRY KISSINGER ordered the CENTRAL INTELLIGENCE AGENCY to destabilize Chile's economy, with the goal of toppling Allende. The illicit campaign was successful, climaxed by a military coup in September 1973 that killed Allende and ended Chile's 46-year record of constitutional government. A four-man junta led by Army Chief of Staff Augusto Pinochet Ugarte instituted brutal military rule, during which thousands of Chileans were arrested, murdered, or "disappeared." In 1977 Pinochet promised elections in 1985; losing that vote, he clung to power by force until January 1990 and then finally stepped down as dictator (though he remained as army chief of staff until March 1998). In October 1998 Pinochet was arrested in England on orders from a Spanish judge for trial in the disappearance and presumed murder of Spanish citizens during his term as dictator. British authorities refused to extradite Pinochet, and he returned to Chile in March 2000. There, the nation's supreme court stripped him of immunity from prosecution in June 2000, but a judge found Pinochet mentally unfit for trial in July 2001. No one has yet been punished for the crimes of Pinochet's regime—nor for U.S. complicity in those atrocities.

CHINA

As one of Earth's oldest civilized nations, China has also suffered more than its share of intrigue, subversion, rebellion, and organized crime. Combative feudal states were first united under Emperor Qin Shi Huangdi (Ch'in Shih Huang Ti; 246–210 B.C.), who started work on consolidating a defensive Great Wall to bar invaders from the North. Manchu invaders from the north succeeded, in 1644, in establishing one more in China's succession of ruling dynasties. Isolation was the nation's byword: By the end of the 18th century, only Canton (modern Hong Kong) and the Portuguese port at Macau were open to European merchants. Narcotics and British ingenuity broke down that barrier at last, as the first OPIUM WAR (1839–42) compelled China to accept addictive drugs for the profit of England. A second Opium War (1856–60) was required to guarantee the Royal dealers' territory, and China lapsed into an era of sociopolitical instability. A disastrous war with JAPAN (1894–95) forced China to cede further trading rights, and Peking's retaliatory Boxer Rebellion of 1900 was crushed by an international force including U.S. Marines.

The death of Empress Dowager Ci Xi (Tz'u-hsi) and the succession of an infant heir in 1908 sparked a nationwide rebellion against the Manchu dynasty, led by Dr. Sun Yat-sen (Sun Yixian). Supported by powerful TRIAD crime lords, Sun triumphed to become the first president of a provisional Chinese Republic in 1911. Soon tiring of politics, Sun resigned in favor of Yuan Shikai (Yüan Shih-k'ai), who promptly crushed the Republican movement to rule as dictator. Yuan's death in June 1916 sparked a long civil war for control of China, finally ending in victory for another Triad ally, General CHIANG KAI-SHEK (Jiang Jieshi), and his nationalist Kuomintang faction. Japan invaded Manchuria in 1931—the first military campaign of what would later become World War II—and the struggle continued until 1945. The mushroom cloud had barely settled over Nagasaki when Chiang declared war on China's communist movement, led by MAO ZEDONG. Despite support from the United States, Chiang was defeated and run out of China in 1949, establishing a tiny "nation" on the island of TAIWAN. Washington refused to recognize Red China, but President Harry Truman learned a bitter lesson when Chinese troops repelled U.S. forces from North KOREA in 1951.

At home, Mao's regime was modeled on the works of Russia's JOSEPH STALIN, emphasizing "progress" over human rights (and sometimes survival itself). China occupied Tibet in 1959, forcing the Dalai Lama and 100,000 of his Buddhist disciples into permanent exile. Meanwhile, a "Great Leap Forward" sought to convert China's agricultural economy forcibly to modern industry—with the result that more than 20 million persons ultimately starved to death. That gruesome failure sparked a power struggle within the Chinese Communist Party, climaxed by declaration of a "Cultural Revolution" in 1966, as young Red Guards killed millions more in violent purges of "old ideas, old culture, old habits and old customs." President RICHARD NIXON reversed his lifelong anticommunist stance in 1971, recognizing China in a bid to capitalize on Beijing's rift with Moscow. Mao's death in September 1976 unleashed more rivalries within the Red regime, prompting imprisonment of Mao's widow and three colleagues (the "Gang of Four") on charges of subversion.

China's trend toward Westernization has continued since the death of Mao, interrupted periodically by saber rattling from Washington and/or Beijing. Student demonstrators were massacred at Beijing's Tiananman Square in May 1989, and U.S.–Chinese relations were further strained 10 years later when Congress accused China of stealing American nuclear secrets during the past two decades. (Some U.S. military officers accused President Bill Clinton of complicity in that alleged "treason.") In general, however, Washington has displayed a fair degree of tolerance toward China—and toward Chinese human-rights violations in particular—when the profits of U.S.-based corporations are at risk.

See also CLINTON, BILL AND HILLARY; COMMUNISM.

CHRISTIAN Front

The brainchild of Detroit's Rev. Charles Coughlin, a CATHOLIC priest known for his radio diatribes attacking Jews and President Franklin Roosevelt, the Christian Front was organized in early 1938. Instructions printed in Coughlin's newsletter *Social Justice*, on May 22, 1938, urged would-be leaders of the movement to

Let your organization be composed of no more than 25 members. After a few contacts with these 25 persons you will observe that two of them may be capable of organizing 25 more. Invite these capable people to do that very thing.

The Christian Front's first and largest chapter was organized in New York City, where it met weekly in the basement of the Church of St. Paul the Apostle. Some members affected Nazi-style uniforms, banding together in "goon squads" that were notorious for their verbal and physical assaults on Jewish merchants. On July 31, 1939, *Social Justice* hailed the front as "the inevitable counteraction to COMMUNISM" and "a protector of Christianity and Americanism." A nationwide membership of five million was predicted for the following year.

On January 14, 1940, journalists were summoned to the FEDERAL BUREAU OF INVESTIGATION's (FBI) New York field office where J. EDGAR HOOVER personally announced the arrest of 17 Christian Fronters who were charged with stealing weapons from a National Guard armory as part of a "vast plot" to overthrow the U.S. government and establish a fascist dictatorship. When one of the reporters asked how such a small group could execute a "vast" conspiracy, Hoover replied (inaccurately), "It only took twenty-three men to overthrow Russia."

At trial in April 1940 the Christian Front defendants were accused of plotting to foment race warfare in America. As outlined by the prosecution, "the ultimate idea was to incite Jews to riot and then have a revolution and a counterrevolution." Despite testimony from FBI informant Denis Healy that the front was "growing by leaps and bounds," training special teams "to eradicate the Jews," hard evidence of criminal conspiracy was slim to nonexistent. Defense attorneys questioned Healy's role and cast doubt on his actions as an agent provocateur. None of the defendants was convicted.

CHRISTIAN Identity

Spawned from the 19th-century "Anglo-Israelism" movement, the modern cult of Christian Identity preaches that Europeans of Anglo-Saxon, Celtic, Scandinavian, and Teutonic origins are the true tribes of Israel described in the Old Testament. In this theology Jews are not only excluded from "Israel," but they are also literal children of Satan, produced when Eve allegedly copulated with the serpent in Eden to produce her evil son Cain. Nonwhite races (or "mud people") allegedly did not appear on Earth until Cain was banished from Eden for slaying brother Abel, whereupon he (Cain) mated with various subhuman females and encouraged his sons to do likewise. Evangelist Edward Hine brought the racist doctrine to North America in the 1880s, and the Brooklyn-based Anglo-Israel Association was founded in 1888. Thirty years later, members of the revived KU KLUX KLAN took Christian Identity's gospel to heart, encouraged by Henry FORD's attacks on "the International Jew." In the 1930s various pro-Nazi groups adopted Christian Identity tenets, a trend that continued for the next half-century, blossoming in the 1970s and 1980s with such groups as the Aryan Nations, POSSE COMITATUS, and the SILENT BROTHERHOOD. In the 1990s Christian Identity tenets provided religious underpinnings for the paranoid American MILITIAS. (Militia convert Timothy McVeigh, executed for the OKLAHOMA CITY BOMBING of April 1995, was a Christian Identity believer.) Ironically, at the same time, many hard-core white supremacists abandoned Christian Identity even as their paramilitary cohorts of the militia movement warmed to its teachings. Today, a majority of neo-Nazis have forsaken Christianity altogether, returning to the primitive Odinist religion of their alleged Nordic ancestors.

CHRISTIAN Reconstructionism

Extreme religious fundamentalism, regardless of its basic creed, is arguably the most divisive force on Earth today. Throughout recorded history, more wars, atrocities, and acts of TERRORISM have been motivated by religion than by all political doctrines combined. From the 1990s to the present day, many ultraconservative Christian spokesmen (including prominent TELEVANGELISTS) have pursued a doctrine known as Christian Reconstructionism that seeks to replace the U.S. Constitution and elected government with a narrow interpretation of "Biblical Law." Reconstructionists advocate dismantling democracy and its various trappings—including public schools, labor unions, and any legislation that protects minority civil rights. Women would be relegated to hearth and home under this system, while capital punishment would expand to include such "crimes" as adultery, blasphemy, heresy, homosexuality, and witchcraft. Extreme proponents of the creed publicly advocate a return to stoning as the official means of execution.

Christian Reconstructionism springs from a work by zealot Rousas John Rushdoony titled *Institutes of Biblical Law.* A rambling 800-page "explanation" of the Ten Commandments and other Old Testament rules, Rushdoony's diatribe professes to reveal "the only true order" on Earth. As Rushdoony viewed life, "Every law-order is a state of war against the enemies of that order, and all law is a form of warfare." An appendix by Rushdoony's son-in-law Gary North offered a crash course in "Christian economics." In that discourse North proclaims: "By what standard can man know anything truly? By the Bible, and only by the Bible." Having thus truncated all debate, Reconstructionists wage "war" against civilized society on every front—and the espousal of their creed by high-ranking politicians posing as "compassionate conservatives" suggest that the cult is no longer strictly marginalized. An unfortunate side effect of such beliefs is that extreme fundamentalists in government—such as Secretary of the Interior James Watt under President RONALD REAGAN—care nothing for preservation of the Earth or its environment. Why should natural resources be conserved, they ask, when the Second Coming of Jesus will wipe out all man's works within a few short months or years? Critics charge that such crusading attitudes are perilous not only to Mother Nature but also to the immediate future of humankind when an overzealous finger on the nuclear trigger can make Armageddon a here-and-now reality of Hell on Earth.

CHURCH Committee

Idaho senator Frank Church served as chairman of the U.S. Senate's Select Committee on Government Intelligence Activities, better known as the Church Committee. Active during the term of the 94th Congress (1975–77), it took public and private testimony from hundreds of witnesses and collected thousands of classified files from the FEDERAL BUREAU OF INVESTIGATION (FBI), the CENTRAL INTELLIGENCE AGENCY (CIA), the INTERNAL REVENUE SERVICE (IRS), the NATIONAL SECURITY AGENCY, and other federal investigative bodies. The committee issued 14 reports before it was dissolved, but much of the original reference material remained secret until 1992 when passage of the JFK ASSASSINATION Records Collection Act declassified more than 50,000 documents.

After interrogating FBI officials, informants, and victims of harassment, the Church Committee had this to say about J. EDGAR HOOVER's motives for initiating illegal COINTELPRO campaigns:

Protecting national security and preventing violence are the purposes advanced by the Bureau for COINTELPRO. There is another purpose for COINTELPRO which is not explicit but which offers the only explanation for those actions which had no conceivable rational relationship to either national security or violent activity. The unexpressed major premise of much of COINTELPRO is that the Bureau has a role in maintaining the existing social order, and that its efforts should be aimed toward combating those who threaten that order.

With respect to FBI claims that COINTELPRO activities were discontinued after May 1971, Senator Church and his colleagues reported:

The Committee has not been able to determine with any greater precision the extent to which COINTELPRO may be continuing. Any proposals to initiate COINTELPRO-type action would be filed under the individual case caption. The Bureau has over 500,000 case files, and each one would have to be searched. In this context, it should be noted that a Bureau search of all field office COINTELPRO files revealed the existence of five operations [conducted after May 1971]. A search of all investigative files might be similarly productive.

More disturbing than concealment of records, however, was the committee's discovery that "[a]ttitudes within and without the Bureau demonstrate a continued belief by some that covert action against American citizens is permissible if the need for it is strong enough." Based on that conclusion, the committee declared in its final report that:

The American people need to be assured that never again will an agency of the government be permitted to conduct a secret war against those citizens it considers threats to the established order. Only a combination of legislative prohibition and Departmental control can guarantee that COINTELPRO will not happen again.

Closing its FBI inquiry on a pessimistic note, the Church Committee noted that "Whether the Attorney General can control the Bureau is still an open question." In fact, as events since 1976 have revealed, neither the JUSTICE DEPARTMENT nor the White House has been able to restrain FBI domestic surveillance—if, in fact, they had any serious inclination to do so.

In examining the CIA the Church Committee uncovered murder plots against Cuban leader FIDEL CASTRO (including CIA collaboration with the MAFIA) and revealed details of the Company's MKULTRA mind-control experiments, along with extensive evidence of domestic spying banned by the CIA's charter. As revealed in the committee's final report:

The CIA conducted four mail opening programs within the United States, the longest of which lasted for twenty years. These programs resulted in the opening and photographing of nearly a quarter of a million items of correspondence, the vast majority of which were to or from American residents. While the programs were ostensibly conducted for foreign intelligence and counterintelligence purposes, one former high-ranking CIA official characterized the Agency's use of this technique as a "shotgun" approach to intelligence collection; neither Congressmen, journalists, nor businessmen were immune from mail interception. With cooperation from the FBI, domestic "dissidents" were directly targeted in one of the programs. . . .

The stated purpose of all of the mail opening programs was to obtain useful foreign intelligence and counterintelligence information. At least one of the programs produced no such information, however, and the continuing value of the major program in New York was discounted by many Agency officials. . . .

The CIA's New York mail intercept project, encrypted HTLINGUAL by the Counterintelligence Staff and SRPOINTER by the Office of Security, was the most extensive of all the CIA's mail intercept programs, both in terms of the volume of mail that was opened and in terms of duration. Over the twenty year course of mail openings, more than 215,000 letters to and from the Soviet Union were opened and photographed by CIA agents in New York. Copies of more than 57,000 of these letters were also disseminated to the FBI, which learned of this operation in 1958, levied requirements on it, and received the fruits of the coverage until the project was terminated.

Despite the absence of clear authorization outside the CIA, despite the generally unfavorable internal reviews of the project in 1960 and 1969, and despite the facts that it was generally seen as illegal and that its primary value was believed by many agency officials to accrue to the FBI in the area of domestic intelligence, the momentum generated by this project from its inception in the early 1950's continued unchecked until February of 1973.

Exposure of such illegal techniques before Congress brought more promises of immediate cessation from CIA headquarters, but critics maintain that no information from Langley (or FBI headquarters) can be accepted at face value. More recently, with passage of the USA PATRIOT ACT in 2001, domestic surveillance in the name of "national security" has been expanded beyond anything envisioned by Hoover during the COINTELPRO years.

CISPES case

The FEDERAL BUREAU OF INVESTIGATION's (FBI) four-year pursuit of the Committee in Solidarity with the People of EL SALVADOR (CISPES) began in June 1981 when Salvadoran native Frank Varelli approached the Dallas field office with a tale of right-wing Central American murder squads roaming around the United States. Agent Gary Penrith, second in command of the Dallas FBI, sent an inquiry to the CENTRAL INTELLIGENCE AGENCY and secured a reply that Varelli's information might be accurate. (In fact, it was false.) By that time, Varelli had expanded his story to include CISPES, a group created to solicit funds for humanitarian aid to war-torn El Salvador. Varelli insisted that CISPES was the leftist counterpart of his mythical right-wing assassins, and the bureau took him at his word. In September 1981 a criminal investigation was opened, seeking evidence that CISPES members had violated the federal Foreign Agents Registration Act. G-men found no evidence of any illegal acts, and the case was officially closed in February 1982.

FBI historian Robert Kessler reports (in *The Bureau*, 2002) that "[b]ecause of poor supervision by headquarters, the Dallas office reopened the CISPES case two years later," but records declassified in January 1988 indicate that the CISPES investigation resumed in March 1983 on direct orders from FBI headquarters, employing Attorney General William

Smith's expanded guidelines for "foreign counterintelligence—international TERRORISM" cases. Kessler further states that the investigation "had no political motives," and while headquarters instructed G-men that "the purpose of the investigation was not to investigate the exercise of First Amendment rights of CISPES members," agents proceeded as they might have done for any COINTELPRO operation ordered by late Director J. EDGAR HOOVER. A headquarters memo issued to all field offices on October 28, 1983, commanded agents to develop "information on the locations, leadership, and activities of CISPES chapters within each field offices' jurisdiction."

Before the CISPES surveillance finally ended on June 18, 1985 (without producing any criminal charges), the FBI had opened new files on 2,375 individuals and 1,330 organizations that were found to have some marginal link with CISPES or its members. The other groups included more than 100 organizations opposed to President RONALD REAGAN's Central American policies, plus local chapters of the United Auto Workers and the National Education Association. The writings of one member of the CISPES clergy were cited in an FBI report as evidence of a "mind totally sold on the Marxist Leninist philosophy." When one G-man reported that a group he had investigated was nonviolent and legitimate, FBI headquarters refused his suggestion to drop surveillance; instead he was ordered to "consider the possibility" that the organization "may be a front org for CISPES." A memo from the New Orleans field office, dated November 10, 1983, advised Director WILLIAM WEBSTER that:

It is imperative at this time to formulate some plan of attack against CISPES and specifically, against individuals . . . who defiantly display their contempt for the U.S. Government by making speeches and propagandizing their cause while asking for political asylum.

New Orleans is of the opinion that Departments of Justice and State should be consulted to explore the possibility of deporting these individuals or at best denying their re-entry once they leave.

A subsequent review of the CISPES investigation by the House Committee on Civil and Constitutional Rights found that all 59 FBI field offices were involved in the futile search for "subversive" activity. The committee also documented 50 unsolved break-ins committed during the same period, targeting churches, homes, and offices of persons opposed to Reagan's Central American policies. FBI spokespersons denied any bureau involvement in those burglaries, and while Director William Sessions confessed that "the scope of the investigation was unnecessarily broadened" in October 1983, he called the case "an aberration" in FBI behavior. One agent was disciplined for his role in the CISPES case: G-man Daniel Flanagan, assigned as Frank Varelli's case officer in Dallas, confessed to stealing money earmarked for Varelli and was resigned after reimbursing the FBI $1,000.

CITIZENS' Councils

Often called the *White* Citizens' Councils despite protests from "respectable" leaders, this network of racist groups had its roots in Sunflower County, Mississippi, where the first chapter was organized following the U.S. SUPREME COURT's 1954 order to desegregate public schools. Early members included many southern business people and politicians, who took care to separate themselves from "low-class" KU KLUX KLAN, but there was no philosophical gap between the Councils and the KKK. Both deemed racial equality a communist scheme to "mongrelize" the white race, and both distributed anti-Semitic literature naming Jews as primary architects of the "race-mixing" conspiracy. While the Councils publicly disclaimed any link to acts of racial TERRORISM, known members participated in race riots and other acts of violence throughout the South. In 1960 council leader Emmett Miller was jailed for attempting to bomb a black school in Little Rock, Arkansas. Three years later Mississippi NAACP leader Medgar Evers was assassinated by council member Byron De La Beckwith. By 1970 with membership fading the council dropped all pretense of moderation and joined Klan members to picket the Memphis school board, protesting new "awareness" programs in local grade schools. The councils disappeared after Alabama governor GEORGE WALLACE's abortive presidential race in 1972, but veteran activists returned 13 years later at the helm of a new Council of Conservative Citizens. That organization boasted a list of allies including Senators Trent Lott and Jesse Helms, teamed with such veteran neo-Nazis as former Klan leader David Duke. The group's racism is no more easily concealed today than in the 1960s, and an infiltrating journalist heard one council spokesperson advise local members to "be a Nazi, but don't use the word." The CCC's Web site may be viewed at http://www.cofcc.org.

CLINTON, Bill (1946–   ) and Hillary (1947–   )

William Jefferson ("Slick Willie") Clinton was born at Hope, Arkansas, in August 1946. As a youth he idolized President John Kennedy and determined to follow in JFK's footsteps, a goal he achieved in several respects. Clinton lost his first political campaign (for Congress) in 1974 but later served as Arkansas attorney general (1977–79) and as governor (1979–81, 1983–92). Despite pervasive hints of scandal, he was elected president of the United States in 1992 and reelected in 1996. With wife Hillary, Clinton was embroiled in controversy almost from the day of his inauguration. Volumes could (and have) been written concerning the various scandals that dogged his administration, climaxed by Clinton's December 1998 impeachment on charges of perjury and obstructing justice. (He was acquitted of all counts by the U.S. Senate.) An alphabetical list of Clinton scandals prepared by Thomas Galvin for the *New York Post* included:

Billing-gate: Hillary Clinton's billing records from her years with the Arkansas-based Rose Law Firm were subpoenaed in 1994 by investigators probing charges of impropriety in various cases. The documents were "missing" until 1996 when they magically appeared in a room adjacent to Mrs. Clinton's office. She denied any knowledge of how they got there or where they had been in the interim.

Castle Grande: A real-estate scheme described by investigators as a fraudulent sham. A federal inspector general's report says Hillary Clinton drafted legal papers that funneled large sums of cash to Seth Ward, father-in-law of her ex-partner Webster Hubbell.

Cattlegate: Prior to arriving in Washington, Hillary Clinton invested $1,000 in cattle futures and scored a swift $100,000 profit. Critics said her huge windfall was "virtually impossible" without use of illegal insider information.

Filegate: Investigative journalists revealed that Clinton White House staffers had improperly reviewed FEDERAL BUREAU OF INVESTIGATION files on 900 Republican officials active in the administrations of Presidents RONALD REAGAN and George H. W. Bush. Clinton spokespersons called the invasion of privacy an innocent "mistake," while opponents feared compilation of a NIXON-style enemies list.

Golfgate: White House aide David Watkins was forced to resign for using presidential aircraft improperly on a private golf excursion. Investigation of that charge also revealed that in 1992 Clinton aides used taxpayer funds to help settle a female campaign worker's lawsuit against Watkins on charges of sexual harassment.

Indonesiagate: This scandal concerned the Lippo group, a firm with longstanding ties to Bill Clinton and his friends in Arkansas. An Indonesian couple with ties to Lippo, though apparently devoid of wealth, donated $452,000 to the Democratic National Committee under Clinton and paid Webster Hubbell another $250,000 for unknown services during a five-month period.

Travelgate: Soon after their arrival in Washington, the Clintons fired various career travel staffers and filled the positions with political cronies. White House memos suggested that Hillary Clinton executed the purge on behalf of Hollywood chum Harry Thomason, who sought a slice of the lucrative White House charter business.

Whitewater: Another Arkansas land deal, this investigation broadened into questions surrounding Clinton associates Jim and Susan McDougal and their Madison Guarantee Savings and Loan corporation, whose collapse cost taxpayers an estimated $60 million. Bill Clinton denied knowledge of an illegal $300,000 Whitewater bail-out payment, but critics claim he lied under oath. Susan McDougal served jail time for refusing to testify in that case.

Those scandals and others forced various Clinton staffers to resign, while other associates and acquaintances faced batteries of criminal charges. President Clinton's impeachment resulted from an investigation into an extramarital affair with White House intern Monica Lewinsky and the subsequent attempt to cover it up. Some pointed to this as the latest in a series of sexual incidents, including sexual assault and harassment, that Clinton and his supporters and various staff members had concealed dating back to his early days in Arkansas. First Lady Hillary Clinton countered by dubbing the investigation the product of a vast right-wing conspiracy to smear the president. One conspiracy theory even purports that Lewinsky was a covert agent trained by a foreign government to compromise the office of the president of the United States. Beyond those cases, conspiracists speak archly of a "Clinton death list," including 60-odd victims of homicide or suspicious "suicides" and "accidents." Some lists include the name of journalist DANNY CASOLARO, but the best-known corpse is that of VINCE FOSTER, a White House attorney enmeshed in the Filegate, Travelgate, and Whitewater cases. Clinton provided further fodder for conspiracy theorists during his final hours as president when he granted 33 pardons to numerous people, including some with connections to his brother-in-law Hugh Rodham Clinton or Clinton financial donors. Hillary Rodham Clinton is today a U.S. senator for the state of New York. Her husband, at last report, remains a member of the COUNCIL ON FOREIGN RELATIONS and the TRILATERAL COMMISSION.

See also BUSH DYNASTY; KENNEDY DYNASTY.

COBAIN, Kurt (1967–1994)

On April 8, 1994, electricians installing a new security system at the Seattle, Washington, home of "grunge" rock star Kurt Cobain found their employer dead in a small apartment above the garage. Authorities declared that Cobain had injected himself with 225 milligrams of HEROIN (three times the fatal dosage) and swallowed a quantity of Valium before placing the muzzle of a shotgun in his mouth and pulling the trigger. Near the almost-headless body, police found a cigar box filled with drug paraphernalia, a plaid hunter's cap, a box of shotgun shells, and a rambling handwritten suicide note. The apartment's door was wedged shut from inside.

Cobain had previously attempted suicide on March 4, 1994, leaving another note before he swallowed 50 Rohypnol tablets in Rome. Based on those facts and evidence at the crime scene, police declared his death a suicide, but conspiracists claim that Cobain was murdered. They advance the following arguments to prove their case:

- The heroin dosage found in Cobain's blood, aggravated by Valium, should have been instantly fatal. Indeed, overdosed addicts are often found dead with the needles still in their arms; yet Cobain was found with the long sleeves of his shirt buttoned at the cuffs. How could he have tidied up his clothing, put the drug kit back in its box, and then shot himself before the drugs rendered him unconscious?

- No "legible" fingerprints were found on Cobain's shotgun, the box of cartridges, the suicide note, or the pen used to write it. Initial reports that Cobain had "marks on his hands" from firing the shotgun also proved false and were later repudiated by police.

- Cobain's wife, rock star Courtney Love, did not produce the note from Cobain's alleged Italian suicide attempt until after his death. That note has since been destroyed, but various persons who read it dispute its contents. Some claiming it was a "rambling diatribe" against Love that mentioned divorce, rather than suicide.

- Seattle coroner Nikolas Hartshorne, who signed off on the suicide verdict in 1994, also booked rock bands (including Cobain's band Nirvana) and was described by acquaintances as a "party friend" of Courtney Love. Hartshorne died in a base-jumping accident on August 6, 2002.

- Eldon ("El Duce") Hoke, lead singer for the Mentors, claimed that Courtney Love offered him $50,000 to kill Cobain in January 1994. Hoke allegedly passed a polygraph test administered by Dr. Edward Gelb on March 6, 1996. Eight days after repeating his story for a filmed documentary, on April 19, 1997, Hoke was struck and killed by a train while walking in Riverside, California. Friends of Hoke called his death "highly suspicious," noting that shortly before the accident, Hoke left his house to buy liquor with "a new friend none of his roommates had ever met before." Hoke never returned from the booze run, and his "friend" remains unidentified. Private detective Tom Grant, hired by Love to find her husband after he fled a Seattle drug rehab program on April 1, 1994, now believes Hoke's story and has publicly named Love as a suspect in her husband's alleged murder. Grant additionally claims that Cobain's drug overdose in Rome was "the first attempt on his life."

COCA-COLA

According to its Internet Web site, "The Coca-Cola Company exists to benefit and refresh everyone it touches." Those who benefit first and foremost, of course, are Coca-Cola's executives and major stockholders. Introduced in 1886, Coca-Cola was initially advertised as "a valuable brain-tonic and cure for all nervous afflictions." The "cure" derived from 60 milligrams of COCAINE found in each bottled serving prior to 1903 (no longer included, though Coke's classic flavor is still derived from South American coca leaves). Today the firm manufactures and distributes materials used in production of 300-plus nonalcoholic beverage brands. From its headquarters in Atlanta, Georgia, Coca-Cola oversees operations in more than 200 foreign countries. With so much ready case and global clout, it comes as no surprise that Coca-Cola has inspired numerous conspiracy theories throughout its 108-year history. From the cold war to modern Third World conflicts, Coke's far-flung empire has been accused of collaborating with the CENTRAL INTELLIGENCE AGENCY and other covert cliques to carry out sundry acts of espionage while exploiting foreign workers in conditions tantamount to peonage. Two cases from the new millennium illustrate Coca-Cola's ongoing fascination for conspiracists.

May 20, 2003—Company spokesmen announced that Coca-Cola was investigating claims by former company auditor Matthew Whitley that the firm engaged in massive fraud to inflate yearly revenue by several million dollars. Whitley, described by Coke publicists as a "disgruntled former employee," filed an 85-page wrongful termination lawsuit in Fulton County (Atlanta) Superior Court, alleging that the firm engaged in: phantom sales recorded "just before midnight at the end of each quarter in 2002"; marketing fraud, including bribery and manipulation of sales data for a failed campaign launched in conjunction with Burger King restaurants; and creation of a "slush fund" to disguise the failure of a new soft-drink dispenser manufactured by Lancer Corporation. Lancer spokesmen insisted that firm's financial reporting was "proper and correct," while the U.S. attorney's office in Atlanta had no comment. Whitley's lawsuit is ongoing.

July 4, 2003—A coalition of labor unions in COLOMBIA announced a nationwide boycott of Coca-Cola products beginning on July 22 in retaliation for the recent murders of eight union leaders at Coke plants around the country.

Coca-Cola's main Latin-American bottler, Panamco, already faced union lawsuits on charges that it financed right-wing terrorist groups that were known to intimidate and murder union activists. Coca-Cola publicists responded that their Colombian employees had merely been "caught in the crossfire of a 40-year-old civil war," insisting that "We treat all our employees in nearly 200 countries in which we do business with fairness, dignity and respect." Union spokespersons in Colombia, meanwhile, noted that more than 1,500 labor activists had been slaughtered in Colombia since 1992, including eight murdered at Coca-Cola factories since 1996. Echoes of the boycott were heard as far away as Australia, where John Robertson, Labor Council secretary for New South Wales, told his constituents, "This multinational has been quite happy to exploit its workers in Colombia."

See also TERRORISM.

COCAINE

Cocaine is a highly addictive drug derived from leaves of the South American coca plant (*Erythroxylon coca*). It has been prized as both a painkiller and a recreational drug since the 16th century. Three hundred years later, fictional detective Sherlock Holmes used a 7-percent solution of cocaine to relieve boredom and depression between murder cases, and U.S. addicts could buy their daily fix without a prescription until 1916. Still, cocaine did not become the "drug of choice" among U.S. and European users until the 1970s when government campaigns against HEROIN and MARIJUANA opened new markets for alternative drugs. By the early 1980s, major cocaine-smuggling operations were active in the Andean nations of COLOMBIA, PERU, and BOLIVIA, with cartels based in Cali and Medellín; Colombia was widely touted as home to the world's most ruthless narco traffickers. Pervasive corruption hamstrings law enforcement in all three countries (as well as the United States), and Colombian cartels are notorious for their resort to TERRORISM, assassinating jurists, prosecutors, police, politicians, and journalists whenever their empires are challenged. In the United States, President RONALD REAGAN declared the first "War on Drugs" in 1981, led by Vice President George H. W. Bush, but federal efforts were so haphazard and so often self-defeating that one U.S. Coast Guard officer called the effort an "intellectual fraud." Appointment of various "drug czars" by Reagan's successors has likewise failed to stem the tide of cocaine across U.S. borders, where drug-enforcement officers freely admit that they capture only 10 percent (or less) of all illegal drugs pouring into the country. In the 1990s a new form of "rock" or "crack" cocaine was introduced in U.S. ghettos, delivering "an intensity of pleasure completely outside the normal range of human experience." Some observers now believe crack was invented by government chemists and unleashed on black America by the CENTRAL INTELLIGENCE AGENCY as a means of social control. Whatever the truth of that theory, crack has claimed millions of addicts while providing a bottomless source of income for STREET GANGS such as the CRIPS AND BLOODS. Today, Colombian cartels deal freely with the MAFIA, the YAKUZA, the TRIADS, and other criminal syndicates to reap multibillion-dollar profits from cocaine sales worldwide.

See also BUSH DYNASTY.

COINTELPRO

The FEDERAL BUREAU OF INVESTIGATION's (FBI) official history, reported on the bureau's Internet Web site, provides the following information on so-called COINTELPRO (counterintelligence program) operations in the midst of a section devoted to "The Vietnam War Era." The description reads as follows:

No specific guidelines for FBI Agents covering national security investigations had been developed by the [RICHARD NIXON] Administration or Congress; these, in fact, were not issued until 1976. Therefore, the FBI addressed the threats from the militant "New Left" as it had those from communists in the 1950s and the KKK in the 1960s. It used both traditional investigative techniques and counterintelligence programs ("Cointelpro") to counteract domestic terrorism and conduct investigations of individuals and organizations who threatened terroristic violence. Wiretapping and other intrusive techniques were discouraged by Hoover in the mid-1960s and eventually were forbidden completely unless they conformed to the Omnibus Crime Control Act. Hoover formally terminated all "Cointelpro" operations on April 28, 1971.

That passage, pretending to describe a campaign against criminal activity under the COINTELPRO label, is a classic piece of FBI misinformation. Within a span of 113 words it rewrites history concerning illegal wiretapping; falsely identifies the targets of harassment as "terrorists"; implies that COINTELPRO campaigns occurred only during the first 28 months of the Nixon administration (that is, January 1969 through April 1971); falsely claims that J. EDGAR HOOVER "discouraged" illegal surveillance techniques; and claims (again, falsely) that such techniques have not been used by G-men since 1971.

The FBI has used illegal techniques, including wiretaps, break-ins, and bugging since its creation in 1908. Other classic techniques employed from the start, including frame-ups and the use of corrupt informants as agents provocateurs to promote criminal activity among surveillance targets, were also staples of various COINTELPRO operations during the 25 years when that label was applied to FBI harassment and disruption campaigns. Also while the embarrassing practice was officially discarded in 1971, evidence from the FBI's own files clearly proves that identical abuses have continued without interruption to the present day.

The first official COINTELPRO campaign was launched by FBI headquarters on August 28, 1956. It targeted the Communist Party, aiming to "bring the Communist Party (CP) and its leaders into disrepute before the American public and cause confusion and dissatisfaction among rank-and-file members." On May 8, 1958, Hoover sent Attorney General William Rogers a progress report on the FBI's effort "to promote disruption within CP ranks," including use of paid infiltrators to spark "acrimonious debates" and "increase factionalism." FBI files later revealed that during the years 1957–60, 266 individual COINTELPRO campaigns were mounted against the Communist Party in America. In the year 1960 alone those campaigns involved 114 illegal wiretaps, 74 warrantless bugs, and 2,342 pieces of private mail read by G-men in violation of federal law. Hoover "discouraged" none of it; in fact, he required that headquarters approve each specific criminal act in advance. One such campaign, launched in October 1966 and dubbed "Operation Hoodwink," used anonymous letters and forged CP fliers in an ultimately futile bid to spark violent conflict between communists and the MAFIA.

Hoover's campaign to disrupt the Communist Party proved so successful that a second COINTELPRO operation was launched in 1960, this one targeting a wide spectrum of Puerto Rican nationalists. He warned field offices that "the Bureau desires to disrupt the activities of these organizations and is not interested in mere harassment." When nationalist leader Juan Mari Bras suffered a near-fatal heart attack on April 21, 1964, FBI memos gloated that one of the bureau's trademark anonymous letters "certainly did nothing to ease his tensions for he felt the effects of the letter deeply." Far from ending in April 1971, illegal disruption campaigns against Puerto Rican nationalist groups and leaders escalated during the next two decades, including bombings, beatings, and murders of nationalist leaders, which were investigated but never solved by the FBI. Sworn depositions taken from G-men in 1985 acknowledged use of illegal bugs and wiretaps, while a former secretary with the San Juan field office blamed agents for a 1978 firebombing at the home of Juan Mari Bras.

The bureau's third formal COINTELPRO target, beginning in October 1961, was the Socialist Workers Party (SWP). Any claim that such tactics were reserved for "terrorists" is laid to rest by Hoover's memo of October 12, 1961, complaining that the SWP "has . . . been openly espousing its line on a local and national basis through the running of candidate[s] for public office." In fact, the "new" COINTELPRO-SWP was not new at all: FBI records, later released under the Freedom of Information Act, reveal that between 1943 and 1963, G-men logged 20,000 days monitoring wiretaps on SWP telephones and 12,000 days monitoring bugs illegally planted in SWP homes and offices. The same 20-year period witnessed 208 FBI break-ins against the SWP, with 9,864 party documents stolen or photographed during burglaries. Separate COINTELPRO records, perhaps including some overlap with the previous statistics, confirm 46 disruptive campaigns against the SWP through 1971, with 80-plus break-ins staged to photograph more than 8,000 documents during the same period.

Next on tap for the COINTELPRO treatment, however reluctantly on Hoover's part, were various factions of the KU KLUX KLAN. Spurred by President LYNDON BAINES JOHNSON, the FBI inaugurated its COINTELPRO—WHITE HATE GROUPS on September 2, 1964. By the time action was suspended in

April 1971, G-men had undertaken 287 separate operations against Klansmen in various states. "Snitch-jacketing"—framing loyal Klansmen as FBI informers—was a favorite technique, apparently prompting Mississippi Klansmen to murder one of their colleagues in 1965, but the KKK was seemingly spared the more aggressive techniques employed against targets on the political left. Informants were encouraged to spread dissension in Klan ranks by any means available, including serial adultery with the wives of brother Klansmen, but G-men often sheltered Klan spies who committed acts of violence against southern blacks or civil rights workers. The bureau had 2,000 Klan informants on its payroll by September 1965 when G-men assisted the HOUSE COMMITTEE ON UN-AMERICAN ACTIVITIES with a public investigation of the Klan.

The bureau's last official COINTELPRO operation, targeting "Black Nationalist-Hate Groups," was launched on August 25, 1967, with a memo from Hoover declaring that "the purpose of this new . . . endeavor is to expose, disrupt, misdirect, discredit, or otherwise neutralize the activities of black nationalist, hate-type organizations and groupings, their leadership, spokesmen, membership, and supporters." The campaign undertaken in 1967 was merely an extension of FBI harassment directed at sundry black activists since 1919. False arrests and frame-ups were routine, as the bureau coordinated its efforts with local police departments throughout the United States. Agents provocateurs encouraged various targets to break the law, often supplying guns or other contraband at FBI expense to facilitate arrests. It mattered not to FBI headquarters that G-men were the true felons in such cases; any excess was permissible in the name of forestalling "black revolution."

FBI files from the late 1960s reveal that Hoover's commitment to "prevent violence" by black militants was a cynical sham. In fact, from southern California to Chicago and New York, G-men did everything within their power to *cause* violence between rival groups, promoting street warfare between the BLACK PANTHER PARTY and various rival groups and encouraging members of the militant Jewish Defense League to attack black spokespersons whom the FBI accused of anti-Semitism. Multiple deaths resulted from the bureau's effort to "exploit conflicts" between militant groups in southern California and elsewhere.

The FBI's last official COINTELPRO campaign was launched on May 9, 1968, against a motley collection of radical groups collectively dubbed the "New Left," focused primarily on opposition to the war in VIETNAM. "The purpose of this program," Hoover wrote, "is to expose, disrupt and otherwise neutralize the activities of this group and persons connected with it. It is hoped that with this new program their violent and illegal activities may be reduced if not curtailed." FBI headquarters missed the irony of committing violent crimes to "reduce illegal activities," but there can be no doubt that bureau informants and agents provocateurs significantly increased violence on the part of various New Left organizations. They provided drugs and weapons, schooled their naive subjects in the fine points of bomb making, and suggested acts of sabotage to groups that were content with lawful protest. The Nixon administration assisted FBI efforts against the New Left with multiple conspiracy charges against movement leaders, resulting in trials described by historian William Manchester as "an unparalleled series of judicial disasters for the government." In terms of curbing leftist violence, the bureau's campaign was a resounding failure. A majority of the 862 alleged bombings or bombing attempts recorded by G-men between January 1969 and April 1970 remain unsolved (perhaps because investigation would expose the crimes committed by agents provocateurs on the FBI payroll). Of 13,400 persons arrested in New Left demonstrations during May 1971, 12,653 were discharged without trial; 122 were convicted, while another 625 pleaded guilty or no contest, but all such pleas were voided and expunged by a federal court in 1974 on grounds of police coercion.

The FBI's harassment network suffered terminal embarrassment in March 1971 after burglars invaded the resident agency located in Media, Pennsylvania, and stole several thousand COINTELPRO documents, which soon found their way to the press. Hoover officially canceled all COINTELPRO activities a month later, although their full scope would not be revealed until several years after his death. According to records exposed by the CHURCH COMMITTEE in 1975, the FBI mounted at least 2,218 separate COINTELPRO actions against various groups and individuals between 1957 and 1971; those illegal campaigns included at least 1,884 illegal wiretaps and 583 warrantless bugs, plus 55,804 pieces of mail illegally opened and read by G-men.

It would be comforting to believe the FBI's claim that such methods have not been used since April 1971, but evidence to the contrary is plentiful. The Church Committee found that during 1972–74, despite the alleged ban on all COINTELPRO techniques, FBI agents installed another 421 illegal wiretaps and 114 warrantless bugs while stealing another 2,042 pieces of personal mail. As embarrassing as those disclosures were (or should have been), they still had no apparent impact on the bureau's dedication to business as usual. Organizations including the AMERICAN INDIAN MOVEMENT (AIM), EARTH FIRST!, the Committee in Solidarity with the People of El Salvador (CISPES), and various Puerto Rican nationalist groups suffered attacks indistinguishable from "banned" COINTELPRO techniques throughout the 1970s, 1980s, and early 1990s. (On November 26, 1973, some 31 months after all such programs supposedly ended, Agent Richard W. Held penned a memo to headquarters suggesting that "Los Angeles and Minneapolis consider possible COINTELPRO measures to further disrupt AIM leadership.") "Terrorism" remains a frequent excuse for extralegal measures on the part of federal agents, and sweeping provisions of the new USA PATRIOT ACT suggest that use of such methods may be increasing, rather than declining in the future.

See also COMMUNISM.

COLOMBIA

Spanish conquistadors invaded present-day Colombia in 1510 and officially established the colony of New Granada in 1538. Simón Bolívar's revolutionary force from VENEZUELA fought a 14-year war to oust SPAIN from the region, finally emerging victorious in 1819. Five years later, Bolívar united Colombia, Venezuela, PANAMA, and ECUADOR as the Republic of Greater Colombia. Ecuador and Venezuela seceded in 1830, and Colombia passed through several political incarnations before stabilizing with its present name in 1885. A brutal civil war erupted in 1899 and dragged on for three years, while the United States usurped Colombia's longstanding claim to Panama. Relative peace was restored until 1946 when a chaotic era dubbed "La Violencia" erupted, claiming several hundred thousand lives during the next 12 years. A military junta restored the illusion of order in 1958, but leftist guerrillas soon initiated a new wave of bloodshed, their vehicles including the M-19 movement.

The rise of a flourishing COCAINE industry in the 1970s made Colombia a world center of drug trafficking, and violence proliferated on all fronts. By 1989 murder was the leading cause of death in Colombia; this was unrestrained by political leaders who were terrorized and thoroughly corrupted. In 1999 some 23,000 persons were murdered across the country; an estimated 2 million Colombians have fled the country during recent years, seeking safe havens elsewhere. Billionaire drug lords remain untouchable while the nation staggers from one crisis to the next.

COLONIA Dignidad

Paul Schäfer was a nurse in ADOLF HITLER's Lüftwaffe during World War II, mourning the THIRD REICH's collapse while he established an orphanage in GERMANY. Fifteen years later, in 1961, he fled to CHILE as a fugitive from charges that he had molested children in his care. Accompanied by a handful of rabid Nazis, Schäfer settled on a 70-square-mile parcel of land in the Andean foothills, establishing a weird "religious" community that he named Colonia Dignidad. Surrounded by barricades, barbed wire, searchlights, and security cameras, Schäfer preached a familiar gospel of anti-Semitism and anti-COMMUNISM, flavored with apocalyptic overtones. As his flock grew to 300, supported by donations from Germany and alleged drug trafficking, Schäfer curried favor with Chile's right-wing military leaders and German immigrants. By the time dictator Augusto Pinochet seized power in 1973, Schäfer ranked among the junta's most favored allies. Chile's intelligence chief, Gen. Manuel Contreras, stashed political prisoners at Colonia Dignidad and supervised their torture during frequent personal visits. By the time democracy was restored in 1990, Schäfer had established what one legislator calls "a state within a state."

Colonia Dignidad lost its "charity" status in 1990, but its real troubles began six years later when a student at the compound's boarding school complained that Schäfer was molesting him. The boy's mother pressed charges, and soon a flood of similar complaints besieged the Nazi enclave. Schäfer—known as "Permanent Uncle" inside the barbed wire—currently faces a dozen charges of sodomy, assault, and child abuse, but authorities have thus far been unwilling to arrest him. Senator Jaime Naranjo Ortiz says that Schäfer has waged "a guerrilla war in the courts," financed by his ever-growing business empire. "They easily control properties and enterprises worth more than $100 million through their various holding companies," Naranjo told the *New York Times*. "They are involved in real estate, mining, commerce and agriculture, just like any of several better-known business conglomerates in this country." Prosecutors say Schäfer favors boys ages eight to 12, whom he entices with appeals to their parents. Attorney Hernán Fernández Rojas told the *Times:* "These are poor kids whose families sent them to live at Colonia Dignidad in hopes of a better life for them. Schäfer thought he could do what he wanted with these boys within the enclave he controls and that they would have no way to defend themselves."

As the standoff continues, that judgment would appear to be correct. In addition to wholesale child molestation, "Uncle" Schäfer and his cultists are suspected in the disappearance of U.S. tourist Boris Weisfeiler, who vanished while hiking near Colonia Dignidad in January 1985. A Chilean military informer later said that Weisfeiler (a Russian-Jewish immigrant) was killed on Schäfer's orders. Prosecutors say that charge is impossible to confirm "without unrestricted access to other eyewitnesses or the Colonia Dignidad premises." A move to expel the cult's German leaders from Colombia was blocked on appeal, with a ruling that accused criminals may only be deported after trial and sentencing. Senator José Vierra-Gallo told the *Times,* "That means we may never be able to get rid of them. This thing just keeps turning around and around in circles. They are so powerful, with so much protection, that they have the ability to keep these cases going in the courts indefinitely."

COLUMBIA shuttle disaster

On February 1, 2003, concluding a 16-day mission in space, the shuttle *Columbia* reentered Earth's atmosphere and disintegrated in midair, 39 miles above Texas. All seven crew members died in the fiery plummet to impact, scattering wreckage and human remains over a wide strip of the Lone Star State. As in the *Challenger* tragedy of 1986, suggestions of enemy sabotage were instantly raised, with fears heightened in this case by the faltering course of President George W. Bush's global "War on TERRORISM." Investigators ultimately blamed the loss on defective insulation tiles, but conspiracists refuse to accept the official verdict. Suspects in the terrorist scenario include AL-QAEDA mastermind Osama bin Laden and Iraqi dictator SADDAM HUSSEIN. And unlike *Challenger,* the *Columbia* did have at least one possible target on board. Crew member Ilan Ramon was ISRAEL's first astronaut and a member of that nation's air force. The son of a HOLOCAUST survivor, Ramon was one of the Israeli pilots who bombed IRAQ's sole nuclear reactor in 1981.

See also BIN LADEN FAMILY; BUSH DYNASTY.

COMMITTEE to Reelect the President

This group, led by former attorney general John Mitchell, was organized to ensure the reelection of President RICHARD NIXON in 1972. Ostensibly its duties included fundraising and advertising plans for Nixon's final campaign, but nothing was ever quite what it seemed in the Nixon White House. From day one, the aptly named CREEP was involved in a range of criminal activity that included solicitation of illegal contributions and pursuit of an elaborate "dirty tricks" campaign against potential Democratic challengers. CREEP's tactics included covert surveillance, wiretapping, bugging, and slander. Ironically, it was the covert committee's own zeal that finally toppled Nixon, with a clumsy break-in at Democratic Party headquarters in Washington's WATERGATE office complex in June 1972. Revelation of the men behind that crime came too late to prevent Nixon's reelection five months later, but the far-ranging investigation finally drove Nixon from office in disgrace two years after the fact.

COMMUNISM

It is curious that communism—a theory and system of sociopolitical organization that dominated much of 20th-century history—still remains ill defined and widely misunderstood by most inhabitants of Earth. To some it means utopia, to others a globe-encircling "evil empire" that enslaved or slaughtered millions. Indeed, the very invocation of its name seems to preclude a calm and rational debate.

Perfect communism, as espoused by theorists Karl Marx and Friedrich Engels in the 1840s, involved revolutionary action against monarchists and capitalist ruling classes to create an ideal classless society that was devoid of exploitation at any level. The guiding motto of communism—"From each according to his ability, to each according to his need"—presumed that all humans would share willingly, without avarice or ambition. No government machine would be used by one group to oppress another; no professional army or police force would be needed in the absence of malicious aggression, and no products would be sold for profit. In fact, however, for all the right-wing railing against communism since the mid-19th century, the system envisioned by Marx and Engels has never existed in any "civilized" nation on Earth. Vladimir Lenin changed the Marxist equation in 1917, declaring that a transitional "dictatorship of the proletariat" would be required to convert RUSSIA's feudal society to perfect communism at some point in the undefined future. Whatever Lenin may have truly intended, his death in 1923 placed brutal JOSEPH STALIN in control of Russia's fate, and no further progress was made toward the Utopian ideal. Other "communist" nations, from Eastern Europe to CHINA, CUBA, and VIETNAM, typically followed Stalin's example with variations, imposing a system of one-party rule on peasants who were previously ruled by kings, colonial powers, or right-wing dictators allied with the United States. In most cases, downtrodden commoners benefited from the imposition of state socialism, but they experienced Communism in name only, trading one autocratic system for another. Despite the collapse of the Soviet Union in 1989–91, bastardized "communist" regimes survive today in China, Cuba, Vietnam, and North KOREA.

Some historians now question whether communism ever truly posed a global threat to the degree claimed by Western leaders in the years 1917–90. If anything, revisionists suggest, the existence of a menacing "Red Bloc," allegedly plotting world conquest behind Iron and Bamboo Curtains, may have been a tool employed by the West's huge MILITARY-INDUSTRIAL COMPLEX to justify vast arsenals, neocolonial military actions in the so-called Third World, and pervasive domestic thought control. Certainly, the U.S. military, the CENTRAL INTELLIGENCE AGENCY, and FEDERAL BUREAU OF INVESTIGATION profited greatly from shadowboxing with "Red" agents at home and abroad. From the PALMER RAIDS to fabricated "missile gaps" and brushfire wars in Asia, the "national security" apparatus we live with today might never have existed without the threat of a Red bogeyman. At the same time the oppressive measures adopted by Stalin, LAVRENTI BERIA, MAO ZEDONG, and other "communist" leaders claimed thousands or millions of lives (depending on the source). Whether left- or right-wing dictators are worse—if, indeed, any difference at all exists between the two—is a judgment left to history.

COMOROS

The four Comoro Islands—Grande Comore (also known as Ngazidja), Anjouan, Mobéli, and Mayotte—were colonized by FRANCE between 1843 and 1904. In 1974 a 94-percent majority voted for independence, opposed only by the Christian minority on Mayotte (which remains a French overseas territory today). The other three Comoros declared themselves independent in July 1975—and lapsed into chaos 30 days later. Nearly two dozen coups have rocked the archipelago since 1975, compounded by several attempts at secession. Anjouan declared independence in August 1997 after months of conflict with security forces and was followed shortly by Mobéli. The three islands were grudgingly reconciled in February 2001, but another coup shattered the peace on Anjouan six months later. A new constitution reunited the Comoros in March 2002, but only an eternal optimist would predict smooth sailing for this troubled republic in the Indian Ocean.

CONFEDERATE Underground

A secret group of racial terrorists, active in the southern United States in the latter 1950s, the Confederate Underground anticipated Nacirema and the SILVER DOLLAR GROUP by using bombs to combat racial integration and the individuals perceived as prime movers in a "race-mixing conspiracy" to destroy the white race. Anonymous telephone calls to news agencies or to local Jewish leaders claimed credit for racist bombings in Atlanta, Georgia, and in Jacksonville, Florida, during March and April 1958. The Confederate Underground's last known message was a phone call to United Press International, following a blast at an Atlanta synagogue on October 12, 1958. The caller identified himself as "General Gordon of the Confederate Underground," saying, "We have just blown up the temple. This is the last empty building I'll blow up in Atlanta." Several members of

the fledgling National States Rights Party were charged in that case, but all were acquitted at trial. No members of the Confederate Underground were ever publicly identified, though racist attorney Jesse Stoner was widely suspected of taking part in the terrorist campaign.

See also TERRORISM.

CONGO (Democratic Republic)

King Leopold II claimed Africa's Congo region for BELGIUM in 1885 and thereafter proceeded to amass a vast fortune from ivory, rubber, and slave labor, killing an estimated 10 million Africans in the process. Belgium maintained its African colony until June 1960 when nationalist agitation secured a grant of independence. The celebration was short lived, as Moise Tshombe's Katanga Province seceded two weeks later followed by the mining province of South Kasai. Belgian troops and mercenaries returned with a vengeance to crush the civil war, followed by a UNITED NATIONS peacekeeping force. President Joseph Kasavubu then staged a coup against popular Prime Minister PATRICE LUMUMBA and delivered Lumumba to Tshombe's camp, where he was murdered. UN Secretary General DAG HAMMARSKJÖLD died in a plane crash en route to a peace conference with Tshombe in September 1961. Seesaw politics and guerrilla warfare brought Gen. Joseph-Desiré Mobutu to power in 1965, and he reigned at the helm of a notoriously corrupt and brutal regime for 32 years. In the process, Mobutu defeated an invasion from ANGOLA (with aid from FRANCE), dissolved parliament, and used Zaire as a launching pad for raids against neighboring countries. Rival Laurent Kabila toppled Mobutu in May 1997, but his own autocratic style soon quelled any celebration of the change in rulers. Rebel forces, aided by troops from RWANDA and UGANDA, launched a new war against Kabila in August 1998. Kabila was assassinated in January 2001 and replaced by his son Joseph, but the grisly civil war drags on. By April 2003 an estimated 3.3 million Congolese were dead, 85 percent of that number lost to AIDS and starvation. In the nation's capital (Kinshasa) some 30,000 children roam the streets, expelled from their homes on accusations of "witchcraft." The UN, meanwhile, is investigating charges that Congolese rebels have systematically killed and devoured forest-dwelling Pygmies in Ituri Province.

CONGO (Republic)

FRANCE added this section of equatorial Africa to its empire by treaty in 1880, uniting it with GABON and Ubangi-Shari as French Equatorial Africa in 1910. Flagrant abuse of black workers sparked international complaints and native rebellions, but the system of virtual slave labor endured until 1930. In 1960 the Congo declared independence without leaving the French community, establishing itself as the Republic of Congo. President Alphonse Massemba-Débat established a communist regime, but he was overthrown by Maj. Marien Ngouabi (a more "moderate" Socialist) in 1968. A four-man commando team assassinated Ngouabi on March 18, 1977, and Col. Joachim Ybombi-Opango assumed the presidency on April 4. A one-party system ruled the nation until 1990, and political leaders renounced Marxism the following year, setting the stage for Congo's first-ever free elections in 1992. Unfortunately, ethnic violence rocked the country during 1993–94, and a four-month civil war devastated the capital (Brazzavile) in 1997. Supported by troops from ANGOLA, former Marxist dictator Denis Sassou-Nguesso toppled President Pascal Lissouba, but vicious fighting continued. After barring his political opponents from the country, President Sassou-Nguesso won reelection in March 2002 with 89 percent of the popular vote. Cliques of so-called Ninja rebels continue their war of attrition against Sassou-Nguesso's regime, fighting for control of Congo's rich OIL reserves, with no end to the mayhem in sight.

See also COMMUNISM.

CONNOR, Eugene ("Bull") (1897–1973)

Born at Selma, Alabama on July 11, 1897, Theophilus Eugene Connor dropped out of high school to work as a railroad telegrapher and radio sportscaster (where he earned his famous nickname for fabricating plays and statistics—that is, "shooting the bull"—during broadcasts). In 1934 he was elected to the Alabama state legislature; three years later he won election as Birmingham's commissioner of public safety, commanding the city's police and fire departments. Connor held that post until 1953, declining to seek reelection that year in the wake of a 1951 sex scandal. He was returned to office in 1957 on a pledge to maintain strict racial segregation in the face of mounting civil rights protests and maintained his post until Birmingham changed its form of municipal government in 1963.

Connor's die-hard commitment to segregation placed him in collaboration with the violent KU KLUX KLAN, protecting nightriders responsible for 40-plus racial bombings between 1948 and 1963. Under Connor, the city was nicknamed "Bombingham," while its largest black neighborhood was dubbed "Dynamite Hill." On the rare occasions when he addressed the problem at all, Connor habitually blamed blacks for the crimes. "We know Negroes did it," he told reporters after three black churches were bombed in January 1962. "Everybody we talk to who knows anything about it says they saw Negroes running away from the churches." A FEDERAL BUREAU OF INVESTIGATION (FBI) memo filed on December 7, 1957, following the demolition of a black-owned home, reported that "Connor did not intend to attempt to solve this bombing." Seven months later on July 24, 1958, FBI headquarters ordered the Birmingham field office "to hold contacts with Connor to a minimum in view of his unsavory background." Connor reciprocated in October 1958 instructing his police to share no information with G-men on pending civil rights cases. (During the last decade of Connor's reign, Birmingham officers were unofficially barred from attending the FBI National Academy.)

The breakdown in communications hardly mattered by that time since FBI informants in the Klan kept G-men fully advised of Connor's negligence where acts of TERRORISM were concerned. One such informant, Gary Rowe, advised agents of Connor's April 1961 agreement to let Klansmen assault participants in the integrated FREEDOM RIDES without police interference. Rather than warn the demonstrators, however, FBI agents provided Birmingham police (including an officer known for his ties to the Klan) with an itinerary of the buses, thereby facilitating violent attacks at Anniston and at Birmingham's Trailways bus depot. Following the latter riot, on May 14, 1961, Connor explained the absence of police by claiming that most officers had gone home to celebrate Mother's Day.

Stripped of his office via popular vote and court orders in 1963, Connor was elected the following year to serve as president of Alabama's Public Service Commission. He held that post until 1972 when a series of strokes left him disabled and forced his resignation. A final stroke claimed Connor's life on February 26, 1973.

CONTRAS See IRAN-CONTRA CONSPIRACY.

COSTA Rica

Sandwiched between NICARAGUA and PANAMA, present-day Costa Rica was inhabited by some 25,000 "Indians" when Christopher Columbus arrived in 1502, but few of them survived the Spanish conquest that began in 1563. The colony won independence in 1821 but was absorbed by MEXICO's expanding empire two years later. Freed at last in 1848, Costa Rica today enjoys "one of the most democratic governments in Latin America." That reputation notwithstanding, Costa Rica has fostered its share of sinister intrigue. Three-time president José Figueres admitted, in 1975, that he had worked for the CENTRAL INTELLIGENCE AGENCY "in 20,000 ways . . . all over Latin America." That did not stop the agency from trying to overthrow Figueres in 1955 and again in 1970–71 when he was deemed "too moderate" on COMMUNISM. Costa Rica's failure to sign an extradition treaty with the United States has marked the nation as a haven for fugitives on the lam, including notorious swindler Robert Vesco.

CÔTE d'Ivoire

Côte d'Ivoire (also known as the Ivory Coast) is another example of African culture destroyed by European incursions. Sixty distinct tribes shared the region when traders from FRANCE arrived in the early 19th century demanding territorial concessions in 1842 and organizing a colonial-style government 51 years later. After World War II, Côte d'Ivoire became an autonomous republic within the French union and then claimed independence in August 1960. Felix Houphouët-Boigny served as president from 1960 until his death in 1993, establishing one of the strongest national economies in Africa. Successor Henri Konan Bédié revised the constitution to enhance his own powers, a move that led to mass demonstrations in 1998. The protesters championed *ivorité* as a slogan of national pride, but it soon lapsed into paranoid xenophobia, driving thousands of ethnic Malians and Burkinans from Côte d'Ivoire in 1999. President Bédié was ousted by a military coup that December in a move that cut off most of Côte d'Ivoire's foreign aid. General Robert Guei permitted an election of sorts in October 2000, with fraud so rife that both sides claimed victory, and violent opposition to Guei soon drove him from the country. Popular candidate Alassane Ouattara was barred from the contest on grounds that he was not a pure-blooded Ivorian, and while Ouattara was finally granted citizenship in 2002 (permitting him to campaign for president in 2005), the two-year dispute cost hundreds of lives in outbreaks of political violence. Guei returned to lead a military coup in September 2002, but he died in the resultant fighting. Bloodshed continued until July 5, 2003, when the military and various rebel forces declared a cease-fire.

COUNCIL on Foreign Relations (CFR)

With the BILDERBERG GROUP and the TRILATERAL COMMISSION this private group commonly appears on lists of "secret rulers" who allegedly control commerce and politics worldwide. The CFR describes itself as a "nonpartisan organization dedicated to improving the understanding of U.S. foreign policy and international affairs through the free and civil exchange of ideas" and (with a slight lapse in modesty) as "the privileged and preeminent nongovernmental impresario of America's pageant to find its place in the world." According to the CFR's Internet Web site the group "is dedicated to increasing America's understanding of the world and contributing ideas to U.S. foreign policy. The council accomplishes this mainly by promoting constructive debates and discussions, clarifying world issues, and publishing *Foreign Affairs,* the leading journal on global issues." Founded in 1921 the CFR pursues four stated goals:

1. To add value to the public debate on international affairs.
2. To energize foreign-policy discussions nationwide by making the council a truly national organization with membership across the country.
3. To identify and nurture the next generation of foreign-policy leaders.
4. To make the council the source for ideas and clear and accurate information on key international issues for the interested public.

Nine years before the CFR was created, founding father Edward Mandell House, a confidential advisor to President Woodrow Wilson, published a book titled *Philip Dru: Administrator* in which he outlined a "conspiracy" within the United States, working for "Socialism as dreamed of by Karl Marx." The plot's goals, as outlined in print, were the establishment of a central banking system, implementation of a graduated income tax, and control of both political parties. Conspiracists note that by 1916 the first two goals had been accomplished (and perhaps the third, as well). Today, critics describe the CFR as a political and financial powerhouse promoting the insidious NEW WORLD ORDER.

Whatever its motives, benign or malignant, there is no denying the CFR's wealth and influence. Initially funded by the Rockefeller and Carnegie Foundations, among others, today the CFR is bankrolled by Xerox, GENERAL MOTORS, Texaco, and other corporate giants. Most U.S. presidents since Franklin Roosevelt (and most unsuccessful White House contenders) have been CFR members, as have all CENTRAL INTELLIGENCE AGENCY directors since the agency was established in 1947. Other identified members, at last count, included 14 secretaries of state, 14 treasury secretaries, 11 defense secretaries, U.S. ambassadors to 18 foreign nations, and "at least a dozen" members of Congress (in 2000).

See also ROCKEFELLER CLAN.

CRIPS and Bloods

The Crips and Bloods are America's two most notorious STREET GANGS and were spawned in the black ghetto of Los Angeles, California, following destruction of the local BLACK PANTHER PARTY by agents of the FEDERAL BUREAU OF INVESTIGATION's illegal COINTELPRO campaign. Black youths impressed by the Panthers' guns, leather jackets, and political rhetoric rallied behind Raymond Washington, a 15-year-old student at Fremont High School, when he organized a new politicized street gang in 1969. Washington initially called his clique the Baby Avenues (in tribute to an older gang, the Avenues), and the tender age of his recruits prompted others to call them Cribs. Standard garb included black leather jackets, earrings (left lobe only), and canes (doubling as weapons) that prompted some enemies to call them cripples or crips. A reporter with the *Los Angeles Sentinel* made the new nickname official in February 1972, and it has endured ever since.

By that time, many Crips were engaged in criminal activity (dubbed "crippin'") that included theft, drug dealing, and turf wars with rival street gangs. Two of those rivals, the Brims and the Piru Street Boys, merged in early 1972 to create a new gang—the Bloods—that would wage ceaseless war on the Crips for the next quarter-century. By 1978 Los Angeles hosted 45 different Crip gangs and 15 Blood factions, some battling each other as viciously as they fought their sworn rivals. Ray Washington was one of the casualties, murdered in 1979 at age 26. A year later the City of Angels reported 355 gang murders in 12 months. In the 1980s and 1990s both gangs spread nationwide with Crip and Blood factions reported in cities from coast to coast. Most were hard-core ghetto cliques that were enriched by trafficking in crack COCAINE, but others were vaguely surreal. (The Crips in Little Rock, Arkansas, consisted of a lone L.A. fugitive surrounded by disaffected white teenagers who adopted black slang and declared themselves "homeys.") A cease-fire between Crips and Bloods was declared in April 1992, followed by a formal merger of the gangs in 1999. While some observers (including the NATION OF ISLAM) hailed the move as a breakthrough for "peace," others noted that the alliance freed Crips and Blood to kill more of their Hispanic and Asian-American rivals while expanding their traffic in drugs.

CROATIA

Once the Roman province of Pannonia, modern-day Croatia was settled by Croats in the seventh century A.D. Byzantine and Frankish invaders were repelled in 925, whereupon the victors established an independent kingdom. Civil war erupted in 1089, paving the way for a Hungarian invasion two years later. The two nations officially united under HUNGARY's king in 1102 while Croatia retained theoretical autonomy. Following Hungary's defeat by TURKEY in 1526, Croatians elected Austrian Archduke Ferdinand of Hapsburg as their king. The Austro-Hungarian Empire, established in 1867, endured with Croatia as a member through the bloody years of World War I, but Croats declared independence in October 1918. They soon combined with residents of Slovenia, SERBIA, and Montenegro to form a single nation (known from 1929 as YUGOSLAVIA). GERMANY conquered Yugoslavia in 1941, whereupon Croatia became a puppet state of the Nazi THIRD REICH. Croatian fascists (the Ustachi) carried out their own

HOLOCAUST during World War II, slaughtering countless Jews and Serbs. With ADOLF HITLER's defeat, Croatia became a republic of Red Yugoslavia, so remaining until the collapse of Soviet COMMUNISM in 1991. A six-month civil war followed Croatia's declaration of independence from Yugoslavia, marked by brutal "ethnic cleansing." Fighting continued through May 1995 despite the presence of a UNITED NATIONS peacekeeping force. In 1999, declaring that "national issues are more important than democracy," President Tudjman imposed autocratic rule and proceeded to destroy the already wounded economy. His death in December 1999 permitted a return of 300,000 ethnic Serbs (banished by Tudjman), while successor Stipe Mesic struggled to patch the nation's bloody wounds. In July 2002 Mesic met with the presidents of BOSNIA and Yugoslavia, forging an agreement to repatriate homeless refugees from the region's latest round of conflict. It remains to be seen whether a treaty can resolve old hatreds spanning generations. Croatia was accepted as a candidate country for the European Union in 2004.

CUBA

Arawak natives inhabited this largest island of the West Indies when Christopher Columbus arrived in 1492, but they were soon wiped out by a combination of savage violence, disease, and slave labor. SPAIN established settlements in 1511, and Havana's excellent harbor guaranteed that Cuba would be a center of trade and military action for the next 400 years. The 19th-century sugarcane industry flourished with importation of African slaves, but an armed struggle for independence erupted in 1867 and lasted until 1878. Reformer José Marti led the struggle that ended Spanish rule in 1898, but the Spanish-American War placed Cuba under U.S. occupation until 1902. By that time the Platt Amendment (1901) had granted Washington the legal right to intervene in Cuban politics, and U.S. troops returned four more times between 1906 and 1920.

As PROHIBITION created modern organized crime in the United States, members of the MAFIA and other bootlegging syndicates (including MEYER LANSKY and CHARLES "LUCKY" LUCIANO) used Cuba as a way station for illicit liquor shipments. Army officers led by Fulgencio Batista toppled President Gerado Machado in 1933 while maintaining Machado's ties

to the U.S. underworld. Batista established a corrupt police state that included support for mob-run casinos and brothels in Havana. His crimes were so flagrant that the CENTRAL INTELLIGENCE AGENCY supported rebel FIDEL CASTRO's uprising in 1956; then it claimed surprise three years later when a victorious Castro declared his allegiance to COMMUNISM. A long war of attrition ensued, marked by a bungled invasion at the BAY OF PIGS in 1961 and multiple attempts on Castro's life. Castro responded by forging close ties with RUSSIA and "exporting revolution" to nations ranging from Latin America to ANGOLA. (Some theorists say he also staged the JFK ASSASSINATION in 1963.) Still manning the nation's helm in 2003, Castro drew his mandate from a popular petition (allegedly signed by 99 percent of the Cuban electorate) that declared Cuba's socialist system "untouchable" for all time. The United States, meanwhile, maintains a military presence at Guantanamo Bay, which since 2001 has also housed "Camp Delta" for unnamed detainees from AFGHANISTAN.

CYPRUS

Cyprus, in the Mediterranean, was the site of Phoenician and Greek colonies in classical times. It fell to TURKEY in 1571 and then was annexed by England soon after the outbreak of World War I. Instead of liberating Cyprus, though, London declared it a British Crown colony in 1925. The island's Greek population craved reunion (*enosis*) with their homeland, and a rebel organization (the EOKA) waged ceaseless war against British occupation troops until August 1960 when Cyprus became an independent nation. Archbishop Makarios, president of Cyprus since 1959, was ousted by a military coup on July 15, 1974. Turkey seized upon the chaos to invade Cyprus five days later, claiming that the move was designed to protect the island's Turkish minority. In fact, Turkish troops overran 40 percent of the island, driving 180,000 Greek Cypriots from their ancestral homes. Makarios returned as president in December 1974 with an offer of self-rule for Turkish Cypriots. In November 1983 the minority declared a Turkish Republic of Northern Cyprus (recognized only by Turkey), but the UNITED NATIONS deemed the move illegal three days later, demanding withdrawal of all Turkish troops. In 1997 and 1999 Turkey protested Cypriot deployment of missiles capable of striking targets on the Turkish coast. Northern Cyprus opened its borders to southern

(Greek Cypriot) visitors in April 2003, but northern leader Raug Denktash demanded that various "undesirable" southerners be banned from entering his self-proclaimed "nation."

CZECH Republic

In the fifth century A.D., Slavic tribes occupied the region of Bohemia, Moravia, and Silesia. Czechs founded the kingdom of Bohemia and the Premyslide dynasty that ruled from the 10th to the 16th century. A Hapsburg, Ferdinand I, claimed the throne in 1526. A Czech rebellion in 1618 touched off the Thirty Years' War, although the rebels themselves were defeated in 1620 and lived for the next three centuries as part of the Austrian Empire. World War I shattered that institution, and the Czech lands merged with Slovakia to create Czechoslovakia in November 1918. GERMANY occupied the nation in March 1939 and ruled it as a "protectorate" of the THIRD REICH through World War II. Elections held in 1946 saw the Communist Party rise to dominance and gain control of the government two years later. RUSSIA brutally suppressed stirrings of independence in the 1960s, but four decades of Red rule ended in 1989 with the election of President Václav Havel. A strong Slovak nationalist movement arose in 1991, climaxed with dissolution of the Czechoslovakian federation on January 1, 1993. Scandal rocked the Czech Republic in 2002 when a senior foreign-ministry official, Karol Srba, was jailed on charges of hiring an assassin to kill investigative journalist Sabina Slonkova.

See also COMMUNISM.

DALEY, Richard Joseph (1902–1976)

Chicago's longtime mayor, known simply as "The Boss," was born in the Windy City on May 15, 1902. He earned a law degree in 1934 but never practiced; instead, like many other sons of Irish immigrants before him, Daley chose politics as a career in one of the nation's most defiantly corrupt cities. He served more than a decade in the state legislature (1936–47) and was four times chosen as a delegate to the Democratic National Convention (1948, 1952, 1956, 1960). Elected mayor of Chicago for the first time in 1955, Daley served until his death in 1976. Daley proved so popular (and powerful) that in three of his six mayoral campaigns (1963, 1967, and 1971) no other candidate opposed his bids for reelection. In 1960, collaborating with the MAFIA, Daley swung the crucial (and fraudulent) votes that allowed John Kennedy to defeat RICHARD NIXON in a hard-fought race for the White House. Daley's outspoken support for President LYNDON JOHNSON's foreign policy in VIETNAM won him the plum assignment of hosting the Democratic convention in 1968—a situation that backfired with antiwar demonstrations, a "police riot," and the long debacle of the CHICAGO 7 conspiracy trial. For Daley, however, such events (and the recurring exposure of widespread corruption inside the CHICAGO POLICE DEPARTMENT) posed no obstacle to landslide reelections. Stricken with a heart attack, he died at his doctor's office on December 20, 1976. The Chicago Democratic machine survived his passing, to elect son Richard Michael Daley mayor in 1989—an office he retains today.

See also KENNEDY DYNASTY.

DALLAS Police Department

In 1962 Michigan State University's Police-Community Relations Institute reported that the Dallas (Texas) Police Department (PD) "has enjoyed for many years a nationwide reputation for outstanding efficiency." That image was shattered a year later by the JFK ASSASSINATION, but further investigation suggests that it was merely a façade that masked pervasive corruption, brutality, and a subculture of racist, ultra-conservative politics. From PROHIBITION onward, illegal gambling and other illicit activities were "protected" by police in the employ of rival gamblers Benny Binion and Herbert Noble. Binion eventually murdered Noble before moving on to a "legitimate" career in LAS VEGAS, but Dallas police ignored the gang war so completely that journalist Holland McCombs pronounced the department "tougher on jaywalkers than on murderers." Chicago mobsters arrived in the 1940s, operating through front man JACK RUBY, whose Carousel Club swiftly became a favorite nightspot for Dallas police (both on and off duty). Ruby's enduring friendship with local police shielded him from prosecution on various charges ranging from pimping to aggravated assault and ultimately enabled him to kill alleged presidential assassin LEE HARVEY OSWALD in the basement garage of police headquarters on November 24, 1963.

Two years before that incident was broadcast worldwide on live TV, the Dallas PD instituted use of "shotgun squads" to deter local burglars. The teams—also called jack-in-the-box squads—hid in various local shops after nightfall waiting to gun down would-be burglars (who, coincidentally, were all black or Hispanic). The tactic of summary execution for attempted theft raised the hackles of civil libertarians, but local police basked in the praise of conservative politicians. Meanwhile, droves of Dallas cops enlisted with the far-right JOHN BIRCH SOCIETY and the terroristic KU KLUX KLAN. Lieutenant George Butler (in charge of the disastrous Oswald transfer) was known as a local Klan recruiter, and he once told journalist Penn Jones that "half the Dallas police were members of the KKK." It is unclear how those political leanings may have affected police performance on the JFK case, but photos clearly reveal that Oswald was beaten in custody. Some conspiracists further allege that Officer J. D. Tippit (allegedly murdered by Oswald on November 22, 1963) was an active participant in the assassination plot. In support of that contention conspiracists cite eyewitness testimony (ignored by the WARREN COMMISSION) alleging that Tippit was seen at the Carousel Club with Ruby and a man resembling Oswald shortly before Kennedy's murder.

That case was not the last black eye suffered by Dallas police. In December 1992 a federal jury convicted officers Swany Davenport and Randy Harris of extorting $50,000 in bribes from local crack COCAINE dealers. A decade later, in July 2002, police informers José Ruiz and Roberto Gonzalez pleaded guilty to framing "numerous" defendants with planted evidence, thereby violating their civil rights. (In return for making phony cases, the two conspirators received $200,000 from police.) And on August 9, 2003, FEDERAL BUREAU OF INVESTIGATION spokespersons announced a federal investigation into the recent death of black merchant Tony Vernon, killed by Dallas undercover detectives when he allegedly threatened them with a weapon outside his clothing store.

DAUGHERTY, Harry (1860–1923)

An Ohio native, born at Washington Court House on January 26, 1860, Harry Daugherty was a lifelong Republican activist known for his talents as a political manipulator. He was also a close friend of WARREN HARDING and served as manager of Harding's presidential primary campaign in 1920. As his reward for that victory, Daugherty was appointed to serve as attorney general on March 4, 1921.

Harding's regime is remembered today as one of the most corrupt in U.S. history, and Daugherty's performance was no exception. He quickly transformed the JUSTICE DEPARTMENT into a "Department of Easy Virtue" that became a national laughingstock. Daugherty's top priority appeared to be concealing crimes committed by Harding's OHIO GANG, including the notorious TEAPOT DOME scandal. To that end, acting in concert with bureau chief WILLIAM J. BURNS and assistant chief J. EDGAR HOOVER, he launched a campaign of surveillance and character assassination against congressional critics, including Senators Thomas Walsh and Burton Wheeler.

Harding's death in August 1923 brought Calvin Coolidge to the White House, and increasing heat from Congress and the courts placed Daugherty in an untenable position. Coolidge demanded his resignation on March 28, 1924, and replaced Daugherty with Harlan Stone 10 days later. Daugherty was subsequently indicted on charges of conspiracy to defraud the U.S. government, but two hung juries spared him from prison, and the charges were dismissed in 1927. He died at Columbus, Ohio, on October 12, 1941.

DAVIS, William Rhodes (1889–1941)

An Alabama native born in 1889, William Davis quit school at age 16 to ride the rails and see the world as a sailor on various tramp steamers. Back in the United States and penniless by 1926, he caught the eye of German diamond brokers Karl and Werner von Clemm, first cousins by marriage to future Nazi foreign minister (and WAR CRIMES defendant) Joachim von Ribbentropp. The von Clemm brothers bankrolled Davis's fledgling OIL company and paid his way to GERMANY in 1933, where he quickly forged personal and economic alliances with leaders of the THIRD REICH. By 1935 Davis Oil was shipping thousands of barrels each week to grease the wheels of ADOLF HITLER's growing war machine. In 1937 Davis and his German backers conspired with Mexican president Lázaro Cárdenas to nationalize Mexico's oil fields and to grant Davis Oil a monopoly on foreign sales. In September 1939 with the outbreak of World War II in Europe, Davis visited President Franklin Roosevelt and tried in vain to sell him on the notion of an alliance with Nazi Germany. Failing at that, in 1940 he served as the conduit for $8 million in Nazi campaign contributions to rival White House candidate Burton Wheeler. Davis also funneled cash into various antiwar groups, including Charles Lindbergh's AMERICA FIRST COMMITTEE. On August 1, 1941, in the midst of a publicity campaign against Roosevelt's Lend-Lease Bill to support Britain against Germany, Davis died of an apparent heart attack in Houston, Texas. Sources close to British intelligence (MI-6) later claimed that Davis was killed by British agents because of his continuing support for Hitler.

DEATH Angels

According to reports issued by California law-enforcement agencies and the state attorney general's office in 1973–74, the Death Angels were (or *are*) a covert splinter group operating within the NATION OF ISLAM, taking the sect's dogma of "white devils" seriously enough to launch a private race war on the streets. Prospective Angels earned their "wings" (full membership) by killing a specified number of whites, based on a point system geared to emotional difficulty—four children, five women, or nine men. Author Clark Howard reports that the cult had 15 "accredited" members by October 1973, presumably responsible for killing 135 men, 75 women, 60 children, or some combination of victims sufficient to make up the "points." California authorities compiled a list of 45 black-on-white murders during the same period, spanning the length of the Golden State, wherein victims were slain with cleavers, machetes, or close-range gunshots. Eight Death Angel prospects were arrested in May 1974, charged with San Francisco's string of "Zebra" attacks that left 15 whites dead and eight wounded over a six-month period, but four Angels were later released for lack of evidence. The trial of the remaining four consumed four years (1975–79), with attorneys supplied by the Nation of Islam, and ended with life sentences for all defendants.

California authorities are strangely silent on the *other* Death Angel cases and what has become of the cult, but its name surfaced again in 1986 on the far

side of the country. This time authorities claimed that Nation of Islam defector Hulon Mitchell, Jr., (also known as Yaweh Ben Yaweh, or "God, son of God") had fielded a team of Death Angels to punish defectors from his Black Hebrew Israelites cult and to kill "white devils" for his personal satisfaction. In all, Miami prosecutors claimed, Yahweh's tarnished Angels were responsible for murdering 17 white victims in Dade County, severing an ear from each on Yahweh's order. Cult enforcer Neariah Israel (formerly pro football player Robert Rozier) confessed to four murders and accepted a life sentence in return for testimony against Yahweh and company. Charged with racketeering and other crimes in a Miami federal court, Yahweh and six codefendants received a curious compromise verdict. All were convicted of conspiracy but acquitted of racketeering; jurors failed to reach a verdict on various other counts. Yahweh was acquitted of murder at a separate trial in November 1986, whereupon additional homicide charges were dropped. The Miami "ear murders"—like the earlier California slayings—remain technically unsolved.

DENVER Police Department

The Denver Police Department (DPD) was heavily infiltrated by KU KLUX KLAN members in the 1920s when Colorado emerged as a surprising KKK stronghold north of the Mason-Dixon Line. Some of that vigilante attitude survived the Klan's collapse and surfaced again in 1954 when a new police intelligence unit was created to spy on local "subversives." In 1969 the unit collaborated with FEDERAL BUREAU OF INVESTIGATION (FBI) agents to harass and arrest members of the BLACK PANTHER PARTY. Unlike the FBI's COINTELPRO operations, however, Denver PD's domestic surveillance campaign was not revealed until March 2002 when its cover was blown by the American Civil Liberties Union. Mayor Wellington Webb admitted that local police had adopted an "overbroad interpretation" of their intelligence duties, resulting in "cases where it may not have been justifiable to include certain individuals or organizations in our intelligence gathering activities." In fact, city spokespersons grudgingly confessed, the DPD had amassed dossiers on 208 different organizations and at least 3,200 individuals. One surveillance target, Glenn Morris of the AMERICAN INDIAN MOVEMENT, was not warned when police discovered that a rival group planned to murder him and two other activists. (DPD did, however, inform FBI headquarters of the plot. G-men likewise did nothing.) Other targets of illegal surveillance in Denver included the American Friends Service Committee, Amnesty International, the Anti-Defamation League of American Indians, the Colorado Coalition for Middle East Peace, Colorado Right to Life, CopWatch, EARTH FIRST!, Greenpeace, Justice for Janitors, the Libertarian Party, Operation Rescue, People for Ethical Treatment of Animals, the Rainforest Action Group, Vail Expansion Opponents, and the Wildland Project. Denver officials, slapped with multiple lawsuits for civil rights violations spanning a half-century, offered the public their promise that all illegal surveillance has been terminated. Skeptics remain unconvinced.

DETROIT Police Department

With the NEW YORK POLICE DEPARTMENT, the Detroit Police Department (DPD) was an early pioneer in "antiradical" activities, collaborating with various local industries to harass and suppress unwelcome labor unions. Detroit police joined in the lawless PALMER RAIDS of 1919 and in 1930 created a Special Investigation Bureau (SIB) "to work on the Bolshevik and Communist activities" in Motor City. Collaborators in that effort included the NYPD, the AMERICAN LEGION, various professional Red-hunters, and a KU KLUX KLAN splinter group called the Black Legion. Police joined the Black Legion and used it to punish "subversives" outside the law, but the cooperative effort proved embarrassing when Black Legion members were indicted for bombing, flogging, and murder. Police Commissioner Heinrich Pickert solved the problem of his own complicity when he "frantically promoted all those police officers who could compromise him." In 1939 a grand-jury probe of police corruption climaxed with indictment of the mayor, the county prosecutor, the police superintendent, and eight officers. The SIB was briefly disbanded and then revived in June 1940 to work with the FEDERAL BUREAU OF INVESTIGATION (FBI) on matters of "national security."

During the next 35 years, Detroit police worked closely with G-men, various corporations, and the HOUSE COMMITTEE ON UN-AMERICAN ACTIVITIES to shadow, harass, and blacklist citizens who were sus-

pected of "disloyalty." In the 1960s the SIB expanded to cover black militant groups, the "New Left," and opponents of the VIETNAM War. Ghetto riots in 1967 left 43 persons dead, nearly all of them shot by police. (Three of the dead were unarmed black men who had been beaten and shot execution style by officers at the Algiers Motel, but the shooters were acquitted by an all-white jury of their peers.) In 1969–70 DPD officers staged a series of raids against the BLACK PANTHER PARTY, acting in conjunction with the FBI. Another program, dubbed STRESS (<u>S</u>top <u>T</u>he <u>R</u>obberies and <u>E</u>njoy <u>S</u>afe <u>S</u>treets), resulted in more ghetto deaths until the team was dissolved for planting weapons on unarmed victims. In 1975 the Michigan Association for Consumer Protection sued the DPD and other police agencies for conducting illegal surveillance on an estimated 110,000 groups and individuals. The SIB was finally disbanded in 1980, but its files were not destroyed; instead, by mayoral order, they were transferred to the Board of Police Commissioners. Two years later, a special order from City Hall banned any investigation of "beliefs, opinions, attitudes, statements, associations and activities" unless the targets were "reasonably suspected" of criminal activity.

Still, problems continue for the DPD. In 2000 after police shot and killed a deaf man "armed" with a rake, the Justice Department launched a probe of 40 fatal shootings in the past five years. (A report published in May 2000 revealed that Detroit led all U.S. cities in fatal police shootings.) In October 2002 a city officer and a civilian department employee were among nine persons indicted on federal charges for stealing 222 pounds of COCAINE from the evidence room and selling it around Detroit. Nine months later 17 cops were indicted on charges of "shaking down precinct prostitutes and drug dealers, theft of huge sums of money and drugs from drug dealers, systematic cover-up of officer abuses and criminal activity, including the planting of evidence, making false arrests and giving false testimony in court."

DIANA, Princess of Wales (1961–1997)

At 12:15 A.M. on August 31, 1997, a black Mercedes S-280 left the Ritz Hotel in Paris with four persons aboard. Driver Henri Paul was joined in the front seat by bodyguard Trevor Rees-Jones. In back, megamillionaire Dodi Fayed sat with his supposed fiancée Diana Spencer, lately divorced from Britain's Prince of Wales and mother of the future King William. The car departed at high speed, pursued by the retinue of tabloid photographers who trailed Britain's most popular and photogenic Royal wherever she went. Four minutes after departure, with the pack of paparazzi trailing a quarter-mile behind, the limousine crashed in the Alma tunnel. Fayed and Paul were killed instantly; Diana died within the hour from her injuries; Rees-Jones survived, but with alleged impairment to his memory. Investigators later claimed that Henri Paul was drunk behind the wheel, pushing the limo to excessive speeds after Fayed ordered him to ditch the photographers.

Within hours of Diana's death, various conspiracy theories surfaced to explain the incident. The three most prominent scenarios include:

1. *Diana faked her death.* Proponents of this theory cite Diana's frequent exasperation with paparazzi and tabloid exposés as a motive for staging the car crash, thus granting her a chance to live in blissful obscurity. As "evidence," conspiracists cite the survival of bodyguard Rees-Jones (defying statements from Mercedes spokesmen that no one could survive a crash occurring at 121 miles per hour) and Henri Paul's last-minute replacement of Fayed's regular driver. Another clue is Diana's statement to journalist Richard Kray, only six hours before the crash, that she planned to withdraw from public life. A variation on the theme suggests that Diana *attempted* to fake her death and then was killed when the stunt spun out of control. Skeptics reject this scenario on grounds that Diana, a famously devoted mother, would never abandon her sons (whose popularity with the same tabloid media renders secret visits virtually impossible).

2. *Diana was killed by* MI6. The British Secret Service (MI6) has a long history of covert/illegal activities on a par with the CENTRAL INTELLIGENCE AGENCY (though rarely as humorous). Some conspiracists believe that MI6 (and perhaps the queen) deemed Diana and her relationship with a Saudi Arabian mogul a threat to "national security." No evidence of

such a plot exists (so far), but Rees-Jones was a former British army paratrooper and officer of the Royal Military Police with two tours of duty in Northern Ireland (land of countless plots and counterplots) behind him. Doubters suggest that while MI6 might kill to protect the monarchy, stripping Britain of its most popular Royal could backfire disastrously for those in power.

3. *Diana's death was "collateral damage."* This scenario assumed that Dodi Fayed was the plot's intended victim, targeted by ruthless enemies of his father (Mohammed al Fayed). As with any holder of fabulous wealth, those potential enemies are legion, including Middle Eastern arms and OIL merchants. In Britain Fayed had recently clashed with the government (which denied Mohammed's bid for British citizenship) and proprietors of Harrods department store (who resisted Fayed's takeover in the 1990s). Some observers viewed the Dodi-Diana romance as a scheme of Mohammed's, a backdoor approach to respectability in England, which his adversaries violently opposed. Skeptics assert that no sane assassin would kill Diana to reach Dodi, thus ensuring a police investigation of unrivaled intensity. As it is, that investigation revealed nothing—which leaves conspiracy theorists predictably unimpressed. (On October 20, 2003, British media reports revealed that a letter Diana wrote to her butler Paul Burrell in October 1996, 10 months before the fatal crash, voiced fears that someone planned to kill her by tampering with the brakes of her car. Specifically, she feared "an accident in my car, brake failure and serious head injury in order to make the path clear for Charles to marry." Spokespersons for the royal family dismiss those fears as absurd.)

DILLINGER, John   See UNDEAD OUTLAWS.

DJIBOUTI

This small, arid nation in northeast Africa was coveted by 19th-century FRANCE because its capital (Djibouti) provided a good port on the Gulf of Aden. Various Somali sultans sold off the land between 1843 and 1886, allowing Paris to create the colony of French Somaliland. Djibouti's inhabitants twice voted to remain under French rule, in 1958 and 1967, but the latter year witnessed a change of title as French Somaliland became the Territory of the Afars and Issas (recognizing Djibouti's primary, bitterly divided tribes). The name was changed again, this time to Djibouti, in June 1977. The harsh policies of dictator Hassan Gouled Aptidon—an Issa who filled his government with fellow tribesmen—sparked armed revolt by the Afars in 1991. A multiparty constitution was approved in September 1992, but Aptidon clung to power by force for another seven years, finally replaced by Ismail Guelleh in 1999. Afar rebels signed a peace accord in March 2000, but sporadic ethnic fighting continues, exacerbated by drought and the presence of countless refugees from neighboring ETHIOPIA and SOMALIA.

DOMINICA

This tiny nation in the Lesser Antilles should not be confused with the larger DOMINICAN REPUBLIC. (Its name is pronounced "Dom-in-EEK-a"), but its 70,000 inhabitants are no strangers to conspiracy and intrigue. Christopher Columbus paved the way in 1493; then England and FRANCE quarreled over property rights until 1763, when Dominica was formally ceded to the British Crown. In 1967 Dominica became a self-governing member of the West Indies Associated States. In June 1981 nine members of the KU KLUX KLAN and U.S. neo-Nazi groups were convicted of plotting to invade Dominica and overthrow its government. The hare-brained scheme to establish a "white bastion" in the Caribbean failed to recognize that 84 percent of Dominica's inhabitants are either black or of mixed race.

DOMINICAN Republic

Christopher Columbus explored this Caribbean island in 1492 and named it Española. His son Diego was the first viceroy, and Diego's capital city (Santo Domingo) is the oldest European settlement in the Western Hemisphere. SPAIN ceded the island to FRANCE in 1795, but an army of African slaves led by Toussaint L'ouverture threw off the French yoke six years later, establishing the Caribbean's first republic. Spain reconquered the island in 1814, but

Spanish troops were expelled in 1821. HAITI next seized power, ruling for 22 years before another rebellion established the Dominican Republic, under Pedro Santana. Ongoing revolts and Haitian assaults prompted Santana to make the island a province of Spain during the U.S. Civil War (1861–65), but the republic was eventually restored. President Buenaventura Báez asked the United States to annex his country in 1870, but Congress rejected the treaty. Instead, when Dominican unrest threatened U.S. investments, Washington dispatched U.S. Marines to occupy the island for nearly two decades (1916–34).

Leathernecks were still on the scene when ambitious Sergeant Rafaél Trujillo Molina toppled president Horacio Vásquez and named himself dictator for life in 1930. Trujillo ruled by force and fear for 31 years until he was assassinated by Central Intelligence Agency-supported opponents in 1961. (More than a year before the murder, President Dwight D. Eisenhower warned his aides, "It's certain the American public won't condemn [FIDEL] CASTRO until we have moved against Trujillo.") Trujillo's son assumed control, but leftist rebels hated him as much as they hated his father. In April 1965 President LYNDON BAINES JOHNSON sent U.S. troops to "protect American interests" on the island, armed forces remaining in place until 1966 when Joaquin Balaguer was elected as president. Balaguer proved so popular with the Dominican army that officers suspended counting of ballots in 1978 when it seemed he might lose his fourth presidential campaign. Threats from Washington persuaded Balaguer to accept defeat, but internal corruption remains a fact of life in the Dominican Republic. In 2002 a UNITED NATIONS report declared that 2 million Haitian children were smuggled into the Dominican Republic, compelled to work as virtual slaves or professional beggars.

DREYFUS affair

The Dreyfus case and its resultant scandal occurred at a time when FRANCE was in turmoil, rocked by government corruption scandals, conflict between monarchists and republicans that threatened to topple the government, and a strong wave of anti-Semitism (encouraged by leaders of the CATHOLIC CHURCH). Against that backdrop Alfred Dreyfus was almost insignificant, an obscure Jewish captain in the French army whose family had fled Alsace when

GERMANY annexed that province in 1871. In 1894 a sheet of paper was retrieved from the wastebasket of Germany's military attaché in Paris, its message listing certain secret documents allegedly delivered to Col. Max von Schwartzkoppen. Dreyfus had access to those documents, and French military authorities declared that his handwriting matched the list found in Schwartzkoppen's trash. A secret court-martial convened in December 1894 convicted Dreyfus of treason in a sham trial where Dreyfus was denied the right to examine the prosecution's evidence. Upon conviction he was stripped of rank and sentenced to life imprisonment on Devil's Island, a French penal colony off the coast of South America, while monarchist and Catholic newspapers heaped further vitriol on Jews and republicans.

There the "Dreyfus affair" might have rested if not for Lt.-Col. Georges Picquart, appointed chief of French military intelligence in 1896. Picquart (although himself a rabid anti-Semite) uncovered evidence that Dreyfus had been framed to protect another traitor in the ranks, Maj. Walsin Esterhazy. Picquart's superiors had no interest in reopening the case, and when Picquart insisted, they transferred him to Tunisia. A court-martial then acquitted Esterhazy in another display of farcical military justice. Novelist Émile Zola next took up the cause, publishing an indictment of the French army under the title *J'accuse!* Convicted of libel and sentenced to prison, Zola fled to England while Catholic leaders and right-wing politicians clamored against the alleged conspiracy of Jews and FREEMASONS to destroy France.

Still, the Dreyfus case would not die. Another army officer uncovered evidence that one Lt.-Col. Hubert Henry had forged papers implicating Dreyfus in acts of treason. Henry committed suicide in the wake of preliminary questioning. Scrambling to save face, the army brought Dreyfus back from Devil's Island for a second trial—and then, incredibly, convicted him again. This time, however, the tribunal found "extenuating circumstances" that facilitated a presidential pardon before year's end. Dreyfus was not finally exonerated of the charges and restored to his former military rank until 1906. Even then the army did not admit its "mistake" in convicting Dreyfus until September 7, 1995. Editors of the Catholic newspaper *La Croix* waited another four months and then apologized for Jew-baiting editorials published 100 years earlier.

DRUG dumping

Drug dumping is the practice of sending defective, outdated or unwanted medicine, or medical paraphernalia to foreign nations where its sale is not legally barred. Often, such shipments occur during times of crisis, disguised as humanitarian relief in the wake of wars or natural disasters. Profit is the motive, as those involved in the practice either sell products banned in the United States to foreign customers or claim a hefty tax deduction for donating products to charity. Donors are allowed by law to claim twice the "cost basis" of donated products—a calculation that includes component materials, labor, warehousing expenses, and accountant's fees. (The same deduction applies to nonmedical donations, thus explaining the bizarre donations of such items as bathing suits and odd-sized women's underwear to Third World countries stricken by famine and earthquakes.) During the 1990s civil war in BOSNIA, so much unwanted medicine was "charitably" donated that officials had to build a special $34 million furnace to dispose of it. ALBANIA received tons of drugs in 1999 with most of the products bearing expiration dates of 1989–90, while others fell within five months of expiration. Spokespeople for the World Health Organization deemed those donations "conspicuous by their size and inappropriateness," but the game continues, encouraged by U.S. politicians who count PHARMACEUTICAL COMPANIES among their largest campaign contributors. In response to public criticism, spokespeople for companies such as Bayer (accused of selling diluted cancer drugs in the Third World) typically reply that they have obeyed prevailing statutes of the nations where sales or donations occurred.

See also BAYER CORPORATION.

DRUG Enforcement Administration

Suppression of "controlled substances" has a long and convoluted history in the United States. As noted elsewhere, most recreational drugs were legal and readily available through the early years of the 20th century. Today they are still readily available, but various statutes and law-enforcement agencies make sale and acquisition a risky game of chance. Responsibility for federal drug enforcement initially lay with the Treasury Department's ultra-corrupt PROHIBITION Bureau (1927–30) and then passed to the Federal Bureau of Narcotics under "reefer madness" zealot HARRY ANSLINGER (1930–68). In his last year as president, LYNDON JOHNSON shifted responsibility to the JUSTICE DEPARTMENT and renamed his unit the Bureau of Narcotics and Dangerous Drugs (1968–73). The Drug Enforcement Administration (DEA) received its present name under President RICHARD NIXON and has struggled ever since to stem the tide of HEROIN, COCAINE, MARIJUANA, and other drugs pouring into the country from all sides. President RONALD REAGAN declared the first "war on drugs" and then cut the DEA's budget and banned FEDERAL BUREAU OF INVESTIGATION (FBI) undercover operations before leaving Vice President George H. W. Bush in charge of the campaign that one U.S. Coast Guard spokesperson dubbed "an intellectual fraud." Bush and subsequent presidents have appointed a series of high-profile "drug czars" to lead the fight (the U.S. Constitution bans royal titles in America), but an endless chain of "record seizures" has failed to win the phony war.

One problem, critics say, is the DEA's endemic corruption and disrespect for law. In 1978 a team of Justice Department attorneys detailed to "investigate allegations of fraud, irregularity and misconduct" at DEA headquarters uncovered details of a June 1975 conspiracy to murder PANAMA's Manuel Noriega (then chief of intelligence, later president, finally kidnapped by U.S. troops in an exercise dubbed "Operation Just Cause"). In 1994 longtime DEA undercover agent Celerino Castillo III resigned and published his memoirs (*Powder Burn*), including revelations of widespread corruption and an expression of personal amazement "that the U.S. government could get away with drug trafficking for so long." Castillo's term of service overlapped the IRAN-CONTRA CONSPIRACY, wherein Reagan-Bush aides smuggled drugs and weapons to support an outlawed terrorist campaign in NICARAGUA. In 2000 journalists revealed that the DEA had allied itself with a Colombian terrorist group, Los Pepes, in a desperate bid to capture or kill cocaine mogul Pablo Escobar. That same year, in Missouri, DEA informer Andrew Chambers was shown to have lied in dozens of cases, sending hundreds of people to prison on false charges during a period of 15 years. In yet another scandal, this one from March 2003, the DEA's associate agent in charge was suspended without pay on suspicion of stealing $150,000. Federal prosecutors charge that 49-year-old Kevin Tamez took the money in 80 installments of $1,000 to $3,000 each, disguised as front money

for undercover drug purchases; he then submitted false documents that claimed that the cash had been spent "on law enforcement business." Ironically, Tamez was also in charge of the New York DEA's Office of Professional Responsibility, which was created to investigate and punish incidents of official misconduct. Other DEA agents told the *New York Post* that Tamez had instituted a system of "rule by terror and went out of his way to jam people up."

See also BUSH DYNASTY; TERRORISM.

DULLES brothers

Few individuals have wielded as much influence over U.S. foreign policy (for good or ill) as brothers John Foster Dulles (1888–1959) and Allen Welsh Dulles (1893–1969). Though sons of a strict Presbyterian minister, the Dulles brothers were influenced more by maternal grandfather John Watson Foster, who served as secretary of state under President Benjamin Harrison, and by uncle Robert Lansing, who filled the same position under President Woodrow Wilson. Both brothers attended Princeton University, John going on to earn a law degree from George Washington University and specializing in international law. Rejected by the army in World War I for his poor eyesight, John Dulles benefited from nepotism when President Wilson appointed him legal counsel to the U.S. delegation at the Versailles Peace Conference in 1918. Afterward, John served as a member of the War Reparations Committee that concocted onerous terms for GERMANY (thus paving the way for ADOLF HITLER's rise to power in the 1930s).

Brother Allen, meanwhile, followed a different path, joining the U.S. diplomatic service, posted variously to AUSTRIA, SWITZERLAND, FRANCE, GERMANY, and TURKEY. In 1922 he was named chief of the Division of Near Eastern Affairs, supervising U.S. diplomatic action in the troubled Middle East. In World War II Allen served with the OFFICE OF STRATEGIC SERVICES (OSS) first opposing the THIRD REICH and then recruiting thousands of Nazis to serve the U.S. intelligence services under terms of PROJECT PAPERCLIP, as the OSS was transformed into the CENTRAL INTELLIGENCE AGENCY (CIA).

While Allen maneuvered on a global scale, John Dulles cast his lot with the Republican Party, serving as an aide and foreign policy adviser to presidential candidate Thomas Dewey in 1944. In 1945 John assisted in drafting the UNITED NATIONS (UN) charter and subsequently served as a delegate to the UN in 1946, 1947, and 1950. Strongly critical of President Harry Truman's foreign policy, Dulles championed the tactic of "containment"—that is, using military force and/or threats of nuclear war to prevent the spread of COMMUNISM. John Dulles found an ally in President Dwight Eisenhower, who appointed him secretary of state in January 1953. During the next eight years, he forged alliances (NATO, SEATO, and so on) that were designed to isolate "iron-curtain" countries and maintain a "balance of terror" with the nuclear arms race. His policy of "brinksmanship" was defined as "the ability to get to the verge without getting into the war." In June 1955 he declared that "neutrality has increasingly become obsolete and except under very exceptional circumstances, it is an immoral and shortsighted conception." Under that philosophy, John Dulles supervised illegal U.S. interventions in various nations ranging from GUATEMALA and CUBA to IRAN and LEBANON.

John's global power plays were ably assisted by brother Allen, whom Eisenhower appointed to lead the CIA in 1953. His agents carried out right-wing coups in Guatemala and Iran, experimented with MIND CONTROL techniques (including LSD and hypnotism), forged alliances with the U.S. MAFIA to murder FIDEL CASTRO, and planned the chaotic BAY OF PIGS INVASION with Vice President RICHARD NIXON. Nixon's defeat in the 1960 presidential campaign left President John Kennedy to carry out the attack on Cuba. Its disastrous failure left Kennedy embittered against the CIA, and Allen Dulles was forced to resign. Ironically, two years later, President LYNDON JOHNSON appointed him as a member of the WARREN COMMISSION created to investigate the JFK ASSASSINATION. It came as no surprise, therefore, that the commission's "lone assassin" verdict failed to find any involvement by CIA agents of their Mafia and Cuban-exile allies in Kennedy's death. Cancer ultimately claimed both Dulles brothers, John in 1959 and Allen 10 years later.

DUPONT dynasty

The DuPont Corporation—one of Earth's largest and richest—headlines its Internet Web site with a logo reading: "The miracles of science." One such miracle launched the DuPont dynasty more than 200 years ago, and some critics say the aroma of that first venture still clings to the family fortune. There is no doubt, as stated by the History Channel, that "DuPont's history is interwoven with the history of the United States. As the manufacturers of gunpowder, DuPont has been a vital part of America's military conflicts. The company's expansion in the 19th and 20th centuries into other products guaranteed its presence in American culture, society and economics."

In 1801, appalled by the inferior quality of American gunpowder, French immigrant Éleuthère Irénée du Pont de Nemours set out to revolutionize the science of destruction. His family had failed to prosper since arriving in the United States two years earlier, but young du Pont was a skilled chemist, tutored by the chief armorer of his native France. Erecting a gunpowder plant beside northern Delaware's Brandywine River, the fledgling DuPont Company turned out a product so impressive that by 1905 it controlled 75 percent of the U.S. black-powder market. After World War I, with Europe's economy in ruins, the company went international, plunging into new chemical endeavors that made simple gunpowder take a backseat. (The company's last black-powder business was sold in 1972). Partners in various up-and-coming ventures included the Rockefeller family's STANDARD OIL Company, GENERAL MOTORS, Germany's I.G. Farben and Krupp Arms.

DuPont links to the THIRD REICH and ADOLF HITLER were not coincidental. In fact, the family/corporation had a history of funding far-right causes, and in 1933 it was a primary supporter of the AMERICAN LIBERTY LEAGUE, which conspired with leading members of the AMERICAN LEGION to stage a military coup d'état against President Franklin Roosevelt and his NEW DEAL. That effort collapsed before the first shot was fired, but the DuPonts kept pouring cash into the league, spending an average $500,000 to support the group's 37 offices nationwide, distributing some 50 million pro-Nazi pamphlets by 1936. The PEARL HARBOR attack failed to sever DuPont's links with Hitler, and corporate spokespeople were seen meeting with Nazi industrial officers in SWITZERLAND as late as March 1942. DuPont escaped prosecution despite such flagrant trading with the enemy, and the family's fortune in FRANCE was carefully protected by German occupation troops.

While financing Hitler abroad, the DuPont machine was instrumental in banning MARIJUANA in

(Upper left) Pierre-Samuel du Pont, comte de Nemours (1739-1817) founded the family dynasty, while (upper right) Éleuthère Irénée du Pont (1771-1834) brought the family business to America and built its first great munitions plant; (bottom left) Henry Du Pont (1812-89) continued the dynasty's tradition of selling munitions and explosives. (Bottom right) Henry Algernon Du Pont's (1838-1926) election to the U.S. Senate merged business and politics. (Author's collection)

the United States. "Demon weed" opponent HARRY ANSLINGER owed his 1930 appointment as director of the Federal Bureau of Narcotics to Andrew Mellon, Herbert Hoover's secretary of the treasury and a major cog in the DuPont financial empire. Conspiracists suggest that DuPont's interest in banning marijuana had less to do with morality and the future of America's youths than it did with simple economics. By 1930 DuPont already dominated the U.S. petrochemical and synthetics industry; it faced potential disaster if the many commercial uses of hemp were realized (at a fraction of the cost for synthetics). Joining forces with Anslinger and various large PHARMACEUTICAL COMPANIES, DuPont thus flexed its corporate muscle to eliminate virtually what hemp advocates call "the nation's most valuable natural resource."

Marijuana was a sideshow, however, compared to the DuPont Corporation's continuing interest in war and political intrigue. Richard du Pont immersed himself in the CENTRAL INTELLIGENCE AGENCY's (CIA) clandestine operation and reaped another megamillion-dollar windfall in the process. Du Pont's Summit Aviation company, founded shortly after the CIA's BAY OF PIGS INVASION in CUBA, was organized with assistance from CIA operative Patrick Foley. During the next decade, Summit furnished "civic action" aircraft for the CIA's AIR AMERICA network and sold converted warplanes to right-wing dictators in GUATEMALA, HAITI, HONDURAS, NICARAGUA, and VIETNAM. The conversion process from civilian aircraft to gunship boosted the sales price of an average Cessna 500 percent. Today, while DuPont explores the "miracles of science" on all fronts, it still profits mightily from war. In 2003, before the gunsmoke cleared in IRAQ from OPERATION IRAQI FREEDOM, President George W. BUSH installed the CEO of

Phillips Petroleum (a DuPont family holding) to supervise extraction of Iraqi OIL from captured fields.

See also FARBEN INDUSTRIES; ROCKEFELLER CLAN.

DZERZHINSKI, Feliks (1877–1926)

Born the son of Polish aristocrats at Vilno in 1877, Feliks Edmundovich Dzerzhinski rebelled against his family by joining the Lithuanian Social Democratic Party and organizing factory workers into trade unions. He was arrested and sent to Siberia in 1897 but managed to escape in 1899 (taking the lessons of incarceration with him). Another arrest in 1908 and then a final one in 1912 sent him back to Siberia for nine years, charged with anticzarist activity, but Dzerzhinski was released in a general amnesty following the Russian Revolution of February 1917. He cast his lot with VLADIMIR LENIN's Bolsheviks and joined in the country's second revolution that October. Lenin rewarded Dzerzhinski in December 1917 with appointment to serve as Commissar for Internal Affairs and head of the All-Russian Extraordinary Commission for Combating Counter-Revolution and Sabotage (Cheka). Thus installed as the first chief of Soviet Russia's SECRET POLICE, Dzerzhinski launched the "Red Terror" of September 1918, following a failed attempt on Lenin's life. Other purges ensued, and Dzerzhinski retained control of the Cheka while expanding his authority as People's Commissar for Transport (1921) and chairman of the Supreme Council of National Economy (1924). In 1922 he transformed the Cheka into the GPU (State Political Administration) without weakening its reputation for TERRORISM. Dzerzhinski died of a heart attack on July 20, 1926, but he was not forgotten. Years later, when the GPU became the KGB, its headquarters was named in his honor.

EARP brothers

History and Hollywood have cast the five Earp brothers—James, Virgil, Wyatt, Morgan, and Warren—as classic heroes of the American frontier, standing firm against ruthless outlaws to make the Wild West a more civilized place. The truth, as usual, is rather different and is glimpsed more commonly between the lines, behind the stage settings and the clouds of gunsmoke that surround this famous family.

The Earps were Illinois natives, James born in 1841, Virgil in 1843, Wyatt in 1848, Morgan in 1851, and Warren in 1855. James was badly wounded as a Union soldier in 1863, and the whole family decamped to California the following year. In the Golden State, Wyatt worked as a stagecoach guard, bartender, and gambler until 1871 when he was jailed for horse theft. Posting $500, he fled the state to hunt buffalo and then drifted to Wichita where James and wife Bessie ran a combination brothel and saloon. Bessie Earp appeared in Wichita police files as a known prostitute between May 1874 and March 1875; Earp critics note that her disappearance from official records coincided with Wyatt's employment (in April 1875) as a Wichita policeman. Wyatt lasted 11 months on the job, was fired, and was fined $30 in March 1876 for assaulting William Smith, a candidate for city marshal.

Moving on to Dodge City, Kansas, Wyatt joined the local police force in May 1876, followed shortly by brother Morgan. James and Bessie soon arrived to

Wyatt Earp led the group of brothers known in certain circles as "the fighting pimps." (Author's collection)

Morgan Earp (top left) was murdered soon after the infamous gunfight at the O.K. Corral, while Virgil Earp (bottom left) survived his wounds from the gunfight to help Wyatt avenge Morgan's murder. Gunfighter and tubercular dentist John "Doc" Holliday (top right) joined the Earp brothers in various shady enterprises, while sometime lawman William "Bat" Masterson (bottom right) was another Earp ally in gambling casinos and brothels. (Author's collection)

resume their familiar trade in flesh and liquor, while Wyatt and colleague William ("Bat") Masterson protected the action. Both were sworn policemen, but Dodge City residents knew them better as card sharks and procurers, dubbed "the Fighting Pimps." Wyatt left Dodge City in May 1879 after he and Masterson beat two drunks so badly that "their own mothers would have had a hard time picking out their sons." A stop-off at Mobeetie, Texas, saw Wyatt collaborate with outlaw/lawman Dave Mather to sell phony gold bricks before he was run out of town by the sheriff. Settled next in Tombstone, Arizona, Wyatt gathered his brothers as usual, enlisting tubercular gambler-gunman John "Doc" Holliday to help out with poker and gunplay. As historian John Faragher described the scene:

> Southeastern Arizona at the time was torn by conflict between the Republican business community and the mostly Democratic ranchers of the arid countryside. The "Cowboys," as the Republican Tombstone Epitaph labeled the ranchers, were led by Newman "Old Man" Clanton and his hot-headed sons and were backed by such violent gunmen as "Curly" Bill Brocius and Johnny Ringo. The trouble in Tombstone was just one episode in a series of local wars that pitted men of traditional rural values and Southern sympathies against mostly Yankee capitalist modernizers. As the hired guns of the businessmen in town, the Earps became the enemies of the Clantons.

Since most of the Earps wore badges, members of the Clanton gang soon found themselves unwelcome in Tombstone, unless they were spending their money in Earp-run saloons, casinos, and brothels. Both sides were suspected in a fatal stagecoach robbery outside town in March 1881, and violent clashes escalated until October 26 when the two factions met in the infamous O.K. Corral shootout. Morgan and Virgil Earp were wounded, along with Doc Holliday, while three members of the Clanton gang were dispatched to Boot Hill. Murder charges were filed against the Earps but then thrown out by a friendly judge. Morgan was killed in a local pool hall on March 17, 1882, and the resultant "vengeance ride" by Wyatt, Warren, Doc Holiday, and others claimed an uncertain number of lives before the last Earps departed Arizona.

Wyatt and Holliday returned to Dodge City in 1883, teaming with Bat Masterson, gambler-pimp Luke Short, and others to create the "Dodge City Peace Commission." In fact, the group was anything but peaceful, launching a reign of terror against reformers who had vowed to close Dodge City's brothels and gambling dens. After successfully defending the corrupt status quo, Wyatt moved on to Idaho Territory, running various saloons with brother James and lending his hand to a claim-jumping gang. Tiring of those pursuits, Wyatt drifted back to California and remained there for the rest of his life, except for four years spent in Alaska (1897–1901), where he banked $80,000 as a gold-rush bartender. Warren Earp returned to Arizona as "a cattle detective" in 1900, but a gunfight in Wilcox claimed his life months later. Virgil died of pneumonia at Prescott, Arizona, in 1906, and James survived another 22 years in San Francisco.

By that time, Wyatt had begun work on his autobiography with author Stuart Lake. He died on January 13, 1929, and thus never saw his strange life become the stuff of all-American legend, revised and inflated beyond all recognition through a long series of novels, films, and television shows. Nor was the process of mythologizing focused solely on Wyatt. Brother Morgan was credited with killing gunman William Brooks at Wichita in 1880 when, in fact, Brooks was lynched for rustling in July 1874. Within a quarter-century of Wyatt's death, the Earp crime family had been transformed into rugged heroes, while their gang war with the Clanton crowd was enshrined as an epic triumph of Good vs. Evil.

EARTH First!

Inspired by Edward Abbey's novel *The Monkeywrench Gang* (1975), Earth First! was organized in 1980 with a motto of "No Compromise in Defense of Mother Earth!" The group's "monkey-wrenching" tactics included removal of surveyor stakes from Forest Service logging roads, vandalism of logging and mining equipment, and "spiking" of trees slated for harvest by loggers. FEDERAL BUREAU OF INVESTIGATION (FBI) agents placed Earth First! under sporadic surveillance almost from its beginning, but interest intensified in May 1987 when a California sawmill employee was maimed after his saw blade shattered on a hidden nail. Henceforth, the bureau regarded Earth First! as a "terrorist" organization and treated its members accordingly.

Between 1988 and 1990 G-men mounted a full-scale effort to infiltrate Earth First! with undercover agents and paid informants. Documents later revealed in response to a lawsuit disclose that the group's Arizona chapter was subjected to a COINTELPRO-style campaign from 1988 to 1990, including use of an agent provocateur who persuaded Earth First! members to cut down a rural power line. G-man Michael Fain provided the necessary tools, instructed Earth First! members in their use, and drove them to the target; then he arrested them as they were acting out his plan. More sinister intentions were suggested by the operation's code name: "Thermcon," which stood for "Thermite Conspiracy" in FBI jargon. Since Earth First! had never used thermite (a military-style incendiary), its members now believe agents planned a frame-up involving illegal explosives, but the plan never came to fruition. Instead, it now appears that G-men decided to try a different approach.

On May 24, 1990, Earth First! activists Judi Bari and Daryl Cherney left Oakland, California, en route to Santa Cruz and a scheduled meeting with fellow environmentalists. Just before noon, a pipe bomb exploded beneath the driver's seat of Bari's car, shattering her pelvis and dislocating her spine, and wounding Cherney in the face with shrapnel. Agents from the BUREAU OF ALCOHOL, TOBACCO, AND FIREARMS launched an investigation of the bombing, but they were soon displaced by G-men and OAKLAND POLICE, after FBI spokespersons declared the bombing to be an act of domestic TERRORISM. On May 25 Oakland police announced the arrest of Bari and Cherney on charges of possessing and transporting a bomb. Sweeping raids throughout the Bay Area failed to reveal Earth First's alleged "bomb factory," and prosecutors dropped all charges in the case on July 17, 1990.

Bari and Cherney, though vindicated, were not content to let the matter rest. Research informed them that Richard W. Held, agent-in-charge of the bureau's San Francisco field office, had a long history of involvement in illegal COINTELPRO operations, including actions against the BLACK PANTHER PARTY, the AMERICAN INDIAN MOVEMENT, and Puerto Rican nationalists. Those campaigns included widespread use of criminal agents provocateurs to incite or commit violent acts, thus leading Bari and Cherney to believe that G-men or their hirelings may have planted the bomb as part of a frame-up or an attempted murder.

On April 8, 1991, Bari and Cherney sued the bureau and the Oakland Police Department, charging false arrest, libel, and violation of their civil rights.

Bari would not live to see the case resolved. She died of breast cancer on March 2, 1997, with the long-running discovery phase still in progress, but executors of her estate kept up the fight. Attorneys for the plaintiffs collected 7,000 pages of FBI and police files, with another 6,000 pages of sworn testimony from official and civilian witnesses. While Agent Held pleaded faulty memory to avoid revealing bureau activities, he could not conceal all of the FBI's moves against Earth First! In one instance, agents had targeted a subject named Mark Berry, whose only link to Earth First! was his friendship with a subject of the Arizona "Thermcon" sting operation. In pursuit of nonexistent crimes, the agents subjected Berry to wiretapping and physical surveillance, read his mail, and circled his home with aircraft. Once, a pregnant woman agent and her male partner visited Berry's cabinet shop in the guise of a married couple seeking baby furniture. It came to nothing, and the Thermcon file was officially closed in January 1990, but Agent Held's San Francisco office kept adding new reports until March—two months before the Bari-Cherney bombing. Earth First! abandoned "monkeywrenching" after 1990, supplanted in that regard by the EARTH LIBERATION FRONT.

On October 15, 1997, a federal judge ruled that six G-men and three Oakland police officers should face trial on the charges, while ex-Agent Held and others were dismissed from the lawsuit on a grant of "qualified immunity." More delays followed, including a postponement occasioned by the terrorist attacks of September 11, 2001, when both sides agreed that the catastrophe might influence jurors.

The Bari-Cherney trial began at last on April 8, 2002. On May 15 Judge Claudia Wilken dismissed two more defendants, former G-men John Conway and Walter Hemje, from the case on grounds of insufficient evidence. Finally, after six weeks of testimony and 11 days of deliberation, the 10-member jury returned its verdict on June 11, 2002. The panel found that six remaining defendants had indeed violated Bari and Cherney's constitutional rights to free speech and protection from unlawful searches, awarding damages in the amount of $4.4 million. Those found guilty by the jury included retired G-men Frank Doyle, John Reikes, and Phil Sena; Oakland police Sgt. Robert Chenault; retired Oakland police Sgt. Michael Sitterud; and former Oakland police Lt. Mike Sims (now with the Tracy Police Department). A seventh defendant, former FBI agent Stockton Buck, was cleared on all counts. The jury's award included $2.9 million for Bari's estate ($1.6 million in compensatory damages, $1.3 million punitive) and $1.5 million to Cherney ($850,000 compensatory and $650,000 punitive). The various defendants filed a notice of appeal on September 6, 2002, claiming that the jury's award was "excessive" and "unsupported by evidence."

EARTH Liberation Front

Unhappy with the moderate course of action charted by the environmentalist group EARTH FIRST! after 1990, more-radical activists met to organize the Earth Liberation Front (ELF) at Brighton, England, in 1992. According to its video *Igniting the Revolution*, ELF sprang from a realization "that to be successful in the struggle to protect the Earth, more extreme tactics must be utilized." The first such actions on record from October 1996 include the burning of a U.S. Forest Service truck in Detroit and the destruction of an Oregon ranger station (causing $5.3 million in damage). Since then, a six-year series of arson incidents claimed by ELF include attacks on a fur breeders co-op ($1 million damage); a fast-food restaurant ($400,000); a ski resort ($12 million); a U.S. Forest Industries facility ($500,000); a Michigan State University research facility ($400,000); Boulder, Colorado's, Legend Ridge mansion ($2.5 million); a Minnesota genetics research lab ($250,000); two houses near Ann Arbor, Michigan ($400,000),

Emergency personnel walk past an automobile destroyed in a predawn arson fire at an auto dealership where Hummers were defaced with antipollution graffiti in West Covina, California, on August 22, 2003. Scrawled on at least one of the vehicles that was not destroyed by the blaze were the letters ELF, the acronym for the radical Earth Liberation Front. (Reuters/Corbis)

plus various other homes, commercial offices, and vehicles. Small-scale activities include roving acts of vandalism and tree spiking.

The FEDERAL BUREAU OF INVESTIGATION (FBI) labels ELF a terrorist organization, but its investigations have produced no noteworthy results thus far. On April 5, 2001, G-men raided the Portland, Oregon, home occupied by ELF spokesmen Craig Rosebraugh and Leslie James Pickering, seeking evidence in recent arson attacks, but they came away empty-handed. Frank Ambrose, a 27-year-old "suspected" ELF activist, was charged with tree spiking in Bloomington, Indiana, at about the same time, but prosecutors dismissed the charges "in the interests of justice" on September 13, 2001, after declaring their suspicion of "a widespread conspiracy" behind the tree-spiking incidents. Defense attorney Richard Kammen took a different view of the dismissal. "It was very clear," he told reporters, "that the state's case was based on wild speculation without any support of the facts. There just wasn't any evidence."

ELF, meanwhile, seemed intent on carrying its battle to the enemy. Protesters picketed the Bloomington FBI office during a "Week of Resistance" in April 2001, and ELF's Web site went further, declaring that the group would henceforth target "FBI offices and U.S. federal buildings," "liberal democracy," and even "industrial civilization" at large. Thus far, no such sweeping attacks have occurred.

EAST Coast Conspiracy to Save Lives (ECCSL)

This self-styled conspiracy was organized by brothers Daniel and Philip Berrigan (both priests of the CATHOLIC CHURCH); its limited membership consisting of nuns and assorted friends who opposed America's involvement in the VIETNAM War. Its actions included sabotage of railroad equipment near a munitions factory and invasion of local draft boards where blood was poured over various files. Some reports also credit the ECCSL (perhaps erroneously) with the 1971 burglary of a FEDERAL BUREAU OF INVESTIGATION (FBI) resident agency in Media, Pennsylvania, that exposed the bureau's illegal COINTELPRO operations to public scrutiny. Before that happened, though, bureau director J. EDGAR HOOVER exposed the group with claims of a deadly plot to undermine U.S. foreign policy—and thus fueled growing ridicule that would hound him to his death in 1972.

On November 30, 1970, Hoover made his regular appearance before a U.S. Senate appropriations committee, pleading for an extra $14.1 million to hire extra agents and clerks in the face of a "radical crime wave." To prove his need Hoover revealed "an incipient plot on the part of an anarchist group . . . the so-called 'East Coast Conspiracy to Save Lives'" to kidnap HENRY KISSINGER while planting bombs at various strategic sites around Washington, D.C. "If successful," Hoover warned, "the plotters would demand an end to United States bombing operations in Southeast Asia and the release of all political prisoners as ransom. Intensive investigation is being conducted concerning this matter." In fact, Attorney General John Mitchell had been aware of the "plot" since June 1970 when Sister Elizabeth McAlister facetiously suggested the kidnapping in a jailhouse love letter to Philip Berrigan. (Their courier was an FBI informer who delivered copies of their private correspondence to the bureau.) Mitchell and President RICHARD NIXON had agreed that there was no danger and refused to prosecute, while Kissinger himself laughed off the "threat" as a daydream concocted by "sex-starved nuns." Hoover's public statements, however, placed Mitchell in a bind where he must either reprimand the longtime FBI director (and keeper of career-destroying secrets) or file conspiracy charges against the "plotters."

On January 12, 1971, a federal grand jury indicted six defendants on charges of conspiring to snatch Kissinger and bomb various Washington landmarks. Those charged included the Berrigan brothers (both already jailed for antiwar activities), Sister McAlister, Father Neil McLaughlin, Father Joseph Wenderoth, Anthony Scoblick (a married priest), and Dr. Eqbal Ahmad. A new indictment on February 8, 1971, added defendant Joseph Glick to the list while expanding the charges to include destruction of government property (draft files) and conspiracy to possess explosives. At trial most of the charges filed against the "Harrisburg 8" proved to be products of fantasy or machinations by an FBI agent provocateur. On April 5, 1972, jurors convicted Philip Berrigan and Elizabeth McAlister on seven counts of smuggling letters in and out of federal prison. The panel deadlocked at 10–2 for acquittal of the other defendants on all charges, and the case was later dismissed. After serving his time, Philip Berrigan left the priesthood and married McAlister, organized a new "Plowshare" pacifist movement, and continued antimilitary demonstrations unabated until his death in 2003.

EAST Timor

Timor, in the East Indies, was first colonized by POR-TUGAL in 1520. Holland seized the western portion of the island in 1613 and fought Portugal for the rest until a treaty divided Timor between them in 1860. Australia and JAPAN fought for the island in World War II, killing 50,000 natives in the process. In 1949 the Netherlands ceded control of West Timor to the fledgling state of INDONESIA, but Portugal held the remainder until 1975 when its sudden withdrawal left the new Democratic Republic of East Timor vulnerable to invasion. To no one's surprise, Indonesia (sanctioned by the United States and other western nations) attacked and annexed the region in July 1976. For the next two decades, largely ignored by the rest of the world, Indonesia's brutal occupation of East Timor killed an estimated 300,000 persons. Human-rights abuses finally went public in the 1990s, and two East Timorese activists won the Nobel Peace Prize in 1996 for nonviolent efforts to liberate their homeland. Violence in East Timor escalated until August 1999 when 79 percent of the population voted for independence in a special referendum sponsored by the UNITED NATIONS. A UN transitional force then governed East Timor until August 2002 when the first new country of a new millennium elected native leaders. In August 2002 former governor Abilio Soares was convicted of crimes against humanity by an Indonesian court. Six other defendants were acquitted at the same time in a verdict widely condemned as a whitewash of Indonesia's WAR CRIMES.

ECHELON

"Echelon" is the code-name applied to a SIGINT (signals intelligence) collection network operated by the U.S. NATIONAL SECURITY AGENCY in conjunction with Britain, Canada, Australia, and New Zealand. Its satellite listening posts reportedly include five in the continental United States, three in Australia, two in Britain, and one each in Cyprus, Germany, Guam, Hong Kong, Japan, and Puerto Rico. Together, as reported in the European press, those stations have a capacity to "record up to two billion telephone messages daily." (Other accounts go further, claiming that Echelon collects every phone call, FAX message, and e-mail on Earth.) Once the signals are collected, "dictionary" computers scan the text at high speed, seeking verbal "warnings"—that is, random words or phrases such as *assassinate, bomb, CIA, C-4, FBI, militia, revolt, terrorism,* and so on ad infinitum. The quality of Echelon's analysis was revealed when Mike Frost, a former Canadian intelligence agent, told CBS News that "one woman ended up in Echelon's database as a possible terrorist because she told a friend on the phone that her son had 'bombed' in a school play." Spying may also have a commercial side, according to the *New York Times*. That newspaper's report on Echelon asserted that information gleaned from SIGINT eavesdropping helped the Boeing aerospace firm to win a lucrative Saudi Arabian contract away from a European competitor and that Echelon data also helped the U.S. firm Raytheon "win a bid for a $1.3 billion surveillance system for the Amazon forest away from Thomson-CSF, a French company." In short, for the right people, Echelon elevates insider trading to a whole new level—as in outer space. In early 2001 the European Union (EU) issued a report condemning Echelon, based on declassified documents and testimony from former intelligence agents, but the EU has no authority to ban the system and no technical means of disabling it. For conspiracists, Echelon is icing on the cake—proof positive that Big Brother has finally arrived.

ECUADOR

Spanish conquistador Francisco Pizarro conquered the Inca rulers of modern-day Ecuador in 1532, and SPAIN controlled the region until 1809 when rebels expelled the colonial rulers, joining COLOMBIA, PANAMA, and VENEZUELA in a confederacy dubbed Greater Colombia. That union collapsed in 1830, and Ecuador declared independence. A seemingly endless series of rebellions and dictatorships then ensued, with 48 different rulers installed during the next 131 years. As if internal conflict were not bad enough, Ecuador was rocked by border wars with neighboring PERU in 1941, 1981, and 1995. A treaty signed in May 1991 finally resolved the territorial dispute, but Ecuador's problems continue, including a nearly bankrupt economy and widespread poverty. A coup toppled President Jamil Mahuad in January 2000, marking South America's first military revolt in a decade. Belated investigations have revealed that most of Ecuador's "leftist" groups in the 1960s were created by the CENTRAL INTELLIGENCE AGENCY either to pacify impoverished workers or to justify continuing dictatorship. According to Quito's chamber of commerce, Ecuador loses $2 billion yearly (11.2 percent of the country's Gross Domestic Product) to flagrant corruption.

EGYPT

Egypt's history dates from around 4000 B.C., its "golden age" occurring between the 16th and 13th centuries B.C. Persia (now IRAN) conquered Egypt in 525 B.C., followed by Alexander the Great (332 B.C.), Rome (30 B.C.), Arab caliphs (A.D. 641), TURKEY (1517), and FRANCE (1801). Mohammed Ali, backed by troops from ALBANIA, became pasha of Egypt in 1805. Britain occupied the country in 1882 and formally declared it a protectorate in 1914. Egyptian nationalism forced England to grant independence in February 1922, though London reserved rights to guard the Suez Canal and to defend Egypt from perceived enemies. British troops were finally withdrawn (except from the Suez Canal Zone) in 1936, but World War II brought them back in full force. Anti-British riots during 1951–52 climaxed with a military coup in July 1952. The Egyptian monarchy was abolished 11 months later, leaving General Mohammed Naguib as provisional president. In fact, a military junta controlled Egypt, and its leader—Gamal Abdel Nasser—ascended to the presidency on June 23, 1956.

Nasser's stubborn refusal to placate the United States and Britain placed him in constant conflict with London and Washington. Accordingly, he sought and received aid from RUSSIA, nationalized the Suez Canal Zone, and expelled British OIL executives from Egypt. In October 1956 ISRAEL invaded the Gaza Strip and the Sinai peninsula, while Britain and France launched attacks of their own against Egypt. Global pressure ultimately halted the attack, UNITED NATIONS (UN) peacekeepers were dispatched to Suez, and foreign troops finally withdrew in spring 1957. Egypt joined SYRIA to form the United Arab Republic (UAR) in 1956, and while a coup forced Syria to withdraw from the alliance in 1961, Egypt continued use of the UAR name for another decade. Israel, meanwhile, launched another invasion in June 1967, occupying Sinai, the East Bank of the Jordan

River, and a zone around the Gulf of Aqaba. Fighting continued around Suez through June 1970, despite a UN cease-fire dating from June 10, 1967.

Nasser died in September 1970 and was replaced by ANWAR AL-SADAT. Angered by Russia's refusal to provide sophisticated weapons, Sadat expelled Soviet advisors in July 1972. Fifteen months later Egypt launched a campaign to expel Israel from occupied Sinai, but the effort failed. Sadat risked his political career in November 1977 with a visit to Israel and pleas for a permanent peace. While Arab nations raged, Egypt and Israel signed a peace treaty on March 26, 1979. Muslim extremists in the Egyptian army murdered Sadat in October 1981. Successor Hosni Mubarak (still in power at this writing) has devoted much of his time to suppressing Islamic extremists, including those responsible for serial attacks on Egyptian Christians (Copts).

EICHMANN, Adolf (1906–1962)

A native of GERMANY, born in 1906, Adolf Eichmann moved to Linz, AUSTRIA, (ADOLF HITLER's hometown) with his family following his mother's death. In Linz, classmates teased him mercilessly about his looks, calling him "the little Jew." He dropped out of engineering school to work various jobs, including a stint as traveling salesman for a U.S. OIL company. Eichmann joined the Austrian Nazi Party in 1932, soon graduating to the "elite" SS and serving at the Dachau concentration camp in 1934. That September, he moved up to the SS security service, first cataloging information on FREEMASONS, then shifting to the Jewish Section where an obsession with Hebrew culture soon earned him recognition as a "Jewish specialist." HEINRICH HIMMLER appointed Eichmann to head a Scientific Museum of Jewish Affairs with the collateral assignment of researching "solutions to the Jewish question." In 1939 Eichmann was chosen to head GESTAPO Section IV B4, tasked with implementing Nazi anti-Semitic policies in all occupied countries (ultimately spanning 16 nations). In July 1940 Eichmann proposed deporting all Jews to Madagascar, but the plan was never implemented. Meanwhile, he supervised the establishment of ghettos in occupied Poland and collected statistics from roving Einsatzgruppen murder teams. Eichmann coordinated the WANNSEE CONFERENCE in January 1942, where Nazi leaders hammered out details of the impending "final solution," and he thereafter served as technical manager of the ensuing HOLOCAUST, a veritable accountant of mass murder. Although he later tried to portray himself as no more than a middle-rank bean counter, Eichmann told one colleague "he would leap laughing into the grave because the feeling that he had five million people on his conscience would be for him a source of extraordinary satisfaction."

The THIRD REICH's collapse left Eichmann at risk of prosecution for WAR CRIMES, but the Allies were slow to close the net, and he escaped to ARGENTINA in 1950 with assistance from the ODESSA network. There, Eichmann lived in ease and affluence as "Ricardo Klement" for a decade when agents of the Israeli MOSSAD learned his whereabouts and kidnapped him on May 11, 1960. Transported to ISRAEL, Eichmann was placed on public trial. He tried to minimize his crimes, asking the court, "Why me? Why not the local policemen, thousands of them? They would have been shot if they had refused to round up the Jews for the death camps. Why not hang them for not wanting to be shot? Why me? Everybody killed the Jews." Eichmann's judges were predictably unmoved by his argument, convicting him on all charges and imposing a sentence of death. He was hanged at Ramleh Prison on May 31, 1962.

ELECTION 2000

The 2000 presidential election takes dubious honors as the most controversial political contest in U.S. history, eclipsing the corrupt bargain struck by RUTHERFORD B. HAYES in 1877 and John Kennedy's narrow (MAFIA-assisted) victory over RICHARD NIXON in 1960. The controversy endures to this day.

By 8:00 P.M. on election day (November 7), all major TV networks forecast that Vice President Al Gore would defeat Republican contender George W. Bush, but late-breaking events in Florida (where brother Jeb Bush reigned as governor) cast the election into chaos. Both sides anxiously awaited tallies from the Florida panhandle, where reports of defective ballots and voting machines vied with rumors of outright fraud in progress. On November 9 Gore's team requested a hand count of votes from four disputed Florida counties, and a circuit judge ordered Palm Beach County not to certify its disputed results. The state's machine count was completed on November 10, giving Bush a microscopic lead of 327 ballots amid 6 million cast. With hand counts proceeding on

November 12, Bush attorneys (led by James Baker, once secretary of state under President George H. W. Bush) filed a federal motion to halt the recount. That motion was rejected on November 13, whereupon Florida Secretary of State Katherine Harris (a Bush campaign leader) announced that she would not extend the 5:00 P.M. deadline on November 14 for receiving all votes. On November 15, while media reports shrank Bush's lead to 286 votes out of 6 million, Harris asked the state supreme court to halt manual recounts. On November 16 Bush attorneys filed their second motion to halt the recounts, and they were again rejected. One day later the Florida Supreme Court blocked Harris from certifying a Bush victory, and on November 21 the judges ordered hand counts to continue. Bush running mate DICK CHENEY suffered his fourth heart attack on November 22 and was rushed into cardiac surgery.

The action shifted to Washington on November 23, 2001, when the U.S. SUPREME COURT agreed to hear Bush's appeal of his lawsuit's two-time rejection. Back in Florida Katherine Harris disqualified all votes from Palm Beach County and then certified Bush's victory by 537 votes. Gore's lawyers filed a new legal action, contending that Harris wrongfully disqualified thousands of mostly black Democratic votes. In Washington the Supreme Court heard oral arguments on December 1. Seven days later the Florida Supreme Court ordered manual recounts in all disputed counties, a ruling canceled one day later by a 5–4 decision of the U.S. Supreme Court. On December 12, 2000, the same five-judge majority (all appointed either by Bush's father or by predecessor RONALD REAGAN) effectively certified Bush as the president-elect. (Even so, Bush *lost* the popular vote by some 539,000 ballots, but his "victory" in Florida assured a majority where it mattered, in the U.S. Electoral College.)

The Supreme Court majority's argument, that a Florida recount would cause Bush "irreparable harm"—that is, loss of the White House—struck many observers as a blatant payoff for the life appointments bestowed by prior Republican presidents. Justice Antonin Scalia proved that suspicion correct when he wrote, in approving Bush's plea for a ban on recounts, that "the issuance of the stay suggests that a majority of the Court, while not deciding the issues presented, believe that the petitioner [Bush] has a substantial probability of success." Furthermore, the Court's majority declared that its "logic" in supporting Bush would have no future application to any other case but was strictly "limited to the present circumstances, for the problem of equal protection in election processes generally presents many complexities." As author Vincent Bugliosi noted, "This point . . . all alone and by itself, clearly and unequivocally shows that the Court knew its decision was not based on the merits or the law, and was solely a decision to appoint George Bush President." Justice John Stevens III affirmed that view in his dissenting opinion when he wrote, "Although we may never know with complete certainty the identity of the winner of this year's presidential election, the identity of the loser is perfectly clear. It is the nation's confidence in [this Court] as an impartial guardian of the rule of law." Unmentioned in that opinion were the blatant conflicts of interest that should have caused two pro-Bush justices to abstain from hearing the case: A son of Justice Antonin Scalia was employed by the law firm that filed suit on Bush's behalf, while the wife of Justice Clarence Thomas worked for the Heritage Foundation, busily vetting future Bush appointees at the time her husband helped appoint Bush to the Oval Office.

See also BUSH DYNASTY; KENNEDY DYNASTY.

EL RUKNS

In the early 1960s Chicago's most notorious STREET GANG was the Blackstone Rangers, founded by a group of 12–15-year-old youths in the Woodlawn ghetto and led by Jeff Fort. By 1967 Blackstone was the first ghetto gang to "go national," with chapters in Cleveland, Milwaukee, and Gary, Indiana. Two years later, during brief political flirtation with the BLACK PANTHER PARTY, the gang became a target of the FEDERAL BUREAU OF INVESTIGATION's (FBI) illegal COINTELPRO operations. G-men used agents provocateurs to incite violent dissension between the two groups, but J. EDGAR HOOVER's plan to have the Rangers kill local Panther boss FRED HAMPTON failed, leaving the job to members of the CHICAGO POLICE DEPARTMENT. Fort later renamed his gang the Black P. Stone Nation and then El Rukns after he converted to Islam while serving time on federal drug charges.

Religious epiphany did not prevent the El Rukns from engaging in criminal activity, however. Sometime in 1985–86, NATION OF ISLAM leader Louis Farrakhan adopted the gang as a kind of personal honor guard, reportedly introducing them to one international audience as his "angels of death" (not to be confused, presumably, with DEATH ANGELS). In due course, El Rukns leaders met agents representing Colonel MUAMMAR AL-QADDAFFI of LIBYA and allegedly accepted $2.5 million in return for a promise to commit acts of TERRORISM in the United States. El Rukns defenders, meanwhile, insist that the streetwise gangsters "didn't know what they were getting into" and were led astray by a mixed bag of foreign extremists, CENTRAL INTELLIGENCE AGENCY (CIA) "moles," and various FBI-police informers. Some versions of the story claim that Qaddaffi shipped a rocket launcher to the gang, but U.S. agents intercepted the package and replaced its trigger mechanism with a tracking device and then followed it to gang headquarters. A different story, advanced by federal prosecutors at trial, was that the gang purchased an "inert" U.S.-made rocket launcher from an undercover FBI agent on July 31, 1986. Five days later G-men raided the gang's headquarters and seized a small arsenal of weapons, including the defective bazooka. Fort and six others were subsequently convicted of conspiracy to commit terrorist acts. Defendant Melvin Mayes evaded arrest and fled into hiding.

Federal officers were still patting themselves on the back for that coup when certain problems with their case leaked to the media. It was disclosed that prosecutor William Hogan, Jr.—reportedly a veteran of both the U.S. Army Special Forces and the CIA—had favored certain prosecution witnesses not only with immunity from prosecution but also with nonstop liquor, drugs, and women while they spun their tales in custody. On at least one occasion, the "witnesses" were also allegedly removed from prison on Hogan's orders to enjoy a respite from confinement at Chicago's Federal Building. Intimations of perjury swirled around the case, while Hogan cast himself as an abused middleman in the proceedings. If any impropriety occurred, he told the press, the wrongful acts had been arranged and supervised by his superiors. That coterie, in turn, included federal judges in Chicago who, according to Hogan, were deeply immersed in corruption themselves. One of the accused jurists, whose estimated net worth topped $140 million in some stories, admitted under oath in an unrelated proceeding that he had not filed a valid income tax return in three decades. No charges were finally filed against Hogan, and despite various expressions of public outrage, all appeals from the convicted El Rukns were denied.

EL SALVADOR

SPAIN conquered the Central American region of modern El Salvador in 1525 and ruled with typical brutality until September 1821. Numerous revolutions and border wars with neighbors consumed most of the years from independence to 1931 when a series of military juntas assumed control through 1979. Civil war erupted in the 1970s between the ruling right-wing Nationalist Republican Alliance (ARENA) and a mixed bag of leftist groups spearheaded by the Farabundo Martí National Liberation Front (FMLN). Despite an abysmal record of human rights violations, "moderate" dictator José Napoleón Duarte (1984–89) received massive infusions of U.S. military aid, justified by President RONALD REAGAN as an attempt "to halt the infiltration into the Americas, by terrorists and by outside interference, and those who aren't just aiming at El Salvador, but, I think, are aiming at the whole of Central and possibly later South America and, I'm sure, eventually North America." Still, despite rural massacres and pervasive use of torture, Duarte failed to crush the insurgents, and he was replaced in 1989 by ARENA strongman Alfredo Cristiani. A cease-fire agreement leaving ARENA firmly in command of the government was signed in January 1992 after 12 years of war and 75,000 deaths. In 2000 President Francisco Flores approved construction of a U.S. military base in El Salvador, presumably to interdict COCAINE shipments bound for North America.

EMPRISE Corporation

On June 2, 1976, Arizona journalist Don Bolles was mortally wounded in Phoenix when a bomb exploded beneath his car. As bystanders rushed to help him, Bolles gasped out, "They finally got me. The MAFIA. Emprise. Find John Adamson." By the time he died on June 13, a crack team of reporters was pursuing the story that led Bolles to his death. The Mafia was already well known, represented in Arizona since 1946 by the Detroit-based Licavoli family. Bolles had been investigating Licavoli ties to an illegal racing wire service and to Kemper Marley, Arizona's top liquor dealer. Stories written by Bolles that exposed Marley's role as supplier of booze served at various dog-racing tracks had forced Marley to resign from the State Racing Commission. Emprise Corporation managed those dog tracks, but as reporters soon discovered, that was only the tip of the iceberg.

Emprise began in 1915 with brothers Charles, Louis, and Marvin Jacobs selling peanuts and popcorn at theaters and minor-league ballparks in Buffalo, New York. By 1930 they were major-league concessionaires, expanding to racetracks in 1939 and airport restaurants two years later. Such rapid advancement in mob-dominated entertainment spheres came with a price tag. In 1966–67 Lou Jacobs "loaned" $712,000 to Michigan Mafiosi Anthony Zerilli and Anthony Giordano (owners of a racetrack where Emprise ran concessions), and the mobsters used that money to buy an illegal hidden interest in a LAS VEGAS casino. Lou Jacobs was dead by 1972 when a federal jury in Los Angeles convicted Emprise of conspiracy and slapped the corporation with a $10,000 fine. That was pocket change to CEO Jeremy Jacobs, who expanded the firm's range into national flea-market concessions four years later. Moved by adverse publicity from the Bolles bombing, Jeremy Jacobs changed the company's name to Delaware North Companies and sought a presidential pardon from President Jimmy Carter in 1977, claiming that the firm had severed all underworld ties. Carter refused to oblige, but the snub proved no handicap to business. In 1992, under President George H. W. Bush, Delaware North inked a lucrative contract to manage concessions in U.S. national parks. By 2001 the company ranked 153rd in the Forbes Private 500, with an estimated $1.5 billion in annual revenue. One of Delaware North's many subsidiaries is Sportsystems, the largest owner–operator of parimutuel facilities in the United States. Estimates of Jerry Jacobs's personal net worth average $400 million, but reporters note that "because his business is so private, the estimate may be low."

Privacy also surrounds the financial and political connections of Emprise/Delaware North. Few casual observers know that the firm is a major stockholder in Bally Manufacturing, world's largest producer of casino slot machines. In Arkansas, where Emprise/Delaware runs dog tracks, the firm and family were once substantial donors to Governor Bill Clinton. The family's Marine Midland Bank of Buffalo, New York, also has extensive business ties to the Bush family—and, according to various Internet conspiracy Web sites, with a "British and Chinese royalty-owned" bank in Hong Kong, directed by "the reputed North American chief of the Red Chinese Secret Police." ("He has a direct link by FAX to the White House," we are warned.) Meanwhile, speaking to the

Boston Globe in 2001, disgruntled ex-employee Larry Moulter said of Jeremy Jacobs, "There's no soul there. He runs his business and his life by the numbers."

Emprise was never directly linked to the Bolles murder case. Phoenix police theorized that Kemper Marley sought revenge on Bolles, employing local contractor Max Dunlap, who in turn hired greyhound breeder John Adamson to plant the bomb (assisted by plumber James Robison). Adamson pleaded guilty to second-degree murder on January 15, 1977, accepting a 20-year prison term in return for testimony against Dunlap and Robison. At their trial in July 1977 Dunlap's attorney fingered Phoenix lawyer Neal Roberts as the plot's mastermind. On November 6, 1977, both defendants were convicted of murdering Bolles and of plotting to kill two more Marley enemies. Both were sentenced to die, but Arizona's Supreme Court overturned their convictions in February 1980. Charges against both men were dismissed in June 1980 when Adamson refused to testify at a second trial. Accordingly, Adamson's plea bargain was revoked, and a jury convicted him of first-degree murder in October 1980. His death sentence was overturned in May 1986, then reinstated, and then reversed again in December 1988. New murder charges were filed against Robison in November 1989 and against Dunlap in December 1980. They were granted separate trials, with Dunlap convicted in April 1993 and sentenced to life with no parole for 25 years. Robison was acquitted in December 1993, despite admissions on the witness stand that he asked a fellow inmate to murder John Adamson. In 1995 he received a five-year sentence for soliciting criminal violence. Adamson was released into the federal witness protection program on August 12, 1996. Kemper Marley, never charged in the case, died of cancer on June 25, 1990.

See also BUSH DYNASTY; CLINTON, BILL AND HILLARY.

ENDOVASCULAR Technologies

EndoVascular Technologies Incorporated is a subsidiary of Guidant Corporation, based in Menlo Park, California. One of its major products was a fabric graft that was surgically inserted through incisions in the human groin to reinforce weak spots or bulges in the aorta. Roughly one-third of the devices shipped by the manufacturer malfunctioned before the product was recalled and corrected in 2001,

claiming at least 12 lives and forcing dozens of other patients to undergo emergency surgery to repair the defects. Federal law required EndoVascular to inform the Food and Drug Administration (FDA) of serious malfunctions in its product, and while the firm reported 172 cases, it illegally concealed 2,628 others. Company sales representatives also entered operating rooms and coached surgeons through untested, unapproved procedures to break off part of the defective device and extract it from various patients. When a subject died during one such operation, seven employees sent an anonymous letter to the FDA, triggering an investigation that led to a recall of the product in early 2001.

While the product was reportedly corrected and returned to the market in 2001 with FDA approval, EndoVascular would not escape prosecution for its offenses. In filing charges, U.S. Attorney Kevin Ryan declared, "Because of the company's conduct, thousands of patients underwent surgeries without knowing the risks they faced, and their doctors—through no fault of their own—were unprepared to deal with those risks." In July 2003 EndoVascular Technologies pleaded guilty on 10 felony charges, including selling a "misbranded" medical device and making a false statement to the Food and Drug Administration. The firm agreed to pay a fine of $92.4 million to settle the case. Parent company Guidant (a 1990s spin off of the Eli Lilly PHARMACEUTICAL COMPANY) declared $612 million in profits for 2002 on total sales of $3.2 billion.

ENRON

Founded in 1985 the Enron corporation began to trade natural-gas commodities four years later and launched the first global commodity-trading Web site in November 1999. Nine months later Enron chairman Kenneth Lay contributed more than $290,000 to the campaign fund of GOP presidential candidate George W. Bush. It came as no surprise, therefore, when Lay was appointed as an advisor to President-elect Bush's transition team in January 2001, while Enron backer Patrick Wood III became Bush's chairman of the Federal Energy Regulatory Commission. Top Bush advisor Karl Rove waited another six months to divest himself of Enron stock worth $100,000, all the while meeting with Enron officials to plan the new administration's energy policy (including tax cuts and expanded drilling in protected

A panel of legal witnesses is sworn in to testify before the U.S. House of Representatives Committee on Energy and Commerce Subcommittee on Oversight and Investigations hearing on the financial collapse of Enron Corporation, focusing on the inside and outside legal advice the company received concerning its business conduct. (Ron Sachs/Corbis)

areas). On October 16, 2001, following conversations between Lay and Commerce Secretary Donald Evans, Enron stunned investors with a report of $618 million in losses and a $1.2 billion reduction in shareholder equity. The SEC launched an investigation into rumored conflicts of interest, while the INTERNAL REVENUE SERVICE revealed Enron's $50,000 campaign contribution to House Majority Whip Tom DeLay.

The scandal spread from there. In November 2001 Enron filed documents with the SEC "revising" its financial statements for the past five years to account for $586 million in losses. A month later the company filed for Chapter 11 bankruptcy protection, dismissed 4,000 employees and borrowed $1.5 billion to keep operating while in bankruptcy. The JUSTICE DEPARTMENT announced a criminal investigation of Enron on January 10, 2002, but Attorney General JOHN ASHCROFT recused himself on grounds that Enron had donated $57,499 to his Missouri political campaigns in 1999–2000. Twelve days later an ex-Enron employee revealed mass shredding of documents after the Securities and Exchange Commission (SEC) investigation was announced in October 2001. Federal Bureau of Investigation (FBI) agents began to pursue that claim on January 23, 2002, and Ken Lay

resigned as Enron's CEO the same day. On January 25 former Enron vice chairman J. Clifford Baxter was found dead in his car, an apparent suicide.

With Attorney General Ashcroft sidelined, the Justice Department instructed President Bush to preserve all documents related to his dealings with Enron, and White House aides agreed. Skeptics questioned whether the warning came too late, but Senate investigators were preoccupied with Kenneth Lay and his associates as past and present Enron executives claimed their Fifth Amendment privilege to avoid giving testimony. The White House also favored stony silence, prompting the General Accounting Office to file an unprecedented lawsuit against Vice President DICK CHENEY on February 23, 2002, demanding release of documents detailing his involvement with Enron and President Bush's energy task force. (At this writing, in January 2003, Cheney was appealing court orders to release those documents.) In March 2002 Army Secretary Thomas White—another ex-Enron executive, holder of 200,000 company shares—publicly denied any improper contact with Enron colleagues; at the same time, he released a list of 44 previously undisclosed phone calls to Enron officials preceding sale of his stock.

In April 2002, while President Bush belatedly called for imprisonment of dishonest corporate executives, the House passed accounting reform legislation including stricter oversight and disclosure provisions. August 2002 saw the first Enron conviction as former executive Michael Kopper pleaded guilty to money laundering and wire fraud. Three weeks later, on September 13, 2002, three British bankers were indicted on wire-fraud charges related to the Enron case. Andrew Fastow, Enron's one-time chief financial officer, was indicted by a federal grand jury on October 31, 2002. His charges included 78 counts of wire and mail fraud, money laundering, and conspiracy to inflate Enron's profits.

Revelation of Enron's illicit activities continued in 2003. On February 4 former Enron trader Jeffrey Richter pleaded guilty on two felony counts in California, including conspiracy to commit wire fraud and lying to the FBI. Prosecutors charged that Richter "was in charge of trading schemes that defrauded California consumers" by manipulating the state's energy market and falsifying information, thereby creating a near-catastrophic power shortage in California during 2000, while Enron's profits increased 15-fold. (State authorities are seeking an $8.9 billion refund in that price-gouging conspiracy.) On March 13, 2003, two more former Enron executives—Kevin Howard and Michael Krautz—surrendered in Houston to face charges of securities fraud, wire fraud, and lying to the FBI. The SEC further charged the pair with falsifying records and quarterly reports on an Internet video scheme that authorities describe as "a sham from its inception." On May 1, 2003, the number of Enron indictees reached 19 as federal prosecutors in Houston charged seven more defendants (including Andrew Fastow's wife) with various counts in the same "pump-and-dump" stock manipulation plot. With trials and additional charges pending, it remains to be seen whether Enron's convoluted plots will further stain the Bush White House.

See also BUSH DYNASTY.

ENVIRONMENTAL Protection Agency (EPA)

Created by President RICHARD NIXON in 1971, the EPA has been a source of controversy ever since. In the agency's own words, it was launched because "[T]he federal government was not structured to make a coordinated attack on the pollutants that harm human health and degrade the environment.

The EPA was assigned the daunting task of repairing the damage already done to the natural environment and to establish new criteria to guide Americans in making a cleaner environment a reality." Its first chief under Nixon, William Ruckleshaus, later served briefly as director of the Federal Bureau of Investigation (FBI) and as deputy attorney general (fired by Nixon for refusal to collaborate in the WATERGATE cover-up).

While any agency started by Nixon is naturally suspect, the EPA ostensibly has no mission other than protecting Earth's environment and thus safeguarding human life. In that pursuit, however, it frequently clashes with the same polluting industries that have supported far-right groups in the United States since the turn of the last century. It is no surprise, therefore, that various MILITIA groups and factions of the "WISE USE" MOVEMENT denounce the EPA as a tool of ZOG, COMMUNISM, or the NEW WORLD ORDER. Cooperation between the EPA and various branches of the UNITED NATIONS provide further "evidence" of some vast, vague conspiracy afoot, and criticism of the EPA is further encouraged by conservative leaders (like George W. Bush) who favor OIL drilling in national parks, relaxation of air pollution standards, and other profit-minded schemes to roll back conservation efforts that span 30 years. Another sore point with far-right conspiracists is the EPA's friendly relationship with private environmentalist groups such as the Sierra Club. As one anonymous Internet scribe summarizes the menace:

> It's really no surprise that many millions of tax dollars go out in grants each year to the very environmental groups wanting every little critter and bug in the world protected by law. In fact, it is quite common in Washington for a department or agency to give funds to private, nonprofit groups, which then turn around and spend the money to advocate and lobby for more funds for the granting agency. That taxpayer funded a merry-go-round is the big joke among eco-whackos. They got us coming and going.

See also BUSH DYNASTY.

EQUATORIAL Guinea

Described by some modern observers as Africa's worst dictatorship, Equatorial Guinea was once the domain of forest-dwelling Pygmies. Portuguese

117

invaders seized control in the 17th century but ceded their colony to SPAIN in the 18th century. Britain briefly supplanted Spanish rule (1827–44) before Madrid regained control, ruling Spanish Guinea until independence was granted in October 1968. President Francisco Nguema—a self-described "Unique Miracle"—ranks among Africa's worst despots of all time. In 1971 a UNITED NATIONS report declared that his regime was "characterized by abandonment of all government functions except internal security, which was accomplished by terror; this led to the death or exile of up to one-third of the population." In August 1979 Nguema was finally ousted and executed by a nephew, Lt. Col. Teodoro Obiang, who remains in power today. Obiang retains many of his uncle's brutal methods, but he has slowly modernized the nation's economy, aided by discovery of off-shore OIL in the 1990s. As recently as 2002, 68 of Obiang's political opponents received stiff prison terms on charges of plotting to overthrow the government.

ERITREA

Eritrea was part of ETHIOPIA until the 16th century when it was occupied by troops of the Ottoman Empire. Italian troops captured a strip of coastal land in 1885, and the Treaty of Uccialli (1889) gave ITALY sovereign power in part of the region. Rome named the land after the Red Sea, Mare Erythraeum, and ruled until Britain captured the land in 1941. The territory was administered as a UNITED NATIONS trust until September 1952 when it was federated with Ethiopia. November 1962 saw Eritrea formally declared an Ethiopian province, but a war of independence instantly erupted, dragging on for the next 32 years. A coup toppled Ethiopia's dictatorship in 1991, and soldiers of the Eritrean People's Liberation Front soon captured the Eritrean capital (Asmara). In 1993 a referendum on Eritrean independence polled near-unanimous votes for a break with Ethiopia. Ethiopia recognized Eritrea's sovereignty in May 1993, but the new era of cooperation was short-

lived. In May 1998 border disputes exploded into military conflict, claiming an estimated 80,000 lives. It remains to be seen if either side will respect the new border established by an international boundary commission on April 2002.

ETHIOPIA

Originally called Abyssinia, Ethiopia was home to the oldest known ancestors of *Homo sapiens*. It is also sub-Saharan Africa's oldest state with a royal dynasty claiming direct descent from King Solomon. Ethiopia's influence peaked in the fifth century before it was weakened by feudal wars and isolated by the rising tide of Islam. Emperor Menelik II routed an Italian invasion in 1896 and thereafter expanded his nation by conquest. A cousin of Menelik's, Tafari Makonnen, was crowned Emperor Haile Selassie I in 1930 (and subsequently worshiped as a living god by members of the Rastafarian sect). ITALY invaded Ethiopia a second time in October 1935 and drove Selassie into exile seven months later. He returned to power at the end of World War II and sparked a bitter 40-year conflict by incorporating ERITREA as part of Ethiopia in 1952. Selassie was deposed in September 1974, with control of the government seized by a Provisional Military Administrative Council (also known as the Derg). In 1977 Lt. Col. Mengistu Haile Mariam assumed dictatorial power, waging ruthless "red terror" against Eritrean rebels and other dissenters. Thousands were killed before the Soviet collapse of 1991 deprived Mengistu of his primary support, and he was driven from office. In April 1996, 68 former military leaders were tried on charges that included genocide and crimes against humanity. New fighting soon erupted between Ethiopia and independent Eritrea (1998–2000) and cost another 80,000 lives before a cease-fire was declared. Meanwhile successive cycles of drought and famine have made Ethiopia an international symbol of natural disasters compounded by humans' inhumanity to fellow beings.

FALSE Memory Syndrome

The label *False Memory Syndrome* (FMS) was coined in 1993 as a means of discrediting various psychologists (and their patients) who were involved in therapy related to childhood sexual abuse. FMS believers maintain, in essence, that while some memories of traumatic events may be unconsciously suppressed on rare occasions, belatedly "recovered" memories of childhood molestation are nearly always "confabulated," typically with the assistance of therapists who are promoting some personal agenda. Despite its scientific sound, FMS remains unrecognized as a "syndrome" today by the American Psychological Association (APA) and its definitive *Diagnostic and Statistical Manual*. Critics note that most FMS proponents are either accused child molesters or well-paid professional defense witnesses, suggesting that they may be somewhat biased. Indeed at a 1993 conference on multiple personality disorder, Dr. Richard Lowenstein (a psychiatrist at the University of Maryland Medical School) denounced the fledgling False Memory Syndrome Foundation (FMSF) as "media-directed, dedicated to putting out disinformation." Some of the foundation's past and present leaders include:

Peter and Pamela Freed, who founded the FMSF after their daughter, University of Oregon psychology professor Jennifer Freed, accused Peter

of molesting her throughout childhood. Jennifer notes that her father "told various people that I was brain damaged," while her mother enlisted Dr. Harold Lief (her personal therapist, later an FMSF board member) to convince Jennifer that her memories were false. "He explained to me," Jennifer recalls, "that he did not believe I was abused. At times I am flabbergasted that my memory is considered 'false,' and my alcoholic father's memory is considered rational and sane." No criminal charges were ever filed against the Freeds.

Dr. Martin Orne, a colleague of Lief's at the University of Pennsylvania and a fellow FMSF board member, was also a participant in MIND-CONTROL experiments carried out by the CENTRAL INTELLIGENCE AGENCY (CIA) in the 1960s. Conspiracist Alex Constantine and others view Orne's FMSF involvement with deep suspicion, charging that the CIA itself perpetrates child abuse and creates cults for various sinister reasons.

Ralph Underwager, another founding FMSF member and longtime professional defense witness in molestation cases, "voluntarily" left the foundation's board of advisors following an interview with the Dutch pedophile journal *Paidika*, in which he stated that pedophilia was not only a "responsible" lifestyle but also "part of God's will." Underwager's wife (and coparticipant in that interview) remained on the foundation's board after his departure.

Richard Ofshe, a psychology professor and professional defense witness in criminal cases, suffered damage to his credibility when his publisher falsely advertised him as a Pulitzer Prize winner. (Ofshe was never nominated, much less awarded a Pulitzer.) With fellow FMSF board member Margaret Singer, Ofshe once filed a $30-million lawsuit against the APA under federal racketeering statutes, claiming that APA spokespersons used "repeated lies" to "discredit them and impair their careers." The case was dismissed.

Elizabeth Loftus, a psychology and FMSF board member, has served as a paid defense witness for such defendants as serial killer Ted Bundy, "Hillside Strangler" Angelo Buono, and Seattle mass murderer Willie Mak, assuring juries that eyewitnesses to the defendants' crimes were either lying or the victims of "false" memories. (Loftus now acknowledges her "error" in those cases.) A *New York Times* review of her memoirs suggested that "Her testimony would be less controversial if she could distinguish between the innocent and the guilty and reserve her help for the former." In April 1983 Loftus faced a lawsuit from U.S. Navy Lt. Nicole Taus (against whom Loftus testified in a child-custody case), accusing Loftus and other parties of "invasion of privacy, defamation, libel per se, negligent and intentional infliction of emotional distress and damages."

There is no doubt that some defendants in divorce and/or criminal cases have been falsely accused of various crimes. Whether the false accusations were malicious or "sincere" (that is, the product of deluded memories) is a matter for courts and qualified psychotherapists to decide. At the same time, organizations created by and for accused criminals and their hired defenders are natural targets of suspicion—particularly when they recruit spokespersons linked to well-documented CIA conspiracies. The controversy in this area will doubtlessly continue.

FARBEN Industries

For decades, I.G. Farben was an industrial colossus of GERMANY and the world at large, dominating much of Earth's chemical business through a formidable array of patents. Its maze of international cartels included such giants as Kuhlmann (in FRANCE), Imperial Chemical Industries (Great Britain), Montecantini (ITALY), Aussiger Verein (Czechoslovakia), Boruta (POLAND), and Mitsui (JAPAN). In the United States, its proud partners included DUPONT, Dow Chemical, and STANDARD OIL. Those prestigious U.S. firms were not put off by Farben's collaboration with ADOLF HITLER, and in some cases their trade continued even during World War II in blatant defiance of federal statutes.

Hitler despised Farben for its international character, but he dared not offend the masters of a chemical empire whose products included synthetics of oil, rubber, nitrates, and various fibers, along with vaccines, sera, and a range of medicines. Before war's end, Farben would also supply the THIRD REICH with much of its gasoline, rocket fuel, and the poison gas used to carry out Hitler's "final solution to the Jewish question" in the HOLOCAUST. Even before Hitler's rise to power, Farben's influence on German politics was so profound that Gustave Stresemann, chancellor and foreign minister during the Weimar Republic, once said "Without I.G. and coal, I can have no foreign policy." In the wake of World War II, Allied investigators preparing briefs for the Nuremburg WAR CRIMES tribunal would say, "Without I.G.'s immense productive facilities, its far-reaching research, varied technical experience and overall concentration of economic power, Germany would not have been in the position to start its aggressive war in September 1939."

Germany's defeat revealed Farben's complicity in Nazi war crimes ranging from slave labor to full-blown genocide. Twenty-four of the conglomerate's executives were indicted for war crimes, branded as the "Devil's chemists." Defendant Max Brüggemann was severed from the case due to illness, while the other 23 defendants faced trial on August 27, 1947. The proceedings consumed 11 months, resulting in a mixed verdict on July 30, 1948. Ten of the defendants were acquitted on all charges; the remainder were convicted on various counts and received prison terms ranging from one to eight years. Most of Farben's assets were seized at war's end, but its shares were traded on the German stock exchange until 1952 when the firm was finally liquidated. Even that was not *really* the end, however: In 2003 while most of Germany's leading industries contributed DM10 billion to a much-belated fund for compensation of surviving slave-labor victims, Farben's trustees remained tight fisted and defiant. On September 17, 2003, chief trustee Otto Bernhardt announced that a possible buyer had been found for the company's property portfolio, which makes up the bulk of its remaining DM21 million ($10 million) of assets. If and when the sale was approved and completed, Farben would finally cease to exist.

FASCISM

Fascism ranks (with COMMUNISM) as one of the "isms" that generated global turmoil during the 20th century, producing vast carnage around the world. With its variant form, NATIONAL SOCIALISM, fascism sparked a series of events that lit the fuse for World War II and that continue causing grief for countless victims to the present day. In essence fascism is a far-right ideology that places loyalty to "nation" (typically defined in racial/cultural terms) above any other sense of duty or obligation. It champions the triumph of a new "elite," motivated by a charismatic leader and supported by brute force to crush opponents (broadly including socialists, feminists, gays, pacifists, and a broad range of racial/religious minorities). While fascist regimes may vary somewhat in their mode of operation, they are typically known for belligerent militarism, overt favoritism for the MILITARY-INDUSTRIAL COMPLEX, curtailment of civil rights, simple-minded scapegoating, jingoistic politics, and general xenophobia. An obsession with "national security" often extends to aggressive military action in the guise of "self-defense," including fabrication of "threats" and "attacks" by smaller, weaker nations.

ITALY was the first nation to adopt a fascist form of government in 1922 under Benito Mussolini. HUNGARY followed two years later with the rise of the brutal Iron Guard. ADOLF HITLER brought National Socialism to GERMANY in 1933 and three years later teamed with Mussolini to support Francisco Franco's right-wing revolt against SPAIN's republican government. Meanwhile, military leaders and the BLACK DRAGON SOCIETY imposed a form of fascist rule in JAPAN. The Great Depression encouraged extreme remedies to global privation, and before World War II erupted in 1939, fascist movements were active throughout Europe and North America, while certain South American nations were openly sympathetic to Hitler.

It might be supposed that the massive destruction and loss of life suffered by so many nations by war's end in 1945 should have buried fascism forever. Sadly, such is not the case. Neo-fascist movements thrive worldwide, taking advantage of racial animosity and economic difficulties to advance their own agendas in nations as diverse as Canada, Great Britain, the United States, Russia, and Poland. In Germany, where public advocacy of Nazi doctrines or display of Nazi symbols was outlawed in 1946, multiple organizations openly agitate for institution of a FOURTH REICH. Wherever they operate, a potential for violence exists, ranging from individual assaults to acts of terrorism like the OKLAHOMA CITY BOMBING of 1995. In the United States, fascist commingling with "all-American" groups such as the KU KLUX KLAN has advanced to the point where many Klansmen have abandoned their nominal faith in Christianity to pursue the Odinist faith of their supposed Nordic ancestors. On a broader scale some critics charge that the United States itself has a kind of fascist government, obsessed with "homeland defense," prone to invading smaller nations for "defensive" reasons that later prove false, corrupt alliances within the military-industrial realm, and traditional support for brutal right-wing dictators throughout the so-called Third World.

FATAH

Organized in 1956, Fatah served for many years as the military arm of Yasser Arafat's Palestine Liberation Organization. A publication of January 1969 described it as "the expression of the Palestinian people and of its will to free its land from ZIONIST colonization to recover its national identity." To that end and depending on the observer's point of view, Fatah guerrillas engaged in numerous acts of resistance or TERRORISM against ISRAEL. At its peak strength in the late 1960s and early 1970s, Fatah had an estimated 10,000 to 15,000 men under arms, supported by contributions from various Middle Eastern nations. In 1970 after Palestinian guerrillas were driven from JORDAN by King Hussein's army, hard-core Fatah members organized the BLACK SEPTEMBER group to carry out acts of vengeance. Fatah suffered another embarrassing defeat in August 1982 when Israeli invaders drove Palestinians out of Lebanon, forcing them to scatter throughout the Arab world. As a result, dissidents left Fatah to organize new groups, including the Popular Front for the Liberation of Palestine and the Fatah Revolutionary Council. Its role in Middle Eastern violence declined steadily thereafter until Arafat was widely viewed (and frequently condemned by former comrades) as a "moderate" in the 1990s.

FEDERAL Bureau of Investigation (FBI)

Prior to 1908 the U.S. JUSTICE DEPARTMENT had no detectives or enforcement agents of its own. Though charged with prosecuting federal crimes, the attorney general had to hire private investigators or borrow agents from the Treasury Department's SECRET SERVICE. That practice was banned by Congress in 1907 following various scandals that left Justice effectively neutered. Attorney General Charles BONAPARTE proposed creation of a small detective force in 1908, but Congress rejected the idea and refused funding. Undeterred by legality, Bonaparte waited for Congress to adjourn and then created the force on his own with approval from President Theodore Roosevelt. When federal lawmakers returned from vacation, they were outraged by Bonaparte's arrogant action, but they reluctantly permitted the small force of "special agents" to survive.

The future FBI had no name until March 1909 when it was christened the Bureau of Investigation. (*Federal* was added in 1935.) Its duties were initially confined to solving crimes committed on federal property, but it received a boost in 1910 with passage of the WHITE SLAVE Act. Ostensibly written to crush organized prostitution, the new law in fact was used primarily against private individuals, casting FBI agents as moral arbiters and filling their files with reams of potential blackmail ammunition. By 1915 the bureau was actively (though illegally) pursuing ANARCHISTS, "radicals," and labor organizers, a practice codified by the Alien and Espionage Acts of 1917. One year later the bureau staged its first mass arrests, as agents joined forces with right-wing vigilantes to jail thousands of alleged draft dodgers across the country. (Only a handful of bona fide "slackers" were found.) In the wake of World War I and RUSSIA's revolution, FBI leaders helped whip up the country's first Red Scare and staged the PALMER RAIDS, jailing thousands of suspected communists and "enemy aliens." (One of every thousand persons

arrested was later deported; the rest were released without charges or apologies.) When not casting dragnets, bureau agents were assigned by Attorney General HARRY DAUGHERTY to harass and frame U.S. Senators investigating the TEAPOT DOME scandal and other corrupt activities of President WARREN HARDING's "Ohio Gang."

By 1924 corruption within the Justice Department was so notorious that Attorney General Harlan Stone was appointed to clean house. Curiously his choice for the FBI's new director was J. EDGAR HOOVER, a man deeply involved in the very corruption and political persecution that Stone sought to erase. During the next 48 years, Hoover would run the bureau as a one-man show (some said a "cult of personality"), largely oblivious to orders from his nominal superiors. His agents would commit as many criminal offenses as they solved, including thousands of illegal break-ins, wiretaps, and frame-ups as well as various acts of harassment that were cast in terms of "neutralizing" groups and individuals that Hoover deemed "subversive." In the 1930s

Theodore Roosevelt, founder of the FBI (Library of Congress)

bureau agents (dubbed "G-men" by the FBI's publicity department) pursued small-time bandits and kidnappers while ignoring organized crime. Indeed until 1961 Hoover publicly insisted that the MAFIA did not exist. Some researchers claim the mob blackmailed Hoover into selective blindness, holding photos of the FBI director in drag at gay parties, while others note his lifelong (very profitable) friendship with a motley collection of gamblers, bootleggers, and corrupt business people who shared his hatred for all things liberal or "Red."

In the 1950s, driven by obsessive enmity against any form of social or political dissent, Hoover launched the FBI's illegal COINTELPRO campaigns, a regimen of surveillance and "dirty tricks" that included anonymous letters and phone calls, burglaries, false arrests, fabrication of evidence, and finally incitement to murder. Agents were commended (and sometimes received "merit pay") for stirring up violent conflict among target groups such as the BLACK PANTHER PARTY and the NATION OF ISLAM. In one bizarre scheme, dubbed "Operation Hoodwink," G-men tried (in vain) to start a shooting war between the Mafia and the Communist Party. In the 1960s, under pressure from President LYNDON BAINES JOHNSON, Hoover reluctantly used similar tactics against the KU KLUX KLAN (although he still suppressed critical evidence in the BAPBOMB case and other racist crimes).

Hoover's death (some say murder) in May 1972 might have permitted some change for the better at FBI headquarters, but President RICHARD NIXON saw the bureau as a potential tool for extending his personal power (or at least deflecting prosecution for the WATERGATE conspiracy), and a half-century of Hoover's influence left most high-ranking FBI officials indoctrinated with his own peculiar standards of "justice." Directors Clarence Kelley (1973–78) and WILLIAM WEBSTER (1978–87) conducted their own illegal covert campaigns against dissident groups including the AMERICAN INDIAN MOVEMENT and the Committee in Solidarity with the People of El Salvador. Director William Sessions (1987–93) was fired by President Bill CLINTON when he refused to step down over charges of abusing his authority. Replacement Louis Freeh (1993–2001) supervised investigation of a series of disasters including the WORLD TRADE CENTER BOMBING, the OKLAHOMA CITY BOMBING, and persistent charges of evidence tampering at the FBI's laboratory. Director Robert

Mueller (2001–   ) has thus far been an active participant with Attorney General JOHN ASHCROFT in undermining civil liberties through endless "terrorist alerts" and the USA PATRIOT ACT. Ashcroft surprised his critics by resigning after President Bush won reelection in November 2004.

See also COMMUNISM.

FEDERAL Emergency Management Agency (FEMA)

President Jimmy Carter created FEMA in July 1979 by means of an executive order (No. 12148) merging various disaster-relief and civil-defense groups into a single entity. With director John Macy at the helm, FEMA began to develop an Integrated Emergency Management System including "direction, control and warning systems which are common to the full range of emergencies from small isolated events to the ultimate emergency—war." In the quarter-century since its creation, FEMA has confronted a full range of crises, ranging from hurricanes and earthquakes to the Cuban refugee crisis of 1980–81, toxic contamination at Love Canal, the Three Mile Island nuclear accident, and the PENTTBOM attacks of September 11, 2001. Along the way, it has also inspired no end of far-right conspiracy theories.

It is sometimes difficult to know whether fringe conspiracists are fabricating "evidence" or they are simply confused. Various Internet Web sites, for instance, cite erroneous numbers for Carter's executive order establishing FEMA. One gives the number as 11051 (an emergency management order issued by President John Kennedy, 18 years before FEMA was born) and then "quotes" nonexistent language empowering FEMA to carry out "the SEIZURE OF ALL AMERICAN PEOPLE for work forces under federal supervision, including SPLITTING UP OF FAMILIES if the government has to." Conspiracist Harry V. Martin calls FEMA "the most powerful organization in the United States," adding that:

Some people have referred to it as the "secret government" of the United States. It is not an elected body; it does not involve itself in public disclosures; and it even has a quasi-secret budget in the billions of dollars.

After noting that FEMA's responsibilities cover "many new disasters [*sic*] including urban forest fires [*sic*], home heating emergencies, refugee situations, urban riots, and emergency planning for nuclear and toxic incidents," Martin goes on to claim that:

Three times since 1984, FEMA stood on the threshold of taking control of the nation. Once under President REAGAN in 1984, and twice under President Bush in 1990 and 1992. But under those three scenarios, there was not a sufficient crisis to warrant risking Martial Law. Most experts on the subject of FEMA and Martial Law insisted that a crisis has to appear dangerous enough for the people of the United States before they would tolerate or accept complete government takeover.

The "experts on FEMA," like those who call it America's "secret government," remain anonymous. Two more specific FEMA conspiracy theories involved malicious tampering with statistics in the January 1994 Northridge (California) earthquake and claims that FEMA response teams stood ready in New York City the night before "9/11." In the first case, conspiracists claim that FEMA and the U.S. Geological Survey falsified the Northridge quake's magnitude, reporting it as 6.7 on the Richter scale, rather than 8.0. The reason: to save Washington billions of dollars in emergency relief funds. In fact, while various other seismologists confirmed the USGS reading of 6.7, the complaints stemmed from an erroneous rumor making the rounds in Los Angeles. According to that story, FEMA was required to hand out home-reconstruction grants (rather than loans) in the event of an earthquake measured at 8.0 or greater. Since no such rule exists, in fact, avoiding it becomes superfluous.

The 9/11 conspiracy theory evolved from a statement by FEMA spokesman Tom Kenney, who told newsman Dan Rather on September 13, 2001, "We're currently one of the first teams that was deployed to support the city of New York in this disaster. We arrived late Monday night [10 September] and went right into action on Tuesday morning [11 September]." Such a statement suggests advance notice of the terrorist attacks, and thus raises the question of U.S. government complicity. FEMA's answer, when it came, was simple and direct: "Tom Kenney simply mixed up his days of the week, saying 'Monday' when he meant 'Tuesday' and 'Tuesday' when he meant 'Wednesday.'" Bland denial carried no weight with conspiracists, but a reporter with the *Boston Herald* called Kenney's home on Cape Cod

and spoke to his wife, who confirmed that Kenney did not leave for New York until September 11. She also "added wryly that it was typical of her husband to confuse dates."

See also BUSH DYNASTY; KENNEDY DYNASTY; TERRORISM.

FIJI

Fiji consists of 332 islands in the South Pacific, located 1,900 miles east of Australia. Only 110 of the islands are inhabited, but the largest have boasted human populations from the second millennium B.C. In 1874 Fijian chiefs "offered" their islands to England, and the British Crown graciously accepted. Large-scale cultivation of sugarcane began in the 1880s with more than 60,000 indentured (slave) laborers imported from INDIA during the next 40 years. De facto slavery was abolished in 1920, but the Indians remained, and racial conflict with indigenous Fijians is a recurring theme of the archipelago's modern history. Fiji was granted independence in October 1970. In October 1987 military leaders staged a coup to forestall election of a coalition government dominated by Indians. Ensuing waves of ethnic discrimination caused thousands of Indian-Fijians to leave during the next decade. A new constitution provided for a multiethnic cabinet in 1998, and Fiji's first Indian prime minister took office the following year, but racial tensions endured, fueled by economic problems. In May 2000 soldiers invaded Parliament and held it captive for two months, demanding a return to government control by ethnic Fijians, but the insurrectionists were captured in July and charged with treason. Coup leader George Speight was sentenced to death in February 2002, but the sentence was later commuted to life imprisonment.

FINDERS

On February 5, 1987, police in Tallahassee, Florida, received an anonymous telephone complaint that two "well-dressed men" were behaving strangely with six unkempt children in a local park. Officers arrived on the scene to find the children milling about a blue van with Virginia license plates, apparently supervised by Washington, D.C., residents Douglas Ammerman and Michael Houlihan. The men refused to answer any questions, instead presenting officers with a card bearing instructions on the Fifth Amendment's right to silence. The children, a mixed group of boys and girls age two through seven, proved more talkative. They claimed to be en route to Mexico for enrollment at a school for "smart kids." Under questioning, the kids could not identify themselves or their custodians. They professed total ignorance of such common devices as toilets and telephones, explaining that they were compelled to live outdoors and received food only as a reward for pleasing their keepers. Officers noted that the children were unwashed, were without underwear, and were covered with insect bites. The van contained maps, books, letters, and a foul-smelling mattress.

Ammerman and Houlihan were jailed on multiple child abuse charges, while Tallahassee police continued their investigation. U.S. Customs agents were summoned on suspicion that the prisoners might be involved in child pornography. In custody, Ammerman and Houlihan claimed they were the children's teachers in transit to Mexico where they planned to erect "a school for brilliant children." Within hours of the arrest, detectives in Washington phoned their Florida counterparts, relating their suspicion that the prisoners and the children might be involved with "a cult group" called the Finders. Washington police had obtained search warrants for two local properties owned by the group, and they invited customs agents to join in the search on February 6. Affidavits filed in support of the warrants included an informant's statement "describing 'blood rituals' and sexual orgies involving children, and an as yet unsolved murder in which the Finders may be involved."

The search proceeded as scheduled on February 6, 1987. The evidence collected included a stockpile of photos, many of them nudes, "at least one of which was a photo of a child 'on display' and appearing to accent the child's genitals." One photo album contained:

a series of photos of adults and children dressed in white sheets participating in a "blood ritual." The ritual centered around the execution of at least two goats. The photos portrayed the execution, disembowelment, skinning and dismemberment of the goats at the hands of the children. This included the removal of the testes of a male goat, the discovery of a female goat's "womb" and the "baby goats" inside the womb, and the presentation of a goat's head to one of the children.

Also seized were "numerous documents which described explicit sexual conduct between the members of the community known as Finders," large quantities of children's clothes and toys, and "numerous files relating to activities of the organization in different parts of the world." (One file bore the label "Pentagon Break-in.") According to a Customs report on the raid, "Cursory examination of the documents revealed detailed instructions for obtaining children for unspecified purposes. The instructions included the impregnation of female members of the community known as the Finders, purchasing children, trading, and kidnapping." In a "computer room," the raiders found a detailed summary of the Tallahassee arrests, while "other documents identified interests in high-tech transfers to the United Kingdom, numerous properties under the control of the Finders, a keen interest in terrorism, explosives, and the evasion of law enforcement." One of the properties contained "a large library, two kitchens, a sauna, hot-tub, and a 'video room.' The video room seemed to be set up as an indoctrination center."

The case seemed promising, even potentially explosive, but no charges were ever filed against the Finders. On April 2, 1987, Washington police advised customs agents that "the investigation into the activity of the Finders had become a CIA internal matter. The [Washington police] report has been classified SECRET and was not available for review." Customs was further informed "that the FBI had withdrawn from the investigation several weeks prior and that the FBI Foreign Counter Intelligence Division had directed [Washington police] not to advise the FBI Washington Field Office of anything that had transpired." In short, as Customs summarized the case, "No further information will be available. No further action will be taken." In the words of one Tallahassee detective, "They dropped this case like a hot rock."

What happened? JUSTICE DEPARTMENT investigators posed that question in December 1993 with the announcement of an "ongoing investigation" into "unresolved matters" surrounding the case. Chief among those questions was the record of interference by the CENTRAL INTELLIGENCE AGENCY. CIA headquarters predictably dismissed the notion as "hogwash," blaming it on "a simple mix-up with D.C. police." Their only link to the Finders, agency spokespersons insisted, was the fact that "a firm that provided computer training to CIA officers also employed several members of the Finders." Florida congressman Tom Lewis remained unconvinced, asking reporters, "Could our own government have something to do with this Finders organization and turned their backs on these children? That's what all the evidence points to. And there is a lot of evidence. I can tell you this: We've got a lot of people scrambling, and that wouldn't be happening if there was nothing here."

Perhaps, but those questions remain unanswered. More than a decade after the Justice Department probe was announced, no reports have been issued, no determinations published. Conspiracists speculate that the Finders case is evidence of U.S. government complicity in founding cults and committing unspecified acts of child abuse, perhaps including youthful indoctrination into SATANISM. Federal spokespeople denounce those claims as paranoid fear mongering, but they do nothing to explain what happened with the Finders or why.

FLUORIDATED water

Fluoride is a mineral that naturally occurs in most water supplies. In the early 1940s U.S. scientists discovered that fluoride may help prevent tooth decay, thereafter theorizing that fluoridation ("adjustment" of fluoride content in water by artificial introduction) might eliminate many dental problems nationwide. In 1945 officials of Grand Rapids, Michigan, volunteered their city as a test site. Local water was fluoridated to a level of one part per million, and an 11-year study found that the cavity rate among Grand Rapids children decreased by 60 percent.

The first conspiratorial alarms over fluoridation were raised in the late 1950s by members of the far-right JOHN BIRCH SOCIETY. Birchers believed that fluoridation was a communist plot to destroy the brains of American patriots and thus sap their will to resist when the United States was finally invaded (by RUSSIA, CHINA, the UNITED NATIONS, or whomever). No invasion was forthcoming, nor did droves of fluoridated zombies suddenly desert the faith of their fathers to champion a Red America (though, theoretically, every unwelcome trend in the past 50 years could presumably be traced to fluoride-damaged brain cells). The furor did not halt fluoridation's progress, and by 1999, 140 million Americans lived in fluoridated communities, where cavities in children decreased 20–40 percent and adult cavities declined 15–35 percent.

At the same time, another 80 million U.S. residents live in communities where fluoridation has been publicly rejected, and the controversy endures. In November 1999 impending fluoridation surfaced as the hot-button issue of local elections in Connersville, Indiana—the state's largest nonfluoridated community—and safe-water activists worldwide have rallied to question (or condemn) the fluoridation process. Perennial White House hopeful Ralph Nader has joined the chorus, declaring that if "the only objective" of fluoridation is to prevent childhood tooth decay, "you don't expose all people to fluoridated water." Sierra Club spokespeople speak of "valid concerns" surrounding fluoridated water, and the Fluoride Action Network (FAN) describes itself as "[a]n international coalition working to end water fluoridation and alert the public to fluoride's health and environmental risks." The FAN's Internet Web site makes the following points:

1. The vast majority of Western Europe has rejected water fluoridation.
2. The fluoride chemical added to water is an unprocessed, industrial waste product from the pollution scrubbers of the phosphate fertilizer industry.
3. A growing body of evidence indicates that water fluoridation is both ineffective and unnecessary.
4. Fluoride's "benefits" are primarily topical, not systemic. Thus, there is no need to swallow fluoride.
5. Two-thirds of U.S. communities, when given the chance to vote, have voted against fluoridation. More than 60 U.S. communities have rejected water fluoridation since 1999.
6. Excessive exposure to fluoride has been linked to health problems, including arthritis, hip fracture, hypothyroidism, cancer, Alzheimer's disease, and reduced IQ.
7. Children are receiving too much fluoride today, not "too little." There is a need to reduce, not increase, current exposures.
8. As a result of excess exposure to fluoride, near-epidemic numbers of children are developing dental fluorosis (a poisoning of tooth-forming cells).

See also COMMUNISM.

FORD Motor Company

Born in 1863 Henry Ford left his family's Michigan farm at age 16 and settled in Detroit, working as an apprentice in a machine shop. He built his first motor car (the "Tin Lizzie") in 1896 and raised enough money to start his own company three years later. Despite financial and technical setbacks, he persevered and in 1907 earned $1.1 million in profits from sales of his Model A car. Two years later he focused on production of the Model T alone, refining assembly-line production until complete assembly of the car required only 1 hour 33 minutes. By 1916 the Model T's retail price had dropped to $360. Ford had achieved a true success and became a hero in the process. One public-opinion poll ranked him as the third-greatest man in history, trailing NAPOLEON BONAPARTE and JESUS CHRIST. Ford was so rich that when son Edsel turned 21, Ford took him to a private vault and gave him $1 million in gold. By 1940 his company controlled more than 50 percent of the U.S. automobile market.

There was, however, a darker side to the American dream-come-true. After his heavy investments in pacifism failed to halt World War I, Ford turned to politics with a bizarre anti-Semitic slant. Beginning in May 1918 his *Dearborn Independent* newspaper published a series of articles headlined "The International Jew: The World's Problem," which repeated and elaborated on charges contained in the fraudulent *PROTOCOLS OF THE ELDERS OF ZION*. Ford's diatribes were later released in book form and enjoyed brisk sales, assisted by the KU KLUX KLAN (and it remains a "classic" volume today among neo-Nazis and white supremacists). Ford donated money to ADOLF HITLER in the 1920s, and he was singled out for special praise in *Mein Kampf,* while a large photo of Ford decorated Hitler's Munich office. In 1923 when rumors of a Ford presidential campaign surfaced, Hitler told reporters, "I wish that I could send some of my shock troops to Chicago and other big American cities to help."

Slapped with an epic libel suit, Ford apologized for the worst of his rants in 1927, blaming them on the *Independent*'s staff, but his devotion to far-right politics and Nazi-related business did not waver. Ford bitterly opposed the NEW DEAL of President Franklin Roosevelt and opposed labor unions in any form. When the United Automobile Workers (UAW) tried to organize Ford plants, the company hired MAFIA goons to battle the union through a series of

Auto tycoon Henry Ford employed mobsters and Nazis in his long-running war against labor unions and "the International Jew." (Author's collection)

bloody clashes that included multiple murder attempts on the UAW's REUTHER BROTHERS. In 1940, after a meeting with Nazi agents, Ford and son Edsel supplied GERMANY with fleets of five-ton military trucks but refused to build aircraft engines for Britain. Edsel served on the board of FARBEN INDUSTRIES's U.S. branch and supervised Ford operations in Nazi-occupied FRANCE. In 1941 Henry Ford resumed his public attacks on Jews, and after the PEARL HARBOR attack he hired Charles Lindbergh, spokesman for the AMERICA FIRST COMMITTEE, as a company "consultant." Ford continued business dealings with the THIRD REICH throughout World War II: A financial statement from occupied France shows a Ford profit of 58 million francs.

Ford died in 1943, but the company he founded has seen no end of controversy and alleged conspiracies in recent years. In the 1960s defective fuel tanks in the Ford Pinto caused multiple deaths and hideous injuries, highlighted by U.S. Senate investigations in 1965. Ford paid out millions to settle civil lawsuits out of court and spent millions more on lobbying against tighter federal safety standards, until a full-blown scandal erupted in the 1970s. (Nearly 9,000 persons burned to death in fiery Pinto crashes by 1972.) Ford's "cost-benefit analysis" determined that safety improvements would make Pintos too expensive for the average buyer—an argument that persuaded successive secretaries of transportation under Presidents RICHARD NIXON and Gerald Ford (no relation to the family). Phrased another way, in the calculation of sales versus lawsuits, Ford placed a $200,000 price tag on each human life, while maimed burn victims were valued at $67,000 per head.

Washington belatedly imposed new safety standards in 1977, and Ford recalled a total of 1,530,000 defective vehicles in June 1978, but further scandals were waiting. In 2001 federal investigators claimed that a lethal combination of Ford Explorer vehicles and Firestone tires had caused "at least five" of 174 deaths and 80 injuries under study from roll-over crashes in four-wheel-drive sport-utility vehicles. Ford and Firestone loudly blamed each other, severing a 95-year business relationship, while Ford ultimately paid out $3 billion to replace 13 million tires on its SUVs, citing "an unacceptable risk to our customers." (Firestone countered with charges that the Explorer's design contributed to explosive tire failure.) A new lawsuit, filed in January 2003 by the National Police Association (representing more than 1,000 police unions nationwide), accused Ford of negligent failure to correct a Pinto-type problem that caused Crown Victoria police cars to explode in flames when struck from behind. Court papers cited the recent death of New York State Trooper Robert Ambrose and seven similar cases, all blamed on the Crown Victoria's fuel tank.

FOSTER, Vince

Arkansas attorney Vince Foster was a longtime intimate of Bill and Hillary Clinton, who served in 1993 as their number-two White House counsel. At 1:00 P.M. on July 20, 1993, Foster left his Washington office, advising one of his aides that he expected to return later and mentioning that he had left some candy on his desk if the aide wanted it. Five hours later Foster was found dead in Virginia's Fort Marcy Park, apparently killed by a gunshot fired into his brain through the mouth. U.S. Park Police quickly declared the death a suicide, but many nagging doubts remain. They include (but are not limited to) the following:

The gun(s): The man who found Foster's body insisted, under FBI grilling, that he saw no gun in either of Foster's hands. Officially, Foster died with a .38-caliber revolver clutched in his right fist, found there by police. The weapon was an 80-year-old army model; it was, in fact, composed of parts from two different revolvers. Its 6-shot cylinder held two cartridges, one of which had been fired. No fingerprints were found on the weapon's outer surfaces, a circumstance that Federal Bureau of Investigations (FBI) lab technicians explained by claiming that Foster had not perspired prior to death. (Body oil, the source of fingerprints, is not dependent on sweat, and the day's temperature topped 95 degrees.) Two fingerprints found *underneath* the gun's removable hand grips were never identified; indeed, no effort was made to trace them. Although the bulky pistol was fired inside Foster's mouth, its recoil did not damage his teeth, and no blood or tissue "blowback" was found on the weapon or on Foster's hand. When Foster's wife went looking for his silver .22-caliber pistol at home, she found it inexplicably replaced with a gun she had never seen before.

Other forensic evidence: FBI experts found no "coherent soil" from the park on Foster's shoes, though he walked 700 feet from his car on unpaved trails to the site of his death. Hairs and carpet fibers found on his clothing were never identified or traced to their source. Although the pistol did not fall from his hand, Foster's glasses were found 19 feet from the body on the far side of dense shrubbery. (Police suggested that they "jumped" when he was shot.) Foster's autopsy report describes an exit wound at the back of his head, though ambulance technicians and the doctor who certified his death saw none. One attendant *did* see a small "entrance" wound in Foster's neck below the jawline, a discovery that is missing from the autopsy report. Missing, too, are all crime-scene photographs and X-rays from the autopsy. Dr. James Beyer, who performed the

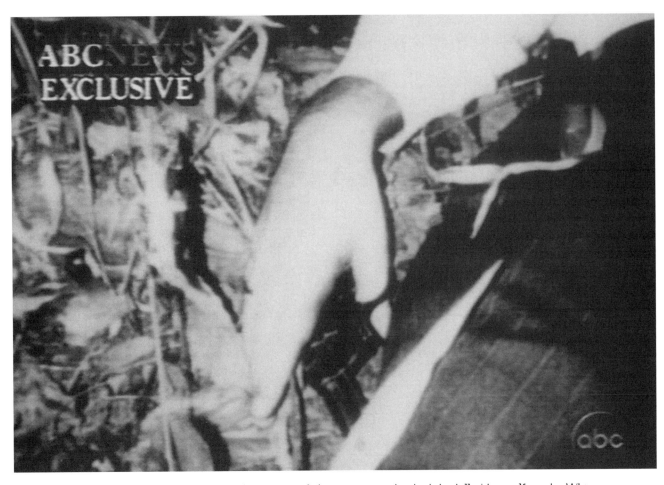

This photo shows Vince Foster's thumb on the trigger of the weapon with which he killed himself as the Whitewater affair was brought to the public's attention. (ABC News/Corbis)

autopsy, initially said that the X-rays showed no bullet fragments inside Foster's head, but he later denied taking X-rays at all.

White House activities: White House spokespersons claim that the Clintons first learned of Foster's death at 8:30 P.M., but Arkansas authorities say that they were notified of the shooting by a minor presidential aide at 6:15 P.M. White House staffers refused a police request to seal Foster's office pending a search, and officers sat passively outside through the night while various aides paraded through the room. In the wake of that sideshow Foster's file index was missing along with an uncertain quantity of documents that were removed from his files and safe while police watched.

Foster's depression: The suicide theory hinges on Foster's state of mind. Police found a short list of

psychiatrists in Foster's wallet, all of whom denied knowing or speaking to Foster. Authorities missed the alleged suicide note the first time they searched Foster's briefcase. A second search revealed the message, torn into 28 pieces (with one piece missing). When reassembled, the note read less like a suicide message than a list of reasons for returning to Arkansas (which, in fact, Foster's wife had requested he write). Its content hardly mattered, though, since no fingerprints were found on the shredded note and three handwriting analysts (one of them from Oxford) declared the note a forgery after comparing it to 12 known samples of Foster's handwriting.

Right-wing conspiracists rank Foster high on the ever-growing "Clinton death list," while other theorists note Foster's suspicious European travels and financial transactions, speculating on a possible link to shady figures outside the Washington Beltway. Whatever the truth about Foster's death, it remains nearly as controversial today as the JFK and RFK ASSASSINATIONS.

See also CLINTON, BILL AND HILLARY.

FOUR Pi movement

In 1969 while gathering material for a book on the Charles Manson case, journalist Ed Sanders encountered reports of a sinister SATANIC cult alleged to practice human sacrifice in several parts of California and to lure youthful members from college campuses throughout the western half of the United States. The cult was allegedly a spin off from the weird Process Church of Final Judgment and took its name—"Four Pi" or "Four P"—from the parent group's "power sign" (four Ps arranged in the shape of a stylized swastika). According to Sanders the group initially boasted 55 members, of whom 15 were middle aged, the rest consisting of men and women in their early twenties. The group's leader—dubbed the "Grand Chignon" or "Head Devil"—was said to be a wealthy California businessman who exercised his power by compelling younger members to act as slaves and murder random targets on command. The central object of the cult was to promote "the total worship of evil."

Organized in northern California during 1967, the Four Pi movement (according to Sanders) held its secret gatherings in the Santa Cruz Mountains, north of San Francisco. Rituals included the sacrifice of dogs as well as human beings. Beginning in June 1968, police in San José, Santa Cruz, and Los Gatos began to find canines skinned and drained of blood without apparent motive. The director of a Santa Cruz animal shelter told reporters, "Whoever is doing this is a real expert with a knife. The skin is cut away without even marking the flesh. The really strange thing is that these dogs have been drained of blood."

That blood, according to Sanders and a self-described member of the cult, was drunk by worshipers in nocturnal ceremonies; so was the blood of human victims slain on a dragon-festooned altar, stabbed to death with a custom-made six-bladed knife. Each sacrifice climaxed with removal of the victim's heart, which cultists divided among themselves and devoured. Victims were chiefly hitchhikers, runaways, and homeless drifters, though Sanders

chronicled one murder of a willing volunteer. Corpses were incinerated in a portable crematorium, mounted on a truck, while armed guards and attack dogs patrolled the ritual sites.

In early 1969 the cult reportedly moved southward, shifting operations to the Santa Ana Mountains near Los Angeles. The following year, a drifter named Stanley Dean Baker was arrested at Big Sur following a hit-and-run accident. In custody, he told police, "I have a problem. I'm a cannibal." Baker produced human bones to prove his statement and directed authorities to the grave of his latest victim, Montana park ranger James Schlosser, whose heart Baker had extracted and consumed. Baker was linked to a second murder by bloody fingerprints at the scene, but prosecutors delayed that trial so long that the case was thrown out of court. From his cell, Baker spoke openly of his activities with the Four Pi cult, but no one cared to listen. He was sentenced to life imprisonment for the Schlosser homicide and paroled to parts unknown in 1985.

Six years before Baker hit the streets, imprisoned serial killer David ("Son of Sam") Berkowitz smuggled a letter out of prison describing *his* intimate knowledge of the Four Pi cult's chapter in New York. Berkowitz claimed that the group was involved in the 1976–77 "Sam" shootings in New York City, as well as the gruesome (still-unsolved) 1974 murder of co-ed Arlis Perry at California's Stanford University. Citing names, dates, and places to confirm his story, Berkowitz also predicted a string of future crimes from his cell, but he stopped talking in July 1979 after a near-fatal incident wherein his throat was slashed by persons unknown. Subsequently the man whom Berkowitz named as the cult's number-one killer— William Mentzer—was sentenced to life in jail for the California murder of millionaire movie producer Roy Radin. Mentzer was also suspected (but never charged) in several other contract killings. (Mentzer denies any knowledge of cults or additional murders.)

Journalist Maury Terry pursued the Berkowitz story and confirmed much of what Ed Sanders wrote a decade earlier. He documented links between the cult and Charles Manson's homicidal "family" and suggested connections to various unsolved murders across the United States. According to Terry the cult had more than 1,000 members nationwide in 1979 and controlled a small (unnamed) college in the Los Angeles area. Various conspiracists have also linked the Four Pi cult to the unsolved Zodiac murders of

1966–70 (a connection suggested by Stanley Baker) and to "Unabomber" Theodore Kaczynski. If Terry is correct, the cult is deeply involved in WHITE SLAVERY, child pornography, and the international narcotics trade. To date, no other living members of the cult have been identified or charged with any crimes.

FOURTH Reich

The collapse of the THIRD REICH in 1945, unfortunately, did not mark the end of FASCISM or NATIONAL SOCIALISM as political ideologies. Thousands of Nazis linked to WAR CRIMES and genocidal actions during the HOLOCAUST escaped prosecution at the end of World War II. Some, like ADOLF EICHMANN and JOSEF MENGELE (and perhaps MARTIN BORMANN), escaped to South America with the aid of ODESSA and other underground networks. Others, including KLAUS BARBIE, were adopted by the U.S. government as anticommunist allies under PROJECT PAPERCLIP. Countless others were simply ignored by postwar German authorities, resuming their normal lives as entrepreneurs, politicians, even police officers and judges. Ambiguous evidence and Russian intransigence raised doubts in many minds as to whether ADOLF HITLER himself had really died in 1945.

Considering the global losses suffered during World War II, it is entirely natural that freedom-loving people everywhere should fear the rise of a "Fourth Reich" in Europe (or anywhere else). In the past half-century, those fears have been exacerbated by a variety of trends and events, including:

1. The slow leak of revelations, from the latter 1940s to the present day, exposing war criminals who slipped through the net in 1945, including some who settled in the United States and others who were actively employed by U.S. government agencies.
2. The survival of prewar fascism in "neutral" Spain until 1975, accompanied by the rise of neo-fascist military juntas (most supported, if not created, with U.S. aide) in nations ranging from Greece to Central and South America.
3. The proliferation of neo-fascist groups in Europe from the 1950s onward, including organizations in Germany (where any display of pro-Nazi sympathy remains a criminal offense) that were seemingly sheltered by sympathetic police and prosecutors.

4. Reports from Nazi outposts, such as Chile's COLONIA DIGNIDAD, where old-school fascists put down roots in the bad old days and have flourished (often with local government protection) ever since.
5. The reunification of Germany in 1990, followed by new waves of neo-Nazi skinhead violence against minorities and increasingly belligerent activity by various far-right political parties.
6. The collapse of Soviet communism in 1991. Though long a goal of anticommunists worldwide, the USSR's dissolution only exacerbated Russia's economic crises while clearing the way for organization of neo-fascist groups in the mold of those found throughout Western Europe.

It seems unlikely, at first glance, that Hitler's Reich will ever rise again, and yet students of history recall the conditions that brought Hitler to power in 1933: economic crises, obsessive fear of "enemy aliens" coupled with demands for "national security" at any cost, erosion of constitutional liberties by crusading leaders, and a final acceptance that "war is the health of the state." Those problems still exist, and if as some suggest that the would-be "saviors" of the nation have traded their brown shirts and jackboots for thousand-dollar suits, the disguise only makes them more dangerous.

FRANCE

Archaeological evidence indicates that France has been continuously occupied by humans since Paleolithic times. Greek and Phoenician invaders arrived in about 600 B.C., followed by Julius Caesar in 57 B.C. Rome then ruled France until the Franks invaded during the fifth century A.D. Successive kings ruled France (or portions of it) from 751 to 1789 when the French Revolution and ensuing Reign of Terror plunged the country into a nightmarish bloodbath. Military hero NAPOLEON BONAPARTE emerged as consul in 1799 and was elevated to emperor five years later. Two catastrophic wars with GERMANY (1914–18 and 1940–45) left French power much diminished worldwide. After World War II, communist members of the wartime anti-Nazi resistance made a strong bid to control the government, opposed by a motley coalition of rightists covertly supported by the United States. In the late 1940s the CENTRAL INTELLIGENCE AGENCY forged an alliance with Corsican gangsters and HEROIN smugglers to crush left-wing unions in France and disrupt pro-Communist meetings. Dismantling its foreign empire was a bloody ordeal for France, including brutal wars of attrition in ALGERIA and Southeast Asia. Right-wing terrorists of the Secret Army Organization (OAS) made several attempts to kill President Charles DeGaulle after he freed Algeria, and President Jacques Chirac survived a similar attack by neo-fascist elements as recently as July 2002. A year later France was rocked by a bizarre sex-and-murder scandal linking politician and antipornography crusader Dominique Baudis to convicted serial killer Patrice Alegre. Testimony from a prostitute alleges that Baudis participated in sadomasochistic orgies in the 1990s and that he murdered a 23-year-old transvestite blackmailer. Baudis denies the charges and has sued the prostitute for slander; Alegre—serving life on five counts of murder and six counts of rape—insists that Baudis was involved (with a judge and several police officers) in the slaying. As revealed so far in "l'affair Alegre," the serial slayer provided drugs and hookers for a series of orgies allegedly involving various prominent Frenchmen. Baudis has demanded an official investigation to clear his name.

See also COMMUNISM; FASCISM; JULIUS CAESAR.

FRANKENFOODS

For years, U.S. scientists have conducted genetic experiments on various fruits, grains, and vegetables, trying to produce crops that are more prolific, less easily spoiled on the shelf or in transit, and (at least presumably) more nutritious. Conspiracists dub the resultant hybrid-mutant products "Frankenfoods," suggesting that corporate "mad scientists" may be on the verge (unwittingly or otherwise) of unleashing a biotechnical catastrophe—indeed, a veritable enemy within. Charges range from the relatively benign (claims that genetically altered produce has less flavor or nutrient value than normal items) to the extremes of science-fiction (fears that consumption of Frankenfoods may produce genetic abnormalities in humans or lead to MIND CONTROL via some method as yet undescribed). Whatever the tone of protest, the controversy shows no sign of abating.

The scientific case was not helped when President George W. Bush joined the fray, denouncing various

European nations for their embargoes on genetically altered foods from the United States. A die-hard friend of agribusiness with no perceptible scientific knowledge (he denies the existence of global warming and has fought to increase the "acceptable" level of arsenic in U.S. drinking water), Bush was seen by many in Europe as pitchman who would say anything in support of wealthy campaign contributors. In June 2003, addressing a biotechnology conference in Washington, Bush criticized the European Union (EU) for refusing to accept genetically modified foods, adding a claim that their refusal somehow contributed to starvation. "For the sake of a continent threatened by famine," Bush said, "I urge the European governments to end their opposition to biotechnology. We should encourage the spread of safe, effective biotechnology to win the fight against global hunger." Reijo Kemppinen, a spokesman for the European Commission, replied: "The fact is that we in Europe have chosen to do some things differently from the United States. As regards [Frankenfoods], we simply believe that it is better to be safe than sorry." Bush countered with threats of a formal complaint to the World Trade Organization, while EU spokesmen declared that Bush's claims concerning African famine "are simply not true." The controversy endures, while prophets of doom await the first evidence of biological disturbance in Frankenfood consumers.

See also BUSH DYNASTY.

FREEDOM rides

The "freedom ride" movement was designed to test court orders that required racial desegregation in interstate transportation. The first rides were organized by the Congress of Racial Equality (CORE) in 1947 after the U.S. SUPREME COURT ordered integrated seating on interstate buses. Several CORE members were arrested in southern states despite the court's ruling, but the demonstrations passed without much fanfare.

Such was not the case in 1961 when a new court ruling ordered desegregation of all terminal accommodations related to interstate commerce. CORE and the Student Nonviolent Coordinating Committee planned a new series of freedom rides, opposed by the KU KLUX KLAN (KKK) and racist police. J. EDGAR HOOVER, meanwhile, insisted that the FEDERAL BUREAU OF INVESTIGATION (FBI) could not protect freedom riders because it was "not a police agency." Instead, Hoover decreed, the bureau would "fulfill its law enforcement function" by keeping state and local police informed of the riders' itinerary—even when those officers were known as members or friends of the KKK.

An integrated team of freedom riders left Washington, D.C., aboard two buses on May 4, 1961. The first violence occurred on May 9 at Rock Hill, South Carolina, where white thugs assaulted three demonstrators. By then FBI headquarters knew that police and Klansmen in Alabama were planning a violent reception for the freedom riders. BIRMINGHAM POLICE commissioner EUGENE ("BULL") CONNOR promised that police would grant the Klan 15 minutes of mayhem at the local bus station when freedom riders arrived on May 14. Connor wanted the riders beaten until they "looked like a bulldog got ahold of them"; he also specifically ordered that black demonstrators be stripped of their clothing so that police could arrest them on charges of indecent exposure when they fled the terminal naked. Police were nowhere to be seen on May 14 when Klansmen attacked the Greyhound bus at Anniston, beat its passengers, and then set the bus on fire. When the Trailways bus reached Anniston, Klansmen rushed aboard and beat several of the riders, permanently disabling Dr. Walter Bergman. FBI agents watched and took notes as the bus, with Klansmen still aboard, proceeded on its way to Birmingham.

Another racist mob was waiting at the Trailways terminal in Birmingham. Police kept their promise, giving the terrorists time to beat the demonstrators, black bystanders, and various journalists before the first squad car arrived. Bull Connor explained his department's failure by noting that May 14 was Mother's Day and claiming most officers were at home with their families. Those riders who were still able to travel, reinforced by others, continued to the state capital at Montgomery on May 20, 1961. Despite FBI warnings of Klan riot plans, Police Commissioner Lester Sullivan stationed no men at the bus depot. Another melee erupted, again with G-men on the sidelines snapping photographs and taking notes. Attorney General Robert Kennedy finally dispatched 500 U.S. Marshals to Montgomery where they held a mob of 3,000 racists at bay outside Rev. Ralph Abernathy's church on the night of May 21. Four Klansmen were arrested on May 22, and federal judge Frank Johnson issued a sweeping injunction against further violence by various Klan factions. On September 1, 1961, a federal grand jury indicted nine

suspects for their role in the Anniston Greyhound attack. Five defendants were convicted in January 1962 and received one year's probation in return for their promise to sever all ties to the Klan. No one was ever punished for the riots in Birmingham and Montgomery.

More than two decades later, in 1983, injured freedom riders Walter Bergman and James Peck sued the FBI for collaborating with Bull Connor and the KKK. A federal court found the FBI liable for injuries suffered by Bergman and Peck. On February 17, 1984, Bergman was awarded $45,000 in damages, while Peck received $25,000.

See also KENNEDY DYNASTY.

FREEMASONS

Freemasonry is an international fraternal order that was founded in England in 1717, though members theoretically trace their group's history to the ancient

Anti-Masonic author William Morgan mysteriously vanished in 1826, while writing an exposé on Masonic ritual. (Author's collection)

"A French Lodge of Freemasons for the Reception of a Master." Copied from the very rare original print, published in 1745 (Bettmann/Corbis)

builders of King Solomon's temple. (Other sources link Freemasonry to the crusading KNIGHTS TEMPLAR, noting that the order's youth division is named for Templar chief Jacques Demolay.) It is organized in "lodges," complete with rituals and recognition signs that are presumably kept secret from the world at large (but widely published through the centuries, sometimes with fictional additions designed to make the group seem sinister). Many U.S. presidents, other officials, and highly placed captains of industry throughout the world have been Freemasons—which, combined with the society's air of nominal secrecy guarantees no end to conspiracy theories surrounding the order.

Anti-Masonic agitation may be dated with some specificity to 1826 and a series of claims made by one William Morgan of Batavia, New York. Depending on the source, Morgan was either a 30-year veteran of Masonic lodges who "broke ranks" or a flagrant liar who conceived plans for revenge after his membership application was rejected. In either case, before his book was published, Morgan was kidnapped by persons unknown and disappeared forever. (Years later, a Mason named Henry Vance confessed on his deathbed that he and two other lodge members had murdered Morgan and dumped his body in the Niagara River.) The book was released in 1827, filled with blood-curdling descriptions of supposed Masonic rituals and vengeance oaths, which prompted an investigation of the order by New York State legislators in 1829. The committee's final report opened with a gratuitous attack on JESUITS and then went on to complain that Freemasons:

have recently made demonstrations of a power, astonishing in its effects, upon the social and political compact of a character such as the friends of free institutions cannot fail to deplore.

A deluge of accusation and condemnation followed, trumpeted by such newspapers as the *Anti-Masonic Beacon* (in New York City) and the *Anti-Masonic Inquirer* (Rochester). Many of the charges were recycled accusations that formerly had been leveled against Jesuits or other institutions of the CATHOLIC CHURCH. Critics of the order also note

Albert Pike, a prominent Freemason, is often credited with drafting the original Ku Klux Klan's constitution. (Author's collection)

that Albert Pike, a high-ranking Mason, helped compose the original KU KLUX KLAN's constitution and may have been the terrorist group's "grand dragon" in Arkansas during RECONSTRUCTION. In more recent times Freemasons have been blamed for carrying out London's JACK THE RIPPER murders of 1888. Author Stephen Knight, who premiered that accusation, buttressed his argument by claiming that the fraudulent *PROTOCOLS OF THE ELDERS OF ZION*—a document forged by czarist secret police to incriminate Jews—was actually a Masonic handbook for world domination. More recently still, Freemasons have been implicated by some critics in cases of satanic ritual abuse against children. Another perennial allegation links the Masonic order to the shadowy ILLUMINATI who have been accused of masterminding every revolution on Earth since the mid-18th century.

See also TERRORISM.

GABON

PORTUGAL "discovered" Gabon in 1472, followed by the NETHERLANDS (1593) and FRANCE (1630). The French established their first permanent colony there in 1839 and absorbed the rest of Gabon as a French territory in 1888. The captive nation finally won independence in August 1960 and elected its seemingly indestructible president, Omar Bongo, in 1967. Through dictatorial means, in the guise of periodic "free" elections, Bongo has remained in power to the present day. Prior to 1990 he ran unopposed in elections staged every five years. In that year strikes and riots forced creation of a "transitional constitution" that legalized multiparty elections, but the move had no effect on Bongo's winning streak (and, in fact, increased the president's term in office to seven years). Bongo's most recent election, in 1998, was marked by claims of fraud from his opponent and general disinterest from the outside world. Gabon is rich in OIL, which fattens Bongo's coffers and the bank accounts of foreign investors. According to the French weekly *L'Autre Afrique,* Bongo presently owns more real estate in Paris than any other foreigner.

GAINESVILLE 8   See LEMMER, WILLIAM.

GAMBIA

PORTUGAL was the first European power to explore present-day Gambia in 1455, but FRANCE edged out the competition in 1681. British slave traders were not far behind, and human bondage was the nation's chief source of revenue before slavery was outlawed in 1807. Gambia became a British Crown colony in 1843 and an independent nation within the British Commonwealth in February 1965. Full independence followed in April 1970, but it brought no semblance of security. In July 1994 a military coup deposed five-term President Jawara, replacing him with Captain Yayah Jammeh. Jammeh suspended the constitution and banned all political parties, easily winning the next rigged election in September 1996. Seven months later, Jammeh returned Gambia to "civilian" rule—with himself as president, empowered to censor the press and impose other autocratic restrictions on dissent. Jammeh crushed a coup by his own bodyguards in January 2000; student riots broke out three months later (also brutally suppressed). Meanwhile, corruption and mismanagement in Gambia's crucial peanut industry caused the export system to collapse, leaving farmers unpaid and unable to sell a bumper crop of the nation's chief commodity. In 2001 Jammeh legalized opposition parties in Gambia, but the move failed to block his reelection for another term as president.

GEMSTONE File

The so-called Gemstone File is said to be a 1,000-page collection of reports or correspondence penned by American gemologist Bruce Roberts between the

1960s and 1975, summarizing a series of supposed conspiratorial events that shaped world history across four decades. (One critic calls it "the most notorious rant in conspiracy history.") According to Roberts—and freelance author Stephanie Caruana, who drafted a "skeleton key" summarizing the larger file—Greek shipping magnate Aristotle Onassis was the key player in a global cast of characters including every U.S. president from 1933 onward, plus supporting players from the CENTRAL INTELLIGENCE AGENCY and a host of other groups operating on both sides of the law. The narrative culminates in 1975, the year before Roberts died of lung cancer, when "[President Gerald] Ford, [HENRY] KISSINGER, and [Nelson] Rockefeller squat like toads on the corpse of America." Other players (or victims) in the ultimate chess game include Franklin and Eleanor Roosevelt, MEYER LANSKY, Joseph Kennedy, billionaire HOWARD HUGHES (allegedly kidnapped by Onassis), LYNDON JOHNSON (ordered by Onassis to ignore conspiracy evidence in the JFK ASSASSINATION), J. EDGAR HOOVER (murdered with a dose of "sodium morphate" in a slice of apple pie), RICHARD NIXON, and the DEATH ANGELS, which was prosecuted for San Francisco's "Zebra" murders in 1974. Some Gemstone believers maintain that British author Ian Fleming used Onassis as the model for fictional supervillain Ernst Stavro Blofeld in three James Bond novels. Most skeptics agree with the judgment of one critic who dismisses the whole narrative as "a big pile of crap."

See also KENNEDY DYNASTY; ROCKEFELLER CLAN.

GENERAL Electric Company

General Electric (GE) is the brainchild of Thomas Alva Edison, inventor of the incandescent electric light. In 1890 Edison consolidated his various businesses into the Edison General Electric Company. Two years later Edison General merged with its primary rivals to become the General Electric Company, headquartered at Schenectady, New York. Today, GE is a huge multinational firm that is involved in a wide variety of markets and activities spanning more than 100 nations. Among other interests, GE is sole owner of the National Broadcasting Company (NBC) and thus a major power in transmission of news and entertainment worldwide. In 2003 GE had the largest market capitalization of any firm on Earth. It employed more than 300,000 persons and reported revenue (in 2001) of $126 billion.

As with all vast multinationals, there is more to GE than we find in raw corporate statistics—and the firm's top executives are unhappy when glimpses of that secret side become public. In 1998 they fought to block publication of author Thomas O'Boyle's book *At Any Cost: Jack Welch, General Electric and the Pursuit of Profit*. That volume revealed, among other things, that members of GE's plastics division were notorious party animals, playing "demolition derby" with rental cars and trashing various hotels so thoroughly that some asked them not to return. Such infantile capers pale by comparison to some of GE's other transgressions, however. Some of those activities include:

1928–1940—GE joined various other U.S. industrial giants in financing ADOLF HITLER's rise to power in GERMANY while providing technological assistance to the Nazi-allied KRUPP ARMS company. GE engaged in price fixing with Krupp to manipulate the price of tungsten carbide, charging U.S. industries 12 times the price per pound that Hitler was required to pay. In 1935–36 a GE subsidiary (the Carboloy Company) made $694,000 in profits from business with the THIRD REICH, while GE received $754,000.

1946—GE vice president Zay Jeffries was charged with conspiracy to monopolize the market in tungsten carbide. Codefendants included W. G. Robbins (president Carboloy Company) and ex-GE trade manager Gustav Krupp (already jailed in Germany for WAR CRIMES). At trial in 1947 the defendants were convicted on five counts. Judge John Knox declared, "Competitors were excluded by purchase and by boycott; prices on unpatented products were fixed, future patent rights were forced into the pool, world markets were divided, and on occasion prices were fixed beyond the scope of any asserted patent protection." Still, Judge Knox ignored the prosecution's request for harsh punishment, fining GE and Carboloy a mere $20,000 each while individual defendants paid a wrist-slap fine of $2,500 each.

1961—GE pleaded guilty in federal court to price fixing and paid a fine of $372,500.

1977—The firm was convicted again of price fixing.

1979—After Alabama authorities sued GE for dumping toxic waste in rivers, corporate lawyers settled the case out of court.

1981—GE was convicted of establishing a $1.25 million fund to bribe public officials in PUERTO RICO.

1985—GE pleaded guilty to 108 counts of fraud on a Minuteman missile contract with the U.S. government. The chief engineer of GE's space systems division was also convicted of perjury. The firm paid a $1 million fine.

1985—In a separate case, GE pleaded guilty to falsifying employee time cards.

1989—GE paid the U.S. government $3.5 million to settle five civil lawsuits on charges of contractor fraud at a jet-engine plant, where company thieves altered 9,000 daily labor vouchers to inflate Pentagon billings.

1990—GE was convicted of criminal fraud for cheating the U.S. Army on a contract for battlefield computers. The firm paid a $16 million fine, of which $11.7 million was used to settle government complaints that GE had padded its bids on 200 *other* military and space contracts. The company was thus "penalized" an average of $58,000 for each fraudulent multimillion-dollar contract it received.

1991—GE led all other U.S. companies in citations received from the Occupational Safety and Health Administration (OSHA). While company spokesman Jack Batty told reporters, "We're always trying to do better," his firm received more than 1,400 citations of federal workplace safety laws spanning a nine-year period. Finally, GE paid a meager $151,003 in penalties for 382 of those violations (25 percent of the total), for an average of $46 per day of violating federal statutes.

1993—GE was among 90 firms and individuals convicted of various felonies in "Operation Ill Wind," a nationwide investigation of corruption in defense industries during the years 1986–90. The final settlement involved $190 million in fines, penalties, and foregone profits (that is, reductions of the usual egregious over-billing).

1999—Soon after George W. Bush announced his presidential candidacy, GE CEO Jack Welch met with key Bush adviser Karl Rove, emerging from that conference to tell associates "a Bush administration would initiate comprehensive deregulation of the broadcast industry, thus resulting in huge new profits for NBC." Various communications companies thereafter funneled at least $9.8 million into Bush campaign coffers. Bush tried to keep his promise, appointing Michael Powell as chief of the Federal Communications Commission to modify FCC regulations (thereby allowing media moguls to own more TV stations without facing antitrust charges), but Congress blocked the move in July 2003. Bush watchers expect the assault on longstanding guidelines of media ownership to continue.

GENERAL Motors Company

This multinational giant was born as the Olds Motor Vehicle Company in 1897 and rechristened with its present name under CEO William Durant in 1908. One year later, bankers rejected Durant's request for a $9.5 million loan to buy out the rival FORD MOTOR COMPANY. That defeat proved no great hardship, however, and in December 1955 General Motors (GM) became the first U.S. company to report profits in excess of $1 billion. Today, it is the world's largest manufacturer of motor vehicles, producing 15 percent of all cars and trucks on Earth in 2002. Its worldwide operations and brands include Buick, Cadillac, Chevrolet, GMC, Holden, Hummer, Oldsmobile (scheduled for closing in 2004), Opel, Pontiac, Saturn, Saab, and Vauxhall. Overseas, GM also owns substantial shares of Alfa Romeo, Daewoo, Fiat, Isuzu, Lancia, Subaru, and Suzuki. Aside from vehicles, GM's subsidiaries include ACDelco, Allison Transmission, General Motors Electro-Motive Division (producing diesel-electric locomotives), and Hughes Electronics (including DirecTV).

By this point in our narrative, it comes as no surprise that various conspiratorial skeletons may be found lurking in GM's closet. Some of its unsavory activities include the following:

1930s—GM's Industrial Relations Department collaborated with the DETROIT POLICE DEPARTMENT and other law enforcement agencies to harass employees deemed "radical" or "communist" for their allegiance to mainstream labor unions. Illegal raids and mass arrests were commonplace in Michigan company towns such as Dearborn, Flint, and Pontiac.

1931—GM formed a business alliance with FAR-BEN INDUSTRIES in GERMANY that would endure beyond the start of World War II. By 1939, GM had invested $30 million in various Farben plants.

1936—Proving that support for ADOLF HITLER was not strictly business, GM executive Alfred Sloan visited Der Führer in Berlin. Upon returning to the United States, he funded national speaking tours by various Nazi supporters, including Governor Eugene Talmadge of Georgia.

1938—GM collaborated with OIL and the DUPONT chemical empire to supply the THIRD REICH and JAPAN with gasoline and other materials critical to their respective war machines. War-related transactions continued beyond the PEARL HARBOR attack, and in fact went on unpunished through 1945. When U.S. troops hit the beach at Normandy on D-day, they met Nazi troops in tanks and other vehicles manufactured by GM's Opel subsidiary. In 1967, after prolonged negotiation, the U.S. government granted GM a $33 million tax exemption in reparation for the "troubles and destruction occasioned to its airplane and motorized vehicle factories in Germany and Austria in World War II."

1940s—GM allegedly conspired to buy and shut down streetcar lines in cities across the United States, thus forcing purchase of their diesel buses as an alternative form of mass transportation. GM apologists deny the charge and term it an "urban legend," but certain facts remain undisputed. National City Lines (NCL), a GM subsidiary, purchased the Los Angeles Railway in 1944 and replaced its famous "red cars" with buses. Nationwide collaboration between GM, Greyhound, Standard Oil, Mack Trucks, and Firestone Tire and Rubber had dismantled 100-plus streetcar systems in 45 cities from coast to coast. In 1947 GM and NCL were charged under the Sherman Antitrust Act with conspiracy to form a mass-transit monopoly and conspiracy to monopolize sales of buses and supplies to companies owned by NCL. In 1949 they were acquitted on the first count but convicted on the second.

Each corporate defendant was fined a paltry $5,000, while their convicted executives were fined one dollar each.

1994—GM and two other corporate defendants paid more than $1 million to settle a federal charge of procurement fraud. As in the 1940s case the penalty amounted to a fraction of their government-contracts profits that were obtained by fraudulent means.

See also COMMUNISM.

GEORGIA

Georgia, on the Black Sea, became a kingdom in about 4 B.C., and by the reign of Queen Tamara (A.D. 1184–1213) its territory included all of Transcaucasia. Tamerlane and the Mongols decimated Georgia's population in the 13th century, and the country has never truly recovered. Through the 16th and 17th centuries, TURKEY and Persia (now IRAN) battled for control of the bloodstained landscape; RUSSIA arrived to "save" Georgia in the 18th century, but the price of protection was virtual slavery. Following the Russian Revolution of 1917, Georgia joined ARMENIA and AZERBAIJAN to form the short-lived anticommunist Transcaucasian Federation. That alliance dissolved in 1918, whereupon Georgia proclaimed independence. Four years later, with its defiant former allies, Georgia was annexed by the Soviet Union as part of a new Transcaucasian Soviet Socialist Republic. It became a separate Soviet republic in 1936, forcibly transformed under JOSEPH STALIN from an agricultural to an industrial, urbanized society. When the USSR collapsed in 1991, Georgia once again declared independence. President Zviad Gamsakhurdia was deposed nine months later (January 1992), amid charges of jailing political opponents, muzzling the press, and generally abusing human rights. Armed conflict with rebels in Abkhazia Province (1992–93) prompted Georgian leaders to seek military aid from Russia, but Russian troops failed to suppress the rebellion. Eduard Shevardnadze was elected president in 2000, winning 83 percent of the national vote, but international observers found the election "marred by irregularities." In 2002 Georgia imported U.S. military advisers, a move sanctioned by President George W. Bush in his pursuit of alleged AL-QAEDA terrorists.

See also BUSH DYNASTY; COMMUNISM.

GERMANY

Based on actual performance, Germany was arguably the most dangerous nation of the 20th century, but its imperial adventures did not begin with the outbreak of World War I in 1914. In the fourth and fifth centuries A.D., German invaders finished off the ailing Roman Empire. In the eighth century, a loose coalition of German warlords (led by the Franks) organized the Holy Roman Empire in conjunction with the CATHOLIC CHURCH, maintaining its grip on Europe at large until 1806. Prussia was the backbone of German militarism, its officers chiefly responsible for the outbreak of World War I. Defeat in that conflict failed to chasten Germany, and ADOLF HITLER soon employed a mixture of racism and xenophobia to launch his fanatical THIRD REICH. Early German victories in World War II might have been permanent but for Hitler's insanity and obsessive pursuit of a HOLOCAUST against Jews and other "inferiors." Defeated once again, Germany was divided after 1945, with the eastern zone under communist control, while the west (under U.S. guidance) restored many "ex"-Nazis to leadership positions. West German chancellor Willy Brandt, winner of a Nobel Peace Prize for his foreign policies, was forced to resign in 1974 after an East German spy was revealed among his top aides. After the collapse of Communism, Germany's two halves were reunited in October 1990. Dedicated Nazi watchers warned that the move might be dangerous in light of recent right-wing terrorist incidents that targeted foreigners and racial minorities throughout Germany. Though banned by law, expressions of pro-Nazi sentiment are increasingly common in the German fatherland, with proponents of a FOURTH REICH found among street-prowling skinhead gangs and "better" elements alike.

See also COMMUNISM; TERRORISM.

GESTAPO

Gestapo is an abbreviation for *Geheime Staatspolizei* ("secret state police" in Germany), arguably the most notorious SECRET POLICE organization of all time. It was created in 1933, after ADOLF HITLER's Nazi Party seized control of GERMANY. Hermann Göring, then Prussian minister of the interior, detached the espionage and political units of the Prussian police to create his new organization, staffed with thousands of zealous Nazis. Göring formally took command of

the force on April 26, 1933, and retained that post until the Gestapo merged with HEINRICH HIMMLER's "elite" SS in April 1936. Under that arrangement, the Gestapo merged with Germany's *Kriminalpolizei* (or *Kripo,* "criminal police") to form a new *Sicherheitspolizei* (or *Sipo,* "secret police"). In 1939 the Sipo merged again, this time with the German army's intelligence unit known as *Sicherheitsdienst* (or *SD,* "security service") to create a new Reich *Sicherheits Hauptamt* (RHSA, "Reich Security Central Office"). New commander Reinhard Heydrich subsequently organized the WANNSEE CONFERENCE where Nazi leaders planned out details of the HOLOCAUST. During World War II Gestapo units known as *Einsatzgruppen* ("task forces") were dispatched throughout occupied nations to round up Jews and other "undesirables," either killing them on the spot or deporting them to concentration camps. Gestapo agents were schooled in torture techniques, and they widely abused the power of *Schutzhaft* ("protective custody") to detain suspects without charges or trial. In effect, Gestapo actions were above the law; as Nazi jurist Werner Best declared, "As long as the [Gestapo] . . . carries out the will of the leadership, it is acting legally." The Gestapo was formally exempted from administrative courts where German citizens could sue the government to compel observance of various statutes. At its peak the Gestapo included some 45,000 agents. Following the THIRD REICH's collapse in 1945, the entire agency was charged en masse with crimes against humanity. Nonetheless, many active members escaped punishment altogether and resumed administrative roles in postwar Germany.

GHANA

Major African civilizations flourished in parts of modern-day Ghana through the 19th century, but they were under constant pressure from European invasion and exploitation. PORTUGAL was first to arrive (1470), followed by Britain (1553), the NETHERLANDS (1595), and SWEDEN (1640). Britain controlled Ghana's "Gold Coast" by 1820, but resistance from the interior's Ashanti rulers was not finally crushed until 1901. Ghana was liberated from the British Empire in March 1957 and became a republic in July 1960. Premier Kwame Nkrumah soon angered the United States by taking policies of "nonalignment" seriously, trading on equal terms with the United States, RUSSIA, and CHINA. In October 1965 he published a book blaming the CENTRAL INTELLIGENCE AGENCY for various coups and other subversive actions throughout Africa and the Third World at large. Washington immediately cut off foreign aid to Ghana, and four months later Nkrumah was deposed by a military coup financed from CIA headquarters. (Right-wing author John Barron later claimed that "the copious files of the Nkrumah regime" revealed that "the KGB had converted Ghana into one vast base for subversion, which the Soviet Union fully intended to use to capture the continent of Africa." Strangely, not one page from those "copious files" has yet been produced.) Coups multiplied during the next 13 years, until Lt. Jerry Rawlings seized power in June 1979 and permitted the election of civilian president Hilla Limann in July. Unsatisfied with the result Rawlings charged Limann with corruption and staged another coup in December 1981. GOLD is Ghana's largest source of foreign exchange, but waffling international prices pushed the industry to near-collapse in 1999 before it was bailed out by investors from SAUDI ARABIA. President John Kufuo, inaugurated in 2001, is the nation's first democratically elected leader, but it remains to be seen whether he can hold office long enough to rescue his country from poverty and corruption. In June 2003 ex-president Rawlings announced publicly that 15 members of Kufuo's parliament had participated directly in the serial murders of 34 women who were slaughtered in Ghana between 1994 and 2000. While pursuing the claim, Ghana's Inspector General of Police, Nana Owusu-Nsiah, said he was "profoundly disappointed with the utterances and conduct of the former president."

GIANCANA, Sam (1908–1975)

A native of Chicago, born in 1908, Sam ("Momo") Giancana was described in one police report as "a snarling, sarcastic, ill-tempered, sadistic psychopath." Those traits served him well as a member of the notorious 42 Gang and later as a contract killer for the PROHIBITION crime syndicate led by Al Capone. A prime suspect in three murders by age 20, Giancana used his ruthless talents to rise swiftly through MAFIA ranks and dominate Chicago's (some say the nation's) underworld by the late 1950s. At the same time he was acutely conscious of the mob's public image and once allegedly issued a murder contract on Desi Arnaz for producing *The Untouchables,* a TV program that portrayed members of the Capone gang as vicious thugs. (The contract was not carried out.)

In 1960 Giancana's influence was critical to the presidential election of John Kennedy. "Momo" guaranteed a Democratic majority in Illinois by means of massive vote fraud and later claimed credit for putting Kennedy in the White House. During the next two years he also collaborated with members of the CENTRAL INTELLIGENCE AGENCY (CIA) on plots to assassinate Cuban leader FIDEL CASTRO. Instead of the rewards he expected, however, Giancana found himself on a mob "hit list" prepared by Attorney General Robert Kennedy, followed day and night by FEDERAL BUREAU OF INVESTIGATION (FBI) agents who also targeted Giancana for illegal bugging and wiretapping. In June 1963 Giancana took the unprecedented step of suing the bureau for harassment. Private investigators filmed G-men in their "lock-step" surveillance of Momo—at church, on the golf course, during cemetery visits—and Judge Richard Austin ruled in the plaintiff's favor, fining Chicago agent-in-charge Marlin Johnson $500 and ordering G-men to track Giancana from a "reasonable distance" in the future.

Giancana's recorded threats against the Kennedy brothers made him a prime suspect in the 1963 JFK ASSASSINATION, but FBI Director J. EDGAR HOOVER's instant "lone-gunman" announcement precluded any serious investigation of mob ties to the killing. Giancana's name was mentioned again in 1968 following the RFK ASSASSINATION, but again the FBI failed to pursue suggestions of conspiracy. Giancana was scheduled as a critical witness when the CHURCH COMMITTEE launched its investigation of FBI and CIA irregularities, but he never had a chance to testify. On June 18, 1975, Momo was murdered in the basement of his Oak Park, Illinois, home by a gunman who shot him seven times in the head.

See also KENNEDY DYNASTY.

GILCHRIST, Joyce

Joyce Gilchrist obtained her degree in forensic chemistry in 1980 while employed in the Oklahoma City Police Department's crime lab. She worked on some 3,000 cases between 1980 and 1999, and in 1985 she was named the department's "civilian employee of the year." Legendary Oklahoma City district attorney Bob Macy dubbed Gilchrist "Black Magic" for her skill in persuading jurors to convict. "It was in reference to a homicide case," Gilchrist later told *60 Minutes II,* "where the defense attorney referred to me in his closing argument as a sorcerer . . . and stated that I seemed to be able to do things with evidence that nobody else was able to do."

And that was the problem.

In 1987 forensic chemist John Wilson of Kansas City warned the Southwestern Association of Forensic Scientists (SAFS) that Gilchrist offered "scientific opinions from the witness stand which in effect positively identify the defendant based on the slightest bit of circumstantial evidence." Convinced that Gilchrist had presented false evidence in court, Wilson ultimately testified against her in three separate murder cases. "When I read the transcripts and saw what she was saying," Wilson told reporters, "I was really shocked. She was positively identifying hair, and there's no way in the world you can do that without DNA."

The SAFS subsequently censured Gilchrist for ethics violations, and in 1988 the Oklahoma Criminal Court of Appeals overturned Curtis McCarty's murder conviction, based on the fact that Gilchrist gave the court "personal opinions beyond the scope of scientific capabilities." In 1989 the same appellate court overturned another murder conviction, finding that Gilchrist had improperly used hair analysis to testify that James Abels had been "in very close and possibly even violent contact" with the victim. Still, Gilchrist was promoted to supervise the Oklahoma City crime lab in 1994 and continued to testify in criminal cases through the remainder of the decade. It was only in August 1999 after her rebuke by federal judge Ralph Thompson that her career began to implode. At issue was the rape-murder conviction of Alfred Brian Mitchell, sentenced to death largely on the strength of Gilchrist's scientific testimony. Judge Thompson labeled her testimony "untrue" and overturned Mitchell's rape conviction. As a result police removed Gilchrist from the lab in March 2000 and assigned her to administrative work. Seven months later the Association for Crime Scene Reconstruction expelled Gilchrist for misrepresented evidence in court. On April 25, 2001, Oklahoma Attorney General Drew Edmondson announced a review of several capital cases that hinged on Gilchrist's testimony. A FEDERAL BUREAU OF INVESTIGATION report published on the same date alleged that Gilchrist

misidentified hairs and fibers or gave testimony "beyond the limits of forensic science" in at least eight felony cases. Most ominous was the reported fact that Gilchrist's testimony had sent 23 defendants to death row, with 11 of those inmates subsequently executed.

On September 25, 2001, Gilchrist was dismissed for "laboratory mismanagement, criticism from court challenges and flawed casework analysis." In October 2001 a federal grand jury subpoenaed evidence from 10 of Gilchrist's murder cases, including nine wherein defendants had been executed. Despite the insistence of Oklahoma's attorney general that "I am personally satisfied that no innocent person was executed," grave doubts remain. No charges have been filed against Joyce Gilchrist for perjury or any other criminal offense, but cases like hers and that of FRED ZAIN have shaken the faith of many Americans in the modern system of capital punishment.

GODFREY, Howard   See SECRET ARMY ORGANIZATION.

GOLD

Prior to the discovery of OIL, gold was the most coveted natural resource on Earth. Explorers risked their lives and fortunes in pursuit of the precious metal, discovering "new" continents in the process and moving swiftly to subjugate their native peoples. When Spanish conquistadors invaded the New World, slaughtering thousands and enslaving tens of thousands more, they openly declared their motive as pursuit of the Three Gs—Gold, Glory, and Gospel (forcibly converting "heathens" to the doctrines of the CATHOLIC CHURCH). Centuries later, the U.S. government pursued a similar policy, violating its "sacred" treaties with aboriginal tribes the moment trespassing prospectors found the smallest trace of gold on "Indian" land. Dutch and British masters did the same in Africa, drafting whole black nations into slavery, herding them en masse into mines that spanned the continent from the Congo to Johannesburg.

The lust for gold was not confined to its pursuit in mines and rivers. Once it was refined and coined, people and nations alike still grappled to corner the market and horde as much of the yellow metal as brute force or trickery would permit. One of the more infamous efforts was the BLACK FRIDAY CONSPIRACY, hatched by robber barons Jim Fisk and Jay Gould, which sparked a nationwide financial panic in 1869. The U.S. government established its gold standard four years later, codified by federal statutes in 1897 and 1900. That standard remained in place until 1935 when President Franklin Roosevelt and Congress discarded the gold standard in favor of "managed" paper currency. Private collection of gold bullion is now banned by law in the United States, though gold remains a medium of exchange between nations. South Africa, the United States, Australia, and Canada are the world's major gold-producing nations: In 1990 they produced 75 percent of the world's total gold supply. By the end of 2000, however, that figure slipped to 58 percent, with dramatic increases from Argentina, Ghana, Indonesia, Mali, Papua New Guinea, Peru, and Tanzania. A World Gold Council, funded by major gold producers around the globe, actively promotes gold to potential buyers in various markets, ranging from industry to personnel apparel.

GRATHWOHL, Larry C.

Ranked among "the most militant members" of the Weatherman Underground terrorist group in the late 1960s, Larry Grathwohl was in fact a FEDERAL BUREAU OF INVESTIGATION informant whose activities, by his own admission, went far beyond simply observing and exposing the criminal acts of others. Habitually armed with a .357 Magnum revolver and a straight razor, Grathwohl advertised himself to fellow Weathermen as a demolitions expert and offered bomb-making classes for radicals of the "New Left." He went further still, in fact, and later confessed to the *New York Times* that he participated in the 1969 bombing of a Cincinnati public school.

On March 6, 1970, a federal grand jury in Detroit indicted Grathwohl and 12 other Weathermen for conspiracy to bomb various military and police facilities. A subsequent indictment, issued on December 7, 1972, dismissed charges against Grathwohl and another defendant, while adding radicals to the list. Despite the serious nature of the charges, including the March 1970 firebombing of a Cleveland police officer's home and a conspiracy to plant bombs in four states, none of the defendants were ever tried. Grathwohl, meanwhile, vanished into the federal witness

protection program and later published a sensational account of his exploits titled *Bringing Down America: An FBI Informer with the Weathermen* (1976).

GREECE

Sophisticated nation-states that were organized in Greece at about 2000 B.C. loosely merged to create the entity known as Classical Greece circa 750 B.C. Greece reached its pinnacle of glory in the fifth century B.C., but foreign wars weakened the union, inviting conquest, and it was reduced to the status of a Roman province by the second century B.C. TURKEY seized Constantinople in 1453 and made the rest of Greece a Turkish province seven years later. Greek rebels rose against the Turks in 1821 and won their independence (supported by Britain, FRANCE, and RUSSIA) in 1827. Under King George I (1863–1920), Greece forcibly expanded its territory by seizures from the crumbling Turkish empire. A failed struggle with Turkey after World War I toppled the Greek monarchy and sent King George II into exile. A short-lived republic was toppled by military coups, and George II returned to lead the country once again—until GERMANY and ITALY arrived to conquer Greece in 1941. Resistance to fascist rule centered around the Greek Communist Party and its military arm, the People's Liberation Army (ELAS). In 1944 ELAS soldiers helped British troops drive German and Italian forces out of Greece.

That victory should have been cause for celebration, but Allied leaders were already focused on the world's next great conflict, that between Communism and the "Free World." At once, British troops and right-wing Greeks turned on the ELAS with a vengeance, driving its leaders into hiding (while telling the world that a "Communist revolt" was in progress). The guerrilla war dragged on through 1946, and that August witnessed an admission from British spokespeople that 228 war criminals of the Nazi SS had been retained by the Crown to hunt leftists in Greece. The "rebellion" was finally crushed with U.S. assistance, reducing Greece to the status of a virtual client state. Washington was alarmed in 1964 when liberal George Papandreou won election as prime minister, but a quiet campaign orchestrated by Greek royalty and the CENTRAL INTELLIGENCE AGENCY drove Papandreou from office in July 1965. He was favored to win reelection in April 1967, but Greek military leaders staged a coup two days before the scheduled vote, imposing martial law complete with censorship, widespread torture, and execution of an estimated 8,000 political prisoners per month. Shortly before that coup, UNITED NATIONS official Gerassimos Gigantes was present when President LYNDON BAINES JOHNSON addressed the Greek ambassador in regard to Greece's ongoing troubles with Turkey in CYPRUS:

> Listen to me, Mr. Ambassador. Fuck your Parliament and your Constitution. America is an elephant. Cyprus is a flea. If these two fleas continue itching the elephant, they may just get whacked by the elephant's trunk, whacked good. . . . We pay a lot of good American dollars to the Greeks, Mr. Ambassador. If your Prime Minister gives me talk about Democracy, Parliament and Constitutions, he, his Parliament and his Constitution may not last very long.

In June 1973 a U.S. Army general called Greece's military dictatorship "the best damn government since Pericles," but it could not last. Another coup ousted dictator George Papadopoulos five months later, and the junta collapsed entirely in 1974 after a failed offensive against Turkey. (At a trial for crimes against humanity in 1975, various defendants testified to the U.S.'s guiding role in the 1967 coup and the atrocities that followed.) Greece has been ruled by elected civilians since 1974 but not without internal strife. Tension with Turkey continues in Cyprus and elsewhere, while the economy lags well behind those of other nations in the European Union. Leftist rebels of the 17 November (17N) movement have waged guerrilla war against the Greek government since 1977 and have been blamed for 20-odd political assassinations. Announcement of a "crackdown" on the group in summer 2002 brought no guarantee of peace.

See also COMMUNISM; FASCISM.

GREEK Orthodox Church

Though divorced from the CATHOLIC CHURCH in the early ninth century, the Greek Orthodox Church shares many (if not all) beliefs of its parent sect. Over time, it has avoided many of the self-inflicted wounds suffered by Roman Catholicism concerning financial irregularities and PEDOPHILE PRIESTS, but the scandal that emerged in spring 2003 was equally serious, involving an alleged assassination plot within the

highest councils of the church. According to a press release of May 23, 2003, the church's Patriarch of Jerusalem, Eireneos I, had filed a lawsuit against his most senior cleric (Metropolitan Timothy of Vostron) for hiring a Palestinian death squad to murder Eireneos. Eireneos cited jealousy as the motive since Timothy had once been a contender for the top slot in Jerusalem's branch of the church. Timothy's Greek attorney Giorgious Alfantakis denied all charges and alluded to plans for a libel suit against Eireneos in ISRAEL. Archbishop Christodoulous, leader of the church in GREECE, appealed for "appropriate solutions" to the case, but no resolution had been found as of press time for this volume.

GRENADA

Grenada occupies 131 square miles of land in the Caribbean. Its original Arawak occupants were slaughtered by rival Caribs, who in turn were decimated when Christopher Columbus arrived in 1498. FRANCE claimed the island in 1672, ruling until British forces captured it in 1762. Slavery flourished until 1833, and Grenada remained a British possession until February 1974. The Marxist New Jewel Movement staged a coup in 1979, replacing Prime Minister Eric Gairy with Maurice Bishop. Alleged to be a protégé of FIDEL CASTRO, Bishop was in turn deposed and killed by military officers on October 19, 1983. Six days later, on orders from President RONALD REAGAN, U.S. troops invaded Grenada and seized control of the island.

Various explanations were offered for that exercise in gunboat diplomacy. First, White House spokespersons claimed that U.S. action was requested by the Organization of Eastern Caribbean States, but that excuse fell flat when Prime Minister Tom Adams (of Barbados) revealed that American agents had approached him on October 15, seeking support for an invasion. Next, Reagan cited the "overriding importance" of evacuating U.S. medical students from Grenada in the face of unspecified "danger"—only to later admit that evacuations aboard charter flights began the day *before* the invasion. Finally, Reagan claimed Grenada was "a Soviet-Cuban colony being readied as a major military bastion to export terror and undermine democracy," asserting that "we got there just in time." No evidence of such a military buildup was forthcoming, and Reagan's press secretary for foreign affairs resigned three days after the invasion, citing "damage to his personal credibility." Leaders of the OECS later admitted receiving CIA payments before the invasion "for a secret support operation."

In the wake of the U.S. assault, Herbert Blaize was elected prime minister, while his party captured 14 out of 15 seats in Parliament. While Blaize and company thanked Ronald Reagan "from the bottom of our hearts," the lone opposition winner resigned in protest against "vote rigging and interference in the election by outside forces." International observers subsequently documented charges of censorship and human-rights violations against the "increasingly authoritarian" Blaize regime. In 1995 Dr. Keith Mitchell became prime minister with a substantial majority vote for his New National Party. Four years later the U.S.-supported NNP won all 15 seats in Grenada's Parliament.

GUARDIANS of the Oglala Nation

Based on South Dakota's Pine Ridge Reservation, the Guardians of the Oglala Nation group, aptly known as GOON, was created in November 1972 by Oglala tribal president Richard Wilson, an outspoken enemy of the AMERICAN INDIAN MOVEMENT (AIM). Initially bankrolled by a $62,000 donation from the Bureau of Indian Affairs, GOON existed (in Wilson's words) to create "an auxiliary police force . . . to handle people like [AIM leader] Russell Means and other radicals." The group came into its own during AIM's siege at Wounded Knee, joining federal officers to fire some 20,000 rounds of ammunition at AIM activists during a one-sided "battle" on March 26, 1973. After the siege was broken they launched a three-year series of reprisals at Pine Ridge, killing at least 69 AIM members or supporters and injuring more than 300 by mid-1976. A series of GOON provocations, followed by FEDERAL BUREAU OF INVESTIGATION (FBI) arrests of AIM members, climaxed on June 26, 1975, with a shootout that claimed the lives of Agents Jack Coler and Ronald Williams. Two AIM members who admitted firing on the agents were acquitted at trial on a self-defense plea, but G-men finally convicted suspect Leonard Peltier with testimony from "witness" Gregory Clifford, who was facing trial for rape until the FBI dismissed those charges in return for his assistance in the Peltier prosecution. Clifford disappeared into the federal Witness Protection Program after Peltier's

trial, but he resurfaced in March 1987, receiving a 45-year prison term for the brutal sex murder of a Colorado woman.

Peltier's incarceration did not end the GOON campaign. In January 1976 GOON members murdered Oglala tribal attorney Byron DeSersa at Pine Ridge. Two suspects in that case, Charles Winters and Dale Janis, plea-bargained for reduced manslaughter charges and received two-year prison terms; their codefendants, Richard Wilson's son and son-in-law, were acquitted on grounds of "self-defense" (though DeSersa was admittedly unarmed when they shot him). Another GOON member, Benny Richards, was suspected in the February 1979 arson slaying of AIM leader John Trudell's wife and three children. That case remains officially unsolved today, along with the majority of crimes committed by GOON vigilantes at Pine Ridge.

GUATEMALA

Once the site of a sophisticated Mayan civilization, Guatemala was conquered by SPAIN in 1524 and would not regain a semblance of independence until 1839. Dictator Manuel Estrada Cabrera ruled the country with an iron hand from 1898 to 1920, followed by General Jorge Ubico Castaneda. Ubico was overthrown in 1944, permitting Guatemala a 10-year glimpse of democracy under liberal presidents Juan Arévalo (1945–51) and Jacobo Arbenz Guzmán (1951–54). Arbenz ran afoul of U.S. investors when he championed land reform in a nation where 2.2 percent of the population owned 70 percent of all land and agricultural workers earned $87 per year for their labors. When the neocolonial United Fruit Company demanded $16 million for its property in Guatemala, Arbenz offered $525,000. Arbenz effectively sealed his own fate with a public statement that "Foreign capital will always be welcome as long as it adjusts to local conditions, remains always subordinate to Guatemalan laws, cooperates with the economic development of the country, and strictly abstains from intervening in the nation's social and political life."

In Washington, President Dwight Eisenhower and the DULLES BROTHERS decided Arbenz was a "communist" and marked him for removal at gunpoint. In March 1953 CENTRAL INTELLIGENCE AGENCY personnel began to funnel arms and cash to right-wing military officers in Guatemala, their efforts climaxed by a coup that deposed Arbenz in June 1954. A year later, the *New York Times* frankly reported that "The United States has begun a drive to scuttle a section of the proposed Covenant of Human Rights that poses a threat to its interests abroad"—specifically a clause that "declares in effect that any country has the right to nationalize its resources." One military junta swiftly followed another in Guatemala after the fall of Arbenz, each new regime more brutal and corrupt than the last. Shortly after one such revolt, in March 1963, journalist Georgie Anne Geyer wrote: "Top sources within the Kennedy administration have revealed that the U.S. instigated and supported the coup." A nonstop reign of terror by the army and its covert death squads wreaked havoc throughout Guatemala, prompting armed guerrilla response from the targets of repression. At least 50,000 persons (some estimates double that figure) "disappeared" or were murdered by government forces between 1966 and the alleged cut-off of U.S. military aid in 1978; countless others were arrested, imprisoned, and tortured. Even without U.S. support, Guatemala's agony dragged on until December 1996 with a minimum of 200,000 reported dead in Latin America's longest-running civil war. In 1999 a Guatemalan truth commission found the army responsible for 97 percent of all atrocities committed since the 1960s, while leftist rebels were blamed for 3 percent. President Alfonso Portillo Cabrera apologized for his nation's brutal history in August 2000 and vowed to prosecute those responsible for WAR CRIMES and to compensate the victims. Still, the process was sluggish at best. Four death-squad members accused of murdering ROMAN CATHOLIC Bishop John Gerardi in 1998 were twice convicted in 2001–02, only to have their verdicts reversed on appeal, while prosecutor Leopoldo Zeissig was driven from Guatemala by death threats. In July 2003 Guatemala's Constitutional Court ruled that former dictator Efrain Rios Montt (blamed for 17,000 murders and the destruction of 400 rural communities during his brief reign in 1982–83) could not be legally barred from seeking the presidency in November.

GUINEA

Susu tribesmen arrived in the region of modern-day Guinea in about A.D. 900, building a sophisticated civilization by the 13th century. FRANCE arrived to "protect" the country in 1849, renaming it French Guinea, and then made it a part of French West Africa in 1895. Independence came in October 1958 under Marxist president Sékou Touré, who suspended diplomatic relations with France in 1965 and aligned his country with RUSSIA. Bauxite exports brought relative prosperity, and Touré was twice reelected to seven-year terms in 1974 and 1981. His death in March 1984 created a power vacuum that was swiftly filled by military rebels under Colonel Lansana Conté. After five years of dictatorship, Conté announced a surprise shift to multiparty democracy, and voters approved a new constitution in 1991. The benefit for Conté was a repeal of presidential term limits, clearing the way for a third-term election in 2003. Despite the outward trappings of democracy, Conté continues to run Guinea with an iron hand while staging military forays into war-torn LIBERIA.

GUINEA-BISSAU

Explorers from PORTUGAL "discovered" modern-day Guinea-Bissau in 1446 and soon transformed the offshore Cape Verde Islands into a center of the brutal slave trade. The first serious revolt against Portuguese colonial rule began in 1956 with foundation of the African Party for the Independence of Guinea-Bissau and Cape Verde. An 18-year guerrilla war ensued, climaxed by a grant of independence for Guinea-Bissau in August 1974. Luis Cabral was installed as president, ruling the country until a military coup deposed him in November 1980. The change brought no relief as new premier João Bernardo Veira was accused of corruption, crony capitalism, and failure to alleviate Guinea-Bissau's abject poverty. Veira aroused further discontent when he imported troops from GUINEA and SENEGAL to combat antigovernment rebels. Even so, by 1998 the insurrectionists controlled most of the country and parts of the capital (Bissau) itself. A cease-fire agreement was crafted in November 1998, but Veira's refusal to disarm his private security guard prompted the rebels to depose him in May 1999. Independence leader Kumba Yalá emerged as Guinea-Bissau's new president in 2000 following a period of military rule, but his popular support thus far has failed to raise Guinea-Bissau from its status as one of the world's poorest nations.

GULF of Tonkin incident

On August 2, 1964, North Vietnamese torpedo boats allegedly attacked the U.S. destroyer *Maddox* while that ship was on routine patrol in the Gulf of Tonkin. Two days later a similar attack was reportedly directed at the USS *Turner Joy*. President LYNDON BAINES JOHNSON appeared on national television that evening to announce that U.S. aircraft would retaliate for the unprovoked attacks by bombing targets in North VIETNAM. On August 7 the U.S. Senate passed the Gulf of Tonkin Resolution with only two negative votes (from Ernest Gruening of Alaska and Wayne Morse of Oregon). That resolution gave Johnson a virtual blank check for military escalation in Southeast Asia, authorizing him "to take all necessary measures to repel any armed attack against the forces of the United States and to prevent further aggression." The rest is tragic history: More than 55,000 Americans and at least 1 million Vietnamese killed during the next decade, while untold thousands more were wounded, maimed, left homeless, or otherwise traumatized forever.

Six years elapsed, and Johnson was retired to private life before investigative journalists and politicians confirmed what antiwar activists had long suspected—that is that the "Gulf of Tonkin incident" was a complete and utter lie, concocted by the Pentagon and the White House as a means of securing approval for a massive military commitment in Southeast Asia. Today, with the benefit of hindsight and multiple exposés, we know the following facts to be true:

1. The USS *Maddox* and *Turner Joy* were not engaged in anything resembling "routine surveillance" of North Vietnam; in fact, those ships were engaged in aggressive intelligence-gathering maneuvers, synchronized with attacks on North Vietnam that were coordinated by the South Vietnamese navy and the Laotian air force. Scholar Daniel Hallin writes that concerted attacks on North Vietnam occurred on August 1, 1964, as "part of a campaign of increasing military pressure on the North that the United States had been pursuing since early 1964." In those circumstances any "aggressive" moves made by North Vietnam would constitute self-defense, and yet . . . .

2. The reported attacks never happened at all. Captain John Herrick, commanding the *Maddox,* informed his superiors that the initial report of a PT-boat attack resulted from "freak weather conditions" and "almost total darkness," coupled with an "overeager sonarman" who "was hearing [the] ship's own propeller beat." Squadron commander James Stockdale later told the press, "I had the best seat in the house to watch that event, and our destroyers were just shooting at phantom targets. There were no PT boats there. . . . There was nothing there but black water and American fire power." Johnson himself acknowledged as much in 1965 when he said, "For all I know, our Navy was shooting at whales out there."

3. The deception was deliberate, not a mistake. Author Tom Wells notes that the U.S. media "described the air strikes that Johnson launched in response as merely 'tit for tat'—when in reality they reflected plans the administration had already drawn up for gradually increasing its overt military pressure against the North." Author Daniel Hallin adds that U.S. journalists possessed "a great deal of information available which contradicted the official account; it simply wasn't used. The day before the first incident, Hanoi had protested the attacks on its territory by Laotian aircraft and South Vietnamese gunboats. It was generally known . . . that 'covert' operations against North Vietnam, carried out by South Vietnamese forces with U.S. support and direction, had been going on for some time."

4. The Gulf of Tonkin Resolution was written *before* the alleged attacks. This revelation comes from George Ball, a member of Johnson's inner circle who served as undersecretary of state in 1964. According to Ball a resolution endorsing "all measures, including the commitment of force" was drafted in June 1964, but it was not submitted for ratification until after Johnson accused North Vietnam of "open aggression." In 1995 ex-Secretary of Defense Robert Strange McNamara recalled a 1964 comment from Ball affirming that "many of the people who were associated with the war . . . were looking for any excuse to initiate bombing."

GULF War

In late July 1990 SADDAM HUSSEIN conferred with April Gillespie, then U.S. ambassador to IRAQ, and informed her that he planned to invade KUWAIT (a part of Iraq's Basra Province until 1899 when Great Britain severed it from Iraq and claimed Kuwait as a colony). Gillespie raised no objections, and the invasion proceeded on August 2. In short order a publicity campaign was mounted by professional advertisers condemning Iraqi WAR CRIMES in Kuwait. The most sensational claim involved allegations that Iraqi soldiers removed infants from hospital incubators and smashed their heads against the wall. Months later, *TV Guide* and other media outlets identified the source of those accusations as a Kuwaiti actress (and, some claimed, the Kuwaiti ambassador's daughter).

True or false, the claims roused public opinion against Iraq. One month after the invasion, on September 6, President George H. W. Bush sent 125,000 U.S. troops to neighboring SAUDI ARABIA. Iraq requested negotiation on specific terms—guaranteed access to the Persian Gulf (cut off when Britain created Kuwait); settlement of border disputes in the Ramala oilfield (95 percent Iraqi territory); and a Kuwaiti plebiscite on possible reunion with Iraq—but Bush refused and sent another 800,000 troops between November 1 and November 8, 1990. (In the United States, meanwhile, public opinion polls showed that 75 percent of the population was opposed to war with Iraq, even if sanctions failed to resolve the conflict.) On November 29, under U.S. pressure, the UNITED NATIONS authorized use of military force to expel Iraq from Kuwait. Six days later, ISRAEL threatened to launch a unilateral attack if the UN failed to move against Iraq. Finally, on January 16, 1991, a coalition dominated by U.S. forces launched "Operation Desert Storm," expelling Iraqi troops from Kuwait in short order.

Or did they?

Soon after the last shots were fired, French philosopher Jean Baudrillard aired his theory that the Gulf War never occurred. The whole sequence of events, in Baudrillard's view, was a media charade concocted to dazzle a global audience "increasingly divorced from the truth." Critics scoffed at Baudrillard's claim, noting that he had also predicted (in 1990) that the war would not occur. His other claims—that the year 2000 never happened and that Disneyland somehow conceals "the unreality of

America"—admittedly did nothing to enhance Baudrillard's credibility. Still, conspiracists of the sort who believe that APOLLO PROJECT technicians faked a series of trips to the Moon were inclined to take Baudrillard more seriously.

Assuming that the Gulf War *did* occur, it still provides fertile ground for conspiracy theories. President Bush clearly coveted Kuwaiti OIL, just as his son's craving for Iraqi petroleum reserves inspired OPERATION IRAQI FREEDOM 11 years later. In the wake of battle, thousands of U.S. combat veterans displayed symptoms of an unknown disease that was soon labeled *Gulf War Syndrome*. Pentagon spokespersons ardently denied that Iraqi troops had used chemical weapons during the brief conflict, but skeptics recalled similar denials in respect to AGENT ORANGE and the VIETNAM War. At length, physicians surmised that the various symptoms displayed by Gulf vets might derive from breathing toxic fumes around Kuwaiti oilfields, allegedly torched by retreating Iraqi troops. Once again, the Pentagon was caught lying, however. Between 1996 and 2003 the American Gulf Veterans Association collected "numerous reports from veterans stating that U.S. forces were responsible for setting the oil well fires at the end of the Gulf War." In March 2003 the AGVA released one veteran's affidavit, which read in part:

We were mustered into the briefing tent at which point a gentleman whom I first had thought to be an American, but I was concerned because he was wearing a UN uniform and insignias, began to brief us on the operation. There was concern that America, the American public, might see this conflict as an unnecessary thing, and we were asked to do this, or we were ordered to do this in order to sway any American public opinion to remove any doubts whatsoever that Saddam Hussein and his regime were a terrible evil that had to be dealt with.

After that briefing, said the anonymous soldier, troops were issued explosives and ordered to detonate specific oil wells, resulting in widespread fires. The soldier admitted, "I carried out my mission parameters and then I withdrew and concealed myself until such a time as the front moved past me." Spokespeople for the George W. Bush administration have thus far ignored the accusations, and members of his father's administration have no comment.

GUYANA

During the age of exploration, Britain, FRANCE, and Holland all established colonies in the region of present-day Guyana. Dutch settlers were dominant by the 17th century, but the Napoleonic wars brought drastic change, and the new colony of British Guiana was created in 1831. Slavery remained legal for another three years, followed by mass importation of cheap labor for large foreign-owned plantations (with the result that 93 percent of Guyana's current population is of African or East Indian descent). British Guiana was made a Crown colony in 1928, with "home rule" granted in 1953. Dr. Cheddi Jagan was elected the nation's first president on a platform of social reform, but talk of workers' rights and public education prompted Britain to unseat the new government by military force five months later with an announcement that "Her Majesty's Government are not prepared to tolerate the setting up of communist states in the British Commonwealth." CENTRAL INTELLIGENCE AGENCY (CIA) personnel infiltrated the country to bribe labor leaders, ensuring that any unions that were permitted to function would rubber-stamp sweetheart contracts proposed by international investors. When Jagan was elected a second time, in 1957, the CIA organized mass demonstrations against him, erupting into widespread strikes and rioting. A change of government in England offered hopes for freedom in 1964, but the *New York Times* reported that the Labor Party, "bowing to United States wishes," had "ruled out early independence for British Guiana." Liberation came two years later, and the country resumed its traditional name. President Forbes Burnham ruled for the next 21 years until his death in 1985. During that time Guyana earned a reputation as a haven for off-beat foreign cultists, climaxed by mass murder and suicide at Jonestown in 1978. In a nation racked by bitter racial antagonism and violence, Cheddi Jagan finally captured the presidency in 1992, but he achieved little in terms of relieving Guyana's grim poverty. Bharrat Jagdeo, an ethnic East Indian, assumed the presidency in 1999, and Guyana's economic stagnation continued. Jagdeo's reelection in 2001, amid accusations of widespread voter fraud, sparked race riots among Afro-Guyanese who consider him the enemy.

See also COMMUNISM; JONESTOWN MASSACRE.

HAARP

HAARP is the High-frequency Active Auroral Research Project that is described by its creators as "a scientific endeavor aimed at studying the properties and behavior of the ionosphere, with particular emphasis on being able to understand and use it to enhance communications and surveillance systems for both civilian and defense purposes." If the prospect of converting Earth's atmosphere into one vast listening device were not alarming enough, conspiracists insist that HAARP's true goal is to "superheat" the ionosphere with potentially catastrophic results. As described on the Internet Web site "60 Greatest Conspiracies," HAARP's huge transmitter (based at a 23-acre complex near Gakona, Alaska) "zaps the earth's ionosphere with high-frequency radio waves" and thus dramatically increases its temperature. Some alarmists have dubbed HAARP "the Pentagon's doomsday death ray," blaming it for a variety of worldwide disasters (including the crash of TWA FLIGHT 800). Theorists charge (and federal sources deny) that HAARP's destructive potential includes disruption of aircraft and missile guidance systems, "weather modification plots and perhaps even MIND-CONTROL experiments." Environmentalists, for their part, question the advisability of tampering with the ionosphere for any reason whatsoever.

HAITI

Haiti was occupied by Arawak natives until Christopher Columbus arrived in December 1492, swiftly annihilating them by the sword, slave labor, and disease. SPAIN ruled the island until ousted by FRANCE in 1697. The island's population of 480,000 African slaves revolted in 1791, led by Pierre-Dominique Toussaint Louverture and declaring independence in 1801. NAPOLEON BONAPARTE briefly suppressed the rebels, but they triumphed in 1804 under leader Jean-Jacques Dessalines, and the new country resumed its original Arawak name. Sadly, the revolution wrecked Haiti's economy, and disputes with neighboring Santo Domingo (now the DOMINICAN REPUBLIC) further retarded development under a series of corrupt dictators. In 1905 Haiti "accepted" a U.S. customs receivership which lasted until 1941 and included 19 years of occupation by U.S. Marines to ensure "stability" on behalf of foreign investors. After World War II Haiti enjoyed four years of democratic government, which was subsequently wiped out in 1949 by the ascension of military strongman Paul Magliore. In 1957 Magliore was eventually replaced by François ("Papa Doc") Duvalier, a sadistic tyrant whose secret police—the Tonton Macoutes—used a mixture of voodoo and raw brutality to suppress dissent. In the early 1960s elements of the MAFIA tried to unseat Duvalier, replacing him with a ruler more amenable to tourism (that is, gambling), but Duvalier hung on with U.S. support until 1971, succeeded by son Jean-Claude (also known as "Baby Doc"). In the 1980s, already one of the world's most crowded nations, Haiti became one of the first to suffer from the spreading AIDS epidemic. When popular rebellion finally drove Baby Doc from the country in February 1986, he fled with satchels of loot aboard a U.S. Air Force jet.

While publicly committed to democracy in Haiti, Washington granted $30 million in military aid to Haitian army in 1986–87. In the 21 months between Baby Doc's flight and the elections scheduled for November 1987, Haitian soldiers killed more people than Duvalier had slaughtered in the past 15 years. Throughout the election campaign, CENTRAL INTELLI-GENCE AGENCY personnel were "involved in a range of support for a range of candidates." Violence post-poned the balloting from November 1987 to January 1988, whereupon the army's candidate declared vic-tory in a process widely viewed as fraudulent. Blood-shed continued for the next two years, climaxed by the election of charismatic reformer Jean-Bertrand Aristide. Elected in 1990, Aristide weathered one coup attempt before his inauguration in February 1991. Seven months later, another military coup massacred Aristide's supporters; U.S. troops returned again to impose "order." UNITED NATIONS peacekeepers fol-lowed American troops and remain in Haiti today. A rebellion in 2004 finally drove Aristide from office, and he remains in exile as of this writing.

HAMMARSKJÖLD, Dag (1905–1961)

Swedish native Dag Hammarskjöld, born in 1905, was an outstanding student at Uppsala University. Fascinated with political economy, he served vari-ously as the governor of Uppland, prime minister of Sweden, a member of the Hague Tribunal, and chair-man of the Nobel Foundation. In 1953 he was elected secretary general of the UNITED NATIONS (UN) and was reelected to a second term in 1957. Much of his time in office was devoted to a futile quest for peace in the Middle East where ISRAEL and her Arab neigh-bors were in constant conflict. In July 1960 the focus shifted toward the Belgian Congo where rebellion and mass murder threatened the stability of all of Africa. On September 18, 1961, while returning from an emergency conference in Leopoldville, Ham-marskjöld's plane crashed near the border separating Katanga and North Rhodesia killing all 16 persons aboard. Three separate inquiries concluded that the crash was caused by pilot error, but the investigators did not exclude "other possibilities."

Conspiracy theories flourished for the next four decades, including a 1992 claim by two former UN officials that Hammarskjöld's plane was shot down by mercenaries hired by a consortium of Belgian, British, and U.S. mining companies with large invest-ments in the Congo. In August 1998 spokespeople for SOUTH AFRICA's Truth and Reconciliation Com-mission announced that official letters dating from the apartheid era described a conspiracy to kill Ham-marskjöld. The letters were written by officers of the South African Institute for Maritime Research, a front for that nation's military intelligence apparatus under the former white-supremacist government, and detailed a murder plot hatched between British Intel-ligence (MI5) and the U.S. CENTRAL INTELLIGENCE AGENCY (CIA). One letter states that "In a meeting between MI5, special ops executive and the SAIMR, the following emerged—it is felt that Hammarskjöld should be removed." The same letter went on to say that "Allen DULLES [then director of the CIA] has promised full co-operation from his people." A sec-ond document outlined plans to sabotage Ham-marskjöld's aircraft with explosives planted in the wheel bay, primed to detonate when the landing gear was retracted on takeoff. In light of past disclosures, few observers were persuaded by a British declara-tion that "intelligence agents of the United Kingdom do not go around bumping people off." Ham-marskjöld, perhaps, had the last word on the subject in a poem penned during his college days. He wrote:

Tomorrow we shall meet,
Death and I,
And he shall thrust his sword
Into one who is wide awake.

HAMPTON, Fred (1948–1969)

An Illinois native, born in 1948, Fred Hampton was by all accounts a remarkable young man. At age 18 he organized and led a successful campaign to deseg-regate Chicago swimming pools under auspices of the National Association for the Advancement of Colored People. A year later he was affiliated with the more militant BLACK PANTHER PARTY, marked by the FEDERAL BUREAU OF INVESTIGATION (FBI) as a dangerous radical. Chicago agent-in-charge Marlin Johnson opened a file on Hampton in late 1967 that expanded to 12 volumes and some 4,000 pages during the next two years. In February 1968 Johnson requested wiretaps on Hampton's mother; three months later Hampton was listed in the bureau's Agitator Index as a "key militant leader." By that time Hampton faced local charges of stealing ice-cream bars valued at $71. He was convicted in that case, drawing a prison term of two to five years, but he was released in August 1969 on an appeal bond.

The FBI was not idle while Hampton fought the theft case in court. Between December 1968 and April 1969 members of the bureau's illegal COINTELPRO team used anonymous letters to provoke a gang war between Hampton's Panthers and members of the Blackstone Rangers. WILLIAM O'NEAL, a bureau informant and agent provocateur, was installed as security chief of the Illinois Panthers in February 1969, later serving as Hampton's personal body-guard. G-men raided the Chicago Panther office on June 4, 1969, ransacking the building and arresting eight persons in an alleged search for federal fugitives (none of whom were found on the premises).

Soon after that raid, FBI leaders approached members of the CHICAGO POLICE DEPARTMENT, asking them to conduct additional Panther raids. A series of violent clashes ensued, leaving two police officers and two Panthers dead by the end of July and nine persons jailed on various felony charges. Following the second police raid on July 30, "mysterious" fires broke out in the Panther office and caused extensive damage. A third raid, on October 21, 1969, left the remodeled office in shambles once again. Throughout that series of attacks, authorities found nothing to support FBI claims that the Chicago Panthers had stockpiled illegal weapons.

On November 9, 1969, Chicago agents learned that Hampton was scheduled for promotion to serve as the Panther Party's national chief of staff if incumbent David Hilliard was imprisoned for threatening President RICHARD NIXON. Accordingly, G-men turned up the pressure on local police to destroy Hampton, a campaign that gathered steam after November 13 when another shootout in Chicago killed two Panthers and two police officers. Eight days later agents met with representatives of Illinois State's Attorney Edward Hanrahan and provided them with information collected by William O'Neal. The package included a detailed floor plan of Hampton's apartment, with various objects helpfully labeled—including "Fred's bed." That same day, November 21, 1969, the Chicago field office reported to FBI headquarters that "[o]fficials of the Chicago police have advised that the department is currently planning a positive course of action relative to this information."

On the night of December 3, 1969, some unknown person sedated Fred Hampton with a dose of secobarbitol before he went to bed. Hampton was unconscious at 4:45 the next morning when state and local police stormed the apartment. Panther Mark Clark was killed by the first police gunshot as officers burst through the door. Dying, he triggered the only shot fired from a Panther weapon that morning, a shotgun blast into the floor. Police swept through the apartment, firing an estimated 90 shots at unarmed targets. Fred Hampton died in his bed, shot twice in the head at close range with a pistol, execution style. Five other Panthers were wounded in the fusillade, and various tenants of the apartment were charged with "attempted murder."

In the wake of Hampton's death, one member of the raiding party (Sgt. Daniel Groth) told reporters, "Our men had no choice but to return fire" during the raid. Ballistic evidence soon gave the lie to that claim while critics dubbed Hampton's killing an assassination. Agent M. Wesley Swearingen supported that claim, later testifying under oath that a member of the bureau's Racial Squad told him, "We gave [police] a copy of the detailed floor plan . . . so that they could raid the place and kill the whole lot."

Agent-in-charge Johnson was blasé in his public statements—"What they did with the information was none of our concern."—but he cabled Hoover on December 11 to boast that "The raid was based on information furnished by the informant. . . . This information was not available from any other source and subsequently proved to be of tremendous value." He requested a $300 bonus payment for William O'Neal, which Hoover personally approved on December 17, 1969, "for uniquely valuable services which he has rendered over the past several months." (In all, O'Neal earned $30,000 from the FBI between 1969 and 1972.)

To preserve appearances, Agent Johnson requested a federal grand-jury investigation on December 13, 1969, to determine whether police had violated anyone's civil rights during the Hampton raid. Attorney General John Mitchell assigned Assistant Attorney

General Jerris Leonard to chair the hearings, which began on December 21. Four months later, an FBI memo of April 8, 1970, disclosed that "AAG Jerris Leonard . . . advised SAC Marlin Johnson in strictest confidence that no indictments of police officers are planned. . . . The above is based on an agreement whereby Hanrahan will dismiss the local indictments against the BPP members." The police, in return for absolution, agreed to keep silent regarding FBI involvement in the raid.

Members of the Clark and Hampton families were not satisfied with the grand jury's findings. In 1970 they filed a $47.7 million lawsuit against Hanrahan and others, charging conspiracy to violate the civil rights of Fred Hampton and Mark Clark. (A new grand jury indicted Hanrahan and 13 police officers for conspiracy in August 1971, but the charges were later dismissed.) Nearly a decade passed before evidence uncovered in that case revealed the bureau's central role in Hampton's death. Attorneys for the plaintiffs persuaded ex-Agent Swearingen to testify, and the defendants finally settled with a payment of $1.85 million in November 1982. One attorney in the case described that settlement as "an admission of the conspiracy that existed between the FBI and Hanrahan's men to murder Fred Hampton."

HANSSEN, Robert (1945–)

A Chicago native, born in 1945, Robert Hanssen was the only son of a brutal police officer who constantly humiliated him while hounding him to become a doctor. After graduating from Knox College, Hanssen enrolled at Northwestern University's dental school in 1966 and studied there for two years and then dropped out shortly after his marriage in August 1968. He ultimately earned a master's degree in business administration from Northwestern (1973) and became a certified public accountant. He then spent two years with the CHICAGO POLICE DEPARTMENT's Internal Affairs division. Hanssen joined the FEDERAL BUREAU OF INVESTIGATION (FBI) in January 1976, spending two years on white-collar crime investigations in Indiana, where his supervisors "thought Bob Hanssen walked on water."

Still he was dissatisfied; he was anxious for a foreign-intelligence assignment to make use of the Russian he studied in college. Transferred to New York City in 1978, Hanssen organized a major sting operation to capture Soviet spies, but he was disappointed once again. As a colleague recalled, "He set up this squad . . . and well over half the FBI guys called in from home. They didn't want to work on Sunday, so the Russians got away." Thereafter, Hanssen apparently resented the bureau and decided to betray it for profit. In 1979 he accepted $20,000 from Russian military intelligence (GRU) to reveal various FBI secrets, including the identity of Russian double-agent Dmitri Polyakov (executed in 1988 after he was betrayed a second time by CENTRAL INTELLIGENCE AGENCY [CIA] traitor ALDRICH AMES). Hanssen's career as a spy was nearly ruined in 1980 when his wife caught him writing a letter to his Russian paymasters and he confessed his illicit activity. In lieu of surrendering to the bureau, however, Hanssen consulted a Catholic priest who advised him to stop spying, seek counseling, and give the Soviet money to charity.

Religious vows notwithstanding, Hanssen kept spying until 1981 when he was transferred to FBI headquarters as a supervisory agent. Two years later he was transferred to the FBI's Soviet Analytical Unit in Washington and then back to New York City as a supervisor in 1985. Aware that G-men did not monitor mail sent to the homes of KGB officers who were stationed in the United States, Hanssen wrote to agent Viktor Charkashin in October 1985 and offered to sell classified data for $100,000. His letter—signed "B"—proved his worth by naming three KGB agents secretly serving the United States. Two were subsequently executed; the third was sentenced to 15 years in a Russian labor camp.

During the next 15 years Hanssen emerged as one of Russia's most valuable spies in the United States. He betrayed entire espionage networks while evading detection by his fellow G-men. Returned to headquarters as an intelligence analyst in 1987, he burrowed deeper, using his spare time and advanced computer skills to expose high-level secrets of the FBI, the CIA, and the NATIONAL SECURITY AGENCY. Moscow was delighted, and his coworkers were none the wiser. G-men had their first clear chance to capture Hanssen in 1990 when brother-in-law Mark Wauck, a Chicago FBI agent, grew suspicious of Hanssen's cash reserves. Wauck told his superiors that Hanssen kept unusual amounts of money at home and that he suspected that Hanssen was spying for Russia. The bureau did nothing, and Hanssen continued his illegal operations for another decade. He earned a small fortune from the Soviets but wisely resisted the urge to indulge in extravagant spending. (One deviation from that cautious pattern was his expensive romance with a stripper, whom he once flew to Hong Kong when there for an inspection tour of the FBI legal attaché's office.)

In the end it was a Russian double-agent who betrayed Robert Hanssen. In the latter part of 2000 a KGB source supplied G-men with some of the material furnished by Hanssen since 1985. The source did not know Hanssen's name, but fingerprints were lifted from one of the plastic bags that contained certain documents. Thus identified, Hanssen was placed under surveillance (with his office bugged) from December 12, 2000, through February 5, 2001, and agents noted the location of a "dead drop" where he left information for his Russian contacts. When Hanssen was arrested en route to make another delivery on February 18, 2001, he asked the agents who surrounded him, "What took you so long?"

Hanssen confessed his crimes in custody and bargained with federal prosecutors to escape the death penalty. On July 6, 2001 he pleaded guilty to 13 counts of espionage; 10 months later, on May 9, 2002, he received a prison term of life without parole. Former FBI/CIA Director WILLIAM WEBSTER was appointed to investigate Hanssen's long career as a spy, producing a report highly critical of the bureau's failures (including laps in reviewing its agents' financial records). A month before his final sentencing, it was reported that Hanssen had provided "valuable aid" in closing some of the bureau's security loopholes against future spies.

HARDING, Warren Gamaliel (1865–1923)

A political product of the corrupt OHIO GANG, Warren Harding served as a state legislator (1899–1903), lieutenant governor (1904–05), and U.S. senator (1915–21) before his inauguration as president. Harding was elected on a promise to restore "normalcy" in America after the turmoil of World War I and the PALMER RAIDS, but instead he brought new levels of corruption to the capital, revealed after his premature death, in the TEAPOT DOME scandal. (Harding's secretary of the interior, Bernard Fall, would be the first cabinet member convicted of crimes committed while in office.)

The Bureau of Investigation's (BI) growth stalled under Harding and new chief WILLIAM J. BURNS, with the agent force expanding from 346 to 401 while support staff was cut from 294 to 189. (The budget also deceased, from $2,342,751 in 1921 to $2,166,997 in 1923.) Many of the new agents were "dollar-a-year men," appointed to the BI by political cronies who were anxious to fill their pockets with graft. Attorney General HARRY DAUGHERTY used the bureau as a blunt instrument to punish striking railroad workers in 1922 and sent agents to raid the offices of his critics in Congress. PROHIBITION enforcement languished while bootleg gangs took their first steps toward establishment of a national crime syndicate.

President Harding, meanwhile, amused himself with mistress Nan Britton (who bore his child out of wedlock in 1919) and his personal bootlegger. Several historians claim (and one reports as fact) that Harding joined the KU KLUX KLAN soon after his inauguration. The Klan's "Imperial Wizard" confirmed those reports, and while his word is naturally suspect, Klan members nationwide held mourning ceremonies in August 1923 after Harding died while traveling. Various accounts of his last hours attribute Harding's death to food poisoning, a stroke, or possible assassination by persons unknown. For years afterward, Ohio Klan leaders posted an honor guard at his gravesite.

HARDY, Robert W.

On August 22, 1971 FEDERAL BUREAU OF INVESTIGATION (FBI) Director J. EDGAR HOOVER joined Attorney General John Mitchell to announce the arrest of 20 anti–VIETNAM War activists in or near the Camden, New Jersey, federal building. Five days later Mitchell announced the indictment of 28 defendants on charges of destroying government property, interfering with the Selective Service System, and conspiracy to destroy records from the Camden draft board, the FBI's resident agency, and the Army Intelligence office. The defendants (including four Catholic priests and a Lutheran minister) called themselves "America's conscience"; critics and defenders alike dubbed them the "Camden 28."

At trial, the government's key witness was Robert Hardy, an FBI informant who approached the bureau in June 1971 with word that a group of "friends" planned to burglarize the Camden draft board. G-men later claimed that they employed Hardy in hopes of capturing the persons who had raided an FBI office at Media, Pennsylvania, three months earlier, removing and publicizing documents that exposed the bureau's illegal COINTELPRO operations, but in fact Hardy's activities went far beyond providing inside information on a criminal conspiracy. At trial, the Camden defendants testified that they had abandoned their burglary plan as hopeless before Hardy joined the group and resurrected the idea. Hardy himself, under oath, admitted proposing a break-in, offering his "expertise at breaking and entering," and providing "90 percent" of the tools used to invade the federal building. Defense attorneys urged the jury to acquit all 28 defendants if the FBI had gone to "intolerable lengths" that were "offensive to the basic standards of decency and shocking to the universal sense of justice." After three days of deliberation, the panel acquitted all 28 defendants on all charges.

HARE Krishnas

The International Society of Krishna Consciousness (ISKCON) was founded in 1966 by Indian "swami" A.C. Bhaktivedanta Prabhupada and American acolyte Keith Ham (also known as Kirtanananda Bhaktipada). From all appearances, Prabhupada was an amiable pacifist who was content to oversee a Manhattan curio shop while his young disciples shaved their heads, donned saffron robes, and begged for money to the tune of "Hare Krishna" chants. Keith Ham ran ISKCON behind the scenes, and in the words of one associate he soon "decided that Swami Prabhupada was an old fart who didn't know as much as [Ham] did about marketing a new idea." In pursuit of that goal Ham purchased 130 acres of land outside Moundsville, Virginia, in 1968 and named it New Vrindaban, expanding the settlement to 2,800 acres by 1983. Local opposition, including several incidents of violence, finally prompted Swami Prabhupada to ask his flock:

When New Vrindaban has been attacked twice, thrice, why are you not keeping guns? Where violence is, there must be violence. We are not followers of Gandhi's philosophy. Ours began on the fields of war. If somebody attacks you, you must protect yourselves to the best of your ability.

Accordingly, Ham began to stockpile weapons and recruiting a team of enforcers more notable for their criminal records than any devotion to prayer.

Swami Prabhupada died in 1977, dividing his global religious empire among 11 gurus, each with his own religious turf. Keith Ham promptly declared his 10 rivals "in *maya*" (that is, living in sin) and launched a latter-day crusade to consolidate the cult under his personal control. The first known ISKCON murder claimed disciple Steve Bovan at Newport Beach, California, in October 1977. Six hours later, another local California ISKCON guru Alexander Kulik was arrested with $1.5 million worth of HEROIN in his possession. In February 1980 police raided another ISKCON compound, north of San Francisco, confiscating an arsenal of illegal weapons and explosives. Back at New Vrindaban, polygamous guru Dennis ("Dharmatma") Gorrick made a killing through fraud, including mass sales of counterfeit sports memorabilia. Between 1983 and 1985 ISKCON banked $10 million from sales of bootleg T-shirts, caps, and other items bearing likenesses of famous (and copyrighted) cartoon characters.

Internal squabbling over those illicit profits sparked further dissension in the cult, resulting in assaults, homicides, and other violent acts. In January 1986 raiders from New Vrindaban stole three cars, 23,000 books, and $15,000 in cash from a rival ISKCON compound at Berkeley, California. Sued for the thefts in court, Ham was forced to pay $40,000 in damages. In 1986 New Vrindaban enforcer Tom Drescher was convicted of killing two wayward disciples. Ham and two cohorts were indicted in May 1990 on three counts of racketeering, six counts of mail fraud, and one count of conspiracy. He dismissed the charges as "absurd," but a jury disagreed, convicting him in 1991. His appeal in that case was successful, but a second jury convicted him again in 1996, and Ham was finally consigned to prison.

HAYES, Rutherford B. (1822–1893)

Ohio native Rutherford Hayes was born in October 1822 and graduated from Harvard Law School at age 22. He entered politics in 1857 as Cincinnati's solicitor general, but his career was interrupted by military service in the Civil War. Back in civilian life, he served in the House of Representatives (1865–67) and as Ohio's governor (1868–72, 1876–77). The Republican Party chose Hayes as its presidential candidate in 1876, but he failed to win a majority of the popular vote in that November's election, which was marked by widespread racist TERRORISM in the

Republican candidate Rutherford Hayes negotiated a bargain to claim the White House after he lost the 1876 presidential election. (Author's collection)

southern states. The final count showed Democratic candidate Samuel Tilden with 4,300,590 votes against Hayes's 4,036,298. Neither candidate had the requisite 185 electoral votes to carry the contest—though Tilden had 184 to Hayes's 165. Twenty critical votes were disputed in three southern states (Florida, Louisiana, and South Carolina) where white supremacists had staged widespread acts of violence and "carpetbag" governments stood accused of fraudulent tabulations. While Congress undertook a recount of the votes, Hayes met secretly with Democratic leaders from the South (including the former "grand dragon" of Georgia's KU KLUX KLAN). A compromise was reached whereby Samuel Tilden surrendered his claim to the White House in return for Hayes's promise to end RECONSTRUCTION in Dixie. Southern state governments thus returned to white rule and the drive for racial segregation began,

while Hayes was inaugurated on March 4, 1877. His single term in office was distinguished by bloody government suppression of labor unions in the country's first significant railroad strike. Hayes declined to seek reelection in 1880, and he subsequently died in January 1893. The next candidate to occupy the White House despite losing the popular vote would be another Republican, George W. Bush in ELECTION 2000.

See also BUSH DYNASTY.

HEROIN

Heroin is a drug processed from morphine, a derivative of the opium poppy (*Papaver somniferum*) which was discovered in 1854. Morphine was widely used as a painkiller during the U.S. Civil War, though its addictive quality was not widely recognized until the postwar years. Heroin was developed in 1874 and initially was marketed as a safe, nonaddictive substitute for morphine. By the time doctors discovered their mistake in that regard, thousands of patients were addicted to the new drug that is widely known today as "H," "horse," "skag," or "junk." Opiates were banned by the Dangerous Drugs Act of 1920, but legislation simply moved production outside the United States without reducing the supply. From the 1920s onward, members of the MAFIA and other syndicated crime groups supplied an ever-growing addict population with their drug of choice. Primary sources of heroin today include Latin America, Southeast Asia (the "Golden Triangle" of LAOS, MYANMAR, and THAILAND), and Central Asia (the "Golden Crescent" or TURKEY, IRAN, and AFGHANISTAN). In 1999 federal authorities acknowledged 104,000 *new* heroin users in the United States. The following year 1.2 percent of the U.S. population—some 3.4 million people—admitted using heroin at least once in their lives. In 2000 Mexican "brown" heroin cost $13,200 per kilogram on average, while pure "China white" from Southeast Asia cost between $50,000 and $200,000 per kilo.

The most alarming aspect of America's heroin epidemic is not the drug's availability, per se, but the role often played by U.S. government agencies in the global narcotics traffic. During World War II Naval Intelligence and the OFFICE OF STRATEGIC SERVICES collaborated with Mafia bosses in the United States and ITALY to defeat America's fascist enemies. One price of that collaboration was protection of Mafia rackets including the heroin trade. In the early days of the cold war, the CENTRAL INTELLIGENCE AGENCY (CIA) worked hand-in-hand with Corsican heroin traders to suppress left-wing activists in FRANCE, a joint effort that opened the United States to the notorious "French Connection." Two decades later in VIETNAM, the CIA struck similar bargains with opium warlords in Asia, transporting shipments of heroin into the United States on protected AIR AMERICA flights. As recently as 2001, when President George W. Bush sent troops to topple the Taliban government of Afghanistan, suppression of heroin traffic was billed as a secondary reason for the invasion. In fact, however, heroin exports have tripled under the new "free" regime in Kabul. Critical observers suggest that such traffic could not exist without protection from highly placed officials on both sides of the Atlantic.

See also BUSH DYNASTY; FASCISM.

HESS, Rudolf (1894–1987)

Rudolf Hess was born at Alexandria, Egypt, in April 1894, the son of a prosperous German exporter-wholesaler. He lived in GERMANY from age 14 and volunteered six years later for military service in World War I. Wounded twice in combat, he emerged from the army to join the right-wing Freikorps, a mercenary force employed to crush communist uprisings in postwar Germany. He also joined the Thule Society, a group of anti-Semitic occultists prominent in National Socialist circles. Hess joined the Nazi Party in July 1920 and three years later participated in ADOLF HITLER's abortive revolution. In prison, Hitler dictated *Mein Kampf* to Hess and soon ranked Hess among his closest friends. When Hitler seized power in 1933, he named Hess Deputy Führer, the third most powerful man in Germany (after Hitler and Hermann Göring). Subsequent titles bestowed upon Hess included Reich Minister without Portfolio, member of the Secret Cabinet Council, and member of the Ministerial Council for Reich Defense. In 1939 Hess was even designated to be Hitler's successor after Göring. Because of his bashful and unassuming nature, however, Hess was sometimes overshadowed by his nominal subordinate, MARTIN BORMANN.

On May 10, 1941, with World War II well underway, Hess boarded a Messerschmitt fighter plane that had been fitted with extra fuel tanks and embarked from occupied France on a 900-mile flight to Great Britain. His alleged intention was to meet the Duke of Hamilton (a brief acquaintance from the 1936 Berlin Olympics) and negotiate peace between England and Germany prior to Hitler's impending invasion of RUSSIA. Hess navigated within 30 miles of the Duke's home near Glasgow, Scotland, and then bailed out of his plane at 6,000 feet and parachuted into a Scottish farmer's field. British authorities dismissed the unauthorized peace plan and clapped Hess in prison, while Hitler denounced Hess as a mentally unbalanced traitor. In 1945 Hess was returned to Germany as a defendant in the Nuremberg trials. He received a life sentence for WAR CRIMES and remained in Spandau prison until 1987 when he allegedly committed suicide at age 92.

Hess's flight to Scotland was so strange that it inevitably spawned a host of conspiracy theories. Nearly two decades after his death, doubts still linger concerning his mission, his motive—and, indeed, his very identity. Some conspiracists claim that Hess was in league with a clique of British Nazi sympathizers who planned to seize the government and dictate peace terms favorable to the THIRD REICH. Others maintain that the *real* Rudolf Hess never left Germany, but rather that a doppelganger made the flight and subsequently maintained the charade for 56 years without blowing his cover. Dr. Hugh Thomas, a consultant surgeon in the Royal Army Medical Corps during 1970–78, looked after Prisoner Number 7 at Spandau and insisted that the man jailed there was not Rudolf Hess. (An alternate doppelganger theory claims that Hess did fly to Scotland himself but died in custody before war's end and was replaced by a look-alike volunteer.) Some scenarios add a twist at the end, suggesting that "Hess" planned to reveal his true identity in 1987, whereupon he was murdered by custodians at Spandau to ensure eternal silence. Various alleged cohorts of Hess in his far-fetched peace plan died during World War II in a series of "accidents" that easily might have resulted from sabotage. British authorities, naturally, deny any knowledge of such a conspiracy.

See also COMMUNISM; NATIONAL SOCIALISM.

HIMMLER, Heinrich (1900–1945)

Born at Munich in October 1900, Heinrich Himmler served in World War I as a teenager and then earned a degree in agriculture from Munich Technical High

School in 1922. After working briefly as a fertilizer salesman, he joined the Nazi Party and participated in ADOLF HITLER's failed revolution of November 1923. Between 1925 and 1930 he served as the party's propaganda minister, interrupted briefly by a failed attempt at poultry farming. In January 1929 Himmler was named to lead the SS, Hitler's "elite" black-shirted bodyguards. By the time Hitler seized control of GERMANY in 1933, SS membership had ballooned from 200 to 52,000, a force that would play a key role in the coming HOLOCAUST. In April 1934 Himmler donned a new party hat as chief of the GESTAPO, while retaining command of the SS. Himmler established the first Nazi concentration camp (at Dachau) in 1933 and afterward supervised the expansion of camps throughout occupied Europe. In 1937 he declared, "There is no more living proof of hereditary and racial laws than in a concentration camp. You find there hydrocephalics, squinters, deformed individuals, semi-Jews: a considerable number of inferior people."

In addition to his racial fanaticism, Himmler was also a dedicated occultist who pursued black-magic rituals at Wewelsburg Castle in a basement chamber constructed by slave laborers. He was a firm believer in such off-beat theories as the notion of a HOLLOW EARTH inhabited by perfect examples of the "superior" Aryan race, and Himmler's agents spent substantial time seeking the entry to that netherworld on the polar ice cap. Back in Germany, meanwhile, he established Aryan breeding centers, declaring in 1939 that "it will be the sublime task of German women and girls of good blood acting not frivolously but from a profound moral seriousness to become mothers to children of soldiers setting off to battle." After the WANNSEE CONFERENCE, Himmler and ADOLF EICHMANN methodically undertook Hitler's final solution to the "Jewish question," supervising the wholesale murder of 6 million Jews and other "undesirables" including Gypsies, Slavs, gays, and the mentally ill. Captured and indicted for WAR CRIMES in 1945, Himmler committed suicide by poison prior to trial. His legacy survives in a speech delivered to an SS audience in 1943:

One principle must be absolute for the SS man: we must be honest, decent, loyal, and comradely to members of our own blood and to no one else. What happens to the Russians, what happens to the Czechs, is a matter of

utter indifference to me. Such good blood of our own kind as there may be among the nations we shall acquire for ourselves, if necessary by taking away the children and bringing them up among us. Whether the other peoples live in comfort or perish of hunger interests me only in so far as we need them as slaves for our Kultur. Whether or not 10,000 Russian women collapse from exhaustion while digging a tank ditch interests me only in so far as the tank ditch is completed for Germany. We shall never be rough or heartless where it is not necessary; that is clear. We Germans, who are the only people in the world who have a decent attitude to animals, will also adopt a decent attitude to these human animals, but it is a crime against our own blood to worry about them and to bring them ideals. I shall speak to you here with all frankness of a very grave matter. Among ourselves it should be mentioned quite frankly, and yet we will never speak of it publicly. I mean the evacuation of the Jews, the extermination of the Jewish people. . . . Most of you know what it means to see a hundred corpses lying together, five hundred, or a thousand. To have stuck it out and at the same time— apart from exceptions caused by human weakness—to have remained decent fellows, that is what has made us hard. This is a page of glory in our history which has never been written and shall never be written.

HINDENBURG disaster

It was the largest airship ever built, 804 feet long, capable of ferrying 158 crew members and passengers across the Atlantic from GERMANY to North or South America. Supported by huge bags of hydrogen gas, the dirigible *Hindenburg* was the pride of ADOLF HITLER's Nazi regime until May 6, 1937, when it exploded and burned during docking maneuvers at Lakehurst, New Jersey. In the space of 37 seconds, 35 of the 97 persons aboard perished in flames while onlookers watched in horror and newsreel cameras captured the disaster for posterity. Investigators on both sides of the Atlantic concluded that the fire was a simple accident, leaking hydrogen ignited by a charge of static electricity—but was it true?

As with most disasters of modern times, conspiracy theories surfaced within hours of the *Hindenburg* explosion. Some theorists believed (and still maintain today) that saboteurs destroyed the blimp in a homicidal bid to embarrass Nazi Germany. Captain Pruss, commander of the *Hindenburg*, was one of those who blamed the disaster on sabotage, but Hitler's regime and the U.S. administration of President Franklin Roosevelt seemed equally eager to close the investigation without pointing fingers. One suspect often named in conspiracy theories is Joseph Spah, a surviving passenger who frequently visited his dog in the *Hindenburg*'s baggage compartment (and thus had ample opportunity to plant a bomb). Another suspect, crewman Eric Spehl, died in the fire and was posthumously credited with anti-Nazi attitudes. No solid evidence indicts either suspect (or anyone else), but speculation on causes of the fire still continues. In 1998 spokespeople for the National Hydrogen Association blamed weather conditions and an "unorthodox" landing for the explosion. As explained in the NHA's publication:

Observations of the incident show evidence inconsistent with a hydrogen fire: (1) the Hindenburg did not explode, but burned very rapidly in omnidirectional patterns, (2) the 240-ton airship remained aloft and upright many seconds after the fire began, (3) falling pieces of fabric were aflame and not self-extinguishing, and (4) the very bright color of the flames was characteristic of a forest fire, not a hydrogen fire (hydrogen makes no visible flame). Also, no one smelled garlic, the scent of which had been added to the hydrogen to help detect a leak.

Conspiracists remain unpersuaded as they have for the past seven decades, noting that a bomb blast would preclude any lingering aroma from a slow leak, with or without garlic.

HISS, Alger (1904–1996)

Baltimore native Alger Hiss graduated from law school in 1929 and four years later joined President Franklin Roosevelt's NEW DEAL as an attorney for the Agricultural Adjustment Administration. In 1935 he shifted to the State Department's Trade Agreements division. By 1944 Hiss was promoted to serve as deputy director of the State Department's Office of Special Political Affairs, in charge of establishing the postwar UNITED NATIONS (UN). A year later he served as secretary general of the San Francisco conference that established the UN. In 1939 former Communist Party member Whittaker Chambers told State Department officials that Hiss and other New Dealers were members of a secret CP cell in Washington, D.C. FEDERAL BUREAU OF INVESTIGATION (FBI)

agents delayed their first interview with Chambers until May 1942 and recorded a series of conflicting statements during the next three years. In all statements Chambers denied any knowledge of spying.

FBI agents tapped the Hiss's telephones from December 1945 through September 1947, but they later admitted that "no espionage activities by Hiss were developed from this source." Hiss was called to testify before the HOUSE COMMITTEE ON UN-AMERICAN ACTIVITIES in August 1948, and when he denied knowing Chambers, HUAC brought them together on August 17. Confronted with his accuser, Hiss admitted knowing Chambers as "George Crossley," a freeloader who rented an apartment from Hiss in the mid-1930s and skipped without paying his bills. Hiss denied any communist ties under oath and challenged Chambers to repeat his charges outside the shelter of Congress. This Chambers did 10 days later on television's *Meet the Press,* and Hiss responded with a slander suit for $50,000.

Chambers had thus far continued to deny any knowledge of espionage, including new denials in a deposition to Hiss's attorneys on November 4, 1948. He changed his story two weeks later, though, producing a sheaf of 69 documents allegedly passed to him by Hiss for later delivery to a Soviet agent. (Chambers failed in the latter part of his mission, allegedly hiding the documents for a decade at the home of a relative in Baltimore.) The stash included 69 typed digests of various State Department reports and four short notes in what appeared to be Hiss's handwriting. Since all the documents were dated between January 1 and April 1, 1938, Chambers was forced to change his testimony once again, now claiming that he left the party on April 14, 1938. FBI headquarters helped by suppressing reports of his earlier contradictory statements.

On December 1, 1948, HUAC member RICHARD NIXON telephoned FBI headquarters to report that Chambers "did not tell the FBI everything he knew" in previous debriefings. There were documents, Nixon reported, that would "substantiate and vindicate his position which have up to this time not become publicly known." That night Chambers led HUAC staffers to a rural property where they extracted five rolls of microfilm from a hollow pumpkin. Two of the rolls revealed various State Department documents, some of them in code. On December 15, 1948, a grand jury indicted Hiss on two counts of perjury. Specifically he was charged with lying under oath when he denied passing documents to Chambers and when he denied knowing Chambers after January 1, 1937.

The prosecution hit a snag in January 1949 when Chambers told G-men that he would not testify that Hiss belonged to the Red cell in Washington since "he was not sure Alger Hiss was in the group." Worse yet, a memo to Hoover (dated February 2, 1949) reported: "It is not clear at this time if Chambers can testify that he received these particular 69 documents from Hiss, but upon establishing the facts of this situation, decision can therefore be reached as to who is in the position to introduce these documents." While Chambers waffled, FBI agents scoured the countryside for Hiss's old typewriter, a Woodstock bearing the serial number 230099. It was finally located in Washington, and members of the Hiss defense team were stunned when a report from the FBI's laboratory matched the machine to 68 of the documents furnished by Chambers. One report had been typed on a Royal machine, the discrepancy never explained since Chambers insisted all 69 had been typed at home by Hiss's wife. (Another FBI report, exonerating Priscilla Hiss as the typist, was illegally withheld from the defense.) Two decades later, reminiscing in the Oval Office, President Nixon confided to aides, "The typewriter was always the key. We built one in the Hiss case."

Hiss's first trial ended with a hung jury in June 1949. He was convicted on January 20, 1950, at a second trial and received concurrent five-year prison terms on each perjury count. Hiss served 44 months and was released in November 1954. While remaining philosophical—he told reporters that "three years in jail is a good corrective for three years at Harvard"—Hiss fought tirelessly for vindication throughout the rest of his life. He was disbarred and divorced but ultimately won reinstatement to the Massachusetts bar in 1975. Hiss died on November 15, 1996, with heated debate still continuing about the details of his case.

See also COMMUNISM.

HITLER, Adolf (1889–1945)

The future champion of GERMANY's "Master Race" was neither German nor visibly superior to any of his peers. Born in Austria on April 20, 1889, Adolf Hitler was a moody, mentally unstable child who left school at age 16 to endure "five years of misery and woe" as a failed would-be artist. During that time he cultivated a pathological hatred of Jews, encouraged by such groups as the mystic-racist Thule Society. Hitler's mental state was not improved by a poison-gas attack that left him hospitalized during World War I, and he fumed impotently over the subsequent Versailles Treaty, blaming Jews, "traitors," and communists for Germany's defeat on the battlefield. Drawn inexorably to the fascist creed of NATIONAL SOCIALISM, Hitler rose by 1919 to command Germany's Nazi Party. He is credited with adopting the swastika as that party's emblem and for leading a half-baked revolution against the Bavarian government in November 1923. That episode sent him to prison, where he spent his time dictating a long-winded political rant (*Mein Kampf*, "My Struggle") to comrade RUDOLF HESS. Back on the street by 1925 Hitler rallied his ever-growing mob of disciples and watched the Nazi Party win increasing power in the German Reichstag (legislature). He was appointed chancellor of Germany in January 1933 and six months later seized absolute power as Germany's dictator.

Despite his predictions that the THIRD REICH would endure for a thousand years, Hitler clung to power (and to life) for only 12 years after his rise to ultimate power in Berlin. Within those dozen years, he captured most of Europe, invaded RUSSIA, and plunged the Earth into World War II. Hidden behind his military adventures, Hitler also planned and carried out the Holocaust, his genocidal plan to rid the planet of Jews and other "undesirables" by means of forced labor, starvation, and mass murder. In his madness Hitler was finally unable to carry out his campaign for world conquest, driven by occult beliefs and racist obsessions to make a series of tactical blunders that ensured Germany's ultimate defeat. On April 29, 1945, with enemies advancing on Berlin from all sides, Hitler dictated his last political testament: "Above all I charge the leaders of the nation and those under them to scrupulous observance of the laws of race and to merciless opposition to the universal poisoner of all peoples, international Jewry." The next day he committed suicide with his bride of 24 hours, Eva Braun. Because their bodies were cremated and the charred remains were found by Russian soldiers, rumors circulated in the West for many years that Hitler had escaped to ARGENTINA (or even to the inside of a HOLLOW EARTH) where he allegedly plotted the rise of a

FOURTH REICH with vanished comrades MARTIN BOR-MANN, ADOLF EICHMANN, and JOSEF MENGELE. The matter of his death is now well settled, but the Holocaust and the Nazi looting of occupied Europe still rank among the most grandiose criminal conspiracies of all time.

See also COMMUNISM; FASCISM; HOLOCAUST AND HOLOCAUST DENIAL.

HOLLOW Earth

Science-fiction authors from Jules Verne to Edgar Rice Burroughs are famous for their novels of elaborate and perilous worlds existing beneath our feet in the hollow bowels of Earth. Their stories have amused generations of readers and moviegoers, but most fans of the genre would be surprised to learn that some persons believe devoutly in the theory of a hollow earth inhabited by anything and everything from living dinosaurs and missing links to fugitive Nazis, genetic supermen, and/or alien visitors from some distant planet. Conspiracists who buy hollow-earth theory commonly tack on a government conspiracy of silence aimed at deflecting the public from knowledge of whatever lurks below.

British astronomer Edmund Halley (of Halley's comet fame) in 1692 was one of the first to propose a hollow earth. His study of Earth's fluctuating magnetic field convinced Halley that the planet was hollow and contained smaller concentric spheres within, swaddled in a gaseous atmosphere whose escape through polar ice created the aurora borealis. Swiss mathematician Leonard Euler revised Halley's theory, replacing the multiple orbs with an internal sun that is 600 miles wide and lights an advanced subterranean civilization. Scottish mathematician John Leslie proposed dual inner suns (named Pluto and Prosperine), while American John Symmes sought money for a polar expedition to find the hidden world's secret gateway. Symmes failed in his quest, but a U.S. expedition to the South Pole sought that entry port in 1838. Its members found no gaping chasms, but they saw enough of Antarctica to name it the Earth's seventh continent. Eight years later, the discovery of frozen mammoths in Siberia sparked author Marshall Gardner's belief that the prehistoric elephants had emerged from a world below ground.

Some theorists apparently believe that Earth's modern civilization exists on the *inside* of a hollow planet. ADOLF HITLER tested that theory during World War II, dispatching a team to the Baltic Sea where Dr. Heinz Fischer aimed a telescopic camera at the sky in hopes of photographing British warships across the hollow interior of a concave Earth. (He failed.) Other unverified stories claim that HEINRICH HIMMLER sponsored Arctic expeditions in search of the portal to inner Earth where, he believed, a race of Aryan supermen waited to join the THIRD REICH's military effort. Postwar author Ernst Zundel, most (in)famous for his role in outspoken Holocaust denial, published a book asserting that Hitler and his entourage had escaped to inner Earth via ARGENTINA and the South Pole, there establishing a secret base from which to launch UFOS. The vast weight of geological evidence refutes the hollow-Earth theories, but hard-core conspiracists assume such "evidence" is fabricated to conceal the buried truth.

See also HOLOCAUST AND HOLOCAUST DENIAL.

John Cleves Symmes (1780–1829) was an early proponent of the hollow-Earth theory. (Author's collection)

HOLOCAUST and Holocaust denial

In 1920 fascist leader ADOLF HITLER promised a German audience that he would someday supervise "the removal of the Jews from the midst of our people." Thirteen years later, on seizing control of the German government, Hitler launched the systematic persecution of Jews that would lead to his "final solution"—the calculated murder of millions within Nazi-occupied territory. That 12-year campaign of genocide is broadly referred to as the Holocaust, or in Hebrew as the *Shoa* ("catastrophe"). Before Hitler killed himself in April 1945, Nazi administrator ADOLF EICHMANN estimated that the THIRD REICH had destroyed 6 million Jews along with lesser numbers of Gypsies, Slavs, homosexuals, the mentally ill, and other "undesirables."

The first Nazi concentration camps were built in 1933, patterned on 19th-century prison camps used in SOUTH AFRICA. (By 1945 the Nazis had established no fewer than 37 different kinds of concentration camps, each with a distinct purpose and class of prisoners.) In 1935 Jews were denied German citizenship and forbidden to marry non-Jews. By the time Hitler started World War II in 1939, Jews in GERMANY were barred from owning land and practicing most professions. Those not penned in camps were confined to urban ghettos. Full-scale mass murder of Jews began in 1941 with Hitler's invasion of Russia. By year's end Nazi reports detailed the slaughter of 1.4 million Soviet Jews, but the killing pace was insufficient to satisfy Hitler. The WANNSEE CONFERENCE of January 1942 formalized plans for the massacre of Jews on an assembly-line basis. While able-bodied prisoners were worked to death as slaves and others were singled out for bizarre medical experiments under perverse physicians such as JOSEF MENGELE, millions more were marked for execution at a series of death camps in occupied Poland. Those camps—Auschwitz, Belzec, Sobibor, and Treblinka—were literal death factories where incoming Jews were routed directly from railroad cattle cars to large gas chambers that were disguised as showers or delousing rooms. Two million were gassed at Auschwitz alone, their corpses trundled into crematoria that blazed around the clock.

Exposure of the Holocaust to public scrutiny in 1945 left various Nazi leaders to face trial for WAR CRIMES, while others escaped through the ODESSA network or made themselves useful to the U.S. intelligence community as anticommunist spies in the cold war era. Adolf Eichmann was kidnapped from South America in 1960 for trial and execution in ISRAEL. In that televised trial Eichmann downplayed his role in the Holocaust but freely admitted that millions were killed under Hitler's regime. Similar confessions had already been obtained from captive Nazi leaders in 1945–47 while tons of documentary records, films, and photographs proved the grim facts of the Holocaust beyond the smallest vestige of a reasonable doubt.

Or so it seemed, at least, until the 1970s when a small but vocal group of "revisionist" authors (chiefly propagandists for one or another neo-Nazi fringe group) launched a wave of Holocaust denial in the world media. Spearheaded by the so-called Institute for Historical Review (IHR), these self-styled scholars mounted a propaganda campaign to downplay Hitler's crimes, in effect "rehabilitating" the Nazi regime while blaming various alleged "distortions" and "lies" on the worldwide "Jewish media." Among the Holocaust-denial movement's primary claims are the following:

1. While some Jews admittedly died in concentration camps, their number has been much exaggerated by anti-Nazi propagandists, inflated from perhaps 100,000 to the "impossible" figure of 5–6 million.

2. Of those who died in Nazi custody, a few were legally executed for various "crimes" (as defined by racist Nazi statutes), while the vast majority succumbed to disease in crowded camps or ghettos. Allied bombing raids on "innocent" Germany left kindhearted Nazis without sufficient food or medicine to properly care for their prisoners.

3. Most evidence of Nazi atrocities is fabricated by Jews or those in their employ. Films and photos of mass graves at various concentration camps *really* depict German civilians killed by Allied bombers at Dresden, while Nazi records of the Holocaust are clever forgeries. Nazi officers who confessed to war crimes were "tortured," "brainwashed," and so on.

4. Finally, where evidence of deliberate murder is undeniable, the crimes occurred without Hitler's knowledge or approval, even in defiance of direct orders to the contrary from Der Führer. Sadly, all such records of Hitler's concern for the Jews and other prisoners have been

lost, presumably destroyed by the very Jews who malign his memory.

While such assertions are patently ridiculous (and banned by law in some countries, including Germany itself), public-opinion polls in the 1980s and 1990s revealed that Holocaust denial was making inroads with the U.S. public at large. One author who never missed an opportunity to minimize Hitler's evil was British historian David Irving, whose works include *The Destruction of Dresden* (1963), *Hitler's War* (1975), *The War Path* (1978), and *Goebbels: Mastermind of the Third Reich* (1996). In 1993 author Deborah Lipstadt labeled Irving "one of the most dangerous spokespersons for Holocaust denial," and he subsequently filed suit for libel in London. After a 10-week trial, in April 2000, Judge Charles Gray agreed with Lipstadt's claims that Irving was "a racist, an anti-Semite, an active Holocaust denier, who associates with right-wing extremists." Judge Gray also found that "Irving has for his own ideological reasons persistently and deliberately misrepresented and manipulated historical evidence. For the same reasons he has portrayed Hitler in an unwarrantedly favorable light, principally in relation to his attitude towards and responsibility for the treatment of the Jews." As the loser in that case, Irving was liable for court costs in the amount of £2 million ($3.7 million). He also faced possible extradition to Germany on criminal charges of racial incitement, following a speech he delivered to a neo-Nazi audience. The IHR remains supportive of Irving and condemns the various attacks on his work as character assassination.

See also FASCISM.

HONDURAS

Honduras was inhabited by Mayan natives when Christopher Columbus arrived on the scene in 1502. Slaughter by Spanish conquistadors followed, and the country remained a colony of SPAIN until 1821 when it declared independence and joined a federation of Central American states. Seceding from the federation 17 years later, Honduras achieved true independence. A clash with neighboring NICARAGUA brought U.S. Marines to "restore order" in 1907, followed by five more invasions to protect American investments in 1911, 1912, 1919, 1924, and 1925. Dictator Tiburcio Carias Andino

finally established "stability" in 1932, with pockets full of U.S. dollars. In 1954 the CENTRAL INTELLIGENCE AGENCY (CIA) used Honduras as a launching pad for the destruction of GUATEMALA's lawfully elected government. EL SALVADOR invaded Honduras in 1969, waging a fierce border war that left 5,000 persons dead before the invaders withdrew. In the 1980s Honduras reprised its role as a CIA staging area for terrorist attacks on a neighbor—this time targeting Nicaragua with raids by CONTRA guerrillas. President Ricardo Maduro, inaugurated in 2002, promised to curb crime and public corruption, but critics regard his beefed-up army and police force, both increasingly oppressive, as a replay of the nation's earlier dictatorships.

HOOVER, J. Edgar (1895–1972)

Long-time FEDERAL BUREAU OF INVESTIGATION (FBI) director J. Edgar Hoover was born in Washington, D.C., on January 1, 1895. He earned a law degree in night school but never practiced. Two months after the United States entered World War I, in July 1917, Hoover accepted a draft-exempt job as a clerk with the JUSTICE DEPARTMENT, assigned to the Alien Enemy Bureau. He was promoted on July 1, 1919, to serve as special assistant to Attorney General A. Mitchell Palmer, a move that placed Hoover in charge of the Red-hunting General Intelligence Division, where he organized and supervised the PALMER RAIDS of 1919–20. On August 22, 1921, Hoover was promoted again, to serve as the bureau's first assistant director under WILLIAM J. BURNS. Scandals surrounding the administration of President WARREN HARDING ultimately doomed Burns, but Hoover emerged unscathed from the wreckage at Justice, and he was appointed acting director of the bureau on May 10, 1924. He became full-time director on December 10, 1924, and held that position until his death on May 2, 1972, almost 48 years later. Under seven presidents and 16 attorneys general, Hoover exercised near-dictatorial power, relying on FBI files to influence, amuse or blackmail his superiors and to guarantee that he remained in office. He briefly cherished higher ambitions, pursuing a failed campaign to become a U.S. SUPREME COURT justice in 1948 and launching an abortive presidential bid in 1956, but Hoover's command of the FBI gave him more covert authority than most public officials in the United States.

While admirers hailed that fact and looked to Hoover as the savior of conservative America, his flaws were both profound and numerous. One obvious problem was strident racism, exemplified by obsessive campaigns to "prevent the rise of a 'messiah'" in the black community. His pathological bigotry was revealed when Attorney General Tom Clark asked Hoover to investigate the attempted murder of (white) labor leader Victor REUTHER in 1949. The strange answer came back: "Edgar says no. He says he's not going to get involved every time some nigger woman gets raped." Hoover was also corrupt, a fact effectively hidden from the public until three years after his death. During his tenure as FBI director he used bureau agents to remodel and maintain his home while ghost writers in the Crime Records Division prepared various books and magazine articles for publication over Hoover's by-line. Income from book and film royalties alone exceeded $200,000, "donated" to the FBI Recreational Association and other funds that Hoover and his top aides used as private slush funds. With constant companion Clyde Tolson, he accepted free vacations and gambling junkets each year (officially described as "inspection tours") with millionaire cronies Clint Murchison, William Byars, Sr., and others picking up the tab. Those same friends also guaranteed no-loss investments for Hoover in oil and natural-gas corporations, while members of organized crime funneled cash into the "nonprofit" J. Edgar Hoover Foundation.

Hoover's mental health was also open to question. A hypochondriac who secretly consulted dozens of physicians for imaginary ailments, Hoover nurtured an obsessive fear of disease on par with that of HOWARD HUGHES, outfitting his home and office with special "bug lights" designed to "electrocute" germs, and he displayed an "almost demented" reaction to flies in his office. Assistant Director WILLIAM SULLIVAN was assigned to scour the media for articles on treatments that were alleged to prolong human life "no matter how farfetched the claim" while Hoover displayed peculiar fear of letting anyone step on his shadow. By the mid-1960s a private nurse was employed to give Hoover daily "massive injections of some substance to keep him going." In 1970 *Time* magazine reporter Dean Fischer found Hoover mentally confused, noting that he "had difficulty in responding to a question . . . without losing himself in a forest of recollections" from the 1930s.

Hoover's death on May 2, 1972, was officially blamed on "hypertensive cardiovascular disease," but rumors persist to this day that he may have been murdered. During the WATERGATE investigation, journalist Mark Frazier reported in the *Harvard Crimson* that a series of break-ins at Hoover's home had been "directed by G. Gordon Liddy," a former G-man and key player in RICHARD NIXON's criminal Committee to Reelect the President. According to Frazier's report the first burglary was intended to "retrieve documents that were thought to be used as potential blackmail against the White House." When that effort failed, a second break-in was staged. "This time," Frazier wrote, "whether through misunderstanding or design, a poison of the thiophosphate genre was placed on Hoover's personal toilet articles." No autopsy was performed, and a death certificate was routinely issued on May 5, 1972. Liddy later denied any knowledge of the Hoover burglaries, much less a murder plan.

See also JFK ASSASSINATION; RFK ASSASSINATION.

HOUSE Committee on Un-American Activities (HUAC)

The House Committee on Un-American Activities, or HUAC, was created in 1938, with Rep. Martin Dies as chairman, to investigate subversive activities in the United States. At the time fascist groups such as the German American Bund and the CHRISTIAN FRONT were a primary concern, but the far-right political leaning of Dies and company ensured that most of those investigated over the next 30-odd years would be suspected members or associates of the Communist Party. HUAC's disregard for law and the U.S. Constitution was revealed a month before its first hearings opened on July 6, 1938: Staff member E. K. Gubin told FEDERAL BUREAU OF INVESTIGATION (FBI) agents that Dies had ordered "certain of the Investigators to confiscate anything that they wanted in any business office to which they may be sent and . . . not worry particularly about legal procedure." A case in point occurred in May 1940 when HUAC raiders illegally seized two tons of documents from the Communist Party and the International Workers Order in Philadelphia. By the time three leaders of the raid were jailed and the documents returned by order of a federal judge, HUAC staffers had already photocopied the papers for future reference.

At about the same time, Chairman Dies made the critical mistake of criticizing J. EDGAR HOOVER and the FBI, suggesting that G-men were less than efficient in their pursuit of Reds. On November 22, 1940, Attorney General Robert Jackson accused Dies of interfering with the bureau's work, but the feud continued for another year until Hoover aide Edward Tamm privately confronted Dies with evidence of a recent $2,000 bribe. Henceforth, while Dies continued his verbal assaults on the New Deal, he never again criticized the bureau; in fact, as described by journalist Curt Gentry, HUAC soon became "almost an adjunct of the FBI," dominated and manipulated by Hoover "for his own purposes."

The pattern emerged most obviously under Chairman J. Parnell Thomas when the FBI provided HUAC with classified files and testimony from such informants as Elizabeth Bentley who had outlived their covert usefulness or failed to make their charges stick in court. Targets including William Remington and Harry Dexter White were subjected to public character assassination by HUAC when G-men found no evidence required for criminal charges, and countless lives were ruined in the process. Rep. RICHARD NIXON joined HUAC in 1947 and subsequently made a national reputation with his pursuit of witness ALGER HISS. Chairman Thomas spoke fondly of the HUAC-FBI partnership in July 1948, telling Congress: "The closest relationship exists between this committee and the FBI. . . . I think there is a very good understanding between us. It is something, however, that we cannot talk too much about." (Nor would it save Thomas in 1949 when he was convicted of padding his payroll and was sentenced to three years in prison.)

HUAC continued to serve the FBI under various chairmen through the years. In 1950, prior to publication of a critical FBI history, the committee grilled author Max Lowenthal's publisher in a failed attempt to find Red connections. During 1965–66, deviating from its pattern of investigating only left-wing targets, HUAC subjected the KU KLUX KLAN to similar treatment. In the process, Chairman Edwin Willis (from Louisiana) deplored Klan violence and underestimated membership by 66 percent, simultaneously praising the FBI's anti-Klan work and exonerating "respectable" segregationists from any involvement in TERRORISM.

In 1969 HUAC was officially renamed the House Internal Security Committee (HISC), but its perform-

ance under Chairman Richard Ichord ran true to form. The committee worked with G-men and Nixon White House aides to investigate "New Left" targets, but the WATERGATE scandal and subsequent exposures of federal corruption left the HISC bereft of public support. One of its last investigations, into charges of alleged FBI malfeasance, may best be described as a whitewash. The 1974 report ignored any mention of illegal COINTELPRO operations, blamed recent FBI problems on "an inept [Nixon] Administration" and warned of the danger presented by any future "severe restrictions placed upon the FBI." The committee was formally abolished by Congress in January 1975, its files transferred to the National Archives under seal for a minimum of 50 years.

HOUSE Select Committee on Assassinations

Public skepticism concerning lone-assassin verdicts in the 1963 JFK ASSASSINATION and the 1968 murder of MARTIN LUTHER KING, JR., was not assuaged by the WARREN COMMISSION's report in 1964 (on the death of President John Kennedy) or by the FEDERAL BUREAU OF INVESTIGATION's (FBI) MURKIN investigation (of King's assassination). Revelations of criminal activity by G-men and agents of the CENTRAL INTELLIGENCE AGENCY, exposed by the U.S. Senate's CHURCH COMMITTEE in 1975–76, added fuel to various conspiracy theories surrounding the murders. Congress responded to those widespread doubts in September 1976, authorizing a new investigation of both crimes by a House Select Committee on Assassinations. The committee was specifically created to answer four questions:

1. Who assassinated President Kennedy and Dr. King?
2. Did the assassin or assassins in either case have assistance—was there a conspiracy?
3. Did the responsible federal agencies perform adequately in sharing information prior to each assassination, in protecting President Kennedy and Dr. King, and in conducting their investigations of the assassinations?
4. Was there a need for new legislation or for amending existing legislation with respect to assassinations?

Chaired by Ohio congressman Louis Stokes, the committee questioned 335 witnesses in public or executive sessions, conducting a total of 4,924 interviews. Immunity orders were secured for 165 witnesses, and two—Chicago mobsters SAM GIANCANA and JOHN ROSELLI—were murdered by persons unknown before they could testify. The committee published its findings in January 1979, and while various questions remained unanswered (including the role of organized crime in President Kennedy's murder), the report found "a high probability" of multiple gunmen in JFK's slaying. "A likelihood of conspiracy" was also found in Dr. King's death, with two deceased suspects named as possible sponsors of an alleged murder contract, executed by confessed assassin JAMES EARL RAY.

The committee's report exonerated both the FBI and the CIA of direct participation in either slaying, but the bureau did not escape criticism. In respect to President Kennedy, committee members found that the JUSTICE DEPARTMENT "failed to exercise initiative in supervising and directing" the FBI's assassination inquiry. Specifically, while the bureau's investigation of LEE HARVEY OSWALD prior to November 1963 was "adequate" and its probe of his role in JFK's murder was "thorough and professional," the FBI was ranked "deficient" in sharing its data with other agencies and furthermore "failed to investigate adequately the possibility of a conspiracy to assassinate the President."

Evidence of federal malfeasance was more voluminous in Dr. King's case where committee members found that the FBI's COINTELPRO campaigns "grossly abused and exceeded its legal authority and failed to consider the possibility that actions threatening bodily harm to Dr. King might be encouraged by the program." The bureau had performed "a thorough fugitive investigation" in pursuit of James Earl Ray, but once again G-men had "failed to investigate adequately the possibility of a conspiracy in the assassination." Beyond that failure, the FBI had "manifested a lack of concern for constitutional rights in the manner in which it conducted parts of the [King] investigation." Specific "investigative excesses" noted by the committee included illegal interception and photocopying of several letters exchanged between defendant James Earl Ray and his attorneys. G-men also interviewed Ray on at least one occasion without legal counsel or mandatory advice concerning his right to stand silent. The committee presumed that those actions were prompted by "pressure from above" in the form of demands from Director J. EDGAR HOOVER.

Ultimately, the House committee's investigation solved nothing. Its 792-page report failed to convince lone-assassin devotees, while its failure to identify living suspects in either assassination rendered its proconspiracy verdicts effectively impotent. None of the committee's recommendations for new legislation were ever enacted by Congress. Controversy surrounding both crimes (and the RFK ASSASSINATION, ignored by the committee's inquiry) endures to the present day.

See also KENNEDY DYNASTY.

HUGHES, Howard (1905–1976)

Future billionaire recluse Howard Hughes was born in Houston, Texas, in December 1905. His father was the founder and president of Hughes Tool Company, a thriving business that accustomed young Howard to luxury from infancy onward. Though Hughes never graduated from high school, timely donations from his father permitted him to audit classes at Cal Tech University. Higher education was abandoned with his father's death in 1924 as Hughes plunged headlong into managing Hughes Tool at age 19. From that financial base he moved on to Hollywood film producing, aeronautics, and construction. (One of his projects, the Texas Theater in Dallas, witnessed the arrest of alleged presidential assassin LEE HARVEY OSWALD in November 1963.) By the mid-1930s, while America wallowed in the Great Depression, Hughes was well on his way to making billions out of millions and rubbing shoulders with countless influential politicians and industrialists in the process. Exposure of a secret loan from Hughes nearly ended RICHARD NIXON's political career in 1952. His ties to the MILITARY-INDUSTRIAL COMPLEX were legion and legendary, including frequent interaction with the CENTRAL INTELLIGENCE AGENCY (CIA) on various covert schemes. At the same time Hughes was no stranger to the MAFIA, cheerfully doing business with anyone who could multiply his already vast fortune. In 1953 Hughes founded the Hughes Medical Institute in Delaware, gifting it with shares of Hughes Aircraft (thus making his lucrative weapons industry a tax-exempt "charity").

By the early 1960s Hughes had developed a paranoid phobia of germs, retreating into near-total seclusion, but his quirks did not prevent him from running his empire with an iron fist. In 1966 he invaded LAS VEGAS and set about purchasing numerous hotel-casinos, perpetuating a myth that he "cleaned up" the town while the former criminal management of his new acquisitions remained intact. Two years later Hughes declared, "I am determined to elect a president of our choosing this year and one who will be deeply indebted, and who will recognize his indebtedness. Since I am willing to go beyond all limitations on this, I think we should be able to select a candidate and a party who knows the facts of political life. . . . If we select Nixon, then he, I know for sure, knows the facts of life." Nixon was in fact selected and emerged victorious in a narrow race marked by the June 1968 RFK ASSASSINATION. By the time Nixon's administration foundered on the WATERGATE conspiracy, Hughes had left the United States for a closely guarded hospital ward in the Bahamas. There he remained until April 5, 1976, when he died en route to a Houston hospital, aboard his private jet.

Or did he?

Conspiracy theories surround Hughes's final days, including allegations in the GEMSTONE FILE that he was kidnapped by Greek shipping magnate Aristotle Onassis. Others contend that Hughes faked his own death and went underground, still clutching the reigns of power in some shadow government that manipulates most major events in America and the world at large. Likewise, his name features in countless conspiracy theories spanning a half-century from the 1920s to his presumed death, including multiple interactions with the FEDERAL BUREAU OF INVESTIGATION, the CIA, organized crime, and various foreign plotters. The billionaire's passion for privacy ensures that most of those theories shall remain speculation, and nothing more.

HUNGARY

The Roman Empire occupied present-day Hungary in 14 B.C., followed by Magyar invaders in 896. In 1241 a devastating Mongol invasion killed roughly half of Hungary's population. The nation rebounded under King Louis I the Great (1342–82), but a century of destructive warfare with TURKEY ensued after 1389. In 1526, after a stunning defeat by Turkish troops, Hungary accepted Hapsburg rule to escape Turkish occupation. Still, sporadic warfare with Turkey continued until 1699. A revolt against the Hapsburg monarch was bloodily suppressed in 1848.

World War I briefly liberated Hungary in 1918, but a short-lived republic was followed by communist rule under tyrant Belá Kun until Romanian troops occupied Budapest in August 1919. Hungary allied with Nazi GERMANY in World War II, but Hungarian failure to participate enthusiastically in ADOLF HITLER's 1941 invasion of Russia prompted Hitler to install a puppet government for the remainder of the war. In 1948 with support from Russian troops, the Communist Party seized control of Hungary and ruled the nation until 1989. An anti-Communist revolt was swiftly crushed in 1956 after 190,000 persons fled the country. Subsequent leaders gradually liberalized their policies until October 1989 when Hungary's constitution was amended to permit multiparty elections. Russian troops withdrew in June 1991, leaving Hungary to struggle with a failing economy. Prime Minister Péter Medgyessy, elected in 2002, was embarrassed by revelations that he had served as a spy in the Communist era, but an official investigation "did not uncover any untoward behavior" during his years as a secret agent.

See also COMMUNISM.

HUSSEIN, Saddam (1937–   )

The man described by President George W. Bush as "Hitler revisited" was born at Tikrit, Iraq, on April 28, 1937. The son of poor farmers, he grew up in Auja, a village of mud-brick huts located northwest of Baghdad. Saddam Hussein joined the socialist Baath Party at age 19 while enrolled at Baghdad's Mustanseriya University, and he made his mark three years later as a participant in the attempted assassination of Prime Minister Abudul Karim Kassim. Saddam was shot in the leg during that escapade, but he escaped Iraq and lived abroad for several years. In 1968 he helped lead the revolt that brought the Baath Party to power under Gen. Ahmed Hassan Bakr, who rewarded his efforts with the vice presidency. In that post Saddam built an elaborate network of SECRET POLICE to weed out dissidents. In 1979 he deposed Bakr and assumed control of Iraq.

The 1980s were a heady decade for Saddam, armed and supported by the United States under Presidents RONALD REAGAN and George H. W. Bush to pursue a ruthless eight-year war against neighboring IRAN. Washington ignored Saddam's WAR CRIMES and flagrant human-rights violations, including near-genocidal suppression of Iraq's Kurdish minority. Washington remained supportive in July 1990 when Saddam informed U.S. Ambassador April Gillespie of his plans to invade KUWAIT (a province of Iraq until British occupation forces severed it from the larger nation in the late 19th century). The invasion proceeded on August 2, 1990, whereupon Bush suddenly reversed himself and prepared to expel Iraqi troops from OIL-rich Kuwait. The first GULF WAR, in early 1991, left Saddam in power but surrounded by hostile forces, his nation subjected to crippling economic sanctions. Tension between Iraq and the United States continued during the next 12 years as leaders in Washington conveniently forgot their role in supporting Saddam's "evil" regime. Rumors of an Iraqi plot to assassinate President Bush in 1991 proved groundless, but Bush's son apparently believed them and would bide his time to seek revenge.

The PENTTBOM attacks of September 11, 2001, exacerbated tensions between the United States and Saddam. President George W. Bush pronounced Iraq one-third of a mythical AXIS OF EVIL, also including its mortal enemy Iran and the completely unrelated state of North KOREA. Additionally, Bush cited Iraqi ties to the AL-QAEDA terrorist network and claims that Saddam had developed various "weapons of mass destruction" for use against ISRAEL and other targets. Neither claim was substantiated after U.S. troops invaded Iraq on March 20, 2003. OPERATION IRAQI FREEDOM toppled Saddam's regime and killed his sons, but Saddam himself proved as elusive as had Osama bin Laden during the earlier U.S. invasion of AFGHANISTAN.

The search for Saddam Hussein in occupied Iraq quickly became a comedy of error with no end in sight. Initial Pentagon reports that Saddam had been killed by a "smart bomb" attack on his command bunker proved false: there was no such bombing, and indeed no such bunker. Iraqi politician Ahmad Chalabi cited "credible information" pointing to Saddam's postwar survival on May 12, 2003, which was confirmed a month later by Iraqi prisoners of war who testified that Saddam had escaped the U.S. bombardment of Baghdad. On June 10 unsubstantiated rumors claimed Saddam had fled with $1.3 billion from Iraq's Central Bank and that he had offered cash bounties for the death of U.S. soldiers from a hideout in northern Iraq. An alleged ultimatum from Saddam surfaced on June 14; it warned "all foreign citizens and those who came with the

cowardly occupiers . . . to leave Iraq." Paul Bremer, head of the U.S.-led administration in occupied Iraq, told reporters two weeks later, "I'm assuming he's still alive, and we will get our hands on him, dead or alive." On July 3, U.S. authorities offered a $25 million reward. Four days after that bounty was posted, an audio tape was broadcast over the Arabic satellite network Al-Jazeera calling Iraqis to continue resistance against U.S. occupation forces. Saddam was finally found alive in a bunker near Tikrit on December 14, 2003. But even as President Bush proclaimed his capture a military triumph, armed resistance against U.S. occupation troops continued at full force.

See also BIN LADEN FAMILY; BUSH DYNASTY.

HUSTON Plan

Named for White House aide Tom Charles Huston, the Huston Plan was an attempt by President RICHARD NIXON to coordinate and consolidate domestic surveillance of his perceived political enemies throughout the United States and abroad. The move began on June 5, 1970, when Nixon met with the four chiefs of U.S. intelligence: FEDERAL BUREAU OF INVESTIGATION (FBI) Director J. EDGAR HOOVER; Director Richard Helms of the CENTRAL INTELLIGENCE AGENCY; Vice Admiral Noel Gaylor of the NATIONAL SECURITY AGENCY; and Donald Bennett, director of the Defense Intelligence Agency. Proclaiming that the nation was beset by an "epidemic of unprecedented domestic TERRORISM," Nixon appointed the four chiefs to an ad hoc committee for development of "a plan which will enable us to curtail the illegal activities of those who are determined to destroy our society." Hoover was placed in charge of the committee, with Huston serving as White House liaison.

Huston's relationship with Hoover broke down three days later when he met with the chiefs and rejected Hoover's bid to prepare "a historical summary of unrest in the country up to the present." Contradicting Hoover before his peers, Huston dismissed any review of "the dead past," instead demanding a list of techniques for use against left-wing radicals in "the living present." While Bennett, Helms, and Gaylor cautiously agreed, Hoover balked at revealing the FBI's illicit methods. In a memo to Assistant Director WILLIAM SULLIVAN dated June 6, 1970, Hoover declared:

For years and years I have approved opening mail and other similar operations, but no. It is becoming more and more dangerous and we are apt to get caught. I am not opposed to doing this. I am not opposed to continuing the burglaries and the opening of mail and other similar activities, providing someone higher than myself approves of it. . . . I no longer want to accept the sole responsibility. [If] the attorney general or some other high ranking person in the White House [approves] then I will carry out their decision. But I am not going to accept the responsibility myself anymore, even though I've done it for many years.

Historian Theodore White praised Hoover's stand as a lone hero's resistance to Nixon's criminal activities, but in fact it was nothing of the kind. Hoover simply refused to place himself at risk for a corrupt administration that might use him as a scapegoat. Coordination of domestic spying through the White House was thus derailed by Hoover's instinct for self-preservation, while the nation's chief practitioner of such techniques became an icon to civil libertarians. It was Hoover's last coup before his death in May 1972. Tom Huston was replaced in Nixon's favors by John Dean, and the Nixon regime moved on to the fatal morass of the WATERGATE scandal.

IBM

The International Business Machines Corporation (IBM) was created in 1924 when leaders of the Computing-Tabulating-Recording Company opted for a less cumbersome title. Four years later, IBM joined in the pseudoscientific eugenics movement, funded by the ROCKEFELLER Foundation and other wealthy benefactors, which aimed at launching a full-scale domestic campaign of ethnic cleansing across the United States. IBM's contribution to the racist movement was the preparation of early computer punch cards that would classify Americans according to such categories as "race descent," "nativity and citizenship," and "kin in institutions." The Carnegie Institution's notorious Jamaica Race Crossing Project introduced the punch-card system in 1928 as a tentative means to purging the Earth of nonwhites. Connecticut authorities subsequently failed in their attempt to index (and forcibly sterilize) 11,900 residents who were classified as "socially inadequate," but the IBM punch-card system was soon adopted by ADOLF HITLER and his SS as a means of eliminating "undesirables" from Europe. Investigative journalist Edwin Black broke the sordid story seven decades later at the dawn of a new millennium in his book *IBM and the Holocaust*. IBM chairman and CEO Lou Gerstner fielded inquiries from various concerned investigators when the corporation's history went public, announcing that his firm had "deposited the relevant archives" with New York University and Hohenheim University in Stuttgart, Germany. In February 2001 five Holocaust survivors living in New York sued IBM on charges

Herman Hollerith invented one of the first adding machines and then became a founder of the IBM corporation. (Author's collection)

that the company "knowingly supplied technology used to catalog death-camp victims and aided in the persecution, suffering and genocide" of Nazi victims during World War II. Attorney Michael Hausfield, speaking for the plaintiffs, said that "Hitler could not have so quickly and efficiently identified and rounded up Jews and other minorities, used them as slave laborers and ultimately exterminated them, without IBM's assistance." The plaintiffs dropped their lawsuit a month later after German authorities established a $5 billion reparations fund for Holocaust survivors and their families.

See also HOLOCAUST AND HOLOCAUST DENIAL.

ILLUMINATI

The original Illuminati ("Enlightened Ones") was founded in 1776 by Adam Weishaupt, a disillusioned JESUIT and professor of canon law at the University of Ingolstadt, Germany. Borrowing heavily from the rituals of Freemasonry, the group was an elitist revolutionary group with strong occult overtones, mingling magic and politics in a scheme to abolish all monarchies and form an "ideal" one-world government—led, of course, by the Enlightened Ones. Debate continues regarding possible links between the Illuminati and the American Revolution (which also began in 1776) with proponents of the theory noting that several founding fathers were also high-ranking Masons. At least one proposed link, suggested by J. Gordon Melton in his *Encyclopedia of Religions*, may now be laid to rest. Melton claims that the Illuminati "was present in England as the Hell-Fire Club headed by Sir Francis Dashwood," himself a personal friend of Benjamin Franklin, but elementary research proves that Dashwood's blasphemous society dissolved in 1762, well before Weishaupt's group was born.

A quarrel between Weishaupt and disciple Baron Von Knigge led to exposure of the Illuminati's revolutionary goals in 1885. Weishaupt fled Germany, and his organization was banned by law in Bavaria (along with the Freemasons). Historians still debate what happened to the group from that point onward, arguing the merits of a Jesuit priest's allegation (published in 1797) that blamed the Illuminati for the French Revolution's "reign of terror." The same publication linked Weishaupt's occultism to the dishonored KNIGHTS TEMPLAR and beyond that to the Islamic ASSASSINS CULT. More recently, author

David Icke found a "remarkable resemblance" between Illuminati documents and the PROTOCOLS OF THE ELDERS OF ZION (forged by Russian SECRET POLICE in the late 19th century).

No date is available for the Illuminati's dissolution, if indeed it ever disbanded. Melton confirmed the group's existence in 1978 with public offices in San Francisco and Nantes, FRANCE, but neither responded to queries seeking information about the organization's activities. Conspiracists, meanwhile, suggest that the Illuminati is active behind the scenes of most (if not all) major world events and institutions. Anti-Semites equate it with the so-called Jewish World Conspiracy, while others speak of SATANISM or a guiding hand behind the NEW WORLD ORDER. A typical Internet broadside, devoid of supporting evidence, insists that:

> The Illuminati are elite men, those on the top, who control the International Bankers to control, for evil purposes, the entire world. Their agent[s] are bred, educated, and trained to be placed behind the scenes at all levels of government. As experts and advisers, they mould government policy so as to further the secret plans of their masters. They lure people away from God by offering them money, the world, the flesh, and the devil.
>
> Those who direct the Illuminati are against Christ and for Satan. They always remain in the dark, unidentified, and generally unsuspected. They use all peoples to serve their diabolical purposes. They divide to conquer, supplying arms and money to both sides, instigating people to fight and kill each other, in order to be able to achieve their objectives. they foster the terrorism of atomic warfare and deliberately cause world famine. Their primary goal is to form a one world government to have complete control of the entire world, destroying all religions and governments in the process.

In short, a one-size-fits-all conspiracy encompassing the Earth and all upon it. What conspiracist could ask for more?

ImCLONE Systems

ImClone Systems is a biotechnology firm, self-described as "dedicated to the development of novel treatments for cancer and cancer-related disorders." Its flagship product, the drug Erbitux, failed to receive approval from the U.S. Food and Drug Administration in December 2001, whereupon the company's stock collapsed. As luck would have it, numerous ImClone executives dumped their stock on unwitting buyers before the FDA's decision was announced after the close of trading on December 28, 2001. ImClone's founder and CEO, Dr. Samuel Waksal, warned his father and daughter of the impending collapse, permitting them to sell shares worth $10.6 million before stock prices plummeted. ImClone vice president Ronald Martell sold $2.1 million in shares before the disaster, and corporate counsel John Landes sold $2.5 million. Celebrity stockholder Martha Stewart (whom Dr. Waksal dated after first enjoying a relationship with her daughter) also managed to unload $2.3 million in shares before the collapse. Dr. Waksal was arrested in 2002 for illegal insider trading. On June 10, 2003, federal judge William Pauley sentenced Dr. Waksal to seven years in prison plus fines and back taxes of $4.3 million. Martha Stewart received a five-month prison term for her role in the scandal.

INDIA

One of the world's oldest civilizations flourished in the Indus Valley between 2600 and 2000 B.C. Aryan invaders introduced new language and religion in 1500 B.C., and King Asoka (269–232 B.C.) forcibly united most of the Indian subcontinent for the first time. PORTUGAL "discovered" India in 1498 and held a virtual monopoly on trade for the next century. Muslim invaders captured Delhi in 1526 and formed the Mogul empire, which lasted until 1857. Their collapse was accelerated by the British East India Company, established at Surat in 1612, which burrowed and subverted from within, finally consolidating England's power throughout the subcontinent. Following the last gasp of independence in the Sepoy Mutiny (1857–58), India was formally declared a British colony.

Indian nationalism blossomed after World War I, spurred by the leadership of Hindu lawyer Mohandas Gandhi and his Indian National Congress Party. Peaceful demonstrations goaded British rulers into cruel atrocities that shamed London on the stage of world opinion. Still, independence was stalled by British intransigence and the onset of World War II when India was menaced by invaders from JAPAN. Britain finally granted India her independence in August 1947, but the victory was tainted by the partitioning of mostly Muslim northern districts into a new nation, PAKISTAN. Bloody religious warfare erupted, leaving thousands dead and millions homeless as refugees sought shelter with their respective coreligionists. At the same time, armed conflict flared over conflicting claims to the princely states of Jammu and Kashmir. Gandhi's assassination brought Jawaharlal Nehru to power in 1949, forging a republican state that angered the United States by standing firm for nonalignment during the cold war.

Religious and political strife persists throughout India. In 1975 an Indian court found Indira Gandhi's 1971 landslide election as prime minister invalid due to fraud. Rather than leave her post, Gandhi declared martial law and arrested many of her opponents. The prisoners were freed in 1977, in time for a new election that unseated Gandhi, but she staged a political comeback in 1980. Four years later Gandhi fielded troops against Sikh guerrillas at Amristar, prompting mass desertions by Sikhs in the army. Two Sikh members of Gandhi's bodyguard assassinated her in October 1984, whereupon she was succeeded by her son. Sikh and Muslim TERRORISM continues while Indian troops sporadically assault guerrilla bases in Kashmir and threaten neighboring Pakistan with nuclear weapons. Suicide bombings are common, including a blast in December 2001 that killed 14 persons in the Indian parliament. Lethal rioting between Muslims and Hindus flares sporadically despite (or because of) the election of a Muslim prime minister, A. P. J. Abdul Kalam, in July 2002. On the religious front, members of the Sadhu sect were jailed in 2003 for multiple acts of human sacrifice, while the AGHORA CULT continues to practice cannibalism without official interference.

INDONESIA

Diverse cultures and religions flourished throughout the Indonesian archipelago's 18,000 islands when Hindu priests and traders arrived in the first and second centuries A.D. Muslim invasions began in the 13th century, and most island inhabitants were forcibly converted during the next 200 years. PORTUGAL "discovered" Indonesia in the early 16th century, holding a near-monopoly on trade until the Dutch arrived to seize the archipelago in 1595. Establishment of the Java-based Dutch United East India Company secured the Dutch stranglehold on exports of coffee and spices. FRANCE, under NAPOLEON BONAPARTE, briefly claimed the islands in

1811 but returned them to Dutch control five years later. Indonesia was made an integral part of the Dutch empire in 1922, a fact ignored by Japanese invaders who craved new OIL resources during World War II. After JAPAN's surrender, nationalist rebels fought their returning Dutch masters for freedom. Full sovereignty through "union" with the Netherlands was granted in December 1949, but Indonesia broke the deal in February 1956, seizing Dutch property throughout the islands.

Thus began the next great struggle for Indonesian hearts and minds. President Sukarno adopted a concept of "guided democracy" (that is, dictatorship) under which the Indonesian Communist Party (PKI) gained dominant influence. Alarmed, CENTRAL INTELLIGENCE AGENCY leaders plotted Sukarno's ouster by means ranging from bungled assassination attempts to circulation of pornographic films starring Sukarno look-alikes. After eight years of false starts, in October 1965, a U.S.-supported military coup deposed Sukarno and slaughtered an estimated 500,000 alleged communists throughout Indonesia. (In 1990 former U.S. diplomats admitted compiling lists of suspected Reds, which they furnished to the Indonesian army's executioners.) General Suharto—a neofascist who had previously served Dutch colonialists and collaborated with Japanese invaders during World War II—imposed a brutal dictatorship (armed and supported from Washington). In 1975 Indonesia invaded EAST TIMOR, ultimately murdering another 200,000 persons. Economic failures prompted antigovernment riots in 1997, chiefly targeting Indonesia's prosperous Chinese minority. Suharto resigned in May 1998, and Indonesia witnessed its first democratic election in June 1999. Ethnic, religious, and political violence continues throughout Indonesia while ex-President Suharto dodges scheduled court dates on charges of corruption. In August 2002 President George W. Bush announced a $50 million grant of military aid to Indonesia to help the chaotic nation "fight TERRORISM." Based on past performance, critics fear the guns and money may be used to inaugurate a new age of brutal repression.

See also BUSH DYNASTY; COMMUNISM; FASCISM.

INTERNAL Revenue Service

The IRS traces its history to 1862 when Congress appointed the commissioner of internal revenue and enacted a wartime income tax to fund the Civil War. That tax was briefly revived in 1894, but the U.S. SUPREME COURT ruled it unconstitutional the following year. That roadblock was dismantled in 1913 when the Sixteenth Amendment to the Constitution empowered Congress to enact an income tax. Tax rates have fluctuated during the past 90-plus years (peaking at a top rate of 77 percent in 1918), and the IRS was overhauled in the 1950s to (theoretically) eliminate political patronage while replacing corrupt hacks with career professional employees. Today, only the IRS commissioner and its chief counsel are appointed by the president, with confirmation from the Senate, but controversy still dogs the U.S.'s primary tax-collection agency.

There is no doubt that the IRS has enjoyed a checkered career. In the 1930s, while J. EDGAR HOOVER and the FEDERAL BUREAU OF INVESTIGATION still denied the MAFIA's existence, IRS investigators used tax-evasion charges to imprison such notorious gangsters as Chicago's Al Capone, Cleveland's Morris Kleinman, and New Jersey's Irving ("Waxey Gordon") Wexler. Unfortunately, the agency's crime-fighting record was sullied on several fronts. Presidents ranging from Herbert Hoover to RICHARD NIXON and RONALD REAGAN used IRS audits to harass political enemies, and the IRS itself was frequently abusive to taxpayers without any evidence of outside motivation. Its ancillary agency, the BUREAU OF ALCOHOL, TOBACCO, AND FIREARMS, enjoys a similar reputation for riding roughshod over civil rights, sometimes with fatal results. Periodic scandals dating from the Truman era to the present day reveal widespread corruption, conflicts of interest, and other unseemly conduct by IRS administrators and agents from coast to coast. Successive efforts at reform have failed to stem the flood tide of complaints. Hard-core conspiracists, meanwhile, insist that the IRS is a tool of ZOG or some other shadow group acting behind the scenes to destroy U.S. freedoms and inaugurate a brutal NEW WORLD ORDER. Among fringe groups of the right, the very concept of an income tax itself is damned as a form of COMMUNISM.

INTERNATIONAL Brotherhood of Teamsters

Arguably the most notorious labor union in U.S. history, the International Brotherhood of Teamsters (IBT) was organized in August 1903 in a convention held at Niagara Falls, New York. Cornelius Shea was elected general president and held that office until 1907 when he was unseated by Boston organizer Daniel Tobin. Tobin, in turn, ran the union and nurtured strong ties with the MAFIA until 1952 when he retired and was succeeded by Dave Beck. (The union honored Tobin by creating a new position, "president emeritus," which paid the same $50,000 yearly salary received by active-duty general presidents.)

Nationwide links between the Teamsters Union and various mobsters were already well known to law enforcement (albeit ignored at FEDERAL BUREAU OF INVESTIGATION [FBI] headquarters, where Director J. EDGAR HOOVER denied the existence of organized crime in America), but those corrupt ties became public knowledge under Dave Beck's regime. Senate investigations of the union propelled brothers John and Robert Kennedy to national prominence in 1957 and sent Beck to federal prison for five years. Beck's replacement, James Hoffa, was questioned in the same public hearings and nurtured a hatred of the Kennedys that may have led directly to the JFK ASSASSINATION of November 1963. Hoffa was sentenced to an eight-year prison term for jury tampering in 1964, remaining at large for three years until his appeals were exhausted with a rebuff from the U.S. SUPREME COURT.

Despite incessant publicity surrounding the union's mob ties, multimillion-dollar "loans" to LAS VEGAS casinos, and felony convictions of numerous Teamster officials, national politicians still courted the IBT's money and 1.4 million voting members. President RICHARD NIXON was elected with Teamster support and rewarded Hoffa successor Frank Fitzsimmons with a private sweetheart contract: To keep Teamster votes and guarantee Fitzsimmons control of the union, Nixon granted clemency to Hoffa in 1972 but barred him from holding any union office for the next 10 years. Hoffa was fighting that restriction when he disappeared in 1975, a presumed gangland murder victim.

Fitzsimmons ruled the Teamsters for another decade, long enough to see another presidential hopeful, RONALD REAGAN, pledge his support to the union in exchange for cash and votes. Reagan named IBT Vice President Jackie Presser (an eighth-grade dropout, racketeer, and FBI informant) as a "senior economic adviser" to his White House transition team, while lavishing praise on the union at large. (Reagan told one IBT gathering, "I want to be in team with the Teamsters.") Fitzsimmons died of cancer in May 1981, replaced as general president by Reagan ally Roy Williams. Less than two weeks after his election Williams was indicted for conspiracy to bribe Nevada Senator Howard Cannon. Convicted of attempted bribery in 1982 he remained free on appeal after resigning his union presidency. (In 1985, still seeking leniency, Williams turned informer and provided details on the IBT's long symbiotic relationship with organized crime.)

Jackie Presser replaced Williams as Teamster president in April 1983, continuing the union's support for President Reagan and successor George H.W. Bush. Presser's links to the bureau finally could not prevent his May 1986 indictment for racketeering and embezzling $700,000 through a "ghost" employee scam. Six months later four Mafia leaders were indicted for rigging Presser's IBT election and controlling his decisions in office. Mounting legal bills and failing health at last persuaded Presser to step down as president two months before his death in July 1988. William McCarthy replaced him as president, while FBI memos continued to describe the union as "substantially controlled" by leaders of organized crime.

In 1988 the JUSTICE DEPARTMENT filed a civil racketeering lawsuit against the Teamsters Union, codenamed "Liberatus" after the FBI investigation that collected information on mob infiltration of the IBT. Union leaders and Justice officials reached a settlement on March 13, 1989, agreeing that the union's next general president would be chosen in 1991 by popular vote of convention delegates (as opposed to rigged election by the union's national committee composed of or influenced by racketeers). The bureau's Web site hails "Liberatus" as a major victory, claiming that it "has been largely successful at removing extensive [underworld] influence" from the IBT, but the 1991 election of president Ronald Carey was overturned six years later, and Carey was barred from seeking reelection in November 1997 on grounds of corrupt campaign funding. Carey was later indicted on seven counts of perjury concerning that campaign, charges alleging that he lied to a federal grand jury and to various other bodies established to end mob control of the union. Though acquitted at trial in October 2002, Carey was barred from IBT office while James Hoffa, Jr., assumed control of the union that was once led by his father from prison.

See also BUSH DYNASTY; KENNEDY DYNASTY.

INTERPOL

Formally known as the International Criminal Police Organization, Interpol was created in 1924 with headquarters in Vienna, AUSTRIA. Austrian police effectively dominated the early organization, and Interpol fell under Nazi control in the 1930s. German general Kurt Daluege was elected vice president of Interpol in 1937 (and subsequently executed for war crimes in 1946). At about the same time, FEDERAL BUREAU OF INVESTIGATION (FBI) Director J. EDGAR HOOVER sent Assistant Director H. Lane Dressler to an Interpol meeting in London. Dressler recommended that the United States join Interpol, and Attorney General Homer Cummings passed the recommendation to Congress in 1938, two weeks after ADOLF HITLER annexed Austria. Congress authorized payment of the $1,500 yearly dues on June 8, 1938.

FBI participation in Interpol was limited by the approach of World War II in Europe. G-men were invited to attend Interpol's 1939 conference in Berlin, which was held under the auspices of SS leader HEINRICH HIMMLER, but the U.S. State Department declined the invitation. Reinhard Heydrich, chief of Hitler's Security Police (SD) became Interpol's new president, and the group's headquarters moved to the Berlin suburb of Wannsee in December 1941, one day after the PEARL HARBOR attack in Hawaii. There, Interpol shared quarters with the GESTAPO and devoted itself primarily to hunting Jews and other refugees from German occupation. Heydrich was assassinated in June 1942 and replaced six months later by Ernst Kaltenbrunner. Despite a pledge to "continue the strictly nonpolitical character" of Interpol, Kaltenbrunner followed Heydrich's example and was sentenced to death for war crimes at the Nuremberg trials.

On the eve of the THIRD REICH's collapse, Interpol officials transferred their files to neutral Switzerland. The organization resurfaced in 1946 with much of its wartime leadership intact, although a new charter barred investigations of a racial, religious, or political nature. Delegates from the U.S. JUSTICE DEPARTMENT were invited to the first postwar conference at Brussels in May 1946, but Attorney General Tom Clark officially declined. Spokespersons for the State Department accepted, however, and the conference elected J. Edgar Hoover as Interpol's vice president. President Florent Louwage of the Belgian Political Police had worked directly under Kaltenbrunner and led Interpol for the next decade.

FBI membership in the "new" Interpol was terminated in 1950 when Hoover learned that Czech police officials had used the organization to track down political defectors in West GERMANY. Unable to tolerate Reds as he did "reformed" Nazis, Hoover resigned his vice presidency of Interpol for "special reasons" on November 26, 1950. The U.S. Treasury Department joined Interpol in 1958 (at an inflated yearly rate of $25,000, which was approved by Congress), but the FBI remained aloof. Echoes of Interpol's Nazi past were heard in 1968 when SS veteran Paul Dickopf became president. By the time he retired four years later Interpol had a new French headquarters and nearly 2 billion Swiss francs in its bank account, most of it contributed by supporters in Switzerland, BRAZIL, and VENEZUELA. Dickopf's vice president was Eugene Rossides from the U.S. Treasury Department. Another T-man on Interpol's executive committee was Edward Morgan, who had been driven from office in 1974 for his role in the WATERGATE scandal.

That same year, Director Clarence Kelley sent Associate Director Nicholas Callahan as the first FBI representative to attend an Interpol conference since 1958. Interpol was reeling from exposure of charter violations in Northern Ireland (where it helped track political terrorists) and in the BAHAMAS (where it helped politicians deport "undesirable" delegates to a Black Power Conference in 1969). FBI leaders resisted the lure of formal membership until January 1985 when Interpol officially repealed the charter ban on political investigations to permit activity in cases of TERRORISM. Four years later Interpol was further embarrassed by news that its Mexican representative, Florentino Ventura, belonged to a drug-dealing voodoo cult that was responsible for 25 gruesome murders around Matamoros. By 1994 when bureau liaison was handed to the FBI's International Relations, officials estimated that 90 percent of international police inquiries bypassed Interpol entirely. One journalist described Interpol as "far from being the slick and sophisticated organization of popular mythology." Another was more cynical, reporting: "They just haven't been the same since *der Führer* died."

IRAN

The land of modern-day Iran was shared by Medes and Persians until 558 B.C. when Cyrus the Great ousted the Medes and founded the Persian Empire.

A series of wars expanded Persian territory into INDIA before GREECE conquered the empire in 330 B.C., followed by the Seleucids (312–302 B.C.), the Parthians (247 B.C.–A.D. 226), and Arab Muslims (641). Britain and RUSSIA fought for control of Iran throughout the Qajar dynasty (1794–1925). Reza Kahn seized power in 1921 and changed his name to Reza Shah Pahlavi four years later. Iran's alliance with the THIRD REICH during World War II prompted British-Russian occupation in 1941, supplanting the Shah with his more pliable son, Mohammed Reza Pahlavi. Prime Minister Mossadegh, elected in 1951, moved to nationalize Iran's OIL industry and drove the young shah into exile, but U.S. troops joined in a coup to topple him in 1953, restoring the shah to his throne. Pahlavi's postwar campaign of Westernization alienated Iran's Shi'ite Muslim clerics, but dissent was ruthlessly suppressed by terrorist secret police (the SAVAAK). A declaration of martial law failed to stifle armed rebellion in 1978, driving the Shah and his family from Iran in January 1979. Exiled cleric Ayatollah Ruhollah Khomeini returned to establish a Muslim theocracy, imposing strict religious laws and banning political parties throughout Iran. In November 1979 Muslim activists seized the U.S. embassy in Tehran and held 52 staff members hostage for the next 14 months. Their release was negotiated by aides to presidential candidate RONALD REAGAN, the OCTOBER SURPRISE arranged to ensure Reagan's election, with release of the hostages stage-managed to coincide with his January 1981 inauguration. During the next eight years, Reagan vilified Iran and funneled military aid to IRAQ for a series of wars with Khomeini's regime, while at the same time arranging secret (and illegal) arms sales to Iran in support of Reagan's (equally illegal) CONTRA raids on NICARAGUA. The resulting IRAN-CONTRA scandal led to indictment of several presidential aides, all of whom were later pardoned by President George H. W. Bush. Khomeini died in June 1989 and was succeeded as supreme leader by Ayatollah Khamenei. Liberal reform candidates won surprising victories in elections held during 1997 and 2000, but Iran's clerical and military rulers have thus far blocked most efforts to relax theocratic rule. Relations with the United States had relaxed somewhat by 2001 when the PENTTBOM attacks of September 11 prompted President George W. Bush to a fresh round of scapegoating. While the terrorist raids were conducted by agents of AL-QAEDA, led by Osama bin Laden and operating from AFGHANISTAN, Bush unaccountably blamed the incidents on a mythical AXIS OF EVIL including Iran, Iraq, and North KOREA. In May 2003 Bush declared that Iran was stockpiling "weapons of mass destruction"—the same allegation falsely leveled against Iraq prior to the U.S. invasion that toppled SADDAM HUSSEIN's regime—and announced plans to "destabilize" the Iranian government. On June 20, 2003, Bush spokespeople announced that Washington "reserves the right to use military action to stop Iran making nuclear weapons," while Tehran accused the United States of waging "a baseless propaganda war."

See also BIN LADEN FAMILY; BUSH DYNASTY; TERRORISM.

IRAN-CONTRA conspiracy

President RONALD REAGAN (1981–89) was dedicated to elimination of leftist governments wherever they were found on Earth, and none crystallized his obsession more clearly than the legally elected Sandinista regime in NICARAGUA. Determined to overthrow that government by any means available, Reagan and Vice President George H. W. Bush funneled cash and military aid to a group of right-wing terrorists (dubbed "contras") that were created by the CENTRAL INTELLIGENCE AGENCY (CIA) in November 1981. Contras staged brutal raids in Nicaragua, slaughtering civilians, raping nuns, and otherwise behaving in the manner of fascist juntas throughout the Third World. Their crimes were so egregious that Congress banned further U.S. aid to the movement in 1984. Reagan and Bush pursued their illegal war in defiance of federal statutes, seeking cash for the costly campaign from various alternate sources. COCAINE sales covered some of the costs, but the White House also arranged illegal sale of arms to IRAN and then engaged in a war with IRAQ (whom the United States also supported), funneling cash from the sales to contra leaders in Central America.

Exposure of the plot began on October 5, 1986, when Nicaraguan soldiers shot down a contra supply plane and captured its American pilot. One month later, on November 3, a Lebanese newspaper broke the story of secret U.S. arms sales to Iran. Reagan issued a series of false denials but then, on November 25, 1986, admitted arms sales to Iran with a diversion of cash to the contras. Reagan, still denying any personal knowledge of the conspiracy, appointed a commission to investigate the scandal. Both houses of Congress soon formed their own committees, while special prosecutor Lawrence Walsh was appointed to seek indictments against Iran-contra principals. CIA chief WILLIAM CASEY died before his testimony was obtained, while others (including Lt. Col. Oliver North) committed perjury in an effort to soft-pedal the plot. Former national security advisor John Poindexter floated the preposterous tale that *he* had initiated the Iran-contra network without consulting President Reagan. Defendants ultimately charged in the case included:

Carl Channell, head of North's covert fund-raising efforts. On April 29, 1987, he pleaded guilty to conspiracy to defraud the United States.

Richard Miller, Channell's public relations consultant. He pleaded guilty to identical charges on May 6, 1987.

Oliver North, indicted on 12 felony counts, including conspiracy to defraud the U.S. government. He was convicted on three counts in May 1989; received a three-year suspended sentence and a $150,000 fine (reversed on appeal).

Robert McFarlane, Poindexter's successor; pleaded guilty, on March 11, 1998, to withholding information from Congress. Subsequently indicted on charges similar to North's, he was convicted in 1989, fined $20,000, and given two years' probation.

John Poindexter, convicted on five counts of lying to Congress in April 1990 and sentenced to six months in prison (reversed on appeal).

Richard Secord, a retired U.S. Air Force general involved in arms sales to Iran; charged with perjury, obstruction, false statements, and conspiracy to defraud the United States. On November 8, 1989, he pleaded guilty on one count of lying to Congress.

Albert Hakim, owner of a company that facilitated arms transfers to Iran; charged with bribery and conspiracy to defraud the United States. On November 21, 1989, he pleaded guilty on one count of "illegally supplementing" a government employee's salary.

Clair George, Fiers's superior at CIA headquarters; indicted on 10 counts of perjury. His case ended in a mistrial; jurors convicted him on two of five counts at his second trial.

Joseph Fernandez, CIA station chief in Costa Rica; indicted for perjury and obstruction of justice. Charges were dismissed when President Bush's attorney general refused to permit disclosure of classified evidence at trial.

Thomas Clines, an ex-CIA agent who funneled arms to the contras; indicted on tax charges. A jury convicted him on four felony counts on September 18, 1990, and he received a 16-month prison term.

Alan Fiers, Jr., chief of CIA covert operations in Central America (1984–86). On July 9, 1991, he pleaded guilty to withholding information from Congress.

Elliott Abrams, assistant secretary of state who pleaded guilty on October 7, 1991, to withholding information from Congress.

Duane Clarridge, another CIA agent; indicted on seven perjury counts in November 1991.

Caspar Weinberger, former secretary of defense; indicted on five counts of perjury and obstruction.

On December 24, 1992, one month before leaving office, President Bush pardoned defendants Abrams, Clarridge, Fiers, George, McFarlane, and Weinberger, thus ensuring that none would serve time or feel inclined to testify against their superiors in Washington. Lawrence Walsh's final report, published in 1994, scored Reagan and Bush (both out of office by then) for their illegal activities, but neither ex-president was ever charged with any offense.

See also BUSH DYNASTY; FASCISM; TERRORISM.

IRAQ

Known in ancient times as Mesopotamia ("land between the rivers"), Iraq occupies most of the land between the Tigris and the Euphrates. Advanced civilization existed here as early as 4000 B.C., conquered by Persia's Cyrus the Great in 538 B.C., then by GREECE (331 B.C.), and finally by Arab Muslims (A.D. 640). Mongols pillaged the country in 1258, followed by repeated Persian and Turkish invasions during the 16th–18th centuries. TURKEY ruled the country from 1831 until World War I when British occupation troops arrived, renaming the region Iraq and granting independence to its monarchy in 1932. Avid Iraqi flirtation with ADOLF HITLER brought British troops back during World War II. Iraq was a charter member of the Arab League in 1945 and three years later joined in an Arab assault on ISRAEL. A military coup led by Abdul Karem Kassim toppled the monarchy in July 1958; a military junta that forged alliances with RUSSIA was installed. Kassim was overthrown and killed in March 1963 in a coup staged by the Ba'ath Socialist Party, followed by a series of juntas and coups that finally installed SADDAM HUSSEIN as president in July 1979.

Hussein's regime soon developed a reputation for ruthless repression and ethnic cleansing of Kurdish minorities. Official U.S. support remained unwavering while Hussein waged war against neighboring IRAN through the 1980s while Presidents RONALD REAGAN and George H. W. Bush turned blind eyes to Saddam's TERRORISM at home. Bush funneled money to Iraq as late as January 1990, flaunting a congressional embargo on further aid to Saddam. On August 2, 1990, Saddam told U.S. Ambassador April Gillespie that he planned to invade Kuwait (severed from Iraq by British fiat in 1899), and Gillespie raised no objection. As the invasion proceeded, however—placing Saddam in control of OIL reserves estimated at 15 percent of the world's total—Bush had a change of heart and rushed troops to Saudi Arabia while ordering Iraq to withdraw. The resultant GULF WAR of January 1991 drove Iraq from Kuwait but failed to topple Saddam's dictatorship. It remained for another Bush to take up that crusade 12 years later in the guise of "Operation Iraqi Freedom." Following the September 11, 2001, PENTTBOM attacks, President George W. Bush accused Iraq of complicity with AL-QAEDA terrorists and named the country as part of a mythical AXIS OF EVIL (also including Iran and North KOREA). In March 2003 Bush accused Iraq of illegally stockpiling "weapons of mass destruction," then he invaded the nation and drove Saddam into hiding, establishing a pliable regime while U.S. petroleum companies (including Vice President DICK CHENEY's colleagues at Halliburton Corporation) began to pump Iraqi oil. No weapons of mass destruction were found in the war's aftermath, leaving Bush to blame his CENTRAL INTELLIGENCE AGENCY director and various foreign sources for providing "faulty intelligence." Likewise, no links between Saddam and al-Qaeda have yet been discovered.

See also BUSH DYNASTY.

IRELAND

Ireland was inhabited by Picts until the fourth century B.C. when Celtic invaders subjugated the native populace. Norse invaders ravaged the country from 795 to 1015. In the 12th century the pope delivered Ireland to the British Crown as a papal fief, and England's Henry II was acknowledged as "Lord of Ireland" in 1171. Religious warfare began in 1690 with Protestant King William III (of Orange) defeating Catholic King James II, and it has continued to the present day. Anti-British agitation and demands for home rule climaxed during World War I with the Easter Rebellion of April 1916. Britain triumphed in that struggle, but guerrilla warfare continued, and Ireland declared itself a republic in 1919. The Irish Free State was established as a British dominion in December 1922, while six northern counties (modern Northern Ireland) were retained by the Crown. The IRISH REPUBLICAN ARMY failed to prevent that partition, but its long war against Britain would continue into the 21st century. Civil war rocked Ireland prior to final acceptance of the Anglo-Irish Treaty, but the republic survived and in 1937 changed its name to Eire, with a new constitution. Corruption and bribery scandals haunted the dominant Fianna Fáil Party at the dawn of a new century, but its candidates still scored major electoral victories in 2002.

IRGUN

The first modern terrorist group in the Middle East was not an Islamic fundamentalist movement but rather the Zionist organization Irgun Tsvai-Leumi ("Military-National Organization," in Hebrew). Created in 1931 the Irgun denounced any moderate efforts to negotiate creation of a Jewish state in Palestine, instead demanding the immediate evacuation of Arab natives and British occupation troops alike. The Irgun was funded secretly by leaders of the Polish government, ironically including anti-Semites who hoped that the establishment of ISRAEL would promote a mass evacuation of Polish Jews. During Palestine's so-called Arab revolt of 1936–39, Irgun members and associates killed 3,112 Arabs (versus 329 Jews murdered by Arabs). Four years later, led by Menachem Begin (later prime minister of Israel), the Irgun merged with the Israeli Defense Force and broadened its criminal actions to target British officials. Its more notorious actions include the following:

The southern wing of the King David Hotel, which was the headquarters of the British army in Palestine, was blown up by the Zionist terrorist organization Irgun in 1946. British personnel disregarded a telephoned warning; as a consequence, 92 people died. (Hulton-Deutsch Collection/Corbis)

April 25, 1946—Seven British soldiers died in an Irgun raid on an arsenal in Tel Aviv.

July 22, 1946—A bomb explosion at Jerusalem's King David Hotel, headquarters of British civil and military authorities, killed 91 persons (including 17 Jews).

September 9, 1946—A Tel Aviv bombing killed two British officers.

October 8, 1946—An Irgun land mine outside Jerusalem killed two British soldiers and wounded 15.

October 31, 1946—Irgun bombers struck the British embassy in Rome.

November 17, 1946—An Irgun mine in Tel Aviv killed three policemen and a Royal Air Force sergeant.

July 12, 1947—Irgun kidnappers abducted two British soldiers. The captives were hanged on July 30.

September 29, 1947—The Irgun bombed a police station in Haifa, killing eight policemen and two Arab civilians.

December 29, 1947—Irgun commanders lobbed grenades into a Jerusalem café, killing 11 Arabs and two British police officers.

Irgun TERRORISM did not end with the creation of Israel in 1948. On April 9 of that year, joined by members of the equally brutal Stern Gang (led by Yitzhak Shamir, another future Israeli prime minister), Irgun gunners invaded the Arab village of Deir Yassin, murdering 100–120 of the town's 750 unarmed residents. Perhaps dissatisfied with the body count, Irgun propagandists' broadcast reported that 254 had been killed (a figure often repeated in later histories, denounced in Israel as an "Arab exaggeration"). Other atrocities followed, with Irgun leaders marching under the motto: "As in Deir Yassin, so everywhere." Chaim Weizmann, first president of Israel, described the action as "a miraculous clearing of the land." Those Irgun terrorists who did not enter politics were absorbed by the new Israeli army.

See also ZIONISM.

IRISH Republican Army (IRA)

The IRA has its roots in the Easter Rising of 1916 when Irish nationalists fought to throw off the yoke of British colonial rule. That effort failed, but agitation for freedom continued, culminating in a declaration of independence from Britain in 1919. The resulting conflict, with troops of the new IRA battling British soldiers and native "loyalists" (mostly Church of England Protestants) dragged on until 1921, climaxing with partition of IRELAND into its present form, while the six counties of Ulster remained British under the name of NORTHERN IRELAND. That disappointment sparked a brutal civil war within Ireland itself that lasted until 1924. The IRA hung on as a dissident organization, pledged to liberating Northern Ireland from British rule, until President Eamon de Valera banned the group in 1936.

Driven underground by de Valera's edict, the IRA carried its fight to Britain with a series of bombing campaigns and other armed actions in England and

This young man in Belfast, Ireland, reads a mural supporting the IRA. (Ed Kashi/Corbis)

Northern Ireland. Sporadic activity, chiefly raids on arsenals, continued throughout the 1940s and 1950s while the IRA's political wing (Sinn Fein) worked to crystallize nationalist sentiment in both parts of divided Ireland. Renewed warfare was conducted during 1958–60, but dissension split the organization during the next decade, as Marxist influence caused some hard-line members of the CATHOLIC CHURCH to challenge their fundamental beliefs. In 1969 the IRA formally split, with a majority following the new Provisional wing toward a new generation of armed struggle, while the Official IRA opted for a more moderate approach (declaring a permanent cease-fire in May 1972). Moderation was the last thing many nationalists craved, however; an armed struggle (or TERRORISM) escalated steadily during the next two decades. As a new millennium dawned, peace talks and cease-fires offered cause for optimism, but radicals on both sides (including Protestant guerrillas from the Ulster Volunteer Force

and similar groups) seemed unable to break the ingrained habit of violence.

ISRAEL

Known until 1948 as Palestine, the region of present-day Israel was ruled by two kingdoms (Israel and Judah) until successive invasions by Assyrians, Babylonians, Egyptians, Persians, Romans, and Greeks drove most Jews from the region by A.D. 135. Arabs seized Palestine from the Byzantine empire in 634–40 and ruled until the 20th century, challenged only by a series of Crusades launched by the CATHOLIC CHURCH between the 11th and 13th centuries. British forces drove the Turks from Palestine in World War I, and a League of Nations mandate granted the region to England in 1923. Leaders of the Zionist movement, seeking a Jewish homeland in the Middle East since 1896, received conditional support from Britain with the 1917 Balfour Declaration, which said:

His Majesty's Government view with favor the establishment in Palestine of a national home for the Jewish people . . . it being clearly understood that nothing shall be done that may prejudice the civil and religious rights of existing non-Jewish communities in Palestine.

Further declarations in 1918 assured Palestinian Arabs of self-rule in their homeland, but those promises fell by the wayside after World War II and the publicized horrors of the Holocaust. While the IRGUN and other Zionist groups mounted campaigns of TERRORISM to drive British forces from Palestine, world opinion called for the immediate creation of a Jewish state. Thus Israel was born in March 1948. This was immediately followed by military "land-cleansing operations" in April and May, driving countless Arabs from their homes. War erupted with Israel's Arab neighbors in May 1948, ending eight months later after Israel had *increased* its land mass by 50 percent. In 1956 Israel invaded EGYPT to support Britain's claim on the Suez Canal. Another "defensive" war in 1967 doubled Israel's size, at the expense of LEBANON and JORDAN. Various Arab groups thereafter launched guerrilla campaigns against Israel, and Israel responded with bombing raids and mechanized invasions of her neighbors, assassinated enemies abroad, and ruthlessly suppressed Arab dissent at home. Supported by the United States and Britain, Israel is presently the only Middle Eastern state permitted unfettered development of nuclear weapons. Various peace negotiations spanning a quarter-century have failed to rescue the troubled "Holy Land" from incessant violence and religious intrigue.

See also HOLOCAUST AND HOLOCAUST DENIAL; ZIONISM.

ITALY

The Etruscan civilization dominated Italy from the ninth century B.C. until it was toppled by Romans 600 years later. For the next seven centuries, until barbarian invaders sacked the Roman empire in the fourth and fifth centuries A.D., Rome essentially controlled the "known world's" history. From 800 onward various feudal warlords and leaders of the CATHOLIC CHURCH struggled fiercely for control of Italy. NAPOLEON BONAPARTE unified Italy and crowned himself king in 1805, but Austria usurped French control 10 years later. Nationalist uprisings were crushed in 1820–21 and 1831, but the impulse for freedom could not be denied.

A series of revolts and royal decrees unified Italy once more between 1860 and 1870. Although allied with the victors in World War I, Italy was disappointed by its small colonial acquisitions and frightened by the rise of COMMUNISM in Russia. In 1919 fascist leader Benito Mussolini organized a militant movement to "rescue Italy from Bolshevism," leading his black-shirted troops in a march on Rome. Named as premier in October 1922, Mussolini soon transformed the Italian government into a dictatorship and forged an alliance with ADOLF HITLER's Nazi GERMANY in 1936. By that time Italy had conquered ETHIOPIA (1935) and craved new targets. A major obstacle to Mussolini and his comrades was the MAFIA, which had been deeply entrenched in Italy since the 13th century through alliances with corrupt politicians. While Mussolini tried to destroy the pervasive crime syndicate, U.S. mobsters (including CHARLES "LUCKY" LUCIANO and MEYER LANSKY) joined forces with the U.S. military on a plan to invade Italy in World War II.

Defeated by the Allies in 1944, Italy rejected monarchy two years later and declared itself a republic. Open elections including Communist candidates did not appeal to the United States, however, and during 1947–48, the CENTRAL INTELLIGENCE AGENCY spent millions of dollars to suppress leftist political groups in Italy, including use of Mafia goons to intimidate "Reds." In the 1970s a rash of terrorist attacks by extreme left- and right-wing groups (including the notorious Red Brigades) destabilized the Italian government, and while most of those cliques were suppressed by the early 1980s, endemic scandal and corruption marked a series of "revolving door" administrations during the next two decades. Mafia influence remains strong throughout Italy, despite periodic show trials and pledges of reform. Right-wing billionaire Silvio Berlusconi was named prime minister in June 2001, while critics aired charges of Mafia ties and challenged the wisdom of placing Italy's number-one media mogul in charge of the government. Berlusconi won acquittal in 2002 at his trial for bribery and tax fraud, but the controversy surrounding his administration endures.

See also FASCISM; TERRORISM.

IT&T

Brothers Hernand and Sosthenes Behn founded the International Telephone and Telegraph Corporation (IT&T) in 1920 as a holding company for their several

Caribbean-based communications firms. It grew rapidly from there and by the 1930s held stock in several German armaments companies, including a 28-percent share of Focke-Wolf which produced fighter planes for ADOLF HITLER's Luftwaffe. At the outbreak of World War II, IT&T leaders refused an opportunity to repatriate their profits earned in GERMANY and continued doing business with the THIRD REICH. According to author Anthony Sutton in *Wall Street and the Rise of Hitler:* "IT&T's purchase of substantial interest in Focke-Wolfe meant that IT&T was producing German planes used to kill Americans and their allies—and it made excellent profits out of the enterprise." Charles Higham adds in *Trading with the Enemy,* that even after the PEARL HARBOR attack, Hitler's military employed IT&T to make "switchboards, telephones, alarm gongs, buoys, air-raid warning devices, radar equipment, and 30,000 fuses per month for artillery shells used to kill British and American troops." Furthermore, Higham writes, "IT&T supplied ingredients for the rocket bombs that fell on London . . . high-frequency radio equipment, and fortification and field communication sets. Without this supply of crucial materials, it would have been impossible for the German air force to kill American and British troops, for the German army to fight the Allies in Africa, Italy, France, and Germany, for England to have been bombed, or for Allied ships to have been attacked at sea."

Those offenses went unpunished while IT&T expanded further in the postwar years. During the 1960s and 1970s it became one of the world's dominant multinational firms, owning a variety of companies that included the Sheraton hotel chain, Levitt home builders, and Hartford Fire Insurance. The company's propensity for backing homicidal right-wing dictators surfaced again in the early 1970s when President Salvador Allende nationalized IT&T holdings in CHILE. Corporate leaders huddled with leaders of President RICHARD NIXON's administration (chiefly HENRY KISSINGER) and the CENTRAL INTELLIGENCE AGENCY, hatching a plan to destroy Chile's economy and foment revolt within the Chilean army. Allende was deposed and murdered on September 11, 1973, and replaced by the brutal junta of General Augusto Pinochet. (Seventeen days later, left-wing activists bombed IT&T's headquarters in New York City, in a gesture of protest.)

IT&T no longer exists in the form that sparked so much scandal and protest during the Nixon years. The firm sold off its telecommunications holdings in 1987 and eight years later split into three companies: ITT Hartford Group Inc. (insurance); ITT Industries Inc. (defense electronics and auto parts); and a "new" ITT Corporation that merged with Starwood Hotels and Resorts in 1997. In theory, at least, the company no longer wields life-and-death power throughout the Third World.

JACK the Ripper

Arguably the most infamous serial killer of all time, London's "Jack the Ripper" murdered and mutilated at least five hard-luck prostitutes (some place the tally higher) in the autumn of 1888. The stalker got his nickname from the signature appended to various taunting letters mailed to police and the press—most (or all) of which are now considered fakes, written by kooks or headline-hungry journalists. After his last confirmed murder—the victim was Mary Kelly—on November 9, the Ripper packed away his knife and left historians to speculate on his identity. It is the mystery that makes Jack so intriguing with new books and articles about his crime spree published every year.

Inevitably, conspiracy theories have grown up around London's notorious bogeyman. The first, proposed in 1928, claimed that the Ripper was a Russian doctor, one Alexander Pedachenko, who committed the murders in league with czarist SECRET POLICE, as a form of anti-British TERRORISM. No solid evidence supports the case, and Pedachenko is now generally dismissed as a viable suspect.

The next Ripper plot, advanced in 1962, involves a royal conspiracy of silence. In this scenario Jack was Prince Albert Victor Christian Edward ("Eddie"), Duke of Clarence and Heir Presumptive to the throne of England. Driven mad by syphilis or homosexuality (theories differ), the would-be king allegedly ran amok in London, whereupon his family

buried the evidence and consigned him to a sanitarium (where he died in 1892). There are at least four major problems with this theory. First, no evidence exists linking Prince Eddie to the murders. There is likewise no proof that he suffered from syphilis, and while he may in fact have been gay, that argues *against* his guilt since gay serial killers typically target same-sex victims. Finally, official records show that Eddie was far from London on the dates of all five Ripper homicides (though one would expect nothing less from a royal cover-up).

A variation of the Eddie theme, proposed by forensic psychiatrist David Abrahamson in 1992, has the prince joining a homicidal tag-team with his alleged gay lover, supposed woman-hater James K. Stephen. (Stephen alone is also named as the Ripper by other researchers.) Abrahamson claimed that files obtained from Scotland Yard betray Edward and Stephen as the killers; yet London police deny providing Abrahamson with any such material. (Another cover-up?) Abrahamson's account is also rife with historical errors—and, once again, no concrete evidence has surfaced linking either suspect to the crimes.

The mother of all Jack conspiracy theories was floated by author Stephen Knight in 1976. According to Knight, Prince Edward (no longer gay) secretly married a Catholic commoner named Annie Crook and fathered a child by her before the royal family intervened. Discovering the prince's faux pas, high-ranking members of the British government moved to clean up the scandal, clapping Annie Crook into a lunatic asylum and murdering the five prostitutes who witnessed the illicit marriage. Those murders were allegedly performed by a three-man team, including Sir William Gull (physician-in-ordinary to the queen), artist Walter Sickert, and coachman John Netley. All three killers were FREEMASONS (as were the police who covered up their crimes), and the victims were disemboweled in accordance with "Masonic ritual." Knight's tale was a sensation in its day, and it inspired the Sherlock Holmes film *Murder by Decree,* but it is full of gaping holes.

First, Dr. Gull was 72 years old when Jack plied his blade and was partially disabled by the first in a series of strokes that would finally kill him in 1890. Further, Knight based most of his anti-Masonic "revelations" on the *PROTOCOLS OF THE ELDERS OF ZION,* a notorious forgery concocted by Russian agents to vilify Jews. (How Knight shifted the focus of the *Protocols* from Jews to the Masonic lodge is not explained.) Further, prevailing law in England at the time permitted the queen to nullify any marriage between a British heir and a member of the CATHOLIC CHURCH. If this were not sufficient to defuse the plot, research revealed in 1988 that Annie Crook was not a Catholic but rather a loyal Anglican from birth. A curious footnote to the Knight-Masonic plot surfaced in 2002 when mystery novelist Patricia Cornwell named Walter Sickert (minus Gull and Netley) as the Ripper in her final solution to the case. Sadly, as in the many other efforts to reveal Jack's true identity, the Cornwell opus was long on speculation and fatally short on evidence.

JACKSON, George Lester

Born in Chicago on September 23, 1941, future black activist George Jackson moved to Los Angeles with his family at age 14. A series of juvenile arrests climaxed in 1957 when Jackson was convicted of stealing $71 from a local gas station. He received an indeterminate sentence of one year to life in state prison, with his case slated for annual review. During the next 13 years, while waiting in vain for parole, Jackson studied the political writings of FIDEL CASTRO, MAO ZEDONG, and other modern revolutionary figures. He also corresponded with leaders of the BLACK PANTHER PARTY and was named a "field marshal" in that organization, working nonstop to

politicize nonwhite inmates at Soledad. For that offense, some say, his jailers marked him for death.

On January 16, 1970, a white guard at Soledad, John Mills, was killed by unknown inmates in retaliation for the recent fatal shooting of three black prisoners. Prison authorities charged Jackson, John Cluchette, and Fleeta Drumgo with the murder, and the case soon became a radical cause célèbre. A pretrial hearing was scheduled for August 7, 1970, at the Marin County courthouse, while sinister maneuvers went on behind the scenes. Louis Tackwood, a black undercover agent of the FEDERAL BUREAU OF INVESTIGATION (FBI) and the LOS ANGELES POLICE DEPARTMENT (LAPD), later testified that his control agents tried to arrange a jailbreak from the courthouse, using informer MELVIN SMITH to arm and encourage a Black Panther raiding party. In fact, the Panthers refused to participate, and Jackson's hearing was canceled. Unaware of the change, Jackson's teenage brother arrived in court with a bagful of guns but saw only strange faces. Frustrated, he seized the courtroom, armed three prisoners unrelated to his brother's case, and left the courthouse with a group of hostages including Judge Harold Haley, prosecutor Gary Thomas, and three jurors. The group had barely entered Jackson's van before a firing squad of guards from San Quentin prison "coincidentally" arrived and riddled the van with bullets. Dead in the wreckage lay Jackson, Judge Haley, and two of the liberated convicts, while Gary Thomas was crippled for life.

Legal maneuvers delayed George Jackson's trial until August 1971. Three days before the proceedings were scheduled to begin, on August 21, violence erupted once again, this time at San Quentin (where Jackson was housed pending trial). According to official statements, Jackson left his cell to meet attorney Steven Bingham and passed through two searches en route to the meeting. Returning from the visitors room, Jackson allegedly drew a .38 caliber revolver (later changed to a large 9-mm automatic pistol) from beneath an Afro wig where the weapon lay balanced on his head. Chaos ensued, with Jackson killed by prison snipers while three guards were murdered by inmates. Steven Bingham, charged with smuggling the gun (or guns) to Jackson in his briefcase (again, despite prison searches), fled into hiding and remained a fugitive until the 1980s. On his surrender, Bingham was tried and acquitted on all charges related to the case. Meanwhile, George Jackson had become a martyr to the black nationalist movement, and his Soledad codefendants were convicted of killing John Mills. Informer Louis Tackwood testified for the defense at that trial. When asked the nature of his last assignment for the FBI and LAPD, he replied: "The assassination of George Jackson."

JACKSON State College massacre

The month of May 1970, following disclosure of President RICHARD NIXON's covert military campaign in CAMBODIA, witnessed demonstrations on campuses and in cities across the United States. The official response was unusually harsh, including the shooting of 13 students (with four killed) by National Guardsmen at KENT STATE UNIVERSITY on May 4 and police shootings of 86 African Americans (six fatally) in Augusta, Georgia, on May 11. Demonstrations at Mississippi's all-black Jackson State College were marked by scattered incidents of rock and bottle throwing on May 13, and tragedy struck on the following day when a squad of local police and Mississippi Highway Patrol officers opened fire on campus, killing two persons and wounding 12 more.

Both police departments involved in the shooting had long histories of racist violence toward blacks and of friendly collaboration with the KU KLUX KLAN, a mindset emphasized when Highway Patrol Inspector Lloyd ("Goon") Jones radioed a call for ambulances to transport wounded "niggers" from the campus. Officers involved in the shooting immediately collected their empty shell casings and reloaded their weapons to make it appear as if no shots had been fired—this, despite the casualties and evidence of 400 bullet holes in the women's dormitory of Alexander Hall, aside from other damage caused by gunfire. When questioned later, each and every officer present initially denied firing his weapon, a circumstance that led the archconservative Mississippi-Louisiana Press Association to pass a resolution condemning the official conspiracy of silence.

FEDERAL BUREAU OF INVESTIGATION (FBI) investigation of the shooting (code-named JACKTWO) quickly identified pellets of No. 1 buckshot at Alexander Hall and confirmed that only Jackson police officers had been armed with shotguns on May 14. All officers involved had denied firing their guns or collecting spent shells at the scene, but the threat of grand jury subpoenas prompted certain highway patrol officers to produce a number of shotgun shells fired by city police. (Meanwhile, the state patrol officers had destroyed their own shell casings.) Confronted with irrefutable evidence, several officers finally admitted firing their weapons but claimed they had done so only in response to "sniper fire" from Alexander Hall. FBI Director J. EDGAR HOOVER made a premature announcement on May 18, reporting that there seemed "to be substantial proof . . . that there was sniper fire on the troops [sic] from the dormitory before the troops fired." In fact, there was none, as confirmed by Hoover's agents when their investigation was completed.

President Nixon, declaring himself "deeply saddened" by the Kent and Jackson shootings, appointed a President's Commission on Campus Unrest—better known by the name of its chairman, former Pennsylvania governor William Scranton—to investigate the incidents. The Scranton Commission's report on Jackson State, published on October 1, 1970, called the shooting "an unreasonable, unjustified overreaction." It also accused the Mississippi law officers of lying and concealing or destroying vital evidence. The report concluded "that a significant cause of the deaths and injuries at Jackson State College is the confidence of white officers that if they fire weapons during a black campus disturbance they will face neither stern departmental discipline nor criminal prosecution or convictions."

That expectation was borne out by subsequent events. Although lying to FBI agents is itself a federal offense, punishable by a maximum $10,000 fine and 10 years in prison, G-men deviated from their normal routine of obtaining signed statements in this case, thereby exempting all suspects from prosecution. A federal grand jury was convened in June 1970 under Judge Harold Cox (a racist known for describing Mississippi blacks as "chimpanzees"), but it returned no indictments after Cox advised the panel that student demonstrators "must expect to be injured or killed." A Hinds County grand jury acknowledged that initial statements taken from police were "absolutely false" but decided that any indictment of police for perjury or worse would be "unwarranted, unjustified and political in nature." Instead, the panel chose a black bystander, 21-year-old Ernest Lee Kyles, and indicted him on October 14, 1970, for arson and inciting a riot. (Charges were later dropped for lack of evidence.)

Despite claims of "sadness" evoked by the shootings in May 1970, President Nixon and company resented any efforts to exonerate the victims. Vice President SPIRO AGNEW denounced the Scranton Report as "pabulum for the permissivists" and called on J. Edgar Hoover for any derogatory material "that can ameliorate some of the impact." Civil rights activist Ralph Abernathy was a particular target of Agnew's wrath, the vice president seeking information to "destroy his credibility." (Hoover agreed with Agnew that Abernathy, successor to Dr. MARTIN LUTHER KING, JR., as chief of the Southern Christian Leadership Conference, was "one of the worst.") Overall, as noted by the Southern Regional Council in *The New South,* "People here think that the way the police handled the students at Jackson State is the way Nixon and Agnew want the students treated."

Litigation arising from the Jackson State shootings dragged on for more than a decade. Relatives of slain victims Phillip Gibbs and James Early Green, assisted by an ad hoc Lawyers Committee for Civil Rights Under Law, sued state and local police for $13.8 million in federal court. At trial, two officers admitted lying in their FBI interviews, and five G-men testified that there was no evidence of sniper fire aimed at police, but an all-white jury ruled in favor of the defendants on March 22, 1972. The U.S. Court of Appeals in New Orleans ratified that verdict with a convoluted judgment in October 1974: The panel ruled that there *was* a sniper on campus; then it deemed that the police reaction "far exceeded the response that was appropriate," finally declaring that "sovereign immunity" exempted Mississippi police from any lawsuits regardless of their behavior. In January 1982 seven justices of the U.S. SUPREME COURT voted against reopening the case.

JAMAICA

Jamaica was inhabited by Arawak Indians when Christopher Columbus arrived in 1492; he decimated the population and claimed the Caribbean island (which he called St. Iago) for SPAIN. Spanish rule endured until 1655 when Britain seized control. Pirates operated freely from the capital, Port Royal, until an earthquake flattened it in 1692. African slaves were imported to replace the slaughtered Arawaks on great sugar plantations, and armed bands of escapees (called Maroons) harassed British

masters until slavery was finally abolished in 1833. Emancipation and a depression caused by falling sugar prices sparked a revolt in 1865 that the British suppressed. Jamaica became a Crown colony in 1866, a status that remained in effect until London granted autonomy in May 1953. Nine years later Jamaica became independent. Poverty, corruption, and rampant crime remain serious problems, including drug exports to the United States and an international proliferation of Jamaican gangs (dubbed "posses"), notorious for their quick-trigger mayhem. Many of the drug-dealing criminals incorporate a variant form of Vodun, called obeah, into their illicit activities; *obeah* used charms and curses to intimidate superstitious enemies. At the end of the day, however, their primary faith resides in firepower and cold, hard cash.

JAMES, Jesse   See UNDEAD OUTLAWS.

JAPAN

Traditional Japanese believe they ordained their first emperor, Jimmu, in 660 B.C., but the nation's recorded history begins in A.D. 400 when Kyoto's Yamato family seized control of central and western Japan. Warrior clans known as samurai soon rose to prominence, and their historic influence survives today in certain elements of Japanese culture. First contact with the West came in 1542 when a lost ship from PORTUGAL found Japan accidentally. Soon, a parade of traders and missionaries deluged the archipelago, but wary shoguns of the Tokugawa period (1603–1867) banned foreigners outside of the Dutch trading post at Nagasaki. Japan's self-imposed isolation was shattered in 1853 when a U.S. fleet arrived in Tokyo Bay to open trade channels at gunpoint. Reluctant acceptance of those extortionate terms doomed Japan's feudal shoguns as the nation rapidly westernized, becoming the dominant power in Asia. Multiple wars with CHINA and RUSSIA proved Japan's military superiority over much larger neighbors. Further expansion into the Pacific followed Japan's alliance with the victors in World War I. Beginning in 1931 Japan embarked on an imperial adventure that led inevitably to the PEARL HARBOR attack of December 1941. A string of early victories in World War II reaffirmed Japan's strength, but the tide turned in 1942–43, and U.S. introduction of nuclear weapons in 1945 sealed the warrior nation's fate. In the wake of that conflict, various Japanese military leaders were prosecuted for WAR CRIMES. With the threat of COMMUNISM looming in China, the United States forged alliances with Japanese YAKUZA gangsters to suppress labor unions and left-wing political parties throughout Japan. Postwar reconstruction ironically placed Japan in a powerful economic position by the 1960s, emerging as a world leader in electronics, automobiles, and computer technology. Amid the bonanza, members of the Yakuza crime syndicates also prospered, expanding worldwide with narcotics, WHITE SLAVERY, and investment in Western commercial properties (including LAS VEGAS casinos). FEDERAL BUREAU OF INVESTIGATION spokespersons estimate that Yakuza mobsters presently outnumber members of the rival MAFIA around the world by a factor of 10 to 1. Straying widely from its traditional Buddhist roots, Japan in recent years has also become a haven for off-beat religious sects, including the homicidal apocalyptic cult known as AUM SHIN-RIKYO ("Supreme Truth").

JESUITS

The Society of Jesus is a religious order of the CATHOLIC CHURCH, founded in 1540 by St. Ignatius Loyola. Its common "Jesuit" name was first applied as a term of reproach by critics who claimed that members of the society invoked the name of JESUS CHRIST with blasphemous frequency. As dictated by various papal bulls that were issued between 1540 and 1585, the Jesuit order is a body of priests organized for apostolic work, adhering to the rules of the Catholic Church and relying on alms for support. Today, the Society of Jesus is among the largest Catholic religious orders, with more than 20,000 Jesuits serving the Vatican in 112 nations on six continents. They are heavily involved in education, as witnessed by the naming of Chicago's Loyola University and Loyola Marymount University (in Los Angeles).

Throughout their history the Jesuits have been accused of plotting various conspiracies against Protestants. The order was not (as some still claim) initially created as a military unit to oppose the Reformation, but repeated exposure of that lie has not laid to rest persistent claims of Jesuit subversion in America and elsewhere. During the 17th century, various wars between Native Americans and British colonists were blamed on "vagrant and Jesuitical priests" who "made it their business . . . to go from Sachem to Sachem to exasperate the Indians against the English." New York ordered all Jesuits out of the colony on November 1, 1700, but their exile only made the specter of an ecclesiastical conspiracy more compelling. Each new frontier atrocity was branded a "popish plot," thus absolving colonists of responsibility for the sorry state of race relations in America. Jesuits were also instrumental (say conspiracists) in creating the original ILLUMINATI movement and promoting revolutions across 18th-century Europe.

Anti-Jesuit (and broader anti-Catholic) sentiment in the United States was not eliminated by the Revolutionary War. Nativist organizations ranging from the KNOW-NOTHING MOVEMENT of the 1840s to the modern KU KLUX KLAN have railed against alleged papal schemes for world domination. Modern critics of the order note that FIDEL CASTRO was educated by Jesuits (along with millions of other students throughout the world), and Jesuit agents have been named as prime movers behind the JFK ASSASSINATION. (When asked why Rome would kill America's first Catholic president, conspiracists reply that John Kennedy had secretly broken with the church and planned to "turn American.") Adopting a tongue-in-cheek view of those wide-ranging conspiracy theories, one Internet Web site facetiously claims that "Jesuits also caused the American Civil War, the Bermuda Triangle disappearances, and the shortage of Green M&Ms." Given the climate of the times, some theorists will doubtless take that joke as gospel truth.

See also KENNEDY DYNASTY.

JESUS Christ

The central figure of the Christian religion is Jesus Christ, a carpenter-prophet allegedly born at Nazareth (in present-day ISRAEL) in about 33 B.C. The dominant event in Christian dogma is his supposed crucifixion and resurrection from the dead at age 33. Given the pivotal (and often violent) role of Christianity in global events since that supposed drama unfolded, it is only natural that a variety of conspiracy theories have grown to surround the figure of Jesus and the crowning moment of his life on Earth.

The earliest Christian conspiracy theories focus on the execution and alleged resurrection of Jesus.

Skeptics note that to this day there is no record of either event outside the four "gospels" that open the New Testament. Those books of unknown authorship, apparently written 50–100 years after the supposed events, contradict each other so frequently and fundamentally that they must be dismissed as sources of fact (vs. myth). To date, among the only extra-biblical references to Jesus' crucifixion and resurrection is that allegedly penned by Orthodox Jewish historian Flavius Josephus in his *Antiquities of the Jews*, written 70–90 years after the event. In one brief passage of that lengthy text, Josephus claims that Jesus was "the Christ" and that he was "restored to life" three days after his public execution. It seems strange that Josephus would accept Jesus as the Christ (that is, Messiah) when a basic tenet of Orthodox Judaism insists that the Messiah has yet to appear on Earth. In fact, all reputable scholars presently regard the passage as a subsequent interpolation (that is, forgery) inserted by some unknown Christian author long after Josephus's death to strengthen the case for their faith.

As for the supposed resurrection, two conspiracy theories prevail among skeptics. The simplest is that Jesus' disciples stole his body from its tomb and later lied about his various posthumous appearances, thus "fulfilling" a prophecy spun from thin air. A twist on that plot, suggested by author Hugh Schonfield in *The Passover Plot* (1967), claims that Jesus was drugged to simulate death during his crucifixion and then was revived afterward in a hoax resurrection.

Debate over the death of Jesus is a moot point if he never lived at all, an argument advanced by various scholars through the years. Persistent skeptic G. A. Wells and others note, once again, that there is no public record of Jesus' birth, life, or supposed miracles outside the four contradictory gospels. (Again, the brief forged passage from Josephus is excluded on the grounds of unreliability.) Biblical critics note that the legend of Jesus, including his unlikely virgin birth and his later sacrifice on Calvary, contain elements lifted from much older myths and religions. Christian apologists were encouraged in 2003 when an ancient ossuary was unearthed in Jerusalem's Old City, bearing the inscription: "James, son of Joseph, brother of Jesus." If authentic, it would have provided the first extra-biblical evidence that Jesus ever lived. Unfortunately for the faithful, archaeologists dismissed the artifact as fraudulent in June 2003.

JFK assassination

At 12:30 P.M. on November 22, 1963, President John F. Kennedy was fatally shot while riding in a motorcade through Dallas, Texas. Governor John Connally, riding in the same limousine, was also wounded but survived his injuries. At 1:15 P.M. DALLAS POLICE officer J. D. Tippit was shot and killed in suburban Oak Cliff before multiple witnesses. Authorities captured Tippit's suspected killer, LEE HARVEY OSWALD, at a nearby theater; they later accused him of murdering President Kennedy. At 12:21 P.M. on November 24 Oswald was shot and killed by nightclub owner JACK RUBY during a "routine" transfer from one jail to another. Ruby was convicted of Oswald's murder and sentenced to die, but cancer claimed his life before he could be executed.

Millions of words have been published about those seemingly straightforward events; yet virtually every detail of the crimes remains a subject of heated debate to this day. Despite three official investigations, two criminal trials, and 40-odd years of journalistic argument, a definitive verdict in the JFK assassination remains elusive.

The first government investigation of the crime was ordered by President LYNDON BAINES JOHNSON and conducted by a "blue-ribbon" panel named after its chairman, U.S. Supreme Court Chief Justice Earl Warren. Other members of the WARREN COMMISSION included Senators Richard Russell and John Cooper, Representatives Hale Boggs and Gerald Ford, former CENTRAL INTELLIGENCE AGENCY (CIA) director Allen Dulles, and former Assistant Secretary of State John McCloy. FEDERAL BUREAU OF INVESTIGATION (FBI) Director J. EDGAR HOOVER was not included, but he guided (some say controlled) the investigation. In fact, Hoover delivered his verdict to the media on November 25, 1963, stating that "Not one shred of evidence has been developed to link any other person in a conspiracy with Oswald to assassinate President John F. Kennedy." He never wavered from that judgment, and the Warren Commission echoed Hoover's findings when its report was completed on September 27, 1964.

Pronouncement of the lone-assassin theory demanded some curious "logic," however. Multiple witnesses had reported gunshots fired from a "grassy knoll" in front of the president's limousine rather than from the Texas Book Depository building behind Kennedy where Oswald allegedly lay in wait.

Physicians at Parkland Hospital seemed to confirm that testimony with their initial description of an "entrance wound" in Kennedy's throat. FBI marksmen, testing the alleged murder weapon, first had to repair its defective telescopic sight, and even then it was incapable of firing three aimed shots within the time frame dictated by films and audio recordings of the murder.

The Warren Commission's greatest leap of faith was seen in its acceptance of the so-called "magic bullet theory." Simply stated, the commission found that lone gunman Oswald fired three shots at Kennedy's limousine. One shot missed the car entirely, while another was the fatal head shot captured in Abraham ZAPRUDER's famous home movie of the assassination. That left one shot to account for all the nonfatal wounds suffered by Kennedy and Connally together—and what a shot it must have been, if we believe the commission's report. Officially, the bullet entered Kennedy's back and exited through his throat; then it pierced Connally's back, came out through his chest, shattered his wrist, and buried itself in his thigh. Later, at Parkland Hospital, the slug was found on an abandoned stretcher, having apparently fallen from Connally's leg wound unnoticed.

That theory had numerous problems. First, physicians had described the hole in Kennedy's throat as an *entrance* wound, while another relatively shallow wound in his back was probed with a finger and found to be empty. If those early reports were accurate, then Kennedy was shot at least three times (including the fatal head shot), while a fourth bullet must have struck Connally—and Oswald could not be the lone shooter. To eradicate that problem, the commission rewrote history, and medical reports were altered or "lost." In the final version the shallow back wound disappeared, and Kennedy's posture was contorted to permit a gunshot in the back to exit through his throat. From there, the slug followed an impossible zigzag course to strike Connally at a different angle and inflict his various wounds. Thus it was written: Oswald's first shot wounded Kennedy and Connally, his second missed, and the third shattered Kennedy's skull.

But more problems remained.

First, Connally and his wife denied that that the first shot inflicted his wounds. Connally heard the first shot, he insisted, and turned to look at Kennedy before a second bullet struck him in the back. (All rifle bullets travel faster than the speed of sound, so Connally could not have heard the shot that wounded him before the bullet struck.) To explain that anomaly, the commission fabricated a "delayed reaction" on Connally's part, but the story still lacked credibility. The bullet in question—Commission Exhibit 399—was "basically intact," according to ballistics experts who examined it. It had not shattered or "mushroomed" on impact; in fact, it was described in several reports as "pristine." And yet, the bullet that struck Connally left fragments in his wrist and thigh—fragments that are not missing from the bullet found at Parkland Hospital.

Having thus "resolved" the central mystery of Kennedy's assassination with an impossible scenario, the Warren Commission had no problem disposing of the other troublesome evidence. It ignored the "grassy knoll" witnesses and others who disputed the description of J. D. Tippit's killer, along with the voluminous evidence of "lone gunman" Jack Ruby's connections to organized crime. It reported Oswald's "communist" activities while failing to mention his apparent role as a paid FBI informant, his close working relationship with a retired G-man in New Orleans, and his association with known members of the right-wing MINUTEMEN organization. Reports of his appearance with still-unknown companions at critical times and places were dismissed as lies or "mistakes." CIA photographs of an unidentified man who used Oswald's name on visits to the Russian embassy in Mexico City were filed and forgotten. Oswald's 1959 defection to the Soviet Union was highlighted, but the commission had no interest in how he was able to return home so easily in 1962 after renouncing his U.S. citizenship and marrying the daughter of a reputed KGB officer. Jack Ruby's offer to reveal a conspiracy in return for safe passage to Washington was rejected.

In fairness to the commission, its final verdict was influenced as much by ignorance as by dishonesty. The FBI and CIA withheld much critical information, only revealed since the 1970s, and more presumably remains unknown today. The commission never learned that both Oswald and Ruby were FBI informants. It had no knowledge of the CIA's long campaign to murder Cuban leader FIDEL CASTRO, acting in concert with leaders of the American MAFIA. Nor was it told that several of those high-ranking mobsters—including SAM GIANCANA (Chicago), CARLOS MARCELLO (New Orleans), and

SANTOS TRAFFICANTE (Miami)—had threatened President Kennedy's life in 1962–63. Similar threats were on record from leaders of the Cuban exile community and at least one prominent member of the KU KLUX KLAN.

In 1967 New Orleans District Attorney Jim Garrison announced that he had uncovered a conspiracy in the Crescent City. Oswald had lived in New Orleans for a time, and Garrison uncovered his links to the city's wealthy far-right political fringe. Some of the suspects were already dead, including Mafia pilot and self-styled superpatriot David Ferrie who "committed suicide" soon after he was interviewed by Garrison. Still, Garrison filed charges against defendant Clay Shaw, a CIA associate with links to Ferrie and others including Klansmen, foreign agents, and a curious sect called the Orthodox Old Catholic Church of North America. Shaw was also a stockholder in the shadowy Permindex company, accused by French president Charles DeGaulle of financing right-wing attempts on his life in 1962. Jurors acquitted Shaw on March 1, 1969, and he died in New Orleans on August 14, 1974. *Life* magazine, meanwhile, accused Garrison of taking bribes from local mobsters in an exposé that failed to prevent his election as appellate judge. Today, students of the JFK assassination remain bitterly divided as to whether Garrison's probe was an honest attempt to solve the case or a "disinformation" campaign to discredit conspiracy researchers.

Calls for a congressional investigation climaxed in September 1976 with the creation of the HOUSE SELECT COMMITTEE ON ASSASSINATIONS. The committee's report, published in 1979, concluded that "acoustical evidence establishes a high probability that two gunmen fired at President John F. Kennedy" and that therefore Kennedy "was probably assassinated as a result of a conspiracy." Investigators accepted Oswald's role as one shooter, but they were "unable to identify the other gunman or the extent of the conspiracy." That said, the panel ruled out various plotters, including the Russian and Cuban governments, anti-Castro exiles "as groups," and organized crime "as a group." The FBI, the CIA, and the SECRET SERVICE were exonerated of murder, but they were found to have "performed with varying degrees of competency in the fulfillment of their duties." Specifically, the Secret Service was "deficient" in protecting Kennedy; the FBI "was deficient in its collection and sharing of information with other agencies and departments"; and the CIA "was deficient in its collection and sharing of information both prior to and subsequent to the assassination."

Today there are at least 10 prominent theories of who killed JFK and why. Oswald figures in all versions, his role varying from that of prime mover to hapless scapegoat. The major theories and suspects include:

1. *Oswald, the lone assassin.* Defended most recently by author Gerald Posner in *Case Closed* (1993), the lone Oswald/lone Ruby scenario can only be accepted by ignoring mountains of contrary evidence.

2. *Oswald and the Secret Service.* This theory, proposed by author Bonar Menninger in *Mortal Error* (1992) keeps Oswald as a would-be lone assassin but calls the fatal Kennedy head shot an accident, triggered by Secret Service agent George Hickey from another car in the president's motorcade. Thus, while the Secret Service did not conspire to kill Kennedy, Menninger finds a plot to hide the truth of the shooting and thus protect the agency's reputation (already tarnished by reports of agents on a late-night drinking spree the night before the shooting). Supporters of the theory note that Menninger was never sued for libel after naming Agent Hickey as the accidental triggerman.

3. *Fidel Castro.* President Kennedy supported the 1961 BAY OF PIGS INVASION and subsequently sanctioned various attempts on Castro's life by the CIA, Mafia leaders, and anticommunist exiles. Author Gus Russo theorized, in *Live by the Sword* (1998), that Castro finally tired of the murder attempts and retaliated with a more successful attack of his own. Oswald was the primary triggerman, linked to Castro via his involvement with the leftist Fair Play for Cuba Committee (FPCC). Acceptance of this theory requires believers to ignore the fact that Oswald's FPCC chapter was a one-man organization that shared office space with retired FBI agent Guy Banister and a host of far-right activists who hated Castro.

4. *The Russians.* Kennedy humiliated Russian Premier Nikita Khrushchev in October 1962 with the Cuban missile crisis, and some theorists believe the Soviet Union struck back a year later in Dallas. Unfortunately for proponents of

this theory, *any* scenario involving Oswald as the primary shooter must first explain how he managed to defeat the laws of physics in Dallas, using an obsolete rifle and an inoperative telescopic sight.

5. *The CIA.* After the Bay of Pigs fiasco, JFK unleashed FBI raids to close guerrilla training camps in the United States where CIA agents and others prepared Cuban exiles for illegal raids on their homeland. CIA director Allen Dulles (later a member of the Warren Commission) resigned in September 1961 while Kennedy reportedly threatened to dismantle the agency itself. It seems entirely logical that "rogue" CIA officers, long accustomed to foreign assassinations and other criminal activity, might have staged a preemptive strike against the president to save themselves (and, in their view, America). Variations on this theme incorporate conspirators from the Mafia, anti-Castro groups, and various far-right organizations.

6. *The Mob.* Leaders of organized crime worked hard to elect John Kennedy in 1960, and he betrayed them two months later by appointing brother Robert as attorney general to mount an unprecedented federal campaign against racketeers nationwide. In addition to the various Mafia leaders, Teamster's Union president Jimmy Hoffa and several of his aides threatened both Kennedy brothers. The mob had centuries of experience with murder and disposal of witnesses. Jack Ruby's long association with the underworld makes nonsense of his original claim that he shot Oswald to spare Jacqueline Kennedy from testifying at Oswald's trial. Variations of the Mafia scenario involve CIA elements who employed the mob to kill Fidel Castro and anti-Castro Cubans who promised resumption of mob-controlled gambling in Cuba should Castro be deposed.

7. *Anti-Castro Cuban exiles.* This angry clique blamed Kennedy for "sabotaging" the Bay of Pigs invasion and disrupting plans to kill Castro. The exiles' capacity for violence has been demonstrated by a series of unsolved murders and terrorist acts committed by such radical groups as ALPHA 66 and Omega 7. Cuban links to the CIA, the Mafia, and far-right paramilitary groups offered no shortage of potential assassins in 1963. Exile leader José Aleman

discussed assassination plans with Florida mobster Santo Trafficante, and a Miami pamphlet dated April 15, 1963 declared: "Only through one development will you Cuban patriots ever live in your homeland again as freemen. . . . [I]f an inspired Act of God should place in the White House within weeks a Texan known to be a friend of all Latin Americans."

8. *The FBI.* J. Edgar Hoover hated the Kennedys and feared that they would dismiss him if John was reelected in 1964. Oswald and Ruby are both identified in FBI files as bureau informants, a fact Hoover concealed from the Warren Commission. Hoover was also friendly with various mobsters on the Kennedy hit list, accepting cash, free vacations, and no-loss guaranteed investment tips for a 30-year period, during which he denied the existence of organized crime in America. On November 24, 1963, he told White House aide Walter Jenkins, "The thing I am most concerned about . . . is having something issued so we can convince the public that Oswald is the real assassin."

9. *The U.S. MILITARY-INDUSTRIAL COMPLEX.* Pentagon leaders and defense contractors were troubled by President Kennedy's rumored plans to disengage the United States from the Vietnam conflict, and his murder came only days after the assassination of South Vietnamese dictator Ngo Dinh Diem in what many observers now consider a coup d'état supported by the U.S. military and CIA. In this scenario, high-ranking generals and the corporate leeches who grow fat on military cost overruns had billions to gain and nothing to lose by killing a president whom they considered "soft on communism." Lyndon Johnson is often cast as a coconspirator in variants of this scenario.

10. *The far-right "lunatic fringe."* The day before Kennedy's arrival in Dallas, associates of right-wing oilman H. L. Hunt purchased a full-page advertisement in a local newspaper declaring that JFK was "Wanted for Treason." That attitude prevailed throughout the right wing nationwide, with groups such as the Minutemen, the KKK, the JOHN BIRCH SOCIETY, the Christian Crusade, and the White CITIZENS' COUNCIL blaming Kennedy for a "communist takeover" in Washington. Proponents of this theory suggest that Kennedy signed his own

death warrant in 1963 when he declared that "no one industry [that is, OIL] should be permitted to obtain an undue tax advantage over all others." Jack Ruby, like Lyndon Johnson and J. Edgar Hoover, was a known crony of Texas oilmen.

See also COMMUNISM; DULLES BROTHERS; KENNEDY DYNASTY.

JOHN Birch Society

The premier organization of America's radical right in the cold-war era, the John Birch Society (JBS) was founded in December 1958 by candy manufacturer Robert H.W. Welch. The group is named for John Birch, a Baptist missionary killed by Chinese communists in August 1945, whom Welch proclaimed "the first victim of World War III." The JBS describes itself as "dedicated to restoring and preserving freedom under the United States Constitution." *Restoring* is the operative term since members of the JBS believe that the United States has been controlled by communists since the early 1950s (if not earlier) and that the traitors ruling Washington, D.C., have turned the U.S. population into virtual slaves.

From its humble beginnings with 11 charter members, the JBS grew rapidly in the early 1960s, drawing financial support from wealthy ultraconservatives in industry. By 1964 when it rallied behind presidential candidate Barry Goldwater and his motto that "extremism in defense of liberty is no vice," the JBS had an estimated annual income of $5 million, with membership estimates ranging from 60,000 to 100,000. The group was influential in several states, including the South (where it joined forces with the CITIZENS' COUNCILS to oppose racial integration as a "Red conspiracy") and California under the right-wing regime of Governor RONALD REAGAN (1967–75). Alabama governor GEORGE WALLACE publicly boasted of JBS membership, and other right-wing politicians of the day were either cordial toward the group or else parroted its propaganda without attribution.

Despite its efforts to seem reasonable, however, the JBS was publicly tarred with the brush of its own extremism. Its spokespeople were among the first to claim that FLUORIDATED WATER was a Russian MIND-CONTROL device, and some JBS publications (shared with groups including the KU KLUX KLAN) lapsed into thinly veiled anti-Semitism. Welch himself charged that President Dwight Eisenhower, CENTRAL INTELLIGENCE AGENCY chief John Dulles, and SUPREME COURT Chief Justice Earl Warren were "dedicated, conscious agents of the Communist conspiracy." The UNITED NATIONS was a tool of that conspiracy, Welsh said, collaborating with the COUNCIL ON FOREIGN RELATIONS, the Rockefeller family, and other suspects to press the dreaded goal of a "one-world government." On his death in 1983, Welsh was succeeded by ex-Congressman Lawrence Patton McDonald (a cousin of World War II general George S. "Blood and Guts" Patton, Jr.). The group remains active today, continuing its "educational" efforts in print and on the Internet, but the society is a shadow of its former self with the glory days of the 1960s (hopefully) lost beyond recall.

See also COMMUNISM; DULLES BROTHERS.

JOHN Paul I (1912–1978)

Albino Luciani was born in Italy, attended various seminaries, and was ordained as a priest of the CATHOLIC CHURCH in June 1935. Thereafter, he rose steadily through the ecclesiastical ranks until Pope Paul named him a cardinal in March 1973. Finally, in August 1978, he was elected pope by the Vatican's college of cardinals. Church watchers described the new pope John Paul I as a compromise candidate, chosen on the third ballot when quarreling factions split between two other candidates, Cardinal Giovanni Benelli and Cardinal Sergio Pignedoli. In the wake of that narrow (and surprising) victory, John Paul reportedly told the assembled cardinals, "May God forgive you for what you have done on my behalf." He declined the pomp and ceremony of a standard papal coronation and thus lost the respect of some high-ranking Vatican officers. British author John Cornwell noted that the pope's subordinates "treated him with condescension," and one critic likened John Paul to the actor Peter Sellers (of bumbling *Pink Panther* fame). In private, he repeatedly asked colleagues, "Why did they pick me?"

Catholics worldwide were shocked when John Paul suddenly died on September 28, 1978, after only 33 days in office. Rumors of foul play immediately circulated throughout Rome and beyond, exacerbated by a series of lies from the Vatican about John Paul's death. Church spokespersons falsified the time his body was found and strangely claimed that it was discovered by a papal secretary when in fact a nun found the corpse while bringing John Paul a cup of coffee. The same announcement claimed his will and other personal effects were never found when in fact the papers were held by his sister's family. His death was blamed on "heavy smoking," but John Paul was a nonsmoker. Strangest of all, the pope's body was embalmed within 24 hours, thus violating Italian law.

Two major conspiracy theories surround the death of John Paul I, though the second is relatively innocuous. Author David Yallop, in his book *In God's Name* (1985), suggested that the pope's murder sprang from corruption in the VATICAN BANK and that institution's involvement with elements that included Freemasonry and the MAFIA (a theme later incorporated as a subplot in the film *Godfather 3*). Two years later, author John Cornwell was invited by the Vatican to investigate (and presumably to debunk) conspiracy theories surrounding John Paul's death. Cornwell's final report (*A Thief in the Night*, 1989) concluded that John Paul *did* die of natural causes but that two aides moved his body in a clumsy bid to make the death seem sudden, thus concealing the pope's chronic illness (and, by implication, their possible "guilt" in failing to provide medical care). Both aides deny Cornwell's supposition, and the Vatican damned his report with faint praise. Calls for exhumation of the pope's body for a full post mortem continue.

See also FREEMASONS.

JOHN Paul II (1920–2005)

On May 13, 1981, while riding in a motorcade through St. Peter's Square in Rome, Pope John Paul II was struck by three bullets fired from the crowd of 20,000 spectators. Two bystanders were also wounded, and the pope barely survived six hours of emergency surgery. The gunman, a 23-year-old Turk named Mehmet Ali Agca, was captured at the crime scene with the pistol used in the shooting. He also carried several notes scrawled in Turkish, one of which read: "I am killing the pope as a protest against the imperialism of the Soviet Union and the United States and against the genocide that is being carried out in El Salvador and Afghanistan."

Police declared that Agca's message reflected the "third position" doctrine of the Gray Wolves, a neofascist organization that denounced both superpowers while engaging in acts of TERRORISM and bloody street fighting with left-wing students in TURKEY. Subsequent investigation showed that Agca was in fact a member of the Gray Wolves, though he claimed that he acted alone in St. Peter's Square. Authorities failed to verify eyewitness claims of a second dark-haired gunman who was seen fleeing the square seconds after the shooting. In July 1981 Agca was convicted of attempted murder and received a sentence of life imprisonment.

The case seemed to be solved, but in 1982 a story surfaced among Western journalists that the Soviet KGB had conspired with Bulgarian assassins to kill John Paul II, out of fear that the Polish-born pontiff would encourage anti-Communist rebellion in his homeland and throughout Eastern Europe. The story came primarily from U.S. intelligence sources and played nicely into new president RONALD REAGAN's view of RUSSIA as an "evil empire." Mehmet Agca soon adopted the new theory, presumably hoping that exposure of the "Bulgarian connection" would win his release from prison as a cooperative witness. Italian authorities launched a new investigation, climaxed by the arrest of four Turks and three Bulgarians, but all were released "for lack of evidence" in 1986 after Agca contradicted himself repeatedly in court (and further claimed that he was JESUS CHRIST). The Soviet-Bulgarian plot was finally debunked in 1990 by Melvin Goodman, a former analyst for the CENTRAL INTELLIGENCE AGENCY (CIA). Testifying before the U.S. Senate, Goodman declared for the record that "the CIA had no evidence linking the KGB to the plot" against John Paul II. In retrospect, the "Bulgarian connection" appears to be one more example of Reagan-era deception on a par with the IRAN-CONTRA CONSPIRACY. No further investigation of the Gray Wolves was pursued, although that group continued terrorist activities throughout the 1990s.

See also COMMUNISM; FASCISM.

JOHNSON, Lyndon Baines (1908–1973)

Texas native Lyndon Johnson won his first election to Congress (financed by OIL tycoons and assisted by flagrant voter fraud) in 1936. He served six terms in the House before he was elected to the U.S. Senate in 1948 (by which time his talent for enlisting the dead to vote alphabetically had earned him the nickname "Landslide Lyndon"). Soon after his arrival in

Washington, Johnson purchased a home across the street from FEDERAL BUREAU OF INVESTIGATION (FBI) director J. EDGAR HOOVER, who shared many of LBJ's wealthy friends and political views.

Hoover provided his first known service to Johnson in 1956 when G-men suppressed evidence of vote fraud in the Texas primary elections. Six years later, while Johnson served as vice president under President John Kennedy, Hoover buried an FBI report detailing the Texan's alliance with various "hoodlum interests." Following the November 1963 JFK ASSASSINATION, Hoover joined LBJ in a concerted effort to suppress conspiracy rumors, producing an overnight judgment that suspect LEE HARVEY OSWALD was the president's lone assassin. Hoover's political service to Johnson included extensive surveillance on critical journalists, civil rights leaders, Republican

Party leaders, and opponents of the VIETNAM War. In return for such favors, Johnson granted Hoover the ultimate reward: exemption from retirement at age 70 as required by federal law. Mounting protest against the Vietnam war persuaded Johnson not to seek renomination in 1968. Stricken with a heart attack on January 22, 1973, Johnson died en route to a San Antonio hospital.

See also KENNEDY DYNASTY.

JONESTOWN massacre

On November 18, 1978, the world was shocked by news emerging from the jungles of Guyana. According to the first reports, 911 members of a cult known as the People's Temple had committed suicide at Jonestown, a community named for their guru, Rev. Jim Jones. Subsequent accounts revealed that some of the cultists—and a group of visitors led by California congressman Leo Ryan—had been shot by Jones's bodyguards, apparently on orders from the demented messiah. Today, while the body count remains unchallenged, little else is certain in the saga of the Jonestown massacre, and some conspiracists describe the event as a case of government MIND CONTROL run amok.

Although he later claimed to be the reincarnation of VLADIMIR LENIN *and* JESUS CHRIST, Jim Jones made an unlikely savior. Born in 1931, the son of an Indiana KU KLUX KLAN member, Jones revealed an early obsession with religion. By age 12 he was preaching to congregations of younger children and practicing faith healing on neighborhood pets. Defrocked by the Methodist Church in 1954, Jones opened his own interracial congregation in Indianapolis, dubbed the People's Temple Full Gospel Church. One of those who helped him found the church was childhood friend Daniel Martine, later a torture instructor for the CENTRAL INTELLIGENCE AGENCY (CIA) in South America. On the side Jones also practiced telepathic communication with extraterrestrials, prophesied imminent nuclear war, and suffered unexplained fainting spells. He also joined the Communist Party but kept that news secret when his congregation joined the Disciples of Christ.

In 1962 Jones led his congregants to Brazil, ostensibly seeking a refuge from Armageddon. It may be coincidence that Dan Martine was then employed as an interrogation specialist by Brazil's SECRET POLICE, but several of Jones's new neighbors suspected him

"Landslide Lyndon" Johnson earned his nickname by rigging Texas elections in which votes were recorded using names of people buried in cemeteries. (Library of Congress)

of working as a CIA agent, noting that he "lived like a rich man" and claimed to receive "a monthly payment from the U.S. government." When Jones tired of Brazil, he moved his church to Ukiah, California, where local government officials strangely permitted Jones to act as legal guardian for numerous state mental patients. Jones's next stop was San Francisco where Mayor George Moscone appointed him to serve on the city's housing board.

In 1973, at about the same time that the CIA allegedly discontinued its "MKULTRA" mind-control program and Jones was detained for propositioning an undercover policeman in a porno theater, the People's Temple paid $650,000 for a 27,000-acre plot of jungle land in Guyana that later became Jonestown. (Years later, some reporters claim the money came from alleged CIA agent Philip Blakely.) Jones delayed moving the cult there until August 1977, two weeks after *New West* magazine published a scathing exposé of his alleged bisexual escapades and financial double-dealing in the cult. The weirdness only worsened in Jonestown, described by the *San Francisco Chronicle* in early 1978 as a "jungle outpost" where "the Rev. Jim Jones orders public beatings, maintains a squad of 50 armed guards, and has involved his 1,100 followers in a threat of mass suicide." Government sources claim that Jones transferred $500,000 to the Soviet embassy in Guyana while promising his flock that their next stop would be RUSSIA. At the same time, he ordered "white night" drills in preparation for raids by "CIA mercenaries." When Congressman Ryan's delegation arrived in November 1978 to investigate claims of human-rights abuses at Jonestown, it triggered the slaughter that claimed nearly 1,000 lives.

In retrospect, conspiracists cannot agree if the Jonestown massacre resulted from a plot by Russian agents or the CIA. Most seem to blame the agency, however, claiming that Jonestown was a mind-control experiment conducted in a venue where pesky civil libertarians could not intervene. One acknowledged CIA agent, Richard Dwyer, was present at Jonestown and survived the holocaust: On one tape recording of Jones's final remarks, the maniac messiah is plainly heard commanding, "Get Dwyer out of here!" Joseph Holsinger, an aide to Congressman Ryan, also believed that Jonestown was a wholly owned subsidiary of the CIA. He based that conclusion in equal parts on Dwyer's presence in Jonestown and on a 1980 report entitled "The Penal

The People's Temple Cult mass suicide, orchestrated by Reverend Jim Jones at Jonestown, Guyana, claimed the lives of 913 people. (Bettmann/Corbis)

Colony" from a professor at U.C. Berkeley. The author of that document contended that the CIA did not abandon its mind-control program in 1973 (as agency spokespersons claimed in sworn congressional testimony) but rather shifted its focus toward creation and manipulation of religious cults and political extremist groups (including the SYMBIONESE LIBERATION ARMY). As Holsinger told the world in 1980, "I believe that it is possible that Jonestown may have been a mind-control experiment, that Leo Ryan's congressional visit pierced that veil and would have resulted in its exposure, and that our government or its agent the CIA deemed it necessary to wipe out more than 900 American citizens to protect the secrecy of the operation." (The CIA denies any involvement at Jonestown or in any other criminal activities.)

JORDAN

The territory of modern-day Jordan was variously held in ancient times by Assyrians, Babylonians, Persians, and Seleucids. Rome conquered the region in A.D. 106 and was supplanted by Arab warlords in 633–36. TURKEY absorbed Jordan and held it until World War II shattered the Ottoman empire. Britain took control under the Palestine mandate of 1920 and then liberated Jordan in 1946 out of gratitude for loyal support in World War II. King Abdullah I was assassinated in 1951 and was succeeded by son Talal, but Talal's mental illness prompted Jordanian leaders to depose him in 1952, replacing him with his son Hussein. King Hussein was forced to perform a delicate balancing act, trapped between the fledgling state of ISRAEL and Palestinian activists who sought the return of their ancestral homeland. Agitation increased after Israel seized Jordanian territory in 1967, and Palestinian guerrillas virtually controlled some sectors of the country until 1971 when Hussein defeated the rebels and drove them into neighboring LEBANON. Jordan's opposition to the GULF WAR of 1991 strained relations with the United States, but Hussein ultimately signed a peace treaty with Israel in June 1994. (A clause naming Hussein "custodian" of Islamic shrines in Jerusalem further outraged Palestinian Arabs.) In January 1998, dying of cancer, King Hussein deposed his brother Hassan (heir apparent for 34 years) and named son Abdullah the new crown prince. Abdullah ascended to the throne when his father died on February 7, 1999. In 2002–03 Jordan faced more heat from the United States for its refusal to collaborate with another invasion of IRAQ.

JULIUS Caesar (100 B.C.E.–44 B.C.E.)

Thanks to William Shakespeare, Roman emperor Julius Caesar ranks with U.S. president John Kennedy as one of the world's most famous assassination victims. Every schoolchild in the English-speaking world knows that Caesar was assassinated on March 15, 44 B.C.E., by a group of aristocratic conspirators including Marcus Junius Brutus and Gaius Cassius Longinus. Ironically, both plotters owed their lives to Caesar, who had pardoned them on capital charges of supporting his rival (Pompey) in a recent civil war. The knife-wielding killers, still smeared with Caesar's blood, rushed from the murder scene to the Forum Romanum where they were hailed as saviors of the republic. Rome's senate hastily passed an amnesty for the assassination, while Caesar's supporters (including Marcus Antonius) hurried to reconcile with the killers and thus save themselves. Ironically, Caesar's dictatorship had produced Rome's era of greatest prosperity and stability, the very conditions his murderers claimed to desire. He had increased the number of Roman senators from 500 to 900, while expanding the empire dramatically through various military campaigns. With Caesar's death the Roman Empire began a slow but irreversible decline into decadence and squalor, climaxed by barbarian invasions that shattered Caesar's dream for all time.

JUSTICE Department

While Congress authorized appointment of a U.S. attorney general in 1789, the department was not created until 1870 in the middle of the tumultuous RECONSTRUCTION era. Even then, federal prosecutions were so rare that the Justice Department required no detective force of its own for another decade. As responsibilities expanded with passage of the Interstate Commerce Act (1887) and the Sherman Anti-Trust Act (1890), various attorneys general used agents of the Pinkerton Detective Agency on a part-time, case-by-case basis. That relationship was severed in 1892 when Pinkerton's brutal strikebreaking activities prompted a congressional ban on temporary hiring of individuals already employed in the private sector. For the next 16 years Justice borrowed SECRET SERVICE agents from the Treasury Department until further abuses led Congress to ban that practice in May 1908. Two months later, in defiance of congressional opponents, Attorney General Charles Bonaparte created a detective force that would become the FEDERAL BUREAU OF INVESTIGATION (FBI).

Passage of the Mann and Dyer Acts in 1910 and 1919 further broadened the Justice Department's authority, but investigations took an increasingly political (and often personal) turn after the Russian Revolution of 1917. Fear of ANARCHISTS and the Communist Party prompted creation of an Alien Enemy Bureau in 1917, closely followed by Attorney General A. Mitchell Palmer's Red-hunting General Intelligence Division and the sweeping PALMER RAIDS of 1919–20. J. EDGAR HOOVER, employed with the Justice Department since 1917, escaped censure for his role in those activities and was appointed assistant director of the bureau under Attorney General HARRY DAUGHERTY. Unfortunately, Daugherty and the rest of President WARREN HARDING's OHIO GANG were so corrupt that Justice soon became known as "the Department of Easy Virtue." Exposure of the TEAPOT DOME scandal nearly sent Daugherty to prison, but Hoover concealed his own involvement in those crimes and was appointed director of the bureau under Attorney General Harlan Stone.

During the next 48 years, Hoover's relationship with his nominal superiors at Justice depended chiefly on the latitude that various attorneys general granted to him in pursuit of his personal agendas. Between 1925 and 1960 most attorneys general avoided exercising any supervision over Hoover and the FBI; a few actively encouraged expanded domestic surveillance in violation of prevailing federal law. Attorneys general who tried to impose some restraint on the bureau, including Robert Kennedy, were opposed and publicly reviled by Hoover at every turn. By the end of Hoover's life, it seemed that history had come full circle, with Justice mired in another morass of corruption under President RICHARD NIXON.

In the wake of Hoover's death and the WATERGATE scandal that toppled Nixon's administration, leaders at Justice have vacillated on priorities and the desirability of continuing widespread FBI spying. Attorneys General Edward Levi and Griffin Bell emphasized prosecution of MAFIA leaders and issued guidelines restricting domestic surveillance on political groups, while successors William Smith, Edwin Meese, and Richard Thornburgh took the opposite approach, condemning "subversives" and "terrorists" while mobsters and white-collar criminals were largely ignored. Attorney General Janet Reno was accused of political partisanship in protecting President Bill Clinton from various investigations, but the same must be said for attorneys general serving Presidents RONALD REAGAN and George H. W. Bush.

In November 2001 President George W. Bush and Attorney General JOHN ASHCROFT announced a "wartime reorganization" of the Justice Department to treat TERRORISM as a top priority. Ashcroft's "blueprint for change" reassigned 10 percent of the departments headquarters staff to "front-line" field offices nationwide while declaring that nonpolitical cases would take a backseat. "We cannot do everything we once did," Ashcroft told reporters, "because lives now depend on us doing a few things very well." Critics suggested that the shift in priorities was not only a response to the PENTTBOM attacks of September 11, 2001, but also meant a retreat from cases that held little interest for the Bush White House, including prosecution of corporate crime.

John Ashcroft announced his resignation from the office of Attorney General in November 2004 and was replaced by Alberto Gonzales, whose nomination was confirmed in February 2005.

See also BUSH DYNASTY; CLINTON, BILL AND HILLARY; COMMUNISM; KENNEDY DYNASTY.

KAL Flight 007

On August 31, 1983, Korean Airlines (KAL) Flight 007 left New York City with 269 passengers and crew members aboard bound for touchdown at Seoul, KOREA. After refueling at Anchorage, Alaska, the Boeing 747 resumed its long journey, flying southwestward toward Seoul-Kimpo Airport. Strangely the pilots plotted a course that would carry them 300 miles off-course to the west, invading Russian air space over the Kamchatka Peninsula, the Sea of Okhotsk, and Sakhalin Island. Another KAL flight had made a similar mistake in April 1978 and was forced by Russian fighter planes to land at Murmansk. This time the Soviet reaction would be more severe. Just before dawn on September 1, two fighter planes from Dolinsk-Sokol airbase intercepted KAL-007 and fired a single air-to-air missile with catastrophic effect. One minute 46 seconds later the airline crashed at sea, 34 miles off Moneron Island, killing all aboard.

President RONALD REAGAN immediately capitalized on the disaster to promote his anticommunist agenda, branding the "Korean airline massacre" an "act of barbarism," "inhuman brutality," and a "crime against humanity [that] must never be forgotten." Soviet spokespeople claimed that their pilots thought the airliner was a military aircraft and that violations of Russian air space justified the shootdown. Investigators from the International Civil Aviation Organization concluded that KAL-007's course

deviation was accidental, a result of human error in setting the automatic pilot. Naturally the incident produced its share of conspiracy theories with two proposed scenarios standing out above the rest.

French aviation expert Michel Brun aired the most outlandish conspiracy theory in 1995 with publication of his book *Incident at Sakhalin: The True Mission of KAL Flight 007*. According to Brun, the jet's course deviation was intentional, and the airliner was accompanied by several U.S. military aircraft when it violated Russian air space. Presumably its mission was to gather some kind of secret intelligence unavailable to the United States via its fleet of spy planes and orbiting satellites. Brun claims that a two-hour aerial dogfight then ensued, during which Soviet pilots shot down 10 U.S. warplanes, killing at least 30 air force and navy personnel. Flight 007, meanwhile, cleared Sakhalin island and flew south over the Sea of Japan for some 45 minutes before it was destroyed off Honshū, Japan "by means and for reasons which remain to be established." Equally vague are the U.S. motives for choosing to risk war with Russia in 1983 and the means by which the epic battle was concealed from public view.

Beside Brun's theory, the dominant alternative scenario seems positively tame. The "no crash" theory apparently sprang from an article written by right-wing author John Barron for *Reader's Digest* magazine in January 1984 contending that KAL 007 did not crash immediately as reported in the press but rather stayed aloft for at least 12 minutes, gradually descending from an altitude of 35,000 feet until its final crash. From that assertion, it was a short step to suggesting that the plane never crashed at all but rather landed safely on Soviet soil. Authors writing for the JOHN BIRCH SOCIETY were first to float that theory, claiming that the aircraft and all 269 persons aboard were being held in Russian custody. The unsolved riddle, then and now, was Moscow's motive for forcing down the plane and imprisoning its passengers. No-crash theorists suggest that only one person aboard KAL 007 was actually targeted on September 1, 1983; the rest were simply witnesses to the abduction who were permanently silenced by confinement to Soviet prisons. More than two decades after the incident, the supposed "real target" remains unidentified and his (or her) mission still undisclosed.

See also COMMUNISM.

KELLY, George "Machine Gun" See UNDEAD OUTLAWS.

KENNEDY dynasty

Often described as "American royalty," the Massachusetts-based Kennedy clan has captivated public opinion in the United States for more than a half-century. Their fabulous wealth, occasional scandals, and heart-rending tragedies played out in the atmosphere of a media circus ensure that the family name (and influence) is recognized throughout the world. Inevitably, given their power and persistent craving for more, the Kennedys have been cast both as villains and victims in a long-running chain of conspiracies and/or conspiracy theories that continue to the present day.

The family's roots lie in Ireland, and its patriarch was Patrick Joseph Kennedy (1858–1929), a child of Irish immigrants born in Boston. At age 22 Patrick borrowed money from his family to buy a run-down saloon in a slum neighborhood. Although himself a teetotaler, Patrick grew wealthy from liquor sales, launching his own wine and spirits importation business (P.J. Kennedy and Company) in 1885. Patrick married the daughter of another wealthy businessman and soon turned his eyes toward politics, winning election to the Massachusetts state senate in 1892. Soon, partnered with fellow state senator and future Boston mayor John Francis ("Honey Fitz") Fitzgerald, Patrick became one of Boston's most influential politicians.

Patrick's son, Joseph Patrick Kennedy (1888–1969), did even better for himself and for the family. In 1914 he married Rose Fitzgerald, daughter of Honey Fitz, and ultimately sired nine children. Named as manager of a prestigious investment firm in 1919, Joseph quickly mastered the tricks of Wall Street and became a megamillionaire, providentially retiring just before the stock market crash of 1929. By that time, Joseph was deeply involved in PROHIBITION-era bootlegging, partnered with the likes of MEYER LANSKY and other MAFIA figures. Joseph also produced motion pictures and blossomed into a Hollywood mogul, making little effort to conceal his romantic liaisons with various starlets. Deeply immersed in Democratic Party politics, Joseph was appointed chairman of the Securities and Exchange Commission in 1934, going on

Questions linger to this day concerning the 1963 assassination of President John F. Kennedy. (Library of Congress)

to ban the very speculative practices that made him rich. In 1937 President Franklin Roosevelt named Joseph ambassador to Britain, but his die-hard isolationism and seeming admiration for ADOLF HITLER led him to resign three years later.

Determined to see his son(s) in the White House, Joseph began to groom firstborn—Joseph, Jr. (1915–44)—as a future president. Eldest daughter Rosemary was a thorn in Joseph Senior's side, threatening embarrassment with her independent and rebellious personality until 1941 when Joseph, Sr., arranged for her to receive a prefrontal lobotomy at a Washington, D.C., hospital. Having concealed the plan from his own family including wife Rose, Joseph, Sr., next had to disguise the results which left Rosemary partially paralyzed and unable to speak coherently. Joe, Sr., spread the tale that Rosemary had gone into seclusion at a midwestern convent, maintaining that fiction until the true story broke in 1958.

Presidential candidate Robert F. Kennedy was assassinated by Sirhan Sirhan, on June 5, 1968. (Library of Congress)

Joe, Sr.'s, presidential plans were threatened during World War II when Joseph, Jr., died in action and FEDERAL BUREAU OF INVESTIGATION director J. EDGAR HOOVER caught next-eldest son John Fitzgerald Kennedy (1917–63) enjoying an affair with a Nazi spy from GERMANY. Joe, Sr., ended that relationship and had John shipped to the Pacific, where he became a decorated hero for saving the crew of his PT-boat in August 1943. Injuries from that incident sent John back to civilian life where he won election to Congress in 1946 followed by a victorious Senate campaign in 1952. Ironically, considering his father's longtime (and ongoing) Mafia connections, John served as a driving force behind Senate investigations of the mob-linked INTERNATIONAL BROTHERHOOD OF TEAMSTERS. Younger brother Robert Francis Kennedy (1925–68) served as counsel for those hearings and performed a similar function for the Red-hunting committee chaired by Sen. JOSEPH MCCARTHY. Despite his membership in the CATHOLIC CHURCH (still controversial in many parts of the United States at midcentury), John Kennedy won the Democratic presidential nomination in 1960 and narrowly defeated RICHARD NIXON in a November election that was marked by charges of wholesale vote fraud. Chicago tipped the balance for JFK with a collaborative effort by Mayor RICHARD JOSEPH DALEY and his Mafia allies.

Prior to John's inauguration, father Joseph insisted that the president-elect choose brother Robert as his attorney general. JFK agreed, despite misgivings, and Robert soon initiated the federal government's first full-scale assault on organized crime. Ironically, at the same moment, the Kennedy brothers and leaders of the CENTRAL INTELLIGENCE AGENCY (CIA) employed Mafia leaders in their campaign to depose or assassinate Cuban leader FIDEL CASTRO. JFK inherited the BAY OF PIGS conspiracy from predecessor Dwight Eisenhower, but he allowed the invasion of CUBA to proceed with disastrous results, prompting Cuban-exile members of such groups as ALPHA 66 to denounce him as a traitor. On other fronts JFK pressed for black civil rights in the South (thus outraging the KU KLUX KLAN and the CITIZENS' COUNCILS), threatened to dismantle the CIA, launched secret bombing raids in LAOS, and reportedly considered withdrawing U.S. military forces from VIETNAM. His private life included many adulterous affairs, including one with actress MARILYN MONROE and another with the sometime lover of Chicago mob boss SAM GIANCANA. Thus surrounded by enemies and intrigue, it was perhaps no great surprise when the JFK ASSASSINATION ended his brief presidency on November 22, 1963.

Successor LYNDON BAINES JOHNSON despised the Kennedy clan and soon dismissed Robert as attorney general. Undaunted, RFK won election to the Senate as a "carpetbag" candidate in New York. Building upon his brother's popularity with young and minority voters, Robert launched a campaign against the Vietnam War which he hoped would propel him into the Oval Office. President Johnson declined to run for reelection in 1968, and Robert Kennedy soon emerged as the Democratic front-runner in a heated campaign. He won the crucial California primary election on June 4, 1968, but gunmen waited for him in the hotel where his victory celebration was held, and the RFK ASSASSINATION ensured that Vice President Hubert Humphrey would become the party's nominee (defeated in November by Richard Nixon).

The youngest surviving Kennedy brother, Edward, had campaigned for JFK in 1960 and took his brother's place in the Senate two years later (where he remains at this writing). Democratic Party leaders considered him a strong candidate for the 1972 presidential election, but those hopes were dashed on CHAPPAQUIDDICK Island in July 1979 after Edward crashed his car in a canal and left female companion Mary Jo Kopechne to drown in the vehicle. Family influence saved him from prison, but he was convicted on the minor charge of leaving an accident scene, and the scandal would haunt him forever, scuttling Edward's last attempted White House race in 1980. Nor do scandals and allegations of conspiracy end with the immediate Kennedy family. In 1991 William Kennedy Smith (grandson of Joseph, Sr., and Rose) was accused of rape in Florida, winning acquittal in a trial where some cynics claim jurors voted for celebrity rather than evidence. A decade later in June 2002 Michael Skakel (a nephew of RFK's widow) was convicted in Connecticut for the 1975 bludgeon murder of 15-year-old Martha Moxley. Critics claim that Kennedy influence stalled the trial for 27 years, but in the end it would not save Skakel from a sentence of 20 years to life in prison.

KENT State University shootings

In May 1970 revelation of President RICHARD NIXON's covert military action in CAMBODIA sparked demonstrations on college campuses across the United States.

Students at Ohio's Kent State University rioted on the night of May 1, prompting Governor James Rhodes to impose an 8:00 P.M. curfew. The National Guard occupied the campus after demonstrators burned the ROTC building on May 2, and another demonstration was in progress on May 4, 1970, when troops opened fire with high-powered rifles, killing four students and wounding another nine.

President Nixon described himself as "deeply saddened" by the deaths at Kent State and others in a similar shooting at Mississippi's JACKSON STATE COLLEGE. FEDERAL BUREAU OF INVESTIGATION (FBI) agents were assigned to investigate the Ohio incident (code-named KENFOUR), while Nixon appointed an independent President's Commission on Campus Unrest (better known by the name of its chairman, former Pennsylvania governor William Scranton) to do likewise. G-men eventually submitted some 8,000 pages of testimony to the Scranton Commission, while Director J. EDGAR HOOVER complained to the U.S. Senate Appropriations Committee that the investigation cost $274,100 in overtime. (Staff members at Kent State complained to their representatives in Congress that G-men spent much of that time examining classroom lesson plans and probing the political beliefs of various professors.) Long before that investigation was finished, though, Hoover telephoned White House aide Egil Krogh to report that "the students invited and got what they deserved."

What they got, according to Hoover's own agents, was an undisciplined and indiscriminate burst of gunfire lasting for 11 seconds, including at least 54 (and perhaps 61) shots fired by 29 of the 78 guard members present. None of the four students killed had been demonstrators; they were shot at distances between 85 yards and 130 yards from the guard members, two with their backs turned and one while lying prone on the ground. Of the nine students wounded, only one appeared to be an active demonstrator, shot while making "an obscene gesture" to the guard member from 20 yards away; the rest were shot at distances ranging from 37 yards to 250 yards from the guns. A JUSTICE DEPARTMENT summary of FBI reports likewise disposed of claims that the guard believed themselves to be under sniper fire.

At the time of the shootings, the National Guard clearly did not believe that they were being fired upon. No Guardsman claims he fell to the ground or took any other evasive action and all available photographs show

201

the Guard at the critical moments in a standing position and not seeking cover. In addition, no Guardsman claims he fired at a sniper or even that he fired in the direction from which he believed the sniper shot. Finally, there is no evidence of the use of any weapons at any time in the weekend prior to the May 4 confrontation.

If the physical evidence were not enough, six guard members (including a captain and two sergeants) also "stated pointedly that the lives of the members of the Guard were not in danger and that it was not a shooting situation." As for the 11 guard members who later expressed mortal fear, the Scranton Report concluded: "We have some reason to believe that the claim by the National Guard that they thought their lives were endangered by the students was fabricated subsequent to the event." A report in the Akron *Beacon Journal,* published on May 24, 1970, corroborated that claim of conspiracy with a quote from one guard member: "The guys have been saying that we got to get together and stick to the same story, that it was our lives or them, a matter of survival. I told them I would tell the truth and couldn't get in trouble that way."

Reactions from Washington were predictably hostile. Vice President SPIRO AGNEW called the Scranton Report "pabulum for the permissivists," while the commander of Ohio's National Guard found the FBI investigation results "just unbelievable." Even J. Edgar Hoover did not seem to trust his own agents in this case, responding to an article in the Akron *Beacon Journal* with a letter that read in part: "I can assure you that any comments you may have seen in the news media to the effect that the FBI drew conclusions indicating guilt on the part of National Guardsmen in the shooting at Kent State University are absolutely and unequivocally false." Despite the FBI's reported conclusions and those of the Scranton Commission, an Ohio grand jury refused to indict any guard members, instead condemning student "agitators" and Kent State professors who encouraged an "overemphasis on dissent." As for the guard members, the panel's report found that they "fired their weapons in the honest and sincere belief . . . that they would suffer serious bodily injury had they not done so."

KENYA

Seafaring Arab traders established settlements along Kenya's coast in the eighth century A.D., thriving until they were overrun by PORTUGAL in the early 1500s. British troops arrived to "protect" the country in 1890, and it was made a Crown colony in 1920 and christened British East Africa. Nationalist stirrings began after World War II and erupted into full fury with the Mau Mau uprising of 1952–56. Kenya won full independence in December 1963, with rebel leader Jomo Kenyatta released from prison to become the nation's first president. One-party rule endured from 1964 until 1992 when riotous demonstrations forced President Daniel arap Moi to permit pluralistic democracy. Subsequent elections have left Moi in power despite rampant official corruption, a faltering economy, and a series of natural disasters that rocked Kenya in 1997–98. In the face of crisis, Moi has become increasingly autocratic, including a 1995 arrest order for anyone who publicly insulted him. In August 1998 suspected AL-QAEDA terrorists bombed the U.S. embassy in Nairobi, killing 243 persons and wounding more than 1,000. In 1999 deepening scandal and recession prompted Moi to name high-profile critic Richard Leakey head of Kenya's civil service, but Moi reversed the move and sacked Leakey in 2001. Parliament rejected anticorruption legislation that same year, prompting most foreign nations to slash or cancel foreign aid payments. Transparency International, a global watchdog group, routinely lists Kenya among the world's 10 most-corrupt nations.

KGB

Every dictatorship requires some form of SECRET POLICE to maintain its power, and Soviet RUSSIA was no exception. Beginning as the Cheka under VLADIMIR LENIN, Moscow's chief intelligence agency later became the Government Political Administration (GPU) and then was renamed the Peoples Commissariat for Internal Affairs (NKVD) in 1934. Under that name, it carried out JOSEPH STALIN's purges of the 1930s. Between January 1935 and June 1941 an estimated 19.8 million persons starved to death. NKVD archives, opened in the 1990s, reveal a total of 799,455 executions in Russia between 1921 and Stalin's death in 1953, but the statistics do not separate political prisoners from common criminals. (Anticommunist authors typically blame Stalin for 5 million to 100 million deaths, but none cite reliable sources.) After World War II the NKVD received its new and most infamous name, branded *Komitet*

Gosudarstvennoy Bezopasnosti (Committee for State Security). Until its dissolution in 1991 it served not only as Russia's internal secret police but also as the nation's primary foreign intelligence and counterintelligence body—in effect, as if the U.S. government had merged the FEDERAL BUREAU OF INVESTIGATION and the CENTRAL INTELLIGENCE AGENCY. One branch of the KGB, known as SMERSH (an acronym of the Russian phrase "death to spies"), carried out assassinations and was publicly exposed in author Ian Fleming's James Bond novels. The collapse of Russian COMMUNISM in 1991 prompted Moscow's new leaders to ditch the KGB label and create a "new" spy agency, labeled the Central Intelligence Service (CSR). That body incorporated most of the old KGB's foreign operations and assets, prompting critics to claim that nothing had changed at headquarters. While various KGB officers faced trial across the former Soviet Union for crimes against humanity, some outside observers maintain that Russia's spies still behave much as they did in the dark cold war years.

KING, Martin Luther, Jr.

Dr. Martin Luther King, Jr., recognized the dangers of his calling as America's foremost black civil rights leader of the 1960s. He was constantly harassed and threatened by the KU KLUX KLAN and by agents of the FBI under director J. EDGAR HOOVER. In 1967 after King broadened his campaign to call for peace in VIETNAM, President LYNDON BAINES JOHNSON complained, "That goddamned nigger preacher may drive me out of the White House." As a prelude to his second march on Washington, King joined a strike by sanitation workers in Memphis, Tennessee. There, at 6:01 P.M. on April 4, 1968, he was killed by a rifle shot on the balcony of the Lorraine Motel.

Seconds after the shot, two witnesses saw a masked man leap from a brushy embankment across the street, running with a rifle-like object in his hand. Around the block on South Main Street Guy Canipe saw a stranger pass his amusement shop and drop a bundle in the recessed doorway. Glancing out, Canipe saw a rifle and other objects as a white Ford Mustang sped from the scene. Memphis police were on alert for the white Mustang by 6:25 P.M., but a series of spurious CB radio broadcasts lured them to the west side of town—while the killer, they would later say, fled southward into Alabama and beyond.

The hunt for Dr. King's killer began on South Main Street with the Remington rifle and other items that had been discarded moments after the shooting. FEDERAL BUREAU OF INVESTIGATION (FBI) agents rushed the weapon evidence to Washington, where analysts later claimed that 26 fingerprints were found on various items, but only three were clear enough for identification. It was April 19, more than two weeks later, when FBI clerks identified the owner of those prints as James Earl RAY, a habitual thief who had escaped from Missouri's state prison on April 23, 1967. Hoover's G-men had no jurisdiction in the case until Ray was charged with the federal crime of conspiring to violate King's civil rights. By definition a conspiracy requires at least two plotters, but government spokespersons later dismissed the charge as a ruse to get FBI agents involved in the manhunt. There was never any evidence, they now insist, of more than one participant in King's murder.

And yet. . . .

For a lifelong bungler who spent 14 of his 40 years in prison, James Earl Ray was suddenly graced with amazing luck. Since his escape from prison, although unemployed, Ray had traveled to Canada and Mexico, studied dancing and bartending in Los Angeles, vacationed in New Orleans, and finally settled in Atlanta near Dr. King's home. The rifle found in Memphis was purchased in Birmingham on March 29, 1968. After the slaying he had fled once more to Canada, renting rooms in the name of Paul Bridgman (a real-life Canadian who physically resembled Ray) and obtaining passports in the names of Ramon Sneyd and Eric Galt (again, living Canadians who both resembled Ray). On May 6, 1968, he flew to London and from there to Lisbon, Portugal. Ray returned to London on May 18, 1968, and was planning to leave for Belgium when British police arrested him at Heathrow Airport.

On his return to Memphis, Ray initially retained attorney Arthur Hanes, Sr., a former FBI agent and one-time mayor of Birmingham who was best known as a defense lawyer for Klansmen charged with murdering civil rights worker Viola Liuzzo. Hanes financed the defense by signing a $40,000 book contract with author William Bradford Huie. As a prelude to his book (_He Slew the Dreamer_, 1969), Huie wrote three articles about the case for _Look_ magazine, published in November 1968 and April 1969. The first two installments described a plot by wealthy right-wing conspirators to kill King "for maximum bloody effect" during the 1968 election campaign, concluding: "Therefore, in this plot, Dr. King was the secondary, not the primary target. The primary target was the United States of America." The third article amazingly reversed Huie's previous claims, insisting that Ray had killed King on his own in a quest for "criminal status." Finally, in a strange attempt to resolve his flip-flop, Huie wrote:

> [T]here are large conspiracies and little conspiracies. In large conspiracies, rich and/or powerful men are involved. Small conspiracies involve only little men. . . . I believe that one or two men other than James Earl Ray may have had foreknowledge of this murder, and that makes it a little conspiracy. But if there was a conspiracy, I now believe that James Earl Ray was probably its leader, not its tool or dupe.

By the time Huie penned those words, Ray had pleaded guilty to King's murder and accepted a 99-year prison term. Ray made his plea on March 10, 1969, and instantly regretted it. He spent the rest of his life in prison, filing fruitless motions for a jury trial, telling anyone who would listen that he had been framed for King's assassination by a shadowy cohort he knew only as "Raoul." Ray died on April 23, 1998, still pleading for a day in court.

In fact, there is copious evidence that Ray had an accomplice in King's murder—if he fired the fatal shot at all. Between April 1967 and June 1968 Ray spent $10,000 on travel and living expenses; yet he held only one short-term job at minimum wage. On March 28, 1968, Ray purchased a rifle in a Birmingham sporting-goods store allegedly to go deer hunting with his brother. He exchanged the gun for a larger .30-06 weapon the next day, explaining that his "brother" had told him he bought the wrong weapon. Eyewitnesses in Memphis described a gunman who bore no resemblance to Ray. After King's murder, while Ray was hiding in Toronto, witnesses saw him with an unidentified man on three occasions. The last time, shortly after a "fat man" visited his apartment, Ray paid cash for an airplane ticket to London. When Ray's car was found in Atlanta, the ashtray overflowed with cigarette butts—but Ray did not smoke.

Beginning in September 1976 the HOUSE SELECT COMMITTEE ON ASSASSINATIONS spent two and a half years investigating the murders of King and President John Kennedy. The committee's final report concluded that "on the basis of the circumstantial evidence available . . . there is a likelihood that James Earl Ray assassinated Dr. Martin Luther King, Jr., as a result of a conspiracy." Ray's argument, meanwhile, was that he did not murder King at all. He claimed to be a "patsy" who was used to buy the rifle which was afterward discarded, complete with his fingerprints, to divert attention from the real killer(s). The House committee acknowledged "the likelihood of a financial motive" behind King's murder, finally blaming a pair of wealthy Missouri racists, John Sutherland and John Kauffmann, who had died in 1970 and 1974 respectively. Proof was sadly lacking, thanks to FBI negligence in 1968–69. As described by ex-Agent Arthur Murtagh, G-men in Atlanta cheered reports of King's murder, and those farther afield were actively discouraged from reporting conspiracy leads. In Los Angeles, Agent William Turner was advised by his superiors that Hoover "didn't light any candles when King was killed," and so the case was closed.

KISSINGER, Henry (1923–)

A German native who was born Heinz Alfred Kissinger on May 27, 1923, America's future secretary of state emigrated to the United States with his family in 1938, to escape ADOLF HITLER's persecution of Jews. On arrival in New York he changed his given name to "Henry" and quickly emerged as an outstanding student in public school. Kissinger earned a Ph.D. in international relations from Harvard University and joined the faculty there in 1958, remaining until he became President RICHARD NIXON's assistant for national security affairs in 1969.

While privately describing Nixon as a "basket case" and "meatball mind," Kissinger reveled in his new powers and never hesitated to enlist FEDERAL BUREAU OF INVESTIGATION assistance in pursuance of his broadly-defined duties. In May 1969, after newspapers reported Nixon's illegal bombing campaign in CAMBODIA, Kissinger ordered Director J. EDGAR HOOVER to "make a major effort" to identify the government sources. He singled out four State Department officials for illegal wiretapping, subsequently using those taps to spy on Secretary of State William Rogers and Secretary of Defense Melvin Laird. In June 1969 after protests disrupted Nelson Rockefeller's tour of Latin America,

Kissinger ordered the bureau to investigate "whether they were spontaneous and came from within the countries . . . or whether there was a pattern of conspiracy initiated from outside of these countries that led to the disturbances." (Hoover, as always, blamed the demonstrations on a global communist plot.)

In September 1970 Hoover warned the White House of a plot by anti-VIETNAM War activists Daniel and Philip Berrigan to kidnap Kissinger. While Kissinger scoffed at the story and Attorney General John Mitchell refused to file charges, Hoover went public with the accusations two months later and forced the JUSTICE DEPARTMENT to pursue a costly, ultimately futile trial. More serious in Kissinger's mind was media exposure of the Pentagon Papers in October 1971. As later described by White House aide H. R. Haldeman, "Henry got Nixon cranked up, then they started cranking each other up until they were both in a frenzy." The ensuing investigation included a series of illegal break-ins that prefigured the administration's WATERGATE scandal.

Kissinger succeeded Rogers as secretary of state on September 22, 1973, and remained to serve under President Gerald Ford after Nixon resigned in disgrace. His "shuttle diplomacy" in Southeast Asia and the Middle East won Kissinger a Nobel Peace Prize, along with such superlative media descriptions as "the 20th century's greatest diplomatic technician" and "the most admired man in America." After Ford's defeat in 1976, Kissinger joined the faculty of Georgetown University and later chaired a committee on Central America for President RONALD REAGAN in 1983 (during the IRAN-CONTRA scandal). In the mid-1980s Kissinger emerged as a "statesman for hire," leading Kissinger Associates with offices in Washington and New York City. Despite "a complete lack of experience in business," he repaid $350,000 in startup loans within two years and earned a handsome profit in the bargain.

Despite the honors heaped upon Kissinger for his diplomatic service, critics have raised serious questions concerning his involvement in the Vietnam War, the CENTRAL INTELLIGENCE AGENCY's role in toppling the elected government of CHILE (1973), and atrocities committed by U.S.-financed forces in EAST TIMOR. A book summarizing his alleged "war crimes"—*The Trial of Henry Kissinger,* by Christopher Hitchens—became a surprise best seller in

2001. A year later President George W. Bush named Kissinger to lead an "independent" probe into the terrorist attacks of September 11, 2001, but the plan was derailed by Kissinger's business interests. Kissinger initially promised to "go where the facts lead us," vowing that "We are under no restrictions and we will accept no restrictions," but he quickly changed his mind when ordered to disclose his list of foreign clients (thus avoiding any real or apparent conflicts of interest). Kissinger met with survivors of the "9-11" attacks on December 13, 2002, and agreed to publish his client list, but he changed his mind hours later and resigned from the commission that same afternoon.

See also BUSH DYNASTY; ROCKEFELLER CLAN.

KMART bankruptcy

When the giant Kmart retail chain declared bankruptcy on January 22, 2002, most observers regarded it as a personal tragedy for laid-off employees and communities where stores were forced to close. By January 2003, however, a somewhat different picture emerged from an internal investigation by Kmart's own law firm (Skadden, Arps, Slate, Meagher & Flom). That review depicted a firm deeply divided, perhaps crippled by misconduct at the highest levels of management. According to a summary of the investigation, Kmart executives had "engaged in a broad pattern of abusive practices—like cutting off payments to suppliers, dispensing generous loans to themselves, and masking personal air travel as 'store visits'" in the months before bankruptcy was declared.

The year-long investigation was sparked by a flurry of anonymous letters to Kmart headquarters detailing alleged abuses within the company, and it revealed "a corporate free-for-all" climaxed by near-collapse of the chain in 2001. Among the specific activities detailed in the law firm's final report, the following stood out:

- *Fraudulent handling of vendors:* Kmart suppliers were pressured for cash, known in the trade as "vendor allowances," but often went unpaid for their merchandise. Those payments finally made were sometimes reduced or delayed in a failing effort to improve Kmart's cash flow. Vendors were "purposefully denied access" to computer programs showing their account status, and "deceptive responses were given to vendors who inquired concerning the reasons they were not being paid."

- *Manipulation of financial statements:* Investigators found that Kmart executives pressured subordinates to make "unrealistic" forecasts of the firm's financial prospects, punishing those who refused with demotions. The same shady dealers hired unqualified aides at excessive salaries and altered company books to conceal their activities. One former executive ordered $850 million worth of merchandise for Kmart stores without authorization, in a flub that "substantially contributed to Kmart's liquidity crisis in the fall of 2001."

- *Travel mania:* Some Kmart officers were apparently obsessed with traveling around the country at company expense, covering their tracks "by loading aircraft with Kmart personnel who otherwise had no need to travel." While Kmart's finances took a nose-dive, travel-happy executives spent $12 million on new jet planes.

- *Tapping the till:* Kmart executives took $24 million in personal loans from the company, while the chain's account books began to fill up with red ink. Investigators found that "management failed to disclose" crucial details of the internal loan program, that actual loans "deviated in certain significant respects from what the committee approved," and that records were altered after the fact to conceal those activities. Kmart's former CEO received a $5 million "retention loan," while the former president was given $3 million, and 23 other executives (all of whom subsequently resigned or were fired) received loans ranging from $300,000 to $2.5 million. At the time the internal report was filed in January 2003, only two loan recipients had repaid the money they received (a total of $1,050,000).

Kmart leaders coupled the shocking revelations with a sweeping reorganization, including assurances that two of its largest investors (ESL Investments and Third Avenue Value Fund) would supply a minimum of $140 million when the chain emerged from bankruptcy on April 30, 2003. By that time it was estimated that some 55,000 Kmart employees would have been dismissed from their jobs. The ink was barely dry on that announcement when Kmart declared, on January 23, 2003, that new CEO Julian

Day would receive a $1 million bonus for service to the firm, as soon as Kmart emerged from bankruptcy. Day's contract further entitled him to use a company plane and to receive four times his base salary if Kmart reached certain financial targets in the future. Day replaced James Adamson, who was scheduled to receive $3.6 million in severance pay in April 2003.

KNIGHTS Templar

The Knights Templar ("knights of the temple") was a monastic military order created by the CATHOLIC CHURCH at the end of the First Crusade (ca. A.D. 1099–1100) to protect Christian pilgrims en route to the Holy Land. As the Crusades dragged on and multiplied, the Templars became a front-line fighting force and graduated from living on alms to collecting loot in battle while drawing financial support from the Vatican and various European monarchies. In part, the Templars' power stemmed from the fact that they were immune to any authority but the pope's. At the same time, their swelling ranks and coffers made the order a kind of principality within itself. They essentially invented modern banking, loaning money to impoverished royals throughout Europe and collecting handsome interest in defiance of a papal ban on "usury." After 200 years in the game the Templars were rich and powerful enough to defy kings and popes alike—and therein lay their weakness.

In 1307 King Philip IV of France needed money to continue his long-running war against Edward I of England. Rather than borrow cash from the Templars, he decided to take it by force, a conspiracy in which he had the full support of Pope Clement in Rome. On October 13, Philip ordered the Templars arrested en masse on charges of heresy. He claimed (and some historians agree) that the order had drifted so far from its Catholic roots that it had adopted a covert form of SATANISM. Specific accusations against the Templars included charges that they held secret rituals in which they spat and trampled on the crucifix, practiced homosexual acts in defiance of Scripture, and worshipped a pagan deity known as Baphomet. (Never clearly defined, Baphomet has been described in various accounts as an Arabic demon, an avatar of Satan, or the mummified head of a deceased Templar grand master). Conviction was a foregone conclusion, and the Templars' sentence included forfeiture of all worldly goods in

This image depicts the Knights Templar being burned at the stake, known as the Death of de Molay, 1314. (Bettmann/Corbis)

addition to mass execution. The order's last grand master, Jacques de Molay, was burned alive on March 19, 1314. Legend has it that he cursed King Philip and Pope Clement from the stake, commanding both persecutors to join him within a year. True or false, history records that Clement died within a month of de Molay's execution, followed by Philip seven months later.

Officially the Templars were no more, but various historians insist that the knights are with us still. Supposed heirs to the Templars' spiritual legacy, proposed in different published accounts, include the ROSICRUCIANS, the FREEMASONS (whose youth auxiliary is named for Jacques de Molay), and the sex-magic cult known as *Ordo Templi Orientis* (Order of the Eastern Temple) that was once headed by self-styled "Great Beast 666"

Aleister Crowley. One version of the story claims that Templars found the Holy Grail (a goblet allegedly used by JESUS CHRIST at the Last Supper), and that modern members of the order are physical descendants of Jesus himself. Another school of thought regards their legacy as Satanic, complete with Baphomet and other Far Eastern deities or demons invoked to work harmful magic in modern society. In fact, a modern body of Knights Templar *does* exist, affiliated with the Masonic lodge as a self-described charity. Its Internet Web site may be found at http://www.knightstemplar.org.

KNOW-NOTHING movement

In the mid-19th century, many white Protestant citizens of the United States were concerned about the rising tide of immigrants. That fear was felt most strongly in cities on the eastern seaboard where large numbers of Irish Catholics arrived during the 1840s. Local nativist societies were soon organized to combat "foreign" influence and uphold "American" standards. In New York, those groups merged to form the American Republican Party in 1843, soon renamed the Native American Party (NAP). The movement went national two years later with a platform that called for immigration bans and elimination of recent immigrants from public office. Since some of their activities were illegal, including physical attacks on immigrants and incitement of full-scale urban rioting, members of the movement were warned to say they "knew nothing" in case of arrest. From that defiant answer came the common nickname of their movement—one that critics found appropriate on an entirely different level. Politically, the movement peaked in 1854 when it swept elections in Massachusetts and Delaware, nearly capturing control of New York State. The same year witnessed Know-Nothing riots against Catholics in Kentucky, Maine, Massachusetts, Missouri, New Hampshire, New Jersey, New York, and Ohio.

The Know-Nothing movement's inherent bigotry backfired in June 1855 when southern delegates seized control of the national council in Philadelphia and passed a resolution calling for the maintenance of slavery. The following year, Know-Nothing spokespeople were among the loudest supporters of the proslavery Kansas-Nebraska Act, a move that cost the party thousands of northern members. Abolitionists defected to the newly formed Republican

Party, and while the NAP attempted to elect Millard Fillmore to the White House, its national power was broken. Its legacy, including paranoid hatred of Catholics and local organization in chapters known as "clans," was transmitted to another generation of terrorists with the rise of the KU KLUX KLAN in the late 1860s.

See also CATHOLIC CHURCH; TERRORISM.

KOREA

Korea's first recognized settlements appeared in about 6000 B.C., and national folklore maintains that the country's first civilization (Choson) was founded in 2333 B.C. CHINA enslaved Korea as a vassal state in the 17th century, isolating it from contact with the outside world until JAPAN defeated China in the Sino-Japanese War of 1894–95. Korea was briefly granted independence but then was annexed by Japan in 1910. Thousands of Korean women were kidnapped to serve the Japanese military as sex slaves during World War II, while nationalists at home continued agitation for freedom. RUSSIA invaded Korea in 1945, and Japan's surrender a few days later left the nation divided along the 38th parallel, with Soviet troops in the north and U.S. forces to the south. The partition was made permanent in 1948 with establishment of a Communist regime in North Korea (under Kim Il Sung) and a "free" government in South Korea (under right-wing dictator Syngman Rhee).

Bitter antagonism between the two Koreas has been constant since that time. In 1949 alone, North Korea blamed the south for 2,617 armed incursions to carry out murder, kidnapping, pillage, and arson as a means of fomenting social disorder. Ambassador Philip Jessup, touring the 38th parallel in April 1950, described a state of "constant fighting" that included "very real battles" of 2,000 soldiers or more. No one knows who fired the first shots on June 25, 1950, before North Korean troops crossed the parallel to invade South Korea. Kim Il Sung later claimed that the attack followed two days of incessant artillery bombardment, while Rhee and U.S. spokespersons called the invasion a "surprise attack" that was launched with Russian complicity. In any case the undeclared Korean War dragged on until June 1953, including WAR CRIMES on both sides and drawing Chinese troops into the battle when U.S. forces advanced on China's border with North Korea in

September 1950. The eventual cease-fire agreement left national boundaries unchanged and did nothing to relieve tension between the two hostile regimes. With Russian and Chinese assistance, North Korea developed a potent nuclear arsenal, while U.S. troops propped up Syngman Rhee's corrupt regime in the South. The collapse of European communism in 1991 and China's increasing westernization left North Korea largely isolated, with leaders still vowing to reunite their ancestral homeland. South Korea, meanwhile, has ample problems of its own, including global condemnation for human rights abuses, bungled military coups, the 1996 conviction of President Roh Tae Woo on bribery charges, and a plummeting economy. In 2001, President George W. Bush named North Korea as part of a mythical AXIS OF EVIL (with IRAN and IRAQ). Whereas baseless charges of stockpiling "weapons of mass destruction" sent U.S. troops to Iraq in 2003, however, Bush showed no such inclination to tangle with North Korea's nuclear arsenal. Combat continues along the 38th parallel, meanwhile: 30 North Koreans and 5 South Koreans were killed in an exchange of fire in June 2002, and fresh fighting was reported in July 2003.

See also BUSH DYNASTY; COMMUNISM.

KRUPP Arms

Born in 1870 Gustav Krupp von Boh-len und Hal-bach built a huge family fortune in GERMANY by manufacturing military arms and munitions. In the chaotic years after World War I Krupp initially remained aloof from ADOLF HITLER's Nazi Party, but he ultimately recognized the profits to be earned from endless conflict and evolved into what some observers have called a "super-Nazi." Although headquartered at Essen, Krupp Arms had factories throughout Germany, and the firm soon followed THIRD REICH troops into occupied Poland. There, as the Holocaust gathered momentum toward a "final solution of the Jewish question," Krupp built a factory at Auschwitz with part of the facility inside the death camp's barbed-wire perimeter. Krupp made extensive use of slave labor during World War II, its factories absorbing 73,000 prisoners of war and foreign captives by September 1944. Treatment of Jews on the assembly lines was particularly brutal, and the risks increased as Allied planes began to bomb German war plants. (At Krupp factories the air raid shelters were reserved for "Aryans.") At war's end, various Krupp executives were among those indicted for WAR CRIMES. Gustav Krupp's senility saved him from trial, but son Alfred was convicted of using slave labor, stripped of his holdings, and sentenced to 12 years in prison. Gustav died in 1950, but his family had nothing more to fear from German justice. In 1951 a general amnesty released the nation's corporate criminals from prison and restored their fortunes. Alfred Krupp resumed control of the family business and finished his life in the affluent style he preferred.

See also COMMUNISM; HOLOCAUST AND HOLOCAUST DENIAL.

KU Klux Klan

America's oldest still-active terrorist group was organized at Pulaski, Tennessee, in spring 1866 as a social club for Confederate veterans of the recent Civil War. The founders chose its name from the Greek word *kuklos* ("circle"), popularized by the southern college fraternity Kuklos Adelphon, and added *clan* spelled with a *K* for uniformity. When drinking—which was often—they pursued the familiar southern sport of frightening blacks and dressing in ghostly costumes to play "pranks" on recently freed ex-slaves. Members flocked to the KKK, and its "harmless fun" acquired political motivations in 1867 with the imposition of Congressional RECONSTRUCTION on an unwilling South. Reorganized along military lines, led by Confederate cavalry leader (and prewar slave trader) Nathan Bedford Forrest, the Klan's "Invisible Empire" soon expanded to include active chapters in 12 states. (The old Confederacy only had 11 states, but Klansmen also organized in Kentucky, a former slave state nominally loyal to the Union during the war.) During the next six years, Klansmen waged ceaseless guerrilla war against blacks, "radical" Republicans, and anyone else who showed the least sympathy for racial equality. Several thousand murders resulted, with many times that number of victims wounded, whipped, castrated, branded, or otherwise assaulted in the name of preserving "home rule." Congress and President Ulysses Grant finally passed new legislation to suppress the KKK, bringing a number of Klansmen to trial for their crimes, but the group emerged victorious in 1877 when a corrupt political bargain placed RUTHERFORD B. HAYES in the White House and ended Reconstruction in the South.

Confederate general Nathan Bedford Forrest was the first "grand wizard" of the Ku Klux Klan. (Author's collection)

Southern historians revered the Klan for its role in "redeeming" Dixie from mythical "black anarchy," and its legend grew over time as veteran Klansmen moved into various high political offices. (By 1915 one of them was chief justice of the U.S. SUPREME COURT.) Director D. W. Griffith's epic motion picture *Birth of a Nation* cast Reconstruction Klansmen as heroes in 1915 and was publicly endorsed by President Woodrow Wilson and other respected officials. In Atlanta defrocked minister William Simmons revived the KKK to cash in on the movie's publicity, but his new fraternal order languished through World War I, recruiting fewer than 5,000 members in Georgia and Alabama. In 1920 Simmons employed a publicity firm to boost Klan expansion, and the group expanded nationwide with a new list of enemies that appealed to bigots in every corner of the nation. Aside from blacks, the modern KKK also despised Catholics, Jews, "radicals," labor unions, most recent immigrants—the list was virtually endless. By 1921 membership had risen to 100,000 with no end in sight. Three years later, Klan watchers pegged the number somewhere between 3 million and 5 million dues-paying Klansmen.

Those numbers gave the KKK substantial political clout, and Klan leaders were not afraid to use it. Various states—from Alabama and Georgia to Oregon, Colorado, and Indiana—were dominated by Klansmen in office during the 1920s. Klan legislators supported PROHIBITION (though rarely observing its tenets) and campaigned to ban parochial schools. At the grass-roots level the KKK was both a social and a vigilante organization, resorting to brutal violence in almost every state where it organized. Whippings, torture, and murders created scandals from California through Texas, Louisiana, Alabama, Georgia,

Florida, and Oklahoma (where the governor was impeached for declaring martial law to fight Klan raiding parties). Such episodes, combined with recurring financial chicanery and sex scandals within the Klan hierarchy, whittled Klan membership during the Great Depression. The KKK was a shadow of its former self by 1944 when a federal tax lien closed national headquarters, but local chapters clung stubbornly to life across the South.

After World War II the Klan revived in an atmosphere of racist resentment against the black civil rights movement. Politicians such as Dixiecrat Strom Thurmond and the Georgia TALMADGE DYNASTY took full advantage of Klan support, ignoring a new rash of violence in the South while the FEDERAL BUREAU OF INVESTIGATION remained largely aloof. Mayhem escalated after 1954 with the Supreme Court's order for desegregation of public schools, but the Klan was also

Bill Wilkinson (in suit) served as an FBI informer while leading America's most violent KKK faction in the 1980s. (Southern Poverty Law Center)

fragmented, its former strength divided among as many as two dozen scattered groups at any given time. In the 1960s Klansmen left their bloody mark on such racial battlegrounds as Birmingham, Alabama (scene of the BAPBOMB murders in 1963); Bogalusa, Louisiana; St. Augustine, Florida; and in Mississippi, where virtual anarchy reigned during 1964–67. President LYNDON BAINES JOHNSON finally forced J. EDGAR HOOVER to investigate the Klan in 1964, and the resultant COINTELPRO harassment campaigns greatly weakened the KKK as an effective force. Once again, however, only a handful of Klansmen were prosecuted for major crimes. It remained for personal scandals and belated public revulsion over Klan brutality to break the movement's back.

Klan influence since the 1970s has been relatively minor and dispersed among a myriad of competing (often mutually hostile) factions, but it is a grave mistake to rate the KKK as harmless or defunct. Since the early 1980s Klansmen have been active in various neo-Nazi terrorist groups, including the ultraviolent SILENT BROTHERHOOD. Inspired by *THE TURNER DIARIES* and other extremist screeds, the Klansmen, "lone-wolf" guerrillas, and affiliated skinhead gangs have been responsible for hundreds of violent acts during the past two decades. Timothy McVeigh, executed for the OKLAHOMA CITY BOMBING of April 1995, was once a Klansman before he drifted into the militia movement. With more than 300 right-wing hate groups active in the United States at last report, there is no doubt that such incidents will continue.

See also CATHOLIC CHURCH; TERRORISM.

KUWAIT

Kuwait belonged to IRAQ's Basra Province until 1897, when Britain arrived to "protect" the region, redrawing its boundaries and installing a military garrison.

Coincidentally or otherwise, petroleum prospectors soon "discovered" that Kuwait sat atop OIL reserves comprising 20 percent of Earth's total supply. Full-scale pumping began at once and continues to the present day. Britain granted Kuwait full independence in 1961, while offering continued military aid on request to members of the ruling al-Sabah family (which received 50 percent of all oil profits). By 1968 the al-Sabah clan felt confident enough, in the words of *Time* magazine, that it "sought to establish dominance among the sheikdoms and emirates of the Persian Gulf."

In July 1990 Iraqi president SADDAM HUSSEIN publicly blamed Kuwait for declining Middle Eastern oil prices. That same month, Saddam informed U.S. Ambassador April Gillespie of his plans to reclaim Kuwait as a part of Iraq. Gillespie offered no objections in the conversation that was secretly taped by Saddam, and that acquiescence proved embarrassing when Iraq invaded Kuwait on August 2, 1990. When President George H. W. Bush demanded that Iraq withdraw, Saddam replied with a list of demands including guaranteed access to the Persian Gulf (cut off by Britain in 1897), settlement of boundary disputes in the Rumala oil field (95 percent inside Iraq), and a Kuwaiti plebiscite on the issue of reunion with Iraq. Bush rejected all terms and in January 1991 launched the GULF WAR to expel Iraq from Kuwait. The effort was successful, though it left Saddam still in power and thereby set the stage for a later Bush to wage OPERATION IRAQI FREEDOM in 2003. Kuwait, meanwhile, remains in the grip of the al-Sabah family and rigid Islamic regulations. In 1999 the emir granted women the right to vote and to seek political office, but Parliament rejected the decree. Three years later, coeducation was banned within the nation's only university.

See also BUSH DYNASTY.

LANSKY, Meyer (1902–1983)

One of America's foremost criminals was born Maier Suchowljansky in 1902 at Grodno, RUSSIA (now in POLAND). As Jews, he and his family were constantly at risk from anti-Semites such as the BLACK HUNDREDS, who mounted bloody pogroms throughout the Polish Pale of Settlement. The Suchowljansky clan moved to New York in 1911 where Maier soon Anglicized his name to Lansky (and where immigration officials arbitrarily pegged his birth date as July 4). While still in school Lansky befriended another young Jew, hoodlum Benjamin ("Bugsy") Siegel. Together, they faced extortion from Sicilian delinquent CHARLES "LUCKY" LUCIANO, but Luciano so admired their fighting spirit that the three became lifelong friends. On leaving school, Lansky ostensibly became an apprentice toolmaker, but his real life was street crime, graduating to organized bootlegging with the advent of PROHIBITION in 1920.

During the next 14 years, Lansky and his partners became millionaires, smuggling liquor in conjunction with illegal gambling, prostitution, and HEROIN traffic. In the process Lansky planted outposts in CUBA that would blossom after World War II into lavish mob-owned casinos. During 1930–31 when Luciano waged war in New York to "Americanize" the MAFIA, Lansky and Siegel did their part by forging national alliances with syndicates of different nationalities. In the Great Depression their empire expanded to include gambling concessions in Florida

and New Orleans, where covert partner HUEY LONG offered protection for a price. Siegel moved west to manage syndicate operations in California during the late 1930s; he planted the mob's flag in LAS VEGAS, Nevada, a decade later. When his first casino failed to prosper there and Siegel was accused of stealing from the combination, Lansky approved his old friend's murder and went on to prosper in alliance with mobsters from Chicago, Cleveland, Detroit, and New York in legalized gambling.

The 1950s and 1960s brought turmoil to Lansky's world when FIDEL CASTRO closed mob casinos in Cuba. Lansky collaborated with the CENTRAL INTELLIGENCE AGENCY in its failed attempts to kill Castro; then he shifted his sights to the nearby BAHAMAS and built lavish gambling resorts around Nassau. He is also considered a prime suspect in the JFK ASSASSINATION of 1963. Throughout his career, he served only one 30-day jail sentence (for gambling), but the INTERNAL REVENUE SERVICE planned to change that in 1970 with an indictment for income-tax evasion. Lansky fled to ISRAEL, claiming sanctuary under that nation's Law of Return, but Israeli leaders finally expelled him. In 1973 a Florida jury acquitted Lansky of ducking his taxes, and additional charges were dropped on grounds of his poor health. Lung cancer claimed his life at Miami Beach, on May 15, 1983. Published accounts of his estate's secret value vary from $4 million to some $400 million. Though known to fellow mobsters since the 1920s as the

"Little Man," Lansky's record of achievement remains nearly unrivaled in organized crime.

LAOS

The Lao people migrated from southern CHINA in the eighth century A.D., founding the Lan Xang kingdom 600 years later. Invaders from THAILAND conquered the region of present-day Laos in the 18th century, followed by conquerors from FRANCE in 1893. French colonial rulers incorporated Laos into the larger realm of Indochina (including modern CAMBODIA and VIETNAM). JAPAN conquered the region during World War II, and its example encouraged a strong nationalist movement against the resumption of French colonial rule in 1946. Semiautonomy was granted in 1949, followed by full independence within the French Union two years later. In 1951 exiled Prince Souphanouvong organized a communist liberation movement, the Pathet Lao, in North Vietnam. In 1957 Pathet Lao forces merged with the Laotian royal army, but the agreement failed two years later, and armed struggle resumed. Beginning in 1961, despite a cease-fire agreement in Laos, President John Kennedy launched covert bombing raids against Pathet Lao bases from South Vietnam, while CENTRAL INTELLIGENCE AGENCY mercenary forces waged war on the ground. A new agreement in 1973 reinstated government collaboration with the Pathet Lao, but Red leaders would not be fooled a second time, seizing control of the country in 1975. The Communist regime retains power today, though a revised constitution (1991) deleted references to socialism while retaining one-party rule. Since March 2000 the Laotian capital (Vientiane) has been shaken by a series of unsolved bombings, generally attributed to anti-Communist Hmong tribal guerrillas. Northern Laos lies within the "Golden Triangle" of Southeast Asia where drug lords affiliated with the Chinese TRIAD syndicates produce and export tons of HEROIN each year.

See also COMMUNISM; KENNEDY DYNASTY.

LAS Vegas

Las Vegas, Nevada, is a city founded, built, and nurtured on conspiracy. Illegal gambling was a mainstay of the local economy before state legislators bowed to the inevitable and legalized "gaming" in 1931, but the town that would someday be known as "Lost Wages" lagged behind Reno in popularity and population for another 16 years. It took the postwar MAFIA to recognize the profit potential of Las Vegas, a five-hour drive from Los Angeles. Casinos had already sprouted downtown along Fremont Street—also known as "Glitter Gulch"—under the stewardship of Texas bootlegger and murderer Benny Binion, but the first great gambling palace on The Strip (Las Vegas Boulevard) was launched by a consortium of New York gangsters in 1946. Bugsy Siegel was the front man, bankrolled with drug money from childhood friends MEYER LANSKY and CHARLES "LUCKY" LUCIANO, building the Fabulous Flamingo as the first true Sin City resort.

Financial problems, skimming from his partners chief among them, sent Siegel to an early grave in June 1947, but the Flamingo prospered, and other crime families soon emulated New York's example. During the next dozen years, Cleveland mobsters built the Desert Inn and Stardust hotel-casinos; Chicago's "Outfit" bossed the Riviera; New England's Patriarca family helmed the Dunes; Lansky and Frank Costello split their take from the Tropicana, while Costello and Brooklyn mobster Joe Adonis shared control of the Sahara. The Sands hotel-casino set a record for being "controlled by more mobs than any other casino in Nevada," hosting silent partners from Boston, Chicago, Cleveland, Detroit, Galveston, Houston, Jersey City, Los Angeles, Miami, Minneapolis, New Orleans, New York, Newark, San Francisco, and St. Louis. Nearly all those casinos and most of the other landmarks in Las Vegas were bankrolled by low-interest loans from the mob-controlled INTERNATIONAL BROTHERHOOD OF TEAMSTERS.

The money game, today as in the 1940s, plays three ways in Vegas. First, where common gamblers are concerned, all odds are weighed heavily in favor of the house so that significant winners are few and far between. Second, the "skim"—that portion of daily receipts stolen from casino counting rooms and spirited away to hidden owners out of state before earnings are reported to the INTERNAL REVENUE SERVICE—puts millions of untaxed dollars in the hands of mobsters and their "straight" front men. Finally, the casino culture serves all comers as a huge cash laundry, devouring billions a year from swindlers, drug dealers, pimps, and other unsavory players, spitting out "clean" cash that finds its way into political coffers, Wall Street transactions, tax-deductible charity donations, and covert operations carried out by various intelligence agencies.

From the early 1950s onward Las Vegas has been a launching pad for presidential campaigns. The city's power brokers were instrumental in financing Presidents John Kennedy, LYNDON BAINES JOHNSON, RICHARD NIXON, RONALD REAGAN, George H. W. Bush, and his son. In the early 1960s, much of the CENTRAL INTELLIGENCE AGENCY's illegal war against FIDEL CASTRO was plotted in Nevada casinos and directed by Mafia collaborators SAM GIANCANA and JOHN ROSELLI. Nixon's notorious "plumbers" funneled WATERGATE hush money through Las Vegas in the early 1970s. Ten years later only the names and faces had changed when the Reagan-Bush team sought covert support for their IRAN-CONTRA CONSPIRACY. In the middle of it all, HOWARD HUGHES arrived to "clean up the town," but his purchase of multiple casinos was mere window dressing, a billionaire playing Monopoly® with real-life buildings. A tarnished innocent of sorts where gambling was concerned, Hughes left known mobsters in charge of the casinos he leased or purchased, seemingly oblivious to the fact that they were robbing him blind while he hid in his Desert Inn penthouse, gobbling gourmet ice cream and obsessing over germs.

The short-lived Hughes invasion (1966–70) was not the only effort to "clean up" Las Vegas. The city goes through cyclic phases, superficially transformed from Sin City to a "family place" and back again. Behind the neon, though, even such family-oriented hotel-casinos as Circus Circus had mobsters, Teamsters, and sundry Wall Street sharks lurking in the background. Occasional FEDERAL BUREAU OF INVESTIGATION raids, prosecutions, and breathless newspaper exposés reveal the "surprise" of mob involvement in the city at predictable intervals, but nothing really changes. In 1998 federal agents cracked an international drug and money-laundering conspiracy that was centered in Las Vegas, resulting in 140 arrests on three continents. A year later Las Vegans turned out in force to elect new mayor Oscar Goodman—a local attorney best known for his ardent defense of notorious mobsters, including the late Chicago hit man Tony ("The Ant") Spilotro. Sociologists have termed Las Vegas "the First City of the 21st century," and mob watchers call it the "shadow capital" of the United States. Based on the city's growth, its wealth, and its sinister connections, both may be correct.

See also BUSH DYNASTY; KENNEDY DYNASTY.

LEBANON

At the close of World War I, FRANCE received a League of Nations mandate to occupy Lebanon and neighboring SYRIA (both previously part of TURKEY). In 1920, France drew a border to separate mostly Muslim Syria from the religious stew of Lebanon (where Christians were then dominant). Lebanon proclaimed independence in November 1941, but French troops remained in place until 1946. A national pact provided for the country to operate with a Christian president, a Sunni Muslim prime minister, and a Shi'ite Muslim as speaker of the National Assembly. That agreement was tested after 1948 by a flood of Palestinian refugees from ISRAEL. In 1954–55 Israeli leaders worked openly to spark violence between Lebanese Muslims and Christians, hoping thereby to weaken one of Israel's Arab neighbors. When a religious civil war erupted in 1958 U.S. troops arrived to quell the fighting. Lebanon survived and flourished in the early 1960s, with Beirut widely hailed as "the Paris of the East."

Unsatisfied with early results Israel intensified its efforts to destabilize Lebanon. In May 1972 after members of the Japanese Red Army killed 26 persons in Tel Aviv, Israel, "retaliated" by bombing Lebanon, killing 100-plus civilians. Four months later, when BLACK SEPTEMBER gunmen killed nine Israelis in GERMANY, Israel bombed Lebanon again, killing more than 400 civilians. Warfare between Lebanese Muslims and Christians resumed in April 1975, eventually reducing the elegant heart of Beirut to a burned-out no-man's land. An estimated 40,000 persons were killed, with more than 100,000 wounded, before a Syrian-dominated Arab Deterrence Force intervened to stop the carnage in November 1976. Citing recent terrorist attacks, Israel invaded Lebanon in March 1978, killing 2,000 persons and driving 250,000 from their homes without the loss of a single Israeli soldier. Protests from Washington ended that "war," but Israeli troops returned in June 1982. By mid-August after 124 air strikes against Beirut in nine days, President RONALD REAGAN called the Israeli bombings "unfathomable and senseless," coercing Israel into a reluctant truce. Before Israeli troops withdrew, Christian guerrillas invaded two Palestinian refugee camps that were surrounded by Israeli troops, and the guerrillas slaughtered hundreds of unarmed civilians. (Israeli spokespersons denied any responsibility for the crimes that they witnessed and permitted.) By the time Israel withdrew once more from Lebanon an estimated 50,000 persons had been killed, 85 percent of them civilians.

Religious warfare between private militias continued until early 1991 when Lebanese and Syrian troops finally disarmed the worst offenders. Still, the isolated Beqaa Valley remained a lawless district occupied by various guerrilla bands and well-armed farmers who cultivated opium poppies for conversion into high-priced HEROIN. Israeli bombing raids were repeated in 1996 and 1999, while occupation forces remained in parts of Lebanon until May 2000. Syrian troops went home in the summer of 2001, but their departure did not signal peace. Old antagonisms survive, and terrorist groups—chiefly Hezbollah—showed renewed strength in Lebanon during 2002–03, massing forces along the nation's border with Israel.

In February 2005 former Lebanese Prime Minister Rafik Hariri was assassinated in an attack widely attributed to Syria. Massive public protests followed calling for the dissolution of Lebanon's pro-Syrian government and the withdrawal of Syrian troops. Counterdemonstrations sponsored by Hezbollah and Syria followed, but the protest movement continued in Lebanon, and international pressure mounted for Syria to remove its military presence. In April, Syria finally agreed, and the last Syrian troops left Lebanon on April 26, 2005.

See also TERRORISM.

LEMMER, William

A mentally unstable military veteran, William Lemmer was threatened with a psychiatric discharge from the U.S. Army before he left the service of his own accord. The turmoil had only begun, however: Lemmer's estranged wife had him held for a sanity hearing after he wrote her a letter blaming VIETNAM Veterans Against the War (VVAW) for the breakup of their marriage, threatening to "get" the group's members silently, in "tennis shoes" and with a "length of piano wire." Police in Gainesville, Florida, detained Lemmer after he was found in possession of two loaded guns, and a local doctor recommended psychiatric treatment.

None of that apparently diminished Lemmer's value as a paid informant of the FEDERAL BUREAU OF INVESTIGATION (FBI) who was assigned to penetrate and disrupt the VVAW. His first action of record occurred on May 4, 1972, when 12 demonstrators

from the War Resisters League were jailed for entering Tinker Air Force Base near Oklahoma City to read an antiwar statement. Lemmer planned the demonstration but did not participate. At trial all 12 protesters were convicted of trespassing on a military reservation; four female demonstrators received probation, while eight male defendants served an average of four months in federal custody.

Lemmer's greatest coup occurred in July 1972 and targeted his enemies in the VVAW. Based on Lemmer's testimony to G-men and a federal grand jury in Florida, eight VVAW activists (thereafter known as the "Gainesville 8") were indicted for conspiracy to disrupt the 1972 Republican National Convention in Miami. According to the charges filed against them the defendants planned to attack the convention with a variety of weapons including crossbows, incendiary devices, homemade grenades, automatic weapons, and bazookas. At trial in 1973, however, U.S. attorneys produced no weapons other than slingshots offered for sale in any American sporting-goods store. Major Adam Klimkowski, chief of the Miami Police Department's Special Investigation Unit further admitted under oath that one of his agents proposed acquisition of machine guns to the defendants, who flatly rejected the offer. Lemmer's exposure as an FBI informant finally doomed the government's case, and jurors deliberated less than four hours before acquitting the defendants on all charges.

LENIN, Vladimir Ilyich (1870–1924)

RUSSIA's first Communist leader was born Vladimir Ilyich Ulyanov at Simbirsk on April 22, 1870. The son of a civil-service officer, he distinguished himself in study of Greek and Latin until May 1887 when his eldest brother was hanged for participating in a plot to kill Czar Alexander III. The execution radicalized Ulyanov, who adopted the revolutionary name Nikolai Lenin (allegedly a reference to the Lena River) and immersed himself in radical politics. Before year's end he was arrested and expelled from Kazan University for leading student protests. Independent study qualified him as a lawyer in 1892, but his devotion to armed rebellion persisted. Arrested again on December 7, 1895, Lenin was held in jail for a year before authorities banished him to Siberia. He used the time to hone his rhetoric and published his first book on Marxism (*The Development of Capital in Russia*) before his exile ended in 1900. Thereafter, Lenin traveled widely through Russia and Europe, publishing radical tracts and newspapers. In 1903 he led the dissident Bolshevik (minority) faction of the Russian Social Democratic Labor Party, and three years later Lenin was elected to the party's presidium. Threats against his life from right-wing monarchists prompted a move to Finland in 1907, and Lenin spent the next decade roaming through Europe, spreading the ideology that Winston Churchill once compared to a plague.

Lenin returned to Russia in April 1917, after Nicholas II was deposed. He fled once more in July after a Bolshevik coup failed to seize control of the nation, but October brought him back to lead a successful revolt against the provisional government. On November 8, 1917, Lenin was elected chairman of the Council of People's Commissars—in effect, he became the new leader of Russia. He urged immediate peace with GERMANY, sacrificing much of Russia's western territory in the March 1918 Treaty of Brest-Litovsk. Five months later Lenin survived his first assassination attempt, carried out by dissident Fanny Kaplan. Undeterred by danger Lenin secured victory over anti-Bolshevik armies and U.S. invasion forces during the Russian Civil War of 1918–20. In March 1921 he crushed a naval mutiny at Kronstadt to consolidate his power. Success was fleeting, though, as a series of strokes between May 1922 and March 1923 left him partially paralyzed and forced into virtual isolation by the Russian Politburo. A fourth stroke claimed his life on January 21, 1924, whereupon the city of Petrograd was renamed Leningrad in his honor. Canny subordinate JOSEPH STALIN filled the Russian power vacuum after Lenin's death. Lenin's corpse was embalmed and placed on permanent display at the Kremlin in a glass coffin.

See also COMMUNISM.

LENNON, John (1940–1980)

A Liverpool native, born October 9, 1940, musician John Lennon organized a rock-and-roll quartet, the Beatles, with friends Paul McCartney, George Harrison, and Pete Best in 1960. The group played various British clubs before cutting its first record in 1962. Soon afterward, drummer Best was replaced by Ringo Starr, and the rest is music history. Between 1963 and early 1970 the Beatles took all honors as the world's most successful rock band, leading the so-called British invasion of the United States in 1964 with an appearance on the *Ed Sullivan Show*

that brought 72 million viewers to their TV sets. Lennon created a flap in March 1966 with an off-hand comment that the Beatles were "bigger than JESUS CHRIST," and more controversy flowed from songs apparently endorsing use of the psychedelic drug LSD. McCartney left the Beatles in April 1970, and the band subsequently dissolved.

Lennon and second wife Yoko Ono, meanwhile, had settled in New York and embarked on a course of public protest against the VIETNAM War. Those efforts and John's continuing flirtation with illegal drugs prompted federal efforts to attempt to expel Lennon from the country. FEDERAL BUREAU OF INVESTIGATION agents shadowed the couple for two years, reporting on their every move and compiling voluminous files that were released to public scrutiny decades later under the Freedom of Information Act. On December 8, 1980, Lennon was shot and killed outside his Manhattan apartment by Mark David Chapman, whom authorities described as an obsessive fan-turned-stalker.

Conspiracists still question Chapman's motives and suggest that he was used by other forces in a plot to silence Lennon's political protests. Officially, Chapman—a long-term mental patient—became convinced that Lennon was "a hypocrite" after reading some of the musician's published poetry. Soon thereafter, Chapman allegedly "became frustrated and decided that the solution to his mental instability would be to kill John Lennon." To that end he flew from Hawaii to New York on October 29, 1980, armed with a pistol but no ammunition. Chapman staked out Lennon's apartment, phoning his wife long-distance on November 11 to confess his murder plan. She persuaded Chapman to come home, but he returned to New York on December 5 and shot Lennon three days later, hours after a previous sidewalk encounter wherein Lennon autographed one of his albums for Chapman. ("Is that all you want?" Lennon asked. Chapman replied, "Thanks, John.") Author Fenton Bresler in *Who Shot John Lennon?* (1989) rejected the lone-nut-assassin verdict, suggesting that the CENTRAL INTELLIGENCE AGENCY played a guiding role in Lennon's death. As Bresler summarized his case:

Lennon, the politically most active rock star of his generation . . . was shot dead outside his own home by a killer who was merely a tool, a human gun used and controlled by others to destroy a uniquely powerful radical figure who was likely to prove a rallying point for mass opposition to the policies soon to be implemented. . . . by the new United States government headed by RONALD REAGAN.

LESOTHO

Entirely surrounded by SOUTH AFRICA, the mountainous nation of Lesotho (formerly Basutoland) was held under British "protection" from 1843 to 1966, when London finally recognized King Moshoeshoe II as sovereign ruler of a parliamentary constitutional monarchy. Ntsu Mokhehle, head of the Basutoland Congress Party, claimed victory in 1970's election, whereupon incumbent prime minister Leabua Jonathan promptly declared a "national emergency," suspended the constitution, and clapped Mokhehle into prison. In February 1990 after King Moshoeshoe II refused to rubber-stamp the dismissal of several officials ousted by Justin Lekhanya, chairman of Lesotho's military council, Lekhanya stripped the king of his executive powers, then drove him into exile a month later. Moshoeshoe was replaced by his son, inaugurated as King Letsie III, but further upheavals brought Moshoeshoe back to the throne in January 1995. New elections in May 1998 sparked accusations of widespread vote fraud, and antigovernment riots erupted that autumn, quelled by troops from South Africa and BOTSWANA. Lesotho's army mutinied at the same time, but it was unable to expel the foreign soldiers. In the still-suspect parliamentary elections of 2002, the ruling Lesotho Congress for Democracy scored 54 percent of the national vote, at least on paper.

LETELIER, Orlando (1932–1976)

A native of CHILE, born April 13, 1932, Orlando Letelier pursued a life of politics and public service in his homeland. In 1971 socialist president Salvador Allende named Letelier as Chile's ambassador to the United States, followed two years later by his appointment to serve first as Foreign Minister, then Defense Minister. Throughout that period, the CENTRAL INTELLIGENCE AGENCY (CIA) was actively involved in a conspiracy to topple Allende's government on orders from President RICHARD NIXON and HENRY KISSINGER. After the military coup that killed Allende on September 11, 1973, Letelier was arrested, tortured, and then dispatched to a political prison in Tierra del Fuego. Released in 1974 he moved his family to Washington, D.C., and began a relentless campaign to restore Chilean democracy. Those efforts marked him for death under a wide-ranging program of assassinations ordered from Concepción, under the code-name Operation Condor (a collaborative mass-murder effort also involving the U.S.-supported dictators of ARGENTINA and URUGUAY).

On September 14, 1976, Letelier's wife received a telephone call in Washington. The anonymous caller asked, "Are you the wife of Orlando Letelier?" When she replied in the affirmative, the man corrected her: "No, you are his widow." Seven days later Letelier and American aide Ronni Moffit were killed when a bomb destroyed their car. Moffit's husband, blown clear of the wreckage, publicly blamed Chilean SECRET POLICE for the crime, but then-CIA Director George H. W. Bush falsely assured FEDERAL BUREAU OF INVESTIGATION (FBI) agents that "reliable sources" in Chile ruled out official involvement. In fact, Bush knew the details of Operation Condor, but his agency still joined in Chilean propaganda efforts, claiming leftists had slain Letelier to make him a martyr for their cause. JUSTICE DEPARTMENT investigators identified the actual killers within weeks, but prosecution was deferred until the CIA's latest terrorist campaign was scuttled by predictable leaks and scandals. The same bombers, including a clique of anti-Castro Cuban exiles who were linked to the BAY OF PIGS fiasco and the JFK ASSASSINATION, subsequently bombed a Cuban airliner, killing all 73 persons aboard. According to FBI sources, that slaughter and Letelier's murder were planned at the same meeting.

Those eventually convicted for killing Letelier included Michael Townley, a U.S. expatriate with close ties to Chile's secret police (DINA); General Manuel Contreras, former head of DINA; and another one-time DINA officer, Brigadier General Pedro Espinoza Bravo. CIA documents released under the Freedom of Information Act revealed that Bush's agency was closely tied to Contreras before and after the murder. Townley and accomplice Armando Fernández were also granted visas by the U.S. ambassador to Paraguay at the urging of CIA agents and Paraguayan officials, despite full knowledge that they traveled on false passports. In 1991 when Chile's Supreme Court asked then-President Bush to answer questions surrounding the Letelier murder, Bush refused to cooperate.

See also BUSH DYNASTY; FIDEL CASTRO; TERRORISM.

LIBERAL media

It is an article of faith among American conservatives that a pervasive and subversive "liberal" news media works ceaselessly to vilify and nullify their "patriotic" goals. The notion dates from RICHARD NIXON's tenure in the White House when investigative journalists exposed the crimes of WATERGATE and helped propel one of the most corrupt executives in modern U.S. history into retirement. Ever since those days right-wing officials and their propagandists feel obliged to blast the media whenever some new scandal is exposed. The fault, they seem to feel, lies not within the individuals revealed as power-hungry criminals but rather with the men and women who expose them. In the heat of that debate, however, few spokespersons for left or right have bothered to discover if the so-called liberal media truly exists.

In point of fact America's media outlets are owned and dominated by corporations whose executives are anything but liberal, and the bias of those owners influences every major policy espoused by newspapers and broadcasting networks. At last count three-fourths of all major stockholders in the ABC, CBS, and NBC networks were banking institutions (including CHASE MANHATTAN and the MORGAN Guarantee Trust), while right-wing mogul Rupert Murdoch owns the Fox network outright. NBC is a subsidiary of GENERAL ELECTRIC, which also has officers on the board of directors for the *Washington Post*. Other controlling voices on the *Post* and CBS include such financial powerhouses as IT&T, IBM, COCA-COLA, AT&T, and the FORD MOTOR COMPANY. Ford also has watchful executives on the boards of the *New York Times* and the *Los Angeles Times*. What effect does that staunch conservative ownership have on news reporting in America? A few examples from the past two decades should suffice.

- Former *Time* magazine reporter Stuart Schoffman described himself in the 1980s as "an apparatchik in the service of the corporation's ideas. It is only in retrospect that I realized I was mouthing opinions not my own."
- After Edward Roby, a reporter for United Press International, reported that U.S. OIL companies were illegally claiming their business expenses in SAUDI ARABIA as tax credits (rather than ordinary deductions), his employers barred Roby from writing any further stories about oil or taxes.

- Associated Press reporters Brian Barger and Robert Parry resigned in disgust after their editors repeatedly spiked or emasculated stories detailing links between CONTRA acts of TERRORISM in NICARAGUA and the CENTRAL INTELLIGENCE AGENCY.
- During the 1984 presidential election, ABC editors suppressed various stories critical of RONALD REAGAN and the Republican Party, including items on the FEDERAL BUREAU OF INVESTIGATION investigation of Labor Secretary Raymond Donovan's ties to the MAFIA.
- In 1991, when NBC stringer Jon Alpert returned from IRAQ with video footage of civilian areas blasted by U.S. air strikes, network president Michael Gartner barred use of the footage and terminated Alpert's 12-year employment with NBC.
- In the wake of ELECTION 2000 a survey conducted by the Pew Charitable Trust Project for Excellence in Journalism revealed that 56 percent of all stories published or broadcast about Democratic candidate Al Gore were negative in tone, versus 49 percent of the stories covering opponent George W. Bush. Positive stories about Bush nearly doubled Gore's figure, with 24 percent versus 13 percent.

Other studies in recent years have shown that more members of the media identify themselves as liberal rather than conservative and that the majority tends to vote Democratic, but these studies have not established a connection between this and biased reporting. Some media assessments of the 2004 election found greater percentages of stories favoring John Kerry, while others depicted a more-balanced picture. Critics on both sides argued against the validity of the research. As for the liberal impact on government policy which is so often condemned by commentators of the Rush Limbaugh–Sean Hannity persuasion, it apparently does not exist. In May 2003 George Bush publicly admitted that he never reads newspapers nor watches news broadcasts on television, preferring instead the positive spin of hand-picked bulletins provided by his staff.

See also BUSH DYNASTY.

LIBERIA

Liberia was founded in 1822 as Africa's first republic when members of the American Colonization

Society began to ship freed slaves from the United States. During the next two decades some 12,000 blacks were "repatriated" to a land that they had never seen before, initially christened Monrovia. In 1847 the name was changed to Liberia (for "liberty"). Although U.S. deportees comprised only 5 percent of the country's population, they have historically dominated its politics and society. Government was modeled after that of the United States until April 1980 when a military coup ousted President William Tolbert, Jr. The junta that replaced Tolbert was notable for its corruption and brutality—traits that prompted formation of a rebel group, the National Patriotic Front of Liberia (NPFL), in 1989. Dictator Samuel Doe was assassinated in 1990, but the civil war raged on until 1997, destroying much of Liberia's infrastructure. Charles Taylor was elected president in July 1997 with 75 percent of the popular vote, and while international observers pronounced the election relatively fair and honest, Taylor behaved as a ruthless dictator in office. When not suppressing dissidents, Taylor supported SIERRA LEONE's Revolutionary United Front (RUF) in a bid to unseat that nation's government. Liberia's economy continued to decline, while nonstop fighting by a mixed bag of government and rebel armies continued at various points throughout the country, including troops from Sierra Leone and GUINEA. Domestic rebels, calling themselves Liberians United for Reconciliation and Democracy (LURD), intensified attacks on Taylor's government in 2002, while Taylor was accused of using black magic and cannibalism to thwart his many foes. The UNITED NATIONS charged Taylor with WAR CRIMES in June 2003, while U.S. President George W. Bush ordered his military chiefs of staff to prepare plans for armed intervention in Liberia. In early July 2003 Taylor agreed to leave Liberia for a life of exile, but he changed his mind on July 18, as rebels shelled the capital (Monrovia), vowing to remain and face his enemies. In August 2003, a comprehensive peace agreement ended 14 years of civil war and prompted the resignation of former president Charles Taylor, who was exiled to Nigeria. The National Transitional Government of Liberia (NTGL), which is composed of rebel, government, and civil society groups, assumed control in October 2003. Chairman Gyude Bryant, who was given a two-year mandate to oversee efforts to rebuild Liberia, heads the new government. The United Nations Mission in Liberia (UNMIL), which maintains a strong presence throughout the country, completed a disarmament program for former combatants in late 2004.

See also BUSH DYNASTY.

LIBYA

The first inhabitants of Libya were nomadic Berber tribes. In the seventh century B.C. Phoenicians occupied the region's eastern half, while GREECE claimed the west. Invaders followed from Carthage and Rome before Libya was sacked by Vandals after A.D. 436. Beginning in the 16th century, while nominally a part of the Ottoman Empire, Libya bred a voracious crop of pirates who terrorized the Mediterranean. The United States rejected demands for tribute in 1805, sending U.S. Marines to "the shores of Tripoli" for a showdown that scuttled the worst of the sea wolves. ITALY occupied Libya in 1911 during hostilities with TURKEY, and resistance was effectively suppressed by the time Libya officially became an Italian colony in 1934. World War II brought liberation from Italian occupation, and the UNITED NATIONS granted Libya independence in 1949. Discovery of OIL in 1958 transformed the impoverished economy but only worsened the corruption of Libya's monarchy. On September 1, 1969, Colonel MUAMMAR AL-QADDAFFI deposed the king and installed himself as dictator, transforming Libya into a pro-Arab, anti-Western state with socialist trappings, aligned with a motley crew of allies that included Idi Amin of UGANDA. Al-Qaddaffi's reputed financial support for TERRORISM made him a target for international condemnation, as well as occasional bombing raids launched by ISRAEL and the United States, where Presidents RONALD REAGAN and George H. W. Bush pursued covert (and unsuccessful) plans to topple al-Qaddaffi's regime. Rumors of Libyan "hit teams" stalking Bush proved false, but two Libyan intelligence agents were indicted for complicity in the December 1988 bombing of an airliner over Lockerbie, Scotland, which killed 259 passengers and 11 persons on the ground. In April 1999 after years of negotiation Libya surrendered the defendants for trial in the NETHERLANDS, where one was convicted of murder and the other was acquitted. In 2003 Libya agreed to pay relatives of the Lockerbie victims $3 million to settle various damage claims. By that time al-Qaddaffi's status as international bogeyman had largely faded, while SADDAM HUSSEIN of IRAQ and the ever-elusive Osama bin Laden claimed headlines as terrorist movers and shakers.

See also BIN LADEN FAMILY; BUSH DYNASTY.

LINCOLN, Abraham (1809–1865)

With one exception, the assassinations and attempted slayings of U.S. presidents and presidential candidates during the past 140 years have been officially explained as the demented acts of solitary social misfits, "lone-nut" gunmen whose crimes had involved no accomplices. The sole exception is the assassination of Abraham Lincoln in April 1865. In that case multiple conspirators were named, convicted, and punished for their plot—yet nagging questions linger. Were the prosecutions thorough and competent, or were they simply part of a larger, sinister whitewash?

The basic, unrefuted facts are these: Lincoln was shot on April 14, 1865, while attending a play at Ford's Theater in Washington, D.C. The gunman, actor and Confederate zealot John Wilkes Booth, also stabbed a friend of Lincoln, Henry Rathbone, in the arm before leaping to the stage below and breaking his leg in the process. Simultaneously, conspirators Lewis Powell (or Paine) and David Herold attempted to kill Secretary of State William Seward. Herold panicked and fled while the attack was in progress, and Seward survived his wounds. A fourth plotter, George Atzerodt, aborted his mission to kill Vice President Andrew Johnson. Booth and Herold escaped from Washington, fleeing to Mary Surratt's tavern in Maryland for traveling supplies. Their next stop was the home of Dr. Samuel Mudd, an apparent innocent, who set Booth's leg in ignorance of his recent crime. Lincoln died of his head wound at 7:22 A.M. on April 15, leaving Secretary of War Edwin Stanton to coordinate the manhunt. Booth and Herold were traced to a barn near Port Royal,

Conspiracy theories abound in the April 1865 assassination of President Abraham Lincoln (left). John Wilkes Booth (right) certainly murdered President Lincoln, but who were his accomplices? (Library of Congress)

220

George Atzerodt (left) was hanged for his role in the Lincoln conspiracy of 1865, while alleged conspirator John Surratt (right) escaped conviction. (Author's collection)

Virginia, on April 26, where Herold surrendered and Booth chose to fight. The barn was torched, and Booth was killed in a chaotic shootout. In days to come eight alleged conspirators were jailed and tried before a military court. All were convicted on June 30, 1865, and four of them—Powell, Herold, Atzerodt, and Mary Surratt—were hanged on July 7. Dr. Mudd was sentenced to life imprisonment for conspiracy but was pardoned by President Johnson in 1869. Samuel Arnold and Michael O'Laughlen received life terms for joining Booth in an abortive plot to kidnap Lincoln before Booth set his mind on murder. O'Laughlen died in prison, while Arnold was pardoned with Dr. Mudd. Defendant Edman Spangler, convicted of helping Booth escape from Ford's Theater, was likewise pardoned in 1869.

And there, officially, the story ends. Predictably conspiracists have long declared that nothing is as simple as it seems. Major alternative scenarios and suspects in Lincoln's murder include the following:

The Confederate plot: With the Civil War lately ended and scattered guerrilla fighting still ongoing in the South, suspicion of a Rebel plot to kill Lincoln was only natural. Coded letters found in Booth's possession linked him to the Confederacy, and George Atzerodt's statement at trial ("misplaced" until 1977) detailed Booth's knowledge of a Southern plot to dynamite the White House. The murder, some feel, was staged in retaliation for a bungled Union effort to assassinate Confederate president Jefferson Davis and his cabinet. Conspiracists note that Judah Benjamin, the Confederate secretary of state, burned his records and fled to England before Richmond fell, remaining there until his death in 1884. In this scenario the abortive Booth kidnapping plot was shelved when Yankee troops took Richmond (the Confederate capital), and Lincoln was slain as an act of revenge.

Dr. Samuel Mudd (left) received a life prison term for setting Booth's leg after the Lincoln assassination. Edwin Stanton (right), Lincoln's secretary of war, remains a prime suspect in some conspiracy theories. (Author's collection)

The Johnson plot: Seven hours prior to the assassination, Booth visited Vice President Johnson's hotel in Washington and left a note for Johnson with the desk clerk, reading: "Don't wish to disturb you. Are you at home? J. Wilkes Booth." Various authors contend that Booth knew Johnson from the latter's days as governor of Tennessee, that Johnson attended Booth's performances in Nashville, and that the two friends kept a pair of sisters as mistresses, frequently appearing in public as a foursome. Lincoln's widow herself suspected Johnson of complicity in the murder, writing to a friend on March 15, 1866: "That miserable inebriate Johnson had cognizance of my husband's death. Why was that card of Booth's found in his box? Some acquaintance certainly existed. I have been

deeply impressed with the harrowing thought that he had an understanding with the conspirators & they knew their man. As sure as you & I live, Johnson had some hand in all this." Certain congressmen shared that suspicion, but a special Assassination Committee created to seek proof of the charge revealed nothing.

The Stanton plot: Edwin Stanton is a popular suspect with modern conspiracy theorists. Author Otto Eisenschiml was the first to publicly accuse Stanton, in 1937, with a claim that war-hawk Stanton despised Lincoln's lax RECONSTRUCTION policies and schemed to implement a more radical program to punish prostrate Dixie. Eisenschiml further alleged that Stanton shuffled Lincoln's bodyguards to deny him adequate protection at Ford's

Theater and that he knew of conspiratorial gatherings held at Surratt's tavern. One version of the theory, filmed as *The Lincoln Conspiracy* in 1977, went further still, claiming that Stanton helped Booth escape from the United States to India while an impostor died in the Virginia barn.

The Vatican plot: In 1886 ex-priest Charles Chiniquy alleged that Lincoln's murder was carried out by the CATHOLIC CHURCH in return for a $1 million payoff from Jefferson Davis. The contract was accepted, Chiniquy claimed, because "the JESUITS alone could select the assassins, train them, and show them a crown of glory in heaven." Booth was thereafter recruited and manipulated to ensure that the pope received his payday. Aside from cash, there was another motive: Lincoln had once successfully defended Chiniquy in court when Chiniquy's bishop slapped him with libel and morals charges in 1856. Lincoln was targeted, Chiniquy thought, for winning a victory over the church. In 1924 author Burke McCarty wrote: "In all the bloody history of the Papacy, perhaps in no one man, as in Abraham Lincoln, was there concentrated such a multitude of reasons for his annihilation by that system." KU KLUX KLAN spokespersons touted the theory for decades, recycling it against Catholic presidential candidate John Kennedy in 1960, but no evidence of a Vatican plot has yet been revealed.

The bankers' plot: This foray into thinly veiled anti-Semitism contends that Lincoln was murdered by a cartel of international bankers, led by Europe's Rothschild family, who opposed his economic policies. In one version Lincoln enraged his future slayers by rejecting their offer of high-interest loans to finance the Union war effort. An alternate scenario claims that the Rothschilds, like Stanton, desired harsh terms for Reconstruction—in this case to forestall a revival of Southern agriculture and ensure continued high prices for European exports to the States. Booth is thus reduced to the status of an expendable hired gun.

Other conspiratorial candidates, advanced over time by largely forgotten theorists, include a coterie of U.S. financiers, the Copperheads (Confederate sympathizers in the North), "radical" Republicans in Congress, the B'nai B'rith, the proslavery Knights of the Golden Circle, and even Mary Todd Lincoln. Historian Thomas Turner fairly summarized the situation in 1999 when he wrote: "Those who continue to hope that the assassination may be 'solved,' in the same manner as a murder mystery may be solved, are destined to be disappointed. The century which has passed, makes any new and definitive solution to the crime doubtful. It is unlikely that a smoking gun will surface even though there may still be new sources which will be discovered."

See also KENNEDY DYNASTY.

LIVESTOCK mutilations

In autumn 1972 Swedish farmers and police were startled by a wave of attacks on livestock, including calves, bullocks, and hogs. In each case the animals' throats were cut, and their hearts were removed. Footprints and tire tracks at some of the crime scenes told investigators that humans were responsible, but the culprits eluded arrest. In March 1973 the ritualistic slaughter began at Shirksville, Pennsylvania, with two sheep killed and drained of blood. By year's end the plague had spread to Minnesota and Kansas; scores of cattle had been killed by unknown means, and various organs—typically eyes, ears, lips, udders, genitalia, rectums, and tails—had been removed with what some observers termed "surgical precision." The carcasses were often bloodless, and some of the wounds appeared to be cauterized. By 1980 an estimated 8,000–12,000 had been killed and mutilated across 21 U.S. states and in the western provinces of Canada. (Much higher estimates, including one of 700,000 mutilations, were fabricated by various authors.) The trademarks of the deaths were mystery and silence. A Kansas law officer reported in December 1973 that "the large majority of these mutilations occurred near occupied houses," without disturbing the tenants. One cow had even been found in a mudhole with no footprints or tire tracks at the scene.

Investigation of the deaths and mutilations produced mixed results. An Oklahoma task force reported in March 1975 that while all the animals examined had died of apparent natural causes, "It is the opinion of the task force members that the human element can be attributed to individuals attempting to get in on a fad or to young people dissecting dead carcasses for biological or experimental

223

purposes. We are of the opinion that the human involvement is a fad generated by publicity and is only temporary." A Colorado report, issued the same year, confirmed death by natural causes but blamed the "surgical" mutilations on scavengers such as coyotes. No explanation for the missing blood was offered in either report.

Farmers and frightened townspeople were not consoled by the government verdicts. Some reported UFO sightings in the vicinity of livestock mutilations, while others saw (and sometimes fired at) black "phantom" helicopters that were devoid of the various markings required by federal law. Sporadic livestock mutilations continue to the present day not only in the United States but also in Europe (where horses have been victimized in brutal knife attacks for the past decade or more) and in Latin America (where residents frequently blame an unknown creature called *El Chupacabra,* the "goat sucker"). Three major conspiracy theories attempt to explain the ongoing death and mutilation of farm animals around the world. They include:

Alien experimentation: Just as extraterrestrial creatures are sometimes accused of abducting, studying, and/or impregnating human beings, so they are suspected in some quarters of conducting long-term experiments on Earth's livestock. Aside from occasional UFO sightings or reports of unexplained lights in the sky above fields where mutilated carcasses are later found, the evidence of alien involvement in such cases is largely negative: no tracks, no blood, no cause of death identified, no evidence of human agency at work. Until such time as aliens are caught red handed at their work, the claim remains unverifiable.

Cult activity: Police in Idaho, Montana, and Alberta, Canada, have reportedly uncovered evidence linking some animal mutilations to the blood rituals of SATANISM. Blood tests reveal that some of the Canadian animals were drugged prior to death and that items of occult ritual paraphernalia have been recovered at certain crime scenes. A handful of confessions from unbalanced individuals (and one imprisoned bank robber) produced no convictions, but authorities remain convinced that small, localized cults are responsible for at least a few of the mutilation cases.

U.S. government experiments: It is a measure of the average American's mistrust of Washington since VIETNAM and WATERGATE that many farmers who have been victimized by livestock mutilations blame their own government for conducting a wave of illicit experimentation, presumably in furtherance of some chemical or biological warfare agenda. Elusive, unmarked helicopters suggest a level of funding typically beyond the reach of drugged-out would-be sorcerers, and official denials only strengthen the conviction of conspiracists that something is amiss. In 1975 a Lincoln County, Colorado, rancher found a blue plastic valise (described in some reports as a "government bag") lying beside his roadside mailbox. Inside the valise was a scalpel, a cow's ear, and part of its tongue, with several arm-length latex gloves that were typically used by veterinarians during artificial insemination of livestock. The bag was found one day after a calf was mutilated on a neighboring ranch, but the ear and the tongue had not come from that animal. Separate investigations by the county sheriff and the Colorado Bureau of Investigation failed to trace the bag's owner. The government conspiracy theory was highlighted and "solved" in a 1982 feature film *Endangered Species* starring Robert Urich, JoBeth Williams, and Peter Coyote.

LOCKHEED-MARTIN Corporation

From the 1950s onward Lockheed Corporation has been one of the U.S.'s top defense contractors, producing warplanes, missiles, guidance systems, and other high-tech tools of mass annihilation. It has profited hugely in the arms trade, often by price gouging at taxpayers' expense—as when a 1990s exposé revealed that Lockheed charged the government $640 for each plastic toilet seat installed on U.S. Navy vessels. Officials in Congress and the Pentagon raised no objections to such overcharging, perhaps because Lockheed also ranked among the nation's top dispensers of political payoffs. The chicanery continued (some say increased) after Lockheed's merger with competitor Martin Marietta to become Lockheed Martin in 1994. Some of the firm's suspect dealings include the following:

1976—Revelation of Lockheed's bribes to various Japanese officials, including Prime Minister Tanaka Kakuei, unleashed the worst corruption scandal in Japanese history since World War II. Lockheed executives escaped punishment, but three Japanese politicians were convicted at trial.

June 1993—Secretary of Defense William Perry and Undersecretary of Defense John Deutch approved government handouts to Lockheed, Martin Marietta, and other defense firms as compensation for "restructuring" costs due to mergers and/or acquisitions. The ruling, which reversed a 40-year ban on such payments, was clearly influenced by the fact that both Perry and Deutch were former Martin Marietta executives. Both appointees of Bill Clinton had received special waivers from the normal ethics code that bars ex-corporate officials from doing business with their former colleagues until 12 months have elapsed from their severance. Under the new rule after its 1994 merger Lockheed Martin submitted $855 million in bills to Washington, including $31 million in "triggered compensation" (that is, corporate bonuses) to various company executives. Norman Augustine, new president of Lockheed Martin and former boss of the new Pentagon leaders, received $8.2 million from the public treasury. (President Clinton subsequently named Deutch to lead the CENTRAL INTELLIGENCE AGENCY. While there Deutch mishandled secret documents so egregiously that he faced criminal indictment. One of Clinton's last official acts was an 11th-hour pardon sparing Deutch from prosecution.)

1994—Lockheed and General Dynamics jointly contributed $1.5 million to various political candidates in this election year, while receiving $1.9 *billion* in domestic and foreign military contracts—a tidy profit of 126,567 percent on their investment.

May 1994—The U.S. Equal Employment Opportunity Commission sued Martin Marietta for illegal age discrimination in the layoffs of 2,000 employees between 1990 and 1994. In November 1996 the firm settled that case with an admission of guilt, payment of $13 million in back salaries for those dismissed, and rehiring of those who had been illegally fired.

June 1994—The U.S. JUSTICE DEPARTMENT indicted Lockheed for bribing an Egyptian politician in 1989. The company allegedly paid $1 million in 1989 to guarantee Egypt's purchase of three cargo airplanes. Lockheed executives pleaded guilty in January 1995 and agreed to pay a $24.8 million fine—roughly one-third of the profit they earned from sale of the aircraft.

December 1994—Martin Marietta pleaded guilty to bribing a different Egyptian official in the 1980s. Their $2.87 million payoff won the firm contracts for radar equipment valued at $124 million per year. The company's fine of $5.87 million was little more than a wrist slap in comparison to its profits.

1995–96—Lockheed Martin dispensed $1.2 million to various political action committees during this round of U.S. elections. Speaker of the House Newt Gingrich received $10,000, thus securing House approval for contracts on "stealth" aircraft that were priced at $160 million each.

March 2001—Lockheed Martin settled a federal lawsuit based on charges that it overbilled the Federal Aviation Administration (FAA) millions of dollars for office space in Maryland. Company executives admitted the charges and agreed to a $10.5 million fine, but no money changed hands. Instead, Lockheed Martin agreed to give the FAA "offset credits" for future rent payments for the same offices.

See also CLINTON, BILL AND HILLARY.

LONG, Huey (1893–1935)

Louisiana native Huey Long was born in 1893 and quit school at age 17 to become a salesman. He later attended the University of Oklahoma and Tulane University, passing the Louisiana bar exam in 1915. After three years in private practice he was elected chairman of the state railroad commission, renamed the Public Service Commission in 1921. Long failed in his first gubernatorial race (1924) but was successful four years later with the campaign slogan "Every man a king, but no one wears a crown." As part of his folksy appeal, Long adopted the nickname "Kingfish" from the popular *Amos & Andy* radio show.

In office Huey Long combined traits of grassroots populism with abject corruption. He raised taxes on the rich to finance public works while collaborating with MEYER LANSKY and members of the MAFIA to protect illegal gambling in Louisiana. In 1929 Long defeated an impeachment campaign and went on to win a U.S. Senate seat the following year. Long supported Franklin Roosevelt's presidential campaign in 1932 but then became a strident critic of the NEW DEAL when FDR failed to offer him a prestigious federal appointment. Long announced his own run for the White House in August 1935, but he would not live to occupy the Oval Office.

On September 8, 1935, en route to a special Sunday session of the state legislature at Baton Rouge, Long was confronted in the capitol lobby by Dr. Carl Weiss, a local physician and son-in-law of Judge Benjamin Pavy, a longtime opponent of the Kingfish. Weiss brandished a pistol and gunfire erupted. When the smoke cleared, Weiss's corpse bore 32 gunshot wounds from Long's bodyguards—29 in the back and two in the head—while Long was shot once in the abdomen. Rushed to Our Lady of the Lake Sanitarium, Long underwent a two-hour emergency surgery by Dr. Arthur Vidrine, but the surgeon overlooked a damaged kidney, and Long died at 4:06 A.M. on September 10. Every aspect of Long's death remains shrouded in mystery. Weiss's motive for the shooting is unknown, and some authors contend that Long was shot—accidentally or otherwise—by one of his own quick-trigger henchmen. At the hospital Dr. Vidrine claimed that a .22-caliber bullet had passed completely through Long's body, but without the slug his estimate of caliber is dubious, at best. Decades later, crime reporter Hank Messick alleged that Meyer Lansky told friends in New York, "The doctors were paid to let him die."

Long's notorious corruption spawned two novels—*All the King's Men* by Robert Penn Warren and Sinclair Lewis's *It Can't Happen Here*. The Kingfish also spawned a political dynasty in the Pelican State. Widow Rose completed Long's term in the Senate, while younger brother Earl Kemp Long served three terms as governor. "Uncle Earl's" regime was marked by strong support for racial segregation, public dalliance with stripper Blaze Starr, and confinement to a mental institution. (Discovering that state law did not bar a governor from holding office in an asylum, Long fired the hospital's director and replaced him with a crony who ordered Long's release.) In 1960 Earl was

elected to the U.S. House of Representatives, but he died before taking office. Meanwhile, from 1948 to 1986 Huey's son Russell Long served Louisiana in the Senate where he opposed civil rights legislation and led the charge in favor of tax breaks for billion-dollar industries. Fellow party members elected Russell as the Senate's Democratic whip in 1965, but they were soon embarrassed by his public drunkenness and stripped him of his leadership position four years later. Actor Walter Matthau portrayed Russell Long in Oliver Stone's film *JFK* (1991), depicting an alleged conspiracy in the JFK ASSASSINATION.

LOS Angeles Police Department (LAPD)

From its beginnings in the late 1880s, the LAPD has harbored deep strains of racism, first against Mexican Americans and then against Asians and blacks. Like most other police departments it has also been historically allied with major business interests to suppress early labor unions in the guise of fighting ANARCHISTS and "radicals." Some critics still maintain that LAPD officers collaborated with the fledgling FEDERAL BUREAU OF INVESTIGATION (FBI) to frame innocent unionists for the 1910 bombing of the *Los Angeles Times*. In the 1920s those agencies (though bitter enemies in later years) cooperated to crush the Industrial Workers of the World.

Chief James Davis ran the LAPD from 1926 to 1938, with a four-year interruption (1929–33) occasioned by exposure of widespread corruption in the ranks. Reform never lasted long in L.A., and when Davis returned to power he promoted Capt. Earl Kynette (lately disgraced for coercing bribes out of pimps and prostitutes) to lead a new Red Squad, devoted to smashing COMMUNISM in the City of Angels. As defined by Davis and Kynette (as well as later LAPD leaders), Reds included anyone who criticized police brutality or corruption. In 1938 Kynette and an accomplice were imprisoned for the near-fatal bombing of a private investigator who had been hired by a local reform group, the Citizens' Independent Investigating Committee. In the wake of that scandal the L.A. city council denied Mayor Frank Shaw's request for $90,000 to continue Red Squad operations, and the team lapsed briefly into inactivity.

Police corruption, however, continued in Los Angeles without interruption, with high-ranking officers enriched by payoffs from the local MAFIA. Gambling, prostitution, and narcotics traffic were protected, while minorities, the unemployed, and the homeless were routinely tortured with "third-degree" tactics and packed off to prison. Chief William Parker had begun his LAPD tenure as a member of the Red Squad in 1927, and he revived the unit as soon as he took charge of the force in 1950. His long-running feud with J. EDGAR HOOVER barred local officers from the FBI's police academy until Parker died in 1966, but Parker needed no help in running L.A. with an iron hand. A hard-drinking reactionary he expanded illegal surveillance of "radicals" on every front, indoctrinated his troops with literature from the JOHN BIRCH SOCIETY, and dismissed residents of city ghettos as "monkeys in a zoo." Legend has it that visiting members of organized crime were beaten and run out of town by Parker's elite gangbusters, but organized crime still flourished in the hands of such mobsters as Mickey Cohen and Jack Dragna.

Thomas Reddin took the helm of LAPD after Parker's death, remaining only until 1969 when he decamped to become a radio commentator for $100,000 per year. Replacement Edward Davis (no relation to James) proved even more extreme than Parker: Mending fences with the FBI, he launched a new wave of oppression against "leftist" groups in L.A., with special attention to militant blacks in such organizations as the BLACK PANTHER PARTY. With help from Washington, Davis used agents provocateurs to spark a deadly shooting war between Panthers and the rival United Slaves, led by police informant Ron Karenga. Another full-time informer, LOUIS TACKWOOD later testified that LAPD and the FBI conspired to murder Panther spokesman GEORGE LESTER JACKSON in prison. Davis updated the Red Squad, renaming it the Public Disorder Intelligence Division, and two PDID detectives were jailed in February 1970 while posing as student radicals at UCLA. While right-wing bombings by the KU KLUX KLAN and allied groups proliferated in Los Angeles with 152 blasts in 1975 alone, Davis ignored the threat and branded peaceful opponents of the VIETNAM War as "terrorists."

In April 1975 L.A.'s police commission announced the destruction of some 2 million SECRET POLICE files compiled on 55,000 groups and individuals during the past half-century. The move earned cautious praise, but widespread spying continued without letup. In February 1978 one month after Chief Davis resigned to launch an ill-fated gubernatorial race, LAPD offi-

cers were caught photographing participants in a city council meeting. New chief Daryl Gates faced a series of lawsuits from surveillance and harassment victims during 1978–81 that exposed further illicit police activities. In July 1983 he sought to defuse civic anger by renaming the PDID the Anti-Terrorist Division, but cosmetic changes brought no reform. In February 1984 the city council approved a $1.8 million settlement with 144 plaintiffs in various lawsuits, while ordering LAPD to refrain from further spying except in cases where "a reasonable and articulate suspicion" suggested that targets were "planning, threatening, attempting or performing a significant disruption of the public order." In a subculture where deception and evasion are routine, civil libertarians find no reason to believe that LAPD surveillance activities are anything short of business as usual.

Pending new political exposures, though, LAPD critics must be satisfied with an unending series of scandals involving bribery, detectives moonlighting as contract killers, sexual abuse of teenagers enrolled in the department's Explorer program, drug thefts and sales, rape of female prisoners, fabrication of evidence against innocent defendants in the Rampart Division, televised beatings of unarmed prisoners—in short, more business as usual. On March 27, 2003, the *Los Angeles Times* reported that three men, once members of the LAPD Explorer program, had accused Deputy Police Chief David Kalish of molesting them in the 1970s. The claims accompanied civil lawsuits which remain unresolved at this writing. Daryl Gates spoke for most of his colleagues when he told reporters, "You have a man with . . . a remarkable, impeccable record and distinguished career; along comes a 20-year-old accusation. You could wait until the investigation is complete. If a decision is made and it's against him—fine. But before a decision is made, it's highly inappropriate."

LSD

The hallucinogenic drug Lysergic acid diethylamide, better known as LSD or acid, was synthesized in 1938 by Albert Hofmann, a chemist employed by Switzerland's Sandoz PHARMACEUTICAL COMPANY, while Hofmann was trying to create a new blood stimulant. Five years later, on April 16, 1943, Hofmann accidentally absorbed some LSD through his fingertips and experienced the world's first "acid trip," which he described as a two-hour "uninterrupted stream of fantastic pictures, extraordinary shapes with intense, kaleidoscopelike play of colors." Dr. Max Rinkel brought LSD to the United States in 1949, and it quickly fell into nefarious hands. By 1951 the CENTRAL INTELLIGENCE AGENCY (CIA) had begun its first LSD experiments under the code-name MKULTRA, and the U.S. Army was not far behind with "Operation Third Chance." Both agencies were anxious to develop new "truth serums" for interrogation purposes, but the CIA went further yet, employing LSD and other hallucinogens in protracted studies aimed at all-out MIND CONTROL of assassins and other human "assets."

The CIA-Army LSD experiments were conducted secretly, and while LSD itself was not an outlawed substance in the 1950s or early 1960s, government use of the drug clearly violated a wide range of state and federal statutes. Numerous subjects, both military and civilian, were drugged without their knowledge or consent and then subjected to abusive interrogation and other manipulative ordeals. On the side, when not attempting to program "Manchurian candidates," the CIA hatched an abortive plot to embarrass FIDEL CASTRO by impregnating his favorite cigars with LSD, thus prompting him to rave incoherently in public. The army, meanwhile, employed LSD as a punitive device, as in the 1961 case of James Thornwell, a 22-year-old black soldier suspected of stealing classified documents in France. After six weeks of confinement, brutal beatings, and near-starvation, Thornwell was fed LSD without his knowledge, after which, army documents reveal, interrogators threatened "to extend [his hallucinatory] state indefinitely . . . even to a permanent condition of insanity." Thornwell proved to be innocent, after all, and in the 1970s he sued the U.S. government for $10 million. The House of Representatives approved a $650,000 "compromise settlement" in 1980.

Meanwhile, Congress was rethinking LSD. In 1962 new federal regulations designated acid an experimental drug and restricted testing, producing the first batch of arrests for unauthorized experimentation. Acid hit the streets of America in 1963, and California became the first state to ban it by law in October 1966. Congress followed suit with federal legislation in 1967, too late to stop the sky-high "Summer of Love" in San Francisco and elsewhere. By 1970 an estimated 1–2 million Americans had tried LSD at least once, while such stars as

JOHN LENNON sang its praises. The CIA's bizarre handling of acid was exposed by the CHURCH COMMITTEE in 1975–76, by which time MKULTRA and similar programs had allegedly been discontinued. Some conspiracists believe that LSD or the equivalent may have been used to produce a robot gunman in the RFK ASSASSINATION of 1968 and that acid may have been a motivating factor in the SYMBIONESE LIBERATION ARMY's peculiar war on affluent society. LSD remains on the international list of controlled substances today, though some purists claim that "true acid" no longer exists. The Drug Enforcement Administration reports that the strength of LSD samples obtained currently from illicit sources ranges from 20 to 80 micrograms of LSD per dose. This is considerably less than the levels reported during the 1960s and early 1970s, when the dosage ranged from 100 to 200 micrograms, or higher, per unit.

LUCIANO, Charles "Lucky" (1897–1962)

A native of Sicily, Salvatore Lucania was born in 1897 and moved to the United States with his family at age 10. He was a racketeer even in childhood, offering "protection" from himself to other youngsters at rates of one or two cents per day. Two who resisted him and thereby earned Lucania's respect were MEYER LANSKY and Benjamin "Bugsy" Siegel, his future partners in organized crime. As Charles Luciano, Lucania joined New York's notorious Five Points gang and was suspected of several murders by the time PROHIBITION arrived in 1920. Working with Arnold "The Brain" Rothstein, Luciano and company grew rich from bootlegging, gambling, and prostitution, with a sideline in HEROIN sales. In the mid-1920s Luciano joined the MAFIA as an ally of New York's ruling *capo,* Joe "The Boss" Masseria. By 1928 Masseria was locked in a war for control of the city with rival Salvatore Maranzano, a circumstance that gave Luciano, Lansky, and Siegel a chance to advance their own agenda. Luciano had a narrow brush with death and earned his "Lucky" nickname when he survived a one-way ride in the middle of that war; also he outlived the "Mustache Petes" who kept the U.S. Mafia mired in Old World traditions. With allies of all nationalities, he first killed Masseria and then Maranzano, a clean sweep that left Luciano effectively installed as New York's "Boss of Bosses." At the same time he surrendered enough power to avert further bloodshed, chairing a series of underworld conventions that spread syndicated crime from coast to coast.

Despite that triumph Luciano's reign was short lived. In 1936 special prosecutor Thomas Dewey charged Luciano with WHITE SLAVERY and secured his conviction at a trial that some historians still regard as a frame-up. Luciano received a sentence of 30–50 years in prison, serving 10 before negotiations with the U.S. military secured his freedom. The key to opening Luciano's prison cell was OPERATION UNDERWORLD wherein Lucky and his mob allies collaborated with the federal government to facilitate a U.S. invasion of Sicily while suppressing Axis TERRORISM on the New York docks. In return for services rendered, Luciano was paroled and deported in 1946, but he soon resurfaced in CUBA, meeting with U.S. mob leaders to coordinate expansion in LAS VEGAS and on other fronts. HARRY ANSLINGER secured Luciano's expulsion from Cuba, but Luciano remained active in the Mafia and international narcotics traffic for the remainder of his life. A murder plot against Luciano failed in Italy when word leaked back to the United States that he was working on his memoirs, but Luciano survived until 1962 when a heart attack in Naples claimed his life.

LUMUMBA, Patrice (1925–1961)

A farmer's son, Patrice Lumumba was born at Katako Kombe in the Kasai Province of the Belgian Congo (now the Democratic Republic of Congo), on July 2, 1925. From age 18 to 33 he worked variously as a nurse's aide, a postal clerk, and a volunteer librarian while immersing himself in organized labor and politics. During the same years Lumumba served as secretary and then president of the Association for African Government Employees and as a member of the Comité de L'union Belgo-Congolaise. In October 1958 he founded the National Congolese Movement, and on June 23, 1960, Lumumba became the Congo's first African prime minister. Seven days later the region declared independence, but freedom hit a snag on July 31, 1960, when Katanga Province seceded under Col. Joseph-Desiré Mobutu. By mid-September Mobutu had neutralized his political opposition in Katanga and looked forward to ruling a larger empire.

Lumumba, meanwhile, pursued a policy of nonalignment with Western colonial powers and openness to aide from RUSSIA that would lead inevitably to his death. On October 10, 1960, nervous Congolese colleagues placed him under house arrest, guarded by officers of the UNITED NATIONS and the AFRICAN NATIONAL CONGRESS. Lumumba bridled at confinement, leaving his residence for Stanleyville on November 27. Five days later he was arrested there and delivered to Mobutu's troops in Leopoldville (now Kinshasa), transferred to a prison camp at Thysville on December 3, and moved from there to Katanga's main prison at Elizabethville on January 17, 1961. There, after an all-night torture session, Lumumba was murdered along with two colleagues named Mpolo and Okito. Mobutu subsequently overran the Congo and ruled it until May 1997 with a regime so corrupt that it drove a nation rich in natural resources to virtual bankruptcy.

Lumumba's assassination clearly was carried out by Mobutu, but conspiracists have long suspected white hands eagerly at work behind the scenes. One early suspect was the U.S. CENTRAL INTELLIGENCE AGENCY (CIA), which was deeply immersed throughout the 1950s and 1960s in similar "executive actions" from CUBA to VIETNAM. It is known that CIA agents worked closely with Belgian military officers and SECRET POLICE in the Congo to forestall the alleged advance of COMMUNISM in sub-Saharan Africa, and when the CHURCH COMMITTEE turned a spotlight on CIA crimes during 1975–76, a memo from former CIA Director Allen Dulles was revealed, reading:

In high quarters here, it is the clear-cut conclusion that if [Lumumba] continues to hold high office, the inevitable result will [have] disastrous consequences . . . for the interests of the free world generally. Consequently, we conclude that his removal must be an urgent and prime objective.

Did the agency arrange Lumumba's death, as it had sought to do with FIDEL CASTRO and so many others? Some modern scholars believe so, while others place the full weight of blame on Belgian officials who collaborated with Mobutu to effect Lumumba's liquidation. Today, we know that Belgian police commissioner Gerard Soete and his brother personally dismembered Lumumba's corpse with a hacksaw and dissolved it in sulfuric acid. Interviewed decades later on Belgian television, Soete proudly displayed two teeth and a bullet that he claimed to have salvaged from Lumumba's remains. CIA station chief Lawrence Devlin was briefed on the events, Belgian sources maintain, because the agency "had actively discussed this thing for weeks," but the guiding hands behind the crime apparently were not American.

See also DULLES BROTHERS.

LUSITANIA

On May 7, 1915, British Cunard Line's passenger steamer *Lusitania* was torpedoed and sunk by a German submarine in the North Atlantic. The nine-year-old "floating palace," considered "the acme of comfort" for transatlantic passengers, was initially rocked by an explosion "like a million-ton hammer hitting a steel boiler a hundred feet high and a hundred feet long." Moments later a second and more-powerful explosion ripped through the ship, and it sank within 20 minutes. Only 764 of the 1,965 persons on board were still alive when rescue boat's responded to the doomed liner's distress signal.

Such events were not uncommon in those months of World War I, but the *Lusitania* sinking was critical since the loss of American lives on board pushed the isolationist United States closer to war with GERMANY. Conspiracy theories flourished within days of the tragic event, and they thrive today, despite the passage of nearly nine decades. First, on May 1—the same day that the *Lusitania* sailed from New York—the German embassy published an unprecedented warning in newspapers across the United States. It read:

> *Travellers intending to embark on the Atlantic voyage are reminded that a state of war exists between Germany and her allies and Great Britain and her allies; that the zone of war includes the waters adjacent to the British Isles; that, in accordance with formal notice given by the Imperial German Government, vessels flying the flag of Great Britain, or of any of her allies, are liable to destruction in those waters and that travellers sailing in the war zone on ships of Great Britain or her allies do so at their own risk.*

Also on May 1 the British Admiralty knew that German submarines were en route to British waters, blocking the *Lusitania*'s path. A conference on May 5, chaired by First Lord of the Admiralty Winston Churchill, examined disposition of those submarines, including the same U-20 that later sank the *Lusitania*. Instead of warning the *Lusitania*'s captain, British leaders withdrew the escort ship *Juno* from harm's way and failed even to tell the *Lusitania* that she had been abandoned. Some documents related to that judgment call were finally released for public scrutiny in 1976, but many more remain classified as top secret to this day.

Another linchpin of *Lusitania* conspiracy theories is the second explosion that doomed the great ship, shortly after the German torpedo struck. Officially, the blast was caused by ocean water striking heated boilers in the engine room, but some researchers claim that the *Lusitania* was illegally carrying arms and ammunition to England in clear violation of U.S. neutrality laws. In addition to her passengers, the *Lusitania* was scheduled to transport a cargo of GOLD bullion, platinum, diamonds, and other precious stones, but no trace of that rich cargo was ever found, and shipping invoices reveal no evidence of treasure on board the liner. Instead, conspiracists allege, the ship was hauling a cargo of three-inch artillery shells and millions of rifle cartridges that were disguised as bales of fur and crates of cheese. If true, Churchill and company possessed a double motive for their secrecy surrounding the *Lusitania*'s fate, simultaneously concealing their violation of U.S. law and their callous sacrifice of some 1,200 lives in a bid to place U.S. troops in the trenches of Europe. Until such time as the last secret files are opened, no definitive solution to the *Lusitania* riddle is possible.

MADAGASCAR

Natives of INDONESIA inhabited this island off the east coast of Africa in about 700 B.C. and established a monarchy that ruled the land until troops from FRANCE arrived to "protect" Madagascar in 1885. The island became an autonomous republic within the French Community in 1958 and graduated to independence two years later. Philibert Tsiranana was elected president in 1959, but a military coup drove him from office in May 1973. In June 1975 leaders of the junta announced their intent to follow a socialist program, nationalizing banks, insurance companies, and most natural resources. The new regime was characterized by censorship and repression of dissent, climaxed by a suspicious election that confirmed dictator Didier Ratsiraka as president in 1989. Riots followed, resulting in formation of a multiparty system, but corruption endures, and the rigged presidential election of December 2001 produced so much protest that martial law was declared in February 2002. For the next five months Madagascar boasted two rival presidents and two capitals until Ratsiraka fled to France. Much of the population remains mired in superstition, highlighted in May 2003 when 42 defendants received life prison terms for looting 300-plus tombs and stealing human remains that they sold to practitioners of black magic.

MAFIA

Deliberate mystery surrounds the origin and operations of the crime syndicate known as the Mafia. No two sources agree on the term *Mafia*'s ethnic roots or definition, and estimated dates of the group's foundation range from the 13th to the 19th century. In any case the Mafia as recognized today is an ethnic crime syndicate composed of oath-bound members of Italian ancestry. (Membership was initially restricted to Sicilians but broadened in the 20th century to include mainland Italians.) The old-line Mafia, or "Honored Society," remains a potent force in Italy, where public murders of judges, prosecutors, and investigative journalists rival the crimes of COLOMBIA's militant COCAINE cartels. Sporadic prosecution has jailed various Mafia leaders throughout Italy, but successive pronouncements of the society's demise have all proved premature. Sicilian mobsters currently play a key role in global HEROIN traffic, serving as middlemen between the Chinese TRIADS, the French UNIONE CORSÉ, and various syndicates in the United States.

The U.S. Mafia is a hybrid organization, often dubbed *La Cosa Nostra* ("Our Thing"). The latter term was first publicized by informer Joseph Valachi in the early 1960s and then adopted by the FEDERAL BUREAU OF INVESTIGATION when J. EDGAR HOOVER could no longer defend his 40-year fable that the United States harbored no organized crime. In fact, the modern American crime syndicate is a product of

PROHIBITION when various ethnic gangs fought for control of bootleg turf and then merged in the interest of peace and mutual profit. Between 1929 and 1934 a series of "crime conventions" were held in major American cities, dividing the nation into territories ruled by local syndicates. In the process Mafia leader CHARLES "LUCKY" LUCIANO killed off his old-line competition (dubbed "Mustache Petes") and modernized the society's structure to permit collaboration with non-Italian criminals such as MEYER LANSKY and Benjamin "Bugsy" Siegel. The new mob's enforcement arm, dubbed MURDER INCORPORATED by the press, was organized to carry out assassinations on a national scale.

Federal prosecution of Mafia leaders has been more successful since J. Edgar Hoover died in early 1972, but as in Italy, periodic announcements of the syndicate's destruction always prove inaccurate. Presidents RICHARD NIXON and RONALD REAGAN both cultivated friendships with known syndicate members and leaders of mob-infiltrated unions, including the INTERNATIONAL BROTHERHOOD OF TEAMSTERS. Ongoing scandals of police and political corruption from California to Washington, D.C., and all points in between clearly demonstrate that organized crime is alive and healthy in the United States of America.

MALAWI

British explorer David Livingstone "discovered" the African region of modern-day Malawi in the 1850s, paving the way for Cecil Rhodes's British South Africa Company to "develop" the region in 1884. Conflict with Arab slavers during 1887–89 prompted Britain to annex the district, dubbed Nyasaland, in 1891. The slavers were soon annihilated, but British "protection" endured through the early 1950s when Nyasaland was merged with Northern and Southern Rhodesia to form a new federation. Black Africans protested the imperial move, and Nyasaland finally emerged as independent Malawi in July 1964. New prime minister Hastings Banda quickly established a policy of "one party, one leader, one government and no nonsense about it," ruthlessly suppressing all dissent. In 1971 Banda became president for life, a post he maintained despite sometimes violent opposition until May 1994 when Bakili Muluzi won the nation's first-ever free election. Despite an easing of repression and a landslide reelection victory in 1999, Muluzi's

regime has been tainted with corruption—including accusations that high-ranking officials illegally sold 160,000 tons of reserve maize in 2000, plunging the nation into famine two years later. In January 2003 residents of rural Malawi were panicked by rumors of vampires at large, using syringes to drain their victims of blood. Dressed like classic MEN IN BLACK, the prowlers spread such terror that mob violence erupted in Balantyre, where rioters stoned the governor and three priests for allegedly collaborating with the night-stalking fiends.

MALAYSIA

Modern Malaysia includes the Malay Peninsula of Southeast Asia plus the states of Sabah and Sarawak on the island of Borneo, for a combined land mass slightly larger than New Mexico. Humans first populated the region in about 2500 B.C.E., dwelling peacefully until the clash between Islam and Hinduism introduced religious warfare in the 15th century A.D. British and Dutch traders arrived in the early 19th century, establishing commerce so lucrative that British troops were sent to "protect" the region in the 1880s. Japanese invasion interrupted British rule during World War II, but colonial rule was reestablished via a "semiautonomous federation" in 1948. Native insurgents fought to expel the Brits, whereupon London declared a state of emergency that lasted until 1960. Malaysia finally won independence in September 1963, but turmoil continued in the form of race riots against wealthy Chinese and Indians. Vietnamese "boat people" arrived to exacerbate the problem in 1978, prompting imposition of stiff new restrictions on immigration. Financial crises and allegations of official corruption continue, as do rumors of widespread black magic—including animal (and human) sacrifice—throughout the rural countryside. Since the 1990s Malaysia has been a major center of high-seas piracy with attacks reported throughout the Indian Ocean and South China Sea.

MALI

Most of arid Mali is consumed by the Sahara. Crisscrossed by caravan routes since A.D. 300, the region was ruled by the Malinke Empire from the 12th to the 16th century. MOROCCO conquered the Timbuktu region in 1591 and ruled it for the next two centuries. French colonists seized control in the late 19th century and ruled French Sudan until June 1960 when formation of the independent Sudanese Republic was announced. After a brief, abortive merger with Senegal, the Republic of Mali emerged three months later. Mali's leaders created consternation on both sides of the cold war by accepting aid impartially from the United States, RUSSIA, and CHINA. In the late 1960s, President Modibo Keita launched a purge of his conservative opponents and dramatically expanded Chinese influence in Mali. A military junta ousted Keita in November 1968 and ruled Mali for the next two decades, waging a short border war with neighboring Burkina Faso in May 1985. Dictator Moussa Traoré was ousted in 1991, followed by Mali's first democratic election the following year.

MAO Zedong (1893–1976)

The communist ruler of CHINA from 1949 to 1976 was born in Hunan Province on December 26, 1893. Mao served in Hunan's provincial army during the 1911 revolution and then went on to graduate from Hunan Normal School as a certified high-school teacher in 1918. Quickly immersed in revolutionary politics, Mao attended the first congress of the Chinese Communist Party in 1921 and was elected to the party's central committee two years later. An abortive Red alliance with nationalist Kuomintang (KMT) leader CHIANG KAI-SHEK (Jiang Jieshi) collapsed in 1927 when Chiang and his TRIAD supporters launched a nationwide reign of "white terror" against communists. Mao found refuge with guerrillas in the Jinggang Mountains of southeastern China where he served as chairman of a fledgling Chinese Soviet Republic during 1931–34. KMT forces killed Mao's first wife in their effort to eradicate the Red bastion and thereby propelled Mao's troops into a 12-month "long march" from Jiangxi to Shaanxi in northwestern China. From his new stronghold Mao led Communist resistance against Japanese invaders from 1937 to 1945 while most Allied support went to Chiang's corrupt KMT regime. War's end brought no peace to embattled China, and Chiang's forces were driven off-shore to TAIWAN in 1949.

For the next 27 years, Mao ruled Red China in the style of Soviet dictator JOSEPH STALIN, ruthlessly suppressing dissent in all forms while driving neofeudal China headlong into the 20th century. Mao's "Great Leap Forward," a campaign to collectivize agriculture and promote small-scale rural industry, was sabotaged in part by withdrawal of support from RUSSIA, coupled with unprecedented droughts that starved millions of Chinese peasants to death by 1960. Red leaders Liu Shaoqi and Deng Xiaoping then tried to strip Mao of his powers while leaving him in office as a figurehead, but Mao struck back with a new "Cultural Revolution," handing power to young and fanatical Red Guards who established kangaroo tribunals and executed thousands of political heretics. Mao announced the end of the Cultural Revolution in 1969, but China's official state history marks the brutal campaign's end at Mao's death from Parkinson's disease on September 9, 1976. More upheaval ensued as rivals sought to fill the power vacuum left by Mao's passing, and while many of his draconian methods are today repudiated in China, Mao himself is widely revered as a quasi-godlike figure, verging on the mythical. For millions of Chinese, Mao remains a hero known as the "Four Greats"—Great Teacher, Great Leader, Great Supreme Commander, and Great Helmsman.

See also COMMUNISM.

MARCELLO, Carlos (1910–1993)

A native of Tunis, born Calogero Minacore on February 6, 1910, teenager Carlos Marcello emigrated to the United States and logged his first arrest (for bank robbery) in New Orleans in 1929. That charge was dropped, but 1930 saw him sentenced to nine years in prison for assault and robbery. Released in 1935 he was jailed again for peddling narcotics three years later. Despite his record, Marcello served only 10 months on that charge and emerged from prison to forge a lucrative partnership with New York MAFIA boss Frank Costello. Together, operating in conjunction with MEYER LANSKY, Marcello and Costello monopolized illegal gambling in Louisiana. By the end of World War II Marcello was the undisputed crime boss of New Orleans, wielding influence throughout the Gulf States.

In March 1959 Marcello appeared before a U.S. Senate committee investigating organized crime. One member of the panel was Senator John Kennedy, whose brother Robert served as the committee's counsel. Two years later, with JFK in the White House and Robert Kennedy serving as attorney general, Marcello found himself on a government hit list of mobsters marked for prison or deportation.

Lacking evidence for trial, in April 1961 the Kennedys had Marcello arrested and forcibly deported to Guatemala (falsely listed as his birthplace on official documents). Marcello soon returned to the United States, seething with hatred for the Kennedys, frequently discussing his plans to murder the president. FEDERAL BUREAU OF INVESTIGATION informant Edward Becker advised federal agents that Marcello "clearly stated that he was going to arrange to have President Kennedy murdered in some way." Another informant reported that Marcello planned to take out "insurance" on the contract by "setting up a nut to take the blame." Shortly before the JFK ASSASSINATION of November 22, 1963, Dallas mobster JACK RUBY telephoned Marcello and Florida mobster SANTOS TRAFFICANTE, ostensibly to discuss union business. Days later Ruby shot and killed alleged assassin LEE HARVEY OSWALD in the Dallas police station, allegedly acting from grief and sympathy for the president's widow.

G-men conducted a perfunctory investigation of Marcello after the assassination, informing the WARREN COMMISSION that they "did not believe Carlos Marcello was a significant organized crime figure." Rather, agents claimed, Marcello earned his living "as a tomato salesman and real estate investor." The commission, accordingly, reported no criminal link between Ruby and Marcello. Three years after Dallas, Marcello was jailed for assault in New York City. A protracted legal fight ended with conviction and a two-year prison sentence, but he served a mere two months and was released in March 1971. The HOUSE SELECT COMMITTEE ON ASSASSINATIONS found no proof of Marcello's involvement in the JFK assassination, but committee counsel G. Robert Blakey later named him as a prime suspect in Blakey's book, *The Plot to Kill the President* (1981). A *New York Post* report echoed that charge in January 1992, naming Santos Trafficante and union boss James Hoffa as coconspirators. Marcello died a free man on March 3, 1993.

See also KENNEDY DYNASTY.

MARCOS, Ferdinand (1917–1989)

The wealthy son of a Filipino politician, born September 11, 1917, Ferdinand Marcos won renown as a public speaker at the University of the PHILIPPINES, where he also distinguished himself on the school's shooting team. His marksmanship became an issue in the 1930s when he was tried and acquitted on charges of murdering one of his father's political rivals. Marcos fought Japanese invaders during World War II, but political biographies hailing his wartime heroism were revealed as gross exaggerations verging on hagiography. Marcos served as an aide to Manuel Roxas, first president of the postwar independent Philippines, and then went on to serve in the House of Representatives (1949–59) and the Senate (1959–65). A suspicious landslide victory installed Marcos as president of the Philippines in 1965, a post he used (with wife Imelda) to suppress dissent and to loot his nation's treasure during the next two decades. A series of terrorist bombings in 1972 prompted Marcos to declare martial law, and he assumed dictatorial powers the following year. Widespread corruption, nepotism, and bureaucratic ineptitude were hallmarks of the Marcos regime—none of which prevented U.S. President RONALD REAGAN from hailing Marcos as a shining example for anticommunist leaders worldwide. The public assassination of rival candidate BENIGNO AQUINO sparked a groundswell of opposition that finally drove Marcos and his wife into exile in February 1986. The fugitives settled in Hawaii, while both were indicted for embezzlement by U.S. authorities. Marcos died from kidney failure, prior to trial, on September 28, 1989. Imelda Marcos was acquitted of all charges in Hawaii during 1990, but a Filipino jury convicted her of bribery in 1993.

See also COMMUNISM; TERRORISM.

MARIJUANA

Used for many purposes throughout recorded history, marijuana (*Cannabis*) was initially cultivated in CHINA for its edible seeds (6000 B.C.E.), then for hemp fibers used in clothing (4000 B.C.E.), and finally as a form of medicine (2727 B.C.E.). In colonial America hemp was deemed so useful that Virginia's House of Burgesses passed legislation in 1762 penalizing farmers who refused to plant marijuana. Future president GEORGE WASHINGTON was an early hemp farmer, but invention of the cotton gin in 1793 ultimately lowered cotton prices to the point that hemp was doomed as America's fiber of choice. Far from vanishing, however, marijuana was soon recognized for medicinal uses, employed by 1840 as a recognized treatment for pain, gout, loss of appetite, migraines, hysteria, depression, and a host of other maladies.

It was marijuana's recreational usage, however, that alarmed religious fundamentalists and the legislators who craved their votes. El Paso, Texas, passed the first law banning sale or possession of marijuana in 1914, followed by California (1915), Texas (1919), Louisiana (1924), New York (1927), and Great Britain (1928). Still, marijuana did not achieve designation as a full-blown "menace" until 1930 when antidrug crusader HARRY ANSLINGER rose to command the Federal Bureau of Narcotics. Anslinger launched a national propaganda campaign denouncing *Cannabis* as a "murder weed" that drove users to frenzied outbursts of homicidal violence. Despite a paucity of evidence, yellow journalists scrambled aboard the bandwagon and joined a groundswell that produced the federal Marijuana Tax Act of 1937. Subsequent legislation, passed in 1951 and 1956, increased penalties to the present level: two years to life in prison and a $20,000 fine.

Public opinion on marijuana remains deeply divided, but most physicians recognize its value in treating glaucoma and the side effects of chemotherapy. In 1972 the Shafer Commission recommended that *Cannabis* should be legalized as a prescription drug, but the suggestion was ignored. In 2001 Attorney General JOHN ASHCROFT took time away from his "War on TERRORISM" to arrest California physicians and their patients who employed marijuana under state legislation permitting medicinal use. Cultivation of illicit marijuana and smuggling of shipments from MEXICO or other countries meanwhile remains a lucrative trade in the United States.

MAURITANIA

MALI's largest western neighbor was "discovered" by PORTUGAL in the 15th century, but FRANCE seized control 300 years later and established the thriving colony of French West Africa. Mauritania won independence in November 1960 and entered the UNITED NATIONS in 1961 over strenuous objections from MOROCCO which claimed the territory as its own. Inevitable ethnic bloodshed followed until Mauritania and Morocco divided the Spanish Sahara region (now Western Sahara) between them in 1975. Indigenous Saharawi rebels, organized as the Polisario Front, instantly declared war on both countries, inflicting sufficient damage to topple the

Mauritanian government of Ould Daddah in 1978. Mauritania withdrew from Western Sahara the following year, but ethnic clashes continued at home. Torn between the dominant Moorish–Arab north and largely black south, Mauritania launched a border war against SENEGAL in 1989. At home, despite legal abolition of slavery in 1980, the practice still thrives among wealthy Arabs who prey on black Mauritanians. By 1993 the U.S. State Department estimated that there were some 90,000 slaves in the country. Nine years later a violent movement demanding greater freedom for blacks in Mauritania was officially suppressed, and its political party—Action for Change—was formally banned.

McCARRAN Act

Passed by Congress over President Harry Truman's veto on September 23, 1950, the Internal Security Act is more commonly known by the name of its primary sponsor, longtime Nevada Senator Patrick McCarran. A product of the Red Scare that followed World War II, the McCarran Act authorized deportation of alien radicals; barred Communist Party members from holding passports or working in defense industries; required communist or communist-front groups to register as "foreign agents" with a newly created SUBVERSIVE ACTIVITIES CONTROL BOARD; required the publications of said groups to be labeled as Communist propaganda; and authorized detention of "dangerous radicals" during national emergencies declared by the president. Such legislation provided an illusion of security by focusing national attention on outspoken leftist groups while ignoring the threat of covert espionage agents. FEDERAL BUREAU OF INVESTIGATION Director J. EDGAR HOOVER enthusiastically supported Senator McCarran not only in his Red-hunting pursuits but in his public denials that the MAFIA existed in the United States.

See also COMMUNISM.

McCARTHY, Joseph (1908–1957)

Wisconsin native Joseph Raymond McCarthy joined the U.S. Marine Corps in 1942 and served in the Pacific theater. An airman who never saw combat, McCarthy later billed himself as "Tail-Gunner Joe," and an accidental injury became a "war wound." Those heroic trappings failed to place McCarthy in the U.S. Senate on his first attempt in 1944, but he was more successful two years later, supported by Wisconsin's Communist Party.

In Washington McCarthy befriended J. EDGAR HOOVER, frequently dining with the FEDERAL BUREAU OF INVESTIGATION (FBI) director and joining Hoover on "inspection tours" of race tracks. In February 1950, after a series of reckless speeches claiming that the State Department was riddled with Communist spies, McCarthy sought help from Hoover to support his fabricated charges. Hoover agreed, ordering his staff to "review the files and get anything you can for him."

McCarthy's habitual lies and exaggerations rendered support for his charges impossible. Assistant FBI Director WILLIAM SULLIVAN recalled, "We didn't have enough evidence to show there was a single Communist in the State Department, let alone 57 cases"—or 205, as McCarthy later claimed. Still, G-men searched for evidence to help McCarthy while Hoover's ghost writers drafted his speeches. Hoover biographer Curt Gentry observes: "'McCarthyism' was, from start to finish, the creation of one man, FBI Director J. Edgar Hoover." Hoover's clandestine support reaped benefits for the bureau including more money, more agents, and broader authority under new laws enacted to curb the "Red menace."

McCarthy launched his last televised hearings in March 1954 with disastrous results for himself. On December 2, 1954, the Senate voted to censure McCarthy for "contemptuous conduct" and abuse of privilege. Though still a senator, he was a broken man thereafter. McCarthy's bid to nominate Hoover for president in 1956 failed to renew his former close ties with the FBI. McCarthy died of an alcohol-related liver ailment on May 2, 1957.

See also COMMUNISM.

MEMPHIS Police Department

Memphis, Tennessee, is often hailed as "liberal" southern city, but its police department has never shared that image. A year after the Civil War, between April 30 and May 2, 1866, Memphis police officers led a bloody race riot that left 46 blacks and two white "radicals" dead, with 90 black-owned homes, four churches, and two schools burned to the ground. Many Memphis officers went on to join the KU KLUX KLAN both during RECONSTRUCTION and the 1920s when Memphis was branded the U.S. "murder

capital;" it boasted a homicide rate in excess of 50 per 100,000 population. Despite their facade of morality, Klan cops were strangely unable to prevent widespread PROHIBITION violations in that era or to shut down the city's wide-open red-light district.

A generation later local police were still more concerned about civil rights protests than organized crime. The department's Domestic Intelligence Unit (DIU) mounted surveillance on groups ranging from the "fairly militant" NAACP and Dr. MARTIN LUTHER KING, JR.'s, Southern Leadership Conference to the BLACK PANTHER PARTY. In 1968 when Dr. King arrived in Memphis to lead protests for the local sanitation workers' union, Memphis P.D. was run by Chief Frank Holloman, a 25-year veteran of the FEDERAL BUREAU OF INVESTIGATION (FBI) who spent his last eight years with the bureau in charge of J. EDGAR HOOVER's private office. Holloman mounted round-the-clock surveillance on King in Memphis and then withdrew it on April 4, 1968, shortly before a sniper murdered King in full view of a recently dismantled lookout post. Diverted by CB radio "hoaxes" and other false leads, Holloman's officers somehow permitted the assassin to escape.

Even then, illegal surveillance of Memphis citizens and visitors continued until 1976 when the American Civil Liberties Union sought access to DIU files. With the case still pending in court Mayor Wyeth Chandler ordered the files destroyed, and some 180 boxes of documents were burned on September 10. Unfortunately for the cover-up, police depositions revealed much of DIU's illicit activity, and another stash of documents was found in the basement of an abandoned police station. In September 1978 Memphis police agreed to dismantle their "Red Squad" and accepted an injunction barring surveillance of legitimate groups.

That settlement brought no end of scandal to Memphis, however. Four high-ranking officers were fired in July 2000 on charges stemming from a joint state and federal probe of alleged police corruption. Three years later in October 2003 federal indictments charged 16 defendants with stealing confiscated money, drugs, and weapons from the police department's "secure" property room. Those arrested included Kenneth Dansberry, a 21-year department veteran serving as shift supervisor in the property room, and senior inventory control clerk Edward Johnson. FBI agents also seized the home and vehicles of a civilian suspect, Eric Brown, who was allegedly involved in sale of contraband pilfered from the police department. "Audit problems" at headquarters reportedly dated from 1999, but the investigation needed four years to produce results. On December 18, 2003, two more indictments were issued, charging police supervisors Alnita Campbell and Jacqueline Layrock with accepting some $148,000 in bribes to conceal the ongoing thefts.

The department suffered yet another black eye in September 2003 when Governor Phil Bredesen granted a surprise stay of execution for convicted cop killer Philip Workman. Workman had robbed a fast-food restaurant in 1983, fleeing as police arrived. Shots were exchanged, killing Lt. Ronald Oliver and wounding a second officer. At trial two police officers and alleged witness Harold Davis claimed that they saw Workman shoot Oliver. Shelby County Medical Examiner O.C. Smith helped the prosecution with a claim that he had matched the fatal bullet to Workman's pistol. Davis recanted his testimony in 2001, admitting that he lied in pursuit of cash rewards and that police coached him to produce his sworn statement and then illegally concealed him from defense attorneys prior to trial. Investigation of those claims revealed "new" X-ray evidence that had been hidden by O.C. Smith for nearly two decades and that cast serious doubt on his trial testimony. Workman's appeal is ongoing, defense lawyers claiming that Lieutenant Oliver was killed by police "friendly fire" and that his fellow officers conspired to hide that fact by sending Workman to his death.

MENGELE, Josef (1911–1979)

The THIRD REICH's "Angel of Death," Josef ("Beppo") Mengele, was born on March 16, 1911. He studied philosophy in Munich and obtained his Ph.D. in 1935 with a dissertation on human racial differences. From there, Mengele went on to study medicine at Frankfurt University, progressing to a post with the school's Department of Hereditary Biology and Racial Hygiene. Mengele secured his second doctorate in 1938 with a dissertation on "clan examinations at lip-jaw-palate-cleft." By that time he was also a member in good standing of ADOLF HITLER's Nazi Party. He joined the "elite" SS in 1938 and served in various units until 1942 when he was wounded in RUSSIA. Pronounced unfit for combat, Mengele volunteered to serve as chief medical officer at the Auschwitz death camp in POLAND. There, he

earned his infamous nickname for a series of sadistic experiments involving twins. He also greeted trains filled with newly arrived inmates and personally selected those marked for execution in the camp's gas chambers.

Mengele was captured in 1945 and held briefly as a prisoner of war; then he was released by careless Allies who failed to recognize him. He remained in Germany for the next four years and then escaped to ARGENTINA with help from the ODESSA network and sympathetic leaders of the CATHOLIC CHURCH. Despite long-running investigations and several failed attempts to capture him for trial on WAR CRIMES charges, Mengele eluded his hunters, protected by various pro-Nazi politicians in Argentina, BRAZIL, and PARAGUAY. He reportedly drowned while swimming on February 7, 1979, but his identity was not confirmed by DNA tests until 1992. While still alive in semipublic exile, Mengele bridged the gap from fugitive to literary villain with fictional starring roles in the films *Marathon Man* (1976) and *The Boys from Brazil* (1978).

MEN in Black

On June 21, 1947—three days before pilot Kenneth Arnold saw a group of UFOS soaring past Mount Rainier, Washington, and coined the term *flying saucers*—harbor patrolman Harold Dahl experienced a similar sighting at nearby Maury Island. Dahl and his son saw six metallic, circular objects 100 feet in diameter, flying over Puget Sound. One of the UFOs wobbled in midair and disgorged a chunk of hot debris that fell to Earth, injuring Dahl's son and killing his dog. The next morning a man dressed in a black suit visited Dahl's home and drove the witness to a local café for breakfast. The stranger described Dahl's experience in graphic detail, as if he had been there himself, and remarked that the accident "should not have happened," adding cryptically: "I know a great deal more about this experience of yours than you will ever want to believe." In parting, the man warned Dahl to keep silent about the event, implying a threat to Dahl and his family if secrecy was not maintained.

During the past half-century, UFO witnesses throughout the United States and around the world have reported similar encounters with menacing black-clad strangers, enshrined today in urban folklore as the Men in Black (MIB). Hollywood cashed in on the stories with a pair of blockbuster science-fiction films in 1997 and 2002, but the reality of MIB visits is far from the comedic experience portrayed by actors Will Smith and Tommy Lee Jones. The several hundred witnesses who have described such interviews by cryptic, vaguely Asian-looking visitors unanimously describe their interrogators as hostile and menacing, threatening injury or worse to those who will not recant UFO sightings.

Is there a secret agency committed to suppressing news of close encounters with UFOs and their occupants? If so, the group is not confined to the United States, for MIB sightings are also on file from various other countries, including BULGARIA, CHINA, England, FRANCE, IRELAND, ITALY, MEXICO, and RUSSIA. Likewise, MIB harassment is not strictly limited to UFO witnesses. In 1966 an MIB who called himself "Jack Brown" visited residents of Point Pleasant, West Virginia, who had reported sightings of a large winged creature nicknamed "Mothman." Two years later in Scotland three MIB grilled researcher Alistair Baxter about his investigation of the Loch Ness Monster. Reports of MIB activity continue to the present day, but no official agency on Earth admits responsibility for any of the incidents.

MEXICAN Mafia

California's first known PRISON GANG, the Mexican Mafia (or "Eme") was organized in 1956–57 by Hispanic inmates from East Los Angeles who were confined at Duel Vocational Institute. Initially the group was formed for self-defense against rival inmates and a racist prison staff. Members of the Mexican Mafia traditionally come from southern California, while Hispanic inmates in northern California align themselves with a hostile gang called NUESTRA FAMILIA ("our family"). The gangs are bitter rivals to this day, with scores of murders linked to their long-running feud. On the side, both alternately fight and collaborate with white and black gangs, including the powerful ARYAN BROTHERHOOD and the BLACK GUERRILLA FAMILY. Warring Hispanic gangs also pioneered the use of "colors" with Eme members wearing red bandanas and Nuestra Familia soldiers sporting blue long before those colors were adopted by the CRIPS AND BLOODS.

From cell-block skirmishes the Mexican Mafia soon expanded into contraband smuggling in prison and from there to criminal operations on the outside. Supported by comrades in the "free world" and corrupt prison guards who clear their shipments for a price, Eme smugglers provide a variety of goods and services to customers behind bars. Drugs are their basic stock in trade, along with alcohol and weapons. Extortion remains a popular racket with all prison gangs, and contract murders may be carried out on either side of prison walls for a price. California gang watchers report that Mexican Mafia members commonly boast tattoos reading "Eme," "Aztlan," "Mexikanemi," "Sur" (South), "Sureño" ("Southerner"), the initials "MM," and the number "13." The gang's symbol is an eagle perched atop a war shield with crossed machetes. A splinter group in Arizona prisons, dubbed the New Mexican Mafia, is considered hostile to the parent clique.

In May 1997 a federal jury in Los Angeles convicted 12 Eme members of running a drug-and-crime ring from prison. Specific charges in the 29-count indictment included five murders, various attempted murders, racketeering, drug trafficking, extortion, and conspiracy. All 12 faced terms of life imprisonment on conviction in that case. Evidence produced at the six-month trial suggested that the Mexican Mafia had 400 identified members who took their orders from inmates confined in maximum security at Pelican Bay. The original charges named 22 defendants, a number that was whittled to 13 after one defendant was killed, seven more pleaded guilty on reduced charges, and one was dropped from the list to face state felony charges in Orange County. A single defendant among the remaining 13 was acquitted at trial. Despite their victory in court, prosecutors warn that the gang remains active and dangerous.

MEXICO

Mexico's original rulers—the Mayas, the Olmecs, the Toltecs, and the Aztecs—were slave-trading warlords who practiced human sacrifice and ritual cannibalism on a wholesale basis. Spanish conquistadors arrived to "civilize" the country at sword point in 1519–21, looting and enslaving Mexico's former elite and peasants alike. "Native" Mexicans revolted against Spanish rule in 1810 and won independence of a sort in 1821. During the next 56 years, Mexico endured two emperors (one of them French) and several home-grown dictators who changed governments every nine months on average. In the process, roughly half of the country's total area was stolen by the United States during the imperial war of 1846–48.

Modern times have been no more peaceful for Mexico. Dictator Porfirio Diaz (1877–80 and 1884–1911) practiced brutal repression, but his ouster brought no peace. Repeated incursions by U.S. troops and a civil war in 1920 failed to bring significant reform. Mexican students rebelled against the country's increasing militarization in the 1960s, resulting in the October 1968 massacre of 300-plus dissidents in Mexico City. (Authorities claimed self-defense but finally admitted—in 2003—that the slaughter had been a calculated act of repression.) Today, pervasive political corruption and a thriving drug trade undermine any claims of progress below the Rio Grande. Federal drug-enforcement agents have participated in assassination of reform presidential candidates and even in a border-hopping cult that practiced human sacrifice around Matamoros in 1985–89. Mexican drug cartels reap an estimated $50 billion yearly from sales in the United States, with 40 percent of all U.S. HEROIN supplies, 70 percent of all South American COCAINE, and 80 percent of the U.S. MARIJUANA inventory flowing through Mexico. While some 20,000 Mexican soldiers are committed full-time to eradicating drugs, the traffic flourishes, and Mexico's first appointed "drug czar"—Gen. Jesús Gutiérrez Rebollo—was fired in 1996, after barely 10 weeks in office, for accepting bribes from Mexico's largest narcotics cartel.

MIAs

When President RICHARD NIXON withdrew U.S. combat troops from VIETNAM in 1972, an uncertain number were left behind, rated either as missing in action (MIA) or as prisoners of war (POW). In 1973, before the WATERGATE scandal drove him from office in disgrace, Nixon assured the U.S. public that all living POWs in Southeast Asia had been safely released. Nonetheless, an additional 717 MIAs were repatriated after 1973, including the remains of 40 deceased servicemen. It was not until 1979 that Vietnamese authorities released U.S. Marine Corps Private Bobby Garwood, who was captured at China Beach in 1965. Garwood maintained that other POWs still survived in custody, but the Pentagon swiftly branded him a traitor, thus discrediting his testimony.

Whatever the truth of Garwood's report, it remains an article of faith with many U.S. citizens that captive service members remain in communist prisons today, secretly suffering while Washington ignores their plight. Officially, the Pentagon lists 1,866 identified MIAs in Indochina as of February 29, 2004—including 620 U.S. Air Force personnel, 591 U.S. Army, 382 U.S. Navy, 239 U.S. Marine Corps, and 35 civilians—but all are presumed to be dead. Between 1973 and 2003, military investigators received 1,952 firsthand sightings of live POWs, with another 5,090 hearsay reports. Of the firsthand accounts, 1,909 are officially "resolved," including 532 dismissed as fabrications and 1,377 allegedly correlated with sightings of known (and recovered) MIAs. No further investigation is planned for the remaining 43 "live sighting" reports logged since 1973.

Official explanations notwithstanding, a body of anecdotal evidence apparently supports the notion of POWs languishing in prison camps scattered across Vietnam, CAMBODIA, and LAOS. Jerry Mooney, an employee of the NATIONAL SECURITY AGENCY who through 1976 tracked POW reports from Indochina, claimed knowledge of some 300 surviving prisoners. In 1986 the *Wall Street Journal* reported that Vietnamese officials had offered to exchange 57 live POWs for $4 million in U.S. foreign aid, but President RONALD REAGAN rebuffed the offer as a form of extortion. (That excuse was especially ironic in light of the OCTOBER SURPRISE ransom deal with IRAN, which helped secure Reagan's election in 1980.) Four years later, in 1990, Truong Chinh—former head of the Vietnamese SECRET POLICE—allegedly told author William Stevenson, "We had thousands of Americans after the release of 1973. Until 1985, I knew about groups of Americans in several locations. It is possible we shall embarrass the American government someday by sending some back."

While Hollywood produced several action films depicting rescue of American MIAs from Southeast Asia—*Uncommon Valor* (1983), *Missing in Action* (1984), *Missing in Action 2* (1985), and *Rambo: First Blood II* (1985)—attempts to find MIAs in real life have proved disappointing. Texas billionaire H. Ross Perot launched the first such expedition in 1973, with additional funding from actors John

Wayne and Clint Eastwood, but his mercenaries came back empty-handed. Perot tried again in 1983, this time with former Green Beret Bo Gritz in charge, but the count of rescued prisoners remained at zero. The Reagan administration confused matters further by denying that any POWs survived in Asia; he then warned private searchers that their efforts "could jeopardize the lives of prisoners still living there." A confrontation with President George H. W. Bush ultimately launched Perot's own abortive race for the White House, with recovery of MIAs a major goal of his candidacy. In their last meeting Perot allegedly told Bush, "I go looking for prisoners, but I spend all my time discovering that the [U.S.] government has been moving drugs around the world and is involved in illegal arms deals. I can't get at the prisoners because of the corruption among our own covert people."

See also BUSH DYNASTY; COMMUNISM.

MI5

Britain's equivalent of the FEDERAL BUREAU OF INVESTIGATION is the Security Service, more commonly known as MI5 (for Military Intelligence). Created in the wake of World War I MI5 is primarily responsible for internal security, while sister agency MI6 handles foreign intelligence matters. Both agencies spun off from the now-defunct Secret Service Bureau, founded in 1909. Collaborating with the Special Branch of London's Metropolitan Police, MI5 soon found itself embroiled in conflict with the IRISH REPUBLICAN ARMY. Its reputation suffered when IRA members penetrated MI5, identified its agents in IRELAND, and killed nearly all of them in a bloody purge of informers. MI5 was more successful at detecting Axis agents during World War II, but emphasis soon shifted to RUSSIA and opposition to COMMUNISM as MI5 acquired responsibility for security operations throughout the dwindling British Empire. For all its wartime success against GERMANY, however, MI5 suffered further setbacks during the long cold war, highlighted by the 1963 revelation that Soviet double-agent ADRIAN "KIM" PHILBY had penetrated the group's highest levels. An official pretense that MI5 does not exist was finally abandoned in the 1990s, and the agency has openly recruited via newspaper advertisements since 1997, but many questions remain concerning its cloak-and-dagger activities, both at home and abroad.

MI6

MI6, also known as the Secret Intelligence Service (SIS), is Britain's equivalent of the U.S. CENTRAL INTELLIGENCE AGENCY, tasked with maintaining external security and collecting intelligence from other nations. It may collaborate with domestic security agents from sister service MI5, but theoretically the operatives of MI6 perform no cloak-and-dagger missions on British soil. Represented in fiction by Ian Fleming's heroic James Bond, Agent 007, the men and women of MI6 generally deal with less dramatic and earth-shaking matters, but they are indeed occasionally licensed to kill.

MI6 began life in 1909 as the Secret Service Bureau. Its first director was Sir Mansfield Smith-Cumming, whose final initial ("C," not "M" as in the Bond novels) became the coded designation for himself and his successors in command. Mixed success against GERMANY in World War I led to reorganization as MI6 in 1921, while domestic security chores were handed off to MI5. "Passport control officers" assigned to each British embassy worldwide served as the eyes and ears of MI6, coordinating espionage against friends and enemies alike. After World War II, the agency's primary focus was RUSSIA and the long cold-war campaign to block global advancement of COMMUNISM. Still, for all its best efforts, MI6 could not prevent the British Empire from being whittled down, with major losses in INDIA, KENYA, Palestine, and MALAYSIA. Since 1994, MI6/SIS activities have been subject to oversight by Parliament's Intelligence and Security Committee, but critics maintain that (as in the United States) much illegal activity has been concealed from or tacitly encouraged by Her Majesty's government. The most serious accusation in recent years involves the charge that MI6 agents may have murdered DIANA, PRINCESS OF WALES on orders from the royal family.

MILITARY-INDUSTRIAL complex

On January 17, 1961, in his farewell address to the U.S. voters who twice elected him president, Dwight Eisenhower sounded a prophetic warning for the future and coined a term still popular among conspiracists. While noting that "Our arms must be mighty, ready for instant action, so that no potential aggressor may be tempted to risk his own destruction," Eisenhower also sounded a cautionary note:

This conjunction of an immense military establishment and a large arms industry is new in the American experience. The total influence—economic, political, even spiritual—is felt in every city, every State house, every office of the Federal government. We recognize the imperative need for this development. Yet we must not fail to comprehend its grave implications. Our toil, resources and livelihood are all involved; so is the very structure of our society.

In the councils of government, we must guard against the acquisition of unwarranted influence, whether sought or unsought, by the military–industrial complex. The potential for the disastrous rise of misplaced power exists and will persist.

Many researchers believe that Eisenhower's warning was too little and too late. They point to huge corporations such as GENERAL ELECTRIC and

President Dwight Eisenhower sounded a warning against the vast "military-industrial complex" in 1961. (Library of Congress)

LOCKHEED MARTIN, repeatedly convicted of defrauding the U.S. government, yet still favored with multibillion-dollar defense contracts, while others (such as the UNITED FRUIT COMPANY and IT&T) have covertly influenced foreign policy to the point of toppling "Third World" governments. America's long nightmare in VIETNAM is seen by some historians as a cynical exercise in war profiteering, and a case can be made that OPERATION IRAQI FREEDOM was in fact a war for OIL, launched by President George W. Bush on behalf of billionaire supporters in the petroleum industry.

See also BUSH DYNASTY.

MILITIAS

In normal terms a militia is any body of citizens enrolled for military service, summoned periodically for drills and training, but who serve full-time only in emergencies. Among the 50 U.S. states, that function is fulfilled by National Guard units, typically mobilized during riots or natural disasters, sometimes federalized as reinforcements for regular U.S. troops as in the VIETNAM War and OPERATION IRAQI FREEDOM. In the 1990s, however, a different breed of "patriot militias" came to prominence in America, driven by antigovernment feelings and sporadically engaged in covert warfare against the very regime that legitimate militiamen are pledged to defend.

The 1960s MINUTEMEN provided a foretaste of far-right militia activity but then collapsed after its leaders were jailed for conspiracy to rob banks and bomb police stations. The FEDERAL BUREAU OF INVESTIGATION (FBI) briefly created its own terrorist militia in 1970, but exposure of the SECRET ARMY ORGANIZATION's federal ties brought no end of embarrassment to Washington. Another quarter-century elapsed before the next outbreak, in 1994, of paramilitary patriotism. Fueled by anger at the loss of life in federal sieges at Ruby Ridge, Idaho, and Waco, Texas, and spiked with paranoia over rumors of a NEW WORLD ORDER, crackpot "patriots" and white supremacists joined ranks from coast to coast, forming "citizen's militias" in various states. The first recognized group was John Trochmann's Militia of Montana, officially inaugurated on January 1, 1994, but the Michigan Militia soon outstripped its competition with an estimated 6,000 members.

At their peak in 1996, 858 "patriot" groups were active throughout the United States, declining to 171

(45 of them overt militias) in 2003. That decline was due in equal parts to false predictions of disaster (ranging from foreign invasions to Y2Kaos) and to prosecution of militia members for various acts of TERRORISM. Militia plots and crimes during the peak of "patriot" activity included the following:

April 19, 1995: The OKLAHOMA CITY BOMBING claimed at least 168 lives. Militia associates Timothy McVeigh and Terry Nichols were convicted for that crime.

September 12, 1995: "Patriot" Charles Polk was indicted for plotting to bomb the INTERNAL REVENUE SERVICE building in Austin, Texas. He received a 21-year prison term in 1996.

November 9, 1995: Oklahoma Constitutional Militia leader Willie Lampley, his wife, and a third defendant were charged with plotting to bomb various targets, including abortion clinics, gay bars, welfare offices, and the Southern Poverty Law Center. The defendants, with a fourth arrested later, were sentenced to prison in 1996.

April 26, 1996: Two leaders of the Militia-at-Large of the Republic of Georgia [*sic*] were jailed for manufacturing bombs. By year's end both were serving eight-year prison terms.

July 1, 1996: Twelve members of Arizona's Viper Team militia were charged with plotting to bomb government offices in Phoenix. At trial 10 defendants pleaded guilty, one was convicted, and the twelfth was acquitted. Sentences ranging up to nine years were imposed.

July 29, 1996: Washington State Militia leader John Pitner and seven followers were arrested for making pipe bombs. Pitner and four others were convicted on weapons charges and sentenced to prison, while charges against the remaining defendants ended with a mistrial.

October 11, 1996: Seven members of the Mountaineer Militia were jailed for plotting to bomb the FBI's national fingerprint center in West Virginia. Four were convicted at trial, with leader Floyd Looker receiving an 18-year prison term.

March 26, 1997: Michigan militia activist Brendon Blasz was charged with plotting to bomb an IRS office, a television station, and federal armories. Blasz plea-bargained for a three-year sentence by renouncing the militia movement and providing evidence against his comrades.

April 27, 1997: An explosion near Yuba City, California, landed seven militia activists in jail on various charges. Leader William Robert—previously convicted of rape, burglary, and assault—received a sentence of 25 years to life.

July 4, 1997: Two militiamen were captured near Fort Hood, Texas, one hour before they planned to invade the army base and kill nonexistent foreign troops said to be quartered there. Five others were arrested later, all linked to a militia group called the Third Continental Congress. All were convicted on various state and federal charges.

March 18, 1998: Three members of the North American Militia were jailed in Michigan. Charges include conspiracy to bomb public buildings and an interstate highway, murdering federal agents and a black radio host, and possessing illegal weapons. Leader Ken Carter, a member of the Aryan Nations, turned state's evidence in return for a five-year sentence. His confederates stood firm at trial and were convicted, drawing terms of 40–55 years.

July 30, 1998: Militiaman Paul Chastain was arrested in South Carolina on various drug, weapons, and explosives charges. In 1999 Chastain received a 15-year prison term, after admitting plots to kill U.S. Attorney General Janet Reno and FBI Director Louis Freeh.

December 4, 1998: Two members of the San Joaquin County Militia were jailed in Sacramento, California, charged with conspiring to bomb two propane tanks containing 24 million gallons of flammable gas. A third defendant, militia leader Donald Rudolph, pleaded guilty to conspiracy in the same case during January 2001. Rudolph also admitted that he plotted to murder a federal judge.

December 8, 1999: Donald Beauregard, leader of a militia coalition called the Southeastern States Alliance, was charged with a terrorist conspiracy to bomb power plants in Florida and Georgia. He pleaded guilty on multiple charges and received a five-year prison sentence.

MILOSEVIC, Slobodan (1941–   )

Born on August 20, 1941, future Serbian strongman Slobodan ("Sloba") Milosevic began his professional life as a globe-trotting banker from Belgrade; then he shifted gears to replace Ivan Stambolic as party leader of Serbia's League of Communists of Yugoslavia in September 1987. May 1989 witnessed his election to Serbia's national assembly, followed by victorious presidential campaigns in December 1990 and December 1992. Milosevic's rise to power coincided with the collapse of Eastern European Communism and the rise of various nationalist movements, complete with neo-Nazi views on "ethnic cleansing." Milosevic's regime enthusiastically pursued genocidal campaigns against various minorities during the civil war in BOSNIA-HERZEGOVINA, a campaign that later saw him and many of his underlings indicted for WAR CRIMES.

Before that happened, though, he stubbornly fought to retain power in Serbia. Defeated in the country's November 1996 presidential election, Milosevic contested the results for three months, finally stepping down on February 4, 1997. Constitutionally barred from seeking a third presidential term in Serbia, he next assumed the presidency of the Yugoslav Federation in July 1997. Opponent Vojislav Kostunica defeated Milosevic in September 2000. Milosevic was arrested on April 1, 2000, and charged with corruption and abuse of power. Serbian authorities delivered Milosevic to the UNITED NATIONS International Criminal Tribunal for the Former Yugoslavia in June 2000, and his charges were soon upgraded to include war crimes and genocide. Milosevic's trial began at The Hague, NETHERLANDS on February 12, 2002, and was still in progress at press time for this volume. Milosevic denounced the ongoing trial as an "evil and hostile attack" by his enemies, while a nonstop stream of media stories detailed bizarre and criminal activities by other members of his family.

MIND control

While various forms of psychological warfare have been used for centuries to disrupt morale among enemy troops, the U.S. CENTRAL INTELLIGENCE AGENCY (CIA) carried experimentation to new levels in the 1950s with its MKULTRA mind-control program. CIA Director Allen Dulles secretly authorized MKULTRA in April 1953, including a variety of experiments using hypnotism, LSD, and other drugs on subjects who were sometimes unaware of their selection to "participate" in covert tests. The project's

goal was to produce some sure-fire means of invading and controlling minds at will, thereby obtaining coveted intelligence, debilitating rivals, or unleashing "robot" assassins. In 1958 a CIA auditor warned his superiors that "Precautions must be taken not only to protect operations from exposure to enemy forces but also to conceal these activities from the American public in general. The knowledge that the agency is engaging in unethical and illicit activities would have serious repercussions in political and diplomatic circles."

The CIA destroyed many MKULTRA documents in 1972 when the program allegedly ended, but enough remained for the CHURCH COMMITTEE to document agency abuses three years later. Today, we are assured, no such programs are operated by the U.S. government. Conspiracists reject that statement as false, some of them maintaining that mind-control experiments continue in the form of religious cults and other fringe groups secretly sponsored from Washington. The 1970s SYMBIONESE LIBERATION ARMY is frequently cited as one such example, along with the People's Temple mass suicide in JONESTOWN, Guyana. Some researchers also claim that government agencies are responsible for acts of ritual child abuse linked to SATANISM, allegedly conducted to produce victims with multiple personalities. As evidence they note that Dr. Martin Orne (a psychologist involved in the MKULTRA experiments) was an early member of the FALSE MEMORY SYNDROME Foundation that was created in the 1980s to defend accused child molesters. Several researchers have also speculated that mind-control techniques may have been used on gunman Sirhan Sirhan in the 1968 RFK ASSASSINATION.

See also DULLES BROTHERS.

MINUTEMEN

A forerunner of the 1990s Militia movement, the paramilitary Minutemen organization was founded in 1959 by Missouri chemist Robert Bolivar DePugh. Members stockpiled weapons in preparation for an expected invasion of the United States by Russian, the Chinese, or the UNITED NATIONS military forces. Many who joined the group were also members of the KU KLUX KLAN or other racist groups, promoting agendas that were not restricted to simple anticommunism. (Dennis Mower, second in command of the California Minutemen, was a close friend of KKK "Wizard" Samuel Bowers, who was later convicted of multiple murder and sentenced to life imprisonment.)

In October 1966, 199 Minutemen were jailed for conspiracy on the eve of scheduled raids against various "leftist" targets in New York. Two years later, the organization was publicly linked to William Hoff and Paul Dommer, two associates of the KKK and National States Rights Party who were convicted of conspiracy and violent acts against blacks. The same year, 1968, found DePugh a fugitive from federal charges in Seattle where he and other Minutemen had plotted to bomb a police station and to rob four banks. Captured in July 1969 DePugh received an 11-year sentence and was paroled in May 1973, declaring that prison had taught him "a little humility." While DePugh was imprisoned, G-men recruited some of his California veterans for a terrorist group sponsored by the FEDERAL BUREAU OF INVESTIGATION, the SECRET ARMY ORGANIZATION, linked to bombings and attempted murders around San Diego.

See also MILITIAS.

MISSISSIPPI Plan

White-supremacist Democrats devised the "Mississippi Plan" to "redeem" the Magnolia State from RECONSTRUCTION in 1875. Federal power had broken the KU KLUX KLAN by that time, and Republicans—some of them black—remained in public offices that ex-Confederates coveted for themselves. Since many Mississippi counties boasted black majorities that were enfranchised under the Constitution's Fifteenth Amendment, racist whites fell back on the time-honored technique of TERRORISM to win the election that they otherwise would have lost.

The plan's goal was to bar blacks from voting. In Vicksburg, blacks staging a Fourth of July parade were mobbed by whites; two of them were murdered. The same month brought rumors of black revolt to Water Valley, where white gunmen turned out to massacre unarmed freedmen. In August two blacks were shot and wounded at a Republican meeting in Louisville. Later that month riders from Alabama joined Macon's white terrorists to kill at least a dozen blacks. Democrats revolted in Yazoo City, driving their Republican sheriff from the county and conducting a "lynching bee" that slaughtered every black Republican leader in the district. At Clinton 500 terrorists stormed a Republican

picnic, killing three whites and an estimated 30 blacks. A "minor skirmish" at Satartia left one freedman dead. Coahoma County witnessed six political murders before the black sheriff fled for his life. Noxubee County's Republican nominee for treasurer was assassinated in broad daylight before scores of witnesses.

On election day, with white terrorists posted as "poll watchers" throughout Mississippi, Republican majorities evaporated. In Yazoo City, where 2,427 GOP ballots had been cast in 1873, only seven were recorded in November 1875. Twelve Republicans were bold enough to vote in Tishomingo, while only four found the nerve in Kemper County, two in Utica, and none at all Auburn. Statewide, Democrats carried the election at gunpoint, while federal authorities raised no significant protest. A year later Mississippi's campaign tactics—renamed the "Shotgun Plan"—were used throughout the South in a bloody bid to defeat Republican presidential candidate RUTHERFORD B. HAYES, forcing an electoral compromise that effectively ended Reconstruction in Dixie.

MOLASKA Corporation

Millionaire bootleggers mourned the demise of PROHIBITION in December 1933—so much, in fact, that some resolved to continue the lucrative trade in untaxed booze even when liquor sales became legitimate once more. The largest single vehicle for such activities was Molaska Corporation, created 10 days before Repeal on November 25, 1933. The owners, masked by front men, included New York mobster MEYER LANSKY and two Cleveland associates, Moe Dalitz and Sam Tucker. Lansky's father-in-law, Moses Citron, served the corporation as assistant treasurer.

Ostensibly created to import Cuban molasses (hence its name), Lansky ensured the steady flow of molasses with a personal visit to Cuba where he bribed and befriended the U.S.-supported dictator Fulgencio Batista. At home Molaska went beyond that legal function to erect giant distilleries at Zanesville, Ohio, and Elizabeth, New Jersey. The Zanesville plant turned out an estimated 20,000 bottles of untaxed 190-proof whiskey per day, while the New Jersey plant worked on a somewhat smaller scale. Treasury agents raided the Zanesville plant on January 19, 1935, pronouncing its equipment worth "at least $250,000." Raiders struck the New Jersey still a short time later, and Molaska quietly declared bankruptcy. None of its owners were touched by the scandal, much less charged with any crime.

MONGOLIA

Sandwiched between Siberia and CHINA, Mongolia comprises an area slightly larger than Alaska, with a population smaller than that of Los Angeles. The name *Mongol* derives from an aggressive tribe, originally led by Genghis Khan, which once ravaged Asia and Europe as far west as the Black Sea and prompted China to build its Great Wall as a means of defense. Chinese Manchu rulers conquered Mongolia in the 17th century and held sway until their expulsion in 1912. Russian troops, aided by Mongolian communist rebels, arrived in 1921 and established a Red republic three years later. Theoretically independent since 1945 Mongolia frequently supported RUSSIA in political and military disputes with the country's traditional Chinese enemies. Mongolia's democratic revolution, launched in 1989, produced a multiparty (though still chiefly Communist) government in August 1990. Current rulers, combined as the Mongolian People's Revolutionary Party, still oppose movements for "radical" reform.

See also COMMUNISM.

MONROE, Marilyn (1926–1962)

Arguably the most famous movie actress of all time, Marilyn Monroe was born Norma Jeane Mortensen on June 1, 1926. After spending two years in an orphanage (1935–37), she moved through a series of foster homes and married for the first time at age 16. She graced her first national magazine cover in April 1944 and signed a contract with Fox studios four months later, officially adopting her world-renowned screen name at the same time.

Monroe was as famous for the details of her personal life as for any work on stage or screen. Biographer Anthony Summers suggests a love affair with rising political star John Kennedy in the early 1950s, and any such liaison would have drawn attention from the FEDERAL BUREAU OF INVESTIGATION (FBI). Ex-agent G. Gordon Liddy told Summers, years later, that "[t]he stuff on the [Kennedy] brothers and Monroe was very, very closely held" in Director J. EDGAR HOOVER's personal files. Monroe certainly enjoyed a brief affair with Kennedy after the 1960 presidential election, reportedly meeting him more than once at the home of Kennedy brother-in-law Peter Lawford. Hoover, in turn, warned President Kennedy that Lawford's home "had very likely been bugged by the MAFIA," but he neglected to mention that G-men were also bugging the actor's residence. JFK reportedly saw Monroe for the last time on May 19, 1962, in New York City.

The break-up did not signal an end to Monroe's links with the Kennedy clan, however. She soon proclaimed herself in love with the president's brother, Attorney General Robert Kennedy, once claiming that Robert had promised to leave his wife and marry Monroe. Recounting other conversations with the high and the mighty, Monroe told friends that the Kennedys wanted to replace Hoover with a new FBI director, but the move had been postponed until after JFK won reelection in 1964. Monroe's housekeeper afterward claimed that Robert Kennedy visited Monroe's home on June 27, 1962. Six weeks later, on August 4, 1962, the actress was found dead from an apparent prescription drug overdose, variously reported as accidental, suicide, or murder.

Monroe's death was rife with suspicious circumstances: enigmatic phone calls to friends in her final hours, canceled dinner plans, and eyewitness reports of Robert Kennedy visiting her home with a man who carried a doctor's bag. Stories about her death conflict and contradict each other. Publicist Arthur Jacobs was allegedly summoned to Monroe's home at 11 P.M. on August 4, told that she was "dead or at the point of death," yet housekeeper Eunice Murray did not call Monroe's doctor until 3:30 A.M. The doctor arrived at 3:40, but police were not alerted until 4:25 A.M. Meanwhile, ambulance attendants claim they carried Monroe from her home to a local hospital at 2 A.M., leaving her death at home unexplained.

Coroner Thomas Noguchi found eight milligrams of chloral hydrate in Monroe's blood and 13 milligrams of pentobarbital (Nembutal) in her liver tissue, both amounts "well above fatal doses." Oddly, though, Noguchi found "absolutely no evidence of pills in the stomach or the small intestine," and a "painstaking" search revealed no needle marks. Noguchi *did* report a "purplish discoloration" of Monroe's colon, prompting speculation by District Attorney John Miner that "some portion of the drugs were introduced into the large intestine rather than being swallowed." Another curious aspect, noted by Noguchi, was a fresh bruise spanning Monroe's lower back and hip which "might have indicated violence." Such oddities notwithstanding, Noguchi concluded that Monroe had committed suicide.

LOS ANGELES POLICE DEPARTMENT (LAPD) Chief William Parker raised eyebrows at headquarters when he removed the case from detectives in the Robbery-Homicide Division and assigned it to the "spooks" in LAPD's Intelligence Division. From that point onward, future chief Tom Reddin recalled, no one outside of Intelligence "knew a bloody thing about what was going on." Mayor Sam Yorty asked to see the police file on Monroe but was told that it "could not be found." Forty years later the file is still missing, its fate officially unknown. Conspiracists speculate that Monroe was murdered to prevent revelation of pillow-talk secrets shared by the Kennedy brothers, including various plots to assassinate FIDEL CASTRO.

See also KENNEDY DYNASTY.

MORGAN dynasty

The patriarch of this dominant clan in international banking was Junius Spencer Morgan (1813–60), a British subject who founded London's house of J.S. Morgan and Company. Son John Pierpont Morgan (1837–1913) was born in Connecticut and educated in Boston and at the University of Göttingen. During 1857–60 J.P. Morgan served a brief apprenticeship at the New York City banking house of Duncan, Sherman & Co. and then moved on to serve as agent and attorney for his father's partner, George Peabody, during 1860–64. A succession of lucrative partnerships followed, climaxed with creation of J.P. Morgan & Co. in 1895. Affiliated banking firms—including Philadelphia's Drexel & Co.; Morgan, Harjes & Co. in Paris; and Morgan, Grengell & Co. in London—made Morgan the first great international banker, a financier with a controlling share of countless enterprises. In the 1890s he funded the creation of the U.S. Steel Corporation, which absorbed Andrew Carnegie's holdings and others to become the world's first billion-dollar corporation. In 1895 Morgan also supplied the U.S. government with $62 million in GOLD to support a bond issue and restore the treasury surplus of $100 million. Seven years later Morgan purchased several Atlantic steamship lines to create the first great transatlantic shipping combine. Morgan's banks were also instrumental in financing America's transcontinental railroads—and

they profited hugely from every scheme the railroads used to swindle landowners and farmers, coast to coast. Morgan's pivotal involvement in industry and the strike-breaking tactics of management made him a primary target of radicals and ANARCHISTS in the early 20th century. In September 1920, a wagonload of explosives shattered windows in the House of Morgan, on New York's Wall Street, but Morgan, Jr., escaped injury and the crime remains unsolved. Modern incarnations of the Morgan dynasty include the global banking house of J.P. Morgan Chase & Co., placed on federal probation in 2001 for its "leading role" in ENRON and other financial scandals. Another branch, Morgan Stanley, was severed from J.P. Morgan to comply with NEW DEAL monopoly statutes in

Banker Junius Morgan (1813–90) founded one of America's great financial dynasties. His son John Pierpont Morgan, Sr., (opposite page, top) (1837–1913) compounded the family's fortune to become one of the richest men on Earth. John P. Morgan, Jr., (opposite page, bottom) (1867–1943) continued in his father's footsteps and survived an anarchist bombing attempt on his life in 1920. (Author's collection)

1935. In 1997, Morgan Stanley merged with Dean Witter Discover & Co., maintaining offices in the Twin Towers complex that was leveled in the PENT-TBOM attacks of September 11, 2001.

See also CHASE MANHATTAN BANK.

MORMONS

Mormonism—or the Church of Latter-Day Saints (LDS)—is an offshoot of mainstream Christianity conceived by "prophet" Joseph Smith, Jr., in the early 19th century. According to Smith, as explained in the 1830s, he experienced a series of visions including personal conversations with Jehovah, JESUS CHRIST, and various angels, all of whom selected him to revive "Christ's true church" on Earth. Their detailed message was found, Smith said, on ancient golden plates unearthed near his home in New York, which he translated with a special "peeping stone." Eight other witnesses allegedly saw the gold plates, which strangely no longer exist. Critics point to court records, documenting Smith's involvement in various fraudulent treasure hunts prior to his great revelation, but believers generally ignore or deny that suspicious history.

Smith formally founded his church in April 1830 and two months later produced a "new translation" of the Bible, which he called the Book of Mormon. His revision of the classic King James text, continuing for the remainder of his life, raised hackles among fundamentalist Christians and sparked persecution of Mormons wherever they settled. From New York, Smith led his flock to Ohio (1831–38), but mob action later prompted his flight to Missouri. There, further anti-Mormon violence—climaxed by the bloody Haun's Mill massacre—drove Smith and company to Nauvoo, Illinois. Smith fared no better there, lynched with his brother by a mob on June 26, 1844. The prophet's mantle fell next upon Brigham Young, who led the faithful on a cross-country trek to find their promised land in the West. They chose present-day Utah, known to Mormons in those days as Deseret, and established a theocracy that soon found itself in conflict with the ever-expanding United States of America.

In the latter 1850s a "Mormon War" erupted between Washington and Young's regime in Salt Lake City. A Mormon militia, the Danites (or "avenging angels") ambushed U.S. troops, assassinated "gentile" travelers, and generally transformed

Joseph Smith (left) abandoned a dubious business career to found the Mormon Church, following "divine revelations," while Brigham Young (right) led the Mormon faithful to Utah and later fought a full-scale war against the U.S. government for territorial supremacy. (Author's collection)

Utah into a free-fire war zone during 1857–58. No final tabulation of casualties is available, but the war's most notorious incident occurred at Mountain Meadows in 1857. There, a wagon train of 140 immigrants bound for California was attacked by Danites and an allied war party of Paiute Indians. The Mormons offered safe passage through their territory but then slaughtered the travelers as soon as they disarmed. Only 17 children were spared, handed off to Mormon families for adoption. While Salt Lake authorities later admitted their responsibility for the massacre, another 17 years elapsed before a single defendant—Danite fanatic John Doyle Lee—was charged with the crime. Convicted alone, Lee was executed in 1877.

One major sticking point between Mormons and the U.S. government was the LDS practice of polygamy, announced by Joseph Smith as "divine will" in the early 1840s. Plural marriage was officially repudiated by Mormon leaders before Utah's admission to the Union, but an uncertain number of Mormons still follow the custom today, strangely unmolested despite their defiance of various bigamy statutes. Some outspoken polygamists have been excommunicated, but that religious punishment has only compounded their difficulty. Several outcast groups now claim a "true prophet" as their leader, waging bloody internecine war against competing rivals across the United States and northern Mexico. One such cult, founded by exiled Mormon Ervil LeBaron, survived via theft and has committed dozens of murders from the 1960s through 1988, prompting journalists to dub LeBaron "the Mormon Manson."

MOROCCO

The Berber homeland of Morocco was annexed by Rome in A.D. 46, overrun by Vandals in the fifth century, and invaded by Muslim Arabs in 685. Native

Berbers accepted the new creed so enthusiastically that they joined the Arabs to invade SPAIN in 711 but then revolted to expel Arab rulers in 1086. For the next 200 years, until their expulsion in the 13th century, Berbers dominated large areas of Moorish Spain. At home, the Alawite dynasty—alleged lineal descendants of the prophet Muhammad—seized control of Morocco in 1660 and rule it to this day. Coveted by both sides during two World Wars, Morocco suffered French meddling in 1953 with the ouster of Sultan Mohammed V, but nationalist upheaval secured his return two years later. In 1956 both France and Spain recognized Morocco's independent sovereignty, freeing the country to quarrel with MAURITANIA over the right to rule and plunder Spanish (now Western) Sahara. Spain withdrew entirely from that territory in 1976, and Mauritania surrendered its final claims three years later. Rebels of the Polisario Front then waged ceaseless war against Moroccan occupation forces until 1991 when the UNITED NATIONS brokered a negotiated cease-fire. Still, in 2002, King Mohammed VI declared that he "will not renounce an inch of" Western Sahara to native rule. In July of that year Morocco flexed its military muscles by invading a small, uninhabited island claimed by Spain off Morocco's Mediterranean coast, but it could not hold the prize and Spanish troops soon routed the usurpers. On May 16, 2003, terrorist bombings killed 40-odd victims at several targets in downtown Casablanca, including the Spanish consulate and a Jewish community center.

See also TERRORISM.

MOSSAD

The Mossad ("institute" in Hebrew) is ISRAEL's secret intelligence service. Created by Prime Minister David Ben Gurion on April 1, 1951, as the Institute for Intelligence and Special Tasks, it was subsequently known as the Central Institute for Coordination and the Central Institute for Intelligence and Security. Headquartered in Tel Aviv the Mossad has primary responsibility for intelligence collection (spying), covert action, and counterterrorism. The institute is naturally secretive about its personnel, but various published membership estimates suggest a headquarters staff of 1,200 or more, with as many as 35,000 agents worldwide (allegedly including 20,000 active spies and 15,000 "sleepers").

Given Israel's history of conflict with her Arab neighbors, the Mossad's primary focus is Arab states and militant organizations worldwide, but the institute also spies on friendly nations (including the United States), and its agents were once well known for pursuit of Nazi fugitives who escaped the defeated THIRD REICH after World War II. (Chief among Mossad's triumphs in that regard was the 1960 capture of ADOLF EICHMANN in ARGENTINA.) Mossad has also conducted state-sponsored terrorist campaigns against Arabs and others who are perceived as enemies of Israel, committing assassinations throughout the world. The institute's WRATH OF GOD was established in 1972 to punish BLACK SEPTEMBER terrorists responsible for slaying Israeli athletes at the Munich Olympics, and while that unit was ostensibly disbanded by 1979, assassinations in the name of "self-defense" continue. More recent victims, acknowledged or alleged, include Abu Jihad (a ranking member of the Palestine Liberation Organization, killed in Tunis, 1988), GERALD VICTOR BULL (murdered in Belgium during 1990 while preparing a "super gun" for IRAQ), and Khalid Meshaal (a leader of the paramilitary group Hamas in JORDAN, injected with poison by an Israeli hit team, 1997).

Mossad's six acknowledged departments include Collections (in charge of espionage), Political Action and Liaison (collaborating with friendly intelligence services), Special Operations (charged with "sensitive" tasks including murder and sabotage), Psychological Warfare (including propaganda and deception), Research (responsible for analysis and collating of raw intelligence), and Technology (development of advanced equipment to assist Mossad).

See also TERRORISM.

MOTORCYCLE gangs

America's first motorcycle gangs were organized in the late 1940s by disaffected veterans of World War II. The most famous of the gangs (or "clubs," as they prefer) is the Hells Angels, borrowing its name from a U.S. bomber squadron in Europe. During the next two decades "outlaw" bikers—so called by legitimate clubs that promote "family-style" outings—were viewed by police and civilians as nomadic bands of drunken, drug-addled hoodlums who roamed the countryside at will, pausing to haze small towns and rape any women unlucky enough to cross their path. By the early 1970s, however, a new vision of motorcycle gangs emerged, depicting them as the latest evolutionary phase of organized crime.

And organized they surely are. With chapters spanning the globe, the "Big Four" motorcycle gangs—Hells Angels, Bandidos, Pagans, and Outlaws—dominate the trade in bootleg methamphetamines ("speed" or "crank") while maintaining lucrative sidelines in illegal weapons distribution and WHITE SLAVERY. Many gang chapters run strip clubs, massage parlors, and similar "sex-work" operations where young women—either from the gang's "old lady" ranks or kidnapped from the streets—are drugged and put to work in circumstances reminiscent of a concentration camp. Murders are frequent in the gang milieu. Hells Angels gunmen wear a patch that reads "Filthy Few" to denote members who have killed "for the club." The various gangs also perform contract murders and "muscle" services for traditional crime syndicates such as the MAFIA. At last count, the major gangs were organized throughout North and South America, Europe, Australia, and parts of Africa.

Although some 900 outlaw biker gangs were recognized in the United States during the 1970s, the following groups achieved dominance in a chaotic field and retain it today:

Hells Angels: Operating with the motto "Three can keep a secret if two are dead," the Angels have expanded from their northern California roots of 1947 to control a multimillion-dollar empire based on illicit, commercial sex and fear. They fight sporadically with other gangs for turf and over insults to inflated egos. No final tally for gang murders is available, but hundreds have died in the long-running war between Hells Angels and rival members of the Outlaws gang. Canadian enforcer Yves ("Apache") Trudeau confessed to 46 murders at his arrest in the early 1980s. In December 2003 state and federal agents staged coordinated raids against Hells Angels in Alaska, Arizona, California, Nevada, and Washington: At least 57 gang members were arrested in the sweep, which climaxed a two-year investigation into drugs and gun smuggling.

Outlaws: This gang, founded in Chicago in 1959, presently maintains an estimated 34 chapters with 900 members in the United States and Canada. Sadistic mistreatment of women is a common theme in Outlaw crimes, coupled with a marathon war against the larger and stronger Hells Angels. Between 1974 and 1984 Outlaw gunmen killed at least 95 persons in the states of Florida and North Carolina alone, according to official estimates. Aside from commercial sex, significant sources of income include drug sales, gun running, mail fraud, and armed robbery. The gang's motto is apt: "God forgives, Outlaws don't."

Bandidos: With 30 chapters and an estimated 500 members, this gang operates throughout the United States and boasts a thriving offshoot in Australia. Its motto—"We are the people our parents warned us about"—seems humorous at first glance, but organized crime has been a deadly serious business for the Bandidos since 1966. Texas-based and steeped in Anglo racism, the gang's constitution includes a provision that "no fat Mexicans" may join the group. Official corruption protects the gang's drug trade in much of the United States, but terror is employed where money fails. Gang members wounded U.S. Attorney Jim Kerr of Texas in a November 1978 machine-gun ambush, and they were also blamed for the assassination of federal judge John Wood, killed by a sniper in May 1979. In September 1984 a skirmish between Bandidos and rival Commancheros left 7 dead and 21 wounded outside Sydney, Australia.

Pagans: This gang evolved from another—the Sons of Satan—in the early 1970s and today has some 900 members in 44 chapters along the Eastern Seaboard. Its war with the rival Warlocks gang claimed 15 lives in Pennsylvania during 1974–75, and the same era saw Pagans linked to the serial murders of six women and a half-dozen Mafia-related bombings in the Keystone State. Prodigious drug profits are supplemented by income from mob "muscle" work in labor racketeering and the pornography trade.

MOZAMBIQUE

PORTUGAL "discovered" Mozambique—already occupied by Bantu tribes and Arab traders—in 1498 and colonized the area in 1505. Lisbon held sway by typically repressive measures until 1963 when a native guerrilla movement arose to challenge the colonial regime. Some 40,000 Portuguese troops were assigned to hunt the "terrorists" by 1973, but they failed at their task, and a cease-fire was arranged in September 1974, followed by full independence in June 1975. Guerrilla leader and first president Samora Moises Machel ran the new republic until October 1986 when a plane crash claimed his life. By that time a new band of native rebels supported by white-racist SOUTH AFRICA—the Mozambique National Resistance—had virtually paralyzed government operations. President Joaquim Chissanó abandoned the state's long-term shift toward socialism in 1989, thereby granting victory of a sort to the rebels (and, some said, to the U.S. CENTRAL INTELLIGENCE AGENCY under President George H. W. Bush). In November 1995 Mozambique became the first non-former British colony to join the British Commonwealth, but its problems continued. Famine and a series of natural disasters during 2000–01 prompted President Chissanó to cancel his reelection campaign, whereupon independence hero Armando Guebuza was chosen to lead Mozambique into a bleak future. In February 2004 a group of Catholic nuns in Nampula complained of receiving "some very clear threats" to their lives after they publicly denounced a ring of criminals trading in the sex organs of murdered children. The Sisters Servants of Mary Immaculate claim to have spoken with intended victims who escaped from the ritual-murder cartel, bearing photos of slaughtered children with their genitals excised for use in black magic ceremonies.

See also BUSH DYNASTY; CATHOLIC CHURCH; TERRORISM.

MURDER Incorporated

Between 1929 and 1934 prominent racketeers and bootleggers from every major U.S. city convened periodically to discuss formation of a cohesive national crime syndicate. As a result of those meetings, leaders of the MAFIA and other ethnic gangs divided the country into "territories"—discrete regions where individual gangs or "families" reigned supreme. As an aide to gangland discipline the mobsters also established a Brooklyn-based team of contract killers, later dubbed "Murder Incorporated" by various reporters.

Murder Inc. grew from the "Bug and Meyer Mob," operated during PROHIBITION by gangsters Benjamin ("Bugsy") Siegel and MEYER LANSKY, who provided non-Italian gunmen during CHARLES "LUCKY" LUCIANO's war to "Americanize" the Mafia. Under the new syndicate, control of the Brooklyn hit team was ceded to labor racketeer Louis ("Lepke") Buchalter, assisted by Mafioso Albert Anastasia (dubbed the "Mad Hatter" and the "Lord High Executioner"). The hit squad's premier gunmen included Frank ("The Dasher") Abbandando, Louis Capone, Martin ("Bugsy") Goldstein, Vincent ("Chicken Head") Gurino, Seymour ("Blue Jaw") Magoon, Harry ("Happy") Maione, Abe ("Kid Twist") Reles, Harry ("Pittsburgh Phil") Strauss, Allie Tannenbaum, and Charles ("The Bug") Workman. All were credited with multiple murders, and Strauss alone is commonly deemed responsible for 100–150 slayings. Gunmen were paid a constant salary plus fees of $1,000 to $5,000 per slaying, with promises of legal representation and support for their families in the event they were arrested.

In 1940 New York district attorney Burton Turkus arrested Goldstein, Reles, and gunman Dukey Maffetore on murder charges. Believing that they would be murdered to ensure their silence, the trio turned state's evidence to save themselves and furnished evidence against their former comrades. Several Murder Inc. gunmen were executed as a result of that testimony, and Lepke Buchalter himself took a seat in New York's electric chair on November 12, 1944—the only leader of organized crime ever executed by judicial process in the United States. Albert Anastasia escaped prosecution—either through official negligence or a corrupt deal with the prosecutor's office; reports vary—and Lepke's execution did not save Abe Reles from mob retribution.

Although held under 24-hour police guard at Coney Island's Half Moon Hotel, Reles still met the fate shared by many informers. On November 12, 1941, he plunged from the window of his room, leaving a dangling rope of knotted sheets behind, and died on impact with another rooftop, several stories lower. No one believed his death was suicide, and Reles had no motive to flee custody, but the detectives on the guard detail had a novel theory: Kid Twist was a practical joker, they said. Perhaps he climbed from his window with intent to sneak in through another room and thus surprise them with his clever wit. Twenty years after the fact Lucky Luciano confirmed what reporters had long suspected: The detectives guarding Reles were paid $50,000 to murder "the canary who sang but couldn't fly."

MUSLIM Brotherhood

Founded in 1928 after the collapse of the Ottoman Empire, the Muslim Brotherhood (or Society of Muslim Brothers) is a fundamentalist Islamic organization with "a political approach to Islam." The group opposes secular trends in Islamic nations, seeking a return to basic principals of the Koran and a complete rejection of Western influence. Its motto reads: "Allah is our objective. The Prophet [Muhammad] is our leader. Koran is our law. Jihad [holy war] is our way. Dying in the way of Allah is our highest hope."

From its beginnings as a youth organization in EGYPT, the Muslim Brotherhood expanded into SYRIA by 1935 and today claims active branches in 70 nations. The group was banned by law in Egypt after a member assassinated Prime Minister Mahmud Nokrashi on December 28, 1948; police killed the group's Egyptian leader two months later. Another member tried to kill Egyptian president Gamal Abdel Nasser in October 1954, resulting in the arrest of some 4,000 Muslim Brothers. Syria's branch of the organization was banned for subversive activities in 1958, revived in 1961, and then banned again in 1963. Still the movement endured, leading strikes and conducting terrorist actions, killing 83 cadets at the Aleppo artillery school in 1979, and attempting to murder President Hafez al-Assad in June 1980. Assad then launched a full-scale military purge of the Brotherhood, killing an estimated 10,000 to 25,000 members and associates by February 1982. While the Syrian branch then dissolved, other members were suspected in the public assassination of Egyptian president ANWAR AL-SADAT. A decade later, authorities in RUSSIA claimed that the Muslim Brotherhood was a key element in the Chechen revolt, and Brotherhood members applauded the establishment of fundamentalist Taliban rule in AFGHANISTAN. Spokespeople for the Muslim Brotherhood claim active chapters in 70 nations worldwide, though some are forced to operate as covert cells.

See also TERRORISM.

MYANMAR

Historically known as Burma, the Southeast Asian country of Myanmar was overrun by Kublai Khan's Mongol raiders in the 13th century. The Burmese resisted incursions by European traders until the 19th century when agents of the British East India Company waged three successive wars to capture natural resources. Britain finally annexed Myanmar in 1886 and bestowed formal colonial status in 1937. A key battleground during World War II, Burma was liberated in January 1948. Leftist general Ne Win staged a coup in 1962, thereafter brutally suppressing opposition as he charted the "Burmese way of socialism." A quarter-century of privation and brutality sparked public uprisings in 1987–88 that were ruthlessly crushed by the State Law and Order Council. Burma's military rulers officially changed the country's name in 1989, but the change brought no reform. Rural guerrilla movements, led by ethnic Karens along Myanmar's border with THAILAND, have fought for decades to secure basic rights. Meanwhile, government troops and the private armies of various HEROIN warlords defend the nation's primary (albeit illegal) cash crop. Despite a self-imposed ban on items manufactured in Myanmar, described as a blow against that nation's dictatorship, President George W. Bush promoted his 2004 reelection campaign with sloganeering T-shirts made in Burmese sweatshops.

See also BUSH DYNASTY.

MY Lai massacre

The most notorious of American WAR CRIMES in VIETNAM occurred on March 16, 1968, when soldiers from Charlie Company, commanded by Lieutenant William Calley, murdered at least 347 Vietnamese civilians at My Lai, one of nine hamlets surrounding the larger village of Song My. None of the victims was armed, most being women, children, infants, and the elderly. Before death some victims were tortured and raped. The slaughter ended only when an army helicopter crew landed and intervened. The pilot, Warrant Officer Hugh Thompson, Jr., threatened to open fire on Calley's soldiers if the massacre continued, and his gunners—Glenn Andreotta and Lawrence Colburn—supported the threat by aiming their machine guns at the killers.

A preliminary "investigation" by Col. Oran Henderson failed to produce any disciplinary action, and there the matter rested for six months until Tom Glen, a soldier from the 11th Light Infantry's "Butcher's Brigade," wrote a letter to his member of Congress detailing various U.S. atrocities against Vietnamese civilians. Maj. Colin Powell—later U.S. commander in the GULF WAR and Secretary of State under President George W. Bush—dismissed Glen's charges with the observation that "relations between American soldiers and the Vietnamese people are excellent." That administrative whitewash suppressed any further discussion of the incident until November 12, 1969, when journalist Seymour Hersh broke the My Lai story in print. Eight days later photos of the massacre in progress appeared in the Cleveland *Plain Dealer* and were broadcast nationwide.

Belatedly, on March 17, 1970, 14 officers were charged with suppressing evidence related to the My Lai massacre. All were eventually acquitted. Lieutenant Calley was convicted of murder and sentenced to life imprisonment, but President RICHARD NIXON ordered his release from prison two days after the verdict was rendered. (Calley ultimately served three and one-half years house arrest for his crime, an average of four days for each victim murdered.) At trial Calley accused his commander, Capt. Ernest Medina, of ordering the massacre, but Medina denied the charge at trial and was acquitted. Thirty years after the case, helicopter crewmen Thompson, Andreotta, and Colburn received the Soldiers Medal—the U.S. Army's highest award for bravery not involving contact with the enemy—for their role in stopping the slaughter. Their intervention was officially credited with saving 11 lives.

NAMIBIA

Portuguese explorer Bartolomeu Dias "discovered" the African region of modern-day Namibia in the late 15th century, but GERMANY seized control of the colony in 1884 and massacred most of the indigenous Gerero tribesmen in 1908. Boer and British forces from SOUTH AFRICA seized the territory during World War I, and the Treaty of Versailles made it a South African mandate in 1920. Ever fond of ruling black masses, the whites-only government of South Africa sought to incorporate Namibia as part of its territory in 1946, but that move was rejected by the UNITED NATIONS (UN). Nonetheless, legislation passed in 1949 drew the country ever closer to Pretoria and under the thumb of apartheid's racist masters. South Africa ignored a 1968 UN order to withdraw troops from Namibia, thereby earning condemnation from the International Court of Justice. Despite empty threats of UN intervention if they failed to institute transfer of power to native Namibians by May 1975, South Africa's leaders hung on for another 14 years, brutally crushing all forms of dissent. Namibia's first-ever free elections were held in November 1989, with Sam Nujoma installed as the country's first president in February 1990. Still, turmoil continues: In 1999 combat erupted between Namibian troops and separatists in the Caprivi Strip, a narrow stretch of land along the Zambezi River; in 2000 Home Affairs Minister Jerry Ekandjo announced government plans to "eliminate gays and lesbians from the face of Namibia," and wholesale arrests of suspected homosexuals began in January 2001.

NATIONAL Security Agency (NSA)

The NSA is America's top official eavesdropper, responsible for collecting and analyzing "signal intelligence" from all forms of public and private communications via radio, telephone, the Internet, "and otherwise intercepted forms." Its covert budget rivals that of the CENTRAL INTELLIGENCE AGENCY (CIA), and it ranks as the world's single largest employer of mathematicians who are hired to digest and crack various codes. Although active under various names since World War II and operating under its current title since 1952, the NSA "puzzle palace" has maintained a much lower profile than the CIA and other U.S. intelligence agencies, and its existence was officially denied by Washington for nearly two decades after the war. (One shopworn joke suggests that the initials *NSA* stand for "No Such Agency.") Directed by a series of generals and admirals since 1952, the NSA collaborated with corresponding agencies in Australia, Britain, and New Zealand to maintain a global web of electronic ears, including the ECHELON network. Civil libertarians condemn the NSA for violating individual and group privacy rights; conspiracists go further, suggesting manipulation or suppression of data, widespread "disinformation" campaigns, and attempts at MIND CONTROL. NSA spokespeople, for the most part, are content to say nothing at all.

NATIONAL Socialism

National Socialism is a variant form of FASCISM, most infamous as GERMANY's political system during the years 1933–45. Its primary vehicle was the National Socialist German Worker's (Nazi) Party, led by ADOLF HITLER. Nazis believe that a nation is the highest creation of a race; therefore, great nations owe their power to great races. More specifically, Hitler and company advanced the Aryan "master race" as predestined rulers of the world, imbued with a divine right to subjugate weaker countries and "inferior" or "mongrel" races. The proof of superiority lay in warfare, in a theoretical world where Might literally makes Right. Races without nations of their own—specifically Jews and Gypsies in the 1930s—were denounced as "parasitic" and marked for extermination during the Holocaust. Despite their espousal of the "Socialist" label, Nazis shunned all trappings of the typical socialist welfare state, dismissing such programs as COMMUNISM. German industrial giants such as FARBEN INDUSTRIES and KRUPP ARMS were not nationalized under Nazi rule, but rather profited hugely from their military contracts with the government while reaping benefits from captive slave labor.

Despite Germany's crushing defeat in 1945 and the exposure of Hitler's WAR CRIMES, National Socialism endures as an extremist political movement in many nations today—including Germany, where it is banned by law. Elements of Nazism have influenced nationalistic and anti-Semitic groups from RUSSIA throughout Europe to the Western Hemisphere. The "100-percent American" KU KLUX KLAN has praised Hitler since the late 1920s, and many Klan factions today are little more than neo-Nazi cliques. The Southern Poverty Law Center reported 65 neo-Nazi groups acting in the United States during 2002. Strangely, Nazism also enjoys a fan base of sorts in the heart of Africa where black leaders in UGANDA and ZIMBABWE have expressed admiration for Hitler.

See also HOLOCAUST AND HOLOCAUST DENIAL.

NATION of Islam

The Nation of Islam (NOI), better known as the Black Muslim sect, was founded in Detroit during 1930 by an itinerant evangelist named Wallace Fard. He preached a curious amalgam of Islam and science fiction, wherein "blue-eyed devils" (whites) were "grafted" from "Original Man" (blacks) by a prehistoric mad scientist. Doubts remain as to whether Fard himself was black or white, and one Chicago newspaper report later described him as "a Turkish-born Nazi agent [who] worked for ADOLF HITLER in World War II."

Fard vanished mysteriously in June 1934 and was replaced by disciple Elijah Muhammad. Muhammad was arrested by FEDERAL BUREAU OF INVESTIGATION (FBI) agents for sedition in 1942, spending four years in federal prison. FBI surveillance on the Nation of Islam continued for the next three decades. In 1963 bureau memos claimed credit for the rift between Muhammad and prominent NOI minister MALCOLM X. Federal harassment intensified in 1967 when FBI Director J. EDGAR HOOVER launched an illegal COINTELPRO campaign "to expose, disrupt, misdirect, discredit, or otherwise neutralize" six black organizations, including the NOI. Hoover's goal was to "prevent the rise of a 'messiah' who could unify, and electrify, the militant black nationalist movement."

The movement split with Muhammad's death in 1974, one faction led by Louis Farrakhan, while Muhammad's son controlled a smaller off-shoot of the NOI. In early 1995 G-men accused Qubilah Shabazz, Malcolm X's daughter, of hiring a killer to slay Farrakhan. Reporters trumpeted allegations that Farrakhan may have plotted Malcolm's death in 1965, but no proof of either conspiracy was forthcoming. Evidence revealed that Michael Fitzpatrick, Farrakhan's alleged would-be killer, actually proposed the plot to Shabazz, while she resisted the suggestion. In the past, it was disclosed, Fitzpatrick had been jailed on cocaine charges and was once expelled from an ANARCHIST group for carrying weapons to meetings and urging the group to plot bombings—in short, the typical behavior of an FBI agent provocateur. Shabazz's attorney William Kunstler told the press, "There's a puppeteer pulling the strings and there are lots of puppets out there." Retired FBI agent Dan Scott, meanwhile, admitted "handling" Fitzpatrick as an informant in the 1970s and called him "a highly credible witness." The charge against Shabazz was dropped, thereby renewing rumors of an abortive FBI frame-up.

NETHERLANDS

After centuries of conquest by various invaders—Rome's JULIUS CAESAR, FRANCE, and SPAIN—the Netherlands (or Holland) finally won independence in 1648. Anxious for profit and payback, it soon developed into one of the world's great trading nations and proceeded to build its own empire in the Dutch East Indies (now INDONESIA). ADOLF HITLER ignored pleas of neutrality during World War II, subjugating the Netherlands along with the rest of Western Europe. In the meantime Japanese troops seized most of Holland's Asian holdings, thus burning imperial bridges that could never be rebuilt. In 1949 Holland granted independence to the Dutch East Indies but retained the western half of New Guinea until 1963 when that, too, was surrendered to Indonesia. Stubborn refusal to liberate the South Moluccas Islands prompted acts of TERRORISM by separatists in Holland during the 1970s, but the Dutch "empire" today stands reduced to the Caribbean islands of Aruba and the Netherlands Antilles (Bonair and Curaçao). In 1999 Holland startled the world by legalizing euthanasia. Two years later WAR-CRIMES trials involving leaders of the former YUGOSLAVIA convened in Holland at The Hague. Some observers called that move ironic, based on the negligence of Dutch UNITED NATIONS (UN) troops assigned as peacekeepers in BOSNIA-HERZEGOVINA. In April 2002 Wim Kok's government resigned following publication of a report that Dutch troops failed to prevent a 1995 massacre of Bosnian Muslims at the UN "safe haven" near Srebrenica. One month later Kok's replacement as prime minister—right-wing anti-immigrant spokesman Pim Fortuyn—was publicly assassinated.

Immigration was also a factor in the November 2004 assassination of Dutch filmmaker Theo Van Gogh, director of *Submission,* a film critical of Islamic culture. Van Gogh's alleged killer, Mohammed Bouyeri, whose trial began in January 2005, was a Muslim with reported ties to Islamic radicals and terrorists who may have had a hand in plotting the murder.

NEW Deal

In U.S. history the term *New Deal* described President Franklin Roosevelt's (FDR) legislative attack on the Great Depression, intended to provide both immediate relief and long-term reforms in American society. Stemming from the stock market crash of 1929, within four years the ensuing depression increased U.S. unemployment from 3 percent to 25 percent, while cutting industry's output by 33 percent. Shockwaves from the Wall Street fiasco spread worldwide with varying effects. While England launched its first experiment with a planned national economy, ADOLF HITLER seized power in GERMANY, and Benito Mussolini tightened fascist controls over ITALY's corporate state. At home, right-wing critics denounced Roosevelt's "new deal for the American people"—announced on the campaign trail in July 1932—as a rush toward Socialism or COMMUNISM on a par with JOSEPH STALIN's ongoing collectivization efforts in RUSSIA. Extremist groups such as the KU KLUX KLAN, meanwhile, deplored FDR's administration for including Jews and members of the CATHOLIC CHURCH in high-ranking positions while making marginal concessions to black civil rights. New Deal initiatives condemned by wealthy industrialists and right-wing propagandists included the following:

President Franklin Delano Roosevelt was accused by many of his critics of using his New Deal programs to create socialism in the United States. (Library of Congress)

U.S. bank holiday (1933), closing all banks until they were certified by federal auditors—a step condemned as "un-American" interference with free enterprise.

Civilian Conservation Corps (1933), created to employ unskilled young adults with the federal government—denounced by social Darwinists as upsetting a "natural balance" of success and failure.

Federal Emergency Relief Administration (1933), providing breadlines and other aid for unemployed Americans in crisis—panned as a leap toward state socialism.

Agricultural Adjustment Act (1933), which stabilized prices by paying farmers not to grow certain crops. While publicly condemned as another assault on "natural order," the act and later farm subsidy programs fattened the bankrolls of some wealthy planters, including many southern congressmen and senators who were opposed to welfare for poor urban families.

Public Works Administration (1933), a counterpart to the Civil Conservation Corps, employing middle-aged skilled workers on public projects—and condemned for identical reasons.

Federal Deposit Insurance Corporation (1933), established to prevent future bank failures and insure personal savings accounts—thus infuriating sticky-fingered bankers.

Security and Exchange Commission (1933), a new watchdog for Wall Street, despised by convicted and suspected inside traders.

Social Security (1935), providing financial assistance to the elderly, disabled, and unemployed—denounced by conservatives as more socialism, while such professional bigots as Eugene TALMADGE condemned the program as a giveaway to "shiftless" African Americans.

National Labor Relations Act (1935), outraging management across the United States by granting labor unions the legal right to exist.

Fair Labor Standards Act (1938), another alleged blow to "free enterprise," establishing a 40-hour work week and the first U.S. minimum wage, fixed at 40 cents per hour.

Right-wing ideologues complain to this day that FDR's New Deal "destroyed" American freedom, although countless wealthy Americans have profited immensely from government programs in the decades since the 1930s. Some crusaders still fight to roll back New Deal programs 70-odd years after the fact. Texas governor George W. Bush, for example, froze his state's minimum wage at $3.35 per hour while federal standards increased to $5.15. As president, he still seeks to "privatize" Social Security and Medicaid by removing taxpayers' money from federal accounts and gambling it on the same stock market whose crash in 1929 unleashed the Great Depression.

See also BUSH DYNASTY; FASCISM.

NEW Haven Police Department

With a population of some 130,000, New Haven, Connecticut, barely qualifies as a "second-tier" city, but its police department was once second-to-none in illegal surveillance of political dissenters and minorities. Illicit wiretapping officially began in 1943, expanded in the late 1950s, and reached its Orwellian apogee under Chief James Ahern during 1968–70. By the time local journalists exposed the illicit eavesdropping in January 1974, an estimated 3,000 targets had been placed under surveillance, with police intercepting more than 10,000 telephone calls. Also implicated in the criminal campaign were agents of the FEDERAL BUREAU OF INVESTIGATION (FBI), officers of the Connecticut State Police, and employees of the Southern New England Telephone Company (headquartered in New Haven). Media exposés prompted a February 1974 investigation by New Haven's Board of Police Commissioners, whose hearings "disclosed irrefuted [*sic*] evidence of a long-standing massive illegal wiretap operation conducted by the New Haven Police Department, during which many thousands of telephone calls were monitored." Board counsel M. Mitchell Moore told reporters, "The number of people whose conversations have been intercepted is absolutely mind-boggling." One of those targets was State Senator Joseph Lieberman, later elected to the U.S. Senate (1988) and chosen as the Democratic Party's vice-presidential candidate (in ELECTION 2000).

The most egregious case of surveillance in New Haven involved the local chapter of the BLACK PANTHER PARTY. Court testimony revealed that police had wired the apartment where FBI informer Alex Rackley was murdered in 1969, but they failed to rescue him from death by torture at the hands of fellow radicals. Attempting to correct that oversight, prosecutors charged Panther boss Bobby Seale with conspiracy in Rackley's slaying, but a judge dismissed all charges against Seale and codefendant Erica Huggins in May 1971. Four other Panthers pleaded guilty to misdemeanor charges, while defendant Lonnie McLucas won reversal of his felony conviction on appeal in 1975.

When New Haven's wiretap network was exposed, the U.S. Department of Justice promptly "investigated" and "exonerated" all FBI agents involved in the campaign. Still, four G-men were included, including Chief Ahern and various other police officers, when 52 surveillance subjects filed federal lawsuits in May 1977. Fourteen months later, Judge Jon Newman ordered release of wiretap records, thereby identifying some 3,000 victims. The case attained "class action" status in 1983 with 1,238 plaintiffs, and Southern New England Telephone quickly settled out of court for $150,000 (while still denying any wrongful acts). New Haven authorities held out until April 1984 when they settled for $1.75 million. Chief Ahern's own commentary revealed the folly of such indiscriminate surveillance, which is still pursued today under the USA PATRIOT ACT. He said:

> We collected very little political data; we were not interested in it. Local police departments don't have the sophistication to gather political information and they wouldn't know what to do with it if they got it. If they pass it on, it's generally useless. Anybody who would listen to their ideas about who's politically dangerous would have to be crazier than they are most of the time.

See also JUSTICE DEPARTMENT.

NEW Orleans Police Department

New Orleans, Louisiana, is known as the "Big Easy" for a reason. Throughout its history an atmosphere of laissez-faire corruption has enveloped the Crescent City, miring politicians, jurists, and police in a morass of payoffs and selective blindness where vice and organized crime are concerned. The city's most notorious lynching, of 11 suspected MAFIA members in 1891, followed the October 1890 murder of Police Chief David Hennessy by unknown assassins. Initially exalted as a martyr, Hennessy is now widely regarded as a crooked cop who backed one mob "family" against another and paid with his life for the error. While that crime caused an acrimonious

rift between the United States and ITALY, it failed to drive the Mafia or graft out of New Orleans.

In the 1930s "Kingfish" HUEY LONG collaborated with New York mobsters MEYER LANSKY and Frank Costello to promote illegal gambling in New Orleans, protected by corrupt police. Organized crime in the Crescent City was later controlled by CARLOS MARCELLO, a mob boss whose reach extended to Texas where he was implicated in the JFK ASSASSINATION and the murder of LEE HARVEY OSWALD by longtime mob member JACK RUBY. Indeed, many leads from President Kennedy's murder led back to New Orleans where District Attorney Jim Garrison filed conspiracy charges against businessman Clay Shaw (a sometime employee of the CENTRAL INTELLIGENCE AGENCY) in 1967. Shaw was acquitted at trial, while the LIBERAL MEDIA devoted itself to branding Garrison as a Marcello employee.

When not engaged in covering for mobsters, New Orleans police were zealous enforcers of racial-segregation statutes through the late 1960s, perennially unable to capture white terrorists affiliated with the KU KLUX KLAN and the CITIZENS' COUNCILS. Women of all races likewise suffered at the hands of New Orleans's finest under a sadistic practice that crime reporter Hank Messick dubbed "rape by rank." As revealed by Messick in his 1971 biography of Meyer Lansky, New Orleans cops often lined up to rape attractive female prisoners, with captains going first, trailed by lieutenants, sergeants, and lowly patrolmen. In the 1960s local police diverted their attention to "radicals," mounting illegal surveillance on hundreds of targets, then (in the words of the city's chief intelligence officer) distributing their information to "every conceivable authority that might have an interest in causing prosecution or further investigation of these persons."

By the 1980s incessant scandals dogged New Orleans police. Aside from mundane corruption, two officers received death sentences in separate murder cases; a third cop was suspected (then exonerated) in the serial murders of 24 black women. Cycles of reform and relapse apparently changed nothing during the next two decades. On July 1, 2003, *USA Today* reported that a local grand jury was assigned to investigate "an overzealous clean-out" of the police evidence room. Missing items included critical evidence in ongoing rape and murder investigations.

See also BUSH DYNASTY; KENNEDY DYNASTY; TERRORISM.

NEW World Order

Various world leaders have been credited with coining this controversial phrase during the past three-quarters of a century. The candidates include dictator ADOLF HITLER (1930s); the Duke of Windsor, formerly King Edward VIII of England (1940); President Dwight Eisenhower (1956); presidential candidate Nelson Rockefeller (1968); President RICHARD NIXON (1972); TRILATERAL COMMISSION member Richard Newton Gardner (1974); presidential candidate Jimmy Carter (1976); and Russian President Mikhail Gorbachev (1988). Despite that confusion, most users of the term today trace its origin to a speech delivered by President George H. W. Bush before the UNITED NATIONS (UN) on September 11, 1990. Addressing concerns raised by IRAQ's recent invasion of KUWAIT before launching the GULF WAR to repel (but not unseat) SADDAM HUSSEIN, Bush told the UN:

A new partnership of nations has begun. We stand today at a unique and extraordinary moment. The crisis in the Persian Gulf, as grave as it is, offers a rare opportunity to move toward an historic period of cooperation. Out of these troubled times, our fifth objective—a New World Order—can emerge. . . . When we are successful, and we will be, we have a real chance at this New World Order, an order in which a credible United Nations can use its peacekeeping role to fulfill the promise and vision of the United Nations' founders.

Conspiracists, chiefly members or adherents of far-right U.S. MILITIAS, saw Bush's statement as a call for establishment of the same "one-world government" that members of the JOHN BIRCH SOCIETY and other reactionary groups had predicted since the 1950s. Researchers debate the significance of such events as COMMUNISM's collapse in RUSSIA and the ratification of free-trade agreements to the progress of a hypothetical New World Order, but no hard evidence of any trend toward one-world government exists today. Likewise, while some researchers viewed the timing of Osama bin Laden's catastrophic PENTTBOM attacks—11 years to the day after Bush's speech to the UN, son and successor George W. Bush seemed intent on isolating the U.S. rather than forging a global alliance. In announcing his invasion of Iraq, curiously dubbed OPERATION IRAQI FREEDOM, Bush, Jr., declared the United Nations "irrelevant" to U.S. military actions abroad—a move that failed to deter some critics from casting him as another agent of the globe-girdling conspiracy.

See also BIN LADEN FAMILY; BUSH DYNASTY; ROCKEFELLER CLAN.

NEW York Police Department (NYPD)

From its establishment in the 19th century, the NYPD has been embroiled in controversy concerning endemic corruption and systematic illegal harassment of political dissenters. Graft and criminal activity by officers at every level of the force were predictable in a city where TAMMANY HALL and the TWEED RING set a national standard for corrupt political machines, enlisting members of the MAFIA and various STREET GANGS to subvert the democratic process while protecting crime of every kind. Full-scale investigations of corruption among New York's "finest" were mounted in 1875 and 1884, with an 1886 report on flagrant vice, declaring that "obviously, such conditions prevailed because of police graft." Police Superintendent William Murray led the pack in those days and blithely refused to explain how he had banked $300,000 ($6 million in today's dollars) on a yearly salary of $3,500. In 1912 Lieutenant Charles Becker was sentenced to death for arranging the contract murder of a gambler who blew the whistle on police shakedowns. PROHIBITION only exacerbated police corruption in the Big Apple, as sticky-fingered cops competed for payoffs from bootleggers, including the leaders of the East Coast's BIG SEVEN combination. In 1941 MURDER INCORPORATED prosecution witness Abe Reles "accidentally" fell to his death from a hotel window while under guard by six NYPD officers; years later, mob boss CHARLES "LUCKY" LUCIANO admitted that the guards were paid $50,000 to give Reles the toss. Investigation of the "French Connection" HEROIN pipeline revealed more crooked cops in 1962, followed by similar revelations in 1970 and a full-scale investigation of cops "on the pad" by New York's Knapp Commission in 1972. Nothing had changed by 1992 when a group of Harlem officers dubbed the "Dirty Thirty" sold protection to ghetto drug dealers, beating and robbing those who declined the "service."

On the political front President William McKinley's murder by an anarchist in 1901 launched the NYPD's first campaign to drive all "radicals" out of the city. The Anarchist Squad, formally established in 1906, soon broadened its attacks to include labor unions of all kinds. The city's first Bomb Squad was created in August 1914 to infiltrate leftist organizations, and two years later newspapers revealed that the NYPD had tapped at least 350 phones since 1895. In 1919 the Bomb Squad collaborated with FEDERAL BUREAU OF INVESTIGATION (FBI) agents and right-wing vigilantes in the PALMER RAIDS. Between 1930 and 1960, the Red Squad and the Bureau of Special Services (BOSS) shared information with the CENTRAL INTELLIGENCE AGENCY and Military Intelligence. In one such case 13 members of the BLACK PANTHER PARTY were accused of plotting terrorist attacks throughout New York City and environs; they were indicted largely on the word of paid informers. The case collapsed at trial in May 1971 when jurors needed only 90 minutes to acquit each defendant on all 156 felony counts.

In fact May 1971 was a turning point for illegal police surveillance and harassment in New York, as plaintiffs in the *Handschu* case accused BOSS (lately the Special Services Division) of countless constitutional abuses. In February 1973 a federal court declared that infiltration of political organizations required a "probability of certain crimes being committed" by the subjects. Thousands of NYPD dossiers on private citizens were then allegedly destroyed, but the case dragged on until March 1985 when Judge Charles Haight approved a settlement package that barred NYPD from further political spying. Nonetheless, old habits die hard, and summer 1987 brought revelations that the illicit surveillance continued, at least in respect to black activists who criticized police racism. Police spokespeople admitted the violations in December 1987, and the new accusations were upheld by court findings in July 1989. Today, in the wake of the tragic PENT-TBOM attacks and passage of the USA PATRIOT ACT in 2001, full-scale political surveillance has resumed in New York City.

See also ANARCHISTS; BUSH DYNASTY; TERRORISM.

NICARAGUA

The U.S. government has long regarded Nicaragua, in Central America, as one of its unofficial possessions. Throughout the 20th century U.S. troops were repeatedly dispatched to invade Nicaragua in support of American business interests and the "friendly" rulers that supported them with tax breaks, kickbacks, and supplies of virtual slave labor. The first such invasion occurred in 1909, followed by arrival of a "small" U.S. Marine detachment that remained in Nicaragua from 1912 to 1925. The troops returned in 1927 to pursue freedom-fighter César Augusto Sandino, this time remaining to wage war through 1933. General Anastasio SOMOZA Garciá finally assassinated Sandino, whereupon he was rewarded with appointment (in 1936) as dictator for life. Few regimes in the Western Hemisphere have been more brutal, more corrupt— or more ardently supported by Washington. At his death in 1967 Somoza was succeeded by his equally corrupt and ruthless brother, Anastasio Somoza Debayle. Twelve years later, an insurgent movement named for Sandino—the Sandinistas—launched a struggle to unseat Somoza, driving him from the country on July 17, 1979. A liberal Sandinista government was installed two days later, but it soon faced opposition from Washington. Three days after taking office in January 1981 President RONALD REAGAN suspended U.S. aid to Nicaragua, citing (false) reports that the Sandinistas (with aid from RUSSIA and CHINA) were fomenting revolution in EL SALVADOR. Reagan's remedy was a long-running campaign of state-sponsored terrorism against Nicaragua, coordinated by the CENTRAL INTELLIGENCE AGENCY and carried out by Somoza supporters dubbed "contras." Congress subsequently banned funding of the contra criminals, but Reagan and Vice President George H.W. Bush continued illegal funding of the campaign via covert channels in the IRAN-CONTRA CONSPIRACY. After nearly a decade of terrorism and economic destabilization anti-Sandinista forces won the general election of 1990 and installed Violetta Barrios de Chamorro as president. Perhaps predictably, the flagrant corruption of that regime soon disillusioned even right-wing business interests in Nicaragua, and new president Arnoldo Alemán was elected in 1996. Alemán lost his reelection bid in 2000 and was indicted two years later on charges of stealing $10 million from the government during his four years in office. Nicaragua remains one of the poorest nations in the Western Hemisphere today.

See also BUSH DYNASTY.

NICOTINE

Diseases related to use of tobacco kill thousands of Americans and millions of persons worldwide every year. The addictive properties of nicotine, a drug naturally occurring in tobacco, have been recognized for generations; yet spokespersons for various tobacco companies and their lobbyists from the Washington-based Tobacco Institute insist to this day that the case against tobacco is "unproved." In the 1990s assembled presidents of the United States' largest tobacco producers went so far as to swear under oath before Congress that they did not believe that their product was addictive. That bizarre performance ended with the publication of internal documents proving that several firms had secretly increased nicotine levels in their cigarettes with the apparent goal of hooking lifelong addicts at a younger age. With those damning documents in hand, President Bill Clinton's Medicaid administration filed federal lawsuits against the tobacco industry in November 1998 to recover tobacco-related health-care costs on behalf of 46 U.S. states. (Four other states settled their claims separately.) Major tobacco firms approved out-of-court settlements totaling $206 billion, but the lion's share of that amount remained unpaid when ELECTION 2000 arrived to make the U.S. safe for nicotine purveyors.

That year's presidential race was critical to U.S. tobacco companies, a fact made clear by the industry's donation of at least $13,954,557 to Republican contender George W. Bush. (Democrats, meanwhile, received a relatively paltry $2,096,881 from two tobacco companies.) Bush's sympathy for big tobacco was suggested by the fact that three of his top campaign staffers—including chief adviser Karl Rove, confidante Charles Black, and business liaison officer Kirk Blalock—were former employees of Bush's top contributor, the Philip Morris tobacco company. The industry reaped its rewards as soon as Bush took office, courtesy of a 5-4 vote by the U.S. SUPREME COURT. As Secretary of Health and Human Services, Bush appointed ex-governor of Wisconsin Tommy Thompson, who cheerfully accepted $72,000 and several free international vacations from Philip Morris while in office (1993–2000). Another Bush appointee, JOHN ASHCROFT, was a friend of big tobacco who in 1998 cast the sole dissenting vote against a U.S. Senate committee's decision to approve debate on a tobacco settlement bill. As attorney general, Ashcroft did everything within his power to scuttle the Clinton-era JUSTICE DEPARTMENT's tobacco litigation. Howard Beales, appointed by Bush to head the Federal Trade Commission's consumer protection bureau, was a former consult-

ant for R.J. Reynolds Tobacco (Bush's fourth-largest contributor in 2000), who once penned an article denying that his company's "Joe Camel" advertisements were directed at minors. Meanwhile, Bush's trade office reversed Clinton's policy of limiting U.S. tobacco exports, attacking South KOREA's tariff on U.S. cigarettes as "unfair treatment" of Philip Morris and R.J. Reynolds.

Those moves might have seemed ill advised in January 2003 when the *Journal of Clinical Investigation* reported that nicotine was not only addictive but also a major cause of lung cancer in smokers. Five months later the Centers for Disease Control announced that Marlboro cigarettes (produced by Philip Morris and ranked as top sellers in 13 foreign countries) contained "significantly higher levels" of the carcinogen nitrosamine than did any other brand. CDC spokespersons called their findings "the latest example of the tobacco industry's reckless disregard for the health" of its customers, but cigarette purveyors and their political allies had no comment. While the American Society of Clinical Oncologists called for an immediate $2-per-pack tax increase on cigarettes to curb smoking, predicting that tobacco-related disease will kill 1 billion victims in the 21st century (compared to a mere 100 million in the 20th), Bush partisans opposed all efforts by the World Health Organization to curb smoking or to stop tobacco advertising aimed at children.

See also BUSH DYNASTY; CLINTON, BILL AND HILLARY.

NIDAL, Abu (1935–)

Before Osama bin Laden captured headlines as the world's preeminent terrorist bogeyman in the mid-1990s, Abu Nidal was the alleged prime mover behind many Arab attacks against ISRAEL and U.S. interests abroad. Born Sabry Khalil Bana in 1935, a son of prosperous middle-class parents in Jaffa, Palestine, Nidal saw his family uprooted with thousands of other Arabs when the state of Israel was established in 1948. The Banas settled in LEBANON where Sabry studied at American University. In 1967 he joined FATAH and quickly rose to a command rank in that militant organization and assumed the name Abu Nidal ("Father of the Struggle," in Arabic). Seven years later doctrinal squabbles with Yasser Arafat led Nidal to create his own Fatah Revolutionary Council, which tried to assassinate Arafat in

1974. Arafat's Palestine Liberation Organization retaliated with a contract on Nidal, and the two groups remained antagonistic through the 1980s. Nidal's agents were ultimately blamed for killing PLO representatives in England, FRANCE, KUWAIT, and PORTUGAL.

That fratricidal conflict did not keep Nidal from his primary targets, however. At various times his guerrillas operated as members of the Arab Revolutionary Brigades, Black June, and the Revolutionary Organization of Socialist Muslims, coupling attacks on Israel with hits on Jews, Egyptians and Jordanians in AUSTRIA, France, and ITALY. All told, some analysts believe that Nidal's hunters may have killed 900 persons in 20 nations. Much of Nidal's financial support in the 1970s and 1980s allegedly came from Libyan dictator MUAMMAR AL-QADDAFFI, but Nidal also maintained guerrilla training camps in Lebanon and SYRIA. With a private army of 500 fighters in 1985, Nidal told a Kuwaiti journalist, "Give me $400 million and in five years I'll change the face of the Middle East." Nidal's fate is uncertain, surrounded by rumor and disinformation. He apparently survived a heart attack and cardiac surgery in 1992, and subsequent reports of his death from cancer are generally dismissed as false. In 2002 another story circulated that Nidal had committed suicide (or had been shot by SADDAM HUSSEIN's police) in Baghdad, IRAQ. Thus far, that tale remains unsubstantiated, but Western intelligence agents no longer regard Nidal as a "player" on the Middle Eastern stage.

See also BIN LADEN FAMILY.

NIGER

An arid land inhabited primarily by nomadic tribes, Niger was annexed by FRANCE in 1896 to become a part of French West Africa. Though often rootless its natives resented the move and rebelled frequently but to no avail. French troops suppressed dissent by any means necessary, and Niger became a formal French colony in 1922. So Niger remained until 1959 when its people successfully opposed assimilation into the French community and declared independence. Uranium mining fattened the country's coffers, while simultaneously luring the greedy to seats of power. Military putschists ousted President Hamani Diori in 1974, but their regime was so corrupt and incompetent that famine ensued, placing two million persons

at risk of starvation. Civilian government was restored in 1976, but another military coup reversed that decision in January 1996. Seven months later a rigged election installed junta leader Ibrahim Baré Maïnassara as head of a corrupt and ineffectual government. Maïnassara's own bodyguards killed him in April 1999, and democratic elections were held in November. In July 2002 mutinous soldiers seized the capital (Niamey) and several army garrisons, demanding back pay and improved work conditions, but their revolt was crushed with three mutineers killed and 220 arrested.

NIGERIA

British forces seized the Lagos region of Nigeria from the Fulani Empire in 1851 and overran the rest of the country by 1886. In 1914 on the eve of World War I London formally announced creation of the Colony and Protectorate of Nigeria. So it remained until the grant of independence, on October 1, 1960, but freedom brought no end of problems to the country. With 250 ethnic and linguistic groups perpetually at odds, there was—and is—no shortage of upheaval in Nigeria. Rioting prompted a military coup in 1966 while Muslim Hausas slaughtered Christian Ibo tribe members in eastern Nigeria. That region declared independence as Biafra in May 1967 but surrendered in January 1970 after 31 months of genocidal civil war. An OIL boom in the 1970s brought prosperity and encouraged a return to civilian government, but another military coup reversed that trend in 1984. Dictator Ibrahim Babangida promised a reversion to civilian rule in 1993, but the results of that year's election displeased him, so he voided the results. The ruling junta's corruption, brutality, and general incompetence prompted UNITED NATIONS inspectors to declare in 1996 that Nigeria's "problems of human rights are terrible and the political problems are terrifying." Still, its strong military established Nigeria as a superpower in West Africa, enabling it to intervene at will in the civil wars of LIBERIA and SIERRA LEONE. Iron-handed repression continues at home, where writer Ken Saro-Wiwa was hanged in 1995 for criticizing the present regime. A general amnesty for political prisoners in May 1999 was closely followed by the suspicious death of opposition leader Mashrood Abiola, jailed since 1993. A return to "democratic" rule in 1999 has not resolved Nigeria's official corruption or extravagance—epitomized by the construction of a $330 million soccer stadium in 2001, consuming the entire national budget for health and education. Incessant fighting between Christians and Muslims has killed more than 10,000 Nigerians since 1999, despite government vows to "crack down" on domestic TERRORISM. The April 2003 presidential election was marked by more bloodshed and widespread accusations of fraud. Abroad, Nigerian gangs are now ranked among the most affluent and brutal HEROIN dealers in Europe and the United States.

NIGHT of the Long Knives

A year after ADOLF HITLER ascended to power as chancellor of GERMANY, conflict developed between Hitler's subordinates for dominant positions in the new THIRD REICH. Aligned on one side of the struggle were Hermann Göring, SS chief HEINRICH HIMMLER, and GESTAPO leader Reinhard Heydrich; opposing that cartel was Ernst Röhm, commander of Hitler's brown-shirted *Sturmabteilung* ("storm troopers," or SA). Already under pressure from National Socialist backers to dispose of Röhm because Röhm and some of his leading SA subordinates were homosexuals, Hitler accepted fabricated evidence from Himmler that Röhm planned a putsch to unseat Hitler and make himself the new Führer of Germany. On the night of June 29–30, 1934, memorialized as the Night of the Long Knives (*Nacht der langen Messer* in German), Hitler led an SS strike force to arrest and execute an uncertain number of SA members. Röhm was among those killed, with estimates of the final body count ranging from 77 victims (the official tabulation) to 400 or more. Hitler legalized the slaughter retroactively with a Law Regarding Measures of State Self-Defense passed on July 3, its single paragraph declaring the "measures taken" against Röhm and company "legal State self-defense." Hitler publicly announced the massacre on 13 July, claiming that 61 persons had been executed, 13 shot while resisting arrest, and three committed suicide. In reporting the purge, he said:

> *If anyone reproaches me and asks why I did not resort to the regular courts of justice, then all I can say is this: In this hour I was responsible for the fate of the German people, and thereby I became the supreme judge of the German people.*

On July 26, 1934, the SS was formally severed from the SA, with Himmler appointed as Reichsführer, answering only to Hitler. Victor Lutze replaced Röhm as chief of the dwindling SA, his unit soon marginalized and effectively emasculated within the Nazi state.

See also NATIONAL SOCIALISM.

NIXON, Richard (1913–1994)

Born in ultraconservative Orange County, California, on January 9, 1913, Richard Nixon was raised as an evangelical Quaker by his mother, who hoped he would become a missionary. Instead, he graduated from law school in 1937 and was threatened with disbarment during his first case by a judge who accused him of mishandling a client's funds. Nixon abandoned his religion's pacifist tenets in 1942 to join the U.S. Navy, from which he was discharged in 1946 with the rank of lieutenant commander. He next found work as an attorney for the Pepsi-Cola Company but soon turned his eye to politics where his dearth of ethics earned him the nickname "Tricky Dick."

In November 1946 Nixon defeated incumbent California congressman Jerry Voorhis in a campaign where Nixon falsely branded his opponent "soft on COMMUNISM." In the House of Representatives (1947–50) he served as a member of the HOUSE COMMITTEE ON UN-AMERICAN ACTIVITIES and earned a Red-hunting reputation in the ALGER HISS case. In 1950 Nixon moved up to the U.S. Senate, defeating incumbent Helen Gahagan (whom he dubbed the "Pink Lady" for alleged Communist sympathies). Republican presidential candidate Dwight Eisenhower chose Nixon as his running mate in 1952, but exposure of Nixon's personal corruption (including a slush fund collected from donors who included billionaire HOWARD HUGHES) threatened the campaign until Nixon offered a tearful quasi-apology on television. As vice president (1953–61), Nixon faced riotous mobs in Latin America and scored points with conservatives for an acrimonious debate with Russian Premier Nikita Khrushchev. Supported by major OIL companies and the INTERNATIONAL BROTHERHOOD OF TEAMSTERS, Nixon ran for president in 1960 and lost narrowly to John Kennedy in an election swayed by the Chicago MAFIA and Mayor RICHARD JOSEPH DALEY's corrupt political machine.

Richard Nixon's long career of financial and political corruption climaxed with the notorious Watergate scandal. (The White House)

1972 election campaign, with a COMMITTEE TO REELECT THE PRESIDENT which specialized in "dirty tricks" including burglary, illegal wiretaps, smear campaigns, and an abortive plot to burn the BROOKINGS INSTITUTION. Nixon's chicanery climaxed in the WATERGATE scandal, which failed to prevent his reelection but nonetheless doomed his presidency. As details of the far-flung political conspiracy emerged and Vice President SPIRO AGNEW resigned to face criminal charges in Maryland, the U.S. House convened to vote on charges of impeachment. Nixon avoided that humiliation by resigning from office on August 9, 1974, and received a preemptive pardon from Vice President Gerald Ford for any and all crimes he may have committed.

Back in semiprivate life, Nixon sought to rehabilitate himself as a public speaker and author of various "nonfiction" books that cast his career in a favorable light. Strangely, many doyens of the so-called LIBERAL MEDIA appeared to accept his new persona, consulting Nixon as a senior statesman on a variety of political and foreign policy issues. Following his death from a stroke on April 22, 1994, Nixon was honored with services in Washington, attended by President Bill Clinton and four predecessors. Significantly, the Richard Nixon Presidential Library in Yorba Linda, California, contains only Nixon's pre- and postpresidential papers. All documents from his White House years remain in Washington, archived as criminal evidence.

See also CLINTON, BILL AND HILLARY; KENNEDY DYNASTY.

Embittered by that loss, Nixon ran for governor of California two years later and in the wake of that defeat told reporters, "You won't have Dick Nixon to kick around any more." Retired to the practice of law (which coincidentally placed him in Dallas, Texas, on the morning of the JFK ASSASSINATION), Nixon forgot his vow in 1968 and opposed Vice President Hubert Humphrey in another race for the White House. Victorious that time, he escalated the U.S. war in VIETNAM while selling ambassadorships to the highest bidders and issuing a near-record number of pardons to members of organized crime. Domestic antiwar protests prompted Nixon to conceive the HUSTON PLAN for sweeping illegal surveillance, but the plot was scuttled by jealous FEDERAL BUREAU OF INVESTIGATION Director J. EDGAR HOOVER. "Tricky Dick" reappeared with a vengeance in the

NOAH'S Ark

Every Jew and Christian knows the Old Testament tale of Noah and the flood that was allegedly unleashed by God to cleanse the Earth of sin. Forewarned of the impending disaster, Noah supposedly built a wooden ship (the Ark) to divine specifications, approximately 425 feet long, 71 feet wide, and 43 feet tall. Within that craft, on three interior decks with a total floor space of some 90,500 square feet (by a generous estimate), Noah collected two specimens "of every living thing of all flesh," male and female, to repopulate Earth after the deluge. Theological debate endures to this day concerning such matters as (a) how animals from distant continents reached Noah's boatyard in the Middle East; (b) how he crowded millions of specimens (many mutually hostile) into the ship, together with six weeks' food for each creature (including carnivores); and (c) how he accommodated thousands of freshwater and saltwater aquatic species. Those arguments do not concern us here since no persuasive evidence suggests that the flood of Genesis ever occurred, but the search for proof of Noah's great adventure now includes a rumor of conspiracy.

In modern times sundry explorers have announced discovery of Noah's moldering ark at various points between TURKEY's Mount Ararat and ETHIOPIA, but each in turn fell short of proving his case. An explanation for those failures was advanced by the Russian newspaper *Pravda* on January 30, 2003. According to that article, Noah's Ark was located by the CENTRAL INTELLIGENCE AGENCY (CIA) sometime in the late 1940s and "secretly delivered to the territory of some U.S. military base." Alleged ex-CIA employee Dino Brugioni was quoted with respect to classified photos of "three huge curved beams" found on Mount Ararat, but the article further alluded to "notorious declassified materials" dating from 1992 that allegedly described a covert operation "supported by the late astronaut James Irvin" that "lasted for several years." Questions unanswered by the breathless exposé include the motive for CIA interest in biblical relics and the simple mechanics of wooden beams surviving some 6,500 years, exposed to harsh weather. *Pravda* itself apparently had doubts about the story, asking its readers: "Could this be true? Goodness knows."

NO Gun Ri massacre

On June 25, 1950, military forces from North KOREA crossed the 38th parallel into the southern half of that once-united country, driving both U.S. and South Korean forces farther southward by the day. U.S. commanders, frightened by the prospect of Communist infiltrators among the hordes of fleeing civilians, issued secret (and illegal) orders to shoot any civilians who approached U.S. military units in the field. Those orders were carried out with a vengeance on July 26–29, 1950, when U.S. armed-service members killed an estimated 400 civilians at No Gun Ri village. Evidence of the slaughter was concealed until September 1999 when U.S. veterans finally confessed the killings to Associated Press reporters. Subsequent official

documentation revealed that 83 percent of the victims were women, children, and elderly men; a full 20 percent were described as infants and children under 10 years of age. While humanitarians worldwide condemned the massacre and the 49-year cover-up, reports of similar events began to surface.

Sung Yong Park, a minister of the Korean Methodist Church and representative of the Congress for Korean Reunification, claims to possess evidence of 37 other massacres committed by U.S. forces in South Korea. Park calls No Gun Ri as "the tip of the iceberg" in U.S. WAR CRIMES of the Korean conflict, citing other cases that include: a U.S. Air Force bombing of Iksan on July 11, 1950, that left 54 civilians dead and 300-plus wounded; killings of 64 victims, with 43 wounded, at Chojang-ri on July 29, 1950; army demolition of bridges spanning the Naktong River that killed hundreds on August 3, 1950; bombings around Bobuk-myon that killed 49 and wounded 90 on January 19, 1951; the slaying of 100 persons, with another 100 wounded, at Jangji-ri on August 20, 1950; air raids on a cavern shelter near Youngchoon that killed 300 victims on January 20, 1951; the bombing of Kumsung-myon that killed 17 and wounded 21 at 1951's lunar new-year celebration; and the shooting of 90 civilians by U.S. troops at Changnyong-up (date uncertain). Park also refers vaguely to "countless massacres" allegedly committed by U.S. and South Korean forces in North Korea before the war's end, but no specific evidence has been produced to document those charges.

See also COMMUNISM.

NORWAY

After ADOLF HITLER's troops invaded Norway in April 1940, Norwegian Maj. Vidkun Quisling earned eternal infamy—and saw his surname shortlisted as a synonym for *traitor*—by collaborating with the THIRD REICH to subjugate his fellow countrymen. That choice sent him to the gallows on October 24, 1945, condemned for treason and WAR CRIMES. In the 1990s Norway was rocked by a series of church fires and grisly murders, apparently by members and fans of various "black metal" rock-and-roll bands committed to the outré tenets of SATANISM. Several defendants were imprisoned in those cases, but the panic inspired by their strange crimes endures.

NUESTRA Familia

The Hispanic PRISON GANG known as Nuestra Familia ("our family") was organized in the mid-1960s by inmates who were subjected to harassment, extortion, or worse by the powerful MEXICAN MAFIA. By the time Puerto Rican convict Robert ("Babo") Sosa was elected "general" of the clique in 1972, an estimated 30 prisoners had died in feuding between the two gangs. Three years later Nuestra Familia created its first free-world "regiment" in Fresno, California (where members sometimes call themselves the Fresno Bulldogs). With coffers fattened by drug sales and contract murders-for-hire, Nuestra Familia sometimes allied itself with the BLACK GUERRILLA FAMILY to battle soldiers of the Mexican Mafia and the ARYAN BROTHERHOOD. General Sosa was deposed in 1980, reportedly for ordering "needless murders," but the gang stayed strong with an estimated 800 members two years later. Various criminal activities, including "cowboy operation robberies" outside prison walls, have resulted in several racketeering prosecutions of Nuestra Familia members. In 2001, 21 alleged members were charged with multiple felonies in a case dubbed Operation Black Widow, wherein 11 defendants pleaded guilty prior to trial. Like their enemies in the Mexican Mafia, Nuestra Familia members observe a "once in, never out" code of honor. Their motto allegedly reads: "If I lead, follow me. If I hesitate, push me. If they kill me, avenge me. If I am a traitor, kill me!"

OAKLAND Police Department

In the 1940s the Oakland Police Department was renowned as one of the most corrupt and brutal law-enforcement agencies in the United States. Black prisoners were routinely beaten in custody, and patrol officers sometimes rolled drunks in broad daylight with witnesses present. An investigation by California's state legislature forced the police chief to quit under fire, while one of his subordinates drew a term in state prison, but broader reform awaited the appointment of reform chief Wyman Vernon. Vernon did his best to weed out grafters while bringing Oakland up to speed on scientific modes of crime fighting. His eventual replacement, Edward Toothman, boasted in 1965 that 40 percent of all Oakland police had one or more years of college education—well above the U.S. average, at the time—but that rosy image of progress concealed grave problems.

Education notwithstanding, Oakland P.D. remained 97 percent Caucasian in a city whose black population was rapidly climbing past 25 percent. African Americans who made the cut still faced discrimination in assignments and promotion, while the department's "elite" motorcycle unit remained a staunch bastion of white supremacy. Despite a departmental ban on political activity, police bulletin boards were routinely covered with crude racist "jokes" and recruiting literature for the far-right JOHN BIRCH SOCIETY. Such views were evidently shared by Toothman, as he ordered officers to infiltrate antiwar groups and to remove "offensive" *Playboy* magazines from Oakland newsstands. On October 15, 1965, while peaceful protests against the VIETNAM War proceeded in cities across the United States, Oakland police formed a human "Berlin Wall" across the Bay Bridge to block approaching marchers from their turf. Strangely, the barrier did not prevent members of the Hells Angels MOTORCYCLE GANG from slipping through to maul demonstrators in full view of police, and the officers moved to "restore order" only after blood was shed.

Public outcry over that episode prompted Chief Toothman's premature retirement, listing his house for sale with a "Caucasians only" rider in the contract, but his emergency replacement was scarcely better. Under Chief Charles Gain, Oakland P.D. regained its reputation as a head-cracking strike force, teeing off with nightsticks and chemical Mace to assault 2,500 protesters and journalists at the Oakland draft board on October 15, 1967. By that time the force was also embroiled in a virtual guerrilla war with the BLACK PANTHER PARTY, with officers harassing party members at every turn (and once riddling Panther headquarters with gunfire in a drunken, midnight, drive-by shooting). That conflict claimed several lives and earned Oakland's "finest" no end of opprobrium, ending only when the Panther Party was reduced by attrition to a ghost of its original size.

Oakland's law-enforcement problems did not end with the tempestuous 1960s. Recent scandals involving the city's police include the following:

Early 1990s—Police sergeant Thomas Alipio, leader of the Oakland P.D. "Wolf Pack," faced multiple accusations of brutality, burglary, and falsifying official payroll records. No criminal charges were filed, but Alipio was fired after claiming Fifth Amendment privileges when questioned under oath about his alleged criminal activities. He went on to serve with the East Palo Alto department and to face new accusations there.

March 1, 2000—Oakland resident Rory Keller-Dean filed a $10 million lawsuit against the Oakland P.D. and individual officers, claiming that one policeman forced her to have sex with him on more than 25 occasions between August 1997 and September 1999, often while his partner was "present as a lookout." Once, in August 1997, the chief offender also allegedly forced Keller-Dean to perform fellatio on a group of on-duty cops near the entrance of Alameda's Coast Guard Island. Trial in that case was pending as this volume went to press.

November 2, 2000—Four Oakland officers known as The Riders (or Rough Riders in some accounts) were charged with 48 felony counts that included kidnapping, assault with a deadly weapon, assault under color of authority, and filing false police reports; another 15 misdemeanor counts were also added to the shopping list. Those charges climaxed a three-month investigation into allegations that rogue cops were beating drug suspects and planting evidence to secure their conviction in court. Police chief Richard Ward recommended dismissal for all four defendants after a rookie cop assigned to the team reported their illegal activities. One of the accused promptly fled to Mexico, while his codefendants remained to face trial on 35 charges. In September 2003 jurors acquitted the officers on eight counts while failing to reach a verdict on 27 other charges. A retrial is planned on those counts but has not yet been scheduled.

April 7, 2003—Reverting to the classic 1960s style, Oakland police fired rubber bullets against unarmed, nonviolent demonstrators protesting President George W. Bush's invasion of IRAQ under the guise of OPERATION IRAQI FREEDOM. No tabulation of injuries was published, but an estimated three dozen marchers were arrested.

October 5, 2003—Relatives and neighbors of 20-year-old Terrence Mearis claimed that he was asleep when police stormed his Oakland apartment and shot him dead in his bedroom. The shooters, members of yet another "crime-reduction team" targeting alleged violent criminals and drug suspects, claim that they possessed a warrant and that Mearis "struggled" with them on his bed before he was shot. No charges were filed in that case.

See also BUSH DYNASTY.

OCTOBER Surprise

At his inauguration on January 20, 1981, President RONALD REAGAN promised "an era of national renewal" in the United States. Within 20 minutes, as if responding to the impact of those words, Iranian authorities released 52 American hostages held in captivity since November 4, 1979. While officials in IRAN had agreed "in principle" to liberate the hostages on November 4, 1980 (election day), their release was delayed an additional 11 weeks, thus robbing incumbent Jimmy Carter of a diplomatic victory that might have secured his reelection. In the climate of post-WATERGATE Washington, rumors predictably blamed the fortuitous timing of the prisoners' release on covert political chicanery by Reagan and Vice President George H. W. Bush (former director of the CENTRAL INTELLIGENCE AGENCY (CIA). Subsequent public and private investigations of the so-called October Surprise—referring to alleged (and illegal) Republican negotiations with Iran's Ayatollah Khomeini—raised more questions than they answered, while revealing the following suggestive facts:

• In 1981, while investigating charges that Reagan staffers stole White House briefing books on the eve of a televised presidential debate, Congress discovered that the GOP had established an elaborate spy network that collected data on the Carter campaign and tracked Carter's efforts to free the hostages. That program was coordinated by Reagan campaign manager William Casey (a veteran of the OFFICE OF STRATEGIC SERVICES, appointed in 1981 to head the CIA).

- In 1988 former Iranian vice president Abolhassan Bani-Sadr spoke from exile in Paris and told reporters that Bush had flown to FRANCE and sealed the hostage bargain on the weekend of October 18–19, 1980. Other alleged witnesses—including a mixed bag of arms dealers, spies, and other shady characters—confirmed Bush's presence in France with William Casey for meetings with Iranian officials. One witness, Iranian arms dealer Jamshid Hashemi, described two earlier meetings with Casey in SPAIN during July and August 1980. According to Hashemi, Bush funneled ransom payments and illicit arms shipments to Iran before the November 1980 election with assistance from ISRAEL. Israeli involvement in the plot was confirmed by ex-MOSSAD agent Ari Ben-Menashe, who served as his nation's military intelligence liaison with Iran during 1979–80.
- With various investigations of the October Surprise underway, self-described Oregon arms dealer Richard Brenneke claimed inside knowledge of the hostage negotiations, including personal sightings of Bush and Bush aide Donald Gregg at a Paris confab with Iranian leaders. While some details of his story were proved false—financial records placed Brenneke in the United States when he claimed to be traveling abroad—he was acquitted of perjury charges in federal court, following indictment by the Bush-Reagan JUSTICE DEPARTMENT.
- Another alleged participant in the hostage negotiations, Oswald LaWinter, was quickly unmasked as a one-time college professor who had been convicted for smuggling narcotics into the United States. Confronted with that fact by journalists, LaWinter declared that Republican plotters had paid him $100,000 "to mount a disinformation campaign" and to "make sure that the media lost interest, and that the [October Surprise] story was discredited."
- Senate investigators sought to question William Casey about his alleged involvement in the plot, but his death from a brain tumor frustrated that inquiry. When Casey's relatives surrendered various documents under subpoena, the late spy's passport and his diary pages for the dates in question were missing.

See also BUSH DYNASTY.

ODESSA

ODESSA is an acronym for the <u>O</u>rganization <u>d</u>er <u>E</u>hemaligen <u>SS</u>-<u>A</u>ngehörigen (Organization of Former SS Members), which aided the escape of Nazis indicted for WAR CRIMES during World War II and the Holocaust. Nazi-hunter Simon Wiesenthal later discovered that the escape apparatus had been created in August 1944 when high-ranking Nazis realized that they were bound to lose the war. Stolen wealth worth billions of dollars at 21st-century rates was first smuggled out of occupied Europe to safe havens in Switzerland and the Americas before fugitives followed their ill-gotten gains into exile. A primary escape course, known to fugitives as the "B-B" route, led from Bremen, GERMANY, through Austria to the seaport of Bari, ITALY. From there, with collaboration from corrupt officials, war criminals escaped to the Middle East or South America. An alternate "Monastery Route" was operated by clerics of the CATHOLIC CHURCH (chiefly Franciscans), who hid Nazis on the run in various European monasteries until they could reach Vatican City and flee Europe from there. ADOLF EICHMANN and JOSEF MENGELE were two of the most notorious runaway Nazis, though some researchers claim an even bigger fish—MARTIN BORMANN himself—also escaped to South America with help from ODESSA. An affiliated network known as *Die Spinne* (The Spider) existed primarily to furnish Nazi fugitives with false passports and other necessary documents.

See also HOLOCAUST AND HOLOCAUST DENIAL.

OFFICE of Strategic Services (OSS)

Prior to World War II, U.S. intelligence activities were carried out on an ad-hoc basis by various departments of the army and the navy with little collaboration and occasional hostility between the rival branches. That changed in June 1942 when President Franklin Roosevelt created the OSS, commanded by New York attorney William ("Wild Bill") Donovan. Even then, however, the OSS did not have total command over foreign intelligence collection, as FEDERAL BUREAU OF INVESTIGATION

(FBI) Director J. EDGAR HOOVER—a bitter enemy of Donovan since the 1920s—was permitted to control U.S. espionage activities in Latin America. Both groups investigated cases of alleged enemy spying inside the United States, but their incessant rivalry jeopardized efficient operations. On one occasion, FBI agents arrived with wailing sirens outside a foreign embassy in Washington, alerting security guards to the presence of OSS burglars inside and nearly costing the prowlers their lives. In another notorious case both agencies burglarized editorial offices of the magazine *Amerasia* to retrieving documents apparently stolen from government files, but the illegal entries scuttled any hope of prosecution. President Harry Truman dissolved the OSS in October 1945, transferring its functions to the State and War Departments. Two years later, those duties were assigned to the fledgling CENTRAL INTELLIGENCE AGENCY. Donovan was once again proposed for leadership, but a malicious whispering campaign orchestrated by G-man Hoover prevented Donovan's confirmation.

OHIO Gang

This nickname describes a group of shady politicians from the Buckeye State, led by fixer HARRY DAUGHERTY, who achieved their greatest triumph with the 1920 election of President Warren Harding. Daugherty managed Harding's campaign and was rewarded with appointment to serve as attorney general, whereupon he transformed the U.S. JUSTICE DEPARTMENT into a laughingstock widely known as the "Department of Easy Virtue." Another member of the clique, Bernard Fall, used his post with the Interior Department to precipitate the TEAPOT DOME scandal. Harding himself was an affable rogue who welcomed his mistress to the White House, savored bootleg liquor during PROHIBITION, and reportedly joined the KU KLUX KLAN (KKK) in a special Green Room ceremony shortly after his inauguration. While Harding's team is generally regarded as the most corrupt U.S. administration prior to RICHARD NIXON's, the scandals were not exposed until after Harding's death on August 2, 1923. Various explanations have been advanced for his sudden demise, and while accidental food poisoning is the most common candidate, some conspiracists believe Harding was murdered. In any case the KKK mourned his passing with motorcades nationwide,

President Warren Harding was the most visible member of the corrupt "Ohio Gang." (Author's collection)

and armed Klansmen long stood guard over Harding's grave at Marion, Ohio. Following his death, successor Calvin Coolidge fired Daugherty, and various members of the Ohio Gang were prosecuted for their crimes.

OIL

Chinese prospectors drilled the first oil wells in A.D. 347, plumbing 800-foot depths with bits attached to bamboo poles. Nine centuries later explorer Marco Polo witnessed mining of seep oil in Medieval Persia (now IRAN). In the 16th century oil was used as fuel in Polish street lamps. The United States lagged behind foreign competitors, reporting its first discovery of oil as an undesirable by-product of Pennsylvania brine wells in 1815, waiting another 35 years before oil from hand-dug pits around Los Angeles was distilled for use in lamps by General Andreas Pico. The first oil well in North America was drilled in 1858 in Ontario, Canada. A year later Edwin Drake drilled the first U.S. well, all of 69 feet deep, at Titusville, Pennsylvania. By 1861 "bulk boats"—the first oil barges—were transporting crude along the Allegheny River.

Today, world governments and industry depend on oil as beating hearts rely on blood. Despite decades of research and U.S. government "initiatives" that were meant to develop alternative energy sources, petroleum—a fossil fuel that produces various toxic pollutants, resulting in a wide variety of long-range calamities including acid rain, global warming, and destruction of the Earth's ozone layer—Big Oil remains supreme on the world stage. In the United States, oil-rich families such as the Bush and Rockefeller clans have dominated politics for decades—through donations, through lobbyists, and often through election of their sons to high political office. In ELECTION 2000, for example, oil companies donated $5,291,212 to "conservative" Republicans versus $1,354,038 to "liberal" Democrats. Both President George W. Bush and Vice President DICK CHENEY have long-standing ties to the oil industry—Bush as the chairman of several failed companies, and Cheney as CEO of Halliburton Corporation, which profited hugely from its White House ties during OPERATION IRAQI FREEDOM.

Aside from the GULF WAR and the subsequent U.S. invasion of IRAQ, oil affects U.S. foreign and domestic policy in a variety of ways. One of the world's primary oil-producing nations, SAUDI ARABIA, is run by a dynastic regime that supports TERRORISM throughout the world. Its native sons include terrorist leader Osama bin Laden (whose father and brothers were business partners of the Bush clan in oil), and 15 of the 19 hijackers involved in the September 2001 PENTTBOM attacks. That catastrophic incident climaxed an eight-year series of attacks on U.S. forces and facilities that began with the 1993 WORLD TRADE CENTER BOMBING, all traceable to Saudi Arabian fanatics bankrolled by petro-dollars. Prior to the 9/11 raid that claimed his life, FEDERAL BUREAU OF INVESTIGATION Deputy Director John O'Neill told reporters: "The main obstacles to investigate [sic] Islamic terrorism were U.S. oil corporate interests, and the role played by Saudi Arabia in it. . . . All the answers, everything needed to dismantle Osama bin Laden's organization, can be found in

Saudi Arabia." Indeed, on September 11, 2001, when all U.S. flights were reportedly grounded, one civilian aircraft was permitted to fly: a jet evacuating members of the bin Laden family from the United States to Saudi Arabia, their passage arranged by FBI officials acting in conjunction with the Bush White House and the Saudi ambassador, Prince Bandar. The bin Ladens were visiting America that day for meetings with the Carlyle Group, an investment firm that is well connected to Republican leaders whose Chairman Frank Carlucci served as RONALD REAGAN's secretary of defense.

See also BIN LADEN FAMILY; BUSH DYNASTY; ROCKEFELLER CLAN.

OKHRANA

Czar Alexander III created the Okhrana ("guard") as his SECRET POLICE force in 1881, hiring thousands of spies to infiltrate and undermine various peasant and worker's organizations throughout RUSSIA. Countless alleged subversives were executed, imprisoned, exiled (like JOSEPH STALIN), or otherwise harassed (like author Leo Tolstoy) on the basis of accusations from Okhrana informers. By the turn of the 20th century, the Okhrana had become the most powerful and feared intelligence service on Earth, with agents operating throughout Europe and elsewhere, frequently engaged in acts of TERRORISM and assassination targeting enemies of the Czar. A deep strain of anti-Semitism also infested the Okhrana, and it was responsible for publication of a malicious forgery titled the PROTOCOLS OF THE ELDERS OF ZION, outlining an alleged Jewish plot for world domination. For all its cloak-and-dagger acumen, however, the Okhrana could not save Czar Nicholas II in 1917, when revolutionaries led by VLADIMIR LENIN toppled the Russian monarchy. Soviet secret police inherited the Okhrana's files and later expanded on its methods, surpassing the efficiency of their old rivals with the new and improved KGB.

OKLAHOMA City bombing

At 9:02 A.M. on April 19, 1995, a Ryder rented truck loaded with 4,800 pounds of homemade explosives detonated outside the Arthur P. Murrah Federal Building in Oklahoma City. It demolished the edifice, killing at least 168 persons (some reports say 169) and injuring 850. After the WORLD TRADE CENTER

BOMBING of 1993 public assumptions first blamed Islamic militants for the crime, but perceptions swiftly altered. Within 90 minutes of the blast, 26-year-old Timothy McVeigh was stopped by a state trooper in Noble County, 60 miles north of Oklahoma City, for driving a car with no license plate. McVeigh was arrested when the officer noticed a pistol concealed under his shirt and jailed McVeigh at Perry, Oklahoma, pending criminal charges. A search of the FEDERAL BUREAU OF INVESTIGATION (FBI) national computer registry disclosed no open warrants on McVeigh.

Meanwhile, a team of 1,000 federal agents combing the blast site found a serial number for the Ryder truck and traced it to renter "Robert Kling," whose name and address both proved to be false. Agents

Jackie Zachmeier from North Dakota reads the description explaining the spray-painted message left by rescuers during the Oklahoma City bombing in 1995, as she toured the Oklahoma National Memorial in Oklahoma City, June 9, 2001. (Reuters/Corbis)

obtained a description of Kling and an unnamed male companion and, searched local motels, discovering that Kling's description matched visitor Tim McVeigh who had rented a room on April 14. A second computer check located McVeigh in his jail cell at Perry and traced his "home address" to a Michigan farm owned by James Nichols. James's brother, Terry Nichols, was a friend of McVeigh's from military service in the GULF WAR, but neither Nichols matched the description of "John Doe No. 2" from Oklahoma City. (That unknown suspect has yet to be identified.)

Investigation of McVeigh's background revealed that he was once a member of the KU KLUX KLAN, later was attracted to the radical Militia Movement, and became obsessed with studying THE TURNER DIARIES, a neo-Nazi novel that depicts truck-bomb attacks against the U.S. government. McVeigh and Terry Nichols were apparently fixated on the FBI siege of a religious cult's compound at Waco, Texas, where 76 members of the Branch Davidian sect died by fire on April 19, 1993. Investigators alleged that McVeigh and Nichols timed the Oklahoma City blast to occur on the anniversary of that tragic event. A search of Terry Nichols's home revealed explosives, blasting caps, blue plastic barrels similar to those used in the truck bomb, and a receipt for 2,000 pounds of ammonium nitrate (used in constructing the bomb).

On August 11, 1995, a federal grand jury indicted both suspects for conspiracy and for the murders of eight federal agents killed in the bombing. Jurors convicted McVeigh on all counts, on June 2, 1997, and recommended a death sentence on June 13. Terry Nichols faced trial in November 1997, but since prosecutors could not place him at the crime scene, he escaped conviction on murder charges and received a life prison term. On May 10, 2001, six days before McVeigh's scheduled execution, FBI spokespersons admitted that the bureau had "inadvertently" misplaced thousands of documents relevant to his case, thereby illegally withholding them from McVeigh's attorney. Attorney General JOHN ASHCROFT granted a 30-day stay of execution, but a court review of the documents revealed no mitigating evidence, and McVeigh was executed by lethal injection on June 11, 2001.

Eight years after the blast in Oklahoma City, conspiracists remain convinced that McVeigh and Nichols did not act alone. Aside from the still-elusive

John Doe No. 2, defense attorney Steven Jones believes that FBI agents deliberately altered or concealed evidence in the case. "They short-circuited the search for the truth," Jones told reporters in February 2003. "I don't doubt Tim's role in the conspiracy. But I think he clearly aggrandized his role, enlarged it, to cover for others who were involved." FBI documents released since McVeigh's execution include records showing that he telephoned Elohim City, an ultra-right-wing compound in Oklahoma, on April 5, 1995—at a time when the camp's residents included fugitive members of the neo-Nazi Aryan Nations. Those fugitives, wanted for bank robbery, reportedly left Elohim City on April 16, 1995, and traveled to a site in Kansas near the point where McVeigh assembled his truck bomb. One of the robbers, Kevin Peter Langan, was interviewed by FBI agents after his arrest in 1996. According to Langan's attorney, Kevin Durkin, "The Justice Department came to us through the assistant U.S. attorney and said, 'We believe your client knows about Oklahoma City and we want to talk to him. We want to work out a deal.'" Langan declined to collaborate, and no other suspects have yet been charged in the Oklahoma City case.

Alternative scenarios, advanced by some Internet theorists, include a possibility that McVeigh and other right-wing activists were hired (or duped) by Muslim militants into planting the Oklahoma City bomb or that federal agents themselves are to blame. The latter theory claims the Murrah bombing was a kind of REICHSTAG FIRE event, coordinated by President Bill Clinton to justify a nationwide crackdown on "patriot" militia groups—which, in fact, did not occur. If others than McVeigh and Terry Nichols were involved in the bombing, those culprits who are still at large were almost certainly members of the neo-Nazi lunatic fringe.

See also CLINTON, BILL AND HILLARY; MILITIAS.

OMAN

Migratory Arabs inhabited the region of modern-day Oman during the ninth century B.C.E. and converted to Islam 1,600 years later. Successive occupations by PORTUGAL (1508–1648) and TURKEY (1648–1741) finally produced a successful revolt against foreign invaders, led by Sultan Ahmad ibn Sa'id, whose descendants rule Oman today with an absolute monarchy. Oman's sultans and imams (Muslim lead-

ers) clashed incessantly during the first half of the 20th century until the last imam was deported in 1959. On July 23, 1970, a palace coup ended the 38-year rule of Sultan Sa'id bin Taimur and placed his son on the throne, accompanied by vows to modernize the government and use Oman's OIL wealth for public benefit. Oman joined the UNITED NATIONS in 1971, but progress at home is difficult to judge. A long border conflict with YEMEN was finally settled in 1997, the same year in which Oman's women were granted suffrage. In 2001 some 20,000 British troops used Oman for a military "training exercise," which some critics viewed as a not-so-subtle act of intimidation against the monarchy and/or its neighbors.

O'NEAL, William (fl. 1968)

Chicago resident William O'Neal was arrested twice in early 1968 for auto theft and for impersonating a FEDERAL BUREAU OF INVESTIGATION (FBI) agent. To avoid prison he joined the bureau's COINTELPRO program as a paid informant inside the BLACK PANTHER PARTY chapter led by FRED HAMPTON. His assignment included provoking dissension between Panthers and various Chicago STREET GANGS, a ploy that produced several shootings. As the chapter's "security chief," O'Neal devised plans to bomb city hall and execute police informers in a homemade electric chair, but Hampton rejected both schemes. In Hampton's absence O'Neal whipped one Panther and encouraged others to commit armed robberies. Finally he helped authorities plan a raid on December 4, 1969, wherein Hampton and comrade Mark Clark were killed by officers of the CHICAGO POLICE DEPARTMENT. Subsequent investigation proved that Hampton was sleeping when shot and that he may have been drugged before raiders arrived. In the wake of that raid O'Neal's FBI handlers paid him a "merit bonus" for his "valuable service" to the Bureau.

OPERATION Iraqi Freedom

According to the testimony of his intimate advisors, President George W. Bush began seeking excuses for a U.S. invasion of IRAQ within hours of his January 2001 inauguration. No excuse for military action then existed—Iraq had been defeated in the GULF WAR 10 years earlier and had been subject to harsh economic sanctions ever since, and Iraq was effectively contained within its borders by hostile neighbors and U.S.-enforced "no-fly zones." Also, while terrorists from the AL-QAEDA network, led by Osama bin Laden, were linked to numerous attacks on U.S. personnel and installations, none of those incidents were traceable to Iraq. Indeed, President Bush—whose family shared lucrative OIL interests with bin Laden's father and brothers—complained that his predecessor, President Bill Clinton, had been "obsessed" with pursuit of al-Qaeda, and Bush reportedly ordered federal agents to "back off the bin Ladens."

One day after the September 11, 2001, PENTTBOM attacks, executed by al-Qaeda terrorists from SAUDI ARABIA, Bush ordered White House counterterrorism coordinator to "Go back over everything, everything. See if Saddam did this." Clarke replied, "But Mr. President, al-Qaeda did this," whereupon Bush replied, "I know, I know, but see if Saddam was involved. Just look. I want to know any shred."

When Clarke reminded Bush that the FEDERAL BUREAU OF INVESTIGATION and CENTRAL INTELLIGENCE AGENCY had already searched in vain for such links, the president "testily" ordered, "Look into Iraq, Saddam." The search for clues was repeated, again in vain, and no excuse for an invasion of Iraq was found. Frustrated in that effort, Bush and company launched a new campaign to portray Iraq as a global threat, based on claims that Saddam had stockpiled "weapons of mass destruction" (WMD). Those claims included the following public statements:

August 26, 2002—Vice President DICK CHENEY told the Veterans of Foreign Wars, "Simply stated, there is no doubt that Saddam Hussein now has weapons of mass destruction."

September 12, 2002—Bush told the UNITED NATIONS General Assembly, "Right now, Iraq is

Deposed Iraqi president Saddam Hussein was found in a hole on property in Al Dawr, near his hometown of Tikrit. "I am Saddam Hussein, president of Iraq, and I am willing to negotiate," were Hussein's words when he was found by members of Special Forces. (Cheryl Diaz/Dallas Morning News/Corbis)

expanding and improving facilities that were used for the production of biological weapons."

September 19, 2002—Secretary of Defense Donald Rumsfeld told Congress, "No terrorist state poses a greater or more immediate threat to the security of our people and the stability of the world than the regime of Saddam Hussein in Iraq."

November 23, 2002—White House press secretary Ari Fleischer told assembled journalists, in regard to Saddam's alleged stockpile of WMD: "If he declares he has none, then we will know that Saddam Hussein is once again misleading the world."

January 9, 2003—Fleischer told another press conference, "We know for a fact that there are weapons there."

January 26, 2003—White House spokesman Dan Bartlett told CNN News, "What we know from UN inspectors over the course of the last decade is that Saddam Hussein possesses thousands of chemical warheads, that he possesses hundreds of liters of very dangerous toxins that can kill millions of people."

January 28, 2003—In his State of the Union address, Bush told America, "Our intelligence officials estimate that Saddam Hussein had the materials to produce as much as 500 tons of sarin, mustard, and VX nerve agent. The British government has learned that Saddam Hussein recently sought significant quantities of uranium from Africa."

February 10, 2003—White House spokesman Scott McClellan told reporters, "This is about an imminent threat."

March 16, 2003—On NBC's *Meet the Press,* Dick Cheney announced, "We believe [Hussein] has, in fact, reconstituted nuclear weapons."

March 17, 2003—Addressing a national audience, Bush declared, "Intelligence gathered by this and other governments leaves no doubt that the Iraq regime continues to possess and conceal some of the most lethal weapons ever devised."

U.S. and British troops launched a full-scale invasion of Iraq on March 20, 2003. Their rapid advance toward Baghdad was accompanied by more confident WMD rhetoric, including these statements from Washington:

March 21, 2003—Ari Fleischer told the press, "Well, there is no question that we have evidence and information that Iraq has weapons of mass destruction, biological and chemical particularly. All this will be made clear in the course of the operation, for whatever duration it takes."

March 22, 2003—General Tommy Franks, commanding the troops in Iraq, declared, "There is no doubt that the regime of Saddam Hussein possesses weapons of mass destruction. And as this operation continues, those weapons will be identified, found, along with the people who have produced them and who guard them."

March 22, 2003—Pentagon spokesperson Victoria Clark told reporters, "One of our top objectives is to find and destroy the WMD. There are a number of sites."

March 23, 2003—Kenneth Adelman, a member of Bush's Defense Policy Board, told the *Washington Post,* "I have no doubt we're going to find big stores of weapons of mass destruction."

March 30, 2003—Donald Rumsfeld assured *ABC News,* "We know where they are. They're in the area around Tikrit and Baghdad and east, west, south, and north somewhat."

April 9, 2003—White House spokesmen Robert Kagan told the *Washington Post,* "Obviously the administration intends to publicize all the weapons of mass destruction U.S. forces find—and there will be plenty."

April 10, 2003—Ari Fleischer told a Washington press conference, "Make no mistake—as I said earlier—we have high confidence that they have weapons of mass destruction. That is what this war was about and it is about. And we have high confidence it will be found."

April 24, 2003—President Bush announced, "We are learning more as we interrogate or have discussions with Iraqi scientists and people within the Iraqi structure, that perhaps he destroyed some, perhaps he dispersed some. And so we will find them."

May 3, 2003—Bush advised journalists, "We'll find them. It'll be a matter of time to do so."

May 4, 2003—Colin Powell told the press, "I'm absolutely sure that there are weapons of mass destruction there and the evidence will be forthcoming. We're just getting it just now."

May 31, 2003—Bush proclaimed that WMD had, in fact, been found in Iraq, telling the press, "You remember when Colin Powell stood up in front of the world, and he said Iraq has got laboratories, mobile labs to build biological weapons. . . . They're illegal. They're against the United Nations resolutions, and we've so far discovered two. And we'll find more weapons as time goes on, But for those who say we haven't found the banned manufacturing devices or banned weapons, they're wrong. We found them."

Within hours of that confident statement, inspectors declared that the "mobile labs" in question contained no evidence of weapons—and indeed, no trace of any Iraqi WMD had been found by the time this volume went to press in 2005. By then, administration spokespersons had begun to backpedal, compounding their earlier misstatements with more distortions. Their disclaimers included the following:

May 4, 2003—Donald Rumsfeld, having detailed where WMD might be found on March 30, now told Fox News, "We never believed that we'd just tumble over weapons of mass destruction in that country."

May 12, 2003—National Security Adviser Condoleezza Rice told Reuters journalists, "U.S. officials never expected that we were going to open garages and find weapons of mass destruction."

May 13, 2003—Maj. Gen. David Petraeus, commanding the 101st Airborne Division in Iraq, told reporters, "I just don't know whether it was all destroyed years ago—I mean, there's no question that there were chemical weapons years ago—whether they were destroyed right before the war [or] whether they're still hidden."

May 14, 2003—Apparently forgetting Dick Cheney's remarks of March 16, (above), Rumsfeld told the U.S. Senate, "I don't believe anyone that I know in the administration ever said that Iraq had nuclear weapons."

May 27, 2003—Concerning other WMD, Rumsfeld told the COUNCIL ON FOREIGN RELATIONS, "They may have had time to destroy them, and I don't know the answer."

May 30, 2003—One day before President Bush declared that WMD labs had been found, Lt. Gen. James Conway—commanding the 1st Marine Expeditionary Force in Iraq—told journalists, "It was a surprise to me then—it remains a surprise to me now—that we have not uncovered weapons, as you say, in some of the forward dispersal sites. Believe me, it's not for lack of trying. We've been to virtually every ammunition supply point between the Kuwaiti border and Baghdad, but they're simply not there."

January 31, 2004—Scott McClellan told reporters at the White House, "I think some in the media have chosen to use the word *imminent*. Those were not words [*sic*] we used. We used *grave and gathering* threat." In fact, McClellan himself had described the Iraqi threat as "imminent" on February 10, 2003 (see above). Others who described the "imminent" threat included Don Bartlett (on January 26, 2003) and Ari Fleischer (on May 7, 2003).

With the supposed Iraqi WMD missing, Bush and company changed tunes again, claiming the war was justified because Saddam had oppressed his own people for decades. The true motive for invading Iraq remains elusive—except, perhaps, to the conspiracists who point out that Dick Cheney's colleagues at Halliburton Corporation received a secret, no-bid contract to provide oil technology in occupied Iraq, a service for which Halliburton admittedly overcharged the U.S. government at least $6.3 million in 2003.

See also BUSH DYNASTY; CLINTON, BILL AND HILLARY; TERRORISM.

OPERATION Underworld

The first official collaboration between elements of the U.S. government and the MAFIA occurred in 1942 when military leaders grew concerned about potential Axis sabotage of Allied ships berthed at the New York City waterfront. Recognizing that mobsters led by CHARLES "LUCKY" LUCIANO effectively controlled all commerce on the New York docks, agents of Naval Intelligence approached "Socks" Lanza, covert lord of the Fulton Fish Market, for an introduction to his boss. Lanza referred the agents to MEYER LANSKY, who in turn carried their offer to Luciano—then imprisoned at Dannemora, New York, on WHITE SLAVERY charges. Thus was born Operation Underworld, in which Luciano promised to assist the Allied war effort in return for certain favors. The payoff for Luciano included immediate transfer to a kinder, gentler lockup in Albany, together with a promise of parole at war's end. In return he mobilized his gangsters to eliminate suspected waterfront saboteurs—and, some say, also provided Mafia contacts to facilitate the 1943 Allied invasion of Sicily.

Most historians today dispute the published claim that U.S. tanks landing on Sicily bore flags emblazoned with the letter *L* (for *Luciano*), but there is no doubt that native Mafiosi led by Don Calogero Vizzini aided occupation forces by eliminating obstacles and executing Fascist leaders. After Sicily was conquered, Don Vizzini and other prominent Mafiosi were appointed to serve as mayors in various towns as a means of preserving "law and order." In that capacity they further served Allied interests—and set the stage for later cold war conflicts in Italy—by liquidating Communists and other left-wing elements of the resistance movement who had risked much in combat with the Nazis. New York mobster Vito Genovese, a Luciano lieutenant hiding in Italy to avoid murder charges at home, made a fortune from U.S. troops in black-market transactions before he was finally arrested and deported to New York for trial. (He was acquitted, after crucial witnesses vanished or changed their stories.)

Naval authorities kept their bargain with Luciano at war's end, arranging his release and deportation to Italy in 1946. After a lavish send-off party in New York, attended by high-ranking mobsters from all parts of the United States, Luciano lived briefly in Italy but then illegally returned to CUBA under the protection of U.S.-supported dictator Fulgencio Batista. From Havana he organized new distribution routes for HEROIN entering the United States, a conspiracy involving the lucrative "French Connection" with members of the UNIONE CORSÉ. Although Luciano was soon forced back to Italy, primarily through the efforts of early "drug czar" HARRY ANSLINGER, his enterprise prospered. In 1946 America harbored an estimated 20,000 heroin addicts—barely 10 percent of the world total that was acknowledged in the 1920s—but the numbers rapidly increased thereafter. In retrospect some analysts suggest that while Operation Underworld helped win the war in Italy, it launched another conflict—the so-called War on Drugs—which continues to the present day with no end in sight.

See also COMMUNISM; FASCISM.

OPIUM wars

With the publicity surrounding modern "wars on drugs" around the world, it seems incredible that any nation would declare war on another to *promote* narcotics traffic. Yet England did precisely that on two occasions in the 19th century. In both cases London's target was CHINA, a vast market where British merchants began to smuggle opium in the 1820s to offset expenses of purchasing Chinese tea for sale in England. Opium was banned by law in China at the time, and Chinese authorities enforced that statute in 1839, destroying a large shipment of British drugs stockpiled at Canton (now Guangzhou). In retaliation for that action Britain launched the First Opium War (1839–42), dispatching gunboats and troops to Canton and other Chinese seaports, overwhelming native forces to "open" forcibly broader trade (including opium traffic) between Britain and China. As a result of that invasion, China signed the Treaty of Nanjing (1842) and the Supplementary Treaty of Bogue (1843), providing full British trading and residency privileges in the ports of Canton, Fuzhou, Jinmen, Ningbo, and Shanghai. Other Western powers soon followed Britain's example, extorting trade rights from China at gunpoint and establishing "spheres of influence" where foreign authorities reigned supreme on Chinese soil.

The Second Opium War erupted in 1856 after an "illegal" search of the British ship *Arrow* at Canton by Chinese authorities seeking smuggled opium. Chinese submission to the Treaty of Tianjin (1858) opened 11 more seaports to Western trade, legalized opium traffic, established Western trade legations in Beijing—and ironically sanctioned the presence of Christian missionaries throughout China. The short-lived peace was broken once again in 1859 when China's vain attempt to bar Western diplomats from Beijing brought a combined force of British and French troops to invade the Chinese capital and burn the imperial summer palace. The Beijing conventions of 1860 that forced China to reaffirm all previous treaties with the West formally ended the Second Opium War in 1860—and thus paved the way for a nationalistic rebellion by "Boxer" guerrillas four decades later. In the meantime, millions of Chinese were addicted to British opium, and London forever surrendered its claim to the moral high ground.

ORANGEBURG massacre

In February 1968 black students from South Carolina State University launched protests against a whites-only bowling alley in Orangeburg. On February 5, police fired on the unarmed demonstrators, killing three and wounding 27 as they fled. Official statements claimed the shooting occurred "only after an extended period of sniper fire from the campus and not until an officer had been felled during his efforts to protect life and property." Yet no weapons were found, and the only police officer injured was accidentally struck by a piece of lumber while trying to douse a bonfire. FEDERAL BUREAU OF INVESTIGATION (FBI) agents found several .22-caliber bullets embedded in the wall of a nearby warehouse but could not determine when they were fired. Examination of the scene *did* prove the slugs originated from a point more than 100 feet away from where the demonstrators had been shot.

The conduct of G-men involved in the case was highly suspect. At least three agents witnessed the shooting but claimed they were elsewhere when questioned by JUSTICE DEPARTMENT investigators. Attorney General Ramsey Clark was "distressed" by the bureau's obstructionist tactics. "It was a shame," he later said, "that we probably had quite a bit of trouble with a number of FBI agents as to what they said at different times and we had trouble getting all the interviews we wanted. We also had a terribly difficult time finding out where the FBI people were on the night of February 8—where they were, what they were doing, whether they were eyewitnesses."

Nine police admitted firing on the demonstrators in their statements to FBI agents. Lt. Jesse Spell—soon promoted to captain—declared, "I ordered my squad to fire their weapons to stop the mob;" yet none of the admitted shooters could recall a verbal order, and most of their 30 victims were shot in the back while running away. A federal grand jury indicted the nine officers on December 19, 1968, for violating civil rights by means of summary punishment inflicted "under color of law." Their trial convened in May 1969. That proceeding was marked by a clash between FBI agents as two of them testified for the defense and another was called to rebut the statements of his fellow G-men. All the defendants were acquitted, prompting further criticism of police and the bureau.

ORGAN theft

A solitary tourist visiting some exotic country unexpectedly meets a beautiful woman, and they spend a romantic evening together. Next morning the traveler wakes shivering in a bathtub filled with ice, gripped by pain from a crudely stitched abdominal incision. On the floor beside the bathtub sits a telephone. A note taped to the wall nearby instructs the victim to call for medical help, explaining that one of his kidneys has been removed.

That story, with variations, has circled the globe countless times via Internet channels, inspired by (or inspiring) a series of novels and Hollywood films in which venal doctors and criminal accomplices steal vital organs from unwilling donors and then sell them to wealthy patients awaiting transplants. Each time the tale surfaces, authorities dismiss it as a hoax, denying that any such thing has occurred in real life.

And yet . . .

On February 18, 2000, the Law Society of Thailand announced its intent to file criminal charges against five doctors at Bangkok's Vachiraprakarn Hospital, claiming that the physicians used false documents to obtain kidneys from brain-dead patients and offered the organs for sale to others awaiting transplants. The racket was exposed after relatives of the unconscious donors discovered that their signatures had been forged on forms granting permission for the surgery. Thai authorities revoked the medical license of Dr. Sirot Kanchanapanchaphol, described in press reports as one of the country's top surgeons, and suspended four alleged accomplices pending further investigation of the charges. On August 30, 2000, two of the physicians and a former hospital administrator were charged with conspiring to murder two comatose patients who died after their kidneys were removed. Charges against a fourth suspect were dropped after he agreed to testify against the others.

Five months before that scandal broke, on September 16, 1999, Turkish prime minister Bulent Ecevit announced an official investigation into press reports that an "organ MAFIA" had performed unauthorized surgery on deceased earthquake victims in Cinarcik. Some 15,500 people died in Cinarcik's earthquake of August 17, followed by claims that corpses in the morgue had been stripped of their organs for sale. If that was not sinister enough, spokespersons for the Turkish Interior Ministry also alleged that an unidentified "30-strong group" was kidnapping young earthquake orphans, along with elderly and disabled persons, to forcibly extract their organs for sale.

In China, even though Beijing authorities declare that "any form of trade in human organs is strictly against related Chinese law," allegations dating from 1996 claim that various organs are routinely extracted from prisoners executed by the state. According to Amnesty International, China—which executes thousands of inmates each year—switched from firing squads to lethal injection in 2001 because chemical deaths "may facilitate the removal of organs from executed prisoners for transplantation." Chinese statutes specify that organs from deceased convicts may be used for medical purposes "if no one claims the body or the family refuses to bury it." In fact, however, U.S. congressional investigators charge that evidence of outright organ sales to "foreigners or wealthy Chinese is substantial, credible and growing." Livers from deceased inmates are reportedly sold for an average price of $43,000.

In a grisly variation on that theme, California's *Orange County Register* reported on April 16, 2000 that corpses donated to nonprofit tissue banks in the United States were being dismantled for piecemeal sale to private research facilities, earning an average of $220,000 per cadaver. While the National Organ Transplant Act of 1984 bars sale of human tissue for profit, it permits an undefined "reasonable charge" for collection and processing of body parts. As Arthur Caplan, a professor at the University of Pennsylvania's Center for Bioethics, told the *Register,* "People who donate [remains] have no idea tissue is being processed into products that per gram or per ounce are in the price range of diamonds."

OSWALD, Lee Harvey (1939–1963)

Alleged double-murderer Lee Harvey Oswald, accused (but never convicted) of the 1963 JFK ASSASSINATION and the peripheral murder of Dallas policeman J. D. Tippit, was a native of New Orleans and was born on October 19, 1939. Before age 18 he lived in 22 different homes and attended 12 different schools, rating a psychological diagnosis of "personality pattern disturbance" when he was 14 years old. After high school Oswald joined the U.S. Marine Corps and learned to speak Russian while stationed in Japan. He subsequently defected to RUSSIA, where KGB agents initially suspected him of spying for the CENTRAL INTELLIGENCE AGENCY (CIA). To forestall deportation from Russia, in 1959 Oswald renounced his U.S. citizenship and then attempted suicide. Russian authorities allowed him to remain in Minsk and granted Oswald permission to marry Marina

Prusakova, reputed daughter of a KGB officer. The marital knot was barely tied, however, when Oswald changed his mind about COMMUNISM and returned to the United States in 1961 with Marina and their infant daughter in tow. Strangely, American authorities raised no objection to his return—yet another piece of circumstantial evidence supporting theories that Oswald was a CIA agent whose defection had been staged for reasons unknown.

Settling in Dallas Oswald quickly found work with a graphic arts firm, Jaggars-Chiles-Stovall, which also did highly classified work for the U.S. government. Oswald later told a friend that the CIA arranged his job specifically to work on maps of CUBA, where the agency was then engaged with members of the MAFIA in plots to murder President FIDEL CASTRO. In April 1963 Oswald moved to New Orleans and found work at the Reily Coffee Company, where employees recall him incessantly questioning Cuban coworkers. On the side he formed a local one-man branch of the pro-Castro Fair Play for Cuba Committee, which strangely shared office space with ex-FBI agent Guy Banister, a right-wing activist involved in the CIA-Mafia plots to kill Castro. About the same time Oswald used the alias "Alek J. Hidell" to purchase two mail-order guns: an obsolete 6.5-millimeter Italian Mannlicher-Carcano and a .38-caliber revolver. He then moved back to Dallas and found work at the Texas School Book Depository, from which he allegedly shot President Kennedy—and where his rifle was found, near a sixth-floor window—on November 22, 1963. Soon after the assassination, Oswald allegedly used his pistol to kill Officer Tippit on a Dallas street before he was cornered and captured in a nearby movie theater.

In custody, Oswald steadfastly denied killing either Kennedy or Tippit, insisting that he was "just a patsy" and that while he was charged with both crimes, he would never stand trial. On November 24 as officers attempted to transport him to the county jail Oswald was shot and killed by transplanted Chicago mobster JACK RUBY in the basement of DALLAS POLICE DEPARTMENT headquarters. Ruby claimed that the shooting was motivated by his sympathy for widow Jacqueline Kennedy and a desire to spare her from testifying at Oswald's murder trial. The WARREN COMMISSION accepted that tale at face value while ignoring Ruby's lifelong involvement in organized crime. Although the commission named both Oswald and Ruby as lone killers, the HOUSE

SELECT COMMITTEE ON ASSASSINATIONS later found that JFK "was probably assassinated as the result of a conspiracy." Evidence supporting Oswald's claim of innocence—or, at least, suggesting that he was manipulated to the point of being charged and then killed by Ruby—includes the following items:

- A famous photograph of Oswald posing with his mail-order rifle, published in *Life* magazine, reveals evidence of possible tampering. Specifically, the divergent angles of shadows seen on Oswald's face and behind his body suggest that Oswald's head was spliced onto the shoulders of some unknown man.
- Substantial published evidence suggests that Oswald was an agent of the CIA and simultaneously served the Federal Bureau of Investigation (FBI) as a paid informant. Both agencies denied any significant knowledge of Oswald during the Warren Commission investigation, and subsequent testimony indicates that files linking Oswald to the bureau were destroyed.
- Between September 27 and October 3, 1963, Oswald visited Mexico City, including an alleged stop at the Cuban embassy where he supposedly requested information on travel to Havana. At that time the Cuban embassy was under constant CIA surveillance, with visitors photographed on arrival and departure. The man identified as Oswald in agency photos from September 1963 bears no resemblance to the real-life Oswald, a discrepancy that remains unexplained to this day.
- Several weeks before the JFK assassination, an unknown man using Oswald's name created a disturbance at a Dallas rifle range, firing repeatedly at other shooters' targets. Witnesses who observed and spoke to the man agreed that he did not resemble Oswald, though he repeatedly identified himself by name. The Warren Commission dismissed the incident as irrelevant.
- Two weeks before the assassination, another unknown man used Oswald's name while paying an Irving, Texas, gunsmith to mount a telescopic sight on an Italian rifle that was similar (but not identical) to Oswald's Mannlicher-Carcano. An anonymous caller informed FBI agents of the event on November 24, 1963, and G-men deemed it "a bona fide transaction," but the Warren Commission once again dismissed the evidence as meaningless.

PACKER, Horace (fl. 1969)

Seattle FEDERAL BUREAU OF INVESTIGATION (FBI) informant Horace Packer was hired in 1969 to infiltrate the STUDENTS FOR A DEMOCRATIC SOCIETY. He later admitted supplying campus radicals (at FBI expense) with drugs, weapons, and the paint used to vandalize Seattle's federal courthouse in February 1970. That incident resulted in federal indictments of defendants known locally as the "Seattle Eight." At their trial Packer testified that his FBI handlers told him to "do anything to protect my credibility" as an informant. Pursuant to those orders, Packer used illegal drugs, including LSD and MARIJUANA, and was jailed several times during violent demonstrations. All charges against the Seattle Eight were eventually dismissed, marking one in a series of judicial defeats for the FBI and President RICHARD NIXON's "law and order" administration during the early 1970s.

PAKISTAN

Pakistan was one of the two original successor states to British INDIA that was created when that former colony split along religious lines in 1947. In theory India became a Hindu nation, while Pakistan—widely split into East and West sections—was a Muslim state. Problem areas remained, including Hyderabad and Junagadh (both predominately Hindu, but with Muslim rulers), but the real bone of contention was Kashmir. India claimed the region in connivance with its Hindu ruler, while the largely Muslim populace sought unity with Pakistan. The dispute has produced four bloody wars thus far, in 1948–49, 1965–66, 1971, and 1999. Further problems arose in March 1971 when separatists in East Pakistan proclaimed their land a new, independent nation called BANGLADESH. Civil war raged, with Indian troops intervening to support the rebels, and Pakistan (no longer West) was defeated in December 1971. The defeat failed to topple Pakistan's rigid military government, and the first experiment with civilian elections failed in March 1977 when Pakistan's junta declared fraudulent the landslide victory of the Bhutto Pakistan People's Party. The resultant protests and riots only tightened military rule, and while President Zulifikar Ali Bhutto was convicted in 1977 for killing a political rival three years earlier, strongman Mohammed Zia al-Huq soon took his place, imposing martial law from September 1978 to December 1985. On August 19, 1988, President Zia died when his air force plane exploded in midair. The state then gave civilian government another try, resulting in a shaky series of ineffective governments climaxed by another military coup in October 1990. While India conducted a series of nuclear tests along Pakistan's border, Pakistan detonated its own A-bomb in May 1998. Former prime minister Nawaz Sharif was convicted of hijacking and TERRORISM in April 2000, receiving dual terms of life imprisonment. A rash of pro-Pakistani suicide bombings erupted in October 2001, killing 38 persons in Kashmir by year's end, while another blast in the Indian parliament left 14 dead. In June 2003 the government of Pakistan's North-West Frontier Province announced plans to segregate women in universities to and "encourage" men to grow beards as symbols of loyalty to Islam.

Despite ongoing U.S. occupation in 2005 and unqualified praise from the White House for General Pervez Musharraf's regime, Pakistan remains a hotbed of alleged conspiracy. In late 2004 a CIA report announced that an arms-trafficking network led by Pakistani scientist A.Q. Khan had provided IRAN with "significant assistance" toward building a nuclear arsenal, including designs for "advanced and efficient" weapons components. Former CIA director George Tenet dubbed Khan "at least as dangerous as Osama bin Laden."

As for BIN LADEN himself, British intelligence sources maintain that at press time for this book, the fugitive terrorist was "being given safe haven with the help of Pakistani officials." Musharraf's vow to stamp out Islamic terrorism within his borders rang hollow, as Taliban factions remained active in several parts of the country and two other militant groups—the Army of Muhammad and the Army of the Pure—escaped official detection by the simple expedient of changing names. Mystery surrounds an alleged attempt to murder General Musharraf in December 2004. The plot's alleged ringleader was killed by Pakistani security forces in what *Time* magazine called "a dubious shoot-out," then a second leading suspect "disappeared" from custody during an unexplained "security lapse." Nationwide manhunts proved unavailing, while international observers questioned the plot's reality.

PALMER Raids

In February 1919 Attorney General Thomas Gregory announced plans to deport at least 7,000 "alien ANARCHISTS and trouble makers" before year's end. The apparent need for such action was reinforced during April and June by a series of bombings that were blamed on unknown radicals. One target was new Attorney General A. Mitchell Palmer, who followed through on the his predecessor's plan. To carry out the purge, he enlisted young J. EDGAR HOOVER, then in charge of the JUSTICE DEPARTMENT's Red-hunting General Intelligence Division.

Hoover staged the first arrests on November 7, 1919, the second anniversary of the Russian revolution. The Labor Department issued 600 arrest warrants for "illegal aliens"; legal niceties were ignored during simultaneous raids in 12 cities nationwide. No figures were published for total arrests, but several thousand persons were detained, most without valid warrants. The *New York Times* reported from Manhattan that "[a] number in the building were badly beaten by the police during the raid, their heads wrapped in bandages testifying to the rough manner in which they had been handled." Of those arrested 249 were deported aboard the SS *Buford* (dubbed the "Soviet Ark") on December 21, 1919.

By that time Palmer and Hoover had planned the next round of arrests, targeting the Communist Party (CP) and the Communist Labor Party. On December 16, 1919, Hoover prepared 3,000 blank arrest warrants and then ordered his spies in the radical movement to arrange party meetings nationwide on January 2, 1920, to "facilitate the making of arrests." Agents were advised to obtain legal warrants "if absolutely necessary"; otherwise, Hoover wrote, "I leave entirely to your discretion as to the methods by which you gain access to such places." On the appointed day at least 10,000 persons were arrested; some 6,500 of them released when they proved U.S. citizenship. Hoover claimed that 3,000 of those jailed made "perfect" deportation cases, but only 556 were finally expelled from the United States Gleeful media reaction to the raids changed sharply in February 1920 with exposure of a Hoover memo warning his superiors that there was "no authority under the law permitting this Department to take any action in deportation proceedings relative to radical activities." In April federal judge George Anderson denounced the bureau for maintaining a "spy system [that] destroys trust and confidence and propagates hate."

Congress investigated the raids between June 1920 and January 1921. Hoover defended the dragnets but later changed his tune. In 1940 one of Hoover's aides told reporters that Hoover "was not in charge of, and had nothing to do with, the manner in which the arrests were made of the so-called radicals under the administration of Attorney General A. Mitchell Palmer." Seven years later Hoover himself told the *New York Herald Tribune,* "I deplored the manner in which the raids were executed then, and my position has remained unchanged."

See also COMMUNISM.

PANAMA

The southernmost Central American nation, Panama has long been a pawn of U.S. interests in the region. Initially ruled by SPAIN (1502–1821) and then by COLOMBIA (1821–1903), Panama struggled in vain to find its own identity. Between 1850 and 1900, the small nation suffered through 40 different regimes, 50 major riots, five abortive secessions from Colombian domination, and 13 U.S. military interventions. At last, after Panamanians agreed to grant the United States rights to dig a shipping canal across their nation, Washington threw its weight behind one last, successful bid for independence from Colombia. Freedom from Washington, however, would not come so easily. Treaties bound Panama to its contract with the United States, and the Canal Zone was officially deemed American soil until December 31, 1999. Meanwhile, the regime of President RONALD REAGAN and Vice President George H. W. Bush supported military dictator Manuel Noriega, head of Panama's SECRET POLICE and a "former" ally of the CENTRAL INTELLIGENCE AGENCY. During the 1980s Noriega installed a series of puppet presidents to do his bidding, but he ultimately quarreled with Washington, whereupon the United States "discovered" his alleged involvement in COCAINE smuggling and indicted him in 1988. In December 1989 former ally Bush sent 24,000 U.S. troops to kidnap Noriega from Panama City and carry him north, where he was later convicted and imprisoned on narcotics charges. In his absence the United States installed compliant successor Guillermo Endara as president. Wholesale smuggling of drugs and weapons continues unabated throughout Panama, while periodic invasions by Colombian guerrillas and security forces have raised concerns for the nation's stability.

See also BUSH DYNASTY.

PAN Am Flight 103

On December 21, 1988, just 38 minutes after taking off from London, Pan America Airlines Flight 103 exploded in midair over Lockerbie, Scotland. The blast and crash killed all 259 persons aboard and 11 more on the ground. On December 28 investigators confirmed that the blast was caused by a bomb in the plane's luggage compartment. In August 1989 President George H. W. Bush created a commission to review the case. The commission's report, which was issued in May 1990, offered no solution but described Pan Am's security lapses and decried the lack of a "national will" to fight TERRORISM. (Pan Am ceased operations on December 4, 1991, and in July 1992 was convicted of "willful misconduct" facilitating the crime.)

Suspicion initially focused on IRAN and SYRIA, two nations said to promote terrorism abroad. Unconfirmed reports persist that British authorities identified two Syrian suspects in 1990 and that Bush intervened with demands that the searchers redirect their attention to LIBYA. On November 15, 1991, authorities indicted two Libyan suspects, Lameen Khalifa Fhimah and Abdelbasset Ali al-Megrahi. Both were employees of Libyan Arab Airlines, but U.S. spokespersons branded them covert intelligence agents of Libyan dictator MUAMMAR AL-QADDAFFI.

A global tug-of-war ensued over the suspects. Qaddaffi announced plans to try them in Libya, while the UNITED NATIONS imposed sanctions to force their surrender. In September 1993 Libya offered to release Fhimah and al-Megrahi for trial in Switzerland, but prosecutors demanded surrender in Scotland or the United States Qaddaffi then proposed that a Scottish court conduct its trial at The Hague, NETHERLANDS. Suppressed U.S. intelligence documents surfaced in January 1995 suggesting that Iran was responsible for the bombing; Washington downplayed the report, and FEDERAL BUREAU OF INVESTIGATION (FBI) spokespeople offered a $4 million reward for capture of the two indicted suspects. In July 1998 all parties finally agreed on trial at The Hague, but negotiations concerning where the suspects would serve time (if finally convicted) stalled the case for another eight months. Fhimah and al-Megrahi were delivered to The Hague on April 5, 1999, but did not enter their not-guilty pleas until February 2000.

The Lockerbie trial, convened on May 3, 2000, spanned nine months. It included review of declassified CENTRAL INTELLIGENCE AGENCY (CIA) files and testimony from a CIA double agent who allegedly saw one of the defendants smuggle a "suspicious" suitcase through British Customs on the evening of the explosion. Prosecutors claimed that the explosives were stashed at the Libyan Arab Airlines office on Malta, and Libyan defector Abdul Majid Giaka solemnly informed the court that Qaddaffi was an "international Freemason." (Defense attorneys countered by noting Giaka's bid for the $4 million FBI reward.) Palestinian guerrilla Mohammed Abu Talb, jailed for bombing a Danish synagogue in 1985, appeared in court and denied any link to the Lockerbie blast. Finally, on January 31, 2001, the court reached a split decision, convicting al-Megrahi and acquitting Fhimah. On March 27, 2004, British Prime Minister Tony Blair announced a new era of friendship with Muammar Qaddaffi as he welcomed Libya's strongman to London for the public signing of an OIL contract worth "several hundred million pounds." In return for the lucrative contract, Qaddaffi vowed to join the "War on Terrorism" and eradicate AL-QAEDA cells in Libya—assuming any could be found.

See also BUSH DYNASTY; FREEMASONS.

PARAGUAY

Initially inhabited by Guaraní Indians, landlocked Paraguay was "discovered" by European explorers in the early 16th century and soon boasted a thriving colony of Spanish JESUITS. The natives rebelled against SPAIN in 1811, expelling foreign masters in favor of 60 years as a "nominal republic" under three successive dictators. The last, Francisco López, waged hopeless border wars with ARGENTINA, BRAZIL, and URUGUAY that wiped out half of Paraguay's male population in 1865–70. A new constitution, adopted in 1870, failed miserably in its goal of preventing bloodshed and dictatorship. Relative stability was not achieved until 1912, followed by the Chaco War (1932–35) that won Paraguay more western territory at BOLIVIA's expense. During and after World War II the country was a haven for fugitive THIRD REICH felons, including Auschwitz "doctor" JOSEF MENGELE. Neo-Nazi dictator Alfredo Stroessner tortured and murdered thousands of persons between 1954 and 1989 with full support from the United States. A military coup finally deposed Stroessner, whereupon Gen. Andres Rodriguez became Paraguay's first elected president in some three-quarters of a century. Raul Cubas Grau won the May 1998 presidential contest, but he was driven from office the following year on charges of complicity in the assassination of Vice President Luis Argaña. The opposition Liberal Party won its first major election in August 2000, but official efforts to try various former officials for human-rights violations have languished. Protracted economic recession sparked rioting in July 2002, which in turn prompted the government to declare martial law under a "state of emergency." Poverty and a legacy of violence hamstring Paraguay's efforts to enter the 21st century.

PEARL Harbor

On December 7, 1941, Japanese aircraft attacked the U.S. Navy base at Pearl Harbor, Oahu, Hawaii, inflicting catastrophic losses on anchored ships of the Pacific fleet. That "day of infamy" propelled the United States into World War II against JAPAN and GERMANY while the country demanded answers about the sneak attack. Officially, investigators placed sole responsibility for the deadly surprise on commanders in Hawaii, Admiral Husband Kimmell and General Walter Short. Subsequent revelations, however, demonstrate that high-ranking officials in Washington either knew or should have known of the impending raid well in advance.

One watchdog who dropped the ball was FEDERAL BUREAU OF INVESTIGATION (FBI) Director J. EDGAR HOOVER. On August 12, 1941, double agent Dusan Popov (serving both the German secret service and Britain's MI6) contacted G-men in New York explaining that his latest assignment for the THIRD REICH involved transmission of data on Pearl Harbor to ADOLF HITLER's Japanese allies. New York's agent-in-charge acknowledged that Popov's information "spells out in detail exactly where, when, how and by whom we are to be attacked," but he found the data "too precise" and opined that "it sounds like a trap." Still, Hoover came to meet Popov—but not to assess his information. Rather, the puritanical FBI leader launched into a tirade against Popov's "playboy" lifestyle, haranguing Popov until his face "turned purple." Hoover declared, "I can catch spies without your or anyone else's help," and as Popov left the office, Hoover shouted after him, "Good riddance!" When Hoover reported a bare-bones outline of the interview to President Franklin Roosevelt on September 3, 1941, he omitted any mention of Pearl Harbor or an impending attack.

While Hoover's FBI clearly failed in its duty to alert the president, some conspiracists claim that FDR was well aware of the impending Japanese raid and that he welcomed it as a sure-fire means of effecting American entry into the war. According to that scenario Roosevelt connived in the Pacific fleet's destruction from 1940 (when he ordered the fleet to Pearl from its secure base at San Diego, California) to February 1941 when FDR told Secretary of State Cordell Hull that he "might not mind losing one or two cruisers" to justify a declaration of war. At least seven other specific warnings of impending attacks on Pearl Harbor reached Washington between January 27 and December 4, 1941. By December 1, 1941 (if not earlier), U.S. cryptologists had cracked Japan's military codes and were thus theoretically able to predict all troop movements ordered from Tokyo.

Instead of "one or two cruisers," the Japanese attack on December 7 sank or badly damaged 18 U.S. warships, including the battleships *Arizona, Oklahoma,* and *West Virginia.* At nearby airfields 188 planes were destroyed on the ground. A total of 2,403 service personnel and 107 civilians died in the raid, but U.S. allies were overjoyed when Washington declared war on Japan the following day.

PEDOPHILE priests

While popes and other leaders of the CATHOLIC CHURCH have been dogged by sex scandals since Medieval times, no amount of consensual philandering by "celibate" clerics produced the explosive reaction engendered by revelations in the latter half of the 20th century. Between 1950 and 2000 church leaders received 10,667 complaints of child molestation by pedophile priests across the United States, involving 4,392 clergymen (4 percent of the total employed). As reported by a committee of 12-member National Review Board in February 2004, 6,700 complaints were substantiated while roughly 1,000 were dismissed as false charges; another 3,300 cases were closed without investigation because the alleged offenders were deceased. By the end of 2002 the American church had spent $573,300,000 on litigation, counseling and other "responses" to the scandal (including hush money for victims bribed into silence). Some 700 pedophile priests were removed from their pulpits during that period, but most were simply transferred to new churches (sometimes after "treatment" by the SERVANTS OF THE PARACLETE), and many of those committed new offenses in successive parishes, protected by their superiors who subverted criminal prosecution at every turn. Eighty percent of the identified victims were male, but some molesters—like Father John Porter, with 125 known victims in four states—raped boys and girls alike. Thus far, no bishops have been prosecuted for aiding and abetting pedophile priests.

The United States is not unique in its problem with pedophile priests. During the past two decades, similar cases involving Catholic clergyman have been reported from Australia, Austria, Brazil, Canada, England, Haiti, Ireland, New Zealand, and the Philippines. In no case to date have church leaders willingly cooperated with civil authorities to prosecute priests for their crimes against children.

PENDERGAST, Tom (1872–1945)

A native of St. Joseph, Missouri, born in 1872, Tom Pendergast moved to Kansas City in the 1890s, learning the basic tenets of corrupt ward politics from his brother James, a saloon keeper and political "fixer." By the time James died in 1911 Tom had a firm grip on the local Democratic Party's reins. Through dealings with the MAFIA and ethnic STREET GANGS, collaborating with corrupt police and politicians, Pendergast ensured that Kansas City remained

President Harry Truman was one of many politicians who owed their allegiance and careers to boss Tom Pendergast. (Library of Congress)

notoriously "wet" throughout PROHIBITION. Illegal gambling also flourished, while votes were bought or fabricated to keep Pendergast's allies in office. In return fat government contracts were awarded to various Pendergast firms, including the Ready Mixed Concrete Company, which profited hugely from NEW DEAL civic-works projects during the Great Depression. By that time Pendergast's political machine dominated the whole Show Me State, with "Boss Tom" hand-picking most of Missouri's successful office holders. Pendergast's great triumph was the selection of U.S. Senator (later President) Harry Truman, a one-time haberdasher from Independence. Reformers sniped incessantly at Pendergast, but their efforts were fruitless until 1939 when he was convicted of evading income tax on some of his gambling bribes. Pendergast served 15 months in prison and then retired to Kansas City, where he lived just long enough to see Truman succeed Franklin Roosevelt as president in 1945.

PENTTBOM

At 8:40 A.M. on September 11, 2001, the Federal Aviation Administration (FAA) informed U.S. military authorities that American Airlines Flight 11, bound from Boston to Los Angeles, had been hijacked. Three minutes later an identical message was broadcast concerning United Airlines Flight 175, also traveling from Boston to L.A. At 8:45 A.M. Flight 11 crashed into Tower 1 of New York City's WORLD TRADE CENTER (WTC), killing all 92 persons aboard. Flight 175 struck Tower 2 of the WTC at 9:03 A.M., killing all 65 persons aboard and precipitating the collapse of both towers for a total estimated death toll of 2,792. And still the grim news kept coming. At 9:24 A.M., the FAA announced that American Airlines Flight 77 had been hijacked while en route from Washington, D.C., to Los Angeles. It crashed into the Pentagon 16 minutes later, killing all 64 persons aboard and another 124 on the ground. At 9:45 A.M. a telephone operator received a cellphone call from United Airlines Flight 93, ostensibly bearing 40 passengers and crew from Newark to San Francisco. The caller reported a hijacking and declared that the passengers were preparing to fight back. The plane crashed near Shanksville, Pennsylvania, at 10:37 A.M., killing everyone aboard.

Those are the raw details of America's worst-ever terrorist attack, a case code-named PENTTBOM by the FEDERAL BUREAU OF INVESTIGATION (FBI). Authorities later identified the hijackers as 19 Arab members of AL-QAEDA, 15 of them from SAUDI ARABIA, presumably directed by fugitive Osama bin Laden. A so-called 20th hijacker, Moroccan citizen Mounir Motassadeq, was arrested in Germany and convicted of conspiracy in February 2003, but an appeals court overturned that verdict in March 2004, citing the refusal of U.S. authorities to supply a key witness. Yet another suspect, Zacarias Moussaoui, was confined in the United States pending trial when this work went to press.

Confusion surrounding the "9/11" PENTTBOM events predictably spawned a host of conspiracy theories, exacerbated by the secretive behavior of President George W. Bush. Within 24 hours of the attacks, Bush ordered White House counterterrorism expert Richard Clarke to seek links between the attacks and SADDAM HUSSEIN in IRAQ. When reminded that no such links had been found, Bush repeated the order. Retired General Wesley Clark confirmed that presidential misdirection in an interview on *Meet the Press*. According to Clark, "There was a concerted effort to pin 9/11 and the terrorism problem on Saddam Hussein. I was on CNN [on September 11], and got a call at my home [from White House staffers] saying, 'You got to say this is connected to Saddam Hussein.' I said, 'I'm willing to say it, but what's your evidence?' And I never got any evidence." After failing to capture bin Laden in AFGHANISTAN, Bush later used the spurious 9/11 argument as one justification for invading IRAQ in OPERATION IRAQI FREEDOM.

Critics cited further evidence of stalling in the 14-month delay between 9/11 and Bush's creation of a special commission to investigate the attacks. On November 27, 2002, Bush named HENRY KISSINGER to chair the commission, but problems arose surrounding Kissinger's secret roster of foreign clients. On December 13, 2002, Kissinger announced that he would publicly identify those clients; then he changed his mind and resigned from the commission. From that day forward the Bush administration was repeatedly accused of "stonewalling" its own commission, withholding crucial documents under claims of executive privilege. Bush and Vice President DICK CHENEY agreed to answer selected questions during a two-hour session in April 2004 but only on condition that no tapes or transcripts were preserved.

That strange performance prompted Ellen Mariani, widow of a 9/11 victim, to file a federal lawsuit against the Bush administration. Mariani's complaint charged that Bush, Cheney, Attorney General JOHN ASHCROFT, Defense Secretary Donald Rumsfeld, and others had possessed sufficient advance knowledge to prevent the PENTTBOM attacks, but they took no steps to avert the disaster. The charge seemed absurd on its face, but a White House security report, grudgingly released in April 2004 (and greatly censored, even then), revealed that the FBI and the CENTRAL INTELLIGENCE AGENCY had warned Bush of suspicious al-Qaeda activity in the United States no later than August 6, 2001. That report bore the unambiguous title "Bin Laden Determined to Attack in the United States."

One of many conspiracy theories surrounding the PENTTBOM attacks contends that Bush and company allowed the raids to proceed—much as Britain allegedly sacrificed the *LUSITANIA* in 1915 and Franklin Roosevelt ignored warnings of the 1941 PEARL HARBOR attack—to advance the timetable of a "war on terrorism" that included the conquest of Iraq and looting of that nation's OIL reserves while distracting Americans from the ENRON scandal, a depressed economy, and other political hot potatoes. Those reaping immense profits from the Bush terror campaign included Dick Cheney's former colleagues at Halliburton Corporation, various petroleum companies, and the U.S. MILITARY-INDUSTRIAL COMPLEX.

PENTTBOM conspiracy theories are not limited to presidential negligence and greed, however. Some go even further, claiming that traitorous elements within the U.S. government engineered the raids and falsely blamed al-Qaeda. French author Thierry Meyssan, in his book *The Big Lie* (2002), asserts that various potential victims of the 9/11 raids were "conveniently invited to a charity lunch in Nebraska" or otherwise evacuated on the day of the attacks, thus reducing the anticipated body count by some 50 percent. Meyssan also questions reports of the Pentagon plane crash. "What became of American Airlines Flight 77?" he asks. "Are the passengers dead? If yes, who killed them and why? If no, where are they?" Meyssan's questions are echoed on various Internet Web sites that claim that Flight 77 is either "missing" or never existed at all.

Another skeptic, Dr. Thomas Olmsted, claims that autopsy reports and other official documents obtained from the Armed Forced Institute of Pathol-ogy (AFIP) via the Freedom of Information Act prove that there were "no Arabs on Flight 77." He cites various discrepancies in published tabulations of the passengers and crew on board (56, 58, or 64) and autopsy reports demonstrating that "no Arabs wound up on the morgue slab." If true, that leaves only two possible explanations: (a) The five al-Qaeda hijackers have posthumously disappeared, or (b) the FBI was less than honest on September 27, 2001, when it televised photos of the five alleged terrorists aboard Flight 77. Olmsted makes no attempt to explain his data, simply presenting it as fact.

See also BIN LADEN FAMILY; BUSH DYNASTY; TERRORISM.

PERU

Once the heart of a vast Inca empire, Peru was conquered by SPAIN in 1531–33. The nation declared independence in July 1821, but Spanish forces resisted expulsion for another three years. Incessant bloodshed stained the next century with frequent revolutions, another war against Spain (1864–66), and the ill-conceived war of the Pacific waged against neighboring CHILE (1879–83). Two decades of dictatorship ended in 1945 with the election of President José Bustamente y Rivero, but a military junta replaced Bustamente in 1948 and ruled Peru for the next 20 years. Quasi-Marxist Gen. Juan Velasco Alvarado seized the reins of power in October 1968, but concessions to U.S. business interests could not save him from another coup in 1975. Democracy of a sort returned to Peru in May 1980, but rebels of the Shining Path continued their guerrilla war against the state, while traffic in COCAINE corrupted government at every level. President Alberto Fujimori, elected in 1990, cited the narcotics trade and TERRORISM as excuses for suspending Peru's constitution, dissolving Congress, and imposing state censorship on the news media. Twice reelected (1995 and 2000), Fujimori waged border war against ECUADOR and watched the climatic disaster of El Niño inflict deadly droughts on Peruvian farms. In September 2000 Fujimori's chief intelligence officer was videotaped in the act of bribing a congressman. Hounded by calls to resign, Fujimori left office in November and fled to JAPAN, where his secret dual citizenship protected him from extradition. "Centrist" Alejandro Toledo was elected president in 2001, but his plans to privatize utilities and court further foreign investments produced widespread rioting by his one-time supporters in 2002.

PHARMACEUTICAL companies

The manufacture and sale of prescription drugs is a megabillion-dollar global industry, dependent in large part on politicians for its continuing wealth. Legislation determines the standards of acceptability for medication in the United States and elsewhere, while likewise regulating patents, testing, foreign sales, and a host of other variables vital to the industry. It comes as no surprise, then, that pharmaceutical companies are huge financial supporters of pliable candidates and friendly political parties. In ELECTION 2000, two U.S. drug companies—Bristol-Meyers Squibb and Glaxo Welcome—gave $2,127,950 to the Republican Party, supporting the campaign of presidential hopeful George W. Bush.

With so much money riding on the line, it also comes as no surprise that pharmaceutical firms engage in a variety of shady or borderline unethical practices to maximize profits. Aside from exposés of DRUG DUMPING in Third World nations and alleged suppression of low-cost CANCER CURES, the following stories made headlines during the first administration of George W. Bush:

- *January 4, 2003:* Writing for the *British Medical Journal,* author Ray Moynihan claimed that drug companies sought to "medicalize" various female sexual problems under the umbrella term *female sexual dysfunction* (FSD) to create a market for remedial drugs—in effect, a female version of Viagra. Spokespersons for the pharmaceutical industry, which has funded all studies of FSD to date, claim that 43 percent of all women suffer from some form of sexual dysfunction. Moynihan noted that the alarming statistic, first reported in 1999, emerged from a survey of 1,500 American women who were questioned regarding sex-related problems (lack of desire, lack of vaginal lubrication, and so on) occurring during the prior two months. Authors of the original study agreed with Moynihan that occasional lack of desire or other sexual problems are completely normal and may spring from countless causes beyond the reach of medication.

- *January 20, 2003:* Republican Party benefactor Glaxo Smith Kline issued an ultimatum to Canadian pharmacists—who sell $1 billion in prescription medicines to U.S. customers each year at prices 20–80 percent below the standard American rates—demanding that the cross-border trade be ended. In effect Glaxo threatened to cut off supplies of U.S. drugs to Canadian retailers if prices were not raised north of the border—a demand that spoke volumes regarding industry "concern" for ailing customers.

- *February 22, 2003:* Documents produced in court revealed that Bayer Corporation executives knew of critical problems with the firm's trademark anticholesterol drug (Baycol) years before the product was pulled from pharmacy shelves in 2001. Baycol was linked to 100 deaths and 1,600 nonfatal injuries before it was withdrawn from sale, thus spawning the lawsuit against Bayer and its British marketing partner, GlaxoSmithKline. A spokesperson for Glaxo told the *New York Times* that "promotion of Baycol was fully consistent with the product label that the (U.S. Food and Drug Administration) approved." Unfortunately, that approved label failed to mention that users of Baycol were placed at heightened risk of contracting a rare and life-threatening muscular disease.

- *June 21, 2003:* As noted elsewhere in this volume, U.S. pharmaceutical giant ASTRAZENECA pleaded guilty in federal court to a felony charge of health-care fraud, settling criminal and civil accusations of illegal marketing with a lump payment of $355 million.

See also BUSH DYNASTY.

PHILADELPHIA Police Department

Civil libertarians mark the Philadelphia Police Department (PPD) as the epitome of law-enforcement agencies that sacrifice law in pursuit of ultraconservative "order." Philly's long war against the Left dates from the late 19th century and spans most of the 20th. It began in earnest during 1902 when Mayor Samuel Ashbridge mobilized his men against ANARCHISTS who recruited from among the unemployed. So successful were police in "the suppression of seditious utterances" that Ashbridge deemed his city "freer from the objectionable class of people than any other large city in the country." A decade later, anarchists and other radicals were routinely denied permits for public gatherings and jailed if they attempted to proceed without the necessary paperwork. In 1919 the PPD organized a "bomb squad" with carte blanche to stem the "mounting tides of Bolshevism in America." Two years later, police commissioner William Mills added a "gas squad" composed of World War I combat veterans who were recruited to tear-gas dissidents and labor unions with an order that "all meetings of a radical character will be prohibited or broken up." From 1930 to 1960 the city's Red Squad collaborated with FEDERAL BUREAU OF INVESTIGATION (FBI) agents to spy on supposed subversives, infiltrating 6,000 "radical" meetings by 1937. In April 1940 the squad joined members of the HOUSE COMMITTEE ON UN-AMERICAN ACTIVITIES to raid Communist Party headquarters without warrants, illegally carting off two truckloads of documents and literature.

Police commissioner Howard Leary was a liberal by most police standards, accepting scrutiny from the nation's first civilian review board in 1958 and creating a Civil Disobedience Squad (CDS) to coordinate peaceful public demonstrations. In 1966 successor Frank Rizzo changed everything with a hard-line, far Right view of law enforcement designed, in his own words, to "make Attila the Hun look like a faggot." Under Rizzo the CDS was converted to a SECRET POLICE surveillance team, targeting a wide range of groups that included the BLACK PANTHER PARTY and STUDENTS FOR A DEMOCRATIC SOCIETY. Brutality was widely recognized and tolerated under Rizzo, whose men favored black "radicals" with public strip searches and marched them nude to paddy wagons in full view of television cameras.

While Rizzo charged various leftist groups with plots against the city and himself (none ever proved in court), he and his staff were strangely unable to cope with organized crime, as practiced by the Angelo Bruno MAFIA family. Bruno reigned supreme in Philadelphia throughout Rizzo's terms as police commissioner (1966–72) and mayor (1972–80). Scandals including rampant police brutality and corruption finally drove Rizzo from office, and he was defeated in two subsequent mayoral races (1983 and 1987). Then he suffered a fatal heart attack before voters could reject him a fourth time, in 1991.

In 1995 a major scandal erupted in the PPD's 39th District where officers were accused of robbing drug dealers, making false arrests, and filing false reports. The usual modus operandi involved corrupt cops raiding drug houses, stealing money from the dealers, and beating anyone who stood in their way. By mid-1997, five officers were convicted on various felony charges in a case where one presiding judge declared that police had "squashed the Bill of Rights into the mud." Thousands of drug convictions are still under review in Philadelphia; some 300 of them overturned at last count. As a result of the scandal, in September 1996 the city reached an agreement with various civil rights groups who threatened class-action lawsuits against the police department. The agreement, supervised by federal judge Stewart Dalzell, mandated two years of independent oversight, coupled with appointment of an Integrity and Accountability Officer to monitor PPD's Internal Affairs Division and the department's rather ineffective Ethics and Accountability Division.

See also COMMUNISM.

PHILBY, Adrian "Kim" (1912–1988)

The son of a British diplomat and born in India on January 1, 1912, Adrian ("Kim") Philby discovered COMMUNISM at Trinity College, Cambridge, and volunteered to spy within England for RUSSIA. His offer was quickly accepted by Soviet intelligence (OGPU), and he became a member of a spy ring dubbed the Cambridge 5, including comrades Anthony Blunt, Guy Burgess, John Cairncross, and Donald Maclean. While working as a journalist in 1940, Philby joined Britain's MI6 intelligence service, working closely with agents of the U.S. OFFICE OF STRATEGIC SERVICES. At war's end he was stationed in TURKEY and later became first secretary at the British embassy in Washington, D.C. Back in England by 1950 he warned Burgess and Maclean of a British "mole hunt" the following year, thereby permitting their escape to Russia. Philby's double life was not exposed until January 1963 with the defection of a high-ranking KGB officer, and Philby too escaped to the Soviet Union. His actions resulted in a shakeup in the British secret service to uncover other "moles," and the tightening of security procedures and protocols in the future. In 1965 he received one of Russia's highest awards, the Red Banner Order, and three years later published a memoir titled *My Silent War*. At his death on May 11, 1988, Philby was honored with a hero's funeral by the Soviet government.

PHILIPPINES

Native tribes occupied this chain of islands in relative harmony before Ferdinand Magellan arrived in 1521. SPAIN claimed the Philippines in 1542 and ruled for the next 350 years until U.S. forces seized the islands in 1898. Filipinos were briefly grateful, until they realized that Washington had no intention of granting them independence. Nationalist leader Emilio Aguinaldo subsequently launched a guerrilla war against the new occupiers, marked by brutal excesses that prefigured America's later performance in VIETNAM. Aguinaldo was captured in 1901, and "peace" was restored the following year, except for pockets of Islamic Moro resistance in the southern islands. In 1934 the Tydings-McDuffie Act

Nationalist leader Emilio Aguinaldo opposed U.S. occupation of the Philippines after the Spanish-American War. (Author's collection)

scheduled transfer of power to a native Filipino government in 1946, and while World War II threatened that schedule, the Philippines still achieved independence in July of the target year. Successive compliant presidents welcomed a strong U.S. military presence on the island and encouraged various forms of vice—including widespread traffic in child prostitutes—that catered to foreign visitors. President FERDINAND MARCOS (1965–86) and wife Imelda were the worst of a bad lot, so brutal and corrupt that even the charade of a revised constitution (1972) and imposition of martial law could not quell domestic upheaval against the criminal regime. Public dissatisfaction peaked in August 1983 with the murder of opposition leader BENIGNO AQUINO, whose widow launched a "People Power" movement to drive Marcos from office. Widespread election fraud tarnished the last Marcos victory in February 1986, and the husband-wife dictators fled into exile three weeks later. New president Corazon Aquino survived several coup attempts and held office until 1992. Her successors have suffered long-running guerrilla warfare with the Moro National Liberation Front, whose rebels seek to establish a separate Islamic state in Mindanao. Another rebel group, Abu Sayyaf, reportedly has ties to AL-QAEDA and fugitive plotter Osama bin Laden. In 2002 President George W. Bush dispatched U.S. troops to the Philippines, ostensibly to train native soldiers for their role in the global "War on TERRORISM."

See also BIN LADEN FAMILY; BUSH DYNASTY.

PHINEAS Priesthood

The neo-Nazi terrorists who call themselves Phineas Priests draw inspiration from an obscure Bible story, reported in Numbers 25:6–13. According to that fable, Phinehas averted divine retribution on ISRAEL and earned his people a "covenant of peace" with God by murdering two mixed-race lovers, an Israelite man and a Midianite woman. Ironically, modern Phineas Priests seek to follow his example (while habitually misspelling his name) by waging a covert guerrilla war against Jews, whom they regard as international conspirators and enemies of the "Aryan" race. Modern Phinean philosophy was first set forth in 1990 by North Carolina white supremacist Richard Kelly Hoskins in his book *Vigilantes of Christendom*. While putting a whites-only twist on the biblical myth,

Hoskins declared: "As the kamikaze is to the Japanese, as the Shiite is to Islam, as the Zionist is to the Jew, so the Phineas priest is to Christendom. . . . [I]t makes little difference whether you agree or disagree with the Phineas Priesthood. It is important that you know that it exists, is active, and in the near future may become a central fact in your life."

Hoskins identified members of the 1980s SILENT BROTHERHOOD as Phineas Priests, though the group itself made no such claims. Mainstream America first heard of the Phineas Priesthood in 1991 when longtime KU KLUX KLAN member Byron De La Beckwith faced his fourth murder trial in the 1963 slaying of Mississippi civil rights activist Medgar Evers. A prospective witness in that case expressed fear of retribution from Phineas Priests if he testified against Beckwith. "You don't know when they're going to strike," the man told reporters. "There is nothing quite so dangerous as a religious fanatic who thinks he's doing the Lord's will." Self-styled Phineas Priests have amply proved that point during the past decade with a series of crimes that include the following cases:

August 1991: Police in Muskogee, Oklahoma, captured gunman Walter Thody in a high-speed chase and shootout after a local thrift shop was robbed for the second time in six weeks. In custody, Thody—a convicted counterfeiter—confessed the holdups to reporters and claimed he was a Phineas Priest. According to Thody some $52,000 stolen in the first robbery was used to fund an impending war against Jews in the United States. Thody received a life prison sentence in 1992.

October 1996: Federal agents arrested four self-described Phineas Priests in Seattle, charged with stealing $108,000 in two local bank robberies. In addition to bombing the two banks they robbed, the Seattle defendants also detonated explosive charges at a local newspaper and at a Planned Parenthood office (demonstrating the group's opposition to legal abortion). Life sentences were imposed on defendants Charles Barbee, Robert Berry, and Jay Merrell, while a fourth accomplice was sentenced to 55 years.

August 1999: Buford Furrow, Jr., a former officer of the Aryan Nations, invaded a Jewish community center in Los Angeles, wounding two adults and three children with gunfire. Hours later Furrow shot and killed a Filipino-American postman who was selected at random. In the wake of his murder conviction, various published reports described Furrow as a Phineas Priest.

September 1999: Gunman Larry Ashbrook stormed a Baptist church in Fort Worth, Texas, killing seven worshippers before he shot himself. Ashbrook left a note that read: "My life has been destroyed by these people—Air Force personnel, Tarrant County sheriff's deputies, the Klan." Early reports from Christian fundamentalist spokespersons described Ashbrook as a raving atheist, but author John Craig informed authorities that he had interviewed Ashbrook during research for his 1997 book on the radical right, *Soldiers of God.* Craig identified Ashbrook as a self-described Phineas Priest, but FEDERAL BUREAU OF INVESTIGATION spokespersons dismissed any thought of investigating Ashbrook's political connections. Local authorities were likewise blasé on the matter, telling the Fort Worth *Star-Telegram* that background research on Ashbrook was pointless since "We're not doing a biography on the subject."

See also TERRORISM.

PHOENIX Program

Until specifically prohibited by law from plotting acts of murder, the U.S. CENTRAL INTELLIGENCE AGENCY (CIA) conducted or "encouraged" homicides around the world. In some cases "executive action" programs (targeting chiefs of state) were launched against foreign leaders whose number included FIDEL CASTRO of CUBA, Africa's PATRICE LUMUMBA, and Rafael Trujillo in the DOMINICAN REPUBLIC. Most CIA killings, however, targeted relative nonentities who were marked as Communist agents or other "enemies" of the United States. The most egregious of all CIA murder campaigns was the Phoenix Program, a long-running guerrilla war carried out in war-torn VIETNAM and neighboring countries from 1968 onward. Phoenix was conceived by CIA leader William Colby to "neutralize" members of the Viet Cong infrastructure—a vague class including known or suspected VC officers, enlisted men, political activists, tax collectors, and any village leader suspected of Communist sympathies. South Vietnamese president Nguyen Van Thieu made the program official and provided native officers to assist the CIA and U.S. Army Intelligence with the campaign of kidnapping, torture, and murder. Field assassins were most frequently recruited from the ranks of Navy SEALS or Army Special Forces ("green berets").

Internal documents, revealed years later, show that leaders of the Phoenix Program set themselves a goal of "neutralizing" 1,800 victims per month during 1969. Official cover-ups make any final body count speculative, but a spokesperson for the U.S. Defense Department, testifying before Congress in 1973, admitted that 26,369 South Vietnamese civilians were killed by Phoenix assassins while the operation was under direct U.S. control between January 1968 and August 1972. According to the same source, another 33,358 persons were seized and detained without trial by Phoenix agents. William Colby offered different figures in 1973, admitting 20,587 Phoenix murders through the end of 1971, with 28,978 persons "captured" and another 17,717 "rallied" to support South Vietnam's corrupt military regime under pain of death if they refused. South Vietnamese agents assumed responsibility for Phoenix—renaming it the Special Police Investigative Service—after President RICHARD NIXON withdrew U.S. combat troops in 1972, but some investigators maintain that CIA agents remained with the Phoenix effort until South Vietnam fell in 1975. Seven years after that defeat, a former Phoenix gunman testified that Phoenix teams had also been assigned to murder U.S. military personnel who were deemed "security risks." The witness opined that those criminal orders did not issue from "division" but from some higher authority within the CIA or the collaborating Office of Naval Intelligence.

See also COMMUNISM.

PIKE Committee

Established on February 19, 1975, the House Select Intelligence Committee—better known by the name of its chairman, New York congressman Otis Pike—was the House counterpart of the U.S. Senate's CHURCH COMMITTEE. While the Church Committee focused primarily on illegal (and frequently sensational) activities of the FEDERAL BUREAU OF INVESTIGATION (FBI)

and the CENTRAL INTELLIGENCE AGENCY (CIA), the Pike Committee took a more subtle approach by reviewing the "intelligence community's" expenses and effectiveness. That angle of attack prompted immediate hostility from President Gerald Ford, as well as leaders of the FBI and CIA. When the investigation was complete, the same Congress that had authorized the probe voted to suppress its findings. The full report has never been published, but CBS newscaster Daniel Schorr was suspended for leaking portions of it to the *Village Voice*. Mainstream newspapers, including the *New York Times* and the *Washington Post*, refused to publish the extracts in deference to "national security."

POLAND

Great Poland was founded in A.D. 966 and merged with Little Poland in 1047. Lithuania was added to the mix via royal marriage in 1386, and the Polish Empire's power peaked during the 15th and 16th centuries with military victories over GERMANY, RUSSIA, and TURKEY. That glory vanished in the 18th century, however, as a weak monarch permitted land grabs by Russia, Prussia, and AUSTRIA between 1772 and 1795. Popular revolts failed to expel the invaders, but Poland was more-or-less reconstituted after World War I—a circumstance that left German Führer ADOLF HITLER seething for revenge. The THIRD REICH's invasion of Poland sparked World War II in September 1939, and Poland soon became the designated killing ground for European Jews during the Holocaust. While concentration camps sprouted throughout occupied Europe, Hitler's dedicated extermination camps—Auschwitz, Belzec, Sobibor, and Treblinka—were all located in Poland. Ravaged by German occupation, Poland fell under Russia's de facto control after 1945, with a Communist government in place and 70,000 square miles of eastern soil ceded to the Soviet Union by treaty. The Polish "people's democracy" persecuted members of the CATHOLIC CHURCH and suppressed organized labor until 1980 when Lech Walesa's union Solidarity wreaked havoc with the already shaky economy. The arrest of Walesa and other Solidarity leaders only delayed the inevitable communist collapse, and Solidarity won a stunning political victory in 1989, seizing effective control of the government. Walesa was elected president in 1990, but his influence waned during the next five years, and a Communist candidate defeated him in 1995. Despite membership in NATO, Poland has lately drawn closer to Russia once more in its ongoing quest for political stability.

See also COMMUNISM.

POLLARD, Jonathan (fl. 1985)

In November 1985 FEDERAL BUREAU OF INVESTIGATION agents arrested U.S. Navy intelligence analyst Jonathan Pollard on charges of selling classified material to Israeli agents. Spokespersons for ISRAEL issued an immediate apology, declaring that the operation was unauthorized. According to that statement, "the close and special relationship of friendship" between the United States and Israel prohibits any covert activities, and "spying on the United States stands in total contradiction to our policy." Joint investigation of the case allegedly proved that Pollard's contacts were not agents of MOSSAD but rather members of "a small, independent scientific intelligence unit" which was subsequently disbanded with return of the purloined documents. At trial on espionage charges, Pollard denied spying against the United States, insisting that he sold only military data vital to Israel's defense (including details of Soviet arms shipments to SYRIA, development of nuclear weapons in PAKISTAN, air-defense systems in LIBYA, and development of chemical weapons in IRAQ). Nonetheless, Pollard was convicted and sentenced to life imprisonment, while his wife received a five-year sentence for assisting him. Despite initial denials of complicity, Israel granted Pollard citizenship and requested presidential clemency in 1988. Pro-Israeli groups and individuals continue agitation for his release, though all appeals to date have been rejected.

PORTUGAL

The Roman Empire conquered Portugal in A.D. 140 but later proved incapable of defending the coastline against Viking raids. In 1143 the nation won independence from Moorish SPAIN, and three centuries later launched its surprising career as a global colonial power. By the mid-16th century, Lisbon's king ruled BRAZIL (where Portuguese remains the primary language), along with major parts of Africa, Indochina, Malaya, and Persia. Spanish troops invaded Portugal in 1581 and occupied it for the next six decades. By the time the Portuguese monar-

chy was restored in 1640, European rivals had usurped most of the nation's colonies abroad. Corrupt King Carlos (1889–1908) named João Franco the nation's de facto dictator in 1906, two years before Carlos and his heir were assassinated in Lisbon. Successor king Manuel II was ousted by revolutionaries in 1910, and Portugal became a French-style republic until 1926 when another rebellion placed Antonio Oliveira Salazar in command. He ruled as virtual dictator until 1970, presiding over the collapse of Portugal's last foreign outposts in India and Africa. That struggle lasted longest and claimed the most lives in ANGOLA, where natives finally won freedom in 1975. Portugal surrendered its last tiny colony, the Chinese port of Macao, in December 1999.

POSSE Comitatus

The Posse Comitatus movement ("power of the county," in Latin) dates from 1969 when two separate groups were founded by far-right extremists Henry Beach and William Potter Gale. Beach, a retired Oregon dry cleaner, had joined the pro-Nazi Silver Shirt Legion in the 1930s, while Gale (a retired army officer who despised and concealed his Jewish heritage) had previously led the California Rangers, a paramilitary group affiliated with the KU KLUX KLAN. Both men espoused a doctrine claiming that the highest level of legitimate authority in the United States is county government, represented by an elected sheriff. Any higher levels of administration—that is, state and federal governments—were deemed illegal, which entitled Posse members to withhold taxes, drive cars without state licenses, ignore various firearms regulations, and otherwise flout established law as they saw fit. Neo-Nazi leaders set the anti-Semitic tone for Posse propaganda, which denounced ZOG—the "Zionist Occupation Government" in Washington, D.C.—and blamed most of the world's financial woes on Jewish financiers.

State and federal authorities predictably disagreed with Posse philosophers, and while the movement spread rapidly among disaffected grassroots Americans—attracting an estimated 50,000 members in 23 states by 1976—Posse members and supporters often found themselves in trouble with the law. FEDERAL BUREAU OF INVESTIGATION agents launched an investigation of the movement in 1975 after Arkansas disciples threatened to kill

Vice President Nelson Rockefeller. Wisconsin Posse leader James Wickstrom staged several abortive political campaigns before he was convicted on a federal counterfeiting charge. Three Colorado members were imprisoned for manufacturing explosives, while others went to jail on tax-evasion and weapons charges. On February 13, 1983, Posse stalwart Gordon Kahl killed two U.S. marshals and wounded three others in a shootout near Medina, North Dakota. Months later, Kahl was traced to an Arkansas hideout where a second pitched battle claimed his life and that of the county sheriff. Posse influence declined in the 1990s, as surviving members defected to join the Militia movement. A survey of American hate groups, published by the Southern Poverty Law Center in spring 2004, found no active Posse groups surviving.

See also ROCKEFELLER CLAN.

PRISON gangs

Ironically, some of the strongest and deadliest criminal gangs in the modern United States were organized behind prison walls and are run today by inmates who are serving long sentences. They are privately acknowledged to control most activities in some large penal institutions, ranging from contraband smuggling and contract murders to inmate job assignments and conjugal visits. Official denials notwithstanding, their continued operation and influence strongly suggests widespread official negligence (at best) or deep-seated corruption (at worst).

The four primary U.S. prison gangs are the ARYAN BROTHERHOOD (combining neo-Nazi politics with drug smuggling and racketeering), the BLACK GUERRILLA FAMILY (sworn enemies of the Aryan Brotherhood since the late 1960s), and two rival Hispanic cliques, the MEXICAN MAFIA and NUESTRA FAMILIA ("Our Family"). Despite their common ethnic roots, the latter groups are bitter enemies, sometimes forging alliances with the Aryan Brotherhood or the Black Guerrilla Family in fratricidal warfare. Racial animosities vie with common greed in the world of prison gangs to produce a never-ending cycle of murder and reprisal. Black Guerrilla Family members have also allied themselves with militant African American groups such as the BLACK PANTHER PARTY, while Aryan Brotherhood members collaborate with outside racist groups including the KU KLUX KLAN and various neo-Nazi cliques.

PROHIBITION

The "noble experiment" of Prohibition—banning alcoholic beverages in the United States—was not a sudden onslaught. Religious groups and nativist factions (who despised foreign-born brewers) began their campaign for a "dry" America in mid-19th century. Three of the 48 states banned booze by 1905 with that number increasing to nine by 1912 and 26 by 1916. The Eighteenth Amendment to the U.S. Constitution, banning liquor nationwide, was ratified on January 16, 1919, and took effect one year later, with penalties for violation imposed by the Volstead Act of October 28, 1919. The first liquor hijacking by bootleggers occurred in Chicago minutes after midnight on January 16, 1920, and the next 14 years witnessed a virtual orgy of illicit drinking that surpassed any temperance worker's wildest nightmares. In most major cities from coast to coast the number of covert saloons (dubbed "speakeasies" after the ostensible need for secrecy) increased 10-fold, while the MAFIA and other ethnic gangs abandoned normal pursuits to grow rich from the proceeds of smuggling. Thus was born America's national crime syndicate, beginning with the East Coast's BIG SEVEN combination and expanding through a series of semipublic "crime conventions" held during 1929–32. Corrupt police and politicians likewise fattened on proceeds from the liquor trade, while hundreds of gangland murders (including Chicago's notorious ST. VALENTINE'S DAY MASSACRE) went forever unsolved. Mob leaders such as CHARLES "LUCKY" LUCIANO and MEYER LANSKY got their start in Prohibition and expanded from illegal alcohol to make fortunes in gambling, narcotics, and racketeering.

A new federal statute, the Blaine Act of February 17, 1933, sounded the death knell of Prohibition in the United States, and the Eighteenth Amendment was repealed by year's end with ratification of the Twenty-first Amendment. Three holdout states—Kansas, Mississippi, and Oklahoma—were still "dry" in 1948, and Mississippi remained the most stubborn, repealing state prohibition statutes only in 1966. A few "dry" towns and counties still remain, scattered across the U.S. map, but the laws have little effect. Strangely, the experiment taught lawmakers little or nothing. The same spirit, reborn as a national (then global) "War on Drugs," has created vast new crime cartels while failing in every respect to curtail trade in MARIJUANA, COCAINE, and HEROIN.

PROJECT Paperclip

Almost before the final shots of World War II were fired, Allied intelligence agencies launched a concerted treasure hunt for German military and scientific inventions, including rocket and jet-engine technology. Both sides in the coming cold war benefited greatly by picking through the ruins of ADOLF HITLER's war machine, but the U.S. War Department's Joint Intelligence Objectives Agency (JIOA) scored a particular triumph with a covert operation known as Project Paperclip, authorized by President Harry Truman in September 1946. Under terms of that project the United States welcomed the technicians who had built Hitler's V-2 rockets and used them to pulverize England. President Truman's original order specifically barred recruitment of anyone found "to have been a member of the Nazi party and more than a nominal participant in its activities, or an active supporter of Nazism or militarism"; yet recruitment of die-hard fanatics proceeded apace. Samuel Klaus, the State Department's JIOA representative, complained that many of the scientists enlisted were "ardent Nazis," but JIOA Director Bosquet Wev overruled that protest, declaring that "the best interests of the United States have been subjugated to the efforts expended in 'beating a dead Nazi horse.'" Furthermore, Wev cautioned, Soviet RUSSIA posed a "far greater security threat to this country than any former Nazi affiliations which they may have had or even any Nazi sympathies that they may still have." Nazis imported under Project Paperclip included:

Arthur Rudolph, director of the Mittelwerk factory at Dora-Nordhausen concentration camp, where 20,000 slave laborers died. A National Socialist since 1931, Rudolph was described in Allied files as "100% Nazi, dangerous type, security threat. . . . Suggest internment." The JIOA found "nothing in his records indicating that he was a war criminal or an ardent Nazi or otherwise objectionable." Rudolph became a U.S. citizen, designed the rocket used in the APOLLO PROJECT moon landings—and fled to West Germany in 1984 when his record of WAR CRIMES was reopened.

Werner von Braun, Hitler's technical director at the Peenemunde rocket research center from 1937 to 1945 and developer of the deadly V-2 rocket. He later worked on guided missiles for the U.S. Army, served as director of NASA's Marshall Space Flight Center, and became a national celebrity in the 1960s as one of Walt Disney's "World of Tomorrow" experts. In the 1970s he served as associate director of National Aeronautics and Space Administration (NASA).

Kurt Blome, another Nazi scientist who admitted experimenting on concentration-camp inmates with plague bacilli. Blome was acquitted of war crimes at Nuremberg in 1947 (although most observers accepted the fact of his guilt). Two months after that acquittal Blome was in Maryland, consulting with the U.S. military on germ warfare. The U.S. Army Chemical Corps hired him in 1951 to continue his life's work and passion.

Walter Schreiber, a Nazi major general who, according to Nuremberg testimony, "assigned doctors to experiment on concentration camp prisoners and had made funds available for such experimentation." Only Schreiber's detention in Russia (1945–48) spared him from trial as a war criminal. He next surfaced at the Air Force School of Medicine at Randolph Field, Texas. Columnist Drew Pearson revealed Schreiber's crimes in 1952, whereupon the U.S. government arranged passage for Schreiber to join his daughter in ARGENTINA.

Hermann Becker-Freysing, convicted and sentenced to 20 years imprisonment at Nuremberg for conducting experiments on Dachau inmates, including force-feeding of seawater that was chemically treated to make it "drinkable." Even before his trial Becker-Freysing was paid by the U.S. Air Force to report on his sadistic experiments.

Siegfried Ruff, a codefendant with Becker-Freysing at the Nuremberg "Doctor's Trial," where he narrowly escaped conviction on charges of killing 80 inmates in a low-pressure chamber designed to simulate altitudes above 60,000 feet. Like Becker-Freysing, Ruff was sought (and paid) by the U.S. Air Force in the interests of "national security."

Reinhard Gehlen, while not a scientist, was one of the THIRD REICH's top intelligence officers who were linked to the torture and murder of countless victims. The CENTRAL INTELLIGENCE AGENCY (CIA) recruited him in 1950 to coordinate its secret war against COMMUNISM in Europe.

KLAUS BARBIE, the Nazi "Butcher of Lyon" and another prized CIA intelligence asset, whose association with the U.S. intelligence service spared him trial and execution for war crimes.

By 1955 more than 760 German scientists were granted U.S. citizenship, their dossiers "sanitized" to remove any taint of active involvement with Hitler's genocidal regime. A 1985 exposé in the *Bulletin of Atomic Scientists* revealed that author Linda Hunt had secured more than 130 files on Project Paperclip immigrants and that she found that every one "had been changed to eliminate the security threat classification." Some conspiracists maintain that the post-war scientific looting of Germany also revealed secrets concerning UFOS which remain classified to this day.

See also NATIONAL SOCIALISM.

PROTOCOLS of the Elders of Zion

Produced by czarist agents of the OKHRANA in 1905, this fraudulent volume pretends to reveal the minutes of a secret Jewish conference held sometime in the late 19th century, wherein conspirators outlined their plans for world domination and destruction of Christianity. In the 1920s anti-Semitic millionaire Henry Ford used the *Protocols* as a basis for his seven-year media assault on "the International Jew," thereby influencing such diverse elements as the KU KLUX KLAN and the National Socialist movement, led in GERMANY by ADOLF HITLER. Various editions of the forgery remain in print today, widely circulated by neo-Nazi groups whose uneducated members accept it as a legitimate blueprint for an ongoing conspiracy helmed by ZOG in Washington, D.C. British author Stephen Knight put a new twist on the *Protocols* in 1976, describing it as a document produced by FREEMASONS and suggesting a Masonic plot behind the crimes of unidentified 19th-century serial killer JACK THE RIPPER. Unaccountably, Knight's tale ignored both the original forger's attribution of the *Protocols* to Jewish authors and seven decades of documentation proving the volume a fake.

See also NATIONAL SOCIALISM.

PUERTO Rico

Christopher Columbus "discovered" the Caribbean island of Puerto Rico in 1493, bestowing the twin plagues of slavery and lethal disease on its peaceful Arawak natives. Spain occupied the island for the next four centuries until U.S. forces seized it for Washington in 1898. It remains an unincorporated U.S. territory today with Puerto Rican residents who officially became U.S. citizens in 1917. Some are outspoken in their wish to have Puerto Rico become the 51st American state, but others are equally passionate in their desire for complete independence. That struggle, long and violent, has included an attempt to kill President Harry Truman (November 1950), a raid on the U.S. Capitol that wounded five congressmen (March 1954), and a protracted series of terrorist acts throughout the United States since the mid-1960s. Conversely, the FEDERAL BUREAU OF INVESTIGATION (FBI) has also waged a long-running illegal campaign to disrupt nationalist organization. That effort included COINTELPRO-style harassment (one FBI memo boasted of provoking a political candidate's near-fatal heart attack) and support for right-wing death squads that assassinated opposition leaders. The struggle continues, with no end in sight.

See also TERRORISM.

QADDAFFI, Muammar al- (1942–)

Libyan dictator Muammar al-Qaddaffi was born in 1942 and as a child came to admire the nationalist creed of EGYPT's Gamal Abdel Nasser. Qaddaffi graduated from the University of LIBYA in 1963 and joined the army two years later, commissioned as an officer. In September 1969 he led a military coup that toppled the monarchy of King Idris I, thus establishing himself as Libya's commander-in-chief and chairman of the Revolutionary Command Council. His regime mixed Arab nationalism, revolutionary socialism, and Islamic fundamentalism in a manner guaranteed to frighten Western leaders and investors. U.S. and British military bases in Libya were closed during 1970, while Qaddaffi seized the property of his nation's Italian and Jewish communities. Strict Koranic law was imposed, including bans on gambling and alcoholic beverages and a statute requiring that the hands of thieves be severed. In 1973 Qaddaffi nationalized all foreign OIL assets, thus earning for himself eternal enmity from multinational petroleum companies. In 1977 Qaddaffi's troops seized a strip of land in CHAD, along Libya's southern border. A full-scale invasion followed two years later. Qaddaffi's proposal to merge the two countries was rejected, and while his troops withdrew in 1981, they returned for another period of occupation during 1983–87.

Since seizing power in 1969, Qaddaffi has been widely accused of sponsoring terrorist activities around the world. Israel is a primary target, but his tastes appear to be eclectic. At various times in the 1970s and 1980s, Qaddaffi was accused of financing the IRISH REPUBLICAN ARMY and other groups unrelated to the Palestinian struggle. In May 1986 a right-wing army officer in SPAIN, Col. Meer de Ribera, claimed that he had negotiated with Qaddaffi for arms and money to carry out attacks on U.S. targets throughout Europe. That assertion came four months after Robert Oakley, head of the U.S. State Department's antiterrorist unit, publicly admitted that no evidence existed linking Libya to recent terrorist attacks in AUSTRIA and ITALY. Some skeptics feel that Col. Ribera's "revelations" were a trifle too fortuitous—perhaps concocted out of thin air by the RONALD REAGAN White House to excuse a 1986 bombing raid that missed Qaddaffi but killed or wounded several of his children.

Whatever the truth of those allegations, two Libyan intelligence officers were indicted for plotting the December 21, 1988, bombing of an airliner that killed 270 persons at Lockerbie, Scotland. Qaddaffi stalled surrender of the suspects—Lamen Khalifa Fhimah and Ali al-Megrahi—until April 1999 whereupon they were tried for mass murder in the NETHERLANDS. (Megrahi was convicted, while jurors acquitted Fhimah.) As a result of that belated cooperation, the UNITED NATIONS lifted its seven-year economic sanctions on Libya, though some U.S. and British sanctions remain in place. In September

2000 Libyan mobs rioted against black Africans living in the country, killing hundreds and prompting several other nations to launch airlifts to repatriate their citizens. The bloodshed struck a telling blow against Qaddaffi's efforts to portray himself as a leading African statesman.

Since the Bush administration's 2003 invasion of Iraq, Qaddaffi has emerged as a surprise favorite of some Western diplomats, professing an abandonment of terror tactics while bringing Libya into closer contact with the world community at large. The permanence of his about-face remains to be seen.

AL-QAEDA

The organization known as al-Qaeda ("the base," in Arabic) was created in 1989 as Soviet troops left AFGHANISTAN and colleagues of U.S.-sponsored guerrilla leader Osama bin Laden searched for new targets. The early members were "Arab Afghans," imported to fight against RUSSIA in the 1980s, armed and trained by the CENTRAL INTELLIGENCE AGENCY with financial support from SAUDI ARABIA. By 1996, al-Qaeda had a dozen training camps scattered across Afghanistan, with agents reputedly active in 40–50 nations worldwide. The group's current targets include ISRAEL and any nation perceived to support Israel's continued survival. Acts of TERRORISM attributed to al-Qaeda by various (often contradictory) sources include the WORLD TRADE CENTER BOMBING in New York (1993); the killing of 19 U.S. soldiers in Saudi Arabia (1996); bombings of U.S. embassies in KENYA and TANZANIA that killed 253 persons (1998); a suicide attack on the USS *Cole* in Yemen (2000); and the catastrophic PENTTBOM skyjackings that killed more than 3,000 persons on September 11, 2001.

The final incident prompted President George W. Bush to invade Afghanistan and overthrow al-Qaeda's allies in the Muslim-extremist Taliban government, but Osama bin Laden slipped through the net and remains at large at this writing (in May 2005), presumably plotting new terrorist actions. Some sources blame al-Qaeda for killing Israeli tourists in Kenya (2002) and for a coordinated spate of bombings in Riyadh, Saudi Arabia (2003). U.S. authorities, engaged in a seemingly endless "war on terror," insist that al-Qaeda remains an active menace to world peace, including threats of "dirty" nuclear weapons. President Bashar Al-Assad of SYRIA, meanwhile, questioned the group's very existence in May

2003. "Is there really an entity called al-Qaeda?" Bashar asked Kuwaiti journalists, rhetorically. "Was it in Afghanistan? Does it exist now?" Bashar questioned how Osama bin Laden "cannot talk on the phone or use the Internet, but he can direct communications to the four corners of the world," deeming the scenario "illogical."

Following the U.S.-led invasion of Iraq in 2003, al-Qaeda contributed to Iraqi resistance forces by coordinating terrorist attacks and supporting insurrectionist elements. Abu Musab al-Zarqawi, a terrorist leader thought to have links to al-Qaeda, was identified as a key leader in the Iraqi resistance movement. He remained free as of this writing.

See also BIN LADEN FAMILY; BUSH DYNASTY.

QATAR

This small but affluent monarchy on the Persian Gulf was once ruled by the sheikhs of BAHRAIN, but natives rebelled against the absentee despots in 1867, prompting helpful British authorities to install wealthy Muhammad ibn Thani al-Thani as the ruling emir. TURKEY's attempted invasion was repulsed in 1893, and in 1916 al-Thani "allowed" his country to become a British protectorate. In the 1940s discovery of OIL beneath Qatar's desert sands brought fabulous riches to some, and today petroleum exports account for 80 percent of the nation's income. Border skirmishes with SAUDI ARABIA were settled via tense negotiations in December 1992. Crown Prince Hamad bin Khalifa al-Thani deposed his father in June 1995, allegedly for his resistance to economic and political reform. Women's suffrage was granted for the first time in 1999. Qatar is home to Al Jazeera, the Arabic satellite television network which has carried many public statements from fugitive terrorist leader Osama bin Laden.

See also BIN LADEN FAMILY; TERRORISM.

QUISLING, Vidkun (1887–1945)

With BENEDICT ARNOLD, Norway's Vidkun Quisling holds the dubious distinction of entering history as a man whose name is synonymous with treason. The son of a Lutheran minister and born July 18, 1887, Quisling was commissioned as a major in the Norwegian army, worked briefly in RUSSIA toward relief of that nation's great famine in the 1920s, and served as Norway's defense minister during 1931–33. During that time he converted to NATIONAL SOCIALISM and in May 1933 joined Johan Hjort to create Nasjonal Samling (National Unity), Norway's fledgling Nazi party. The party enjoyed modest success in that year's elections, garnering 27,850 votes nationwide, but a strong shift toward anti-Semitism and support for ADOLF HITLER during the next two years cost the group critical support. By the time Hitler invaded Norway in April 1940, membership in Nasjonal Samling had dwindled to about 2,000, but Quisling was the only member who counted. On April 9, 1940, during a news broadcast about the invasion, Quisling announced formation of a pro-German government in Oslo with himself at its head. Quisling's expectations of an endorsement from Berlin were dashed five days later, however, when German occupation troops installed Josef Terboven as the new Reichskommissar of Norway, answering directly to Hitler. Quisling lingered on as Terboven's prime minister, recognized as a front man and puppet for the German regime. At war's end Quisling was charged with treason, convicted, and executed on October 24, 1945.

RABIN, Yitzhak (1922–1995)

Yitzhak Rabin was born in Jerusalem in March 1922, the son of militant Zionists who were active in the Haganah guerrilla movement. Rabin in turn joined ISRAEL's army and served in uniform for 27 years, retiring as chief of staff. Among other actions, he commanded Israeli troops in Galilee during the 1956 war with EGYPT, later admitting that his soldiers illegally deported between 3,000 and 5,000 Arab citizens of Israel to SYRIA during that conflict. Retiring from the army, Rabin was appointed to serve as Israel's ambassador to the United States (1968–73); then he returned to seek elective office as a candidate of the Israeli Labor Party. From a seat in the Knesset (legislature), he advanced to serve as minister of labor under Golda Meir, and then won election as prime minister on June 2, 1974. Elective defeat in May 1977 sent him back to the Knesset (1977–84, 1990–92), and he rebounded with election to a second term as prime minister in June 1992. At the behest of U.S. President Bill Clinton, Rabin reluctantly entered negotiations with Palestinian leader Yasser Arafat in 1993 and agreed to tentative cease-fire plans which secured him a joint Nobel Peace Prize (with Arafat and Israeli Foreign Minister Shimon Peres) in 1994. Rabin's plans to regain control of the Israeli government were cut short on November 4, 1995, when an extremist Israeli gunman shot him down at a rally in Tel Aviv.

See also CLINTON, BILL AND HILLARY; ZIONISM.

RASPUTIN, Grigory (1872–1916)

Czarist RUSSIA's most notorious "holy man" was born Grigory Yefimovich Novykh, a son of Siberian peasants, in 1872. Illiterate throughout his life, he enjoyed a religious conversion at age 18 and joined the Khlysty sect, a cult convinced that communion with God was best achieved during marathon bouts of sexual intercourse. Enthralled by that doctrine, Novykh promptly changed his surname to Rasputin ("debauched one," in Russian) and embarked on a quest for further enlightenment that carried him through GREECE and Jerusalem. Back in St. Petersburg by 1905 Rasputin won an introduction to Czar Nicholas and Czarina Alexandra and somehow persuaded them that he alone could heal their hemophiliac son Alexis. A fringe benefit of his presence in the royal court was Rasputin's abrupt "discovery" that wealthy women could be healed of any ailment by a tumble in his bed. Czar Nicholas, initially disgusted by Rasputin's semipublic excess, banished the "mad monk" from court, but Alexandra demanded his return and cherished his advice so zealously that some critics suspected Rasputin of dictating royal policy.

The problem came to a head in 1916, midway through World War I, when Nicholas declared his intent to take personal command of Russia's failing army. Convinced that Rasputin's nefarious influence would soon propel matters from bad to worse, a clique of military officers led by Felix Yusupov plotted the monk's assassination as a means of rescuing the monarchy. The plotters struck on December 29, 1916, when Yusupov invited Rasputin to dine at his home. There, poisoned cake and wine failed to drop Rasputin in his tracks, so Yusupov drew a pistol and shot his victim at close range. After collapsing briefly to the floor, Rasputin rose again and lurched into the garden, where conspirator Vladimir Purishkevich met him with a second burst of pistol fire. Noting that the monk still lived, the would-be killers pushed his body through an ice hole on the Neva River, where Rasputin finally drowned. Sadly for Nicholas and Alexandra, Rasputin's exit came too late to save them from the wrath of revolutionaries led by VLADIMIR LENIN.

RAY brothers

Despite humble beginnings, the Ray brothers—James, John, and Jerry—emerged in later life as pivotal figures (or scapegoats) in the assassination of Dr. MARTIN LUTHER KING, JR. Today, some conspiracists believe the brothers murdered Dr. King, while others insist they were framed for that crime (and others) as part of an elaborate whitewash.

James Earl Ray was born in 1928, followed by brother John in 1933 and Jerry in 1938. All compiled criminal records in the 1950s, including convictions for auto theft, grand larceny, and armed robbery. James was serving 20 years for a Missouri holdup when he escaped from prison on April 23, 1967. Ten years later, authorities noted that John paid a visit to James on April 22 and surmised that he somehow had a hand in the escape. A routine wanted poster was issued for James; then authorities promptly forgot about him until April 19, 1968 when FEDERAL BUREAU OF INVESTIGATION (FBI) spokespersons named him as a suspect in King's murder. Arrested in London on June 8, 1968, Ray returned to the United States and pleaded guilty to King's slaying on March 10, 1969, receiving a 99-year prison term. (Ray's first attorney, supplanted by Percy Foreman, was Arthur Hanes, a former FBI agent and ex-mayor of Birmingham who represented members of the KU KLUX KLAN charged with murder.)

The story might have ended there, but James refused to disappear quietly. He proclaimed himself a patsy, set up by conspirators and coerced into a guilty plea by Texas lawyer Percy Foreman (former counsel for JACK RUBY), who loaned money to brother Jerry contingent on a guilty plea with no

"unseemly conduct" from James. On March 12, 1969, an FBI agent visited James, seeking "cooperation" in a broader conspiracy investigation. When he declined to help, the G-man threatened that James "should expect his brothers to join him in prison."

Jerry Ray was subsequently tried and acquitted of a Georgia shooting, but John was less fortunate. G-men arrested him for bank robbery in October 1970, claiming that he gave a lift to three bandits who stole $53,000 in a Missouri holdup, between the time they ditched their first getaway car and then picked up another. Charged with the robbery itself were James Benney, Ronald Goldstein, and Jerry Miller. Police killed Benney in Oregon, and Miller remains at large, but Goldstein was captured and returned to Missouri for trial. Convicted, he received a 13-year sentence, while John Ray got 18 years from Judge William Webster (later head of the FBI and the CENTRAL INTELLIGENCE AGENCY) for the lesser crime of aiding Goldstein's escape. Stranger still was that Goldstein was acquitted of the charges at a second trial while John languished in prison through 1977, describing himself as "the only prisoner . . . serving a sentence for picking up a person who was found not guilty of robbing a bank."

Soon after John's release, the HOUSE SELECT COMMITTEE ON ASSASSINATIONS questioned all three brothers, concluding that the Rays conspired to kill Dr. King in expectation of a financial "bounty" offered by two wealthy St. Louis racists, John Kauffmann and John Sutherland. Both alleged plotters were already dead, and no hard evidence of their involvement in the murder was produced. No additional charges were ever filed in the King assassination.

REAGAN, Ronald (1911–2004)

Actor Ronald Reagan signed with Warner Brothers studios in 1937 and spent World War II making propaganda films for the U.S. Army. During the 1940s and 1950s he also served as an FEDERAL BUREAU OF INVESTIGATION (FBI) informant (code name "T-10"), reporting on alleged Communist activities in Hollywood. In 1947 he appeared as a friendly witness before the HOUSE COMMITTEE ON UN-AMERICAN ACTIVITIES. Reagan announced his switch to the Republican Party in 1962, and he was subsequently twice elected governor of California (1967–75).

Reagan's tenure in Sacramento was a preview of his later performance as president. Already linked to various MAFIA figures, he established a pattern of appointing ultraconservative friends to high office and persecuting political dissenters. Reagan proclaimed his willingness to crush campus demonstrations with violence—"If they want a bloodbath, let it be now!"—and declassified FBI documents later revealed his collaboration with the bureau and the CENTRAL INTELLIGENCE AGENCY (CIA) in illegal domestic surveillance campaigns at the University of California. Those activities included harassment of students, faculty, and regents, coupled with a drive to oust UC President Clark Kerr. To that end derogatory information was fabricated and leaked to the press with several reports dispatched to the White House. Assistant FBI Director Cartha DeLoach said that Reagan was "very helpful" to the FBI, while insisting that the bureau gave Reagan "no special treatment."

Running for president in 1980, Reagan solicited aid from various members of organized crime, including the corrupt INTERNATIONAL BROTHERHOOD OF TEAMSTERS. Reagan and running mate George H. W. Bush held closed-door meetings with Teamster officials—most of them under indictment—and Teamster vice president Jackie Presser (also an FBI informant) was a "senior economic adviser" to Reagan's transition team, despite his status as an eighth-grade dropout facing federal charges of corruption.

While Reagan announced a "vigorous war" on crime in and a parallel "war on drugs," his actions belied public statements. Reagan's courtship of the Teamsters continued unabated, while Nevada mob investigations by the FBI and the INTERNAL REVENUE SERVICE were sharply curtailed. Raymond Donovan, a New Jersey contractor with known mob connections who raised $600,000 for Reagan's 1980 campaign, was nominated to serve as Secretary of Labor. Reagan took credit for the conviction of 1,100 mobsters indicted under President Jimmy Carter, but he refused to allow any new undercover operations against organized crime in 1982. The White House also slashed budgets for federal law enforcement across the board, forcing dismissal of 434 employees from the DRUG ENFORCEMENT ADMINISTRATION, and Reagan tried to eliminate the BUREAU OF ALCOHOL, TOBACCO, AND FIREARMS. Overall, federal investigative agencies lost a total of 19,609 employees in 1981–82, prompting sources as diverse as the U.S. Coast Guard and the American Civil Liberties Union to dub the White House war on crime and drugs "a fraud."

Only in the field of political repression did Reagan favor aggressive investigations. His administration escalated illegal FBI harassment tactics against Puerto Rican nationalists and mounted widespread surveillance on critics of the IRAN-CONTRA scandal. One of Reagan's first official acts was pardon of two FBI members who were convicted in 1980 of authorizing illegal break-ins. On March 30, 1981, would-be assassin, John Hinckley, Jr., shot President Reagan. The president survived the shooting, but a tenuous link between the Hinckley family, who were donors to President Reagan's campaign, and Neil Bush, the son of Vice President George Herbert Walker Bush, fueled theories that Hinckley was a brainwashed pawn in a coup attempt meant to install former CIA director Bush as president.

See also BUSH DYNASTY; COMMUNISM.

RECONSTRUCTION

President ABRAHAM LINCOLN and successor Andrew Johnson initially sought lenient terms for readmission of secessionist states to the Union following Dixie's defeat in the Civil War. Instead of displaying contrition, however, the South elected former Confederate leaders to Congress, passed a series of draconian "Black Codes" that returned newly freed slaves to a state of de facto bondage and gloated over the death toll of bloody race riots in Memphis and New Orleans. Furious Republicans in Congress passed a series of Reconstruction Acts between March 1867 and March 1868 that dissolved all-white state governments below the Mason-Dixon Line, mandated black civil rights in a new federal statute (passed over President Johnson's veto), divided the conquered South in to five military districts, and demanded ratification of two constitutional amendments (upholding black citizenship and suffrage) from any state that wished to rejoin the Union.

Southern Democrats responded with a wave of TERRORISM, carried out by members of the KU KLUX KLAN (KKK) and similar night-riding groups. While cast in the role of reluctant vigilantes devoted to preserving "order" and "protecting white womanhood" from lecherous freedmen, the KKK and its allies were overtly political, attacking (and frequently murdering) white Republicans—dubbed "carpetbaggers" or "scalawags"—as often as they did alleged black "criminals." All Southern states were readmitted to the Union by July 1870, but self-styled "conservatives" still plotted to "redeem" the South from what Democratic Party leaders called "black rule." In 1874 the paramilitary WHITE LEAGUE staged a coup d'état in New Orleans and toppled the city's Republican administration, but federal troops quickly restored the lawful government. It remained for presidential candidate RUTHERFORD B. HAYES to end Reconstruction with the Compromise of 1877, exchanging a promise to scuttle black aspirations for a ticket to the White House after he failed to secure a majority vote in the 1876 election. (Modern conspiracists frequently compare that corrupt political bargain to the outcome of ELECTION 2000.)

Withdrawal of troops from the South still left the problem of black citizenship to be resolved by fair means or foul. The U.S. SUPREME COURT effectively revoked the gains of Reconstruction between 1873 and 1896 with a series of rulings that repealed civil rights legislation, permitted racial segregation at every level of society, and limited enforcement of the Fourteenth Amendment to actions undertaken by state officials (rather than private parties). Thus, until the 1960s no conspiracy to strip blacks of their civil rights, no matter how extensive or well organized, would merit federal prosecution unless it included officials acting "under color of law"—and even in those cases, the JUSTICE DEPARTMENT proved extremely reluctant to file charges against white offenders in state government. It would remain for a new climate and a "Second Reconstruction" to dismantle "Jim Crow" legislation in the latter half of the 20th century, with southern politicians and terrorists fighting progress every step of the way.

REICHSTAG fire

Less than one month after ADOLF HITLER took office as chancellor of GERMANY, fire gutted the Reichstag (Parliament) building in Berlin. Hitler called the blaze "a God-given signal" and hastened to meet with President Paul von Hindenburg on February 28, emerging from their confab with near-dictatorial powers for the "defense" of Germany. Immediately, Hitler decreed a suspension of all rights to personal liberty, including freedom of speech and the right to assemble. Blame for the fire fell on suspect Marinus van der Lubbe, a mentally defective Dutchman arrested at the scene on February 27. At trial, van der Lubbe was accused of joining in a Communist conspiracy to destabilize the German government, and conviction brought him a sentence of death. A second "suspect," a Berliner named Bernstein, was spared execution but received 50 lashes for membership in the Communist Party, with another 50 added because he was "also a Jew."

Modern historians are divided as to whether Hitler and his National Socialists lit the Reichstag fire themselves or if it was simply a fortuitous accident. In either case the blaze and subsequent show trial led inevitably to the Holocaust and World War II. A similar fabricated event in 1964, the GULF OF TONKIN INCIDENT, led to dramatic escalation of America's military role in the VIETNAM War. Some 21st-century conspiracists also accuse President George W. Bush of plotting or permitting the September 11, 2001, PENTTBOM attacks as a modern Reichstag fire, thus facilitating passage of the USA PATRIOT ACT, pursuance of an unproductive "War on TERRORISM," and the acquisition of huge OIL profits via OPERATION IRAQI FREEDOM.

See also BUSH DYNASTY; COMMUNISM; HOLOCAUST AND HOLOCAUST DENIAL; NATIONAL SOCIALISM.

REUTHER, Walter (1907–1970)

With younger brothers Roy and Victor, Walter Reuther was the son of a socialist brewer in West Virginia who migrated to Detroit and found work with the Ford Motor Company. In 1932 he was fired for his efforts to organize a chapter of the United Auto Workers (UAW), subsequently affiliated with the Congress of Industrial Organizations (CIO). After Walter's dismissal he spent time in RUSSIA with brother Victor (ironically working at a Ford plant in the Soviet Union) and then returned to the United States to carry on the fight for labor. Ford's management fought back with every weapon available, including MAFIA thugs employed to intimidate union members. In May 1937 Reuther and several dozen UAW members were beaten by mobsters on the Ford payroll. A year later in April 1938 two masked gunmen invaded Reuther's home, tried to abduct him, and were foiled when a guest escaped and summoned help. Another decade passed before the mob struck again, wounding Reuther in his home with shotgun blasts during April 1948. Victor, the next target, was shot in the head at his home in May 1949, one day after corrupt Detroit police ordered him to dispose of his "noisy" watchdog.

Two days after Victor was wounded the U.S. Senate adopted an unprecedented and unanimous resolution calling for a Federal Bureau of Investigation (FBI) investigation of the crimes. Attorney General Tom Clark ordered Director J. EDGAR HOOVER to pursue the case but took no action when Hoover refused. (In a conversation with UAW attorney Joseph Rauh, Clark explained, "Edgar says no. He says he's not going to get involved every time some nigger woman gets raped.") Instead of firing Hoover on the spot for insubordination (and possible insanity), Clark failed to pursue the matter. Years later, after Clark had been appointed to a lifetime seat on the U.S. SUPREME COURT, his acceptance of Mafia bribes was revealed in the press.

Under Walter Reuther the UAW grew into America's largest union with 1.2 million members by the early 1950s. Despite false accusations of COMMUNISM during the Red Scare promulgated by Senator JOSEPH MCCARTHY and Representative RICHARD NIXON, Reuther was elected president of the CIO in 1952 and negotiated its merger with the powerful American Federation of Labor (AFL) three years later. FBI agents continued routine (and illegal) surveillance of the Reuther brothers, adding their support for black civil rights and a global nuclear test-ban treaty to the family's list of "radical" sins. Agents of the CENTRAL INTELLIGENCE AGENCY (CIA) also monitored Reuther's foreign travel, recording any comments that "might be construed as contrary to the foreign policy of the United States."

While most published accounts claim that Reuther's life was relatively peaceful from the 1950s onward, some conspiracists believe that he was marked for death by powerful forces inside the United States. In October 1968 Walter and Victor Reuther narrowly escaped death when their small private plane crashed on its approach to Dulles Airport in Washington, D.C. Investigators blamed a malfunctioning altimeter for that incident, and a similar verdict was announced in May 1970 when Walter, his wife, and four others died in a plane crash near Michigan's Emmet County Airport. In the wake of that tragedy Victor Reuther told author Michael Parenti, "I and other family members were convinced that both the fatal crash and the near-fatal one in 1968 were not accidental." According to Parenti and

colleague Peggy Norton, "disturbing evidence" of conspiracy in Reuther's death includes the following points:

- In January 1970, White House staffer Egil Krogh (later convicted in the WATERGATE conspiracy) requested a copy of Reuther's FBI file for President Nixon. When questioned about the request in 1985, Krogh "couldn't remember" the incident.
- An examination of Reuther's plane by the National Transportation Safety Board revealed *seven* "coincidental" defects in the aircraft's altimeter, including (a) a screw with "torn and broken threads," detached from the unit's critical calibration arm; (b) an "incorrect pivot" installed at one end of a rocking shaft; (c) a rocking stone missing from the same shaft's opposite end; (d) a ring jewel installed off-center inside the altimeter; (e) an "incorrect" rear support pivot on a second rocking shaft; (f) a wrong-sized link pin installed on the altimeter's pneumatic capsule; and (g) an end stone on another internal shaft that had been installed upside-down. As noted by Parenti, the simultaneous accidental occurrence of so many problems in one device is "close to impossible."
- Earlier on the day Reuther died, singer Glen Campbell flew to Detroit aboard the same aircraft with no reported malfunctions.
- The runway selected by Reuther's pilot, while lit, had no identifier lights and no visual approach path indicator (VAPI), which informs approaching fliers of their proper flight angle. Since no warning of the defect was issued, Parenti suggests that the VAPI light was broken a short time before Reuther's plane arrived, presumably without the knowledge of airport officials.

See also DULLES BROTHERS.

RFK assassination

Robert Francis Kennedy ranks among America's most controversial attorneys general. Nepotism was one issue, after newly elected President John Kennedy named his brother to the post in January 1961. Another problem was the gap between Kennedy's liberal ideals and his actions in office—approving illegal FEDERAL BUREAU OF INVESTIGATION

(FBI) surveillance not only against corrupt union officials and MAFIA leaders but also supposed allies such as Dr. MARTIN LUTHER KING, JR.

Kennedy is remembered for his pursuit of organized crime, ironic in light of the role mobsters played in securing JFK's 1960 election. Teamster's Union president Jimmy Hoffa was a special target, finally imprisoned for jury tampering, and he threatened RFK's life on several occasions. Similar threats were made by Mafia bosses SAM GIANCANA (Chicago), CARLOS MARCELLO (New Orleans), and SANTOS TRAFFICANTE (Florida). FBI Director J. EDGAR HOOVER, who despised the Kennedys and feared they would dismiss him, filed the threats without reporting them to the White House or the JUSTICE DEPARTMENT. President Kennedy was murdered on November 22, 1963, and his alleged assassin was killed two days later by mobster JACK RUBY. Moments after the JFK ASSASSINATION, Hoffa gloated, "Bobby Kennedy is just another lawyer now."

His judgment was correct. President LYNDON BAINES JOHNSON was a close friend of Hoover's who also loathed Robert Kennedy. Johnson retained RFK in office until September 3, 1964, but Mafia prosecutions declined by 72 percent in the wake of JFK's death. Robert Kennedy won election to the U.S. Senate in November 1964, and in 1968 he ran for president as an opponent of the VIETNAM War. Some observers believed RFK would use his presidential powers to punish his brother's killers. Kennedy moved one step closer to that goal on June 4, 1968, when he won California's Democratic primary election. At midnight he delivered a victory speech at the Ambassador Hotel in Los Angeles. Fifteen minutes later, his entourage passed through the hotel's kitchen en route to a scheduled press conference, but Kennedy never made it.

In the kitchen a gunman intercepted the procession, mortally wounding Kennedy and injuring five others. More than 70 witnesses watched as Kennedy's bodyguards tackled the shooter, SIRHAN SIRHAN. Unlike the chaotic JFK murder five years earlier, the Los Angeles crime seemed to be open-and-shut. Sirhan was captured at the scene with gun in hand, leaving a journal filled with maniacal scrawls of "RFK must die!" Convicted at trial he was sentenced to die; that sentence was commuted to life imprisonment in 1972.

Open-and-shut . . . but not quite. The second public murder of a Kennedy produced immediate suggestions of conspiracy, and study of the evidence provided ample fuel for speculation.

Ballistics was an instant problem, as in Dallas. Sirhan's 22-caliber revolver held eight cartridges, but victims and walls at the scene displayed marks from at least 13 shots. LOS ANGELES POLICE resolved that issue with a modified "magic bullet theory"—claiming that one slug had drilled two different ceiling panels before striking a bystander—and by stripping the kitchen of bullet-scarred panels and door frames. Photographs remained, however, forcing yet another wriggle when authorities dismissed the bullet marks as "nail holes." In 1975 ballistics expert DeWayne Wolfer testified under oath that he had matched the murder bullets to a revolver with the serial number H-18602, whereas the serial number on Sirhan's weapon was H-53725. Wolfer blamed a bystander in his lab, whose name he could not recall, for giving him the "incorrect" serial number. By the time he admitted his error, both guns had been destroyed.

Aside from the number of gunshots, there was also a critical problem of range and direction. Kennedy's autopsy revealed three wounds: on behind his right ear (the fatal shot) and two below his right arm, 1.5 inches apart; a fourth shot pierced the right rear shoulder of his jacket without striking flesh. All four shots were fired from behind, at a right-to-left angle. The head shot was fired at "a muzzle distance of approximately one inch," marking his flesh with a gunpowder tattoo. Meanwhile, eyewitnesses insist that Sirhan fired from *in front* of Kennedy, never coming closer than "three to six feet" from his target. Furthermore, Sirhan was tackled after firing just two shots, the rest fired wildly while bystanders grappled for his gun.

Conspiracy leads multiplied with the statements of witnesses who recalled Sirhan stalking Kennedy in the days before his murder. Several campaign volunteers recalled Sirhan visiting Kennedy's office in May 1968, accompanied by a blonde woman and a man who looked enough like Sirhan to pass as his brother. Similar sightings were logged from the Ambassador Hotel spanning several hours before the assassination. Finally, within seconds of the shooting, multiple witnesses reported a blonde woman in a polka-dot dress running from the scene, shouting, "We killed the senator!" The woman was never identified, but witness to her existence was "discredited" by L.A. police in a marathon interview best described as intimidating and coercive.

If Sirhan did not act alone—if, in fact, he was never in position to fire the fatal shots at all—who was the second gunman in RFK's murder? A candidate named in several published accounts is Thane Eugene Cesar, a security guard employed at the Ambassador Hotel. In a 1969 interview Cesar claimed he was standing behind Kennedy and to his right when Sirhan opened fire. He also admitted drawing his gun but denied firing it. That statement was contradicted by Donald Schulman, a reporter who stood behind Cesar in the kitchen and gave the following account to reporter Jeff Brent moments later:

Schulman: *A Caucasian gentleman [Sirhan] stepped out and fired three times; the security guard hit Kennedy all three times. Mr. Kennedy slumped to the floor. They carried him away. The security guard fired back.*
Brent: *I heard about six or seven shots in succession. Is this the security guard firing back?*
Schulman: *Yes, the man who stepped out fired three times at Kennedy, hit him all three times, and the security guard then fired back . . . hitting him.*

Schulman's report was admittedly confused since Sirhan fired eight times and suffered no wounds from return fire, but he stuck to his story of Cesar returning the would-be assassin's gunfire. Months after the fact he confirmed that "the guard definitely pulled out his gun and fired."

Cesar's credibility took another hit when he was interviewed by police. He claimed that the gun he drew (but did not fire) was a standard .38-caliber revolver; yet authorities learned that he also owned a .22-caliber weapon of the same brand as Sirhan's. Cesar told investigators that he had sold the .22 three months before the shooting, but a bill of sale later surfaced bearing a date of September 6, 1968, three months to the day *after* Kennedy died in Los Angeles. The gun was found in 1993, dredged from an Arkansas pond, but no ballistics tests have been performed thus far.

Who was Thane Cesar? On the night of June 4, 1968, he was assigned to the Ambassador Hotel by Ace Guard Service, which carried him on its books as a temporary employee. Private investigator Alex Bottus reports that prior to the murder, "months and months" had passed since Cesar last worked for Ace. According to Bottus, Cesar had been jailed several times in Tijuana, Mexico, but the charges were "fixed" in each case by California mobster John

Alessio. Bottus further claimed that Cesar's "whole track record" demonstrated links to organized crime and that Cesar had "connections like crazy."

Conspiracy theories in the RFK assassination focus on most of the "usual suspects" from his brother's slaying, including members of organized crime and the CENTRAL INTELLIGENCE AGENCY (CIA). Conspiracists suggest that Sirhan was "programmed" to kill Kennedy using CIA MIND-CONTROL techniques, and several published accounts name the late Dr. William Joseph Bryan, Jr., (a hypnotist with agency connections) as the likely culprit.

See also KENNEDY DYNASTY.

ROCKEFELLER clan

John Davison Rockefeller (1839–1937) was a native of Richford, New York, whose family moved to Ohio in 1853. Two years later he began work as a bookkeeper in Cleveland, graduating to the produce commission business in 1858. OIL investments followed, the first in 1862, and brother William Rockefeller launched his own refinery in 1865; the brothers teamed with other investors to create the STANDARD OIL Company in 1870. Employing cutthroat methods in the classic "robber-baron" style, Standard Oil soon gained a virtual monopoly on U.S. oil production, reaping fabulous profits for the Rockefeller clan. Rockefeller retired from the crude trade in 1895, earning additional millions when he sold his iron interests (including mines and Great Lakes ore ships) to U.S. Steel. By 1901 John D. Rockefeller was proclaimed the world's richest man, his fortune estimated in the neighborhood of $900 million.

Some of that wealth was returned to the people via philanthropic donations, including Rockefeller's establishment of the University of Chicago (1892) and the Rockefeller Institute for Medical Research (1901), but enough remained to keep the family in regal style. Rockefeller's only son, John, Jr., (1874–1960) inherited most of his father's vast fortune when the elder Rockefeller died in 1937, but it remained for his heirs to put the family's stamp on American politics. Grandson Nelson Aldrich Rockefeller (1908–79) worked in various family firms before Dwight Eisenhower appointed him to the President's Advisory Committee in 1953. He subsequently served as New York's governor (1959–73) and as vice president of the United States under Gerald Ford (1974–77), but his lifelong pursuit of the presidency

John D. Rockefeller (left) founded the Standard Oil empire, and later, financier William Rockefeller (right) helped to expand the family dynasty. (Author's collection)

was frustrated by Republican primary defeats in 1960, 1964, and 1968. Nelson Rockefeller suffered a heart attack on January 20, 1979, while engaged in sex with mistress Megan Marshak and died when she fled the apartment without summoning aid.

Other political Rockefellers include Nelson's brother Winthrop (1912–73), who served as governor of Arkansas in 1967–71; Winthrop Paul Rockefeller (son of Winthrop, born in 1948), elected lieutenant governor of Arkansas in 1999; and John Davison Rockefeller IV (b. 1937), who has served successively as West Virginia's secretary of state (1969–72), governor (1977–85), and U.S. Senator (1985 to present). Both Nelson Rockefeller and John D. IV were members of the TRILATERAL COMMISSION. During his lifetime Nelson Rockefeller also promoted widespread Christian evangelical work in South America and a "pacification" campaign that reaped millions in new oil leases from the territory of converted and dispossessed Indian tribes.

ROMANIA

Most of modern-day Romania lay within the Roman province of Dacia until A.D. 271 when the first of many barbarian invasions overran the territory. Looting and sporadic massacres continued for the next 900 years while the Romanian district known as Transylvania was annexed by neighboring HUNGARY in the 11th century. TURKEY dominated the principalities of Moldavia and Wallachia by the 16th century, despite bloody resistance from the likes of Vlad Tepes (alias "Dracula"), who impaled thousands of his enemies while they were still alive. RUSSIA seized control of Moldavia and Wallachia during the Russo-Turkish War of 1828–29, and Romania did not win independent nation status until 1881 after the Congress of Berlin. Romania began World War I as a neutral but then joined the Allies in 1916, thereby doubling its size at war's end with territorial acquisitions from Russia and the Austro-Hungarian Empire. King Carol II abolished Romania's democratic constitution in 1938 and proclaimed a royal dictatorship. Two years later, the government was reorganized on fascist lines with the brutal Iron Guard forming the nucleus of a new totalitarian regime. Russian incursions during June 1940 prompted Romania to forge an alliance with the THIRD REICH five months later. Romanian troops participated in ADOLF HITLER's invasion of Russia, while the Iron Guard massacred an estimated 270,000 Jews during the Holocaust. Hitler's defeat brought Romania back into the Russian orbit, and a communist government was installed in 1946. Dictator Nicolae Ceausescu ruled his nation in the style of JOSEPH STALIN from 1967 to 1989, looting the Romanian economy to leave the country virtually bankrupt. A military coup deposed Ceausescu in December 1989, whereupon he was tried and executed for various crimes against humanity. The collapse of Soviet communism in 1991 left Romania to flounder on its own, and while the country applied for membership in Europe's Economic Union (EU) during 1995, inept baby steps toward financial reform make it unlikely that EU membership will be granted before 2007.

See also COMMUNISM; FASCISM; HOLOCAUST AND HOLOCAUST DENIAL.

ROSELLI, John (?–1976)

MAFIA celebrity John Roselli was born Filippo Sacco in Italy, date uncertain. He worked for Chicago mobster Al Capone during PROHIBITION but then migrated to LAS VEGAS after World War II as an ally of gambling czar MEYER LANSKY. In September 1960 Roselli colleague SAM GIANCANA met with Allen Dulles, director of the CENTRAL INTELLIGENCE AGENCY (CIA), to discuss collaboration in plans to assassinate Cuban leader FIDEL CASTRO. Roselli persuaded Florida mob boss SANTOS TRAFFICANTE to join in the plot, but several failed attempts on Castro convinced Roselli that killing Castro would not necessarily liberate CUBA. Still, he played along with the scheme to protect himself from federal prosecutors, a scheme jeopardized when Attorney General Robert Kennedy marked Roselli for deportation.

That threat was erased by the JFK ASSASSINATION of November 1963, and Roselli lived in peace until he was subpoenaed by the CHURCH COMMITTEE in 1975. Before that panel Roselli detailed CIA-Mafia plots against Castro, along with his theory that a

CIA hit team in Cuba had been captured and "turned" to kill President Kennedy. After the hearing Roselli told columnist JACK ANDERSON: "When Oswald was picked up, the underworld conspirators feared he would crack and disclose information that might lead to them. This almost certainly would have brought a massive U.S. crackdown on the Mafia. So JACK RUBY was ordered to eliminate Oswald." While authorities ignored Roselli's theory, the mob did not. Roselli vanished from his Florida home in July 1976 and was found 10 days later, floating in an oil drum on Miami's Dumfoundling Bay. He had been strangled; his legs had been hacked off and shoved into the drum atop his corpse. The crime remains officially unsolved.

See also DULLES BROTHERS; KENNEDY DYNASTY.

ROSENBERG, Julius and Ethel (1918–1953; 1915–1953)

The cold war's most sensational espionage case began in September 1945 when cipher clerk Igor Gouzenko defected from the Soviet embassy in Ottawa, Canada. Gouzenko brought with him a cache of documents and names of numerous Russian agents: twenty one were ultimately prosecuted, nine of them were convicted, and 50 more resigned from various government posts or were transferred to nonsensitive positions. While searching the home of suspect Israel Halperin, officers of the Royal Canadian Mounted Police discovered a notebook containing the name and address of Klaus Fuchs, a German physicist living in Scotland. Copies of the notebook were sent to FEDERAL BUREAU OF INVESTIGATION (FBI) headquarters and Britain's MI5; yet four years elapsed before Fuchs was jailed as a spy.

According to FBI spokespeople, G-men followed the trail from Fuchs to Philadelphia chemist Harry Gold and from there to David Greenglass, a soldier at the Los Alamos nuclear test site. Greenglass, in turn, implicated his wife and his sister Ethel Rosenberg, together with Ethel's husband Julius. Greenglass also named Julius Rosenberg as the head of a vast Russian spy ring inside the United States

In fact, however, Greenglass was suspected of stealing uranium samples—a common pastime for soldiers at Los Alamos—and he confessed that relatively petty crime one day *before* Klaus Fuchs named Harry Gold as his American contact. FBI agents showed Greenglass's photo to Gold by pure chance, mixed with pictures of other members of the Los

Alamos staff, and they were surprised when Gold picked him out as a spy. Greenglass subsequently fingered Rosenberg as the agent who seduced him into treason, but he denied Ethel's involvement until February 25, 1951, 10 days before commencement of her trial.

Julius Rosenberg was arrested on July 17, 1950. That same day, a JUSTICE DEPARTMENT memo urged the FBI to "consider every possible means to bring pressure on Rosenberg to make him talk . . . including careful study of Ethel Rosenberg, in order that charges may be placed against her, if possible." Two days later, J. EDGAR HOOVER informed his superiors that "[t]here is no question that if Julius Rosenberg would furnish the details of his extensive espionage

activities it would be possible to proceed against other individuals." Hoover added that "proceeding against his wife might serve as a lever in this matter." The only stumbling block to that scenario was a total lack of evidence against Ethel Rosenberg. Still, agents arrested her on August 11, 1950, and she was held in lieu of $100,000 bond.

Once committed to the frame-up, authorities spared no energy in concocting their case. Twenty high-ranking officials discussed the matter on February 8, 1951, with Justice spokespersons confessing that the case against Ethel was "not too strong." Still, they declared, it was "very important that she be convicted too and given a stiff sentence." Prosecutors sought "the strongest judge possible," finally

Julius Rosenberg (with glasses) and his wife Ethel are escorted into U.S. court in New York for the opening of their trial as key figures in the Klaus Fuchs atomic spy ring. The Rosenbergs received the death penalty for their role in this case. (Bettmann/Corbis)

choosing Irving Kaufman, a former U.S. attorney who reportedly "worshipped J. Edgar Hoover."

David Greenglass made the case in February when he changed his story to implicate Ethel. Forgetting his original statement, Greenglass now "remembered" sessions at his sister's apartment where she watched him pass notes to Julius and afterward "typed them up" in the bedroom. Agents granted Greenglass a private meeting with Harry Gold to coordinate their statements, and both men promptly turned state's evidence against the Rosenbergs, thereby escaping the electric chair. Ruth Greenglass also joined the prosecution team, contradicting her previous statements to support David's newborn memories.

The Rosenbergs and codefendant Morton Sobell faced trial for their lives in March 1951. Defense attorney Emanuel Block refused to cross-examine Harry Gold but then tackled David and Ruth Greenglass without knowledge of their earlier conflicting statements. Julius and Ethel were the only defense witnesses; both denied spying. Then Julius torpedoed their case by pleading the Fifth Amendment to questions concerning his alleged Communist ties. All three defendants were convicted on March 29, 1951. Four days later, Hoover wrote to Attorney General Howard McGrath, recommending death for Julius Rosenberg and Sobell, with 30 years imprisonment for Ethel. In retrospect it seems that no one believed that the executions would be carried out. The electric chair was simply one more "lever," intended to squeeze names and secrets out of Julius Rosenberg. As retired Hoover aide Robert Lamphere confessed in June 1978, "We didn't want them to die. We wanted them to talk."

Judge Kaufman had other ideas. On April 5, 1951, he condemned both Rosenbergs and sentenced Sobell to 30 years in prison. All appeals were denied, and the double execution was scheduled for June 18, 1953. Six G-men invaded Sing Sing Prison that morning, waiting in cells on death row for a last-minute confession, but Julius Rosenberg kept silent and the executions proceeded on schedule.

See also COMMUNISM.

ROSICRUCIANS

The origins of Rosicrucianism are obscured by legend and deliberate obfuscation, but most accounts link it directly to the mystical KNIGHTS TEMPLAR.

French documents dating from the mid-17th century claim that the Order of the Rosy Cross was founded in 1188 by Jean de Gisors, an ex-Templar, a vassal of King Henry II, and first grand master of a Templar splinter group called the Order of Sion. Conflicting reports name the movement's founder as German occultist Christian Rosenkreuz (d. 1484), while other accounts claim that *Rosenkreuz* was merely the pseudonym of a more famous historical figure. (Proposed candidates include Sir Francis Bacon.) Whatever its beginnings, the Rosicrucian order did not surface publicly until the 17th century, with publication of various "manifestos" during 1614–16. By 1623 when elusive members of the Rose-Croix plastered Paris with posters announcing their presence "visibly and invisibly in this city," most observers deemed the movement affiliated with (if not identical to) Freemasonry.

That association prompted allegations of conspiratorial activity that endure to the present day, crediting Rosicrucians with a leading role in momentous events from the breakup of the Holy Roman Empire to the Protestant Reformation to the French Revolution. Known members of the order include Dante Alighieri (author of *The Divine Comedy*), Dr. John Dee (British scientist and spy for Queen Elizabeth I), and Robert Fludd (a principal translator of the Holy Bible for King James I). Modern incarnations of the Rosicrucian order worldwide include the Confraternity of the Rose Cross, Fraternitas Rosae Crucis, Societas Rosicruciana, Rosicrucian Order Crotona Fellowship, Societas Rosicruciana in Anglia, Rosicrucian Fellowship, Order of the Temple of the Rosy Cross, and Lectorium Rosicrucianum.

See also FREEMASONS.

ROTHSCHILD family

Whenever anti-Semitic conspiracists gather to rail against international bankers and the "Jewish world conspiracy," discussion swiftly and inevitably turns to the European Rothschild family. The clan's patriarch, Mayer Amschel Rothschild (1744–1812), was born in the ghetto of Frankfurt-am-Main, GERMANY, and became a self-made millionaire with the establishment of the family's first finance house. In the latter 18th and early 19th centuries the Rothschild empire spread throughout Europe as Mayer stationed his sons in various capital cities, keeping their money in the family with a series of arranged marriages to close relatives.

Those sons and their financial headquarters included Amschel Rothschild (1773–1855) in Frankfurt-am-Main, Saloman Rothschild (1774–1855) in Vienna, Nathan Rothschild (1777–1836) in London, Kalmann Rothschild (1788–1855) in Naples, and Jakob Rothschild (1791–1868) in Paris. The family's role in financing European industry, railroads, and the Suez Canal produced royal titles that were bestowed by rulers of the British and Austro–Hungarian Empires. The Rothschild name became synonymous with luxury, and in the process it inspired hatred from thousands of bigots who regarded Judaism as the root of all worldly evil.

The Rothschilds were also ardent supporters of ZIONISM, with Baron Edmond James de Rothschild standing as a patron of the first Zionist settlement in Palestine at Rishon-LeZion). In 1917 Lionel Walter Rothschild was the addressee of Britain's Balfour Declaration, which committed England to support creation of a Jewish homeland in the Middle East. The advent of ADOLF HITLER and his THIRD REICH saw the Rothschilds hunted and harried throughout occupied Europe, their estates looted of artwork and other property valued in the millions of dollars. Some of that stolen property was never recovered, and it presumably resides today in the same Swiss banks where Nazi looters stashed their swag between 1933 and 1945. Some conspiracists—particularly anti-Semites—see the Rothschild dynasty's hand at work in epic events spanning the past two centuries. The family is variously accused of financing America's Civil War and the assassination of Abraham Lincoln, bankrolling World Wars I and II (despite crushing family losses to Hitler's Third Reich), and has emerged as a prime mover in some descriptions of the "New World Order." Most such theories boil down to a claim of Jewish plans for world domination, as outlined in the bogus *Protocols of the Elders of Zion*. Despite that persecution, the family endures and retains its lavish lifestyle. Modern incarnations of the Rothschild financial empire include London's N.M. Rothschild and Sons, La Compagnie Financière Edmond de Rothschild in Paris, plus the premier Bordeaux wineries of Château Lafite Rothschild and Château Mouton Rothschild. In the 1980s before his conviction for fraud, far-right U.S. presidential hopeful Lyndon LaRouche accused the Rothschilds of financing the global HEROIN traffic, but his evidence was ephemeral, at best.

RUBY, Jack (1911–1967)

Chicago native Jacob Rubenstein was born in 1911, variously claiming birth dates between March and June. That deception set the tone for a life of crime, beginning with teenage apprenticeship to MAFIA bookies and corrupt labor unions. His friends and business partners in Chicago comprised a rogue's gallery of gamblers, racketeers, and contract killers known to law-enforcement agencies from coast to coast. As Jack Ruby, he served in World War II without seeing combat and then celebrated his return to civilian life by relocating in Dallas, Texas. There, Ruby ran a series of nightclubs where drugs and prostitutes were readily available. Several arrests on assault and concealed-weapons charges failed to curb his friendship with officers of the DALLAS POLICE DEPARTMENT. In 1959–60 Ruby was active in the CENTRAL INTELLIGENCE AGENCY's campaigns against FIDEL CASTRO, and he visited Florida mobster SANTOS TRAFFICANTE while Trafficante was briefly detained in CUBA.

Ruby would surely be forgotten today but for his role in the 1963 JFK ASSASSINATION. A week before President John Kennedy was murdered in Dallas, Ruby visited LAS VEGAS, Nevada, and spent time at the Stardust casino, then owned by Cleveland mobster Moe Dalitz. During the same period his telephone records reveal calls to Santos Trafficante in Florida and to Mafia boss CARLOS MARCELLO in New Orleans. On November 24, 1963, Ruby shot and killed alleged assassin LEE HARVEY OSWALD in the Dallas police station, his act beamed worldwide by television cameras at the scene. In custody, Ruby claimed that he shot Oswald in a fit of grief and sympathy for JFK's widow to spare Jacqueline Kennedy the ordeal of testifying at Oswald's trial. Later, he expressed fear for his life and offered proof of a conspiracy to the WARREN COMMISSION in exchange for safe passage to Washington, D.C., but the commission refused to see Ruby outside of Dallas.

Conspiracists dismiss Ruby's "sympathy" motive and regard Oswald's slaying as a mob-type execution that was designed to silence the accused assassin. As evidence, they point to Ruby's lifelong Mafia associations and eyewitness testimony of his movements during November 22–24, 1963. Witnesses reported seeing Ruby at Parkland Hospital while JFK was undergoing futile surgery in an attempt to save his life, and Ruby also surfaced at a police press conference held on November 23. There, when District Attorney

Henry Wade incorrectly identified Oswald as a member of a nonexistent Free Cuba Movement, Jack Ruby—captured again on camera—spoke up from the back row to correct Wade. "Fair Play for Cuba," Ruby called out, and Wade quickly agreed. The Warren Commission subsequently ignored witnesses who placed Ruby and Oswald together in the weeks prior to Kennedy's murder. Convicted of Oswald's murder on March 14, 1964, Ruby was sentenced to death, but that verdict was overturned on appeal, citing pretrial publicity. Ruby died in jail on January 3, 1967, while awaiting retrial. Conflicting reports blame his death on cancer and a pulmonary embolism.

See also KENNEDY DYNASTY.

RUSSIAN Mafia

This generic name is commonly applied to various gangs of organized criminals operating from RUSSIA since the fall of COMMUNISM with outposts all over the world. Comparison with the Italian MAFIA is habitual but not entirely accurate. While the Russian syndicates are hierarchical and ruthless in their discipline, many consist primarily of former military men or agents of the "defunct" KGB. In addition to the normal Mafia rackets—drugs, prostitution, gambling, extortion, wholesale theft, and fraud—the several Russian Mafias are said to deal in heavy military weapons bought or stolen from impoverished states of the former USSR. Some investigators fear that the merchandise may include chemical or nuclear weapons that are offered for sale to the highest bidder in a world overrun by fanatical terrorists.

During the past decade, Russian mobsters have reportedly waged brutal war against Italian Mafia families and the Japanese YAKUZA while forging close alliances with South American COCAINE cartels. Inevitably, though, gang warfare yields to collaboration for mutual profit, and the FEDERAL BUREAU OF INVESTIGATION reports several Russian crime syndicates presently active on U.S. soil. They reportedly smuggle illegal immigrants along with arms and other contraband, a traffic that (at least theoretically) opens America's borders to penetration by terrorists or international fugitives. At last count, U.S. authorities estimated that the several Russian Mafias possess 100,000 hard-core members and a larger but unspecified number of associates cooperating on illicit deals in various nations.

See also TERRORISM.

RUSSIA/USSR

Vast Russia has historically straddled the fence between "civilized" Europe and the "inscrutable" East. Its name derives from Viking raiders who penetrated the region in the latter part of the ninth century A.D. Mongol invaders followed in 1240, ravaging the landscape and leaving control of the nation fragmented among rival dukedoms. Duke Ivan III expelled the Mongols in the 15th century, leaving his son—Ivan the Terrible—to rule united Russia as the country's first czar (a post that combined dictatorship with "divine" leadership of the Russian Orthodox Church). Successive despots expanded Russia's territory to include the Crimea, Ukraine, part of POLAND, Finland, Bessarabia, and Siberia. Czar ALEXANDER I defeated NAPOLEON BONAPARTE's invasion of Russia in 1812–13 and then created the Holy Alliance to suppress Europe's rising liberal movement. ALEXANDER II expanded Russia's borders to the Pacific and into central Asia, while launching widespread persecution of Russian Jews by the BLACK HUNDREDS and similar organizations.

The stress of World War I highlighted czarist corruption and the weird influence of mystic "prophet" GRIGORY RASPUTIN over the Russian royal family. Revolutionaries forced Nicholas II to abdicate in March 1917, and the royal family was massacred in July 1918. By that time VLADIMIR LENIN's Bolshevik movement had overthrown the provisional government of Alexander Kerensky to make Russia the first nominally Communist state on Earth. In fact, however, the new Union of Soviet Socialist Republics (USSR) never progressed beyond "temporary" Communist Party dictatorship to achieve true communism as conceived by theorist Karl Marx (nor, for that matter, has any other nation). President Woodrow Wilson was worried enough by developments in Russia to order an invasion of that country in 1918, and U.S. occupation troops remained in some far-northern regions as late as 1920 without achieving their goal of toppling Lenin's regime. That unprovoked invasion (ignored in most U.S. history books) doubtless did much to influence Russia's relations with the United States in decades to come.

Dictator JOSEPH STALIN emerged triumphant from the power struggle following Lenin's death in January 1924, and he ruled the USSR with an iron hand until his own demise in 1953. During that period Stalin first signed a nonaggression pact with ADOLF HITLER and then fought a desperate war against

Hitler's THIRD REICH after German troops invaded Russia in 1941. Although an ally of the United States, FRANCE, and Britain during the remainder of the war, Stalin was understandably mistrusted in the West where many leaders—including FEDERAL BUREAU OF INVESTIGATION (FBI) director J. EDGAR HOOVER regarded Stalin as a greater threat than Hitler's Axis of Steel. FBI agents devoted much of their wartime effort to tracking alleged Russian agents inside the United States while Nazi spies—and many real-life Soviet "spooks"—were ignored. The 1945 YALTA CONFERENCE granted Stalin permission to dominate much of Eastern Europe after World War II, a strategic decision which in retrospect did much to launch the subsequent cold war. For the remainder of his life, Stalin was blamed (sometimes inaccurately) for every Communist advance or outbreak on the planet, including civil war in divided KOREA and the "loss" of CHINA to COMMUNISM under MAO ZEDONG. While he was clearly brutal and corrupt, employing KGB agents abroad just as Washington used the CENTRAL INTELLIGENCE AGENCY, there is likewise no doubt that Stalin's global influence was exaggerated by Western states leaders, intelligence leaders, and fiction writers to advance their personal agendas.

Stalin's death brought a change to the cold war, but tension between the United States and the USSR never ceased. Each step forward in the form of treaties and accords was countered by some crisis in HUNGARY, GERMANY, CUBA, VIETNAM, CZECHOSLOVAKIA, or AFGHANISTAN. Committed to opposing every "Russian" move around the world, Washington supported many Third World despots as brutal as Stalin himself, while arming bands of "freedom fighters" who would later be denounced as terrorists when they turned on their former benefactors and demanded true independence. President RICHARD NIXON, himself a one-time congressional Red-hunter, surprised the world by improving diplomatic relations with Russia in the early 1970s, but any progress made during that decade was reversed by President RONALD REAGAN in the 1980s. Committed to a simplistic view of Russia as a worldwide "evil empire," Reagan pursued his anticommunist agenda with a series of illegal campaigns that included covert arms deals in the Middle East and a long-running program of state-sponsored terrorism in Central America. Some historians credit Reagan and successor George H. W. Bush with the collapse of Russian communism in 1991, but in fact Russia's economy had been teetering on the brink of implosion for years. Its final breakdown had little or nothing to do with Reagan-Bush foreign policy.

President Boris Yeltsin led the new Russia from 1991 to 1999, despite attempted coups, brushfire wars in various provinces, and his own declining health that was exacerbated by alcoholism. The Chechen-Russian war of 1994–96 ended in a bloody stalemate, while a newly emboldened RUSSIAN MAFIA flagrantly corrupted every level of business and government in the country. In the new millennium, as President George W. Bush seemed intent on turning back U.S. policies to those of his mentor Ronald Reagan, Moscow is increasingly at odds with Washington. Some observers feel that Bush's rejection of long-standing nuclear-weapons treaties with Russia foretell a new cold war in the making—or worse. Meanwhile, Russia is plagued by sinister problems at home. In April 2003 police reported that 88,000 persons were currently listed as missing nationwide. During the past 15 years authorities acknowledged the discovery of 41,292 corpses—one for every 3,500 Russians in a nation of 145 million people. In the first six months of 2002 Russian police identified only 13,000 of the 57,000 corpses under study by the Ministry of the Interior.

See also BUSH DYNASTY; TERRORISM.

RWANDA

The original inhabitants of Rwanda were Pygmies who now comprise only 1 percent of the nation's population. European explorers arrived in 1854, and Rwanda was annexed as part of German East Africa in 1890. During World War I, Belgian troops occupied the country and remained to rule it with a postwar mandate from the League of Nations, along with BURUNDI, as Ruanda-Urundi. The region became a UNITED NATIONS trust territory in 1946, administered as part of the Belgian Congo until that country won independence from BELGIUM in 1960. Ethnic tension between the rival Tutsi and Hutu tribes (which curiously share a common language, cultural traditions, and prior history of intermarriage) sparked civil war after the Belgians departed, driving many of the formerly dominant Tutsi into exile. When Rwanda finally became an independent nation on July 1, 1962, Hutus held the reins of power. Tutsi opposition materialized as the Rwandan Patriotic

Front (RPF) organized in UGANDA to overthrow Hutu rule. RPF guerrillas invaded Rwanda in October 1990 touching off another civil war that theoretically ended with peace accords in August 1993. A coalition government was planned, but ethnic violence exploded once more in April 1994 after a plane crash killed the presidents of Rwanda and Burundi. (Most analysts now believe the plane was shot down by Hutus who opposed the impending political coalition.) Hutu officials launched a genocidal campaign against Tutsi tribes members in Rwanda, led by the Interahamwe militia, which slaughtered at least 800,000 victims in 100 days. While global superpowers remained aloof and United Nations (UN) forces withdrew entirely after losing 10 men in combat, RPF soldiers fought back in a 14-week civil war that routed the Hutu government and sent 1.7 million Hutus into exile. Hutu militia, in turn, staged guerrilla raids into Rwanda from Zaire (now the Democratic Republic of Congo) (DRC). In September 1998 a UN tribunal belatedly sentenced former prime minister Jean Kambanda to life imprisonment for genocide—the first-ever conviction obtained under the Genocide Convention of 1948. A four-year war between Rwanda and the DRC was settled by peace accords in July 2002. On July 31, 2003, 105 defendants were convicted of genocide in a mass trial held at Gikongo, southern Rwanda. Another 100,000 genocide suspects are currently in jail awaiting trial.

SADAT, Anwar al- (1918–1981)

Egyptian president and martyr Anwar al-Sadat was born in 1918 in a village 40 miles north of Cairo. EGYPT in those days was a British colony, and Sadat inherited a hatred of imperial rule. His early heroes were a mixed group that included Turkish liberator Kemel Ataturk, Indian pacifist Mohandas Gandhi, and ADOLF HITLER, whom Sadat admired for challenging Britain. In the mid-1930s Sadat trained at a British military school in Egypt, learning battle tactics while he forged a lifelong friendship with nationalist classmate Gamal Abdel Nasser. Together, Nasser and Sadat founded a revolutionary group that toppled British rule in Egypt two decades later. With Nasser installed as Egypt's first president, Sadat served as minister of public relations, helping Nasser to chart a course of nonalignment with the West and frank hostility toward ISRAEL. On Nasser's death in September 1970 Sadat ascended to the presidency as a relative unknown. He angered many Arabs by proposing peace with Israel (in return for the withdrawal of Israeli troops from captured lands) and by expelling Soviet advisors after RUSSIA spurned his pleas for military aid. When Israel refused to abandon the occupied Sinai peninsula, Sadat struck on October 6, 1973, and regained a portion of the lost territory by force.

Economic problems ultimately led Sadat to seek a new accord with Israel, traveling to the United States in 1978 for negotiations that forged a peace treaty between the two nations a year later. That effort won Sadat a Nobel Peace Prize—and the undying enmity of Muslim fundamentalists at home. As Sadat had once schemed against British colonial rulers, so elements of his own army now plotted to destroy him. On October 6, 1981—a date chosen to commemorate the Suez attack of 1973—assassins struck while Sadat reviewed a military procession in Cairo. Four soldiers led by Lieutenant Khaled el-Sambouli opened fire on the reviewing stand with automatic weapons, killing Sadat and seven others and wounding an additional 28 victims. Police investigation of the slaughter uncovered a widespread conspiracy with 24 defendants placed on trial between November 1981 and March 1982. Twenty-two of the defendants were convicted, 17 were sentenced to life imprisonment, and five were condemned to death. Sambouli and codefendant Abbas Mohammed were shot by a military firing squad on April 15, 1982, while three other defendants—Abdel Farag, Ataya Reheil, and Abdul Salam—were hanged.

ST. BARTHOLOMEW's Day massacre

This 16th-century religious slaughter of Protestant Huguenots in FRANCE sprang from a failed assassination plot. Catherine de Médicis, a royal member of the CATHOLIC CHURCH, opposed the influence of Huguenot leader Comte Gaspard de Coligny on her son, King Charles IX. Never one to shrink from bloodshed in pursuit of power, Catherine plotted to murder Coligny on August 22, 1572, but the initial plan was foiled by faulty marksmanship, leaving Coligny with a nonfatal bullet wound. Two days later, on St. Bartholomew's Day, prominent Huguenots gathered in Paris for a wedding celebration—and, perhaps, to plot revenge against Coligny's would-be killers. Catherine opted for a preemptive strike, sending thugs to invade Coligny's sickroom; he was stabbed to death there, dragged through the streets, and then dismembered under the supervision of a high-ranking Catholic leader, Henry, duc de Guise. At the same time other prominent Huguenots were massacred at the Louvre where they were ostensibly lodged under King Charles's protection. At that point a royal call for peace failed to stop the bloodshed, and religious mayhem continued for the next three days, spilling beyond Paris into neighboring provinces. At least 3,000 Huguenots were killed in Paris and an estimated 50,000 murdered nationwide. Coligny's head was sent to Pope Gregory XIII, who ordered a special medal struck in honor of the occasion.

The sectarian violence ordered by Catherine and Charles on St. Bartholomew's Day continued long after, like a Frankenstein monster running out of control. The massacre triggered France's Fourth War of Religion between Catholics and Protestants (1572–73) during which Huguenots gained political ascendancy in southwestern France. Henry de Guise became one of the most powerful men in France, wielding more power than Catherine de Médicis herself, briefly honored with the title "King of Paris" during the Eighth War of Religion (1585–89), also known as the War of the Three Henrys. On December 25, 1588, Henry was waylaid and murdered by members of King Henry III's royal guard, who also killed his brother, Cardinal Louis of Lorraine, the following day. Henry III, in turn, was stabbed to death by a Dominican monk, Jacques Clement, in 1589. French Catholic leaders hailed Henry's murder as "the noblest of God's doings since the Incarnation of JESUS CHRIST," while Clement's mother was honored for giving birth to the assassin.

ST. VALENTINE'S Day massacre

Chicago recorded 703 gangland murders during PRO-HIBITION, while countless other victims disappeared on "one-way rides" or were slain in Chicago's suburbs. Even CHARLES "LUCKY" LUCIANO, boss of New York's MAFIA, described Chicago in the 1920s as "a goddamn crazy place." The heart of the problem was "Scarface" Al Capone and his endless war to suppress rival bootleggers. Capone killed numerous competitors, but his longest-running campaign involved the North Side gang run by George ("Bugs") Moran. Finally, Capone took advantage of Moran's larcenous nature to set a trap that would wipe out the North rival leadership once and for all.

The bait was a shipment of whiskey, supposedly stolen from Capone en route to Chicago. An intermediary offered the load to Moran, and delivery was scheduled for the morning of February 14, 1929—St. Valentine's Day—at Moran's primary warehouse on North Clark Street. Capone imported two members of Detroit's Purple Gang to watch the garage and telephone a waiting strike team when Moran arrived. Unfortunately, the spotters had Moran's description but no photograph. Around 10:30 A.M. on D-Day, they marked the arrival of a man resembling Moran and made the fatal call.

In fact, the visitor was actually Dr. Reinhard Schwimmer, a Chicago optometrist and "gangster groupie" who enjoyed spending time with the North Side crowd whenever possible. Also present were brothers Frank and Pete Gusenberg, Adam Meyer, James Clark, Al Weinshank, and John May. Moran had overslept and was running late to the meeting. As he approached on foot, shortly before 11:00 A.M., Moran saw a police car stop in front of his garage and fled the scene, thus saving his own life. Inside the garage, two men in police uniforms brandished weapons and ordered all present to stand against a brick wall. Next, two or three other men dressed in civilian garb entered the warehouse. Before the victims recognized their peril, a storm of fire from .45-caliber Thompson submachine guns cut them down. Two of the dead or dying men were also blasted in the face at close range with a sawed-off shotgun.

While Moran and Capone traded public accusations in the slaughter's aftermath, Chicago Prohibition administrator Frederick Silloway aired an alternate theory, claiming that the shooters were corrupt police officers, threatened with exposure by Moran after they stole a shipment of his whiskey. In any case, the massacre effectively destroyed the North Side gang. One of the Tommy guns used on St. Valentine's Day was found in December 1929 after police arrested hitman Fred ("Killer") Burke in Michigan. Burke denied any part in the slaughter and was never charged with the crime, instead receiving a life sentence for the murder of a Michigan police officer.

SAMOA

Polynesians settled on the Samoan islands around 1000 B.C.E., and they remained unspoiled by civilization until traders from FRANCE and the NETHERLANDS arrived some 2,800 years later. In the late 19th century an international treaty between the United States and GERMANY recognized the "paramount interest" of both nations in Samoa (naval bases), thereafter dividing the archipelago into American Samoa and Western Samoa (ruled by Germany). Surprise competitor New Zealand seized Western Samoa in 1914, and in 1946 those islands became a UNITED NATIONS trust—still ruled from Auckland. By that time a native resistance movement called *Mau* ("strongly held view") had taken root in Samoa, agitating for full independence and winning that goal on January 1, 1962. Forty years later New Zealand formally apologized for the injustices suffered by Samoans under foreign rule. Germany and the United States have yet to follow suit.

SAN Francisco Police Department

From PROHIBITION through the 1940s, the San Francisco Police Department (SFPD) harbored as many corrupt officers as any other force in the country. Chief Frank Ahern vowed to change that image in the 1950s, cracking down on local gambling so zealously that his officers soon found themselves raiding senior citizens' bridge clubs. Thomas Cahill was appointed chief on Ahern's death in 1958 and soon shifted the department toward an emphasis on political surveillance and harassment of supposed leftists and "radicals." The first salvo in that battle was fired on May 13, 1960, when police used clubs and fire hoses against nonviolent students protesting a local appearance by the HOUSE COMMITTEE ON UN-AMERICAN ACTIVITIES. Of 64 persons arrested in that melee, all but one were later released without charges.

Cahill failed to learn his lesson, driving SFPD ever farther to the right. Throughout the 1960s more police were assigned to political surveillance in San Francisco than to investigation of organized crime, and Cahill created a special two-man "obscenity squad" to harass local theaters and rock-concert promoters. Persistent reports of racist brutality were filed against SFPD, while KU KLUX KLAN posters blossomed on departmental bulletin boards, and some high-ranking officers boasted of membership in the JOHN BIRCH SOCIETY. San Francisco suffered three days of rioting in September 1966 after a white police officer shot and killed an unarmed teenage car thief in the Hunters Point ghetto. A bloody police assault on student protesters against the VIETNAM War, staged on January 10, 1968, went largely unnoticed because both local newspapers were on strike. The following year, SFPD tear-gassed and raided BLACK PANTHER PARTY headquarters, arresting 16 persons on various petty or trumped-up charges.

Complaints against San Francisco's "finest" continue to the present day. The sampling of cases listed below is representative.

- *January 1999:* Police captain George Stasko received a hero's funeral after he died in a single-car crash. Following the ceremony, journalists revealed that Stasko's blood-alcohol content was three times the legal limit when he crashed into a redwood tree. Critics denounced the cover-up.
- *August 1999:* An inspector was suspended for 90 days when he pleaded guilty to charges arising from a 1997 testing scandal that wreaked havoc with department promotions. Dismissal was held in abeyance for five years, "pending good behavior."
- *March 2003:* Ten officers were indicted on felony charges arising from a November 2002 off-duty brawl at a fast-food restaurant. Those charged with obstructing justice and other counts included Police Chief Earl Sanders; Assistant Chief Alex Fagan and his son Alex, Jr.; Deputy Chief David Robinson; and Deputy Chief Greg Suhr. Alex Fagan, Jr., and two other cops were involved in the original fight, after which department brass sidelined the case. Charges were filed only after FEDERAL BUREAU OF INVESTIGATION agents announced their own investigation of the incident. All counts against Chief Sanders were dropped on March 11, but the other cases were unresolved at press time for this book.
- *September 2003:* A federal court overturned the 1989 murder conviction of alleged STREET GANG member John Tennison. That ruling accused police and prosecutors of illegally

suppressing exculpatory evidence and coaching two witnesses to lie under oath. The buried evidence included memos authorizing a $2,500 payment to one witness, videotaped interviews with an alternative suspect, polygraph tests indicating that another prosecution witness lied in court—and the confession of the actual killer, obtained two weeks after Tennison was convicted.

SATANISM

While Satanism is technically defined as worship of the Biblical Satan (also known as Lucifer), the label has been applied throughout history—often erroneously—to a wide variety of non-Christian religions. Early popes branded any deviation from their dictates as satanic heresy and often punished such transgressions with death. Celebrations of a lewd and sometimes violent "black mass," commonly inverting and deriding rituals of the CATHOLIC CHURCH, have been reported throughout Europe from Medieval times, expanding into the New World with the march of colonialism. Britain's 18th-century "hellfire clubs" were more concerned with drunken sex than demonology, but thousands of human bones supported the confessions of Catherine Deshayes, executed at Paris in February 1680 on charges of sacrificing infants for wealthy clients. In 1912 Spanish authorities executed Marti Enriqueta, a self-styled witch, for slaying children and using their remains as ingredients for love potions. Cult leader Sila Wongsin was shot in 1959 in Thailand for sacrificing children during devil-worship ceremonies. Two decades later, suspect Laxman Giri died in jail while awaiting trial on similar charges in INDIA.

In the 1980s various U.S. jurisdictions were rocked by allegations of satanic ritual abuse involving numerous children, some of them supposedly molested and otherwise menaced with cult mumbo-jumbo in nursery schools and day-care centers across the country. The most famous such trial, involving staffers from the McMartin Preschool in Manhattan Beach, California, ended with acquittal of one defendant and a mistrial for another, but other defendants were convicted or pleaded guilty as charged in Bakersfield, California; Boston, Massachusetts; Carson City, Nevada; Denver, Colorado; El Paso, Texas; Miami, Florida; San Diego, California; and Wenatchee, Washington. Similar convictions were recorded in Canada, England, and Australia. Roughly one-third of those verdicts were overturned on subsequent appeals, but defendants in the remaining cases are still imprisoned in various states. Controversy surrounding the charges endures, sparking allegations of "witch hunts" or a global satanic conspiracy involving drugs, child pornography, and thousands of human sacrifices each year.

SAUDI Arabia

Saudi Arabia is the ancestral home of both the Arab people and the Islamic religion. Those distinctions have not spared it from turmoil and conspiracy, however; quite the reverse, in fact. A long succession of foreign invasions and jihads (holy wars) between divergent Muslim sects have made the Arabian Peninsula one of the Middle East's bloodiest battlegrounds. The modern kingdom of Saudi Arabia was created from scratch by King Ibn Saud (1882–1953), a descendant of Wahhabi rulers who were driven from power by EGYPT and TURKEY in 1818. Saud seized Riyadh in 1901 and established himself as the head of the Arab nationalist movement, expanding from his base of power to conquer most of present-day Saudi Arabia by 1932. OIL was discovered four years later, enriching the Saud family beyond its patriarch's wildest dreams. Ibn Saud's successor, simply Saud, was deposed by Crown Prince Faisal in 1967. Faisal, in turn, was murdered by a relative in 1975. As a leading member of Organization of Petroleum Exporting Countries (OPEC), Saudi Arabia shares responsibility for manipulation of oil prices on a global scale. It has also supported (albeit passively) many past attacks on ISRAEL that were carried out by Palestinians and other Arab nations. Still, the kingdom enjoys a close relationship with Western oil companies, and it provided a base of operations for military action against IRAQ during the 1991 GULF WAR. That same support was not forthcoming in 2003 when President George W. Bush launched an unprovoked assault on Iraq under the sobriquet of OPERATION IRAQI FREEDOM.

See also BUSH DYNASTY.

SAVINGS and Loan scandal

Described by some observers as the greatest theft in U.S. history, the Savings and Loan scandal of the 1980s sprang from government deregulation of savings-and-loan institutions, steadily relaxing government controls on lending until corrupt leaders of various S&L firms were caught looting their companies. In 1989 President George H. W. Bush began a federal bailout of the failing firms, a move sparked in part by familial self-interest, which will ultimately cost U.S. taxpayers $1.4 trillion by 2033.

S&L deregulation crept up on America by slow degrees through a series of federal statutes passed between 1978 and 1981, permitting broader investments in land-development, construction, and education loans, providing tax incentives for real-estate investment, and undercutting federal supervision of S&L firms. The real S&L rip off bonanza began under President RONALD REAGAN in September 1981 when the Federal Home Loan Bank Board granted failing S&L's permission to issue "income capital certificates" that made insolvent firms appear to be financially sound. Between 1981 and 1985 Reagan also slashed the Bank Board's regulatory and supervisory staff while S&L assets increased by 56 percent during the same period (and some firms, notably in California and Texas, expanded by 300 percent). In January 1982 the Bank Board cut S&L net worth requirements from 4 to 3 percent of total deposits. Prior to Reagan, federal law required a minimum of 400 stockholders for any S&L, including at least 125 from the "local community," while barring any individual ownership exceeding 10 percent and any "controlling group" with more than 25 percent—all rules discarded by Reagan's Bank Board in April 1982. Deregulation was completed in December 1982 with passage of the Garn–St. Germain Depository Institutions Act, further expanding the power of S&Ls to invest in risky ventures. That plan was coauthored by the Garn Institute of Finance—named for Senator Jake Garn—which received $2.2 million from S&L industry executives.

The bubble burst in March 1984 with the failure of Empire Savings in Mesquite, Texas, costing investors—and later taxpayers—an estimated $300 million. Reagan's Bank Board responded in April with a bid to eliminate federal deposit insurance on S&L brokered deposits—thus leaving investors to sink unaided—but the courts rejected that attempt to off-load government responsibility. S&L failures in Ohio prompted a "bank holiday" in March 1985—America's first since the Great Depression—but S&L failures spread to Maryland by May, costing investors another $185 million. By 1987 Texas S&Ls represented more than 50 percent of all national losses, with 14 Texas firms among the top 20 losers. In February 1988 the Bank Board introduced a "Southwest Plan" to consolidate and package failing Texas S&Ls for sale to the highest bidder, thus (theoretically) minimizing government losses from deposit insurance payments. Under the Southwest Plan, the Bank Board ultimately sold 205 S&Ls with assets (on paper) of $101 billion.

Still, the financial hemorrhage continued nationwide, and the S&L scandal became a major campaign issue in 1988 when George H. W. Bush was elected president. By that time son Neil Bush had run the Silverado S&L Company into bankruptcy after only three short years as director, and Neil's brother Jeb had defaulted on a $4.56 million loan from Broward Federal Savings in Sunrise, Florida. President Bush unveiled the federal bail-out plan within a month of his January 1989 inauguration, shifting regulation of S&Ls to a new Office of Thrift Supervision, while a Resolution Trust Corporation was created to "resolve" insolvent firms. Silverado's CEO received 3.5 years in prison on pleading guilty to theft of $8.7 million from investors, but Neil Bush settled his case for $50,000 (40 percent of one year's salary at Silverado) while taxpayers bore the brunt of the losses. In Florida, auditors examined the office building that Jeb Bush had financed with his $4.56 million loan, deciding its fair market value was $500,000. Bush and other investors repaid that amount, leaving taxpayers to cover the remaining $4,060,000. Despite that record Bush was elected governor of Florida, later helping brother George win the White House in ELECTION 2000. Today, some conspiracists suggest that President Bush, Sr., may have launched the GULF WAR in 1990 to distract attention from the S&L scandal and more specifically from the role his sons played in that fiasco.

See also BUSH DYNASTY.

SCHOOL of the Americas

The School of the Americas (SOA)—dubbed the "School of Assassins" by critics—has trained more than 60,000 Latin American soldiers and SECRET POLICE officers in various "security" techniques since it was founded in Panama in 1946. Specialized courses include sniping, psychological warfare, commando tactics, and interrogation techniques (that is, torture). Panama ousted the school in 1984, whereupon its campus was relocated at Fort Benning, Georgia—home of the U.S. Army Special Forces ("Green Berets"). At the time Panamanian President Jorge Illueca denounced the SOA publicly as the single "biggest base for destabilization in Latin America." Its grim work continues today under a new name, the Western Hemisphere Institute for Security Cooperation.

The SOA's most traveling tutor was Daniel Mitrione, Sr., who operated in the guise of a spokesman for the U.S. Office of Public Safety. First assigned to BRAZIL, Mitrione ended his career in URUGUAY, where he was kidnapped and executed by Tupamaro guerrillas in August 1970. While the RICHARD NIXON White House praised Mitrione's "devoted service to the cause of peaceful progress in an orderly world," details of his double life began to surface. Manuel Hevia described a torture class for Uruguayan police officers that Mitrione conducted in the basement of his home, where several unnamed victims were brutally murdered.

Mitrione's son, Daniel, Jr., followed his father's footsteps into law enforcement as an agent of the FEDERAL BUREAU OF INVESTIGATION. On March 14, 1985, he pleaded guilty to possessing and distributing 92 pounds of COCAINE as well as taking bribes to ignore other drug shipments. He received a 10-year prison sentence, which was waived on condition that he return $1 million in illegal assets and testify against various accomplices. Mitrione ultimately spent three years in a monastery maintained by the CATHOLIC CHURCH for discipline of wayward priests.

SCIENTOLOGY

Volumes have been written on the history and theology of this controversial cult, founded by science-fiction author L. Ron Hubbard in 1952 as the Hubbard Association of Scientologists and later renamed the Church of Scientology. Best known for recruiting a stellar celebrity cast that includes Tom Cruise, Lisa Marie Presley, Kelly Preston, and John Travolta, Scientology offers a curious blend of fantasy and pop psychology, with devotees striving to "clear" themselves of prenatal infestation by "Thetans" (defined as alien spirits banished from Earth some 75 million years ago by the intergalactic despot Xenu). Achieving "clear" status via long-term "auditing" is a costly process, estimated by *Time* magazine in 1991 to average $300,000 per client. By 1987—again, according

to *Time*—the church allegedly banked $503 million per year from its faithful adherents (a figure hotly disputed by church spokespersons). Without further debating on Scientology's religious merits, any survey of conspiracies would be remiss in omitting the following facts, documented from court records and law-enforcement agencies worldwide:

1969—The church was stripped of its tax-exempt status by the INTERNAL REVENUE SERVICE (IRS). Three years later, T-men announced that Hubbard's church owed $1 million in unpaid taxes for the years 1970–72. By March 1980 the bill (with penalties) had increased to $1.5 million.

July 1977—FEDERAL BUREAU OF INVESTIGATION agents raided church offices in Los Angeles and Washington, D.C., seizing 48,000 documents stolen from the IRS and other agencies by Scientology's covert "moles." In August 1978 nine leaders of the church were indicted for stealing government files and bugging federal offices. All were convicted in October 1979, receiving prison terms of four to five years and $10,000 fines.

1980—L. Ron Hubbard was indicted in Tampa, Florida, for an alleged conspiracy to take over the town of Clearwater via fraudulent real estate purchases and a bizarre plot to frame Mayor Gabriel Cazares on hit-and-run charges after Cazares opposed the land grab. Hubbard could not be found, but estranged son Ronald DeWolff presented evidence that his father had skimmed $100 million from church coffers between 1970 and 1982.

1983—Canadian police raiders seized 250,000 documents from the church office in Toronto. In 1992 Scientology became the first church ever tried for criminal offenses in Canada, charged with infiltrating Ontario's provincial government and three police departments in the 1970s. The church and three members were convicted at trial and fined $250,000.

November 1996—Jean-Jacques Mazier, once the top-ranking Scientologist in FRANCE, was convicted of fraud and manslaughter, receiving an 18-month prison sentence for his role in the suicide of cult member Patrice Vic. Fourteen other Scientologists were also convicted of embezzlement and fraud, receiving suspended sentences.

SEATTLE 8   See PACKER, HORACE.

SECRET Army Organization

In February 1970 members of the disintegrating MIN-UTEMEN organization created a new "Secret Army Organization" (SAO) based in San Diego, California. In autumn 1971 the SAO launched a local terrorist campaign, beginning with a spate of anonymous phone calls and threatening letters. On November 13, a car was firebombed at the home of Peter Bohmer, a college professor who participated in protest rallies against the VIETNAM War. On January 6, 1972, SAO gunmen fired rifle shots into Bohmer's home, wounding a female visitor. The attacks continued until June 1972 when an SAO bomb wrecked a local porno theater.

Police then arrested William Yakopec, a former member of the JOHN BIRCH SOCIETY, soon unraveling the SAO's curtain of secrecy. Identified member included San Diego firefighters and police officers, some of them serving as paid FEDERAL BUREAU OF INVESTIGATION (FBI) informants. The real shock came at Yakopec's bombing trial when SAO member Howard Godfrey testified that he had been an FBI informant since 1967. Godfrey testified that FBI agents had approved all his SAO activities, including delivery of illegal weapons and explosives used in the theater bombing (supplied to Godfrey by the bureau). In fact Godfrey had planned the theater bombing himself with FBI encouragement, and he drove the getaway car when colleague George Hoover shot up Professor Bohmer's house. After the shooting Godfrey gave the rifle and his jacket to FBI Agent Steve Christiansen, who destroyed the garment and hid the weapon for six months before delivering it to local police. Another informant, retired San Diego cop John Raspberry, claimed that his FBI contacts ordered him to "eliminate" and "get rid of" Bohmer, whom they deemed a threat to national security. Obliging to a fault, Raspberry said he would have gladly murdered Bohmer if his orders had been more specific.

The SAO fiasco ultimately had no consequences for the FBI. While Yakopec, George Hoover, and a third terrorist went to prison, Howard Godfrey was rewarded for his "service" with a job in the California fire marshal's office. (He was later indicted for planting a bomb on a busy road near his home, phoning a threat to authorities, and then volunteering to lead the investigation.) Agent Christiansen

escaped prosecution and retired to Utah. He refused to discuss the case with reporters but told them, "The FBI is taking good care of us."

See also TERRORISM.

SECRET police

Throughout history, all autocratic regimes—and many "democratic" ones—have employed secret police agencies to collect intelligence on enemies and often to go further still, harassing, imprisoning, torturing, and sometimes murdering opponents of the state. Whether the government in question is a monarchy, a military junta, or some version of democracy, secret police share certain universal traits. By definition they operate clandestinely, often exceeding their lawful authority and engaging in activities that might be prosecuted if they were not shielded by the power of the state. Seldom satisfied for long with mere collection of data, most such agencies progress in time toward proactive (and often illegal) harassment of perceived enemies. "Disinformation"—that is, deception of adversaries, the general public, and even their own masters—is a nearly universal trait of secret police agencies. In extreme cases the sworn upholders of law become criminals themselves, committing acts of sabotage and personal violence, sometimes collaborating with covert vigilante groups or elements of organized crime to suppress their opponents.

Americans are long accustomed to hearing reports of secret police activities in other countries. Familiar examples include the OKHRANA of czarist RUSSIA and the Soviet KGB; the GESTAPO of Nazi GERMANY; CHILE's brutal DINA; SOUTH AFRICA's Bureau of Special Services (BOSS); BRAZIL's Department of Political and Social Order; Britain's MI5; East Germany's Stasi; the MOSSAD of ISRAEL; and IRAN's homicidal SAVAK. They may not be aware that many agents of military regimes in Latin America have been trained in torture and assassination techniques at the U.S.-sponsored SCHOOL OF THE AMERICAS. Likewise, most Americans would probably deny the existence of secret police organizations inside the United States, but they would be mistaken.

Nationwide, most large U.S. cities have harbored police units that are dedicated to surveillance and harassment of "subversives." Examples covered in this volume include the BALTIMORE POLICE DEPARTMENT, CHICAGO POLICE DEPARTMENT, DENVER POLICE

DEPARTMENT, DETROIT POLICE DEPARTMENT, LOS ANGELES POLICE DEPARTMENT, NEW HAVEN POLICE DEPARTMENT, NEW YORK POLICE DEPARTMENT, OAKLAND POLICE DEPARTMENT, PHILADELPHIA POLICE DEPARTMENT, and SAN FRANCISCO POLICE DEPARTMENT. Various police departments and officials in the South have historically collaborated with the racist CITIZENS' COUNCILS and KU KLUX KLAN to persecute African Americans, including the ATLANTA POLICE DEPARTMENT, Birmingham's public-safety commissioner EUGENE ("BULL") CONNOR, and Alabama's state police under Governor GEORGE WALLACE. The CENTRAL INTELLIGENCE AGENCY (CIA), though barred from domestic spying by its 1947 charter, frequently engaged in illegal activities on the home front, and any bar to such behavior was lifted in 2001 with passage of the sweeping USA PATRIOT ACT.

A prime offender, throughout its 95-year history, has been the FEDERAL BUREAU OF INVESTIGATION (FBI). From harassment of minorities, labor unions, and "radicals" in the years before World War I, through collaboration with the vigilante American Protective League in 1920, through the far-ranging COINTELPRO campaigns launched by J. EDGAR HOOVER in 1956 and continuing until his death, the bureau has committed thousands of illegal break-ins, planting microphones and tapping telephones, stealing and reading private correspondence, harassing and entrapping suspected "revolutionaries" on various minor or trumped-up charges. At its worst, the FBI facilitated Klan assaults on civil rights workers during the 1961 FREEDOM RIDES; framed members of the BLACK PANTHER PARTY and alleged associates of organized crime for murders they did not commit; tried to orchestrate an all-out war between the MAFIA and the Communist Party; and created a right-wing terrorist group, the SECRET ARMY ORGANIZATION, which planted bombs and attempted to murder liberal college professors. The 1970s CHURCH COMMITTEE exposed much illegal activity by the CIA and the FBI, but more recent incidents involving EARTH FIRST!, the CISPES CASE, and similar examples of "overzealous" law enforcement suggest that little has truly changed.

See also COMMUNISM.

SECRET Service, U.S.

The U.S. Secret Service was created in July 1865 as a branch of the Treasury Department designed to suppress counterfeit currency. During RECONSTRUCTION,

some Secret Service agents were also dispatched to investigate terrorist acts committed by the KU KLUX KLAN. Its better-known assignment, guarding the president against assassins, began after an ANARCHIST shot President William McKinley in 1901. That role expanded to protection of major presidential and vice-presidential candidates in 1968 after the RFK ASSASSINATION in Los Angeles. Additionally, Secret Service agents sometimes guard the president against embarrassment by removing peaceful protesters from public gatherings (as when several students were removed from an Ohio State University graduation ceremony for silently turning their backs on the speaker, George W. Bush). Perennial hostility between the Secret Service and the FEDERAL BUREAU OF INVESTIGATION was exacerbated by the JFK ASSASSINATION in 1963, when both agencies failed to detect alleged threats from accused killer LEE HARVEY OSWALD. A quarter-century later, those failures were highlighted by the HOUSE SELECT COMMITTEE ON ASSASSINATIONS. On June 17, 2002, an article in the conservative news magazine *U.S. News and World Report* detailed numerous allegations of illegal, incompetent, or negligent behavior by Secret Service agents. Nine months later the agency was transferred from Treasury to the Department of Homeland Security, ostensibly in the interest of streamlining and coordinating liaison with other departments. As this book went to press, the Secret Service had 5,000 employees, including 2,100 "special" agents, 1,200 uniformed employees, and 1,700 technical or administrative personnel.

See also BUSH DYNASTY.

SENATE Internal Security Subcommittee

Established in January 1951 as the U.S. Senate's version of the Red-hunting HOUSE COMMITTEE ON UN-AMERICAN ACTIVITIES, the Senate Internal Security Subcommittee (SISS) enjoyed a close working relationship with the FEDERAL BUREAU OF INVESTIGATION's (FBI) Crime Records Division, which created a "special squad" to assist with various investigations. FBI Assistant Director Louis Nichols deemed the relationship "very satisfactory," operating "to the mutual benefit of both the [JUSTICE] DEPARTMENT and the bureau, as well as Congress and the general public."

Those benefits were realized in various ways. The FBI provided files on various "disloyal" groups and individuals, including a March 1953 list of "subversive persons" at 56 American universities. In May 1958 as part of a new campaign against "use of lawyers and courts to further Communist Propaganda," the bureau furnished details on "pertinent subversive activities" by 70 lawyers who had represented Communist Party members. Investigation of "un-American activities" fell out of favor in the 1970s, following exposure of lawless domestic surveillance in the WATERGATE scandal and before the CHURCH COMMITTEE. In 1977 the SISS was quietly merged with the Senate Criminal Activities Subcommittee and thereafter ceased to exist.

See also COMMUNISM.

SENEGAL

Portuguese traders "discovered" Senegal in the 15th century, and French rivals moved in to stir the pot 200 years later. By the early 1700s offshore Gorée Island was a major shipping center for the Atlantic slave trade, launching millions of African captives on unwelcome one-way trips to the New World. A seesaw struggle for control of Senegal, fought between Britain and FRANCE, ended with French victory in 1840, and Senegal was merged into the larger colony of French West Africa in 1895. In 1946 it graduated to the status of a French "overseas territory," the same legal fiction used to perpetuate colonialism in ALGERIA and Indochina. Granted independence on June 20, 1960, Senegal joined an ill-fated federation with MALI that collapsed four months later. The colonial legacy lingers in economic stagnation and "flawed" elections that have sparked rebellion in Senegal's southern Casamance Province, where the Movement of Democratic Forces waged a bloody campaign for independence. In 1998 Amnesty International reported that numerous citizens have been murdered by the government and buried in secret mass graves. Negotiations held in the following year produced a tentative Casamance cease-fire, but 80 percent of the province's arable land is presently seeded with land mines.

SERVANTS of the Paraclete

Organized in the 1960s to provide refuge and treatment for troubled priests, the Servants of the Paraclete (holy spirit) describe themselves as "the M.A.S.H. unit of the CATHOLIC CHURCH." Head-

quartered at Jemez Springs, New Mexico, the group has offered therapy to hundreds (or thousands) of priests suffering from such maladies as alcoholism, depression, drug addiction, and simple loss of faith. Sadly for all concerned, the Paracletes have also treated numerous PEDOPHILE PRIESTS, shipped to New Mexico from parishes across the United States and Canada, but their success rate in such cases leaves much to be desired.

Not that the Paracletes themselves admit to any failures: In 1986 group therapist, Dr. Jay Feierman, wrote to Rev. Michael Jamail in the Diocese of Beaumont, Texas, claiming that "Our recidivism rate for behavior which would be considered criminal is 0 percent to the best of our knowledge." That assertion, unrivaled by any other psychiatric facility on Earth, somehow ignored the fact that Paraclete alumni included such serial offenders as Father James Porter (125 victims in four states) and Father David Holley (serving 275 years in prison for molesting 10 New Mexico children *after* his release from the Jemez Springs facility). At the time of his arrest in 1989 Holley was identified as the fifth Paraclete graduate jailed for multiple sex crimes in New Mexico alone.

Indeed, it had by then become traditional for pedophile priests to remain in the Land of Enchantment following their "cure" at the Paraclete center, with reassignment to some New Mexico parish accepted as standard procedure. An exception was Father Porter, who made his first stop at Jemez Springs in 1967 and then transferred to a parish at Bemidji, Minnesota. A spokesperson for the Servants of the Paraclete advised Porter's new bishop that Porter had suffered an unspecified "breakdown," including "some moral problems . . . for which he was not responsible," but no mention was made of his molesting 68 children in Massachusetts. Porter's subsequent crimes were likewise forgiven, sending him back to the Paraclete center twice more. Neither visit helped, and his long record of felonies somehow slipped Doctor Feierman's mind when he claimed a recidivism rate of "0 percent."

Attorney Bruce Pasternak, with 39 civil actions filed against the Archdiocese of Santa Fe and various pedophile priests by 1993, described New Mexico as "the ecclesiastical dumping ground of the Catholic Church." He also dubbed the Paraclete center a "pervert pipeline," used by Catholic leaders to obstruct justice in numerous cases of child molestation. Santa Fe Archbishop Robert Sanchez retired with the exposure of his five adulterous affairs, explaining that he had covered for pedophile priests because he "didn't know it was a crime" to violate children. In November 1993, 17 of David Holley's victims settled out of court with the Paraclete center for an undisclosed "very substantial amount" of cash. In December 1994, six Catholic properties in New Mexico were sold to pay off 135 damage claims, expected to top $50 million.

SEYCHELLES

The Seychelles Archipelago, comprising some 100 islands in the Indian Ocean, northeast of MADAGAS-CAR, was uninhabited when agents of the British East India Company dropped anchor in 1609. Soon the islands became a favorite refuge for pirates, a problem allegedly resolved when French authorities claimed dominion in 1756. Britain seized control of the islands in 1814, finally granting independence in 1976. First president James Mancham was deposed a year later by Prime Minister France-Albert René, who proclaimed a one-party socialist state. Returning to its pirate roots, Seychelles has catered openly to criminals and fugitives since 1996 when its Economic Citizenship program offered passports to all comers at a price of $25,000. At the same time, another statute granted immunity from criminal prosecution to any person who invested $10 million or more in Seychelles.

SHABAZZ, Qubilah   See NATION OF ISLAM.

SHAMIR, Yitzhak (1915–   )

A native of POLAND, born in 1915, Yitzhak Shamir was an early convert to the tenets of militant ZION-ISM. In 1935 he abandoned legal studies in Warsaw and emigrated to British-controlled Palestine, enrolling at Hebrew University in Jerusalem. Between classes he joined the terrorist group known as IRGUN Zvai Leumi, participating in various anti-British paramilitary actions during the next five years. In 1940 Shamir left the Irgun and followed comrade Avraham Stern into a new clique variously known as Lohamei Herut Yisrael (Freedom Fighters of Israel) or the Stern Gang. Decades later, in January 1983, the Israeli newspaper *Ha'aretz* revealed that Shamir and other Stern Gang leaders had attempted

to negotiate with ADOLF HITLER in 1941, offering to form a Jewish state in Palestine "on a national and totalitarian basis, which will establish relations with the German [THIRD] REICH" and protect Nazi interests in the Middle East against Britain and U.S. allies. Hitler's preoccupation with the Holocaust scuttled that bargain, but Shamir and company continued their intrigue against Britain regardless.

Imprisoned in 1941 Shamir escaped two years later and resumed his duties as a Stern Gang leader. In November 1944 his assassins killed Lord Moyne, Britain's minister of state in EGYPT. With Hitler's defeat in 1945, the Stern Gang joined Irgun agents to "recruit" homeless European Jews for immigration to Palestine. Their methods were forceful, to say the least, and Israeli archives name 40 Jews who were murdered by Zionist thugs for resisting the move. British authorities arrested Shamir again in 1946 and exiled him to a prison camp in Eritrea, but he escaped once more in 1947 and resumed command of the Stern Gang. In September 1948 he ordered the assassination of Count Folke Bernadotte, a savior of 20,000 Jews during World War II, who had lately been appointed as UNITED NATIONS mediator between ISRAEL and Arabs in the Middle East. Shamir remained as the Stern Gang's leader until it disbanded in 1949; then he moved on to a post with the MOSSAD. A member of fellow terrorist Menachem Begin's Likud party, Shamir was elected to the Knesset (Parliament) in 1973. Ten years later he succeeded Begin as prime minister of Israel. In and out of power during the next decade, Shamir announced an "unrelenting" quest for peace in October 1991 but scuttled negotiations one day later with a verbal assault on leaders of SYRIA—who responded by producing old "Wanted" posters from the Bernadotte assassination, naming Shamir as a fugitive terrorist. Defeated for reelection in 1992, Shamir stepped down as leader of his party and resigned from the Knesset four years later.

See also HOLOCAUST AND HOLOCAUST DENIAL; TERRORISM.

SIERRA Leone

Though barely half the size of Illinois, Sierra Leone has problems enough to agitate heads of state all over the world. Portuguese explorers were first on the scene to abuse and corrupt aboriginal peoples; then British troops arrived in 1787 to make Freeport a haven for runaway slaves and black veterans of Britain's armed forces. That "altruistic" effort evaporated in 1808 when London claimed the Senegal coast as a British colony, extending royal "protection" to the interior by 1896. Independence was granted in April 1961, followed by military overthrow of the elected civilian government six years later. In 1991 the fledgling Revolutionary United Front (RUF) demanded multiparty elections within 90 days, but the corrupt regime declined to dismantle itself and a guerrilla war erupted, spanning the next decade. By the time peace was formally declared in 2002, at least 50,000 persons had been slaughtered, while thousands more were systematically raped, blinded, and mutilated in a long-running campaign of TERRORISM. Both sides in the war used children as soldiers, with UNITED NATIONS (UN) observers reporting that 25 percent of all government troops were teenagers below age 18. On the rebel side, many children across Sierra Leone have told Human Rights Watch that they were forced at gunpoint to torture, kill, and cannibalize helpless victims. The UN presently maintains its largest peacekeeping force (17,000 troops) in Sierra Leone, where theoretically some 45,000 combatants have been disarmed. President Ahmad Kabbah, responsible for many atrocities in his own right, was reelected in May 2002 with 70 percent of the popular vote. An economic sidebar to the bloody conflict in Sierra Leone involves RUF capture of the nation's fabulous diamond mines. So many "conflict diamonds" have in fact been sold abroad to finance rebel campaigns that U.S. traders are now barred by law from purchasing gems from Sierra Leone—a restriction that has thus far done nothing to end the trade in "hot ice."

SILENT Brotherhood

Spawned by decades of racist propaganda, the Silent Brotherhood (also known as The Order) was America's first hard-core neo-Nazi terrorist group. Its leaders publicly declared war against ZOG—the "Zionist Occupation Government" in Washington, D.C.—and supported themselves by armed robbery, distributing their loot to like-minded fanatics around the country.

The Silent Brotherhood's founding father, Texas native Robert Jay Mathews, drew his inspiration from THE TURNER DIARIES (1978), a racist novel that also prompted Timothy McVeigh to carry out the

OKLAHOMA CITY BOMBING of a federal building in April 1995. Mathews recruited his followers from the KU KLUX KLAN (KKK), the Aryan Nations, and similar groups. Organized in October 1983 the group soon robbed a Seattle video shop and then cranked out stacks of counterfeit $50 bills so inferior that member Bruce Pierce was arrested on his first attempt to pass the money.

Next, the brotherhood turned to bank robbery and armored truck holdups, with greater success. Between December 1983 and July 1984 members stole more than $3.9 million, donating much of the loot to the KKK, Aryan Nations, White Aryan Resistance, and various CHRISTIAN IDENTITY sects. Brotherhood members also murdered Alan Berg, a Jewish radio host in Denver, and killed one of their own as a suspected informer.

FEDERAL BUREAU OF INVESTIGATION agents discovered the Silent Brotherhood's existence on July 16, 1984, when Mathews dropped a pistol registered to sidekick Andrew Barnhill at the scene of a California heist. Another member, Thomas Martinez, agreed to betray his comrades in October 1984, thus avoiding counterfeiting charges. Martinez arranged a meeting with Mathews for November 29 in Portland, Oregon, but Mathews shot his way out of the trap and escaped. Furious at the betrayal, Mathews penned a declaration of war against the U.S. government, signed by nine of his cohorts.

Instead of launching new offensives, though, the "warriors" fled into hiding. Mathews and four others were cornered by G-men at a compound on Whidbey Island, Washington, on December 7, 1984. His companions surrendered, but Mathews fought to the death, incinerated when flares set fire to his ammunition stockpile. Twenty-eight members of the brotherhood were indicted for various crimes. Of those, 15 pleaded guilty; five received suspended sentences, while 10 others faced prison terms ranging from six months to 20 years. Twelve were convicted at trial, their sentences ranging from five years to 250 years in prison.

A copycat group, the Order II, surfaced in early 1986. Its members were affiliated with the Aryan Nations and their activities—counterfeiting, several bombings, and at least one murder—were confined to the vicinity of that group's Idaho headquarters. Five members were indicted on federal racketeering charges in October 1988. All pleaded guilty and received prison terms ranging from six to 20 years.

SILKWOOD, Karen (1946–1974)

In 1972 Karen Silkwood worked as a lab technician at the Kerr-McGee Nuclear Corporation's Cimarron River plutonium plant in Oklahoma. As a member of the Chemical and Atomic Workers Union (OCAW), she was assigned in August 1974 to study the plant's health and safety standards. Silkwood soon found evidence of hazardous leaks, spills, and missing plutonium; then she suffered an unnerving series of "accidental" exposures to dangerous radiation at her workplace—and, strangely, in her home. One day after the third such incident, on November 13, 1974, Silkwood scheduled a secret meeting with her union supervisor and a reporter from the *New York Times*. She claimed to have incriminating documents lifted from Kerr-McGee's files, but Silkwood never reached the rendezvous. At 8:00 P.M. Silkwood died in a single-car crash on Highway 74, seven miles south of Crescent, Oklahoma.

Police found no documents in Silkwood's car and no evidence of a collision with another vehicle. An autopsy revealed .35 milligrams of methaqualone (Quaalude) per 100 milliliters of Silkwood's blood—nearly twice the recommended dosage for inducing sleep—at the time she died. Another 50 milligrams of undissolved methaqualone was found in her stomach. Relatives and OCAW spokespeople charged that Silkwood was murdered, presumably by someone acting on Kerr-McGee's behalf, but the accusations remain unsubstantiated. The OCAW further charged Kerr-McGee with producing faulty fuel rods, falsifying inspection records, and jeopardizing employee safety. The Cimarron plant closed in 1975 after journalists reported that 44–66 pounds of plutonium had been "misplaced." Silkwood's family sued Kerr-McGee on a wrongful-death complaint, and while jurors awarded her estate $10.5 million in 1979, that verdict was subsequently overturned on appeal. Seven years later, with a new trial pending, Silkwood's family accepted a $1.38 million settlement. Two books on Silkwood's case and a 1984 feature film made a case for murder and conspiracy, but no suspects have been identified to date.

SIMPSON, O.J. (1947–)

On the night of June 12, 1994, a knife-wielding assailant slaughtered Nicole Brown Simpson and a friend, Ron Goldman, outside Simpson's home in the affluent Brentwood district of Los Angeles, California.

In the course of that attack, the killer was also apparently injured, leaving traces of his or her own blood at the murder scene. DNA tests identified that blood as belonging to Nicole's estranged husband, ex-football player and actor Orenthal James Simpson. Further investigation revealed bloodstains containing DNA from both victims in O.J. Simpson's car and home. Coupled with a history of domestic abuse, that forensic evidence should have been sufficient to convict Simpson, but jurors (described by prosecutor Marcia Clark as "moon rocks") chose to ignore the DNA tests, acquitting Simpson at trial in 1995. Apparently the panel accepted Simpson's argument that he was framed by the LOS ANGELES POLICE DEPARTMENT while the "real killer" escaped.

Simpson was later found responsible for the double slaying in a civil lawsuit, filed by Goldman's family, but frame-up theories persist. One alternate explanation for the murders, floated during Simpson's trial, claims that Nicole owed money to unnamed COCAINE dealers from COLOMBIA, who killed her as an object lesson to future rip-off artists. Another theory blames convicted serial killer Glen Rogers for the slayings. Author and private investigator Joyce Spizer states the case against Rogers in her book *The Cross Country Killer* (2001). Spizer's evidence includes the following items:

- In January 1994 Rogers was hired to paint Nicole's Brentwood home.
- In June 1994 Rogers telephoned a friend to say that he was "partying" with Nicole and that he planned "to take her down."
- Rogers allegedly confessed the murders to another friend, claiming that he killed Nicole because she "dropped him to go back to O.J." When asked about the missing murder weapon, Rogers drew a knife from his boot and said, "I've got it right here."

No one has yet explained how Rogers could have placed O.J.'s blood at the crime scene and then planted items stained with the blood of both victims inside Simpson's car and home on the night of the slayings.

SIRHAN, Sirhan (1944–)

A Palestinian Arab born in Jerusalem on March 19, 1944, Sirhan Sirhan was four years old when the creation of ISRAEL uprooted his family from their ancestral home. Settled in the United States eight years later, the Sirhans kept abreast of Middle Eastern events, and young Sirhan apparently despised ZIONISM. Prosecutors later claimed that he was outraged by Israel's easy victory over her Arab neighbors in the 1967 Six-Day War and that he seethed with resentment over Senator Robert Kennedy's public support for Israel. A year later, in June 1968, Sirhan was captured at the scene of the RFK ASSASSINATION with a smoking pistol in his hand. Dozens of witnesses agreed that he had fired a burst of shots at Kennedy. Further supporting that case—and overriding critical anomalies in the ballistics evidence—was a diary filled with endless repetition of the phrase "RFK Must Die!" and other odd scribblings, such as "Pay to the order of of of of of . . . this and that."

At trial, Sirhan denied any memory of Kennedy's murder or various events preceding it, including the manic jottings in his diary. Jurors were unimpressed, convicting Sirhan of murder and recommending execution. He was formally sentenced to die, but his sentence was commuted to life imprisonment in 1972. Although legally eligible for parole, Sirhan has seen his bids for freedom rejected 13 times.

See also KENNEDY DYNASTY.

SKULL and Bones

Skull and Bones is a secret society based at Yale University, reportedly established in December 1832. The vast wealth of its members established the Russell Trust Association, which manages the society's real-estate holdings (including "The Tomb," adjacent to Jonathan Edwards College). According to Skull and Bones tradition, member Prescott Bush and a group of fellow "Bonesmen" pillaged the grave of Apache warrior Geronimo, stealing his skeletal remains and bringing them back to The Tomb. Members are purportedly forbidden to discuss the group, but some sport a Skull and Bones lapel pin by which they are identified. Prospective members are selected during their junior year at Yale, often as "legacies" of established Skull and Bones families, and rumors persist that each member receives a large cash bequest at graduation that binds him to the society and its orders in perpetuity.

While membership in Skull and Bones is supposed to be a closely guarded secret, various prominent members have been identified in the media during recent years. They include ultraconservative journalist William F. Buckley, Jr., Presidents George H. W. Bush and George W. Bush, Senator John Chaffee, Russell Davenport (editor of *Fortune* magazine), Henry Davison (senior partner of Morgan Guaranty Trust), Artemus Gates (president of *Time,* Union Pacific, and Boeing Corporation), Senator John Kerry (Democratic presidential nominee in 2004), and Harold Stanley (founder of Morgan Stanley). George W. Bush, in a February 2004 interview, described the society with his usual eloquence: "It's so secret, we can't talk about it." Given that secrecy and the tendency of Skull and Bones members to win command positions in the CENTRAL INTELLIGENCE AGENCY, the society has become a focus of conspiracy theories on a par with the TRILATERAL COMMISSION and the COUNCIL ON FOREIGN RELATIONS. A Hollywood send-up of the society, in *The Skulls* (2000), includes the blanket observation of one excluded character: "If it's elite and secret, it's got to be bad."

See also BUSH DYNASTY; MORGAN DYNASTY.

SMERSH

Ex-spy and best-selling novelist Ian Fleming exposed the Russian intelligence group known as SMERSH (from *smyert shpionam,* "death to spies") in his 1953 novel *Casino Royale.* During the next decade, fictional SMERSH agents kept Fleming's Agent 007 busy with schemes for global domination or annihilation, but few readers knew that the agency truly existed as the KGB's Fifth or Ninth Division (accounts vary), tasked with chores including espionage, sabotage, and murder. In fact SMERSH was divided into five sections, with duties including (1) detection of dissidents in the Red Army, (2) intelligence collection, (3) collation and dissemination of intelligence, (4) investigation and apprehension of civilian suspects, and (5) summary tribunals whose authority allegedly included imposition of death penalties without appeal. While the grandiose schemes of Fleming's SMERSH—including robbery of Fort Knox and long-distance diversion of U.S. guided missiles—existed only on paper or celluloid, it is generally accepted that the agency's killers claimed hundreds or thousands of victims worldwide throughout the cold war. Their most prominent victim may have been fugitive Bolshevik Leon Trotsky, killed in Mexico on orders from JOSEPH STALIN, in August 1940.

SMITH, Melvin (fl. 1969)

On December 8, 1969, four days after police killed FRED HAMPTON and Mark Clark in a raid on the Chicago office of the BLACK PANTHER PARTY, officers of the LOS ANGELES POLICE DEPARTMENT staged a similar raid on the Panther office in L.A. Six party members were wounded, and a total of 13 were arrested, including local leader Elmer ("Geronimo") Pratt and his security chief, Melvin ("Cotton") Smith. Police claimed that they were looking for a cache of automatic weapons, recently stolen from the Marine Corps base at Camp Pendleton, but none were found. Still, the L.A. Panthers were charged with conspiracy to possess illegal weapons, plus conspiracy to assault and murder police.

At trial in 1971 Melvin Smith testified for the state against his comrades. Prosecutors claimed that he had only turned state's evidence since his arrest, but informer LOUIS TACKWOOD revealed that Smith had been his FEDERAL BUREAU OF INVESTIGATION contact in the Panther Party since early 1969. Smith's lie damaged the prosecution's case, winning acquittals on the assault and attempted-murder charges, but Pratt and eight other defendants were still convicted of conspiring to stockpile nonexistent weapons. Suspicion lingers that Smith may have coordinated the December 1969 raid, as informer WILLIAM O'NEAL did in Chicago the night Fred Hampton was slain.

SMITH Act

Although the Declaration of Independence guarantees U.S. citizens an "unalienable right" to overthrow their government by armed force, America's elected leaders forbid any such action under penalty of prison or death. One such law, the Alien Registration Act (more commonly known by the name of its author, Virginia congressman Howard Smith), was passed by Congress on June 28, 1940. It imposed a five-year prison term (later increased to 20 years) on anyone who "knowingly or willfully advocates, abets, advises or teaches the duty, necessity, desirability or propriety of violently overthrowing" the U.S. government or any state government. The law was initially used against Nazi sympathizers during World War II, but none of the 56 defendants indicted during 1942–44 were convicted.

With the onset of the cold war, FEDERAL BUREAU OF INVESTIGATION Director J. EDGAR HOOVER presented Attorney General Tom Clark with a 1,350-page history of the Communist Party, seeking Smith Act prosecution of party leaders. In February 1948 the HOUSE COMMITTEE ON UN-AMERICAN ACTIVITIES contacted Clark, demanding to know why no indictments had yet been filed. A federal grand jury indicted 12 members of the party's national board on June 29, 1948, but Clark sealed the indictments for a month and announced them on July 20 when five of the 12 were arrested in New York City. Hoover freely admitted that the arrests were "a political move . . . timed to break just before the [Henry] Wallace for President convention in Philadelphia" as an embarrassment to Wallace. Eleven defendants faced trial in January 1949 and were convicted nine months later. Their convictions were upheld by the U.S. SUPREME COURT in 1951, and another 126 party members were charged during the next three years, with 93 convicted at trial.

The Supreme Court unexpectedly reversed its view on Smith Act prosecutions in 1957, overturning all but the original 11 convictions with a judgment that mere advocacy of revolution should not be prosecuted. The JUSTICE DEPARTMENT thereafter agreed that future indictments must include "an actual plan for violent revolution" instead of mere theory. A later attempt to prosecute neo-Nazi leaders for sedition, relative to their involvement with the SILENT BROTHERHOOD, resulted in the April 1988 acquittals of all defendants. Still, the Smith Act remains in effect today, reminding Americans that the Declaration of Independence has no practical relevance in modern society.

See also COMMUNISM.

SNUFF films

A topic of enduring controversy in the media and law-enforcement community, "snuff" films—cinematic records of actual murders—allegedly represent the ultimate obscenity, combining homicide and pornography for a select, perverted audience. Reports of such movies and videotapes have circulated since the late 1960s, including claims that members of organized crime and practitioners of SATANISM profit by recording gruesome deaths. Skeptics acknowledge that certain sadistic predators have filmed the slaughter of their victims, but they maintain that no commercial snuff films exist. Believers counter that assertion with a body of anecdotal evidence suggesting the existence of an affluent, sadistic clientele for whom mundane pornography lacks the requisite "kick."

As far back as June 1977, Sgt. Lloyd Martin, chief investigator for the LOS ANGELES POLICE DEPARTMENT's sexually abused children's unit, described a network of kidnappers who smuggled Mexican boys into the United States for sale to violent pedophiles. According to Martin, specially designed vehicles carried human prey across the border in hidden compartments. "They bring them in eight at a time under the floorboards," Martin told reporters. "Then they take them to a motel and clean them up. It's getting more violent. It's as if the kids aren't enough. Now there's a need for blood."

Dr. Judianne Densen-Gerber, founder of the Odyssey House refuge for abused children, agreed that foreign victims were being smuggled into the United States and sold "primarily for the purpose of killing. An American youngster has a school record and a family. But if a child has been taken off the streets of Guadalajara or Acapulco, it's much easier. There are thousands of these nameless, faceless children whose parents may have been told that the child is going for adoption and whose parents may agree simply because they want to afford that child a better life than they had. So here is a man in a Cadillac who looks nice. And they never hear from that child again."

In 1980 the NEW YORK POLICE DEPARTMENT reported persistent rumors of eight-millimeter snuff films selling for $1,500 each or screening for $300 per head at private showings. No movies were seized, but at about the same time, Associated Press reports noted the unsolved mutilation-murders of several prostitutes in ARGENTINA, where local police suggested that the crimes may have been filmed. Detective Joseph Horman of NYPD's Organized Crime Control Bureau explained that some of the films may only simulate murder, while others depict real events. Unconfirmed reports are on file of such films being shot in New York, Los Angeles, Miami, New Orleans, and Houston.

Do snuff films exist?

In 1970 Charles Manson, Bobby Beausoleil, and other members of the Manson "family" freely admitted that films were made of homicidal cult activities in southern California. An informant from that era, speaking to author Ed Sanders, claimed personal knowledge of Manson films depicting both animal and human sacrifice. One reel allegedly portrayed the slaughter of a dog, while another featured a cat blown apart with powerful "M80" firecrackers. The final reel depicted a nude, decapitated woman lying on a beach while hooded, black-robed figures circled the corpse, "throwing blood all over."

A decade later, in 1981, convicted "Son of Sam" gunman David Berkowitz told prison confidants that at least one "Sam" attack—the July 1977 shooting of Robert Violante and Stacy Moskowitz—was recorded on videotape for the private collection of a Satanic "Mr. Big," later identified by Berkowitz as New York millionaire Roy Radin. In October 1981 Berkowitz accurately predicted the Halloween murder of photographer and suspected drug dealer Ronald Sisman, allegedly killed because he planned to trade the Moskowitz tape for judicial leniency in a pending COCAINE case. The tape was never found, and Roy Radin was himself murdered before police could question him.

In June 1988 Satanists John Jones and Jason Rose were charged with the murder of victim Melissa Meyer in Springfield, Oregon. Both killers were convicted, thanks in large part to the videotape they preserved of their sacrifice, found when police searched Rose's home.

In 1993 investigative journalist Yaron Svoray infiltrated a gang of West German neo-Nazis and reported their activities—including collection of sadistic snuff films—in a subsequent book (*In Hitler's Shadow*, 1995). A viewing of one such film set Svoray on the trail of its producers, and he later claimed (in *Gods of Death*, 1997) to have found snuff films on sale in Europe, produced using female victims from war-torn BOSNIA-HERZEGOVINA. Svoray's account was dramatic, but it produced no indictments and the films remained elusive.

See also SATANISM.

SOLOMON Islands

Anthropologists believe the Solomons Archipelago has been inhabited since roughly 2000 B.C.E. Spanish explorers dropped by in 1568, but they found the climate so inhospitable that no other Europeans returned for two centuries. Britain and GERMANY divided the islands in 1886, but Germany's defeat in World War I left London solely in charge. JAPAN captured the islands in 1941, and the Solomons subsequently witnessed epic battles on land and sea during World War II. Britain regained control of the islands in 1945, finally granting independence 21 years later. Since 1999 the large island of Guadalcanal has suffered a bout of ethnic cleansing, with some 20,000 Malaitan tribe members expelled by the dominant Isatabus. Tension peaked in June 2000 when the Malaita Eagle Force stole a cache of police weapons, seized control of Honiara, and forced Prime Minister Bartholomew Ulufa'alu to resign. Civil war was narrowly averted by a shaky cease-fire agreement, but the Solomons still suffer from widespread banditry and general lawlessness.

SOMALIA

Arab and Persian trading posts dotted the coast of modern-day Somalia from the seventh century onward, while nomadic tribes populated the interior. TURKEY seized the northern coast in the 16th century, while sultans of Zanzibar captured the south. Britain and FRANCE vied for control between the mid-19th century and World War I. In 1920 England and ITALY joined forces to "protect" the region, but Italy's defeat in World War II left London to control the whole nation. An active nationalist movement forced Britain to institute representative government in 1957, followed by a grant of independence three years later. President Abdi Rashid Ali Shermarke was assassinated in October 1969 as the army seized power, dissolved the legislature, and jailed all government leaders. New president Mohamed Siad Barre leaned heavily toward RUSSIA and aided insurgents fighting to topple the rulers of neighboring ETHIOPIA. Defeated in an eight-month war with Ethiopia that wiped out most of his army, Barre fled the country in January 1991 while anarchy ensued. The country had no working government between 1991 and August 2000, a decade of chaos ruled by rival warlords and militias, marked by carnage which UNITED NATIONS (UN) forces and some 30,000 U.S. troops could not control. An estimated 50,000 Somalians died in combat during 1992–94, while another 200,000 starved to death. Fugitive terrorist Osama bin Laden found Somalia inviting as a headquarters for his AL-QAEDA network in the 1990s before moving on to AFGHANISTAN. Unhampered by a $25 million reward for his capture or death, bin Laden used Somalia as the launching pad for attacks on U.S. embassies in KENYA and TANZANIA. Ameri-

can troops withdrew from Somalia in March 1994, leaving 19,000 UN peacekeepers behind. A fragile new government was seated in August 2000, but after a full year in office, it controlled only 10 percent of the Somalian countryside. The nation's blighted economy was further stricken in November 2001 after Washington froze Somalian assets in the United States to prevent financing of al-Qaeda. Few observers find any reason for hope that conditions in Somalia will improve.

See also BIN LADEN FAMILY; TERRORISM.

SOMOZA dynasty

Anastasio Somoza was born at San Marcos, NICARAGUA, in 1896. The son of a rich coffee planter, educated in the United States, he returned home in his twenties as an ardent supporter of the U.S.-supported regime. Fearing a leftist victory in the Nicaraguan elections of May 1926, President Calvin Coolidge sent troops to "protect" U.S. citizens and property, sparking a seven-year civil war capped by an uneasy truce between President Juan Bautista Sacasa and rebel leader Augusto Sandino in January 1933. Although Sandino and his comrades were granted amnesty, Somoza plotted to kill them, a goal he achieved without President Bautista's knowledge on February 21, 1934. Three years later Somoza led a military coup that deposed Bautista, installing himself as dictator of Nicaragua. He remained in that post, supported by U.S. money and military aid, until he was assassinated in Léon by poet Rigoberto López Pérez, on September 21, 1956.

Somoza's elder son, Luis Somoza Debayle, succeeded his father as dictator of Nicaragua with Washington's stamp of approval. Terminal illness prompted his resignation in 1967, whereupon younger brother Anastasio Somoza Debayle ascended to the presidency via a suspicious electoral landslide. Anastasio, Jr., was a 1946 graduate of New York's West Point Military Academy, appointed by his father to lead the Nicaraguan National Guard in a classic example of Somoza nepotism. Newly enacted legislation barred Somoza from succeeding himself as president in 1972, but he remained a corrupt power behind the scenes, effectively seizing control of the country on December 23, 1972, after martial law was declared in the wake of a catastrophic earthquake. That shake-up killed 10,000 Nicaraguans, but Somoza was more concerned with personal profit, skimming millions of dollars from the flood of international aid pouring into his country. Incidentally, the quake also placed Somoza in contact with billionaire recluse HOWARD HUGHES, whose home in Managua was leveled. Somoza was pleased to install Hughes as a guest at his country villa, while picking the tycoon's brain and pockets.

Despite cautious opposition from the CATHOLIC CHURCH, Somoza was elected to another term as president in 1974. He soon faced opposition from an army of Sandinista rebels (named for the murdered Sandino), and increased U.S. military aid this time failed to dam the hostile tide. On July 17, 1979, Somoza fled to exile in Miami and later moved from Florida to PARAGUAY. Assassins found him there on September 17, 1980, effectively canceling any plans for resurrection of the Somoza dynasty in Nicaragua.

SOUTH Africa

The Dutch East India Company landed South Africa's first European settlers on the Cape of Good Hope in 1652, thereby inaugurating a dynasty of racism and violence against indigenous peoples. Known as Boers or Afrikaners, the new arrivals tried to establish an independent state in 1795, but British forces arrived that same year to seize control of the colony, making the "protectorate" permanent in 1814. Liberation of black slaves in 1833 prompted 12,000 Boers to begin a "great trek" into the interior, driving native tribes before them on their way to establish an Orange Free State and the republic of Transvaal. Discovery of diamonds in 1867 and GOLD in 1876 drove Cape Colony prime minister Cecil Rhodes to plot annexation of the Boer territories, fabricating an "outlander" rebellion and military "rescue" mission in 1895. Defeat forced Rhodes to resign, but Britain was victorious in the Boer War of 1899–1902, uniting its captured lands as South Africa in 1910. Organized political activity among native Africans began two years later, with formation of the AFRICAN NATIONAL CONGRESS (ANC).

South Africa fought with the Allies in World War II, but it simultaneously welcomed Nazi fugitives from the THIRD REICH and refused to sign the postwar Universal Declaration of Human Rights. White "nationalists" soon established a cradle-to-grave system of apartheid (racial separation) that reduced South Africa's true natives to de facto slave status,

subject to humiliating discrimination, police brutality, and systematic exile or assassination of resistance leaders. Blocked at every turn from achieving reform through democratic channels, the ANC finally turned to armed struggle, thus resulting in imprisonment of its leaders as "terrorists." Racist prime minister H. F. Verwoerd was assassinated, but his successors proved no more compassionate. Another quarter-century of persecution and bloodshed followed before F. W. de Klerk inaugurated a system of cautious reform in 1989. Two years later Parliament scrapped the country's apartheid statutes, and former ANC leader Nelson Mandela became South Africa's first black president in 1994. In 1997 a Truth and Reconciliation Commission opened hearings on South African human-rights violations committed between 1960 and 1963, permitting those responsible to escape punishment via public confession. Some who refused, like the police physician labeled "Dr. Death" and a detective chief dubbed "Prime Evil," played dumb on the witness stand and were sentenced to life terms in prison for multiple murders. At the same time, social upheaval in South Africa turned the tables on one-time oppressors as roving black gangs looted white-owned farms and murdered their proprietors. A sweeping AIDS epidemic, acknowledged for the first time in 2000, spread largely unchecked as President Thabo Mbeki rejected Western medicine, complaining that the plague had been exaggerated by PHARMACEUTICAL COMPANIES in pursuit of profit.

See also TERRORISM.

SPAIN

Spain was conquered by the Roman Empire in 206 B.C.E., and then by Visigoth barbarians in A.D. 412, and by Muslims in 711. Christian incursions from FRANCE and dissent among Islamic warlords combined to oust the last Muslim rulers in 1492. At the same time, Jews were expelled from Spain, and the Roman CATHOLIC CHURCH monopolized religion under pain of death for "heretics." Spanish explorers "discovered" the Western Hemisphere in the late 15th century, launching a brutal conquest of aboriginal peoples that overwhelmed Central and South America. Spain's empire soon girdled Earth, but capturing territory proved easier than holding it. A series of revolutions in the Western Hemisphere drove Spain from most of its possessions there by the

1830s, while a war with the United States in 1898 cost Madrid its colonies in CUBA, PUERTO RICO, and the PHILIPPINES.

At home, Gen. Miguel Primo de Rivera proclaimed himself dictator of Spain in 1923. King Alfonso XIII revoked the dictatorship seven years later, but strong military opposition forced him to flee the country in 1931. A new left-wing constitution declared Spain a workers' republic, breaking up large estates, secularizing schools, and wholly separating church from state, but the reform was too much for some Spaniards to bear. In July 1936 fascist army officer Francisco Franco Bahamonde led a mutiny against the government, sparking a three-year civil war that claimed nearly a million lives. Nazi GERMANY and fascist ITALY supported Franco, using Spain as a proving ground for their new armies and weapons, while JOSEPH STALIN sent troops from RUSSIA to aid the republic. Most other nations remained aloof and kept silent as FASCISM triumphed in Spain. Franco ruled with an iron hand in the name of the Falange Party until his death on November 20, 1975. Reforms proceeded then, but many Spaniards were impatient with their sluggish pace. In the Pyrenees region, Basque separatists launched a guerrilla war for independence that continues to this day, with thousands killed in acts of TERRORISM spanning the past 30 years and no end to bloodshed in sight.

SRI Lanka

Indo-Aryan immigrants from India populated the island of Ceylon, now Sri Lanka ("resplendent island"), in the fifth century B.C.E., forming the Sinhalese ethnic group that dominates the country today. Migrants from the Tamil region of India, Sri Lanka's second-largest ethnic group, began to arrive in the third century B.C.E. Struggles for power between those factions engulfed the island until PORTUGAL took possession in 1505, followed by the NETHERLANDS (1658–1796) and Britain (1796–1948). Centuries of colonial domination failed to eliminate the old ethnic rivalries, however, and fighting began anew with the advent of independence after World War II. Prime Minister S.W.R.D. Bandaranaike championed Sinhalese dominance from 1956 until his assassination by a Buddhist monk in 1959. Still, the Sinhalese controlled Sri Lanka's government, prompting an outbreak of bloody Tamil resistance in 1983. During

the next 18 years, Sri Lanka's civil war claimed at least 62,000 lives. Rebel groups including the Tamil Tigers were relentless in their opposition to the reigning government, while oppressive countermeasures resulted in still more bloodshed. Negotiators from NORWAY brokered a fragile cease-fire agreement in February 2002, followed by an August announcement lifting a legal band on the Tamil Tigers. Peace talks continue in an atmosphere fraught with mistrust and deep-seated hostility.

SS

ADOLF HITLER created the *Schutzstaffel* ("Protective Corps") or SS as an elite paramilitary unit of GERMANY's Nazi Party in 1925 under commander Julius Schreck. Successive leaders of the group included Joseph Berchtold (1926–27), Erhard Heiden (1927–29), and HEINRICH HIMMLER (1929–45). The SS had only 280 members when Himmler took command, but membership increased to 52,000 by December 1932 and topped 250,000 the following year, as dedicated Nazis closed ranks to do their part for the fatherland and racial purity. Adopting the motto "My honor is loyalty," SS members paraded in the same brown-shirted uniforms as their rivals in Hitler's Storm Troop (SA), but Himmler changed the dress code to jet-black in 1932 with a grinning silver skull featured on caps and other accessories. More than a quarter-million zealots had enlisted with the SS by the time World War II began in September 1939.

The SS performed multiple functions within Hitler's THIRD REICH. Reinhard Heydrich, Himmler's second in command, organized an intelligence service (the *Sicherheitsdienst*, or SD), whose agents were among the best in Europe, some of them later recruited by the U.S. CENTRAL INTELLIGENCE AGENCY as part of PROJECT PAPERCLIP. Members of the Waffen ("armed") SS divided their time between front-line combat and mass murder of "inferior races" in occupied Europe. Heydrich chaired the WANNSEE CONFERENCE in 1941, charting a detailed blueprint for the Holocaust, and SS members staffed the various Nazi concentration camps where wholesale murder was carried out with assembly-line efficiency. SS doctors such as JOSEF MENGELE performed all manner of "scientific" experiments on camp inmates—both Jews and captured prisoners of war—in pursuit of methods to expand the so-called master race. Under Himmler's supervision, the SS also established breeding facilities where "ideal" Aryan females (blond, blue-eyed, and healthy) engaged in marathon sex with members of the elite corps, hoping to increase Aryan numbers by sheer perseverance.

Near the end of World War II, with German defeat clearly inevitable, a group of SS officers fled to ARGENTINA and established the well-funded ODESSA network, which subsequently helped Mengele, ADOLF EICHMANN, KLAUS BARBIE, and many others (perhaps including MARTIN BORMANN) escape advancing Allied forces. Himmler boldly moved to strike a bargain with the Allies in April 1945 and was declared a traitor, but Hitler could not reach him from the Führerbunker in Berlin. Karl Hanke briefly replaced Himmler as chief of the SS, but the ink was barely dry on that proclamation when Czech partisans killed Hanke outside Breslau. Himmler was captured and charged with WAR CRIMES, but he escaped trial via suicide in custody. Allied judges at Nuremberg declared the SS a criminal organization rather than a military unit, noting in their verdict that a presumption of guilt attached to anyone "who had been officially accepted as members of the SS . . . who came or remained members of the organization with knowledge that it was being used for the commission of acts declared criminal by Article 6 of the [London War Crimes] Charter."

President RONALD REAGAN created an international controversy in April 1985 when he visited West Germany and laid a floral wreath at a cemetery in Bitburg where certain SS troops were buried. White House spokespersons initially claimed that both German and Nazi troops were buried in the graveyard, but that claim was quickly disproved by a survey of the headstones. In the face of mounting criticism, Reagan defended his act as "morally right," claiming that German soldiers "were victims, just as surely as the victims in the concentration camps." Reagan added, "I know all the bad things that happened in that war. I was in uniform for four years myself" (making army training films in Hollywood). Finally, Reagan named the inspiration for his Bitburg visit as 13-year-old Beth Flom, the alleged author of a letter that "urged me to lay the wreath at Bitburg cemetery in honor of the future of Germany." In fact, Flom's letter had asked Reagan *not* to make the cemetery visit.

See also HOLOCAUST AND HOLOCAUST DENIAL.

STALIN, Joseph (1879–1953)

RUSSIA's most notorious dictator was born Iosif Wissarionovich Dzhugashvili at Gori, in Georgia, on December 21, 1879. His initial calling to the Orthodox priesthood was scuttled at age 20 when he was expelled from a seminary in Tiflis for espousing Marxist politics. Thereafter, he allied himself full-time with revolutionary communists and took the surname *Stalin* ("steel") to symbolize his unyielding resolve. Exiled as a strike organizer from 1903 to 1917, Stalin returned to take part in the Russian revolution led by VLADIMIR LENIN and emerged in 1922 as secretary-general of the Russian Communist Party. At Lenin's death, he vied with rival Leon Trotsky for control of the Soviet Union, driving Trotsky to exile in MEXICO (where he was subsequently slain by Stalinist assassins).

As Russia's undisputed ruler, Stalin presided over a series of five-year plans to expand industry and collectivize farms. The latter campaign, like that pursued in CHINA under MAO ZEDONG a generation later, resulted in countless deaths from starvation. At the same time Stalin and chief henchman LAVRENTY PAVLOVICH BERIA instituted a series of party "purges" and show trials that decimated opposition to Stalin's autocratic rule. In 1939 Stalin signed a nonaggression pact with German dictator ADOLF HITLER, thereby freeing Russian troops to invade Finland and POLAND, but Hitler broke the thieves' bargain to attack Russia in 1941. Millions more died during the next four years before the THIRD REICH was defeated and Stalin used concessions from the YALTA CONFERENCE to extend Russian domination over much of Eastern Europe. The ensuing cold war cast Stalin (at least in Western propaganda) as the bogeyman behind a communist conspiracy to dominate the planet. On March 1, 1953, Stalin collapsed after dining with Beria and Nikita Khrushchev and other party leaders. He died four days later, ostensibly of a cerebral hemorrhage, though some conspiracists believe that he was poisoned. Khrushchev emerged victorious from the new power struggle and presided over a "de-Stalinizing" process that effectively erased the man of steel from official Russian history.

Debate continues over Stalin's role as a global conspirator and domestic mass murderer. Various published accounts claim that Stalin (deliberately or otherwise) starved some 6 million people to death during Russia's great famine of 1932–33 and that another five million died (either executed outright or in labor camps) during the Stalinist purges of 1936–38. Author Olga Shatunovskaia blames Stalin for 19.8 million deaths during 1935–40, while Arthur Koestler places the Russian body count at 20–25 million, and William Rusher cites "100 million people wantonly murdered" between 1917 and 1996. Those undocumented estimates were challenged by the release of Russian SECRET POLICE archives in 1993, revealing a total of 799,455 legal executions throughout Russia between 1921 and 1953. That total included nonpolitical defendants (murderers, bandits, and so on), as well as Nazi prisoners of war and Russians who collaborated with German invaders during World War II. Labor-camp deaths are more difficult to calculate, but the same Russian archives reveal a total of 2,022,976 political prisoners incarcerated in January 1939. About one million of those were released to fight German invaders in 1941, while in-camp deaths averaged 92 per 1,000 prisoners in 1944. By the year of Stalin's demise, that rate had declined to three deaths per 1,000 inmates.

See also COMMUNISM.

STANDARD Oil

The Standard Oil refining company was founded by John D. Rockefeller and a group of partners in 1863. Within five years it was Earth's largest refiner of crude OIL, and by 1870 Standard had launched a campaign of buying or breaking all competitors. By 1878 Rockefeller's company owned 90 percent of all U.S. refining facilities. It reorganized as the Standard Oil Trust, one of America's greatest (and most infamous) monopolies, in 1881. Eleven years later Ohio's state attorney general won the first antimonopoly case against Standard Oil, but two more decades passed before the Rockefeller petroleum empire was broken up by federal courts under terms of the Sherman Antitrust Act.

That drastic legal action was preceded by countless complaints and journalistic exposés of Standard's ruthless methods. Author Ida Tarbell wrote a 19-part series on Standard Oil for *McClure's* magazine, running from November 1902 to October 1904, published in book form as *The History of the Standard Oil Company* during the latter year. Her final assessment—"They had never played fair, and that ruined their greatness for me"—struck a chord with countless readers, and Tarbell's book placed

fifth on a list of the 20th century's top 100 works of journalism, compiled in 1999.

Division of the Standard empire created a bewildering pack of smaller (but no less lucrative) firms, including Standard Oil of California, Colorado, Connecticut, Illinois, Indiana, Iowa, Kansas, Kentucky, Louisiana Minnesota, Missouri, Nebraska, New Jersey, New York, Ohio, and Brazil (owned by Standard Oil of New Jersey). A total of 32 companies sprang from the break-up of Standard Oil, and even under federal scrutiny their methods were often ruthless. In April 1914, during a strike by employees at the Rockefeller-owned Colorado Fuel and Iron Company, state militia forces surrounded a strikers' tent city at Ludlow and sprayed the unarmed civilians with machine-gun fire, killing six persons. The strikers armed in self-defense, and by the time President Woodrow Wilson sent U.S.

Journalist Ida Tarbell's "muckraking" reportage helped dismantle the Standard Oil monopoly. (Author's collection)

troops to Colorado on April 29, 1914, 74 persons had been killed.

In the latter half of the 20th century, Standard Oil's various companies evolved into Atlantic Richfield Oil (Arco), Continental Oil (Conoco), Exxon, Mobil, and Esso. Their influence is strongly felt from Congress and the White House to Latin America, the Middle East, Africa, and Asia. In the late 1990s U.S. journalists revealed that ExxonMobil had paid President Jose Eduardo dos Santos millions of dollars for oil concessions in ANGOLA, money used to prolong that shattered nation's epic civil war. In 2003 ExxonMobil paid the U.S. government $50,000—a pittance—to settle accusations of illegal trading with SUDAN.

See also ROCKEFELLER CLAN.

STREET gangs

Street gangs are as old as urban civilization, typically recruiting children of immigrant, minority, and/or low-income families. In many cases gangs themselves become surrogate families for orphans and offspring of abusive or absentee parents. Where poverty breeds crime, street gangs have traditionally practiced theft and then graduated to extortion from local merchants. In many cases ethnic rivalries and battles for control of a specific "turf" produce violent gang wars, escalating in lethality as new weapons become available.

Street gangs in the United States graduated from nuisance status in the 19th century when New York's TAMMANY HALL and other political machines enlisted street toughs for various errands. The gangs' most common service was provided on election day when they haunted polling places, stuffed ballot boxes, and harassed their employer's rivals. In return, political bosses protected the gangs from police and allowed their daily criminal activities to proceed within prescribed limits. Gang influence grew exponentially with the advent of PROHIBITION in 1920, as former small-time hoodlums turned bootleggers and soon became millionaires. Gang warfare continued, but regional and then national collaboration increased under leaders such as CHARLES "LUCKY" LUCIANO and MEYER LANSKY. By the mid-1920s a gangland consortium called the BIG SEVEN dominated East Coast liquor traffic, and the combination was transformed into a national crime syndicate by the advent of repeal in 1933.

As 19th-century gangsters aged and grew wealthy, turning the tables on politicians who had once commanded and corrupted them, new generations of street toughs sought an opportunity to follow that example. As their elders profited from outlawed alcohol, younger criminals turned to the drug trade as a source of profit. By the early 1970s two black gangs spawned in southern California—the CRIPS AND BLOODS—were ready to expand nationwide and battle for control of the ghetto COCAINE trade. By the 1990s, 750 gangs claimed 80,000 members in Los Angeles alone; Albuquerque, New Mexico, had 43 Hispanic gangs with 5,000 known members; Cleveland had 100 active gangs; and the U.S. JUSTICE DEPARTMENT found gangs operating in 80 percent of all cities with 100,000 or more residents. Between 1993 and 1996 federal racketeering charges were filed against 225 members of 11 New York City gangs. In July 1995 the arrest of 10 youths from the 142nd Street Lynchmob cut Harlem's murder rate by an astounding 54 percent. Still, mayhem continues with no end in sight: Minneapolis had 19 murders in the first six months of 2002, with 17 described by police as gang-related killings.

STUDENTS for a Democratic Society (SDS)

Foremost among countless "New Left" groups of the 1960s, the SDS was founded in 1960 to advance liberal-left ideology throughout American society. Communist Party leader Gus Hall described the SDS as a group the party had "going for us," and FEDERAL BUREAU OF INVESTIGATION (FBI) Director J. EDGAR HOOVER henceforth never mentioned SDS without including Hall's comment as "proof" of a sinister conspiracy. The organization grew from 10,000 members in October 1965 to 80,000 in November 1968 and led its first student demonstrations at Columbia University in April 1968. A full-scale FBI COINTELPRO operation was launched against the New Left on May 9, 1968, with the SDS and founder Tom Hayden named as key targets of the illegal disruption campaign.

It is impossible to say how much credit the FBI deserves for the final SDS break-up in June 1969. More than 2,000 members attended the group's national convention in Chicago, split by arguments over the role of women and racial minorities in the "worldwide fight against U.S. imperialism." The result was a fatal rift, with militant members seceding to join a new Weather Underground faction, while others gravitated toward the Progressive Labor Party. The SDS clung tenuously to life for a few more months, but it had essentially ceased to exist by the time aides to President RICHARD NIXON named it a priority target of the abortive HUSTON PLAN in June 1970. A year later the burglary of an FBI resident agency at Media, Pennsylvania, revealed bureau investigation and harassment of the SDS, along with many other groups and individuals.

The Weather Underground Organization (WUO)—more commonly known as the Weathermen—was one of four factions surviving the 1969 SDS. The group took its name from the lyrics of a popular Bob Dylan song, *Subterranean Homesick Blues:* "You don't need a weatherman to know which way the wind blows." Having pledged themselves to revolution, members of the WUO wasted no time putting their program in action. The group's semiofficial history claims credit for Chicago's "Days of Rage" riots in October 1969 and for 17 bombings in seven states.

Despite those claims of violent action, questions remain concerning the WUO's responsibility for various crimes. Subsequent trials and release of documents under the Freedom of Information Act show that the group's more outrageous crimes were often planned and carried out by FBI or police agents provocateurs. One such, FBI hireling HORACE PACKER, provided Seattle Weathermen with drugs, weapons, and the ingredients for Molotov cocktails; he also furnished the paint that was used to deface a federal courthouse in February 1970. At trial Packer testified under oath that G-men knew of his crimes and told him to "do anything to protect my credibility." Another FBI provocateur, LARRY C. GRATHWOHL, was ranked among the WUO's "most militant members" in Detroit where he gave bomb-making lessons to fellow radicals. Yet another bureau agitator, THOMAS TONGYAI, recruited rioters for the Chicago "Days of Rage," provided other radicals with weapons, and volunteered to plant various bombs.

The WUO suffered a fatal rift in the summer of 1976. Gender, race, and organizational issues prompted a split in the ranks, producing the Central Committee and its rival the Revolutionary Committee. At year's end the Revolutionary Committee expelled its more "conservative" critics and three months later created a Prairie Fire Organizing Com-

mittee to speak for the WUO "above ground." Five members surrendered in New York in November 1977, and others slowly surfaced throughout the next two decades, with the last arrest reported in 1996. The federal campaign backfired in 1978 when FBI officials Edward Miller and W. Mark Felt were indicted for authorizing illegal break-ins. Both were convicted in 1980 but then were pardoned months later by President RONALD REAGAN.

See also COMMUNISM.

SUBVERSIVE Activities Control Board

Created by the MCCARRAN ACT in September 1950, the Subversive Activities Control Board (SACB) existed to identify and register the members of "Communist-action, Communist-front or Communist-infiltrated" organizations. To that end the SACB relied primarily on FEDERAL BUREAU OF INVESTIGATION files and hearings that featured a variety of bureau informants, professional ex-Communists and hostile witnesses subpoenaed from suspect groups. Although bound in theory by federal rules of evidence, SACB hearings mimicked those of the HOUSE COMMITTEE ON UN-AMERICAN ACTIVITIES (HUAC) and the SENATE INTERNAL SECURITY SUBCOMMITTEE by providing a forum for rumor, innuendo, and character assassination.

A series of U.S. SUPREME COURT rulings in 1956–57 curtailed the SACB's perceived campaign of "outlawing the Communist Party without becoming involved in the constitutional complications of actual outlawry," and while its influence faded thereafter, the board persevered in its heavy-handed efforts through the 1960s. On occasion it was able to assist kindred spirits, as in its investigation of the National Committee to Abolish HUAC, but the SACB generally failed to intimidate "New Left" activists and organizers of VIETNAM War protests. Public discontent with domestic surveillance and the broadening WATERGATE scandal prompted abolition of the SACB in 1973. The attorney general's list of subversive organizations was abolished the following year.

SUDAN

This troubled African nation shares a history of conquest with its neighbors, successive military and religious invasions stirring the pot from 2600 B.C.E.

until the 19th century when first EGYPT (1874) and then Britain (1898) conquered the region. Known as Anglo-Egyptian Sudan from 1898 to 1955, the country won independence in January 1956. Old rivalries endured, however, with endemic bloodshed occurring between Muslim Arabs in the north and a mixed bag of Christians and black animists to the south. Matters went from bad to worse when Gen. Ibrahim Abboud seized power in November 1958, suspending the nation's fragile democracy in favor of a hard-line military junta. That move touched off a 17-year civil war, highlighted by another military coup in 1969. The latest strongman, Col. Jafaar Mohammed al-Nimeiry, permitted presidential elections (which he easily won) in 1972. Uneasy peace descended on Sudan, enduring until 1983 when Nimeiry proclaimed the nation an Islamic fundamentalist state, instituting a rigid code of law lifted directly from the Koran. Osama bin Laden and AL-QAEDA found the new atmosphere congenial for plotting acts of foreign TERRORISM, but Christian and animist resistance continued. Another civil war erupted, dragging on for 19 years and claiming an additional two million lives. A cease-fire was announced between the government and the Sudan People's Liberation Army in July 2002, but peace seems unlikely to last. A separate problem in Sudan is the question of widespread, continuing slavery. According to a BBC report issued in May 2003, at least 11,000 persons have been kidnapped in slave raids across Sudan in the past 20 years. About 10,000 of those victims are still missing and presumed to be enslaved by unknown masters. Protests from the UNITED NATIONS and various foreign countries have failed to curb the trade in human flesh.

See also BIN LADEN FAMILY.

SULLIVAN, William (1912–1977)

William Sullivan joined the FEDERAL BUREAU OF INVESTIGATION (FBI) in August 1941, winning promotion three years later to supervise foreign operations of the bureau's Special Intelligence Service during World War II. Nicknamed "Crazy Billy" by fellow G-men, he subsequently transferred to the Domestic Intelligence Division, and in 1956 he penned the monograph that launched the FBI's first illegal COINTELPRO campaign against the Communist Party. In his post at Domestic Intelligence (Division 5) Sullivan ran the intelligence side

of the JFK ASSASSINATION case, the 1968 investigation of Dr. MARTIN LUTHER KING, JR.'s, slaying, and most of the FBI's COINTELPRO operations against black militants, the "New Left" and the KU KLUX KLAN. He was a pivotal figure at headquarters, regarded by many observers as Hoover's heir apparent to command of the bureau. His reply: "I'm not a Judas, Mr. Hoover, and you certainly aren't Jesus Christ."

Fired on the spot for insubordination, Sullivan chaired the new Office of National Narcotics Intelligence from May 1972 to June 1973 and then retired to a New Hampshire farm. His testimony before the CHURCH COMMITTEE and the PIKE COMMITTEE in 1975–76 exposed FBI chicanery spanning three decades, but any possibility of Sullivan addressing the HOUSE SELECT COMMITTEE ON ASSASSINATIONS was canceled on November 9, 1977, when he was shot and killed in New Hampshire. Authorities named the shooter as a policeman's son and called Sullivan's death a hunting accident. Conspiracists question that verdict.

See also COMMUNISM.

SUPREME Court, U.S.

As the only federal court required by the U.S. Constitution, the U.S. Supreme Court has original jurisdiction in "all cases affecting ambassadors, other public ministers and consuls, and those in which a State shall be a party." Appellate jurisdiction extends to all cases, arising from state or lower federal courts, in which some issue of federal law is asserted. Supreme Court justices are appointed by the president, with mandatory confirmation by the U.S. Senate. Unless impeached by Congress, they serve for life.

The Court achieved its current influence under Chief Justice John Marshall (1801–35), whose ruling in *Marbury v. Madison* (1803) was the first to declare a federal law unconstitutional. Marshall met his match in President Andrew Jackson when the Court barred Jackson's policy of Indian removal. "John Marshall has made his decision," Jackson declared. "Now let him enforce it." No other president has thus defied the Court, although RICHARD NIXON came close in 1974 with his desperate attempts to suppress the WATERGATE scandal. Most presidents now seek to fill Court vacancies with ideological comrades to advance their domestic agendas.

Chief Justice Roger Taney issued the Supreme Court's endorsement of slavery. (Author's collection)

During the NEW DEAL era, Franklin Roosevelt hatched a "court-packing" scheme to increase the Court's size, but Congress rebuffed the idea. More recently, Presidents RONALD REAGAN, George H. W. Bush, and George W. Bush have defied the Constitution's ban on religious tests for federal appointees by imposing a "litmus test" that requires judicial nominees to uphold "Christian values" and oppose legal abortion.

Supreme Court decisions are frequently controversial. During and after RECONSTRUCTION, the Court systematically undermined federal civil rights laws, restricted the privileges of nonwhite citizens, and finally approved wholesale racial segregation in *Plessy v. Ferguson* (1896). A half-century later, the Court reversed its stand on race, declaring school segregation unconstitutional and moving on from there to strike down most forms of discrimination in public accommodations. The Court's most controversial judgment of modern times was rendered in

Bush v. Gore, which effectively appointed George W. Bush as president in ELECTION 2000.

The Court has also been a target of various illegal plots in modern times. FEDERAL BUREAU OF INVESTIGATION Director J. EDGAR HOOVER coveted appointment to the Court and campaigned secretly for presidential loser Thomas Dewey in 1948, based on Dewey's promise to make him chief justice. Failing that, Hoover bugged, wiretapped, and burglarized court offices while recruiting informers on the clerical staff and filing covert reports from at least one justice (Lewis Powell, 1972–87). Hoover also aided the Nixon administration's unsuccessful bids to impeach Justices William Douglas (1939–75) and Abe Fortas (1965–69). Douglas outlasted both Hoover and Nixon, later revealing that he had penned his resignation in 1969 before the clandestine assault persuaded

Chief Justice Edward White was an admitted member of the Reconstruction Ku Klux Klan. (Author's collection)

him "to stay on indefinitely until the last hound dog had stopped yapping at my heels."

See also BUSH DYNASTY.

SUPPRESSED inventions

Aside from alleged CANCER CURES discussed elsewhere in this volume, conspiracy literature is replete with examples of miraculous inventions and discoveries that have reportedly been suppressed via collusion between industry and corrupt government officials, chiefly to safeguard the profit margins of OIL producers, PHARMACEUTICAL COMPANIES, and other greedy capitalists. A partial list includes:

- Lester Hendershot's "fuel-less generator" or "free energy machine," invented circa 1927–28. Three decades of foiled patent attempts and alleged government harassment ended with Hendershot's death (a supposed suicide) on April 19, 1961.
- Henry Moray's "radiant energy device," developed in the 1920s to tap a global "sea of energy" for unlimited power at little or no cost to consumers. From 1927 onward, Moray's plans were rejected by the U.S. Patent Office, allegedly at the behest of legislators bribed by public utility companies. By 1939 Moray had reportedly produced a 55-pound unit that produced enough electricity to run a large factory. When buyers from RUSSIA expressed interest in Moray's designs, he suffered threats, sabotage, and attempts on his life by unknown assassins.
- Charles Pogue's 200-mile-per-gallon carburetors, patented in Canada during 1935–36. Oil companies allegedly conspired to suppress the invention, though stories persist that Pogue carburetors were installed on some U.S. Army tanks during World War II—and then were swiftly removed from circulation when that conflict ended.
- Ivor Newberry's high-mileage carburetor, patented in October 1940, which allegedly "delivers a truly dry vapor to the engine and produces very little, if any, exhaust pollutions." Again, oil companies are blamed for suppressing the invention.
- Hans Coler's "Magnetotromapparat," another "free-energy" device constructed in 1946 from magnets, copper coils, and condensers. British

intelligence agents reportedly visited Coler and questioned him about his invention, but its fate is unknown.
- Joseph Bascle's carburetor, invented in the 1950s and reportedly installed as standard equipment on a fleet of taxicabs in Baton Rouge, Louisiana. It reportedly increased mileage by 25 percent while reducing pollution 45 percent.
- Robert Shelton's high-mileage carburetor, patented in May 1961. The device—allegedly enhancing mileage 800 to 1000 percent—was never commercially produced.
- Norman Colton's "gravity electric engine," designed to "draw electricity from the atmosphere without the use of any fuel" beyond Earth's gravitational field. Announced to the media in July 1961, the device subsequently vanished without a ripple.
- Oliver Tucker's high-mileage carburetor, patented in April 1972. The device reportedly offered 60–100 miles per gallon, another obvious threat to oil company profits.
- A gas-water additive, presented to navy officials by chemist John Andrews in May 1974. The chemical allegedly permitted the mixture of water and gasoline without reducing combustibility, thus promising gas prices in the neighborhood of two cents per gallon. When navy buyers tried to follow up with Andrews, they allegedly found him missing from home, with his laboratory ransacked.
- Guido Franch's "water-to-gas miracle," pioneered around the same time as the Andrews water additive. Franch's invention was a "green powder," derived from soaking coal in some unspecified liquid, which then transformed tap water into a fuel more efficient than gasoline.
- Joseph Yater's rooftop heat-to-electricity converter, built to capture "fluctuation voltage" (the static heard on radios and amplifiers) for conversion into electric power while employing solar heat. Government scientists allegedly took custody of Yater's invention in September 1975, promising a working model within six months; then they dismissed the project as "impractical."
- Tom Ogle's "vapor fuel system," created to bypass traditional carburetors and to offer 100 miles per gallon with "no exhaust pollution

emission." Ogle reportedly sold his invention to Seattle's Advance Fuel Systems in 1981, and nothing more has been heard of it since.

SURINAME

Named for its original inhabitants, the Surinen Indians, Suriname was "discovered" by SPAIN in 1593 and subsequently settled by invaders from the NETHERLANDS and Britain. African slaves furnished free labor for large plantations until slavery was banned in 1863. As Dutch Guiana, the realm was granted self-government in 1950, followed by full independence in 1975. Between those two events, a series of brutal race riots, exacerbated by unemployment and inflation, rocked the country. A military coup toppled Suriname's civilian government in 1980, and Holland severed foreign aid two years later after the junta massacred 15 journalists, politicians, lawyers, and union officials. A racial insurrection led by the mostly black Jungle Commando organization threatened destabilization before new elections were held in May 1991. The junta surrendered most of its power, and longtime dictator Dési Bouterse announced a series of economic reforms in 1997. By year's end Dutch authorities announced Bouterse's indictment for COCAINE smuggling, a move that highlighted Suriname's role as a center of international drug trafficking. Bouterse fled into hiding with his considerable bankroll, but he was convicted and sentenced in absentia by a Dutch court. He remains at large today.

SYMBIONESE Liberation Army

In March 1973 black ex-convict Donald DeFreeze settled in Oakland, California, and proclaimed himself "field marshal" of a new radical group, the Symbionese Liberation Army (SLA). The name apparently derived from a novel by Sam Greenlee, *The Spook Who Sat by the Door* (1959), which portrays an armed insurrection in Chicago's ghetto and uses the term *symbiology* in passing to describe collaboration among disparate organisms. Befitting the occasion, DeFreeze renamed himself "Cinque," after the leader of a 19th-century slave revolt.

The SLA's battle plan involved Cinque giving orders to a handful of naive young radicals. Despite its professed dedication to oppressed minorities, the SLA apparently had no black members other than DeFreeze. His disciples were unanimously white and thoroughly ashamed of it, to the extent that they shunned their given "slave names" and adopted more exotic monikers. Female recruits—comprising seven of the SLA's 11 members—went even further in rejecting their ethnicity, affecting dark makeup and Afro wigs to make themselves "look black."

The SLA made its first move on November 9, 1973, when two members ambushed Oakland's black school superintendent Marcus Foster and killed him in a fusillade of cyanide-tipped bullets. The gunmen were captured on January 10, 1974, charged with murder, and sentenced to life imprisonment. FEDERAL BUREAU OF INVESTIGATION agents took over the SLA's case on February 5, 1974, when four masked members kidnapped 19-year-old Patricia Hearst (granddaughter of newspaper magnate William Randolph Hearst) from her Berkeley apartment. Ransom letters from the SLA demanded that Hearst's family provide free food for ghetto residents in northern California, but compliance failed to end the nightmare. Authorities and Hearst's relatives were stunned on April 15, 1974, when SLA members robbed a San Francisco bank of $10,960. Security cameras captured the event—and revealed one of the armed bandits to be Patricia Hearst. Federal arrest warrants named Hearst as a material witness to the robbery; those named as active participants included DeFreeze, Nancy Perry, Patricia Soltysik, and Camilla Hall. On the same day state authorities indicted SLA members William Wolfe, Angela Atwood, William Harris, and Emily Harris for giving false information on their California driver's license applications.

While the Hearsts insisted that Patricia had been brainwashed by her captors, an audio tape arrived on April 24. In that recording Hearst identified herself as "Tania," called her father a "pig," and denounced the brainwashing claims as "ridiculous." Randolph Hearst dismissed the tape as a product of coercion, but a federal grand jury disagreed, indicting Patricia for bank robbery on June 6, 1974.

By that time half of the SLA's soldiers were already dead. Authorities traced DeFreeze and company to Los Angeles on May 17, 1974, surrounding the gang's rented hideout. A pitched battle erupted and the house caught fire. Hours later, police and firefighters removed the charred remains of DeFreeze, Wolfe, Perry, Hall, and Soltysik from the rubble. "Tania" Hearst remained at large for another 15 months, during which the SLA robbed another

California bank, stealing $15,000 and killing customer Myra Opsahl. On September 18, 1975, G-men captured William and Emily Harris in San Francisco's Mission District. Moments later agents raided a nearby apartment where they found Patty Hearst and fugitive Wendy Yoshimura (wanted for conspiracy to bomb a Naval ROTC center in 1972). After psychiatric testing found her competent for trial, Hearst was convicted of bank robbery and sentenced to seven years imprisonment but was paroled after serving 28 months.

SLA survivors William and Emily Harris were convicted in August 1976 of snatching two hostages during the April 1974 robbery of a Los Angeles gun shop. Two years later they pleaded guilty to a reduced charge of "simple kidnapping" in Hearst's case. With credit for time served, William Harris was paroled on April 26, 1983; his wife was released one month later on May 27. SLA fugitive Kathleen Soliah remained at large until June 1999 when she was finally captured in Minnesota. A guilty plea on charges of attempted murder earned Soliah a sentence of 20 years to life, imposed on January 18, 2002. The sole remaining SLA fugitive, James Kilgore, was arrested in Cape Town, SOUTH AFRICA on November 8, 2002. News of Kilgore's capture was "coincidentally" announced by G-men one day after four of his SLA comrades—Sarah Olson, Michael Bortin, William Harris, and his ex-wife Emily Montague—pleaded guilty to the Opsahl murder in Sacramento. Those defendants received prison terms ranging from six to eight years.

The SLA's politics and criminal antics were so peculiar that some modern conspiracy theorists believe the group was a U.S. government creation, organized specifically to embarrass left-wing activists and to justify repressive police action. In that scenario DeFreeze-Cinque was allegedly subjected to MIND-CONTROL experiments at Vacaville, presumably conducted by the CENTRAL INTELLIGENCE AGENCY or a similar clandestine group, and "programmed" to follow the course that led to his fiery destruction.

SYRIA

Between 1500 B.C.E. and A.D. 1516 Syria was conquered by Egyptians, Hebrews, Assyrians, Chaldeans, Persians, and Greeks, Romans, Arabs, Mongols, and Turks. The country remained a Turkish province until World War I when it became a French mandate via the League of Nations. Nationalist demonstrations in 1939 prompted FRANCE to suspend the constitution and impose military rule. The end of World War II saw British troops installed to preserve "order," finally departing after a revolution broke London's power in September 1961. A perennial enemy of ISRAEL, Syria lost territory to the Jewish state in 1967 and 1973, regaining some of it via negotiations chaired by HENRY KISSINGER in 1974. At about the same time, Syria sent troops to intervene in LEBANON's religious civil war, a commitment of some 25,000 soldiers that would endure until summer 2001. (Some Syrian troops remain in the Lebanese hinterlands today, though all were withdrawn from Beirut.) In the meantime, Syria acquired a reputation for supporting TERRORISM throughout the Middle East and abroad, a circumstance that led U.S. President George W. Bush to threaten economic sanctions (with a hint of possible invasion) during 2003. Thus far, those threats have not been realized, and Syria has adopted a more moderate course—at least for public consumption.

See also BUSH DYNASTY.

TACKWOOD, Louis

An African-American resident of southern California, Louis Tackwood was hired in 1969 to serve as an informant for LOS ANGELES POLICE DEPARTMENT's Criminal Conspiracy Section (CCS), acting in collaboration with the FEDERAL BUREAU OF INVESTIGATION (FBI). He was assigned to infiltrate the BLACK PANTHER PARTY and to report on its activities while disrupting the group by any means available, frustrating its proposed alliances with other "New Left" organizations, and entrapping Panthers in various criminal acts. Tackwood's first assignment was to spark a shooting war between the Panthers and Ron Karenga's United Slaves, an effort that claimed several lives within a year.

When not fomenting murder in the streets, Tackwood disrupted Panther alliances with the STUDENTS FOR A DEMOCRATIC SOCIETY and joined police in framing party members for murders they did not commit. One such victim, Elmer ("Geronimo") Pratt, served more than a quarter-century in prison before he was finally vindicated and released. During the same period Tackwood also had contact with Donald DeFreeze, a black prison inmate and alleged subject of government MIND-CONTROL experiments who later formed the SYMBIONESE LIBERATION ARMY.

Tackwood describes his final CCS-FBI mission before he went public in 1971 as a plot "to kill GEORGE LESTER JACKSON," a Panther Party spokesman who was serving time in San Quentin Prison. Tack-wood was not the triggerman, but he allegedly participated in an official conspiracy to slay Jackson during a staged prison break, occurring on August 21, 1971. According to Tackwood, "It was a plot, see, between the CII and the guards. The guards hate him, they hate his guts. He's accused of killing a guard, remember that. And they hate him, at least some of them do. They harass him at all times, give him all the hell they can, illegally. Then they kill him. Poor old George." Tackwood blew the whistle on his employers in autumn 1971 with sworn courtroom testimony and a published memoir, *The Glass House Tapes*. He subsequently passed a polygraph test, administered by former FBI agent Chris Gugas, suggesting (if not absolutely proving) that his tale was true.

TAIWAN

Chinese settlers first inhabited this offshore island in the seventh century A.D., displacing its Malayan aborigines. PORTUGAL dispatched explorers in 1590, naming the island Formosa ("the beautiful"), but SPAIN and the NETHERLANDS divided its territory in 1624. Dutch forces drove the Spaniards out in 1641 and ruled alone until Chinese troops captured Formosa 20 years later. JAPAN took a turn in 1895, remaining until their defeat in World War II handed the island back to CHINA. Four years later, after his defeat by communist forces under MAO ZEDONG, Generalissimo CHIANG KAI-SHEK retreated to Formosa with his nationalist followers and proclaimed his shrunken stronghold the Republic of China. A succession of U.S. presidents honored that fiction, treating Taiwan as the only "real" China while Chiang and his 600,000 soldiers schemed in vain to recapture the mainland. Despite repeated terrorist raids into China, Chiang saw his dreams collapse in October 1971 when his rivals were belatedly admitted to the UNITED NATIONS and Taiwan was expelled. Throughout Chiang's belligerent reign (1949–87), Taiwan served as a haven for TRIAD mobsters engaged in narcotics smuggling, money laundering, and various other criminal activities. Little changed with the advent of his son, Chiang Ching-kuo, and to this day Taiwan has enjoyed only two "free" presidential elections (in 1993 and 2000). Chiang's far-right Kuomintang Party remains dominant on Taiwan, committed to separation from the People's Republic of China at any cost. Sporadic saber rattling continues on both sides. On March 18, 2004, while riding in a campaign motorcade, President Chen Shui-bian and Vice President Annette Lu were wounded by unknown gunmen in an apparent assassination attempt.

See also COMMUNISM; TERRORISM.

TAJIKISTAN

Mountainous Tajikistan was part of the Persian Empire until Alexander the Great arrived to take charge in 333 B.C.E. Arab invaders appeared on the scene 300 years later, converting the populace to Islam at sword point. Uzbeks and Afghans next tried their hand at ruling the region before RUSSIA struck with overwhelming force in the 1860s. Tajikistan was still a Russian property in 1924 when the communist masters of Moscow declared a new Tajik Autonomous Soviet Socialist Republic. Six decades later, with Russian communism teetering on the brink of collapse, Tajikistan declared its sovereignty in August 1990. The following year, its leaders supported an attempted coup against Soviet president Mikhail Gorbachev, but that faux pas did not exclude Tajikistan from the Commonwealth of Independent States, organized in December 1991. Establishment of a parliamentary republic in November 1992 brought no end to conflict, however, as Islamic rebels and democratic forces rose in arms against the Red-dominated government. Some 60,000 persons died in the ensuing civil war, which officially ended

on June 27, 1997. Despite that cease-fire, sporadic bloodshed continues while the war-ravaged country suffers in abject poverty.

See also COMMUNISM.

TALMADGE dynasty

Eugene Talmadge was a stereotypical racist demagogue of the American South, born in Monroe County, Georgia, to a family of wealthy planters on September 23, 1884. He earned a law degree in 1907 and combined legal practice with farming until 1920 when he plunged headlong into Democratic Party politics. Any Georgian candidate of promise in the 1920s was a member of the KU KLUX KLAN (KKK), and Talmadge was no exception. Unlike many political Klansmen, however, "Old Gene" took his bigotry seriously, admitting years later that he had personally flogged at least one African-American victim. During his first term as Georgia's governor (1933–37) Talmadge assailed President Franklin Roosevelt's NEW DEAL as a socialist campaign that favored "niggers" over rural whites, and he declared martial law to crush a strike by the United Textile Workers. Financial scandals dogged his second term in the governor's mansion (1941–43), but rural "wool hats" and "crackers" remained fiercely loyal, empowered beyond their numbers by a Georgia statute that granted equal voting strength to each county regardless of total population. True to form, Talmadge pardoned convicted Klan floggers and appointed a KKK leader to serve as the chief of his state police, the Georgia Bureau of Investigation. In 1946, running hard for a third term as governor, Talmadge confronted black voters for the first time. A Klan delegation visited his office, seeking advice on the best way to frustrate black suffrage, whereupon Talmadge scrawled a one-word note: "Pistols." Elected once more on a tide of Klan TERRORISM, Talmadge died unexpectedly on December 21, 1946, three weeks before his scheduled inauguration.

Georgia Klansmen mourned Old Gene's passing and furnished the largest floral wreath at his funeral. Within hours of his death, KKK Grand Dragon Samuel Green declared that "the Klan has lost one of the best friends it ever had." Fortunately for the white knights, 23-year-old Herman Talmadge was ready and willing to take his father's place, assisted by a coup of sorts when state legislators (including many Klansmen) voted to install him as governor under terms of an obscure Georgia statute. Grand Dragon Green subsequently appeared as an honored guest at Herman's 1948 birthday party and received a standing ovation when he delivered a racist tirade to state lawmakers. Talmadge served as governor until 1955 and as one of Georgia's U.S. senators from 1957 to 1981. In both offices he maintained family tradition by opposing any expansion of black civil rights. Fellow senators censured Talmadge for financial improprieties in 1979 in a scandal that produced his first electoral defeat one year later. He thereafter returned to Georgia and practiced law until his death on March 21, 2002.

TAMMANY Hall

Tammany Hall is the popular name given to a Democratic political machine that ruled New York City politics from 1854 until the election of Mayor Fiorello LaGuardia 80 years later. Its origins date from 1786 when the Tammany Society of New York City was founded as a social and fraternal organization and became increasingly politicized during the next 12 years until it emerged as the chief vehicle of Jeffersonian ideals in the Big Apple. Tammany's bonds to the Democratic Party tightened through the early 19th century, and it emerged as the controlling factor in local ward politics under President Andrew Jackson. William ("Boss") Tweed and his cronies in the notorious TWEED RING ruled Tammany from 1858 to 1871, their flagrant corruption sparking a reform movement that failed to unseat the society's power brokers. Under leaders John Kelly (1872–86), Richard Croker (1886–1902), and Charles Murphy (1902–24), Tammany forged enduring bonds with the MAFIA and various ethnic STREET GANGS to buy or coerce votes in crucial elections, paying off with cash, political patronage, and immunity from arrest. That protection was especially vital during PROHIBITION when bootlegging profits filled political coffers in New York and nationwide. Tammany Hall suffered a dual setback in 1932 when corrupt Mayor James Walker was forced out of office and rival Franklin Roosevelt was elected president of the United States, while repeal of Prohibition dried up much of the society's illicit income in 1933. Despite its waning influence under the NEW DEAL and the Second World War, however, Tammany enjoyed a minor

"Boss" Richard Croker ran Tammany Hall for 16 years. (Author's collection)

renaissance under boss Carmine DeSapio (1949–61). Its final defeat was administered by Eleanor Roosevelt, who blamed DeSapio for defeating her son (Franklin Roosevelt, Jr.) in his 1954 campaign to become New York's attorney general. With wealthy friends, Mrs. Roosevelt created the New York Committee for Democratic Voters, opposing DeSapio and Tammany Hall, and the society dissolved in the mid-1960s.

TANZANIA

Arab traders were the first outsiders to settle this East African country in A.D. 700, supplanted by PORTUGAL in 1500 and OMAN in the 17th century. German troops arrived in 1885, merging Tanzania with BURUNDI and RWANDA to become German East Africa. That colony survived until World War I when Britain occupied the region as a League of Nations mandate and later as a UNITED NATIONS trust territory. As Tanganyika the country won independence from Britain in December 1961. Its name was changed in October 1964, following a merger with the offshore island of Zanzibar. UGANDA invaded Tanzania in November 1978, provoking a two-year war that killed thousands on both sides. On August 7, 1998, agents of the terrorist group AL-QAEDA bombed the U.S. embassy in Dar es Salaam, killing 10 persons in an attack that was coordinated with an even more destructive bombing in KENYA. More than 1 million citizens of Tanzania are presently infected with AIDS, and the lethal epidemic shows no signs of abating. In July 2003 Tanzanian authorities announced the nation's latest crime wave: a thriving trade in human skin. According to police reports, supported by a grisly public display of body parts in Dar es Salaam, southern Tanzania had suffered a two-year rash of brutal murders in which victims were skinned and their hides sold to black-magic practitioners outside the country. As Gloria Machube, spokeswoman for the chief chemist's office, told BBC News on July 6, "People are skinned and the skin is used for their rituals." In 2001 police filed murder charges against 13 members of one skin-smuggling ring, but the crimes continue unabated.

See also TERRORISM.

TAYLOR, Zachary (1784–1850)

A cousin of founding father James Madison and born in Virginia on November 24, 1784, Zachary Taylor served as a U.S. Army major in the War of 1812, as a colonel in the Black Hawk War (1832), and as a general in the Mexican War (1846–48). Those campaigns earned him the nickname "Old Rough and Ready," while securing his election as president in 1848. Taylor occupied the White House at a critical juncture in U.S. history, with the nation bitterly divided over slavery. Although himself a slaveholder, he denounced the institution as "a social and political evil," opposing expansion of slavery into new territories or states. He condemned the Compromise of 1850, which removed interstate slave trading from federal jurisdiction and permitted expansion of slavery into western territories, responding to southern threats of secession with a pledge that he would hang defecting traitors "with less reluctance than I hanged spies and deserters in Mexico." On June 17, 1850,

Taylor threatened use of U.S. troops in Texas if slaveholders there attempted to invade the Territory of New Mexico.

Just more than two weeks later, on July 4, 1850, President Taylor attended a groundbreaking ceremony for the new Washington Monument. Journalists noted that he was "to all appearances, sound in health and in excellent spirits . . . in the full enjoyment of health and strength participating in the patriotic ceremonies." That evening, however, he suddenly sickened, dying on July 9 under circumstances that sparked rumors of poisoning. Official spokespersons blamed Taylor's death on a combination of overexposure to "broiling sun," combined with a meal of cherries and iced milk to produce a fatal case of gastroenteritis. In fact, however, reports of the event describe Taylor seated in shade "under [a] broad awning," and nothing on his final menu qualified as dangerous. No autopsy was conducted prior to Taylor's burial at Louisville, Kentucky.

The immediate reaction of Taylor's political enemies encouraged speculation that he may have

Conspiracists dispute the official verdict that President Zachary Taylor died from eating cherries and milk. (Author's collection)

been assassinated. Henry Clay, a key author of the pending compromise on slavery, wrote to relatives, "I think [Taylor's death] will favor the passage of the Compromise bill." Co-author Daniel Webster agreed, confiding to friends that "I think the country has had a providential escape from very considerable dangers." A decade after Taylor's death, President Abraham Lincoln received letters suggesting that Taylor was poisoned, urging Lincoln to be careful what he ate and drank in Washington. Despite strident opposition from the so-called LIBERAL MEDIA, a forensic examination of Taylor's remains was finally made in 1991. On June 26, of that year Kentucky state medical examiner George Nichol told the press that Taylor died of "natural" causes, despite traces of arsenic found in his remains; in fact details of Nichol's report ignored by the media include findings that Taylor's hair contained 1.9 parts per million of arsenic (three to nine times the modern "acceptable" level), while Taylor's nails contained 3.0 parts per million of arsenic (five to 15 times the modern

normal level). Nichol's report also contained the following passage, universally ignored in media accounts of Taylor's "natural" death:

The symptoms and duration of Zachary Taylor's disorder are historically and medically compatible with acute arsenic poisoning and many natural diseases. Symptoms begin within 30 minutes to 2 hours after ingestion. The symptoms include nausea, vomiting, severe abdominal cramping, pain, burning epigastric pain, and bloody diarrhea. Death usually results within 24 hours to 4 days. . . . Lastly, the symptoms which he exhibited and the rapidity of his death are clearly consistent with acute arsenic poisoning.

The leap from that finding to a conclusion that Taylor died from "natural" causes rival the WARREN COMMISSION's "magic-bullet theory" in the JFK ASSASSINATION. It would be unfair to say that the case against cherries and iced milk has been proved in Taylor's death.

Senators Henry Clay (left) and Daniel Webster (right) hated Taylor for opposing Clay's "great compromise" on slavery in the United States. (Author's collection)

TEAPOT Dome conspiracy

In 1920 Congress passed the Oil Land Leasing Act, permitting private companies to lease oil-drilling rights on reserves owned by the U.S. Navy. The following year, on May 31, 1921, President WARREN HARDING issued an executive order transferring control of those reserves from the navy to the Interior Department, which was controlled by Secretary Albert Fall, a member of Harding's corrupt OHIO GANG. Two months later, without competitive bidding (and in return for a $100,000 bribe), Fall granted drilling rights on the 40,000-acre Elk Hills, California, reserve to an old friend, Edward Doheny of Pan American Petroleum. In April 1922 another of Fall's cronies, Mammoth Oil boss Harry Sinclair, obtained exclusive drilling rights to the 9,481-acre oil reserve at Teapot Dome, Montana. Fall's payoff in that case included $70,000 in cash and $233,000 in Liberty bonds.

Rumors of Fall's corruption soon reached the ears of Montana senators Thomas Walsh and Burton Wheeler, but Attorney General HARRY DAUGHERTY sidetracked requests for a JUSTICE DEPARTMENT investigation. There matters rested until August 2, 1923, when President Harding died unexpectedly in San Francisco. Senator Wheeler opened a formal investigation of the suspect oil leases in October 1923, while Walsh launched a Senate probe of the Justice Department three months later. Daugherty and FEDERAL BUREAU OF INVESTIGATION Director WILLIAM J. BURNS did their best to obstruct the investigation, with help from Assistant Director J. EDGAR HOOVER.

Walsh and Wheeler became primary targets. G-men orchestrated a frame-up of Wheeler on false corruption charges, but he was acquitted and pressed on with the inquiry, scoring a major coup against Daugherty and Burns with the testimony of ex-Agent Gaston Means. President Calvin Coolidge fired Daugherty on March 28, 1924, while Harry Sinclair was fined $1,000 and sentenced to three months in jail for contempt of Congress. Still, another three years elapsed before the U.S. SUPREME COURT annulled Sinclair's and Doheny's oil leases in 1927.

Doheny and Fall faced trial for conspiracy in November 1926, but both were acquitted. Fall and Sinclair faced identical charges in October 1927, with agents from the Burns Detective Agency harassing jurors. That activity produced a mistrial, and Fall was deemed too sick for trial when Sinclair was retried and acquitted in April 1928. Fall was finally convicted of bribery on October 25, 1929, fined $100,000, and sentenced to a year in prison.

TELEVANGELISTS

Televangelists are the ministers who preach and plead for cash around the clock on various TV networks, reaching—and sometimes swindling—millions of viewers around the world. Controversial at best, sometimes outrageous, they have parlayed religion into a multibillion-dollar broadcasting empire during the past half-century while making their influence felt in right-wing political circles. Wealth and power, however, do not protect God's self-proclaimed spokespersons from human failings. Even as they were courted by Presidents RONALD REAGAN, George H. W. Bush, and George W. Bush, various stars of the "Christian Right" found themselves mired in scandals involving fraud and corruption, adultery, and extremist politics verging on TERRORISM. Prominent examples include the following:

Oral Roberts: In the 1980s Roberts told his audience of private talks with God, including threats from the Almighty that Roberts would be "called home" unless he raised $8 million by March 31, 1987. Two months later he claimed powers to raise the dead. Son Richard Roberts, himself a televangelist, vouched for Oral's claim of having resurrected a dead child, but proof remains elusive at this writing.

Jim Bakker: Bakker launched TV's PTL ("Praise the Lord") Club with wife Tammy Faye in the 1970s, selling lifetime "partnerships" in a religious theme park while squandering the cash on perks that included $200,000 yearly salaries, a $4 million "bonus" for Jim, a $600,000 California home, four condominiums, a Rolls Royce, and an air-conditioned doghouse. Exposure of Jim Bakker's sexual affairs forced Bakker to resign in March 1987, and he was later convicted of fraud in North Carolina, receiving a 45-year prison sentence. Paroled in 1993, he is back on TV today with new wife Lori, selling a revised message of faith.

Jimmy Swaggart: Louisiana's Jimmy Swaggart ranked among Jim Bakker's most outspoken critics in early 1987, but his own TV empire was rocked by scandal a year later after Swaggart

347

was found consorting with prostitutes. Swaggart broadcast a tearful apology to his family and flock, vowing to accept any disciplinary measures imposed by his church but then reneged on that promise when church governors banned him from further lucrative TV broadcasts. When police caught Swaggart with another prostitute, he warned the congregation, "God says it's none of your business!"

Benny Hinn: Faith-healer Hinn has been a lightning rod for controversy since the 1980s, dogged by accusations of fakery in healing ceremonies and misuse of funds. In 1997 he hired Mario Licciardello to investigate charges of "wrongdoing and corruption concerning the handling of offering money" received from TV viewers, but Licciardello soon turned the tables by "demanding money to keep him from revealing what he knows about allegations of theft and corruption at Hinn's World Outreach Center." A court gag order silenced Licciardello, pending resolution of that dispute, but a new scandal erupted in December 1998 with media revelations that two of Hinn's aides had died from HEROIN overdoses.

Robert Tilton: Tilton built a lucrative TV empire in the 1980s based on faith healing, speaking "in tongues," and pay-as-you-go prayer requests. The business collapsed in 1991 when reporters followed tips to Tilton's trash bins and found thousands of prayer requests his staff had discarded after removing cash and checks. ABC's *PrimeTime Live* reported that Tilton earned $80 million a year from gullible donors, sparking lawsuits and investigations that drove him off the air. Divorced from his first wife in 1993, journalists found him in May 2003 living "comfortably" in Florida, broadcasting again, and collecting mail-in donations to the tune of $1,000 per hour.

Jerry Falwell: Falwell founded the "Moral Majority" in 1979 and threw its weight behind Republican presidential candidate Ronald Reagan the following year. That effort veered so far from charity that the INTERNAL REVENUE SERVICE stripped Falwell of his tax exemption, but he still heads one of North America's largest churches, and his penchant for controversy keeps his name in headlines. In the 1990s Falwell accused President Bill Clinton of drug trafficking and murder. A decade later, he claimed that the PENTTBOM attacks of September 2001 were God's judgment against "the pagans, and the abortionists, and the feminists, and the gays and the lesbians who are actively trying to make that an alternative lifestyle" in America.

Pat Robertson: Biographer Rob Boston describes televangelist Pat Robertson as "the most dangerous man in America." Robertson established the Christian Broadcast Network in 1960, expanding into 180 nations and 71 languages by the close of the 20th century. He subsequently founded the Christian Coalition as a thinly veiled political machine and launched an abortive campaign for the Republican presidential nomination in 1988. At last report, Robertson's net worth was estimated between $800 million and $1 billion, a fortune that shields him against most consequences of his eccentric behavior. In 1985 and 1995 Robertson claimed that his prayers alone had shielded Virginia from hurricanes. In 2001 he joined Jerry Falwell in blaming the September PENTTBOM attacks on God's wrath, and in October 2003 the U.S. State Department condemned Robertson for advocating terrorism. Specifically, he told his audience, "If I could just get a nuclear device inside Foggy Bottom [a Washington, D.C., neighborhood and sobriquet of the U.S. State Department], I think that's the answer. It looks like Congress had better do something, and maybe we need a very small nuke thrown off on Foggy Bottom to shake things up."

TERRORISM

No two "experts" agree on the precise definition of *terrorism,* though a broad consensus typically applies the term to any use of violence or intimidation to influence political, religious, or ethnic events. Some authors distinguish between *terrorism* (practiced by fringe elements to destabilize society or illegally persecute minorities) and *terror* (identical tactics employed by a state, such as the THIRD REICH), but semantic nitpicking is irrelevant to the victims and has no place in our present discussion.

The broad problem of terrorism is a matter of perspective. Simply stated, one person's terrorist is another person's freedom fighter, heroically battling

348

for a worthy cause against hopeless odds. America's founding fathers were deemed terrorists in 18th-century London, and President RONALD REAGAN reversed the formula 200 years later, comparing U.S.-supported CONTRA murderers in NICARAGUA to George Washington and Patrick Henry. The same conflict of interest is seen wherever political, racial, or religious violence occurs. Members of the night-riding KU KLUX KLAN (KKK) were once hailed as heroes who "redeemed" the South from RECONSTRUCTION. The IRISH REPUBLICAN ARMY waged a long war for "freedom" in Northern Ireland, opposed by contract killers from the ULSTER LOYALIST CENTRAL COORDINATING COMMITTEE. The modern Middle East has seethed with violence for more than a half-century, beginning with attacks by the IRGUN on behalf of ZIONISM and continuing to the present with a seemingly endless war between ISRAEL and various Arab groups from FATAH and BLACK SEPTEMBER to AL-QAEDA.

Problems arise when politicians and/or law-enforcement leaders tailor definitions of terrorism to suit a specific agenda and then skew their actions to support a predetermined outcome. In the 1960s certain southern governors condemned nonviolent civil rights activists as "terrorists" and "extremists" while ignoring (or actively supporting) the KKK's defense of white supremacy. A decade later President RICHARD NIXON applied the terrorist label to critics of the VIETNAM War, whether or not their protests turned violent. In the 1980s and early 1990s under "pro-life" Presidents Reagan and George H. W. Bush, the FEDERAL BUREAU OF INVESTIGATION (FBI) refused to investigate bombings of women's clinics on grounds that such acts did not constitute "domestic terrorism."

Indeed, while hailing itself as America's first line of defense against terrorist threats, the bureau has a mixed record (at best) in cases of political violence. Various bombings perpetrated by ANARCHISTS in 1918–20 remain unsolved today, and many 1970s radicals were never captured despite their placement on an expanded version of the FBI's famous "Ten Most Wanted" list. Author James Moore, once an agent of the rival BUREAU OF ALCOHOL, TOBACCO, AND FIREARMS, describes the FBI's performance in terrorist cases:

FBI "achievements" in the field of terrorism generally fall into two categories: cases they "adopt" without disclosing that the most critical aspects of the case were actually accomplished by other agencies; and instances where the "accomplishment" is described as "preventing a terrorist act." The latter, translated into what the FBI actually did, consists of having received a tip and interviewing the alleged would-be terrorists—informing them that "we know what you're planning" and warning of the consequences, should they choose to carry out the reported plot. Receiving tips is no accomplishment—considering the $3.5 million the FBI paid to informers in 1975 and their mandate, which makes it every police agency's duty to report such rumors to the FBI. "Resolving" the situation through aggressive questioning and dire warning is something any officer could do. Result: No one knows whether there really was a plot, so no one goes to jail.

Granting that Moore's opinion of the bureau may be skewed by longtime rivalry between federal agencies, there is still no denying that the FBI has also been responsible for acts of terrorism on U.S. soil. Under J. EDGAR HOOVER's illegal COINTELPRO programs, launched in 1956, FBI agents have encouraged and facilitated violent actions committed by or directed against such groups as the Communist Party, the MAFIA, the BLACK PANTHER PARTY, STUDENTS FOR A DEMOCRATIC SOCIETY, and the AMERICAN INDIAN MOVEMENT. A brutal vigilante group active on various midwestern Indian reservations, GUARDIANS OF THE OGLALA NATION (GOON), was financed in large part by the FBI, and FBI informants led several violent KKK factions between 1969 and 1981. Worse yet, in 1970 the FBI created its own right-wing terrorist group, the SECRET ARMY ORGANIZATION, which detonated bombs and attempted to murder "radical" college professors in southern California. Such crimes pale in comparison to the PENTTBOM attacks of September 11, 2001, but they still raise fundamental concerns about the nature and operation of SECRET POLICE agencies.

See also BUSH DYNASTY; COMMUNISM.

TEXAS suicide

Texas suicide is a term once applied to the suspicious deaths of individuals involved with notorious con man Billy Sol Estes in the Lone Star State. Estes, a close friend and financial supporter of future president LYNDON BAINES JOHNSON, bilked the U.S. government for $20 million in 1960 via federal crop subsidies on nonexistent produce. An agent from the

Department of Agriculture, one Henry Marshall, was dispatched to investigate the case in 1961, but he "committed suicide" by shooting himself five times—with a bolt-action high-powered rifle. Three businessmen linked to Estes subsequently died in their cars, from carbon monoxide poisoning, and those deaths were likewise ruled suicides. While Estes ultimately went to prison, the string of deaths received no further official scrutiny. Lyndon Johnson survived the scandal to become president in 1963 after the JFK ASSASSINATION. That event, in turn, was followed by another series of suspicious deaths, including several that fit the mold of classic "Texas suicide."

THAILAND

Formerly known as Siam, Thailand is rare among Third World nations in having escaped protracted rule by foreigners. Britain gained a brief foothold in 1824 but granted Thailand full independence in 1896 as part of a treaty with FRANCE to create a buffer zone between Britain's colony in MALAYSIA and French Indochina. Japanese invaders seized control of the country in 1941, but their puppet state collapsed three years later, whereupon Bangkok repudiated its tenuous bonds to the Axis. During the war in VIETNAM, Thailand served as a well-paid staging area for U.S. raids against various neighbors, including illegal strikes at CAMBODIA and LAOS. At the same time, large-scale HEROIN production and exportation made Thailand part of the infamous "Golden Triangle," also including Laos and MYANMAR. That multibillion-dollar trade continues to the present day in concert with Thailand's flagrant (though technically illegal) role as a center of global sex-tourism, including ready availability of child prostitutes. Prime Minister Thaksin Shinawatra, himself a billionaire telecommunications mogul, was indicted on corruption charges in December 2000 but won acquittal at his trial eight months later. At the same time, an aggressive new antidrug campaign was launched from Bangkok, resulting in an estimated 2,300 deaths by June 2003. Critics of the government program complain that many suspects are summarily executed by covert death squads, often gunned down on the streets or in their homes. Predictably, the victims in the killing sprees have all been addicts or small-time street dealers, while wealthy Thai drug lords remain securely under guard with private armies and protection from corrupt police. A thriving black-magic subculture also exists in Thailand, exposed for the first time in 1959 when self-styled sorcerer Sila Wongsin was executed for performing human sacrifices of at least six children. In August 2003, 28-year-old Kittisak Laoprasert was indicted for stealing human fetuses for sale to ritual practitioners around Bangkok.

THIRD Reich

Nazi propagandists coined the term *Third Reich* ("empire" or "kingdom") to describe their regime in GERMANY during the years 1933–45. According to the National Socialist mythology espoused by ADOLF HITLER, the First Reich was the Holy Roman Empire (800–1806), while the German Empire established in 1871 comprised the Second Reich. Teutonic glory was betrayed in World War I and languished under the Weimar Republic (1919–33) until Hitler seized power and embarked on a suicidal course of world conquest; in fact much of Nazi philosophy was based on occult studies of the Thule Society and other groups whose mystic trappings smacked of SATANISM. Der Führer also referred to his regime as the "Thousand-Year Reich," but that title proved grossly overoptimistic when Allied forces conquered Germany in April 1945. Hitler's sole "achievement," in retrospect, was the ignition of a world war that claimed some 20 million lives, including five to six million Jews and other "inferiors" slaughtered in the Holocaust. Today, neo-Nazis in Germany and elsewhere still dream of establishing a FOURTH REICH to continue Hitler's genocidal work and "get it right this time."

See also HOLOCAUST AND HOLOCAUST DENIAL; NATIONAL SOCIALISM.

THUGGEE

A cult devoted to the Hindu death goddess Kali arose in India during the 12th century and flourished during the next 600 years with acolytes known as *thags* ("deceivers") ranging far and wide in search of human sacrificial victims. Typically, the cultists disguised themselves as holy pilgrims and befriended travelers on rural highways, later strangling their victims and mutilating their bodies before making off with any valuables from the crime scene. British colonial authorities tackled the cult in the 19th century, convicting 4,500 identified members of various crimes between 1830 and 1848—including 110 defendants convicted of murder. While no definitive body count is available, official estimates blamed the cult for 40,000 murders in 1812 alone, and one cultist named Buhram confessed to 931 slayings at his trial in 1840. Taking 1812 as the sect's banner year, with a murder rate 10 times the hypothetical norm, it is evident that *thags* must have killed at least 2.4 million victims during six centuries of homicidal activity. British colonists mispronounced *thag* as *thug*—now used in common parlance for any violent criminal—and dubbed the ritual strangling process *thuggee*. While the cult was theoretically eradicated in the late 1840s, rumors of its survival circulated around Calcutta in the late 1980s.

TITANIC

One of history's great maritime disasters occurred on the night of April 14–15, 1912, when the British ocean liner *Titanic* struck an iceberg and sank in the North Atlantic, claiming an estimated 1,512 lives. Ironically, the huge ship that was deemed "unsinkable" did not survive its maiden voyage, thanks in part to faulty "watertight" compartments below decks. Aside from spawning countless books and films (including 1997's box-office blockbuster), the *Titanic* disaster has also spawned a predictable crop of conspiracy theories. The most prolific theorist, with three books published so far, is British author Robin Gardiner. His works raise various unanswered questions about the *Titanic* catastrophe, ranging from mundane negligence (a fire burning unchecked in one of *Titanic*'s coal bunkers before the ship sailed) to a bizarre bait-and-switch plot involving the liner's sister ship *Olympic*.

Gardiner outlines the conspiracy as follows: On September 20, 1911, the *Olympic* collided with a Royal Navy cruiser HMS *Hawke*, resulting in extensive damage to both ships. Two weeks of hard work were required before the *Olympic* could sail to its shipyard at Belfast for further repairs. *Titanic* remained unfinished at that time, with her maiden voyage scheduled to begin on April 10, 1912, and the lack of a functional ship had already cost the White Star Line some £250,000 in lost fares ($18.6 million at current exchange rates). Gardiner maintains that White Star's owners chose to hastily repair *Olympic* and pass it off as the new *Titanic* to meet their deadline and then dispose of it at sea to cover

up their fraud. No loss of life was anticipated, Gardiner claims, because the rescue ship *Californian* was dispatched in advance to a North Atlantic rendezvous point, there to await *Titanic*'s prearranged distress signal and safely offload those aboard. On the night of April 14, Gardiner says, *Titanic*'s lookouts were so distracted by their search for icebergs that they overlooked a second (unnamed) rescue vessel sitting in their path, and that collision sent *Titanic* to the bottom. The original *Titanic*, meanwhile, allegedly returned to service as the "repaired" *Olympic* and spent another quarter-century at sea without further incident.

TONGYAI, Thomas (fl. 1960s)

Nicknamed "Tommy the Traveler" after his penchant for rambling around New York State, Thomas Tongyai posed as a "New Left" radical when he visited various college campuses in the late 1960s. Financed simultaneously by the FEDERAL BUREAU OF INVESTIGATION and local police departments, Tongyai furnished leftist student groups with radical speakers and literature, urging each audience in turn to kill police, build bombs, and demolish selected targets. At one point Tongyai tried without success to organize a Rochester chapter of STUDENTS FOR A DEMOCRATIC SOCIETY, and he encouraged New York students to visit Chicago in October 1969 for the Weather Underground Organization's riotous "Days of Rage." An obsessive proponent of illegal violence, Tongyai habitually traveled with firearms and hand grenades, instructing campus dissidents in marksmanship and counseling them on construction of bombs. Students at Hobart College apparently took his advice and bombed the campus ROTC office, whereupon Tongyai's activity as an agent provocateur was revealed. Even so, he escaped indictment by the grand jury that charged nine of his followers, and Tongyai retired from undercover operations to become a policeman in Pennsylvania.

TRAFFICANTE, Santos, Jr. (1914–1987)

The son of a high-ranking MAFIA member, Santos Trafficante, Jr., was born at Tampa, Florida, in November 1914. In the 1940s he joined MEYER LANSKY, CHARLES "LUCKY" LUCIANO, and other mobsters to establish gambling casinos in CUBA under corrupt dictator Fulgencio Batista. In 1954, with his father's death from throat cancer, Trafficante won control of the Florida "family," but the Cuban mother lode of untaxed cash dried up five years later when FIDEL CASTRO seized control of the Caribbean island. Thereafter, Trafficante joined SAM GIAN-CANA, JOHN ROSELLI, and other mobsters in attempts to murder Castro, encouraged and aided by members of the CENTRAL INTELLIGENCE AGENCY. Despite collaboration with the U.S. government, however, Trafficante soon became a major target of Attorney General Robert Kennedy, and the Florida gangster remains a prime suspect in the 1963 JFK ASSASSINATION. A few weeks before the president's murder in Dallas, Trafficante allegedly told Cuban exile leader Jose Aleman, "Mark my word, this man Kennedy is in trouble, and he will get what is coming to him. Kennedy's not going to make it to the election. He is going to be hit." A longtime acquaintance of Trafficante's, JACK RUBY, shot and killed supposed assassin LEE HARVEY OSWALD on November 24, 1963, leaving telephone records that show calls to Trafficante shortly before the Kennedy slaying. Two decades later Trafficante reportedly joined in the IRAN-CONTRA CONSPIRACY organized by President RONALD REAGAN and Vice President George H. W. Bush. The HOUSE SELECT COMMITTEE ON ASSASSINATIONS questioned Trafficante in 1978, but he denied any knowledge of the JFK murder and the committee's final report leveled no accusations. Trafficante died in March 1987 at age 72.

See also BUSH DYNASTY; KENNEDY DYNASTY.

TRENCHCOAT Mafia

The original Trenchcoat Mafia—completely unrelated to the MAFIA crime syndicate—was a group of disaffected students at Columbine High School in Littleton, Colorado, self-named for their favorite style of clothing. Two fringe members of the outcast clique, Eric Harris and Dylan Klebold, invaded the campus on April 20, 1999, armed with guns and homemade bombs, killing 12 fellow students and one teacher before they committed suicide. Because the massacre occurred on ADOLF HITLER's birthday, some observers blamed the crime on neo-Nazi attitudes, but no link to organized racist groups such as the KU KLUX KLAN was ever proved. Likewise, rumors that Harris and Klebold specifically targeted athletes, Christians, or racial minorities seem to be false. (The tale of one female victim allegedly shot

after the killers asked if she loved JESUS CHRIST has been revealed as a hoax.) In the wake of the Columbine murders, numerous Internet Web sites sprang up purporting to represent the "real" Trenchcoat Mafia.

TRIADS

Modern Triad crime syndicates, often described as the Chinese MAFIA, began as resistance groups opposing the Ch'ing Dynasty that ruled CHINA from 1644 to 1911, seeking restoration of the previous Ming Dynasty. Along the way, they practiced robbery, gambling, extortion, and murder, while learning from China's OPIUM WARS that illicit drugs are a source of great wealth. Triad leaders supported military ruler CHIANG KAI-SHEK (described by some researchers as an oath-bound Triad member), and they profited immensely under his corrupt regime. When MAO ZEDONG's revolution drove Chiang from China in 1949, many Triad loyalists followed him to TAIWAN, while others operated throughout Southeast Asia and farther afield.

The Triads (or "Tongs") discovered North America in the mid-19th century when thousands of Chinese were imported to build U.S. railroads and labor in mines. The opium trade followed them, with strong sidelines in gambling and prostitution (often dubbed WHITE SLAVERY). By the turn of the 20th century, gang wars raged in major cities from San Francisco to New York between powerful Chinese cliques including the Hop Sings, Suey Sings, and Kwong Ducks. Vigilante riots and a federal Chinese Exclusion Act curbed Triad influence for a time, but the VIETNAM War provided vast new markets for Asian HEROIN in the United States, and Triad smugglers seized the opportunity, soon expanding into other areas of vice and "legitimate" investments in LAS VEGAS, Nevada. Other illicit enterprises favored by the Triads are smuggling undocumented aliens and weapons on a global scale.

As with any secret criminal society, hard data on Triad membership is difficult to obtain and is rarely trustworthy. In 1989 the U.S. JUSTICE DEPARTMENT named Hong Kong as the epicenter of Triad activity with an estimated 100,000 members divided among 50 gangs. The largest Hong Kong syndicates are known as 14K and the Wo Group. On Taiwan the United Bamboo gang boasts some 15,000 members, while the Four Seasons Triad lags behind with an estimated 3,000. Triad groups reported active in the United States with varying numbers include 14K, Leun Kung Lok, Sun Yee On, Wo Hop To, and Wo On Lok. Their presence is strongly felt in Chinese-American communities from coast to coast where special law-enforcement task forces have thus far failed to stop invaders from the East.

TRILATERAL Commission

Founded in 1973 by wealthy private citizens from the United States, Canada, Japan, and various European nations, the Trilateral Commission was created (in its own words) "to foster closer cooperation among these core democratic industrialized areas of the world with shared leadership responsibilities in the wider international system." Established for a three-year period (and renewed by its members for successive triennia to the present day), the group's self-described initial purpose was:

to draw together—at a time of considerable friction among governments—the highest level unofficial group possible to look together at the key common problems facing our three areas. At a deeper level, there was a sense that the United States was no longer in such a singular leadership position as it had been in earlier post-World War II years, and that a more shared form of leadership—including Europe and Japan in particular—would be needed for the international system to navigate successfully the major challenges of the coming years.

During the past three decades membership in the Trilateral Commission has been broadly expanded to include representatives from Mexico, other Pacific-Asian nations, and the growing cast of European Union countries. "Globalization" is the goal espoused by the commission's Internet Web site, and therein lies the problem for conspiracists of sundry political shadings, who lump the Trilateral Commission with the COUNCIL ON FOREIGN RELATIONS and the ephemeral NEW WORLD ORDER as a form of global shadow government. Critics note that a founding member was David Rockefeller, heir to STANDARD OIL billions and a longtime president of CHASE MANHATTAN BANK. Plans for establishment of the Trilateral Commission were allegedly conceived at gatherings of the BILDERBERG GROUP. According to critic and ex-Senator Barry Goldwater, "The Trilat-

eral organization created by David Rockefeller was a surrogate—the members selected by Rockefeller, its purposes defined by Rockefeller, its funding supplied by Rockefeller. David Rockefeller screened and selected every individual who was invited to participate." The presumed goal is stated by an anonymous Internet theorist as follows:

The Commission's purpose is to engineer an enduring partnership among the ruling classes of North America, Western Europe and Japan—hence the term "Trilateral"—in order to safeguard the interests of Western capitalism in an explosive world. The private commission is attempting to mold public policy and construct a framework for international stability in the coming decades. To put it simply, Trilateralists are saying: The people, governments and economies of all nations must serve the needs of multinational banks and corporations.

See also ROCKEFELLER CLAN.

TURKEY

Between 1900 B.C.E. and the 12th century A.D., the region of modern-day Turkey was overrun and occupied by Hittites, Phrygians, Lydians, Persians, Romans, and troops of the Byzantine Empire. Turning the tables between the early 13th century and World War I, the Ottoman Turkish Empire expanded to devour much of Central Asia, North Africa, and Eastern Europe, challenging the strength of mighty RUSSIA. That empire's strength began to falter with the Russo-Turkish War (1877–78), suffered another blow with the Young Turks' revolt (1909), and endured serious setbacks in losing wars with Italy (1911–12) and in the Balkans (1912–13). The last in a string of bad choices saw Turkey allied with GERMANY and the Austro-Hungarian Empire in World War I, where crushing defeat brought an end for all time to imperial dreams. Turkey's modern boundaries were drawn by the victors in 1923, with Kemal Atatürk installed as president (1923–38). A quarrel with GREECE led Turkey to invade CYPRUS in July 1974, seizing 40 percent of the island. By that time Turkey was a well-established source of HEROIN that flowed to Europe and the Western Hemisphere, a trade established in the 1920s that flourishes to the present day. Home-grown rebels, including the Turkish People's Liberation Army and the Kurdistan

Worker's Party (PKK), have conducted long-running guerrilla campaigns against the ruling government in Ankara, campaigns that are regarded as TERRORISM or struggles for liberation, depending on the observer's point of view. During the 1980s and 1990s an estimated 35,000 persons died in clashes between the PKK and Turkish military forces. Abdullah Ocalan, a PPK leader, was sentenced to death on June 2, 1999, following his conviction on charges of treason and separatism. Two months later a catastrophic earthquake left 17,000 Turks dead and 200,000 homeless—a tragedy blamed in large part on corrupt cost cutting by construction companies and government officials who were paid to look the other way.

TURNER Diaries, The

The Turner Diaries is a futuristic racist novel published in 1978 by William Luther Pierce, under the pen name "Andrew Macdonald." It portrays a United States dominated by ZOG—the Zionist Occupation Government—in which white separatists wage guerrilla warfare to preserve their bloodline and the basic tenets of the U.S. Constitution. One such warrior is Earl Turner, the novel's narrator, who participates in various acts of TERRORISM including a massive truck bombing in Washington, D.C. Prosecutors identify *The Turner Diaries* as the direct inspiration (or "blueprint") for various neo-Nazi crimes committed across America since the early 1980s. The SILENT BROTHERHOOD (1983–85) took its alternate name—"The Order"—directly from Pierce's novel, and likewise emulated its tactics from armed robbery to counterfeiting. A decade later, MILITIA activist Timothy McVeigh studied the novel while he plotted the OKLAHOMA CITY BOMBING with accomplice Terry Nichols. In June 1998 three would-be members of the KU KLUX KLAN in Texas dragged black victim James Byrd, Jr., to death behind a pickup truck after telling him, "We're starting *The Turner Diaries* early."

William Pierce was a curious character, born in Atlanta on September 11, 1933. He earned a B.A.

Dr. William Pierce, author of *The Turner Diaries*, sits before the Nordic Rune symbolizing white power. (Scott Houston/Corbis)

The reconstructed part of TWA Flight 800 sits in a hangar in Calverton, New York. Investigation of the explosion was the most expensive crash probe ever conducted by U.S. safety and law-enforcement investigators. (Reuters/Corbis)

in physics in 1951 and then worked at Los Alamos Scientific Laboratory before completing his Ph.D. in 1962. At about the same time he joined the JOHN BIRCH SOCIETY, but its conspiracy theories proved too tame for Pierce's taste. In 1965 he abandoned teaching and any semblance of rational behavior, plunging headlong into the racist world of NATIONAL SOCIALISM. After stints with the American Nazi Party and the neofascist Liberty Lobby, Pierce formed his own National Alliance in 1974. Six years after publishing *The Turner Diaries,* he wrote another novel, *Hunter,* dedicated to racist serial killer Joseph Paul Franklin. In 1984–85 Pierce received donations from the Silent Brotherhood, accepting cash looted from armored cars, but he escaped prosecution on those charges and amused himself with a series of mail-order brides from Eastern Europe. On the side Pierce established a near-monopoly on sales of European "white power" music in the United States and fraternized with a

Who's Who of American racist leaders, including "former" Klansman David Duke. Pierce died on July 23, 2002, his dreams of a FOURTH REICH still unfulfilled, but his fictional musings continue to inspire racists around the world.

See also FASCISM.

TWA Flight 800

On July 16, 1996, TWA Flight 800 crashed in the sea off Long Island killing all 230 persons aboard. Eyewitness reports of a midair explosion and a "streak of light" pursuing the plan from ground level raised the possibility of TERRORISM, whereupon a FEDERAL BUREAU OF INVESTIGATION (FBI) investigation was initiated in conjunction with the standard crash review conducted by the National Travel Safety Board (NTSB). Nearly a decade after the event, many facts about the case remain obscure, contributing to charges of an official cover-up.

One sticking point with critics of the FBI verdict is the acknowledged presence of a "mystery boat" near the crash site. Radar plots contained in the NTSB's final report place an unknown vessel 2.9 nautical miles from crash scene, tracked for 16 minutes while speeding out to sea. Despite 16 months of investigation, including some 7,000 interviews, FBI headquarters reported that the bureau "has been unable to identify this vessel."

Crash investigators found chemical traces of explosives on various fragments of Flight 800, but FBI officials attributed them to a canine bomb-detection exercise allegedly conducted on the aircraft five weeks earlier. In addition to trace evidence, at least 89 crash victims had foreign objects resembling shrapnel embedded in their corpses. FBI agents seized all such fragments and submitted them for laboratory analysis, but the objects *and* the lab reports have disappeared. In October 2000 an FBI affidavit declared that the evidence could not be found despite a "thorough search."

The NTSB held hearings on the crash in December 1997, but FBI spokesmen objected to public disclosure of "any interviews or reinterviews of the 244 eyewitnesses whose reports were examined by the CIA in connection with its analysis and to calling any eyewitnesses to testify at the public hearing." Without objection, NTSB Chairman Jim Hall agreed to the bureau's demand for secrecy and excluded all eyewitness testimony from the hearing. Nor was the FBI's suppression of evidence limited to public hearings. For 13 months after the crash, G-men withheld statements of 278 witnesses from the NTSB itself—including *all* statements from witnesses who claimed they saw a "streak" shoot upward from the ground or sea toward Flight 800 on the night it fell. Likewise, a FBI letter dated August 25, 1998, declared that agents were "unable to locate" results of their study to determine the origin of an alleged surface-launched object seen by witnesses before the crash.

In November 1996 ABC News reporter Pierre Salinger suggested that a U.S. Navy missile was responsible for the disaster. Salinger cited radar images and documented naval maneuvers in the area on July 16, 1996, but the FBI and NTSB jointly dismissed his theory. A January 1997 report from the BUREAU OF ALCOHOL, TOBACCO, AND FIREARMS concludes that Flight 800 crashed after a mechanical flaw caused its central fuel tank to explode. In May 1999 ATF spokesman Andrew Vita told the U.S. Senate that he "met resistance" from the FBI when he tried to submit that report, but G-men later endorsed the findings. Senator Charles Grassley termed the crash investigation "a model of failure, not success"; he further dubbed the FBI's performance "a disaster" and charged that the bureau "risked public safety" by manipulating crash-site evidence.

TWEED Ring

The Tweed Ring takes its name from William Marcy Tweed (1823–78), a political "fixer" and boss of New York City's TAMMANY HALL in the mid-19th century. A bookkeeper and volunteer firefighter who graduated into corrupt ward politics in the early 1850s, Tweed ended that decade as Tammany's undisputed boss, a master of patronage and shady deals throughout the Big Apple. In the process he served at different times as an alderman, a member of Congress, and a New York State senator, but

"Boss" William Tweed of Tammany Hall created the notorious Tweed Ring. (Author's collection)

Tweed's true gift lay in making deals behind the scenes. Collaboration with robber barons James Fisk and Jay Gould made Tweed a director of the Erie Railroad, but his principal source of income was the bottomless well of New York City graft. The so-called Tweed Ring—including Tweed, Mayor A. Oakey Hall, city chamberlain (treasurer) Peter Sweeny, and comptroller Richard Connolly—ultimately bilked New York City of an estimated $30 million via skimming from taxes and padded or fictitious charges. While reformers failed to break his hold on the city, in 1870 Tweed pressured the state legislature to expand Tammany's charter and powers. Tweed's downfall came about when new county bookkeeper, M. J. O'Rourke, uncovered massive fraud and took his story to the *New York Times*. Crusading articles and a series of scathing cartoons by Thomas Nast produced a groundswell of revulsion, climaxed by Tweed's indictment on corruption charges. A hung jury spared Tweed at his first trial, but a second panel convicted him, and Tweed received a 12-year prison sentence. That term was reduced on appeal, and he served one year in custody before emerging to face further charges. This time, Tweed fled to CUBA and then to SPAIN, but he was extradited for trial in 1876 and died in prison two years later. Tammany survived him and remained the dominant force in New York City politics until 1934.

UFOs

Reports of unidentified flying objects—UFOs—span the full range of human history from biblical times to the present day. Ancient witnesses spoke of fiery "wheels" and chariots, while luminous "airships" filled the skies over North America in 1896–97, and Allied pilots recorded midair encounters with "foo fighters" during World War II. Our modern fascination with UFOs properly dates from June 24, 1947, when pilot Kenneth Arnold reported a formation of unknown aircraft over Mount Rainier, Washington, and compared them to "flying saucers." Barely two weeks later, on July 8, a UFO allegedly crashed outside Roswell, New Mexico, strewing the desert with debris—and, some say, tiny not-quite-human corpses.

The first known UFO investigation by the U.S. government began one day after the supposed Roswell crash when Brig. Gen. George Schulgen of the Army Air Corps requested FEDERAL BUREAU OF INVESTIGATION (FBI) assistance to determine if the "saucers" were part of a communist plot "to cause hysteria and fear of a secret Russian weapon." Director J. EDGAR HOOVER approved the inquiry, with one proviso: "I would do it, but first we must have access to all disks recovered." On July 30, 1947, a memo from FBI headquarters to all bureau field offices ordered G-men to "investigate each instance which is brought to your attention of a sighting of a flying disc in order to ascertain whether or not it is a bona fide sighting, an imaginary one, or

a prank." Some two dozen reports reached Washington during the next 60 days, most stamped with the heading "Security Matter—X."

Thus began the FBI's real-life X-Files, but Hoover was not alone in pursuing the elusive saucers. On September 23, 1947, the U.S. Air Force launched Project Sign with an identical goal. Active investigation began on January 22, 1948, and culminated in a February 1949 air-force report, admitting that 20 percent of the sightings reviewed could not be explained in terms of known aircraft or natural phenomena. Perhaps disgruntled by those findings, the air force named its next UFO investigation—begun on February 11, 1949—Project Grudge. That unit's classified 600-page report, released six months later, grudgingly listed 23 percent of all UFO sightings as inexplicable. Having said that, however, the air force investigation strangely "lapsed more and more into a period of almost complete inactivity," according to one member of the team.

The same could not be said for Hoover's agents. On March 25, 1949, a memo from Washington advised all FBI field offices: "For your confidential information, a reliable and confidential source has advised the Bureau that flying discs are believed to be man-made missiles rather than natural phenomenon [*sic*]. It has also been determined that for approximately the past four years the USSR has been engaged in experimentation on an unknown type of flying disc." Twelve months later, in March 1950,

Agent Guy Hottel—commanding the Washington, D.C., field office—informed Hoover that an unnamed "investigator for the Air Force" had admitted recovery of three disabled UFOs in New Mexico, containing nine corpses of three-feet-tall alien beings. On December 8, 1950, an "urgent" cable to Hoover from the Richmond, Virginia, FBI declared that agents of Army Intelligence "have been put on immediate high alert for any data whatsoever concerning flying saucers."

Those startling bulletins notwithstanding, it was March 1952 before the air force opened its last known investigation of UFOs, code-named Project Blue Book. This time around, air force researchers claimed that only 1.8 percent of known sightings remained unexplained, but their "explanations"—including swamp gas, mass delusions, and mistaken sightings of the planet Venus—left many readers unconvinced. Project Bluebook officially ended in December 1969 when Maj. David Shea declared that further study of the phenomenon "cannot be justified either on the ground of national security or in the interest of science." J. Edgar Hoover, meanwhile, had washed his hands of the saucer problem in July 1966, advising one curious correspondent that "the investigation of unidentified flying objects is not, and never has been, a matter within the investigative jurisdiction of the FBI." (In fact, the last known FBI report on UFOs was filed on January 18, 1967, reporting an alleged ALIEN ABDUCTION at Chesapeake, Virginia.) Still, official denials frequently fell on deaf ears. A 1997 *Time*-CNN poll determined that 17 percent of U.S. residents believe in UFO abductions, while a 1992 Roper survey found 2 percent of the population (some 3.7 million Americans) convinced that they had been kidnapped by aliens.

Alien abductions, whether carried out as medical experiments, for purposes of racial hybridization, or

Four brightly glowing, unidentified objects appeared in the sky at 9:00 P.M. on July 15, 1952, above a parking lot in Salem, Massachusetts. (Corbis)

for some other still-unfathomable motive, represent only one tier of conspiracy theories attached to the UFO phenomenon. Others include (but are by no means limited to) the following:

- Nazi UFOs emerging from a HOLLOW EARTH. In 1976 author Ernst Zundel—a leading Canadian proponent of Holocaust denial—published a claim that fugitive leaders of the THIRD REICH retreated to ANTARCTICA in 1945, there establishing subterranean bases replete with secret technology. UFOs are their airships, used to keep surface dwellers under surveillance pending establishment of a FOURTH REICH. Such claims have not forestalled Zundel's conviction and imprisonment under Canadian hate-speech statutes.

- LIVESTOCK MUTILATIONS. Since the mid-1960s, throughout the United States and elsewhere, UFO sightings have been reported in conjunction with discovery of dead and mutilated domestic animals, including cows, horses, sheep, and various other species. As with alleged abductions of human victims, the motive remains obscure, but most theories presume an alien interest in studying life forms on Earth—a kind of intergalactic biology class.

- Alien domination of Earth with collaboration from human race-traitors. A common theme in the popular *X-Files* TV series, this scenario was pioneered (or at least refined for widespread public consumption) by author George Andrews in his 1986 book *Extra-Terrestrials Among Us*. According to Andrews, aliens with an appetite for conquest control earthly affairs through a "privileged elite class" that includes the U.S. CENTRAL INTELLIGENCE AGENCY, created specifically to administer a global form of "corporate FASCISM."

- Covert adoption of alien technology on Earth. A year after Andrews published his treatise on alien rule of the planet, other researchers countered with publication of supposed Top Secret documents labeled *MJ-12* (sometimes referred to as *Majic-12* or *Majestic-12*). The papers in question comprise—or simulate—correspondence between President Harry Truman and his secretary of defense, James Forrestal, relating to the Roswell crash of July 1947. Presented as smoking-gun proof that alien

spacecraft and corpses are in fact held by the U.S. government, at AREA 51 or elsewhere, the MJ-12 documents are cited in support of various theories involving adaptation of otherworldly technology to produce "stealth" airplanes, and so forth. Critics dismiss the papers as clever fabrications, including too-precise copies of Truman's signature photocopied from more mundane documents.

- Alien mimicry of humankind. Finally, if aliens are not controlling humans, or at least contributing scientific marvels to our store of knowledge, perhaps they have *become* human beings to rule Earth directly. A small but ardent body of conspiracists believe that extraterrestrial beings pass for humans on a daily basis, while holding leadership positions in government and industry. Some theorists go further yet, suggesting that scaly creatures called "reptilians" have donned false faces (after the fashion of invaders in the TV science-fiction series *V*) to pose as men and women at the pinnacle of power on Earth.

See also COMMUNISM; HOLOCAUST AND HOLOCAUST DENIAL.

UGANDA

Bantu tribes occupied the region of present-day Uganda around 500 B.C.E., dividing the territory among three kingdoms (Ankole, Buganda, and Bunyoro) by the 14th century A.D. Arab traders and European explorers arrived almost simultaneously in 1844, and Uganda fell within the British "sphere of influence" a half-century later by treaty agreement between England and GERMANY. Unlike other British possessions, Uganda attracted few white settlers, but large numbers arrived from INDIA and PAKISTAN, sowing the seeds for future ethnic rivalry. Uganda won independence in October 1962, with Edward Mutesa installed as the first president; Milton Obote became prime minister. Four years later, aided by young army officer Idi Amin, Obote deposed Mutesa and seized control of the nation. Amin, in turn, ousted Obote in January 1971, immediately expelling Asian residents while he launched a reign of terror against native opponents. In 1976 Amin declared himself president for life. His tactics—including claims of cannibal feasts with Amin's ranking opponents on the menu—

claimed an estimated 300,000 lives by 1977 according to Amnesty International. A curious sideshow of Amin's dictatorship included flirtation with Palestinian terrorist groups, culminating in the 1976 hijacking of a Lufthansa airliner from Europe to Entebbe airport where a flying squad from ISRAEL subsequently freed the hostages. Exiled ex-president Obote launched an invasion of Uganda in 1980, whereupon Amin fled to SAUDI ARABIA. Obote reclaimed the presidency, but another military coup drove him from the county in July 1985. A major anti-Obote group, the National Resistance Army, found itself excluded from the new regime, and its troops seized Kampala in January 1986, installing leader Yoweri Museveni as president. Museveni is hailed for transforming postwar Uganda into "an economic miracle" and for pursuing a largely successful campaign against AIDS. Nonetheless, struggle continues with another rebel group, the Lord's Resistance Army (LRA), based in SUDAN. That long war is now in its 18th year, with an estimated 8,000 to 10,000 Ugandan children kidnapped to serve as LRA troops under "prophet" Joseph Kony.

See also TERRORISM.

UKRAINE

Until the 16th century A.D., Ukraine was known as Kievan Rus, from which the name RUSSIA derives. Its power peaked in the 10th century, crumbling with Mongol invasions in 1240. POLAND dominated Ukraine from the mid-13th century until the Union of Brest-Litovsk divided the region between Orthodox and Ukrainian Catholics. In 1654 Ukraine granted sovereignty to the Duke of Muscovy in return for protection against Poland. The end result was annexation into Russia and the subsequent declaration of a Soviet republic in 1922. Coveted by GERMANY for its vast stores of grain, Ukraine was ravaged by ADOLF HITLER's troops in World War II. Four decades later, in 1986, it suffered one of Russia's worst disasters at the CHERNOBYL nuclear plant. An independent nation since the collapse of Russian COMMUNISM in 1991, Ukraine agreed to destroy its stockpile of nuclear weapons three years later, but some observers claim that those warheads have in fact been sold by members of the RUSSIAN MAFIA and other outlaw groups on the international black market. Violent protests rocked the country in winter 2001 as rioters demanded the resignation or impeachment of quasi-dictator Leonid Kuchma.

President Kuchma was accused of plotting to murder a journalist who exposed government corruption, a charge supported by Kuchma's voice on tape discussing terms for the assassination. Kuchma's party failed to win a clear majority in the April 2002 elections, but his refusal to step down prompted another round of violent demonstrations, continuing sporadically to the present day. In 2003 Kuchma devised a scheme to make Parliament responsible for future presidential elections, thereby disarming the broader electorate, but he dropped the plan under U.S. pressure in February 2004.

See also CATHOLIC CHURCH.

ULSTER Loyalist Central Coordinating Committee

In 1998 Irish author Sean McPhilemy reported that a private organization, the Ulster Loyalist Central Coordinating Committee (ULCCC), had collaborated with police officers of the Royal Ulster Constabulary (RUC) to carry out terrorist murders of various Catholic residents in Northern Ireland. Most of the victims were members of organizations opposed to continued British rule in Northern Ireland, including the IRISH REPUBLICAN ARMY and its Sinn Fein political arm. McPhilemy's report on the ULCCC, updated in 1999, alleged that rogue police officers and a pair of professional killers hired by the committee—Robin ("The Jackal") Jackson and Billy ("King Rat") Wright, both deceased—murdered at least 166 victims between August 1973 and May 1997. Of those murders, 101 were committed personally by Robin Jackson, sometimes acting with accomplices. Cancer claimed Jackson's life in 1998, and while he is thus unavailable for questioning, McPhilemy concludes that The Jackal "undoubtedly committed many more murders" that remain unknown today.

A defecting ULCCC member, Ken Kerr supplied McPhilemy with 48 alleged committee members or associates "who fully supported its murderous activities." Those named in print by McPhilemy—none of whom filed defamation actions when the charge was published—include: Frazer Agnew, ex-mayor of Carrickfergus and member of the Ulster Unionist Party; Bill Abernethy, an Ulster banker, former RUC reserve officer, and ULCCC chairman; Sammy Abraham, a businessman in Tandragee, County Antrim; Alec Benson, a gunman for the loyalist Retaliation and Defence Group; Philip Black, a staff member in the computer science department at Queen's University, Belfast; Alan Clegg, an RUC inspector and former head of the department's Lurgan station; Trevor Forbes, retired RUC assistant chief constable and head of the RUC's Special Branch; Robin Jackson, assassin; Alec Jamison, of the RUC's "Inner Force"; Ken Kerr, ex-British soldier and a paramilitary loyalist; Cecil Kilpatrick, a former RUC reservist and member of the Ulster Independence Committee; Graham Long, ex-British soldier and a paramilitary loyalist; Nelson McCausland, a Belfast city councilor and member of the Ulster Unionist Party; John McCullagh, of the paramilitary Ulster Resistance; Isobel McCulloch, ULCCC secretary; Dean McCullough, member of the paramilitary Ulster Volunteer Force; Charles Moffett, an accountant who laundered money for illegal arms shipments; Richard Monteith, a Belfast attorney; Drew Nelson, attorney; Albert and David Prentice, brothers and private businessmen; Hugh Ross, a Presbyterian minister and president of the Ulster Independence Committee; James Sands, a member of the RUC "Inner Force," later turned informant; Lewis Singleton, attorney, partner of Drew Nelson, and member of the Ulster Independence Committee; William Trimble, member of parliament and leader of the Ulster Unionist Party since 1995; Ian Whittle, of the RUC "Inner Force"; and Billy Wright, assassin. RUC detectives report that all alleged ULCCC members have been questioned and deny any involvement in illegal activities. None has been charged with any crimes to date.

See also CATHOLIC CHURCH; TERRORISM.

UNDEAD outlaws

Americans adore flamboyant badmen—and bad women, for that matter. Law-and-order protests notwithstanding, eccentric and "romantic" outlaws are revered in the United States, especially those cast as "social bandits" who outwit authorities while engaged in David-and-Goliath contests with despised institutions—Old West railroads, Depression-era banks, even the U.S. government itself. Some lawbreakers transcend headlines and pass into legend. They are too colorful to die, spawning reports of survival even after very public deaths. The most famous immortal antiheroes include:

Jesse James (1847–1882): Arguably America's most famous outlaw of all time, Jesse followed elder brother Frank into a Confederate guerrilla unit at age 17 and never truly acknowledged the Civil War's end. In 1866, back in civilian life, the James brothers and their cousins from the Younger clan pioneered daylight bank robbery and soon branched out to rob trains. A disastrous raid in Northfield, Minnesota, shattered the James-Younger gang in 1876, but Frank and Jesse escaped the trap and resumed their criminal activities with the Ford brothers, Bob and Charles, in 1879–81. On April 3, 1882, after negotiating a $10,000 reward with Missouri's governor, Bob Ford allegedly killed Jesse at his home in St. Joseph.

Jesse was barely in the ground before a procession of impostors surfaced, each in turn claiming to be the "real" Jesse James. The most persuasive of the lot, 103-year-old J. Frank Dalton, died at Lawton, Oklahoma, in 1951, four decades before the invention of DNA tests that might have proved (or disproved) his claim. In 1966 author Rudy Turilli published an account of James-Dalton's life, outlining a conspiracy that included Jesse's wife and mother, Bob Ford, and Missouri governor Thomas Crittenden. Turilli claims the plotters arranged Jesse's disappearance, while Ford shot another gang member, Charlie Bigelow, to take Jesse's place in the casket. In October 2003 DNA testing ruled out another Jesse candidate, known in life as Jeremiah James of Neodesha, Kansas. Still, controversy over Jesse's life and death continues, exacerbated in 1978 when the outlaw's corpse was exhumed and the bullet still lodged in his skull was identified as .38 caliber—not the Colt .45 claimed by Bob Ford in his own account of the murder.

Billy the Kid (1859–1881): More than 120 years after his alleged death in New Mexico, every aspect of this Old West gunman's life remains controversial, from his birth name (William Bonney or Henry McCarty) to his final body count (somewhere between 6 and 21 victims). Most of that carnage occurred during New Mexico's infamous Lincoln County War (1878–81) when Billy allied himself with cattle baron John Chisum against county boss Lawrence Murphy and his cohorts. Sheriff Pat Garrett, himself a former friend of Billy's allegedly tracked down the Kid and shot him from ambush at Fort Sumner on the night of July 14, 1881. As with Jesse James, however, stories quickly circulated that Bonney–McCarty was still alive. The best-known Billy, one Ollie ("Brushy Bill") Roberts, died at Hico, Texas, in 1950. After decades of controversy, in 2003, Lincoln County's sheriff petitioned the courts for an exhumation order on Billy's mother, Catherine Antrim, to compare her DNA with that of Roberts and the body planted under Billy's headstone at Fort Sumner. New Mexico governor Bill Richardson approved the plan in November 2003, but legal wrangling left the tests in limbo at press time for this volume.

Butch Cassidy (1866–?): Utah native Robert LeRoy Parker, alias Butch Cassidy, differed from Jesse James and Billy the Kid in his reluctance to use deadly force. It hardly mattered, though, since other members of his rustling and train-robbing "Wild Bunch"—including Har-

vey Logan, Harry Tracy, and "Sundance Kid" Harry Longbaugh—were certified killers. Wells Fargo detectives and local law officers decimated the gang by 1905 when Cassidy and Longbaugh fled to Bolivia, accompanied by Longbaugh's lover, Etta Place. Six years later, after another series of holdups and narrow escapes, Butch and Sundance were allegedly trapped and killed by Bolivian troops in a small rural village. Various accounts claim both were shot by soldiers, or that gravely wounded, Cassidy first killed his friend and then himself. The bodies were identified by Percy Siebert, who briefly employed Butch and Sundance at his Bolivian mine—but did he tell the truth?

In 1975 Cassidy's sister, Lula Parker Berenson, published a book claiming that her brother returned to the United States in 1910, traveling as William Thadeus Phillips. According to Berenson, Butch kept that pseudonym for the

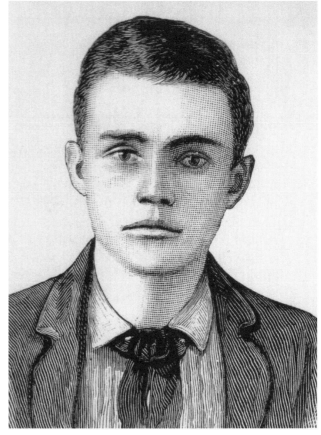

Stories persist that outlaw Jesse James (left) survived his alleged murder in 1882; Bob Ford (right) is variously credited with killing James or helping him fake his death. (Author's collection)

Some theorists believe that Billy the Kid (left) was killed by Sheriff Patrick Garrett (right) in New Mexico. (Author's collection)

remainder of his life, meeting frequently with relatives and friends, fighting briefly as a mercenary in the Mexican revolution, and then marrying and settling down in Spangle, Washington, where he finally died in 1937. Some historians find the story persuasive, but no DNA tests have confirmed it thus far. As related by Berenson, Butch claimed that Percy Siebert misidentified the Bolivian corpses "to give him and Sundance another chance" at life. No credible reports of Harry Longbaugh's survival have surfaced to date.

John Dillinger (1903–1934): Depression-era bank robber John Dillinger was born in Indiana, eight years before Butch Cassidy allegedly met his fate in Bolivia. Unlike most of his felonious contemporaries in the 1920s and 1930s, Dillinger's flamboyant career lasted only 11 months, but he crammed those days with daring holdups, jailbreaks, and shootouts with law officers in six states. He was a living legend at age 31 when a treacherous "woman in red" betrayed him to FEDERAL BUREAU OF INVESTIGATION (FBI) agents, and he was riddled with bullets outside Chicago's Biograph Theater on July 22, 1934.

Or, was he? In 1970, author Jay Robert Nash claimed that Dillinger had paid a group of mobsters and corrupt police officers to fake his death, substituting look-alike Jimmy Lawrence at the Biograph. In support of that claim, Nash produced "Dillinger's" autopsy report, noting discrepancies in height, eye color (brown, versus Dillinger's blue), and a chronic heart condition unknown from Dillinger's navy and prison medical records. Nash also traced the serial number of a pistol allegedly retrieved from Dillinger's corpse and then displayed for decades at FBI headquarters, and he found that the gun was manufactured months after the Biograph shooting. Finally, Nash produced letters written by the "real Dillinger" in 1959 and 1963, together with a photo of their author, but he never traced the suspect for an interview. Skeptics maintain that 1930s-era coroners' reports were often filled with errors, making them unreliable for the most part. As for Dillinger's missing gun, author William Helmer suggests that J. EDGAR HOOVER claimed the weapon as a personal keepsake, replacing it with a "ringer" in the FBI trophy case.

"Machine Gun" Kelly (1895–1954): Chicago native George Barnes, Jr., changed his surname to Kelly in 1926 between arrests for bootlegging. Paroled from Leavenworth federal prison in 1930, he graduated to bank robbery and allegedly received his famous nickname from

Some authors believe 1930s bandit John Dillinger faked his own death with help from the FBI and organized crime. (FBI)

wife Katherine—who (legend has it) bought George a Tommy gun and nagged him into becoming a proficient marksman. In July 1933, with accomplice Al Bates, Kelly kidnapped Oklahoma oilman Charles Urschel and collected $200,000 ransom. At his arrest on September 26, 1933, Kelly supposedly gave FBI agents their own headline tag, cowering before their guns and pleading, "Don't shoot, G-men!" (In fact, he was captured by Memphis police, with the remark, "I've been expecting you.") Sentenced to life imprisonment, Kelly reportedly died of a heart attack, at Leavenworth, on July 18, 1954.

That version of events remained unchallenged until 1988 when authors Jim Dobkins and Ben Jordan published *Machine Gun Man: The True Story of My Incredible Survival into the 1970s.* "Incredible" was the operative word, as Dobkins and Jordan served up memoirs of the late John H. Webb—allegedly Machine Gun Kelly in the flesh. Webb, conveniently deceased by the time his story went to press, advanced a far-fetched tale of prison identity theft, wherein he (that is, George Kelly) switched names with another inmate who resembled him and then claimed the other man's parole after his death. To accept the fable, readers must believe that guards, clerks, and administrators at the federal lockup either did not notice Kelly's switch or simply did not care.

UNION Carbide

Union Carbide is a chemical manufacturer, since February 2001 a subsidiary of Dow Chemical Company (the world's leading producer of napalm). Founded in 1898 Union Carbide is best known for INDIA's Bhopal disaster of December 3, 1984, when 40 tons of deadly methyl isocyanate (MIC) gas escaped from a pesticide factory located in the heart of town. More than 2,000 residents of Bhopal died immediately, while at least 150,000 more (some reports say 600,000) suffered grievous injury from the toxic fumes. Another 6,000 victims ultimately died from exposure to the lethal fumes.

Investigation of the tragedy revealed that leakage occurred when water was introduced into MIC holding tanks at the Union Carbide factory, generating large volumes of gas and forcing an emergency release of pressure. Chemical "scrubbers" that should have captured and detoxified the MIC were off-line for repairs at the time, one of many safety procedures bypassed at the plant. Indian officials charged that those vital safeguards were ignored in the interest of cost cutting, and while Union Carbide still denies that allegation, documents admitted during litigation in a New York federal court reveal that Union Carbide frequently exported "untested technology" to its Bhopal facility.

Victims of the Bhopal disaster sued Union Carbide for $3 billion, and while the firm settled that case out of court in February 1989 with a payment of $470 million, corporate spokespersons still deny complicity in the deaths. (Officially, Union Carbide blames the leaks on TERRORISM or acts of "industrial sabotage" by persons unknown.) Warren Anderson, Union Carbide's CEO in 1984, was charged with culpable homicide and was declared a fugitive from justice by Bhopal's chief judicial magistrate on February 1, 1992. Extradition hearings were threatened but never pursued, leaving Anderson to enjoy his retirement in America while denying any role in the disaster. Meanwhile, journalists report that little of the $470 million settlement ever reached survivors of the incident. Union Carbide sold its Bhopal plant to an Indian battery manufacturer in 1994; Dow Chemical purchased the rest in 2001 for $10.3 billion in stock and debt settlements. At last report, several hundred tons of toxic waste remain untouched at the Bhopal factory, threatening residents to this day with new ailments in an area where cancer rates are already higher than normal.

UNIONE Corsé

The French crime syndicate commonly known as the Unione Corsé or Corsican MAFIA is based in Marseilles, but its tentacles extend worldwide. Spawned on the island of Corsica—the French equivalent of Sicily, in terms of criminality, blood feuds, and an oppressive code of silence—the Unione Corsé established profitable drug-dealing outposts wherever France had colonies during the 20th century, including Indochina and North Africa. In the 1930s French fascists hired syndicate thugs to battle communist demonstrators in the streets. A decade later, under Nazi occupation, the Unione Corsé hired out to Red resistance fighters for the GESTAPO. In the postwar era strategists from the U.S. CENTRAL

INTELLIGENCE AGENCY continued that tradition, using French mobsters to harass and disrupt left-wing labor unions. The U.S.-Corsican connection swiftly established Marseilles as a center of HEROIN production and export, obtaining morphine base from covert labs in LAOS, THAILAND, and VIETNAM. Corsican dominance of the Asian drug trade was challenged after 1954 when French troops were replaced by American forces in Vietnam, but the Unione Corsé retained a strong presence throughout Southeast Asia and established a close relationship with U.S. mobsters to complete the "French Connection" to New York.

An alleged *Unione Corsé* connection to the 1963 JFK ASSASSINATION surfaced 25 years after the fact, in 1988, when the British Broadcasting Company aired a television series titled *The Men Who Killed Kennedy*. One episode of that speculative series detailed California author Stephen Rivele's interviews with Christian David, a Corsican gangster imprisoned in the United States for drug trafficking. According to Rivele and the BBC, David agreed to share his knowledge of President Kennedy's murder in exchange for Rivele's help in obtaining a lawyer. David claimed that in May or June 1963, he was offered the contract on JFK's life in Marseilles by Unione Corsé leader Antoine Guérini. David declined the offer, but he subsequently learned details of the murder while traveling in Argentina on mob business in 1965. Three shooters were involved, he told Rivele, but syndicate "honor" prevented David from naming those still alive. He offered the first name of a deceased participant—"Lucien," whom Rivele later identified as Corsican mobster Lucien Sarti, killed in a shootout with Mexican police in 1972.

After providing technical details of the Kennedy assassination—secret flights and border crossings, triangulated rifle fire in Dallas's Dealey Plaza—David urged Rivele to grill another Corsican, Michel Nicoli, then hiding in the U.S. federal witness-protection program. Rivele located Nicoli with help from Agent Michael Tobin in the Drug Enforcement Administration (DEA) and obtained statements corroborating David's story. Nicoli also added a twist with his declaration that the killers of JFK were paid off in heroin, which they sold for cash with Nicoli's help in Brazil. Agent Tobin described Nicoli to Rivele as the most reliable informant Tobin had known during 30 years with the DEA, opining that if Nicoli said something,

"You could go to the bank on it." Rivele concluded that New Orleans mobster CARLOS MARCELLO—a bitter enemy of the Kennedys who was illegally deported by Attorney General Robert Kennedy in 1962—contracted the JFK murder through Marseilles to divert suspicion from himself.

See also COMMUNISM; FASCISM.

UNION Station massacre

No event in FEDERAL BUREAU OF INVESTIGATION (FBI) history had a more profound impact than the "massacre" at Kansas City's Union Station on June 17, 1933. It propelled Congress to expand bureau authority and powers, launching the "war on crime" that would make J. EDGAR HOOVER an international celebrity. Another 30-odd years elapsed before the legend was exposed as fiction.

The story begins with fugitive Frank Nash, captured by G-men at Hot Springs, Arkansas, on June 16, 1933. Because they lacked arrest powers, the agents recruited an Oklahoma police officer to give their raid tenuous legitimacy. More agents and local police waited to meet the party at Kansas City's Union Station escort Nash the final 30 miles to Leavenworth Prison along back roads. The train with Nash and company aboard arrived at 7:00 A.M. on June 17. Moments later, as they piled into a pair of waiting cars, the law officers were ambushed and gunfire erupted. Nash was killed, along with FBI Agent Raymond Caffrey, Police Chief Otto Reed, Officer W. J. Grooms, and Officer Frank Hermanson. Agents Francis Lackey and Reed Vetterli were wounded; Agent Frank Smith escaped harm.

Patrolman Mike Fanning witnessed the ambush and fired at one of the shooters, a "fat man" who fell as if wounded. "I don't know whether I hit him or whether he fell to escape," Fanning told reporters. "In any event he got up, fired another volley into the car, and ran toward a light Oldsmobile car, which roared west toward Broadway. As the car raced out of the parking lot I saw three men in it, but there may have been more." As the Oldsmobile escaped, Fanning said, "A 1933 Chevrolet car with more gunners swooped past [Caffrey's] parked car and riddled it from the rear. I ran into the street, fired two shots into the back of that car, and rushed to the parked Chevrolet. I still didn't know the men in it were officers." Thus, if Fanning was correct, there were two cars involved in the attack and at least six men—

three in the Oldsmobile, plus a driver and "more gunners" in the Chevrolet.

The problem for investigators was identifying those responsible and running them to earth. Eyewitnesses were hopelessly confused. Surviving agents Smith and Lackey disagreed on the number of assassins involved, but both initially reported that they had not seen the shooters' faces. Agent Vetterli identified one triggerman as Robert Brady, an escaped convict and partner of bandit Harvey Bailey. That statement meshed with testimony from two bystanders who named Bailey as one of the gunmen. One of those witnesses, Samuel Link, also named the gang's wheelman as bandit Wilbur Underhill, but FBI reports described Link as delusional. Another shaky witness, Lottie West, identified one of the gunmen as bank robber Charles ("Pretty Boy") Floyd, but her claim was contradicted by others who named the man she saw as a Union Station employee.

Ballistics evidence was problematic. Souvenir hunters looted the crime scene before police secured it, leaving only a handful of cartridge cases behind, and those were useless without weapons for comparison. There were *other* shells, though, found inside the FBI vehicle where Agent Lackey had fired two rounds from a 16-gauge shotgun, its cartridges loaded with steel ball bearings in place of the usual buckshot. Lackey's first shot, whether accidentally or by design, had killed Frank Nash. Steel shotgun pellets also caused the fatal head wounds suffered by Agent Caffrey and Officer Hermanson, but G-men swiftly buried that evidence. Chief Reed was struck twice in the head—once by a .45-caliber slug, and once by a .38-caliber round. Either wound was potentially fatal, but the order of impact was never determined, and none of the five .38s carried by law officers that day were test-fired for comparison. The others killed or wounded at Union Station (Grooms, Lackey, and Vetterli) were all struck by 45-caliber bullets from submachine guns or pistols—but who did the shooting?

Telephone records revealed conversations between Nash's wife and Missouri mobster Vernon Miller on June 16. Miller was long gone when G-men searched his home, but fingerprints discovered there were checked in vain against a list of fugitives including Harvey Bailey, Wilbur Underhill, Pretty Boy Floyd, and frequent Floyd accomplice Adam Richetti. Much later, on February 13, 1934, agents "found" new fingerprints at Miller's home and matched one to

Richetti a month later. Assuming that Floyd must be involved with any action of Richetti's, FBI headquarters named Miller, Richetti, and Floyd as the Union Station killers. The second carload of assassins was never thereafter discussed.

Verne Miller was already dead by that time, beaten to death in Detroit on November 29, 1933, but agents arrested his girlfriend and held her incommunicado until she signed a statement naming Miller, Floyd, and Richetti as the killers. Floyd was wounded in the left shoulder, she said, thus explaining bloody rags found at Miller's home. In October 1934 Floyd and Richetti surfaced in Ohio. Richetti was captured on October 19; Floyd was cornered by G-men three days later and killed in what one witness described as a summary execution.

FBI ballistics experts allegedly matched one of Floyd's .45 automatics to a single shell casing found at Union Station, but his autopsy raised new problems. There was no shoulder wound, as described by Miller's girlfriend, so agents extracted a new statement: This time the woman "remembered" that the bloody rags belonged to an entirely different fugitive. As for the rest of her story, she swore that Floyd's shoulder wound "was the only part I wasn't telling the truth about in the first statement."

Hoover was satisfied, and Richetti was indicted for killing Officer Hermanson. The only physical evidence offered at trial in June 1935 was the fingerprint from Miller's basement. Agents Vetterli and Smith changed their original statements and identified dead suspects Floyd and Miller as their assailants. Agent Lackey—Hermanson's actual killer—named Richetti as one of the assassins and falsely denied firing any shots himself. Richetti was convicted on June 17 and executed on October 7, 1938. The truth about his frame-up was revealed by author Robert Unger in 1997, including an FBI agent's admission to federal judge William Becker: "Our agent sitting in the back seat pulled the trigger on Nash, and that started it. The machine gunners didn't shoot first. Our guy panicked."

UNITED Fruit Company

Organized in 1899 the United Fruit Company provided a classic example of neocolonialism, ranking among the earliest multinational corporations whose (often destructive) influence deeply penetrated the internal government and policies of various Third World nations. It is from United Fruit and its predecessors—including Boston Fruit and Cuyamil Fruit—that we recognize the term *banana republic* as denoting a corrupt and brutal regime wherein pursuit of profit and power override concerns for human rights and quality of life.

United Fruit owned vast plantations throughout Central America, where it corrupted governments by means of brute force and wholesale graft, becoming a virtual law unto itself. Its first overt display of power came in 1910 when the president of HONDURAS refused United Fruit's demands for favored tax status. In short order a shipload of mercenary thugs sailed from New Orleans and toppled the Honduran government, installing a new president who instantly granted the firm a 25-year exemption from any taxation.

GUATEMALA was another stronghold of United Fruit, known locally as *Mamá Yunay* ("Mommy United"). There, while erecting schools for children of company employees, the firm effectively blocked government construction of highways throughout the country, thus preserving its lucrative railroad monopoly. In 1954, when President Jacobo Arbenz Guzman planned to nationalize company land for redistribution to peasant farmers, United Fruit and its bankers persuaded President Dwight Eisenhower that Arbenz was a dangerous Communist. At the company's behest, Eisenhower mobilized the CENTRAL INTELLIGENCE AGENCY to support a coup d'état against Arbenz, resulting in the overthrow of his regime and a long-running civil war that claimed at least 100,000 lives.

United Fruit dissolved in 1970, but its successors still maintain powerful influence in COLOMBIA, COSTA RICA, CUBA, Guatemala, Honduras, and PANAMA, where "dollar diplomacy" and suppression of human rights often go hand in hand.

See also COMMUNISM.

UNITED Nations

During World War I President Woodrow Wilson conceived the notion of a League of Nations, organized to keep the peace and mediate global disputes without bloodshed. Wilson lobbied hard for the league and succeeded in winning the cooperation of Europe's leading postwar powers, but isolationists in the U.S. Senate refused to approve its country's participation. While the resultant league successfully resolved minor border disputes in the Balkans and Central Asia, it had no military forces of its own and no legal authority to act against sovereign nations. In the 1930s it was thus unable to prevent aggressive actions by the military governments of GERMANY, ITALY, and JAPAN that lit the fuse for World War II and claimed an estimated 30 million lives in 1939–45.

With that conflict still in progress, Allied leaders began negotiations for a new and more powerful peacekeeping organization to solve the world's problems. President Franklin Roosevelt suggested the name *United Nations* (UN), officially aired for the first time in January 1942. From August to October 1944 representatives of the United States, FRANCE, CHINA, Britain, and RUSSIA met at the Dumbarton Oaks Estate in Washington, D.C., to outline the UN's structure and duties. One participant in those meetings, U.S. State Department employee ALGER HISS, was later accused of espionage by the HOUSE UN-AMERICAN ACTIVITIES COMMITTEE, a circumstance that prompted right-wing activists to denounce the United Nations as a procommunist organization. Officially founded in San Francisco on October 24, 1945, the United Nations held its first general meeting (with 51 nations represented) in London on January 10, 1946. Membership is open to all "peace-loving states," a label sometimes honored more in the breech than in observance. As this volume went to press, 191 nations belonged to the United Nations, many of them (including the United States, Russia, and ISRAEL) anything but peaceful.

From its beginning the United Nations has figured prominently in a host of conspiracy theories. Some, like the allegations that sabotage caused UN Secretary DAG HAMMARSKJÖLD's fatal plane crash, involve plots against selected individuals. Most such theories, however, paint conspiracies on a grand scale. Since the 1950s, members of the JOHN BIRCH SOCIETY and similar far-right groups have maintained that UN leaders (including "traitors" in Washington) plot day and night to subvert U.S. sovereignty in favor of an insidious "one world government." Those theories were revived in the 1990s, principally by paramilitary militia groups, which cast the United Nations as the advance guard of a shadowy NEW WORLD ORDER. Also, while the modern United Nations does have military units that are engaged as peacekeepers at various points around the world, no

evidence has been produced thus far of any plot to dominate the planet. In fact, as President George W. Bush prepared to launch OPERATION IRAQI FREEDOM and topple the SADDAM HUSSEIN regime in 2003, UN opposition fell on deaf ears, and Bush declared the United Nations "irrelevant" in terms of U.S. foreign policy.

See also BUSH DYNASTY; COMMUNISM; MILITIAS.

USA PATRIOT Act

It was inevitable that the PENTTBOM attacks of September 11, 2001, would produce new federal legislation aimed at future acts of TERRORISM. Critics charge, however, that the law enacted by Congress and signed by President George W. Bush on October 26, 2001, is a leap toward erosion of basic civil rights. The law's authors titled it the Uniting and Strengthening America by Providing Appropriate Tools Required to Intercept and Obstruct Terrorism (USA PATRIOT) Act. Its major provisions include expansion of wiretaps and bugging; broader authority to search computers, increased FEDERAL BUREAU OF INVESTIGATION access to confidential records; revival of banned domestic surveillance by the CENTRAL INTELLIGENCE AGENCY; detention of foreign "suspects" without charges; official designation of "terrorist" groups linked to deportation of alien members; secret searches of private property; removal of the long-standing legal barrier between foreign intelligence gathering and domestic criminal cases; increased federal access to banking records; expansion of border surveillance; and broadened definitions of *domestic terrorism* including any attempt "to influence the policy of a government by intimidation or coercion."

As administered by Attorney General JOHN ASHCROFT, the Patriot Act has already sparked a series of lawsuits. Mass detention of Muslim immigrants who registered with immigration authorities as required by post-"9/11" regulations have prompted class-action litigation by the American Civil Liberties Union and other groups (still unresolved as this work went to press). It seems certain that various provisions of the law will face challenges in court for years to come. Such criticism notwithstanding, Ashcroft appeared before Congress in 2003 and 2004 with complaints that he needed *more* power to perform his duties.

See also BUSH DYNASTY.

URUGUAY

Charrúas aborigines inhabited Uruguay before invaders from PORTUGAL arrived to "settle" the region in 1680; nearly all indigenous people had been exterminated by the time SPAIN seized control of the country in 1778. Uruguay threw off the Spanish yoke in 1811, but Portuguese invaders from BRAZIL returned to assert dominance six years later. Final independence was won with help from ARGENTINA in 1825, but the establishment of a republic failed to quell domestic bloodshed. A rebellion in 1836 touched off a half-century of mayhem, including a brutal civil war (1839–51) and a war with PARAGUAY (1865–70), sporadically interrupted by military incursions from Argentina and Brazil. In 1973 a military coup toppled Uruguay's civilian government, and for the next 12 years a military junta ruled the nation by means of TERRORISM and oppression, jailing or executing thousands of political prisoners. Finally, to avert a popular uprising, the junta restored elections in November 1984 and relinquished power four months later, leaving the country a legacy of runaway inflation and crippling national debt. At press time for this volume Uruguay was still mired in recession. A commission established in August 2000 to investigate the disappearance of 160 dissidents under the defunct military regime has yet to report its findings.

VATICAN Bank

Few institutions on Earth possess more wealth—most of it untaxed—than the CATHOLIC CHURCH. That wealth is managed and manipulated by Rome's Institute for Religious Works, more commonly known as the Vatican Bank. Throughout the latter half of the 20th century, recurring scandals rocked the Vatican Bank as it was accused of hoarding GOLD and other treasures stolen by agents of the THIRD REICH during World War II, collaborating with fugitives accused of heinous WAR CRIMES, paying hush-money to countless victims of PEDOPHILE PRIESTS, and working with the MAFIA to reap vast profits from illicit enterprises. Some critics go so far as to suggest that Vatican bankers and their criminal cohorts conspired to murder Pope JOHN PAUL I and replace him with a more pliable pontiff.

Public scandals surrounding the Vatican Bank initially sprang from its relationship (and partial ownership) of Banco Ambrosiano, an Italian financial institution. Ambrosiano's president, Roberto Calvi, was convicted on corruption charges in 1981 but remained free on bail pending appeal of that verdict. On June 11, 1982, Calvi fled ITALY with a suitcase full of documents. Those papers were missing eight days later when authorities found Calvi's body hanging under Blackfriar's Bridge in London, his pockets stuffed with bricks and $15,000 in cash. Calvi's death was ruled a suicide in July 1982, but a second inquest 12 months later returned an "open" verdict, admitting the possibility of foul play. Investigators disclosed that Calvi had ties to the Mafia, the CAMORRA, and "P2," a secretive right-wing group of FREEMASONS in Rome. Twenty years after his death, a new forensic report officially declared Calvi's death a murder. At press time for this volume, four suspects—including a known Mafioso and Calvi's Austrian lover—faced homicide charges in that case. Other allegations against the Vatican Bank during the past quarter-century include the following:

1986—Italian police issued arrest warrants for Catholic Archbishop Paul Marcinkus (president of the Vatican Bank from 1971 to 1989), charging financial irregularities. The felony counts were later dismissed under a 1929 statute barring Italian courts from prosecuting Vatican officials. Pope JOHN PAUL II sheltered Marcinkus in Vatican City for seven years and then packed him off to the United States, where he remains at press time for this work, serving as a parish priest in Arizona.

1990—Media reports linked the Vatican Bank to a bribery scandal in Milan. As reported in the press, private corporations had paid out $105 million in bribes to various local officials, some $63 million of that amount laundered through the Institute of Religious Works in Rome.

VENEZUELA

2001—Investigative journalists accused the Vatican Bank of hiding more than $55 billion in illicit funds from various criminal cartels in Italy. Reporters for the *London Telegraph* and *Inside Fraud Bulletin* called the Vatican a leading "cut-out" country with financial operations active in Macau, Mauritius, and Nauru. According to those reports, the Vatican "ranked well ahead of such offshore havens as the Bahamas, Switzerland, and Liechtenstein" in terms of global money laundering for swindlers, drug dealers, and other felons.

2002—Insurance commissioners in five U.S. states filed a $600 million federal racketeering lawsuit against the Vatican Bank alleging that Catholic leaders aided and abetted insurance frauds committed by convicted swindler Martin Frankel. The lawsuits challenged Vatican sovereign immunity—a concept that permits Vatican City, as the world's smallest "nation," legally to conceal wrongdoing by its financial agents. Trial is pending in that case.

VENEZUELA

Christopher Columbus "discovered" Venezuela on his third New World voyage in 1498, and later Spanish explorers coined the name which means "Little Venice." Simón Bolívar, who later liberated much of South America from SPAIN, was born at Caracas in 1783 and joined in Venezuela's successful war for independence (1810–21). Initially merged with COLOMBIA and ECUADOR as the Republic of Greater Colombia, Venezuela became an independent state in 1830. A string of unstable dictatorships followed, financed by the discovery of OIL in the early 20th century. Leftist leader Rómulo Betancourt and his Democratic Action Party won control of the government and drafted a new constitution in 1946, installing Rómulo Gallegos as Venezuela's first democratically elected president a year later. Gallegos lasted all of eight months in office before a military coup replaced him with dictator Marcos Peréz Jiménez. Peréz, in turn, was ousted by another band of rebels in 1958, and since that time oil-rich Venezuela has ranked among the more stable regimes of Latin America. The United States was

alarmed when President Rafael Caldera Rodriguez (1969–74) legalized the Communist Party, established diplomatic relations with RUSSIA, and nationalized foreign-owned oil and steel companies, but no armed intervention was forthcoming. Economic recession prompted President Hugo Chavez to expand government authority in 1999, prompting criticism that he had imposed a leftist dictatorship. Widespread strikes have swept the country since December 2001, including a massive antigovernment demonstration in April 2002 wherein 12 protesters were killed by police. A coalition of business and military leaders next illegally drove Chavez from power, but he recaptured control of the government two days later. Strikes continue in the oil industry and other vital areas, while SECRET POLICE harass labor leaders across the country.

See also COMMUNISM.

VIETNAM

Portuguese explorers "discovered" the region of modern-day Vietnam in the 16th century to establish trading posts that were supplanted by French colonists 300 years later. Despite brief interruption by JAPAN in World War II, FRANCE ruled Indochina—including the present nations of Vietnam, CAMBODIA, and LAOS—from the 1880s until 1954. Rebel leader Ho Chi Minh requested U.S. aid in liberating his country from French imperial forces, but President Harry Truman preferred to support France against Vietnam's native people. When that effort failed and France was defeated, negotiators agreed that Vietnam would be divided until nationwide elections were held in 1955 to select the next president. Ho Chi Minh won an overwhelming majority, whereupon Washington and puppet ruler Ngo Dinh Diem reneged on the agreement, declaring that North and South Vietnam should be permanently separated. Thus began the hopeless U.S. struggle to "save" Vietnam from itself by means of supporting one corrupt tyrant after another. After eight years of brutal totalitarian rule, Diem lost U.S. favor and was assassinated on November 1, 1963. His replacements encouraged broader U.S. involvement in Vietnam's civil war, while they grew rich from HEROIN exports facilitated by the CENTRAL INTELLIGENCE AGENCY. Dissent at home finally compelled President RICHARD NIXON to withdraw U.S. combat troops from Vietnam in 1972, but the southern regime fought on until April 1975. All told, the war claimed at least 58,000 U.S. lives, while killing an estimated 1.3 million to 3 million Vietnamese.

Ho's victory in 1975 reunited Vietnam, but it did not end the nation's conflicts. Border fighting with CAMBODIA escalated through 1977, while CHINA complained that its people were subjected to racist persecution in Vietnam. Sixty thousand Vietnamese troops invaded Cambodia and toppled the regime of genocidal dictator Pol Pot, while Chinese forces invaded northern Vietnam in 1979. Vietnamese troops began to withdraw from Cambodia and Laos in 1988, though final peace accords between Cambodia and Vietnam would not be signed until October 1991. The collapse of Russian COMMUNISM that same year left Vietnam as one of the few avowedly "Red" states remaining on Earth. Even there, however, economic problems and a breakdown in Marxist theory prompted trends away from traditional Communist measures. Some critics insist that Vietnam still conceals an uncertain number of U.S. POWs, for reasons unknown, but 30-odd years since the end of overt hostilities, the case is increasingly difficult to prove.

VOTESCAM

Election fraud is a serious concern in any jurisdiction where a pretense of democracy exists. Throughout the world election outcomes are routinely challenged on grounds of vote rigging, intimidation, and other corrupt practices that effectively negate popular suffrage. In some nations, particularly in the so-called Third World, rigged elections sometimes spark armed rebellions, toppling regimes that claim legitimate authority even as their candidates are driven into exile or are dragged to the gallows. It would be comforting to think that the United States is immune to such foibles, but sadly, that is not the case.

From the TWEED RING and TAMMANY HALL to ELECTION 2000, U.S. political contests have been marred by accusations of wholesale fraud and corruption—often with sufficient evidence to justify imprisonment of those responsible, though prosecutions are extremely rare. Two American presidents—RUTHERFORD B. HAYES and George W. Bush—"won" their office in contests where their opponents received clear majorities of the popular vote, while most historians today concede that John Kennedy stole the 1960 presidential election from RICHARD NIXON with help from the MAFIA and corrupt Chicago mayor RICHARD JOSEPH DALEY. Kennedy's running mate, LYNDON BAINES JOHNSON, was known in Texas as "Landslide Lyndon," for the frequency with which dead voters rose to cast their eleventh-hour ballots in alphabetical order. Southern whites, meanwhile, complained of Republican electoral malfeasance throughout RECONSTRUCTION, and they formed the KU KLUX KLAN to eradicate black suffrage by means of TERRORISM. A century later, the TALMADGE DYNASTY still ruled Georgia by night-riding terror, while Missouri boss TOM PENDERGAST groomed Harry Truman for the White House. Political bosses from coast to coast rose or fell on their ability to deliver blocs of votes—from immigrants, saloons, graveyards, or lunatic asylums—variously "stuffing" or "losing" ballot boxes according to their needs.

The mechanics of election fraud changed radically with the demise of paper ballots and the introduction of electronic voting machines in the 1970s. From that day to the present, some observers have alleged the existence of a national "Votescam" conspiracy, in which both major parties are accused of stealing or fabricating votes in their pursuit of power. In 1988 Harvard University computer expert Howard Strauss remarked to CBS News on the subject of electronic vote counting: "Get me a job with the company that writes the software for this program. Then I'd have access to one-third of the votes. Is that enough to fix a general election? When it comes to computerized elections, there are no safeguards. It's not a door without locks, it's a house, without doors." In short, U.S. voters may never really know how many votes were cast in any given election or which candidate secured a legitimate majority.

Ironically, the scandals surrounding Election 2000 actually may have exacerbated vote fraud in America. The uproar over Florida's "illegible" ballots and "hanging chads" in November 2000 prompted a new wave of "reform" under President Bush, including passage of the federal Help America Vote Act, which delivered thousands of new electronic voting machines to precincts across the United States. Votescam critic Victoria Collier described those "Touch Screen Trojan horses" as follows:

These machines are not just unverifiable, they are secretly programmed (their software is not open to scrutiny by election officials or computer experts), equipped with modems, accessible by computer, telephone, and satellite. They are the final product of decades of work by the election rigging industry. When they are installed in every precinct in America, our elections will finally become completely meaningless, nothing more than charades behind which criminal thugs will wield the power of this nation.

The 2004 presidential election took place without the controversy that had marred the 2000 vote. Afterward scattered claims of voting fraud were made around the nation, but no evidence emerged to support specific claims relevant to "votescam."

At press time for this volume, there are still no safeguards on the system, a fact that encourages conspiracists to fear the worst—and, perhaps, with good reason.

See also BUSH DYNASTY; KENNEDY DYNASTY.

WALKER, John, Jr.

John Walker, Jr., was a communications specialist and chief warrant officer in the U.S. Navy who sold himself as a spy for RUSSIA in the 1960s, afterward recruiting friends and relatives to continue theft of classified data even after Walker himself retired from the service in 1975. As a cover for his spying on behalf of Communists, Walker cultivated a right-wing image by joining the KU KLUX KLAN and the JOHN BIRCH SOCIETY—both of which were suitably embarrassed by his arrest in 1985. Before FEDERAL BUREAU OF INVESTIGATION agents finally bagged Walker and his ring of accomplices, the network deciphered more than one million secret messages for Moscow, earning Walker recognition as one of the 20th century's most effective and dangerous spies. Federal authorities completely overlooked Walker's activities and relatively lavish lifestyle, fueled by more than $1 million in payoffs for stolen intelligence. It finally required a tip from Walker's wife to crack the ring, whereupon Walker and several cohorts were convicted of espionage and imprisoned for life. Son Michael Walker, a relatively minor player in the network, turned state's evidence to save himself and was released from custody in February 2000.

See also COMMUNISM.

WALLACE, George (1919–1998)

Alabama's premier racist demagogue of modern times was born in Barbour County on August 25, 1919. After serving in the U.S. Army Air Force during World War II, Wallace plunged headlong into the Cotton State's one-party (Democratic) political system, winning election to the state legislature (1947–53) and a circuit judgeship (1953–58). Wallace set his sights on the governor's mansion in 1958, challenging racist hard-liner John Patterson from the posture of a racial moderate, condemning Patterson's open alliance with the violent KU KLUX KLAN (KKK). Crushing defeat in that contest taught Wallace the most important lesson of his political career. "They out-niggered me that time," he remarked to friends, "but they'll never do it again."

In 1962 Wallace courted Klan support and handily won the election. Returning the favor, he appointed Klan members to various high-ranking posts (including command of Alabama's state police) and streamlined parole for Klansmen convicted of castrating a black man in 1957. Wallace's inauguration address in January 1963 (written by former Klan chief ASA EARL CARTER) hinged on a single promise to his white constituents: "Segregation today, segregation tomorrow, segregation forever." To that end, he subverted federal investigations of Klan TERRORISM (including the notorious BAPBOMB case of 1963), denounced state attorney general Richmond Flowers for "wasting time" on investigations of KKK murders and vetoed legislation that would have imposed harsh penalties for illegal possession of dynamite by Klan bombers.

State law barred Wallace from a second term in 1966, so wife Lurleen campaigned for governor in a thinly veiled charade to keep George in power. It worked, and while Wallace busied himself with a run for the White House in 1968—polling 9.4 million votes for the American Independent Party (organized by members of the KKK, the CITIZENS' COUNCILS, and the JOHN BIRCH SOCIETY) that November—loyal state legislators expunged the statutory ban on successive gubernatorial terms. Wallace returned to the governor's mansion in 1971, serving as Alabama's chief of state through 1978 and again from 1983 to 1987. His second run for the White House as an AIP candidate was scuttled on May 15, 1972, when would-be assassin Arthur Bremer shot Wallace at a political rally in Maryland. Thereafter confined to a wheelchair, Wallace subsequently retreated from his

Alabama governor George Wallace forged a close alliance with the terrorist Ku Klux Klan in the 1960s. (Florida State Archives)

hard-line racist and ultraconservative views, prompting one Klan leader to complain in 1976 that Wallace "is not as white as he was in 1968. His mind has deteriorated, I'm sorry to say, along with his body." Wallace died at a Montgomery, Alabama, hospital on September 13, 1998.

WANNSEE Conference

This key event in the Holocaust occurred at Grossen Wannsee, near Berlin, on January 20, 1942, when leaders of the THIRD REICH met to plan details of ADOLF HITLER's "final solution to the Jewish question." Attendees included SS-Obergruppe führer Reinhard Heydrich (chief of the GESTAPO); SS-Obersturmbannführer ADOLF EICHMANN; Dr. Alfred Meyer (Reich Ministry for the Occupied Eastern Territories); Dr. Wilhelm Stuckart (Reich Ministry for the Interior); Dr. Roland Freisler (Reich Ministry of Justice); SS-Gruppenführer Otto Hofmann (Race and Settlement Main Office); Dr. Erich Neumann (Head of the Four Year Plan Office); Dr. Martin Luther (Foreign Office); Friedrich Wilhelm Kritzinger (Reich Chancellery); Dr. Josef Buhler (Governor of occupied Poland); Dr. Karl Eberhard Schongarth (commander of the Nazi intelligence service); Dr. Rudolf Lange (commanding the intelligence service in Latvia); Reichsamtleiter Dr. Georg Leibbrandt; SS-Oberführer Gerhard Klopfer; and SS-Gruppenführer Heinrich Muller (Gestapo). Surviving minutes of the meeting indicate that Nazi leaders planned to eliminate an estimated 11 million Jews from Europe. While no mention of mass murder was recorded on paper, the minutes refer to mass deportation of Jews to the East for "appropriate labor . . . in the course of which action doubtless a large portion will be eliminated by natural causes." Furthermore, the "final remnant will . . . have to be treated accordingly, because it . . . would, if released, act as the seed of a new Jewish revival." Eichmann and other attendees, when tried for WAR CRIMES after World War II, admitted that "extermination" of Jews and persons of "mixed blood" was bluntly discussed during the conference.

See also HOLOCAUST AND HOLOCAUST DENIAL.

WAR crimes

All warfare includes some measure of atrocity, but leading nations of the Earth have tried for the past 150 years to make mortal combat more "civilized."

A code of maritime law was established in April 1856, followed eight years later by the Lieber Code, dictating proper behavior for the U.S. Army in the midst of America's great Civil War. The first of many Geneva Conventions occurred in August 1864, producing guidelines for "the Amelioration of the Condition of the Wounded in Armies in the Field." Successive conclaves renounced the use of certain explosives (December 1868); limited the use of toxic gas and expanding "dum-dum" bullets (July 1899); banned the discharge of projectiles and explosives from balloons (October 1907); established laws of naval warfare (February 1909); banned toxic gases and bacterial weapons (June 1925); codified treatment of captured soldiers (July 1929); banned attacks on historic monuments and artistic or scientific institutions (April 1935); and protected civilian populations from "new engines of war as introduced" (1938).

Observance of those treaties was limited to signatories, and even they might violate the terms at any time without fear of repercussions since no tribunal existed to try war-crimes cases. The first such tribunal was established in August 1945 by the victors in World War II to prosecute defeated Axis leaders for war crimes. First in the dock were 21 high-ranking officials of the THIRD REICH, tried at Nuremberg, GERMANY, between November 1945 and December 1946, for various crimes against humanity. Other trials followed, including both German and Japanese defendants. Inspired by the horrors of the Holocaust, on December 11, 1946, the UNITED NATIONS (UN) General Assembly voted unanimously to make genocide (extermination of a race or ethnic group) a crime under international law. That resolution was formally codified on December 9, 1947, when the UN unanimously adopted the Genocide Treaty.

A surprise holdout on ratification of that groundbreaking treaty was the United States. Citing various "omissions and inherent dangers" in the document, members of the U.S. Senate delayed approval of the treaty until October 14, 1988. It was finally signed by President RONALD REAGAN on November 11, 1988. Meanwhile, in 1949, the UN's International Law Commission labored to establish an International Criminal Court, but opposition from the United States and other nations finally doomed that effort in 1954. Another 53 years elapsed before the international court was finally created, without U.S. participation, in April 2002. By that time, the U.S.

Congress and President George W. Bush had created a new international furor, demanding immunity from war-crimes prosecution for any U.S. troops assigned to a UN peacekeeping mission. Congress went further yet, passing a statute dubbed the Hague Invasion Act, which authorized use of military force to free any U.S. soldiers arrested for war crimes. The law also barred any U.S. agency from cooperating with the International Criminal Court and blocked U.S. military aid to any non-NATO signatory of the ICC treaty. Critics suggest that the Bush administration's actions were calculated to give U.S. troops free rein in OPERATION IRAQI FREEDOM, planned from the moment of Bush's January 2001 inauguration and carried out two years later in defiance of UN opposition. In May 2004 U.S. soldiers faced courts-martial for torture of Iraqi prisoners, while inquiries were opened into the deaths of 37 detainees held by American forces in Afghanistan and Iraq.

See also BUSH DYNASTY; HOLOCAUST AND HOLO-CAUST DENIAL.

WARREN Commission

Formally known as the U.S. Commission to Report upon the Assassination of President John F. Kennedy, the "blue-ribbon" Warren Commission was established by executive order from President LYNDON BAINES JOHNSON on November 29, 1963. Its chairman and namesake was Earl Warren, then chief justice of the U.S. SUPREME COURT. Other members included U.S. Senators John Cooper (R–KY) and Richard Russell (D–GA); U.S. Representatives Hale Boggs (D–LA) and Gerald Ford (R–MI); Allen Dulles, former director of the CENTRAL INTELLIGENCE AGENCY (CIA); and John McCloy, former president of the World Bank. U.S. Solicitor General James Rankin served as the commission's chief counsel, with 14 assistant counsels and 12 additional staffers. Proceedings began on December 3, 1963, and the commission delivered its findings to LBJ on September 24, 1964. After hearing testimony from 552 witnesses and reviewing reports from 10 federal agencies (including the CIA, the FEDERAL BUREAU OF INVESTIGATION (FBI), the SECRET SERVICE and military intelligence), the Warren Commission declared that no evidence existed linking either alleged assassin LEE HARVEY OSWALD or his slayer JACK RUBY to any conspiracy.

Various critics condemned the Warren Commission's findings as a "whitewash," and in fact numerous

Supreme Court chief justice Earl Warren led the Warren Commission to its "lone gunman" verdict in the JFK assassination. (National Archives)

discrepancies (deliberate or otherwise) have been revealed in the commission's report and appended volumes of supporting evidence since 1964. Among the more egregious examples are the following:

- Apparent manipulation of the commission by FBI Director J. EDGAR HOOVER, who announced a "lone-assassin" verdict in the case within hours of JFK's murder and manipulated commission hearings (with help from FBI informant Gerald Ford) toward that end throughout the proceedings.
- Suppression of evidence that both Oswald and Ruby were paid FBI informants, each with significant links to violent right-wing extremist groups and the MAFIA.
- Suppression of testimony from numerous witnesses who placed multiple gunmen at the JFK ASSASSINATION scene on November 22, 1963.

- Manipulation of the ZAPRUDER FILM, which included removal and rearrangement of critical frames depicting bullet impacts on the president.
- Inexplicable rejection of Jack Ruby's offer to document a criminal conspiracy if the commission would transport him safely from Texas to Washington, D.C. They refused, and he subsequently died in jail, his story untold.
- Suppression of FBI evidence that proved that Oswald's obsolete bolt-action rifle was incapable of firing three shots within the commission's mandatory lone-assassin time frame and further demonstrating that its telescopic sight could not be focused on a target.
- Fabrication of a "magic-bullet theory" to explain mismatched wounds allegedly inflicted on Kennedy and Texas Governor John Connally by a single projectile, thereby defying the known laws of physics.

Scores of books—ranging from scholarly tomes to virtual science fiction—have been published since 1965, dissecting the commission's many errors, omissions, and misstatements of fact. Still, leading spokespersons for the so-called LIBERAL MEDIA still champion the Warren Report as the final solution to Kennedy's slaying.

See also DULLES BROTHERS; KENNEDY DYNASTY.

WASHINGTON, George (1732–1799)

George Washington was a man of many parts: planter, surveyor, FREEMASON, slaveholder, early MARIJUANA grower, revolutionary hero, first U.S. president, and Father of His Country all rolled into one. Additionally, Washington's account books brand him as one of America's first war profiteers—and a very creative one, at that. In June 1775, when Washington was appointed to serve as commander in chief of the Colonial Army, Congress offered him a salary of $500 per month. Major generals, the next closest rank to Washington's, received only $166 monthly, and they (along with all other military personnel) were required "to furnish their own Arms and Clothes." Washington, all patriotic magnanimity, declined the offer with the following remarks to Congress:

As to pay, Sir, I beg leave to Assure the Congress that as no pecuniary consideration could have tempted me to have accepted this Arduous employment (at the expense of my domesttic [sic] ease and happiness) I do not wish to make any Proffit [sic] from it. I will keep an exact Account of my expenses. Those I doubt not they will discharge, and that is all I desire.

Eight years later to the month, in June 1783, Washington submitted his expense account to Congress for reimbursement. Instead of the $48,000 he would have earned for that period (at $500 per month, with no allowance for clothing or weapons), Washington billed Congress for a whopping $449,261.51—more than nine times the original salary offered. Among the items reimbursed by Congress, we find the following:

- $175,754.39 for "household" expenses, including servants' pay, groceries, laundry, and "sundries"
- $40,975 paid to spies for "secret service"
- $27,665.30 for Martha Washington to visit her husband in winter quarters at Valley Forge, Pennsylvania, (where his soldiers spent the season starving, often without coats or blankets)
- $9,607.74 for horses and supplies
- $5,411.86 for visits to Congress in Philadelphia
- $1,837.55 for wine
- $1,439 for a custom-made carriage
- $1,407.41 paid to barbers
- $1,274 for a French telescope
- $468 to purchase 20 pounds of tea "for public use"

The latter item, while relatively trivial, is reminiscent of later excesses committed by corrupt entrepreneurs of the MILITARY-INDUSTRIAL COMPLEX. When Congress approved the purchase of tea at $23.40 per pound in 1783, it paved the way for $300 bolts and $1,200 plastic toilet seats.

General George Washington turned a huge profit by declining a flat salary for his service in the Revolutionary War. (Author's collection)

WATERGATE

The mother of all U.S. political scandals began on June 17, 1972, when five burglars were captured in the Democratic National Committee headquarters, located in the Watergate Office Building in Washington, D.C. The five prowlers—Bernard Barker, Virgilio Gonzalez, Eugenio Martinez, James McCord, Jr., and Frank Sturgis—had broken into the same office on June 16 and planted listening devices; they returned one night later to repair defective bugs and/or photograph Democratic Party documents (reports vary). Police searched the prisoners and found a telephone number for E. Howard Hunt, an ex-employee of the CENTRAL INTELLIGENCE AGENCY (CIA), more recently engaged as a strategist with the Republican COMMITTEE TO REELECT THE PRESIDENT (CREEP), a "dirty-tricks" unit organized by President RICHARD NIXON's White House staff. Nixon's press secretary, Ron Ziegler, dismissed the affair as a "third-rate burglary," but it would not be so easily forgotten.

At his arraignment, burglar McCord identified himself to the court as a CIA agent, thus intriguing *Washington Post* reporters Carl Bernstein and Bob Woodward. Their investigation of the break-in, spanning several months, revealed that Nixon had asked the CIA to retard FEDERAL BUREAU OF INVESTIGATION (FBI) investigation of the burglary with spurious claims of a "national security" risk. In fact, Bernstein and Woodward discovered that the Watergate burglary was only one of many illegal actions carried out by CREEP under the direction of Hunt and ex-FBI agent G. Gordon Liddy. Those conspiracies included an abortive plot to burn the BROOKINGS INSTITUTION, a bungled plan to murder journalist JACK ANDERSON, burglaries and wiretaps targeting suspected leakers of Pentagon files to the *New York Times,* collection of illegal campaign donations, and funneling of "hush money" to the Watergate burglars. An anonymous informant, known as "Deep Throat" and recently identified as former assistant director of the FBI, Mark Felt, exposed new dimensions of the plot that were essentially designed to undermine American democracy.

Nixon won a second White House term before most of his staff's criminal activity was revealed,

but he could not forestall the unfolding scandal. The five Watergate burglars, with codefendants Hunt and Liddy, faced trial in Washington on January 8, 1973. All except Liddy and McCord pleaded guilty on reduced charges; the two hold-outs were convicted of burglary, wiretapping, and conspiracy. Angered by evidence that the defendants were bribed to keep silent, Judge John Sirica pronounced 35-year prison terms for the defendants, with an offer of leniency if they decided to cooperate. That offer broke McCord, who promptly implicated CREEP and confessed to perjury.

McCord's admission guaranteed further investigation of the broadening scandal. A committee of the U.S. Senate, chaired by Senator Sam Ervin, was

This diagram depicts the six members of Richard Nixon's staff who resigned as consequences of the Watergate scandal, with President Nixon at the center. (Bettmann/Corbis)

impaneled to probe the Watergate morass. As exposures continued, including testimony that Nixon had secretly recorded every conversation with his staff, high-ranking administration members were implicated in the Watergate crimes. On April 30, 1973, Nixon demanded resignations from his two top aides, H. R. Haldeman and John Ehrlichman—both of whom were subsequently indicted, convicted, and imprisoned. White House counsel John Dean was sacked for testifying honestly before the Ervin Committee, and he went on to turn state's evidence against the president. While assuring the nation that "I am not a crook," Nixon fought disclosure of the White House tapes and then released edited transcripts with a curious 18.5-minute gap in one recording (officially blamed on an "accidental" erasure by Nixon secretary Rose Mary Woods).

The toll of Watergate-related convictions continued, unrelenting. Vice President SPIRO AGNEW resigned in disgrace on October 10, 1973, subsequently pleading guilty to corruption charges dating from his term as governor of Maryland. The conspiracy indictments naming Haldeman and Ehrlichman on multiple counts of perjury and obstructing justice expanded to include Nixon staffers John Mitchell (once Nixon's attorney general and in 1972 his campaign manager); Charles Colson (alleged mastermind of the Brookings Institution arson plot); CREEP boss Jeb Magruder; and a team of White House "plumbers"—Egil Krogh, Robert Mardian, Kenneth Parkinson, and Gordon Strachan—who never let legality obstruct their pursuit of whistleblowers or other White House "enemies." Most pleaded guilty on reduced charges, while the stubborn few were convicted and sentenced to prison.

That left Nixon, resolved to "fight like hell" for his tarnished reputation. On March 1, 1974, a federal grand jury secretly named Nixon as an "unindicted co-conspirator" with seven CREEP stalwarts. On July 24 the U.S. SUPREME COURT overruled Nixon's claims of "executive privilege" and ordered immediate release of all White House tapes. By the time Nixon complied on July 30, the House Judiciary Committee had voted three articles of impeachment, including abuse of power, contempt of Congress, and obstruction of justice. With conviction in the Senate virtually guaranteed, Nixon resigned on August 9, 1974. One month later, on September 8, successor Gerald Ford issued a blanket presidential pardon shielding Nixon from prosecution for any crimes he

may have committed during his term as president. That pardon, in turn, was a major factor in Ford's defeat by Jimmy Carter when he sought election to the White House in 1976.

WEBSTER, William (1924–)

William Webster served with the U.S. Navy in World War II and then practiced law in St. Louis from 1949 to 1969, with an interval of naval duty during the Korean War and brief service as a federal prosecutor in Missouri (1960–61). President RICHARD NIXON appointed Webster a federal judge in 1970, his cases including the peculiar bank-robbery prosecution of defendant John Larry Ray. In 1973 Nixon elevated Webster to the 8th Circuit Court of Appeals, where he remained until President RONALD REAGAN chose him to serve as FEDERAL BUREAU OF INVESTIGATION (FBI) director in February 1978.

Webster's tenure as director was marked by a mixture of reform and repression. He emphasized diversity in hiring and expanded the FBI's range of undercover operations, stressing pursuit of white-collar crimes and the MAFIA until President Reagan curtailed those activities. Webster once boasted that since J. EDGAR HOOVER's death in 1972, there had not been "a single proven case of a violation of constitutional rights" by FBI agents, but he ignored the bureau's persecution of Puerto Rican nationalists and the AMERICAN INDIAN MOVEMENT. Likewise, at the time he made that statement, Webster's G-men were pursuing an identical campaign in the CISPES CASE and harassing other critics of Ronald Reagan's foreign policy in Central America. Reagan, for his part, admired Webster enough to name him director of the CENTRAL INTELLIGENCE AGENCY in 1987. Webster left the FBI on May 26 and spent four years in his new post, retiring in May 1991.

WHITE League

An unmasked successor to the KU KLUX KLAN (KKK), the White League was a racist paramilitary group organized in Louisiana to "redeem" the state from RECONSTRUCTION and restore "home rule" by white Democrats. The movement's epicenter was New Orleans, first city in the South to integrate its police force, while 240 black ex-slaves served in various political posts. A typical recruiting flyer for the White League read:

This cartoon from *Harper's Weekly* depicts the White League's alliance with surviving factions of the early Ku Klux Klan. (Florida State Archives)

Can you bear it longer, that negro [sic] ignorance, solidified in opposition to white intelligence, and led by carpet-bag and scalawag impudence and villainy, shall continue to hold the State, your fortunes and your honor by the throat, while they perpetuate upon you indignities and crimes unparalleled?

Unlike the KKK, whose nightriders generally contented themselves with individual slayings and assaults, the White League staged a full-dress coup d'état in New Orleans on September 14, 1874. Various accounts of the battle between White Leaguers and state MILITIA list between 11 and 27 Republican defenders killed and at least 60 wounded, while the insurrectionists lost 16 dead and 45 injured. Legitimate forces were routed, and the White League seized control of state offices, but Governor William Kellogg had telegraphed President Ulysses Grant while the fight was in progress. Grant dispatched federal troops and a naval squadron of six warships to contain the rebellion, whereupon the White League surrendered and Governor Kellogg resumed his office on September 19. It would require the dubious election of President RUTHERFORD B. HAYES in 1877 to finally restore white rule throughout the South and inaugurate a system of racial discrimination that endured through the mid-20th century.

WHITE slavery

On July 6, 1885, Britain's *Pall Mall Gazette* ran the first installment of a series titled "The Maiden Tribute of Modern Babylon," detailing the alleged abduction and sale of young Englishwomen as sexual slaves in the Middle East. The series sparked outrage throughout Europe and the United States, while popularizing *white slavery* as a synonym for compulsory prostitution. By the early 1900s the term was used without regard for a victim's race, although visions of white virgins subjected to rape by nonwhites touched the rawest possible nerve in a racist society. On June 25, 1910, Congress passed the White Slave Traffic Act, better known as the Mann Act (after its primary sponsor, Illinois representative James Mann). The statute imposed a maximum 10-year prison sentence and/or fines for anyone convicted of transporting females across state lines "for the purpose of prostitution or for any other immoral purpose."

The latter phrase granted FEDERAL BUREAU OF INVESTIGATION agents free rein to investigate the sex lives of various public and private figures with no link to any prostitution syndicate, including black boxer Jack Johnson, KU KLUX KLAN leader Edward Clarke, and musician Chuck Berry. Ironically, the statute was rarely (if ever) used against pimps or others who maintained stables of prostitutes (sometimes enforcing discipline by force or by dosing their "stable" with HEROIN). State laws were used to prosecute MAFIA leader CHARLES "LUCKY" LUCIANO for compulsory prostitution in 1936, and he spent 10 years in New York prisons before he was liberated in the wake of OPERATION UNDERWORLD.

Despite the best efforts of J. EDGAR HOOVER and various local police chiefs, white slavery was not eradicated in America, and in fact it remains a global problem to the present day. During World War II Japanese forces kidnapped and enslaved an estimated 200,000 "comfort women" throughout the Far East, most of them dragooned at gunpoint from occupied CHINA, KOREA, and the PHILIPPINES. A half-century later, "ethnic cleansing" in BOSNIA-HERZEGOVINA included the kidnapping of at least 30,000 women and girls, who were confined in officially sanctioned "rape camps" by Serbian soldiers. Other victims from the fractured former state of Yugoslavia were shipped abroad as prostitutes—more than 1,400 sent to England in 1998 alone, according to the British Home Office. In 1997 Russian authorities estimated that 10,000 females from the former Soviet Union had been enslaved since 1991 by members of the RUSSIAN MAFIA posing as legitimate entrepreneurs.

In the United States, meanwhile, members of various MOTORCYCLE GANGS are known to kidnap young women or "turn out" their own "old ladies" for service in strip clubs, massage parlors, and brothels. In 1978 the Texas House Select Committee on Child Pornography investigated reports of "slave auctions" conducted in Dallas, Houston, and elsewhere across the state, where children transported from Mexico were allegedly sold to wealthy pedophiles. At about the same time author Robin Lloyd informed the U.S. House Select Committee on Education and Labor of a reverse traffic in Anglo children sold to Mexican pornographers, sometimes for use in SNUFF FILMS. As recently as January 2003, police in Detroit broke up a ring that kidnapped victims as young as 13 years of age and forced them into prostitution.

WICCA letters

Allegedly intercepted by police after a 1981 meeting of the Witches International Coven Council in Mexico, the so-called Wicca letters are a bizarre outline for global domination by occultists, similar in many respects to the fraudulent *PROTOCOLS OF THE ELDERS OF ZION*. Widely published—and presumably believed—by fundamentalist Christians, the document is dubious at best. No such organization as the WICC has been uncovered to date, and enumeration of conspiratorial goals in this manner would seem to be a risky proposition. As normally presented, the "letters" read:

1. *To bring about the covens, both black and white magic, into one, and to have the arctress to govern all—ACCOMPLISHED;*
2. *To bring about personal debts causing discord and disharmony within families—ACCOMPLISHED;*
3. *To remove or educate the "new age youth" by:*
   a. *infiltrating boys/girls clubs and big sister/brother programs*
   b. *infiltrating schools, having prayers removed, having teachers teach about drugs, sex, freedoms*
   c. *instigating and promoting rebellion against parents and all authority*
   d. *promoting equal rights for youth—ACCOMPLISHED;*
4. *To gain access to all people's backgrounds and vital information by:*
   a. *use of computers*
   b. *convenience*
   c. *infiltration—ACCOMPLISHED;*
5. *To have laws changed to benefit our ways, such as:*
   a. *removing children from the home environment and placing them in our foster homes*
   b. *mandatory placement of children in our day-care centers*
   c. *increased taxes*
   d. *open drug and pornography market to everyone—NOT YET ACCOMPLISHED;*
6. *To destroy government agencies by:*
   a. *overspending*
   b. *public opinion*
   c. *being on the offensive always, opposing, demonstrating, demoralizing—NOT YET ACCOMPLISHED;*
7. *Not to be revealed until all else has been accomplished. Target date for revelation—June 21, 1986—the beginning of the Summer Solstice and great feast on the Satanic calendar.*

Author Art Lyons reportedly traced the Wicca Letters to a police "cult expert" in San Diego, California, but there the trail ended. Some ultraconservatives might say that the listed goals were now "accomplished;" yet no black magic Renaissance has yet occurred in the United States.

WINTER Hill Gang

Boston's mostly Irish Winter Hill Gang was organized by James ("Whitey") Bulger in the early 1960s after his parole from federal prison on a bank-robbery charge. By the decade's end Bulger's syndicate dominated racketeering, gambling, and drug sales in Boston and environs, edging out the local MAFIA's Angiulo family for control of lucrative turf. Bulger's ascendancy was aided in equal parts by his ruthless temperament, his brother's election to serve as president of the Massachusetts state senate, and collaboration from the FEDERAL BUREAU OF INVESTIGATION's

(FBI) Boston field office. G-man John Connolly, Jr., was a boyhood acquaintance of the Bulger brothers, and he welcomed the chance to recruit Winter Hill gang leaders for the bureau's "Top Echelon Informant Program," ignoring various criminal activities in return for tips about the Mafia. For the next three decades, as detailed by FBI historian Robert Kessler, "the FBI ran a protection racket for the Winter Hill Gang in return for their information on the New England Mafia and the ego gratification of recruiting informants."

Connolly and other agents also accepted cash from the gang while joining in the frame-ups of four defendants for a 1965 murder they did not commit. The victim in that case, small-time mobster Edward Deegan, was killed by FBI informants Joseph Barboza and Vincent Flemmi, with the bureau warned of their plan in advance. After failing to prevent the murder, Connolly and other G-men assisted Barboza and Flemmi in accusing four innocent suspects—Louis Greco, Peter Limone, Joseph Salvati, and Henry Tameleo—of killing Deegan. All four were convicted at trial on perjured testimony and received life prison terms. Greco and Tameleo died in custody, while Limone and Salvati were finally exonerated and released in 2000. By that time Barboza was dead, John Connolly was retired from the FBI, and Whitey Bulger was a globe-trotting fugitive from justice on narcotics charges. Barry Mawn, new agent in charge of the FBI's Boston office, discovered in 2000 that Connolly had warned Bulger of pending federal indictments in 1995, permitting his old friend to flee Boston. (As of November 2004 Bulger remains a "Top Ten" fugitive, with a $10 million price on his head.)

At Connolly's trial in May 2002, prosecutors described him as "a Winter Hill Gang operative masquerading as an FBI agent." Jurors convicted him on bribery and other charges, resulting in a 10-year prison sentence. Another ex-agent from Boston admitted similar crimes on the witness stand, but the legal statute of limitations saved him from prosecution. At last report, Connolly and the FBI still faced wrongful-death lawsuits for some $35 million, filed by relatives of murder victims John Callahan, Richard Castucci, and Brian Halloran. Plaintiffs in those cases charge that Connolly and other G-men leaked information to Bulger's crew, which resulted in their loved ones being murdered.

"WISE Use" movement

Wise use is the deceptive term applied to a network of groups and individuals active since the 1980s in a campaign to roll back environmental protection legislation in the United States and western Canada. Activist Ron Arnold, often named as the father of Wise Use and a self-styled follower of Mohandas Ghandi, once said of environmentalists, "We're out to kill the fuckers. We're simply trying to eliminate them. Our goal is to destroy environmentalism once and for all." To that end various groups including the American Legislative Exchange Council, People for the West, the American Farm Bureau Federation, the Fairness to Land Owners Committee, the "Share" groups of British Columbia, and others are funded by industries involved in logging, mining, OIL or gas drilling, and agribusiness to oppose environmental legislation at the state and federal levels. An example of the movement's honesty is seen in the misnamed Environmental Conservation Organization, a group created by leaders of the Land Improvement Contractors Association to lobby *against* conservation laws. Wise Use spokespersons typically denounce organizations such as the Sierra Club and the Wilderness Society as "hate groups," while labeling individual environmentalists as "tree huggers," "eco-Nazis," "pagans," and so forth.

In essence, Wise Use leaders are industry front men (and women) pursuing two broad goals: First, removal of all constraints on the use of private property, including present limits set for reasons of public health, safety, and environmental protection; second, unlimited access to all public lands for unrestricted logging, mining, drilling, motorized recreation (off-roading, snowmobiles, etc.), and any other commercial enterprise. Henry Yake, president of the Blue Ribbon Coalition (supporting off-road motorcycle racing and similar activities), spoke for his colleagues in July 1990 when he told the press, "Wilderness has no economic value, no timbering, no oil and gas production, no mining, no livestock grazing, no motorized recreation."

In 2001 Wise Use found champions in President George W. Bush and his Secretary of the Interior, Gale Norton (a millionaire former lobbyist for logging and strip-mining companies). Norton's hand-picked "ambassador to the West" is Deputy Secretary J. Steven Giles, formerly an energy industry lobbyist in Washington. The Bush-Norton-Giles regime has pursued a list of antienvironmental policies that includes widespread logging in national forests ("to prevent forest fires"), oil and gas drilling in national parks ("for national security"), passage of a federal "Clear Skies Initiative" that permits *higher* levels of industrial air pollution, increased levels of arsenic in drinking water, and reinstatement of an 1872 mining law that allows mining on public lands even in cases where "substantial or irreparable harm" to the environment may result.

In addition to their political efforts, Wise Use groups do not shrink from criminal activity. In 1990 unknown terrorists tried to kill EARTH FIRST! leaders Judi Bari and Daryl Cherney with a car bomb. When that attack failed, agents of the FEDERAL BUREAU OF INVESTIGATION and the OAKLAND POLICE DEPARTMENT next tried to frame Bari and Cherney for planting the bomb themselves—a conspiracy exposed in federal court when Earth First! sued the agencies responsible. Other environmentalists have also suffered threats, assaults, arson, and attempted murder by individuals espousing Wise Use rhetoric; G-men and some police departments remain curiously aloof, focused single-mindedly on "eco-terrorists" of the EARTH LIBERATION FRONT and similar groups. In April 1992 a group of Wise Use thugs attacked Florida environmentalist Stephanie McGuire, raping her, slashing her with razors, and brandishing firearms. McGuire's life was saved when her dog attacked the rapists and drove them away, but Taylor County sheriff's deputies dropped the case after perfunctory investigation, and spokespersons for the Florida Department of Law Enforcement hinted that McGuire's wounds were "self-inflicted."

A curious sidebar on the Wise Use movement is its link to the Unification Church, led by KOREA's Rev. Sun Myung Moon. The controversial Rev. Moon—once convicted of tax evasion in the United States, publicly linked to operations of South Korea's SECRET POLICE, and also involved in the IRAN-CONTRA CONSPIRACY—supports the Wise Use agenda in his ultraconservative newspaper, the *Washington Times*. Moon's American Freedom Coalition played a pivotal role in the early Wise Use movement. Ron Arnold himself felt compelled to deny "Moonie" ties in 1989. Far-right politics aside, Moon's interest in the Wise Use movement may be explained by a 1990 survey of the minister's financial empire, published by the conservative *U.S. News & World Report*. According to that piece, at least 335 international companies were affiliated with Moon's church,

producing everything from military weapons and computers to clothing and soft drinks. In the United States, Moon owned at least 150 companies involved in media, real estate, and commercial fishing—including boats, canneries, processing, wholesale distribution, and 65 sushi restaurants. In 1984 a report from JAPAN's national bar association declared that Moon's various high-pressure sales schemes had bilked consumers out of some $165 million.

See also BUSH DYNASTY; TERRORISM.

WORLD Trade Center bombing (1993)

At 12:18 P.M. on February 26, 1993, a massive explosion rocked the World Trade Center in Lower Manhattan. The blast killed six persons, injured more than 1,000, and trapped thousands more in the Twin Towers office complex while emergency workers swarmed over the scene. Initial speculation centered on transformer explosion, but agents of the FEDERAL BUREAU OF INVESTIGATION (FBI) and the BUREAU OF ALCOHOL, TOBACCO AND FIREARMS discovered remains of a car bomb in the basement garage. A vehicle identification number led G-men to Jersey City, where the Ford van had been rented on February 23 to Mohammed Salameh, a 25-year-old Palestinian from Jordan. Soon after the bombing, Salameh had reported the van stolen and demanded a refund of his $400 fee. A background check on Salameh identified him as a follower of Sheik Omar Abdel Rahman, a cleric expelled from Egypt in 1981 for advocating overthrow of the Egyptian government.

G-men were waiting on March 4, 1993, when Salameh returned to the rental office. A search of his apartment and a storage unit yielded chemicals similar to those used in the bombing. The FBI lab, meanwhile, had problems analyzing the crime-scene evidence. Technicians squabbled over the bomb's composition, and one employee complained that "mistakes were made" in the process. Lab supervisors pressured the dissenters to keep silent while street agents searched for more suspects. One of those, Ahmed Mohammed Ajaj, had been incarcerated since his arrest with bomb-making manuals at JFK Airport on September 1, 1992, but G-men still named him as part of the plot. Another defendant, Mahmud Abouhalima, was captured in Cairo and returned to the United States for trial. Together, the accused were charged with conspiracy, explosive destruction of property, and interstate transportation of explosives. Their trial began in September 1993 and lasted five months and included testimony from 207 witnesses. Jurors convicted the defendants on March 4, 1994; two months later Judge Kevin Duffy sentenced them to matching 240-year prison terms.

With that victory behind them and two more suspects still hiding abroad, FBI leaders sought more conspirators in New Jersey. They were encouraged by Emad Salem, a former Egyptian Army officer and confidant of Sheik Rahman, who was also an informant for the FBI and NEW YORK POLICE. Salem had spied on the mosque's congregation for nearly two years, and he now reported a series of terror attacks in the planning stage; targets included the UNITED NATIONS building, the FBI's New York field office, the George Washington Bridge, plus the Holland and Lincoln Tunnels. He arranged for his comrades to rent a "safe house" bugged by G-men, where their every word was captured on tape. Raiders arrested five of the would-be terrorists on June 24, 1994, allegedly while building bombs. Sheik Rahman and seven others were picked up later, all 14 charged with conspiracy to bomb New York landmarks and murder various prominent persons in the United States and EGYPT.

The eight-month conspiracy trial began on January 30, 1995. FBI lab technician Fred Whitehurst testified as a witness for the defense, describing various forensic reports as fraudulent. When Emad Salem took the stand, he admitted taping many conversations with his FBI and NYPD handlers. Among the startling revelations on those tapes were a New York police officer's suggestion that Salem should demand a $1.5 million informant's fee from the FBI and "settle" for $1 million. Most shocking, however, was the dialogue indicating that FBI agents knew of the Trade Center bombing in advance and did nothing to stop it.

On one tape, Agent John Anticev is heard telling Salem to learn where the defendants stored their explosives, explaining, "We'll just know where stuff exists and where it is, and then we'll make our move. There's no danger, you know. We can be sneaky and take our time."

After the Trade Center blast, on April 1, 1993, Salem rebuked Anticev for failing to prevent the bombing. "They told me that 'we want to set this,'" he declared. "'What's the right place to put this?' You were informed. Everything is ready. The day and the time. Boom. Lock them up and that's that. That's why I feel so bad."

According to Salem, Anticev's FBI supervisor proposed a plan to arrest the bombers without damage to the World Trade Center. "He requested to meet me in the hotel," Salem reminded Anticev on tape. "He requested to make me to testify and if he didn't push for that, we'll be going building the bomb with a phony powder and grabbing the people who was involved in it. But since you, we didn't do that." Later, speaking to Agent Nancy Floyd about Anticev, Salem told her, "He [Anticev] said, 'I don't think that the New York [FBI] people would like the things out of the New York office to go to Washington, D.C.'" Agent Floyd replied, "Well, of course not, because they don't want to get their butts chewed." Salem told Floyd, "Since the bomb went off I feel terrible. I feel bad. I feel here is people who don't listen." Her response: "Hey, I mean it wasn't like you didn't try and I didn't try. You can't force people to do the right thing."

Of the 15 defendants on trial, four pleaded guilty, one turned state's evidence against his friends, and the rest were convicted on October 1, 1995. Three months later Rahman and defendant El-Sayid Nosair received life sentences with no parole; the rest drew prison terms ranging from 25 to 57 years. While the trial was still in progress, on February 7, 1995, fugitive Ramzi Yousef was captured in Pakistan and returned to the United States. The last alleged plotter, Eyad Najim, was caught in Jordan and delivered to U.S. authorities on August 2, 1995. The pair faced trial together in August 1997, and both were convicted on November 12. Najim and Yousef received 240-year prison terms; they were also slapped with uncollectable $250,000 fines and ordered to pay $10 million in restitution to their victims.

WRATH of God

In the predawn hours of September 5, 1972, Palestinian terrorists from the BLACK SEPTEMBER group invaded the Olympic compound in Munich, GERMANY, where they killed two Israeli athletes and took nine more hostage. Subsequently, while the invaders attempted to flee with their captives in helicopters provided by German authorities, police opened fire and a shootout ensued, killing all nine hostages, five Palestinians, and one police officer. ISRAEL retaliated three days later with air strikes against suspected terrorist camps in LEBANON and SYRIA, killing at least 66 Arabs and wounding hundreds more. Israeli troops also invaded Lebanon, ostensibly to engage Palestinian guerrillas hiding there. Unsatisfied with that broad and rather indiscriminate response to the Munich massacre, Israeli Premier Golda Meir and Defense Minister Moshe Dayan created a secret retaliation force, officially known as Committee X, more commonly dubbed the Wrath of God (WoG). Its goal, simply stated, was to find and kill Palestinian resistance leaders—or failing that, to render them helpless in exile.

To carry out that mission, Committee X drafted members of the MOSSAD's *kidon* ("bayonet") assassination unit, led by Mike Harari. Operating from a covert base in Geneva, Switzerland, the Wrath of God set out to liquidate 11 specific targets, including: Kamal Adwan, FATAH's chief of sabotage operations in Israeli-occupied territories; Hussein al-Chir, alleged liaison between the KGB and the Palestine Liberation Organization (PLO) in CYPRUS; Dr. Basil al-Kubaisi, logistics officer of the Popular Front for the Liberation of Palestine (PFLP); Mohammed Boudia, a PLO agent in Europe; Abu Daoud (Black September); Dr. Wadi Haddad, alleged "chief terrorist" of the PFLP; Mahmoud Hamshiri, a PLO member and suspected coordinator of the Munich raid; Kamal Nassir, chief spokesman for the PLO Executive Committee; Ali Hassan Salameh, chief planner of the Munich attack; Abu Yussuf, a high-ranking PLO leader; and Wael Zwaiter, a cousin of PLO leader Yasser Arafat, allegedly responsible for terrorist acts in Europe.

Zwaiter was the first to die, gunned down by Israeli assassins outside Rome on October 16, 1972. A telephone rigged with explosives killed Mahmoud Hamshiri on December 8, 1972. During the next few months, Israeli counterterrorists killed al-Kubaisi, al-Chir, Boudia, and Zaid Muchassi (a late addition to the list, who had replaced al-Chir on Cyprus). The Geneva hit team was then recalled to Israel, but the Wrath of God campaign was not finished. In April 1973 Israel launched "Operation Spring of Youth," a wholesale murder campaign that killed at least 100 Palestinian activists (while sending two Israeli hit men home in caskets). Ali Hassan Salameh was finally traced to Lillehammer, NORWAY, on July 21, 1973, but the assigned shooters killed an innocent Moroccan waiter, Ahmed Bouchiki, by mistake. Six months later, on January 12, 1974, three Israeli assassins were killed during a second bungled attempt on Salameh, this time in Switzerland. On the third attempt to snare Salameh, in London, one member of the *kidon* team was killed in his hotel room by a female assassin masquerading as a prostitute. Other WoG members avenged that slaying on August 21, 1974, when they tracked the woman down and killed her at her home near Amsterdam. Mike Harari then aborted the order to kill Salameh, but his insubordinate shooters pressed to a fourth botched attempt wherein armed sentries routed a three-man Israeli team from Salameh's hideout on Gibraltar. It would be 1979 before Mossad hunters finally overtook Salameh, killing him with a car bomb in the heart of strife-torn Beirut.

That murder was supposedly the last contract carried out by Wrath of God assassins, but rumors persist that the unit was never demobilized—or, at least, that it remained active much longer than Israeli leaders will admit. One victim often mentioned (but never confirmed by Israeli sources) is GERALD VICTOR BULL, murdered in Brussels during 1990 while engaged in manufacturing a huge "super gun" for IRAQ.

See also TERRORISM.

X, Malcolm (1925–1965)

The son of an outspoken black separatist, Malcolm Little was born in Omaha on May 19, 1925. The family moved later to Michigan where Malcolm's father was killed by a streetcar on September 28, 1931. (Malcolm suspected that the accident was really murder, planned by a faction of the KU KLUX KLAN.) Convicted of larceny in January 1946, Malcolm converted to the teachings of Elijah Muhammad while in prison. Released in 1952 he joined the NATION OF ISLAM (NOI), adopting the name *Malcolm X*. Three weeks later, on September 23, 1952, the FEDERAL BUREAU OF INVESTIGATION (FBI) began surveillance of Malcolm that continued for the rest of his life. G-men reported his 1961 meeting with Georgia KKK leaders, his subscription to newsletters published by the Fair Play for CUBA Committee, and his description of the 1963 JFK ASSASSINATION as a case of "chickens coming home to roost." Elijah Muhammad expelled Malcolm from the NOI over that episode, and the rift became irreparable in February 1964 when a former aide in New York warned Malcolm of an NOI plot to bomb his car.

In March 1964 Malcolm told *Ebony* magazine that Muhammad's Black Muslims have "got to kill me. They can't afford to let me live. . . . I know where the bodies are buried, and if they press me, I'll exhume some." Death threats were by now routine, but they struck close to home when Malcolm's house was firebombed at 2:46 A.M. on February 14, 1965. One week later, on February 21, Malcolm was shot and killed while speaking at Harlem's Audubon Ballroom. Early reports declared that three gunmen were captured at the murder scene, but police later claimed only two were arrested (with a third jailed two days later). All three suspects were linked to the Nation of Islam. On the night of Malcolm's death, an FBI informant gave G-men one of the pistols used in the murder.

Suspects Talmadge Thayer, Norman 3X Butler, and Thomas 15X Johnson were indicted for murder on March 10, 1965. At trial in March 1966, Thayer admitted that he and three others were hired to kill Malcolm, but he insisted that Butler and Johnson were innocent. Johnson's wife swore he was not present at the shooting, but jurors convicted all three defendants on March 11. A month later, all three were sentenced to life imprisonment. Conspiracy theories suggest that Malcolm was slain by some combination of the FBI, the CENTRAL INTELLIGENCE AGENCY, and MAFIA leaders who resented his June 1964 call for "an all-out war against organized crime" in black communities across the United States.

YAKUZA

Like the Sicilian MAFIA which they emulate in many ways, JAPAN's Yakuza crime syndicates sprang from uncertain origins, obscured today by fantasy and folklore. Some researches claim that the name *Yakuza* is numerical, deriving from Japanese terms for the numbers 8 (*ya*), 9 (*ku*) and 3 (*za*). Together, they make 20, a worthless hand in the card game *oicho-kabu* wherein players strive for a maximum hand of 19. Thus, the Yakuza welcomes recruits deemed worthless misfits by society at large, providing them with a strong and lucrative "family."

Various published accounts date the Yakuza's beginnings anywhere from 1612 to the mid-19th century. In the earlier version Yakuza pioneers were freelance samurais known as *ronin* or *kabuki-mono* ("crazy ones"), who formed roving bands of outlaws in the manner of America's Wild West two centuries later. Another version holds that early Yakuza were actually drawn from the ranks of *machi-yakko* ("city servants"), who armed themselves to defend their rural communities against the *kabuki-mono*. Yet another version of history described the Yakuza as rooted in a 17th-century alliance of urban gamblers (*bakuto*) and street vendors (*tekiya*) who swore loyalty among themselves and prospered in defiance of prevailing law. All sources agree that rival Yakuza syndicates were well established throughout Japan by the mid-to-late 19th century, flourishing in support of various right-wing nationalist groups between the 1920s and the end of World War II.

After Japan's defeat in 1945, Allied occupation forces found it useful to collaborate with right-wing Yakuza (*unyoke*) in opposition to leftists of communist political parties and labor unions. As elsewhere throughout the world, the Pentagon and the CENTRAL INTELLIGENCE AGENCY forged alliances with organized criminal groups to harass, torment, or murder individuals perceived as tools of RUSSIA or CHINA in the cold-war game of world domination. Between 1958 and 1963 an estimated 5,200 Yakuza gangs operated throughout Japan, boasting an estimated total membership of 184,000, which exceeded the manpower of Japan's postwar army. Modern membership estimates, admittedly imprecise, typically range between 90,000 and 100,000 active syndicate mobsters. Yakuza sources of profit run the full gamut of organized criminal activities, including prostitution and narcotics, smuggling of contraband (ranging from stolen property and weapons to illegal immigrants), extortion, gambling, and all manner of theft and fraud. Widespread corruption keeps the syndicates in business, with a twist. Whereas the Mafia and other ethnic syndicates usually operate behind the scenes in legitimate business, it is not uncommon for Japanese corporate leaders to be identified as friends or active members of the Yakuza.

Two things that set Yakuza mobsters apart from their peers around the world are the practice of full-body tattooing and the finger-cutting ritual called *yubitsume*. Tattoos tell a gangster's life story while identifying his Yakuza gang or clan. Courage is demonstrated by insistence that the tattoos be applied with primitive bamboo needles, an agonizing process that may take years to complete a neck-to-ankles "suit" of colored images. In *yubitsume*, mobsters who have failed at some task or embarrassed their clan offer apology be severing joints of their fingers one at a time, presenting the bloody appendages to their commanding officer. Police and journalists thus find it possible to identify Yakuza members—and to chart their relative ineptitude—by counting fingers that remain.

Worldwide today, the Yakuza is recognized as collaborating with the Chinese TRIADS, the Mafia, and various other syndicated criminal groups to transport HEROIN, COCAINE, illegal weapons, sex slaves, and other contraband items in a 21st-century world where boundaries have little meaning and money speaks louder than ever to corrupt police and politicians. From LAS VEGAS to Toronto, London, Paris, and Hong Kong, the Yakuza have made their presence felt without significant interference from law-enforcement agencies.

YALTA Conference

Often cited as the unofficial beginning of the cold war, the Yalta Conference of February 4–11, 1945, was a strategic meeting of the "Big Three" leaders in World War II—U.S. President Franklin Roosevelt, British Prime Minister Winston Churchill, and Soviet Premier JOSEPH STALIN. Convened at Yalta in the Russian Crimea, the meeting (whose full minutes remained classified until 1947) essentially outlined Allied plans for the remainder of the war and disposition of the postwar world. The attendees confirmed their insistence on GERMANY's unconditional surrender, with division of that nation into four zones governed by Britain, FRANCE, the United States, and RUSSIA. Plans were also laid for a postwar UNITED NATIONS organization, including France and CHINA as dominant members. Stalin agreed to declare war on Japan within three months of Germany's surrender, in return for which Russia was granted joint control (with China) of occupied Manchuria. As part of the Yalta agreement, U.S. and British forces in Germany slowed their advance west of the Rhine and permitted Russian troops to capture Berlin, where ADOLF HITLER committed suicide in April 1945. Sub-

sequent Russian advances in Eastern Europe, the "loss" of China to COMMUNISM, and allegations of a U.N. plot to impose "one-world government" encouraged speculation that the Yalta Conference was part of a global "sell-out" to Stalin and the theoretical Red conspiracy to dominate planet Earth. President Roosevelt, discouraged and in failing health, said of Yalta in the weeks before his death, "It wasn't perfect, but it was the best I could do."

YEMEN

Roman legions invaded ancient Yemen in the first century A.D. to capture the lucrative trading post at Aden. Ethiopians and Persians followed in the sixth century, and Yemen converted to Islam in 628. The Rassite dynasty of the Muslim Zaidi sect dominated politics in northern Yemen from the 10th century until 1962, while TURKEY occupied the land from 1538 until 1918. In 1962 a pro-Egyptian military coup captured the country's northern half and proclaimed a Yemen Arab Republic, supported by EGYPT and RUSSIA in its civil war against royalists in the south (aided by JORDAN and SAUDI ARABIA), ending with defeat of the royalists in 1969. A new Republic of Yemen was born in May 1990, but traditional north-south conflicts flared again four years later with the outbreak of another civil war. Once again the superior northern forces emerged triumphant, but their victory brought no semblance of peace. Yemen's first free election in decades was held in April 1997 and witnessed an overwhelming victory for a party known as the General People's Congress. Unsatisfied with that result, a radical Islamic group—the Aden-Abyan Islamic Army—began to kidnap Western tourists in 1998–99. That struggle continues today, with rebel leader Zein Al-Abidine al-Mihdar battling to overthrow the parliamentary government and establish a fundamentalist Muslim state on the pattern of IRAN. Meanwhile, in October 2000, 17 U.S. sailors aboard the destroyer *Cole* were killed and another 37 wounded in a suicide attack by terrorists of AL-QAEDA, led by Osama bin Laden.

See also BIN LADEN FAMILY; TERRORISM.

Y2KAOS

"Y2Kaos" was the nickname assigned by some conspiracists to a chain reaction of disastrous events predicted for January 1, 2000 (Year 2000 or Y2K). Prior to the event, it was presumed that many computers would be unable to distinguish dates in the year 2000 from those in 1900 since both are represented by a double 0 in mathematical shorthand (for example, 1/1/00). That failure, theorists declared, would cause a global "crash" of vital computers that control every aspect of modern life from credit and finance to utilities and military defense systems. The predictions for New Year's Day 2000 ranged from worldwide economic breakdowns and sweeping shortages of various commodities to invasions of the United States carried out under cover of the presumed security blackout. While disaster was widely predicted, principal spokespeople for the Y2Kaos theory included U.S. MILITIA groups, right-wing Christian TELEVANGELISTS (led by Pat Robertson), and various computer firms hawking software designed to prevent breakdowns on New Year's Eve. In fact, nothing happened, either on January 1, 2000, or a year later when the 21st century actually began on January 1, 2001. Thus, Y2Kaos slapped latter-day prophets with their greatest disappointment since Seventh-Day Adventists predicted the second coming of JESUS CHRIST in 1844.

ZAIN, Fred

Serologist Fred Zain was employed for 13 years at the West Virginia State Police crime laboratory and later in Texas before investigators turned up problems with his work. Like JOYCE GILCHRIST, Zain now stands accused of faking test results and testifying falsely under oath in felony cases, sending numerous innocent defendants to prison. Once revered as "a god" by West Virginia prosecutors, Zain was discredited in 1993 when West Virginia's Supreme Court ordered a review of every case on which he worked, ruling that "as a matter of law, any testimonial or documentary evidence offered by Zain at any time should be deemed invalid, unreliable and inadmissible."

Zain began his forensic career in 1977, building a reputation as an expert who could solve the most difficult cases and assure prosecutors of convictions. Those prosecutors were presumably unaware of his tactics, but his supervisors should have been suspicious. In some cases Zain testified to positive results for tests the lab could not perform since it lacked the proper equipment, and yet none of his superiors objected. In 1985 FEDERAL BUREAU OF INVESTIGATION lab directors warned Zain's boss that Zain had lied about his credentials to obtain his job, but Zain was not dismissed. At least two other lab employees also complained about Zain's methods and were likewise ignored. Zain's reputation began to unravel in 1991 after an alleged rapist

convicted on Zain's testimony was exonerated by DNA evidence.

Zain, meanwhile, had left West Virginia for Texas in 1989. Alerted by the West Virginia controversy, Texas prosecutors charged Zain with perjury and jury tampering in one case, but the charges were dismissed because the statute of limitations had expired. In 1994 Zain was indicted for perjury in West Virginia. One count of the indictment was dismissed prior to trial; jurors acquitted Zain of a second charge and deadlocked on the third. Another West Virginia grand jury indicted Zain for fraud in March 1998, but a judge dismissed the case nine months later on grounds that the state could not be a victim of fraud. That ruling was reversed in 1999, and Zain also faces a new charge in Texas, though legal delays have postponed both trials beyond press time. If he avoids prison time, Zain must answer a $10 million civil lawsuit from Jack Davis, a Texas resident falsely convicted of murder on Zain's testimony.

ZAMBIA

British empire-builder Cecil Rhodes gained his first foothold in modern-day Zambia in 1889 when he won mining concessions from King Lewanika of the Barotse tribe. White settlers quickly invaded the region and seized control from indigenous peoples, ruling first in the name of the British SOUTH AFRICA

Company and after 1924 as the British colony of Rhodesia. Between 1953 and 1964 Northern and Southern Rhodesia were joined with Nyasaland (now MALAWI) as the Federation of Rhodesia and Nyasaland. On October 24, 1964, Northern Rhodesia became the independent state of Zambia, affiliated with the British Commonwealth of Nations under President Kenneth Kaunda. Severance of ties to Britain in 1965 severely damaged Zambia's economy, a crisis exacerbated 10 years later by the collapse of global copper prices. Meanwhile, in 1972 President Kaunda outlawed all opposition parties, establishing himself as Zambia's de facto dictator. Thus he ruled by brute force until 1991 when a series of riots and popular uprisings forced Kaunda to permit multiparty elections, thus ensuring his own defeat by reform candidate Frederick Chiluba. Barred by law from seeking a third term in 2001, Chiluba handpicked successor Levy Mwanawasa and saw him installed as president in January 2002, despite loud complaints of wholesale election fraud. Six months later, Mwanawasa asserted his independence by accusing Chiluba of stealing millions from the public treasury. (No criminal charges were filed.) Famine threatened Zambia in 2002, but Mwanawasa refused foreign donations of genetically engineered FRANKENFOODS, which he denounced as "poison."

ZAPRUDER film

Dallas dressmaker Abraham Zapruder was one of several hundred eyewitnesses to the JFK ASSASSINATION on November 22, 1963. Unlike most of those present, however, Zapruder had a Bell & Howell 8-millimeter movie camera with a telephoto lens, and his 22-second film of President Kennedy's murder is regarded by many observers as the most compelling evidence of a conspiracy involving multiple snipers. In its original form, the Zapruder film posed two crucial problems for the WARREN COMMISSION's lone-assassin verdict. First, it shows Kennedy struck by two separate shots within a time frame impossible for LEE HARVEY OSWALD's antique bolt-action rifle. Likewise, the explosive impact of the second shot—with blood and brain tissue bursting from the back of Kennedy's head—seems to indicate beyond doubt that at least one shot came from in front of the presidential motorcade, while Oswald (allegedly) fired from the rear.

Further suggestions of conspiracy were raised when the Warren Commission, in its final report, scrambled the order of frames from Zapruder's film to show JFK's head jerking *forward* on impact from the second shot, a blatant manipulation of evidence which Federal Bureau of Investigation director J. EDGAR HOOVER dismissed as an innocent "printing error." Further tampering occurred after Time-Life Corporation purchased the Zapruder film for $150,000, keeping the master copy under wraps and out of public view for years after the assassination. On December 6, 1963, after Dallas physicians reported finding a bullet entry wound in JFK's throat—a physical impossibility if Oswald was the

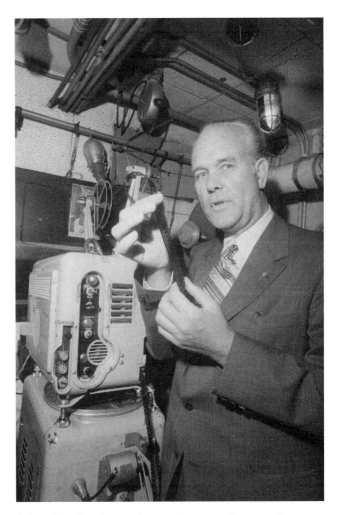

Col. L. Fletcher Prouty, former Pentagon liaison officer, reviews the Zapruder film of the assassination of President Kennedy, prior to a press screening where afterward he urged Congress to reopen the investigation. (Bettmann/Corbis)

only gunman—*Life* magazine retorted that Zapruder's film "shows the President turning his body around to the right as he waves to someone in the crowd. His throat is exposed—toward the sniper's nest [behind him]—just before he clutches it." In fact, the film shows nothing of the kind. The *Life* report was a complete fabrication, unchallenged while the film remained in Time-Life's sole possession.

In 1971 researcher David Lifton viewed a copy of the Zapruder film at Time-Life's Los Angeles office. He found "splices on the film that had never been mentioned by Time-Life," and reported that JFK's head was "blacked out" in frames following the lethal head shot. Five years later, a lawsuit under the Freedom of Information Act forced the CENTRAL INTELLIGENCE AGENCY (CIA) to release various documents, including an admission that the CIA had taken custody of the Zapruder film "within days of the assassination." Lifton later wrote:

In my view, previously unreported CIA possession of the Zapruder film compromised the film's value as evidence: (1) the forward motion of Kennedy's head, for one frame preceding frame 313, might be the result of an altered film, and if that was so, it made the theory of a forward high-angle shot . . . completely unnecessary; (2) an altered film might also explain why the occipital area [of JFK's skull], where the Dallas doctors saw a wound, always appears suspiciously dark, whereas a large wound appears on the forward, right-hand side of the head, where the Dallas doctors saw no wound at all.

See also KENNEDY DYNASTY; JFK ASSASSINATION.

ZIMBABWE

Once known as Southern Rhodesia, the region of present-day Zimbabwe was settled by British colonists and missionaries in the 1850s, displacing Nguni and Zulu tribes. The colony took its name from Cecil Rhodes, mogul of the British South Africa Company and a dominant figure in 19th century colonization of southern Africa. After World War II the white rulers of Southern Rhodesia (or simply Rhodesia) voted to remain a British colony, while neighboring states clamored for independence. Another 20 years passed before the white-minority government of Rhodesia declared

independence from Britain, in November 1965. Its harsh racist policies mirrored those of neighboring SOUTH AFRICA, and the two states frequently collaborated to suppress their black majorities. Insurgent movements included the AFRICAN NATIONAL CONGRESS, the Zimbabwe National Union (ZANU) and the Zimbabwe African People's Union (ZAPU). In March 1978 Rhodesia's white rulers finally agreed to a transfer of power, with black Africans assuming control of the state at year's end. A strange dual government ruled Rhodesia until 1980 when the first-ever biracial elections finally ousted white leaders from power. Still, at press time for this volume, one-third of Zimbabwe's arable land was still owned by white farmers—an endangered species increasingly under attack by black raiders who are openly encouraged by President Robert Mugabe. Claiming victims of both races in a long campaign of domestic TERRORISM, Mugabe has declared: "I am still the HITLER of the time. This Hitler has only one objective, justice for his own people, sovereignty for his people, recognition of the independence of his people. If that is Hitler, then let me be Hitler tenfold. Ten times Hitler, that is what we stand for." His "Green Bomber" youth militias are the spearhead of a ruthless domestic campaign that has seen thousands of opponents jailed, tortured, and killed while orchestrated acts of "random" violence purge whites and black dissidents alike.

ZIONISM

Prior to the early 1880s most European Jewish intellectuals agreed that the solution to anti-Semitism and related problems lay in full assimilation of Jews into the various countries where they resided. A shift in that viewpoint began with publication of Leon Pinsker's *Self-Determination* in 1882 and accelerated with the release of Theodore Heizl's *The Jewish State* in 1896. Both authors proposed the creation of a Jewish nation, preferably in Palestine, where they claimed a "divine right" of occupancy dating from Old Testament times. The political movement toward that end is termed *Zionism*, and it culminated 52 years later in the creation of ISRAEL.

Theodore Heizl became president of the Zionist World Congress in 1896, and he soon approached the sultan of TURKEY, requesting leave for Jews to occupy Palestine. Rejected on that front, he next turned to Britain, but the offer of UGANDA as a Jewish homeland failed to excite much Zionist enthusiasm. During the late 19th century, some 20,000 Jews emigrated to Palestine in a movement dubbed the First Aliya ("ascent"). A Second Aliya followed RUSSIA's abortive revolution of 1905, and Zionists kept their sights fixed firmly on Palestine. In 1914 at a Zionist meeting in London future Israeli president Chaim Weizmann declared Palestine "a country without a people for a people without a country"—somehow ignoring the fact that Palestine was fully occupied by Arab residents of long standing. Three years later, Weizmann was largely responsible for the British government's Balfour Declaration, which stated that:

His Majesty's Government view with favor the establishment in Palestine of a national home for the Jewish people . . . it being clearly understood that nothing shall be done that may prejudice the civil and religious rights of existing non-Jewish communities in Palestine.

Therein, however, lay the problem. Two years later in the wake of World War I, investigators of President Woodrow Wilson's King-Crane Commission reported that 90 percent of Palestine's inhabitants were non-Jews who opposed establishment of a Jewish state. If granted Palestine, the commission declared, "Zionists looked forward to a practically complete dispossession of the present non-Jewish inhabitants . . . nor can the erection of such a Jewish State be accomplished without the gravest trespass upon the civil and religious rights of existing non-Jewish communities in Palestine." Furthermore, "No British officer consulted by the Commissioners believed that the Zionist program could be carried out except by force of arms. That of itself is evidence of a strong sense of injustice of the Zionist program." Finally, the commission declared, "The initial claim, often submitted by Zionist representatives, that they have a 'right' to Palestine, based on an occupation of two thousand years ago, can hardly be seriously considered."

And yet, it was. In 1920 the League of Nations made Palestine a British "mandate." That April anti-Zionist riots erupted, claiming the lives of 51 Jewish settlers. A British commission of inquiry blamed that outbreak on "Arab disappointment in the non-fulfillment of promises of independence [dating from 1915] and to their fear of economic and political subjugation to the Zionists." Arthur Ruppin, head of the Jewish National Fund, spoke clearly for the Zionists when he declared, "Land is the most necessary thing for establishing our roots in Palestine. Since there are hardly any more arable unsettled lands in Palestine, we are bound in each case of the purchase of land and its settlement to remove the peasants who cultivated the land."

In fact by the time ADOLF HITLER seized power in GERMANY, few Palestinian Arabs were willing to entertain Zionist offers for land. Nonetheless, between 1933 and 1935 another 133,000 European Jews fled the impending Holocaust and settled in Palestine. In 1938, a full year before the start of World War II, Zionist spokesman David Ben Gurion spoke with surprising candor on his movement's intentions. "In our political argument abroad," he said, "we minimize Arab opposition to us, but let us not ignore the truth among ourselves. We are the aggressors and they defend themselves." Another Israeli leader of the future, Menachim Begin, was equally frank: "If this is Palestine and not the land of Israel, then you [Zionists] are conquerors and not tillers of the land. You are invaders. If this is Palestine, then it belongs to a people who lived here before you came."

July 1938 witnessed the first wave of Zionist TERRORISM in Palestine as members of the IRGUN paramilitary group detonated a series of bombs, killing 76 Arabs. British authorities jailed an Irgun leader in the wake of those attacks, whereupon the group murdered another 52 Arabs. In 1939 after Britain fixed Jewish immigration to Palestine at 15,000 new arrivals per year the Irgun slaughtered another 27 Arabs. After World War II Zionist attacks extended to British officials themselves. The most prominent victim was Count Folke Bernadotte, head of the Swedish Red Cross who saved thousands of Jews from Nazi concentration camps, appointed by the UNITED NATIONS on May 20, 1948, as a mediator between Jews and Arabs in Palestine. Bernadotte was murdered by Zionist gunmen in September 1948 on direct orders from future Israeli statesman YITZHAK SHAMIR, then head of a terrorist organization known as the Stern Gang. Other Zionist crimes from that era include the April 1948 massacre of 254 Arabs in the village of Deir Yassin. Irgun commanders issued an order to their assassins—"As in Deir Yassin, so everywhere"—while first Israeli president Chaim

Weizmann called the act "a miraculous clearance of the land."

It must be noted that Zionism does not represent the sole Jewish viewpoint in regard to Palestine or the question of a Jewish state. Many religious Jews interpret God's promise of a Jewish homeland as referring to events *after* the advent of the Messiah—an occurrence which all orthodox Jews agree has not yet occurred. One contrary organization, Neturei Karta, issues fliers with a header addressed to Zionists: "Why do you violate God's order? It will not succeed!"

See also HOLOCAUST AND HOLOCAUST DENIAL.

ZOG

ZOG is an abbreviation for "Zionist Occupation Government," a name applied by modern neo-Nazis since the early 1980s to the U.S. federal government in Washington, D.C. According to such groups as the KU KLUX KLAN, the SILENT BROTHERHOOD, POSSE COMITATUS, and various militia factions, Jewish conspirators based in ISRAEL or elsewhere have captured control of the United States, including the presidency, Congress, and the SUPREME COURT, dictating subversive policies which threaten white supremacy and otherwise conform to the broad terms of world domination outlined in the fraudulent *PROTOCOLS OF THE ELDERS OF ZION*. No evidence supports this fascist fantasy, but it persists regardless, finding new adherents in the ranks of gullible skinheads and other disaffected youth who seek scapegoats for personal failure.

See also FASCISM; MILITIAS; ZIONISM.

ZOMBIES

Best known to moviegoers as rotting reanimated corpses, slow on their feet and hungry for human flesh, zombies occupy a rather different place in the culture of their native HAITI. To worshipers of voodoo, any person may be subject to a curse that kills and then allows the victim's enemy to resurrect his prey, the undead zombie forced to work forever as a mindless slave. Of course, enlightened persons understand that no such creatures actually exist.

Or do they?

On May 2, 1962, 40-year-old Clairvius Narcisse died at a Haitian hospital. He was buried the following day—then resurfaced in his native village during 1980. Fingerprints confirmed his identity, but physicians could not explain his belated resurrection. Narcisse claimed that his brother hired a Vodun priest to curse him in 1962 and that his "corpse" was unearthed within hours of burial, after which he spent two years as a plantation slave in northern Haiti. With other zombies his brother rebelled and escaped in 1964, but he spent the next 16 years hiding in fear for his life until news reached him of his brother's death.

Similar cases are well documented by Haitian physicians, but they remained mysterious until 1982 when Harvard botanist Wade Davis launched a three-year study of zombification, tracing the practice back to its native roots. Davis emerged from his study with malaria, hepatitis, and enough material for two books on voodoo, including a detailed breakdown of various "zombie" potions derived from toxic plants and fish. Abrasive ingredients, ranging from ground glass to caustic plant resins, permit the toxins to penetrate human skin (as when victims walk barefoot over treated soil). The concoctions simulate symptoms of death without inducing full unconsciousness so that victims are aware of their own "death" and interment. Traditional belief in voodoo provides a supernatural explanation when the victims are unearthed and revived with chemical antidotes, sometimes including drugs that promote amnesia and overcome physical resistance.

Z/R Rifle

Z/R Rifle was the code name for one of several plots hatched by the U.S. CENTRAL INTELLIGENCE AGENCY (CIA) in its campaign to murder Cuban leader FIDEL CASTRO. Apparently hatched in the summer of 1961, Z/R Rifle involved CIA recruitment of MAFIA leaders including SAM GIANCANA, JOHN ROSELLI, SANTOS TRAFFICANTE, and others. (Some researchers also describe New Orleans mob boss CARLOS MARCELLO and syndicate mastermind MEYER LANSKY as integral members of the plot.) Those notorious gangsters apparently joined in the conspiracy with full knowledge of Attorney General Robert Kennedy and presumably with the collaboration of President John Kennedy. Despite recruitment of such lethal talent, however, all efforts at liquidating Castro failed. Author Gus Russo contends that the multiple murder attempts, albeit unsuccessful, drove Castro to plot and execute the JFK ASSASSINATION of November 22, 1963, as an act of retaliation. Other researchers disagree, suggesting that the Z/R Rifle team itself was more likely responsible for Kennedy's murder in Dallas. In 1979 the HOUSE SELECT COMMITTEE ON ASSASSINATIONS officially absolved both Castro and the CIA of any role in JFK's murder. The same committee declared that "the national syndicate of organized crime, as a group, was not involved in the assassination of President Kennedy, but . . . the available evidence does not preclude the possibility that individual members may have been involved."

See also KENNEDY DYNASTY.

Bibliography

Allen, Gary. *None Dare Call It Conspiracy.* Rossmoor, Calif.: Concord Press, 1971.

Anson, Robert. *They've Killed the President.* New York: Bantam, 1975.

Archer, Jules. *The Plot to Seize the White House.* New York: Hawthorn Books, 1973.

Austin, John. *Hollywood's Unsolved Mysteries.* New York: Ace Books, 1970.

Bainerman, Joel. *The Crimes of a President: New Revelations on Conspiracy & Cover-Up in the Bush and Reagan Administrations.* New York: S.P.I. Books, 1992.

Baird-Windle, Patricia, and Eleanor Bader. *Targets of Hatred: Anti-Abortion Terrorism.* New York: St. Martin's Press, 2001.

Balsiger, Davie, and Charles Sellier, Jr. *The Lincoln Conspiracy.* Los Angeles: Schick Sun Classic Books, 1977.

Barkun, Michael. *A Culture of Conspiracy.* Berkeley: University of California Press, 2003.

———. *Religion and the Racist Right.* Chapel Hill: University of North Carolina Press, 1997.

Beals, Carleton. *Brass-Knuckle Crusade—The Great Know-Nothing Conspiracy: 1820–1860.* New York: Hastings House, 1960.

Begich, Nicholas, and Jeane Manning. *Angels Don't Play This HAARP.* Anchorage, Alaska: Earth Pulse Press, 1996.

Berman, Jerry, and Morton Halperin, eds. *The Abuses of the Intelligence Agencies.* Washington, D.C.: Center for National Security Studies, 1975.

Bishop, Patrick, and Eamonn Mallie. *The Provisional IRA.* London: Corgi, 1987.

Black, Edwin. *IBM and the Holocaust: The Strategic Alliance Between Nazi Germany and America's Most Powerful Corporation.* New York: Crown Publishing, 2001.

Blackstock, Nelson. *COINTELPRO: The FBI's Secret War on Political Freedom.* New York: Vintage, 1975.

Blum, William. *Killing Hope: U.S. Military and CIA Interventions Since World War II.* Monroe, Maine: Common Courage Press, 1995.

Blumenthal, Sid, and Harvey Yazijian. *Government by Gunplay: Assassination Conspiracy Theories from Dallas to Today.* New York: Signet, 1976.

Boston, Rob. *The Most Dangerous Man in America?: Pat Robertson and the Rise of the Christian Coalition.* New York: Prometheus Books, 1996.

Boyle, Patrick. *Scout's Honor: Sexual Abuse in America's Most Trusted Institution.* Rockland, Calif.: Prima Publishing, 1994.

Breitman, George, et al. *The Assassination of Malcolm X.* New York: Pathfinder Press, 1976.

Bresler, Fenton. *Who Killed John Lennon?* New York: St. Martin's Press, 1989.

Brian, William. *Moongate: Suppressed Findings of the U.S. Space Program and the NASA-Military Cover-Up.* Portland, Ore.: Future Science Research Publishing, 1982.

Brodeur, Paul. *Outrageous Misconduct: The Asbestos Industry on Trial.* New York: Pantheon Books, 1985.

Bryan, C. D. B. *Close Encounters of the Fourth Kind.* New York: Penguin Arcana, 1995.

Bunting, Brian. *The Rise of the South African Reich.* Baltimore: Penguin Books, 1964.

Burnham, David. *Above the Law: Secret Deals, Political Fixes and Other Misadventures of the U.S. Department of Justice.* New York: Scribner, 1996.

Cantwell, Alan, Jr. *AIDS and the Doctors of Death.* Los Angeles: Aries Rising Press, 1998.

———. *Queer Blood: The Secret AIDS Genocide Plot.* Los Angeles: Aries Rising Press, 1993.

Case, Carroll. *The Slaughter: An American Atrocity.* Asheville, N.C.: FBC, Inc., 1998.

Castleman, Barry. *Asbestos: Medical and Legal Aspects.* Englewood Cliffs, N.J.: Aspen Law and Business, 1996.

Charns, Alexander. *Cloak and Gavel: FBI Wiretaps, Bugs, Informers, and the Supreme Court.* Urbana: University of Illinois Press, 1992.

Churchill, Ward, and Jim Vander Wall. *Agents of Oppression: The FBI's Secret War against the Black Panther Party and the American Indian Movement.* Boston: South End Press, 1988.

———. *The COINTELPRO Papers: Documents from the FBI's Secret War against Dissent in the United States.* Boston: South End Press, 1990.

Clark, Jerome. *The UFO Book: Encyclopedia of the Extraterrestrial.* Detroit: Visible Ink, 1998.

Clawson, Patrick, and Rensselaer Lee III. *The Andean Cocaine Industry.* New York: St. Martin's Press, 1998.

Coates, James. *Armed and Dangerous: The Rise of the Survivalist Right.* New York: Hill & Wang, 1987.

Colby, Gerard, and Charlotte Dennett. *Thy Will Be Done—The Conquest of the Amazon: Nelson Rockefeller and Evangelism in the Age of Oil.* New York: HarperCollins, 1995.

Collier, James. *Votescam: The Stealing of America.* New York: Victoria House, 1993.

Colodny, Len, and Robert Gettlin. *Silent Coup: The Removal of a President.* New York: St. Martin's Press, 1991.

Conason, Joe, and Gene Lyons. *The Hunting of the President: The Ten-Year Campaign to Destroy Bill and Hillary Clinton.* New York: Thomas Dunne Books, 2000.

Constable, Pamela, and Arturo Valenzuela. *A Nation of Enemies: Chile Under Pinochet.* New York: W.W. Norton, 1991.

Constantine, Alex. *Psychic Dictatorship in the U.S.A.* Portland, Ore.: Feral House, 1995.

———. *Virtual Government: CIA Mind Control Operations in America.* Venice, Calif.: Feral House, 1997.

Coogan, Tim Pat. *The IRA: A History.* Niwot, Colo.: Roberts Rinehart, 1994.

Cook, Fred. *The FBI Nobody Knows.* New York: Macmillan, 1964.

Corson, William. *Armies of Ignorance: The Rise of the American Intelligence Empire.* New York: Dial Press, 1977.

Courtney, Phoebe. *How Dangerous is Fluoridation?* New Orleans: Free Men Speak, 1971.

David, Ron. *Arabs & Israel For Beginners.* New York: Writers and Readers Publishing, 1996.

Davis, James. *Spying on America: The FBI's Domestic Counterintelligence Program.* New York: Praeger, 1992.

Davis, Wade. *Passage of Darkness.* Chapel Hill: University of North Carolina Press, 1988.

Dees, Morris. *Gathering Storm: America's Militia Threat.* New York: HarperCollins, 1996.

Diamond, Sigmund. *Compromised Campus: The Collaboration of the University and the Intelligence Community.* New York: Oxford University Press, 1992.

Dobson, Christopher, and Ronald Payne. *The Terrorists: Their Weapons, Leaders and Tactics.* New York: Facts On File, 1982.

Domanick, Joe. *To Protect and Serve: The LAPD's Century of War in the City of Dreams.* New York: Pocket Books, 1995.

Donner, Frank. *The Age of Surveillance.* New York: Knopf, 1980.

———. *Protectors of Privilege: Red Squads and Police Repression in Urban America.* Berkeley: University of California Press, 1990.

Drosnin, Michael. *Citizen Hughes.* New York: Holt, Rinehart and Winston, 1985.

Druffel, Ann. *How to Defend Yourself Against Alien Abduction.* New York: Three Rivers Press, 1998.

Earley, Pete. *Family of Spies: Inside the John Walker Spy Ring.* New York: Bantam, 1988.

Eatwell, Roger. *Fascism: A History.* New York: Penguin Books, 1995.

Eisen, Jonathan. *Suppressed Inventions & Other Discoveries.* New York: Perigree Books, 1999.

Ellerbe, Helen. *The Dark Side of Christian History.* Orlando, Fla.: Morningside and Lark, 1995.

Emerson, Steven, and Brian Duffy. *The Fall of Pan Am 103.* New York: Putnam, 1990.

Flynn, Devin, and Gary Gerhardt. *The Silent Brotherhood.* New York: Free Press, 1989.

Foerstel, Herbert. *Surveillance in the Stacks: The FBI's Library Awareness Program.* Westport, Conn.: Greenwood Press, 1991.

Frazier, Thomas, ed. *The Underside of American History*. 2 volumes. New York: Harcourt Brace Jovanovich, 1971.

Galvin, Thomas. "The A to Z Guide of Clinton Scandals." *New York Post,* 16 October 1996.

Gardiner, Robin. *The Riddle of the Titanic*. London: Onion, 1996.

——. *The Titanic Conspiracy*. New York: Citadel Press, 1997.

——. *Titanic: The Ship That Never Sank?* London: Ian Allan, 2001.

Garrow, David. *The FBI and Martin Luther King, Jr.: From Memphis to "Solo."* New York: W. W. Norton, 1989.

Gelbspan, Ross. *Break-ins, Death Threats and the FBI*. Boston: South End Press, 1991.

Gentry, Curt. *J. Edgar Hoover: The Man and the Secrets*. New York: W. W. Norton, 1991.

Gilmore, Christopher. *Hoover vs. Kennedy: The Second Civil War*. New York: St. Martin's Press, 1987.

Goldman, Albert. *Grass Roots: Marijuana in America Today*. New York: Warner Books, 1979.

Goldstein, Robert. *Political Repression in Modern America*. Cambridge, Mass.: Schencken, 1978.

Good, Timothy. *Above Top Secret: The Worldwide UFO Cover-up*. New York: Quill William Morrow, 1988.

Gutman, Roy, and David Rieff, eds. *Crimes of War: What the Public Should Know*. New York: W. W. Norton, 1999.

Halperin, Morton, et al. *The Lawless State: The Crimes of the U.S. Intelligence Agencies*. New York: Penguin, 1976.

Hamm, Mark. *Apocalypse in Oklahoma: Waco and Ruby Ridge Revenged*. Boston: Northeastern University Press, 1997.

Hanchett, William. *The Lincoln Murder Conspiracies*. Chicago: University of Illinois Press, 1983.

Hanley, Charles, Sang-hun Choe, and Martha Mendoza. *The Bridge at No Gun Ri*. New York: Henry Holt, 2001.

Harclerode, Peter. *Fighting Dirty: The Inside Story of Covert Operations from Ho Chi Minh to Osama Bin Laden*. London: Cassell & Co., 2001.

Helms, Harry. *Inside the Shadow Government: National Emergencies and the Cult of Secrecy*. Los Angeles: Feral House, 2003.

Helvarg, David. *The War Against the Greens*. San Francisco: Sierra Club Books, 1997.

Henze, Paul. *The Plot to Kill the Pope*. New York: Charles Scribner's Sons, 1985.

Herer, Jack. *The Emperor Wears No Clothes: Hemp and the Marijuana Conspiracy*. Van Nuys, Calif.: Hemp Publishing, 1992.

Herman, Edward, and Noam Chomsky. *Manufacturing Consent: The Political Economy of the Mass Media*. New York: Pantheon Books, 1988.

Hersh, Seymour. *The Target is Destroyed*. New York: Random House, 1986.

Higham, Charles. *American Swastika*. New York: Doubleday, 1985.

——. *Trading with the Enemy: The Nazi-American Money Plot, 1933–1949*. New York: Barnes & Noble, 1983.

Honegger, Barbara. *October Surprise*. New York: Tudor Publishing, 1989.

Howard, Clark. *Zebra*. New York: Berkley, 1980.

Huberman, Jack. *The Bush Hater's Handbook*. New York: Nation Books, 2003.

Jardine, Matthew. *East Timor: Genocide in Paradise*. Tucson: Odonian Press, 1995.

Jensen-Stevenson, Monika, and William Stevenson. *Kiss the Boys Goodby: How the United States Betrayed Its Own POWs in Vietnam*. New York: Dutton, 1990.

Johnson, R. W. *Shootdown*. New York: Viking Penguin, 1987.

Johnston, David. *Lockerbie: The Tragedy of Flight 103*. New York: St. Martin's Press, 1989.

Jones, Stephen, and Peter Israel. *Others Unknown: The Oklahoma City Bombing Case and Conspiracy*. New York: Public Affairs, 1998.

Kagan, Daniel, and Ian Summers. *Mute Evidence*. New York: Bantam, 1983.

Kaiser, Robert. *RFK Must Die!* New York: E. P. Dutton, 1970.

Kaysing, Bill. *We Never Went to the Moon: America's Thirty Billion Dollar Swindle!* Soquel, Calif.: Holy Terra Books, 1991.

Keith, Jim. *Casebook on the Men in Black*. Lilburn, Ga.: IllumiNet Press, 1997.

——, ed. *The Gemstone File*. Atlanta: IllumiNet Press, 1992.

——. *OKBOMB!: Conspiracy and Cover-up*. Lilburn, Ga.: IllumiNet Press, 1996.

Kelly, John, and Phillip Wearne. *Tainting Evidence: Inside the Scandals at the FBI Crime Lab*. New York: Free Press, 1998.

Kerry, John, and Hank Brown. *The BCCI Affair: A Report to the U.S. Senate Committee on Foreign Relations.* Washington, D.C.: U.S. Government Printing Office, 1992.

al-Khalil, Samir. *Republic of Fear: The Inside Story of Saddam's Iraq.* New York: Pantheon Books, 1989.

Kiernan, Ben. *The Pol Pot Regime: Race, Power, and Genocide in Cambodia under the Khmer Rouge, 1975–79.* New Haven, Conn.: Yale University Press, 1996.

Kilduff, Marshall, and Ron Javers. *The Suicide Cult.* New York: Bantam Books, 1978.

Klaber, William, and Philip Melanson. *Shadow Play: The Untold Story of the Robert F. Kennedy Assassination.* New York: St. Martin's Press, 1997.

Kohn, Howard. *Who Killed Karen Silkwood?* New York: Summit, 1981.

Kornbluh, Peter, and Malcolm Byrne, eds. *The Iran-Contra Scandal: The Declassified History.* New York: New Press, 1993.

Kornweibel, Theodore, Jr. *"Seeing Red": Federal Campaigns Against Black Militancy, 1919–1925.* Bloomington: Indiana University Press, 1998.

LaFeber, Walter. *Inevitable Revolutions: The United States in Central America.* New York: W. W. Norton, 1983.

Lane, Mark. *Rush to Judgment.* New York: Holt, Rinehart and Winston, 1966.

Laqueur, Walter. *Fascism: Past, Present, Future.* New York: Oxford University Press, 1996.

Lardner, James, and Thomas Reppetto. *NYPD: A City and Its Police.* New York: Henry Holt, 2000.

Lavigne, Yves. *Hell's Angels.* Seacaucus, N.J.: Lyle Stuart, 1996.

Lee, Martin. *The Beast Awakens.* Boston: Little, Brown, 1997.

Lewis, Charles. *The Buying of the President 2000.* New York: Avon, 2000.

Linedecker, Clifford. *Children in Chains.* New York: Everest House, 1981.

Lowther, William. *Arms and the Man: Dr. Gerald Bull, Iraq, and the Supergun.* Novato, Calif.: Presidio Press, 1991.

Lukas, J. Anthony. *Nightmare: The Underside of the Nixon Years.* New York: Viking, 1976.

Maccabee, Bruce. *UFO-FBI Connection: The Secret History of the Government's Cover-up.* St. Paul, Minn.: Llewellyn Publications, 2000.

Marrs, Jim. *Crossfire: The Plot That Killed Kennedy.* New York: Carroll & Graf, 1989.

———. *Rule by Secrecy.* New York: HarperCollins, 2001.

Matthiessen, Peter. *In The Spirit of Crazy Horse: The Story of Leonard Peltier and the FBI's War on the American Indian Movement.* New York: Penguin, 1992.

Meager, Sylvia. *Accessories After the Fact: The Warren Commission, the Authorities, and the Report.* New York: Bobbs-Merrill, 1967.

Melanson, Philip. *The Murkin Conspiracy: An Investigation Into the Assassination of Dr. Martin Luther King, Jr.* New York: Praeger, 1989.

———. *The Robert F. Kennedy Assassination: New Revelations on the Conspiracy and Cover-Up.* New York: S.P.I. Books, 1994.

Mendelsohn, Jack. *The Martyrs: Sixteen Who Gave Their Lives for Racial Justice.* New York: Harper & Row, 1966.

Messerschmidt, Jim. *The Trial of Leonard Peltier.* Boston: South End Press, 1983.

Messick, Hank. *John Edgar Hoover.* New York: David McKay, 1972.

Michel, Lou, and Dan Herbeck. *American Terrorist: Timothy McVeigh & the Oklahoma City Bombing.* New York: Regan Books, 2001.

Miller, Nathan. *Stealing from America: A History of Corruption from Jamestown to Reagan.* New York: Paragon House, 1992.

Moldea, Dan. *Dark Victory: Ronald Reagan, MCA, and the Mob.* New York: Viking, 1986.

———. *The Hoffa Wars: Rebels, Politicians and the Mob.* New York: Paddington Press, 1978.

Morrow, Robert. *The Senator Must Die.* Santa Monica, Calif.: Roundtable Publishing, 1988.

Morton, James. *Gangland International.* London: Little, Brown, 1998.

Neff, James. *Mobbed Up: Jackie Presser's High-Wire Life in the Teamsters, the Mafia and the FBI.* New York: Atlantic Monthly Press, 1989.

Nelson, Jack. *Terror in the Night: The Klan's Campaign Against the Jews.* New York: Simon & Schuster, 1992.

Nelson, Jack, and Jack Bass. *The Orangeburg Massacre.* New York: World Publishing Co., 1970.

Nelson, Jack, and Ronald Ostrow. *The FBI and the Berrigans: The Making of a Conspiracy.* New York: Coward, McCann and Geoghegan, 1972.

Newton, Michael. *Bitter Grain: The Story of the Black Panther Party.* Los Angeles: Holloway House, 1980.

———. *Black Collar Crimes.* Port Townsend, Wash.: Loompanics Unlimited, 1998.

———. *A Case of Conspiracy: James Earl Ray and the Assassination of Martin Luther King, Jr.* Los Angeles: Holloway House, 1980.

———. *The FBI Encyclopedia.* Jefferson, N.C.: McFarland, 2003.

———. *Raising Hell.* New York: Avon, 1993.

North, Mark. *Act of Treason: The Role of J. Edgar Hoover in the Assassination of President Kennedy.* New York: Carroll & Graf, 1991.

Nunnelley, William. *Bull Connor.* Tuscaloosa: University of Alabama Press, 1991.

O'Reilly, Kenneth. *Hoover and the Un-Americans: The FBI, HUAC, and the Red Menace.* Philadelphia: Temple University Press, 1983.

———. *"Racial Matters": The FBI's Secret File on Black America, 1960–1972.* New York: Free Press, 1989.

Parenti, Michael. *Blackshirts and Reds: Rational Fascism and the Overthrow of Communism.* San Francisco: City Lights Books, 1997.

———. *Dirty Truths.* San Francisco: City Lights Books, 1996.

———. *Inventing Reality: The Politics of News Media.* New York: St. Martin's Press, 1993.

Parry, Robert. *Trick or Treason: The October Surprise Mystery.* New York: Sheridan Square Press, 1993.

Pearson, Hugh. *The Shadow of the Panther: Huey Newton and the Price of Black Power in America.* Reading, Mass.: Addison-Wesley, 1994.

Pepper, William. *Orders to Kill: The Truth Behind the Murder of Martin Luther King, Jr.* New York: Warner Books, 1995.

Pizzo, Stephen, Mary Fricker, and Paul Muolo. *Inside Job: The Looting of America's Savings and Loans.* New York: HarperCollins, 1991.

Plate, Thomas, and Andrea Darvi. *Secret Police: The Inside Story of a Network of Terror.* Garden City, N.Y.: Doubleday, 1981.

Ranalli, Ralph. *Deadly Alliance: The FBI's Secret Partnership with the Mob.* New York: Harper-Torch, 2001.

Randles, Jenny. *Alien Contacts and Abductions.* New York: Sterling, 1993.

———. *The Truth Behind Men in Black.* New York: St. Martin's Press, 1997.

Rappaport, Jon. *AIDS Inc.: Scandal of the Century.* Foster City, Calif.: Human Energy Press, 1988.

Rashke, Richard. *The Killing of Karen Silkwood.* Boston: Houghton Mifflin, 1981.

Reed, Terry, and John Cummings. *Compromised: Clinton, Bush and the CIA.* Granite Bay, Calif.: Clandestine Publishing, 1995.

Reiterman, Tim. *Raven: The Untold Story of the Reverend Jim Jones and His People.* New York: E. P. Dutton, 1982.

Ridgeway, James, and Jeffrey St. Clair. *A Pocket Guide to Environmental Bad Guys.* New York: Thunder's Mouth Press, 1998.

Riebling, Mark. *Wedge: The Secret War between the FBI and the CIA.* New York: Knopf, 1994.

Rosie, George. *The Directory of International Terrorism.* Edinburgh: Mainstream Publishing, 1986.

Salinger, Pierre, and Eric Laurent. *Secret Dossier: The Hidden Agenda Behind the Gulf War.* New York: Penguin Books, 1991.

Sancton, Thomas, and Scott MacLeod. *Death of a Princess: The Investigation.* New York: St. Martin's Press, 1998.

Sanders, James. *The Downing of TWA Flight 800.* New York: Zebra Books, 1997.

Scheim, David. *Contract on America: The Mafia Murder of President John F. Kennedy.* New York: Shapolsky Publishers, 1988.

Shenkman, Richard. *Presidential Ambition: Gaining Power at Any Cost.* New York: HarperCollins, 1999.

Sick, Gary. *October Surprise: America's Hostages and the Election of Ronald Reagan.* New York: Times Books, 1991.

Sifakis, Carl. *The Encyclopedia of American Crime.* New York: Facts On File, 1984.

———. *Encyclopedia of Assassinations.* New York: Facts On File, 1991.

———. *The Mafia Encyclopedia* 2nd edition. New York: Checkmark Books, 1999.

Sklar, Holly, ed. *Trilateralism: The Trilateral Commission and Elite Planning.* Boston: South End Press, 1980.

Smith, Brent. *Terrorism in America: Pipe Bombs and Pipe Dreams.* Albany: State University of New York Press, 1994.

Speriglio, Milo. *The Marilyn Conspiracy.* New York: Pocket Books, 1986.

Steinberg, Alfred. *The Bosses.* New York: Macmillan, 1972.

Stevenson, William. *The Bormann Brotherhood.* New York: Bantam Books, 1973.

Stone, I. F. *The Killings at Kent State: How Murder Went Unpunished.* New York: Vintage Books, 1970.

Sullivan, William. *The Bureau: My Thirty Years in Hoover's FBI.* New York: W. W. Norton, 1979.

Summers, Anthony. *Conspiracy.* New York: Paragon House, 1989.

———. *Official and Confidential: The Secret Life of J. Edgar Hoover.* New York: G.P. Putnam's, 1993.

Swearingen, M. Wesley. *FBI Secrets: An Agent's Exposé.* Boston: South End Press, 1995.

Tackwood, Louis. *The Glass House Tapes.* New York: Avon Books, 1973.

Terry, Maury. *The Ultimate Evil.* New York: Doubleday, 1987.

Theobald, Robert. *The Final Secret of Pearl Harbor.* Old Greenwich, Conn.: Devin-Adair, 1954.

Theoharis, Athan. *Spying on Americans: Political Surveillance from Hoover to the Huston Plan.* Philadelphia: Temple University Press, 1978.

Theoharis, Athan, and John Cox. *The Boss: J. Edgar Hoover and the Great American Inquisition.* Philadelphia: Temple University Press, 1988.

Thomas, Ken, and Jim Keith. *The Octopus: Secret Government and the Death of Danny Casolaro.* Los Angeles: Feral House, 2003.

Toobin, Jeffrey. *A Vast Conspiracy: The Real Story of the Sex Scandal That Nearly Brought Down a Presidency.* New York: Touchstone, 1999.

Turner, William. *Hoover's FBI: The Men and the Myth.* Los Angeles: Sherbourne Press, 1970.

———. *The Police Establishment.* New York: G.P. Putnam's Sons, 1968.

Turner, William, and John Christian. *The Assassination of Robert F. Kennedy: A Searching Look at the Conspiracy and Cover-Up, 1968–78.* New York: Random House, 1979.

Vankin, Jonathan. *Conspiracies, Coverups, and Crimes.* New York: Dell Books, 1992.

Vankin, Jonathan, and John Whalen. *The 70 Greatest Conspiracies of All Time.* New York: Citadel Press, 1998.

Walsh, Lawrence. *Firewall: The Iran-Contra Conspiracy and Cover-up.* New York: W. W. Norton, 1997.

Washington, George, and Martin Kitman. *George Washington's Expense Account.* New York: Ballantine Books, 1970.

Weisberg, Harold. *Case Open: The Unanswered JFK Assassination Questions.* New York: Carroll & Graff, 1994.

———. *Frame-Up.* New York: Outerbridge & Dienstfrey, 1969.

———. *Never Again! The Government Conspiracy in the JFK Assassination.* New York: Carroll & Graff, 1995.

———. *Oswald in New Orleans: Case for Conspiracy with the CIA.* New York: Carroll & Graff, 1967.

———. *Photographic Whitewash: Suppressed Kennedy Assassination Pictures.* Hyattstown, Md.: The Author, 1967.

———. *Whitewash: The Report on the Warren Report.* New York: Dell, 1965.

———. *Whitewash II: The FBI–Secret Service Cover-up.* New York: Dell, 1967.

———. *Whitewash 4: Top Secret JFK Assassination Transcript.* Frederick, Md.: The Author, 1974.

Wilson, Kirk. *Unsolved Crimes: The Top Ten Unsolved Murders of the 20th Century.* New York: Carroll & Graff, 2002.

Yallop, David. *In God's Name.* New York: Bantam Books, 1984.

Zepezauer, Mark, and Arthur Naiman. *Take the Rich Off Welfare.* Tucson: Odonian Press, 1996.

Index

Presser, Jackie 174, 302
Price, Richard 10
Principi, Anthony 4
prison gangs **294**
    Aryan Brotherhood 26
    Black Guerrilla Family 45
    Mexican Mafia 238
    Nuestra Familia 266
Prohibition 20, 40, 54, 91, 93, 99,
  141, 154, 199, 212, 232, **294**
Project HARP 53
Project Paperclip 37, 63, 131,
  295–296, 332
    and Allen Dulles 100
Protocols of the Elders of Zion
  171, 271, **296**, 311, 396
    and Henry Ford 127
    and Freemasons 135
    and Illuminati 171
    and Jack the Ripper 183
    and Wicca letters 383
Puerto Rico **296**
    Alpha 66 10
    Echelon network 110
    FBI in 83, 302
    General Electric 138
Purple Gang 316
Purvis, Melvin 72

Q

al-Qaddaffi, Muammar 219-220,
  297–298
    and Carlos the Jackal 62
    and El Rukns 113
    invades Chad 68
    and Pan Am Flight 103
    283–284
al-Qaeda 59, 86, 139, 176, 274,
  298
    in Afghanistan 2, 42–43
    and Iraq 168, 177
    in Kenya 202
    PENTTBOM attacks 286–287
    in the Philippines 290
    and Somalia 330
    in Sudan 337
    in Tanzania 345
    in Yemen 390
Qatar **298**
Quisling, Vidkun 265, **298–299**

R

Rabin, Yitzhak **300**
Rasputin, Grigory **300–301**
Raubal, Geli 49
Raybestos-Manhattan 27

Ray brothers **301**
    James Earl 166, 203–204
    Jerry 301
    John 301
Reagan, Ronald 42, 53, 57, 79, 81,
  192, 197, **301–302**, 338
    and Carlyle Group 271
    and William Casey 63
    foreign policy 78, 114
    and "Evil Empire" 193
    honors SS dead 333
    invades Grenada 144–145
    Iran-contra conspiracy
    176–177, 348, 352
    and IRS 173
    and Israel 214
    and KAL Flight 007 198
    and Henry Kissinger 205
    and Libya 219, 297
    and Ferdinand Marcos 234
    and Nicaragua 260
    October Surprise 176
    pardons convicted FBI agents
    336
    and Russia 313
    supports Manuel Noriega 283
    supports Saddam Hussein 167,
    177
    Supreme Court appointees 112
    and Teamsters Union 174
    and televangelists 347
    vs. BATF 54
    "War on Drugs" 57, 81–82,
    100
    and James Watt 76
Reconstruction 43, 135, **302–303**
    and Rutherford B. Hayes
    155–156
    and Justice Dept. 196
    and KKK 209
    and White League 381–382
Red Army faction 62
Red Brigades 181
Reichstag fire **303**
Reno, Janet 28, 61, 197, 242
Republican Party 5, 57, 70–71, 79,
  155–156, 194, 209, 215, 263,
  301–302, 305–306
    Enron scandal 115–116
    and "liberal media" 218
    and oil companies 271
    and pharmaceutical companies
    288
    and televangelists 348
    and tobacco companies 261
Reuther, Victor 164
Reuther, Walter **303–304**
    and Ford Motor Co. 127

RFK assassination 130, 141, 166,
  167, **304–306**, 327
    and CIA 67, 243
Rhode Island
    and Benedict Arnold 25
Rhodesia 50
Rice, Condoleezza 276
Rife, Royal 62
Rizzo, Frank 289
Roberts, Bruce 136
Rockefeller clan 192, **306–307**
    anarchist plots against 15
    and Bohemian Club 47
    Chase Manhattan Bank 69
    David 41
    John D. 14-15, 69, *307*
    Nelson 47, 137, 204, 294
    William *306*
Rockefeller Foundation 90, 170
    Standard Oil 101, 271
    and Trilateral Commission 353
Romania **307–308**
Roper, Sam 29
Roosevelt, Eleanor 137
Roosevelt, Franklin 11, 74, 95,
  137, 256–257, *256*
    and Council on Foreign Rela-
    tions 90
    "court-packing" plan 338
    and gold standard 143
    and Henry Ford 127
    and *Hindenburg* disaster 159
    New Deal 159
    and OSS 269
    and Pearl Harbor attack
    284–285
    plot to depose 13, 101
    and United Nations 369
    Yalta Conference 390
Roosevelt, Theodore 14, *122*
    and Bohemian Club 47
    and FBI 122
Roselli, John 166, 214, **308**, 396
Rosenberg, Julius and Ethel
  308–310, *309*
Rosicrucians **310**
    and Knights Templar 207
Rothschild family **310–311**
    and Lincoln assassination 223
Rove, Karl 115, 138, 261
Rowe, Gary 88
Rubin, Jerry 73
Ruby, Jack 188-192, 279, 308,
  311–312, 377–378
    and Dallas police 93–94
    and Mafia 234
Ruckleshaus, William 117
Rudolph, Eric 25